THE MOST TRUSTED NAME IN TRAVEL

Frommer's®

PORTUGAL

By Paul Ames and Célia Pedroso

FROMMER'S STAR RATINGS SYSTEM

Every hotel, restaurant, and attraction listed in this guide has been ranked for quality and value. Here's what the stars mean:

★	Recommended
★★	Highly Recommended
★★★	A must! Don't miss!

AN IMPORTANT NOTE

The world is a dynamic place. Hotels change ownership, restaurants hike their prices, museums alter their opening hours, and buses and trains change their routings. And all of this can occur in the several months after our authors have visited, inspected, and written about these hotels, restaurants, museums, and transportation services. Though we have made valiant efforts to keep all our information fresh and up-to-date, some few changes can inevitably occur in the periods before a revised edition of this guidebook is published. So please bear with us if a tiny number of the details in this book have changed. Please also note that we have no responsibility or liability for any inaccuracy or errors or omissions, or for inconvenience, loss, damage, or expenses suffered by anyone as a result of assertions in this guide.

Vineyards and villages in the Douro Valley.

CONTENTS

Lisbon's Monument to the Discoveries (see p. 105) in the marina of Belém.

A LOOK AT PORTUGAL

Portugal is a mystery. As a culture, it's far harder to pin down than other western nations. Say the word "Italy" and a slew of images—pasta, hand gestures, suave clothing, and more—pop to mind. The same with "France," "Germany," or the "United States." But to understand Portugal, one must travel there. And listen to the nation's plaintive fado music, gorge on grilled sardines, and wander over rocky cliffs, through cutting-edge contemporary museums, winding cobblestoned alleys, and churches glittering with colonial-era gold. This book tells you how to do all of that and much more. In the following pages are just a few of the spectacular sights you'll see.

Go… and be dazzled.

—Pauline Frommer

Praia do Camilo beach, near Lagos in the Algarve (p. 224).

LISBON

Lisbon is set on seven hills, meaning there's a gob-smacking view around most every corner. Pictured is the atmospheric Alfama district, which has some of the oldest buildings in the city (built on stronger stone, it wasn't as badly damaged as other neighborhoods during the 1755 earthquake).

A foodie mecca, Lisbon has a number of outdoor cafes, though few climb the hills as adeptly as this one does.

With so many ups and downs, catching a vintage cable car is a calf-saving, and delightful, way to see the city's highlights.

Open at one end to the sparkling Tagus River, the Praça do Comércio (p. 67) is considered one of the most majestic, harmonious town squares in Europe. At its heart is a bronze statue of King José I.

Lisbon's cathedral or Sé (Sedes Episcopalis) is said to contain the relics of St. Vincent, the city's patron saint.

Fado music, the soulful heartbeat of Portugal, is usually performed by a singer accompanied by a guitarist. Lisbon's fado clubs are the best in the nation.

The Jerónimos Monastery (p. 102) is a masterpiece of late Gothic Manueline architecture. Tip: To avoid the line to visit the cloister, get a ticket to the inside museum, which will allow you to visit both without waiting.

The Museu Calouste Gulbenkian (p. 107) has a head-spinning variety of art and design, from Rembrandt portraits to Grecian urns to exquisite jewelry by René Lalique. It's considered one of the finest private collections on the planet.

The MAAT (Museum of Art, Architecture, and Technology), p. 102, which opened in late 2016, has transformed the cityscape with its sail-like roof jutting out over the river.

The village of Obidos is so pretty King Afonso II gave it as a wedding gift to his queen. It's a short day trip from Lisbon.

In the suburbs of Lisbon, Sintra (p. 164) holds the Pena National Palace (pictured) along with a number of other royal retreats.

The Sintra-Cascais National Park is an easy escape from Lisbon.

NORTHERN PORTUGAL

Known as the "River of Gold," the Douro wends its way from north-central Spain to Porto. In Portugal, its often-steep banks are terraced with the vineyards that produce the area's famous fortified wine.

Porto's Avenido dos Anados runs through the heart of Porto, flanked by imposing Belle Epoque–era structures. Pictured is *Juventude* by sculptor Henrique Moreira, and it's a fountain, meaning that, yes, it's the "fountain of youth."

Livraria Lello (p. 337) in Porto is as much tourist site as it is bookstore. It has been peddling tomes since 1906.

The most visited museum in the country, the Fundação Serralves (p. 339) houses an important collection of modern Portuguese art, as well as hosting changing exhibitions.

A view of Porto's colorful Ribeira neighborhood. It has clung to this hillside since the Middle Ages.

The exuberant Salão Árabe (Arabian salon, p. 335) is a ceremonial room in Porto's mid-19th-century stock exchange building.

The city's largely Romanesque Sé (Cathedral, p. 336) was begun in the 12th century.

Pop by for a cimbalino (shot of espresso) at the 1920s-era Café Majestic (p. 338).

It seems like every inch of the Sao Francisco church (p. 333) is gilded in gold.

You can't say you've been to Porto until you've tippled your way through a port tasting (p. 335).

Guimarães' castle, site of an important siege, is considered the birthplace of the nation.

Guimarães' Largo de Oliveira (Olive Tree Square, p. 378) is rich in history... and taverns. It's the place to be in the evenings.

A rococo fantasia of a church, Santuário de Nossa Senhora dos Remédios (p. 366) in Lamego is the site of one of the country's largest pilgrimages and festivals each September.

SOUTHERN PORTUGAL

Near Lagos (p. 222) the coast is a wonderland of hidden lagoons, jutting rocks, and grottoes.

A falconer participates in a medieval festival in Silves.

From the heady heights of the parapets of Marvao Castle (p. 269), visitors feel like they can see all of Portugal, and a good swatch of Spain, too.

Évora's Sé (p. 278) is the largest medieval cathedral in the country. The cathedral's greatest treasure is a piece of wood said to be from Christ's cross.

Among the cathedral's many treasures is a sculpture called *Our Lady of Mothers*, where women come to pray for fertility.

Igreja Real de São Francisco (p. 278) in Évora contains a chapel decorated with hundreds of human and other bones.

Students at the Universidade de Coimbra, Portugal's oldest university, wear the same sorts of ceremonial robes that scholars have worn here for centuries.

The stately library at Coimbra's university (p. 292) is viewable on tours of the school.

The Algarve's cliff-shaded beaches draw tourists from across Europe.

Sagres (p. 219) was once considered the edge of the world. Hike to the lighthouse for a view of the vast Atlantic and you'll understand why.

The Castelo dos Mouros (p. 235) in Silves was the center of the Moorish empire until the Reconquista. All that's left are ruins.

Throughout Portugal, you'll see important works from the many civilizations that once ruled this land. Pictured is a still-standing Roman-era bridge in Tavira.

THE BEST OF PORTUGAL

1

Portugal is Europe's West Coast. Its 1,000 miles of shore are bathed in a California-style climate. The lifestyle is laid back, the food and wine among Europe's great gourmet secrets. History has left one of the world's oldest nations packed with heritage sites from prehistoric graffiti to medieval city centers and forests filled with romantic palaces. The land that sent explorers to open the world 500 years ago is now waiting to be discovered.

Mainland Europe's westernmost nation has few rivals as a land where climate, landscape, and history combine so effectively to satisfy travelers' wish lists. Atlantic breezes waft over beaches for every taste, from sheltered, family-friendly coves to strands of endless sand offering the continent's best surf. **Lisbon** has emerged as one of Europe's hippest capitals, a place where the plaintive songs of traditional fado music echo down medieval alleys leading to riverside nightclubs throbbing with the latest DJ sensations.

Foodies can feast on a rich and varied cuisine that's rooted in tradition and dominated by superlative seafood and world-beating wines. Crammed into a country the size of Maine are 18 UNESCO World Heritage Sites, ranging from the rolling hillside vineyards above the **River Douro** and the mysterious stronghold of the Knights Templar in **Tomar,** to historic cities like **Porto, Évora,** and **Guimarães.** If your goal is relaxing in a year-round subtropical springtime, **Madeira** Island is the place.

Those seeking a more active break can hike the mountain wildernesses of the **Peneda-Gerês National Park** or **Serra da Estrela** highlands; race speedboats to watch dolphins frolic off **Algarve** beaches; or play a round on world-class, year-round golf courses. All that combined with its reputation for safety, low crime, and warm hospitality have made Portugal one of Europe's hottest destinations.

CITIES Spread along the broad estuary of the River Tagus, **Lisbon** is the country's political, economic, and cultural heart. It enjoys more sunshine than Madrid, Rome, or Athens. Commuter trains run from downtown to Atlantic beaches in minutes. There are gilded theaters, treasure-packed museums, and atmospheric old neighborhoods that recall the 15th-century golden age of Portuguese Discoveries. Second city **Porto** is fast catching up as a city-trip destination, thanks to its UNESCO World Heritage riverside heart, cultural scene, and growing reputation as a capital of cool. The ancient university city of **Coimbra** is regarded as Portugal's most romantic, while regional centers like **Guimarães** and **Braga** in the far north, **Évora** in the **Alentejo** region, and **Angra do Heroísmo** in the Azores are treasure houses of tradition and culture.

COUNTRYSIDE For a small country, Portugal boasts a richly diverse landscape. The southern **Algarve** region is redolent of the Mediterranean, with balmy beaches, almond groves, and citrus plantations. Further north in the vast rolling plains of the **Alentejo,** black pigs roam feasting on acorns under forests of cork oaks to produce fabulous hams. The land is punctuated by picture-perfect whitewashed villages. In the rugged interior of the central **Beiras** region, mainland Portugal's highest peaks are found in the **Serra da Estrella** mountain range, home to the country's only ski resort. Vine-covered slopes surround the **River Douro** inland from Porto, arguably the world's most beautiful wine region. Beyond, the northwest **Minho** region is verdant and dotted with elegant manor houses, while **Tràs-os-Montes** to the northeast is marked by starkly beautiful high plateaus and a cuisine as robust as its climate.

EATING & DRINKING The Portuguese love to eat. Restaurant attendance is among Europe's highest. Fortunately, eating out costs less here than just about anywhere in Western Europe. Portuguese cuisine isn't as well known as it should be, perhaps because it depends heavily on fresh local ingredients—fish newly plucked from the Atlantic, a multitude of seasonal fruit and vegetables that ripen in the warm climate, beef raised on lush northern pastures, lamb nourished on spring flowers.

COAST The **Algarve** is Portugal's premier vacation region, its sheltered south coast is strung with beaches that range from flat, gently sloping sandbar islands (reached by bridge or boat close to the border with Spanish Andalusia), to the iconic coves hidden between honeycomb cliffs near the towns of **Lagos** and **Albufeira.** Unfortunately, some of the resorts in the Algarve's central strip suffer from the excesses of mass tourism with strips of ugly high-rise and bargain-booze bars, but beyond the dramatic headland of Europe's most southwesterly point at **Sagres,** the coast changes. Wind and waves make the wild west a paradise for surfers and sailors. The world's biggest surfed waves crash ashore near the picturesque fishing port of **Nazaré.** Even along the west coast, however, there are sheltered beaches: the soft white sands and gentle bays just south of Lisbon at **Comporta** and **Arrábida** are a delight.

PORTUGAL'S best AUTHENTIC EXPERIENCES

- **Fado:** There are many places to experience Lisbon's unique fado music: from backstreet dives where the cook may step out of the kitchen to give voice to her emotions by bursting into song, to fancy clubs where you'll pay dearly to dine accompanied by a renowned diva, to concert halls packed with thousands of fans gathered to hear one of the genre's big stars. Fado's bluesy blend of voice and guitar strives to capture the pain of lost love and longing for homelands left behind, all bound up with the untranslatable feeling they call *saudade*, which is deeply bound up with Portugal's national character.

- **Market shopping:** Portugal's daily food markets have suffered from superstore competition, but most showcase an array of fresh products that make them a must for anybody interested in food. They are not for the fainthearted: Butchers' stalls proudly present glistering arrays of offal and fishmongers cheerfully gut and scale the day's catch. Naturally grown fruits and vegetables may lack the shine and same-shape regularity of supermarket goods, but will taste oh so much better.
- **Hitting a hot tub:** Hot springs bubble up from Portugal's hills and plains. Spa resorts are scattered about the country. Some have roots going back to Roman times; many maintain an old-world elegance with splendid Belle Epoque hotels or Art Deco baths in marble, brass, and painted *azulejo* tiles. The charm can be a little faded in some places, but plenty have been restored to their full glory.
- **Downing a bica:** In a country whose former colonies included Brazil, Angola, and East Timor, it's no surprise that the country is hooked on coffee. Although you can find local equivalents of lattes and flat whites, the Portuguese mostly get their caffeine fix through tiny espresso shots known as *bica*, or simply *café*. If you want to blend in, eschew pavement terraces and join the locals lined up at the counter in countless cafes to knock back their *bicas*, quite possibly with a custard-filled *pastel da nata* or another treat from the selection of pastries on show. See p. 40.
- **Chilling on a beach:** While the English complain "it's not my cup of tea," the Portuguese say "*não é a minha praia*"—"it's not my beach." The phrase shows how central the beach is to Portuguese life. Inhabitants of Lisbon and Porto will rush out to the cities' suburban shores at weekends, even in mornings and evenings before and after work. Most beaches have cool bars or restaurants that serve up wonderful fresh shellfish or grilled fish. Surfers from around the world flock to ride the rollers along the west coast at places like Aljezur, Ericeira, and Peniche.
- **Wine tasting at a quinta:** Port wine from the Douro region has been a major Portuguese export for centuries, but the world has only recently woken up to the wonders of the country's other wines: darkly brooding reds, playful white *vinho verdes* from the Minho, bubbly *espumantes*, sweet *moscatels*. Excellent tipples are produced the length and breadth of the country, but the Douro region's terraced hills stand out for their beauty. Sampling wines in one of the Douro's historic estates (*quintas*) while gazing out over the landscape is unforgettable.

- **Watching the sun set at the end of the earth:** The ancients believed the remote Sagres Peninsula at the southwestern tip of Europe was the end of the earth. Prince Henry the Navigator set up his school for mariners there to plot the Age of Discoveries. There are few better places to watch the sun go down. Crowds gather around the cliff-top fort and lighthouse at nearby Cape St. Vincent to see the sun turn the sky orange before sinking beneath the waves. There's nothing but the Atlantic between here and New York. The cocktails served in the fortress café help keep out the sometimes chill winds.
- **Party with the saints:** Lisbon's biggest party comes on July 12. To honor Saint Anthony (*Santo António*), its patron, the city engages in all-night revelry. The streets in the oldest neighborhoods fill with the whiff of sardines on the barbeque and the sound of guitars and accordions. Hordes of revelers quaffing beer and red wine dance into the wee small hours. Celebrations are most intense in the district that wins for the best performance in the *marchas populares*, a singing costumed promenade down the capital's main boulevard. Eleven days later it's Porto's turn, on the night of Saint John (*São João*). The second-city's party includes a spectacular fireworks display over the Douro.
- **Walking a levada:** The island of Madeira is crisscrossed with more than 2,092km (1,300 miles) of hiking trails that follow narrow stone irrigation channels known as *levadas*. Walking them offers wonderful views of the island's mountainous interior and out over the deep blue Atlantic all around. Many lead though the *Laurisilva* forest, what's left of the semitropical native vegetation that covered the island before Portuguese explorers arrived in 1419. It is now a UNESCO World Heritage Site. Among the most scenic is Levada do Caldeirão Verde, which snakes 4 miles though verdant glades and tumbling ocean views before arriving at a 91-meter (300-ft.) waterfall.
- **Taking to the waves in the Tagus:** Lisbon's cutest mode of public transport are the tiny streetcars that weave through the narrow streets. But the famed Tram 28 has fallen victim to its reputation and is now swamped with tourists. A more authentic journey would be to join the thousands of Lisbonites who commute from the south bank of the River Tagus into the city on little orange ferry boats called *cacilheiros*. For 1.20€ you can admire an unrivaled view of the Lisbon skyline as the boat chugs across for the 10-minute voyage to the dock at Cacilhas, where there's a welcoming row of riverside seafood restaurants.

PORTUGAL'S best VILLAGES & SMALL TOWNS

- **Tavira:** While much of the central Algarve coast has been scarred by mass tourism, the region's eastern and western extremities retain their charm.

Nowhere more so than this little town, where noble 17th-century homes line the riverside, narrow streets are filled with restaurants and cafes, and small boats can whisk you to near-deserted island beaches. See p. 258.

- **Óbidos:** Clustered around its 12th-century castle, this is one of Portugal's best-preserved medieval towns. Its maze of cobbled lanes connects whitewashed houses with bright blue or yellow trim. The town is also famed for its bookshops, its sweet cherry liqueur, and the white sands of its lagoon that opens out into the Atlantic nearby. See p. 193.
- **Belmonte:** Birthplace of the explorer who discovered Brazil and home to a Jewish community that preserved its faith in secret through centuries of persecution, Belmonte is built from granite hewn from the remote central highlands. Among the rough stone buildings are a 13th-century castle and the ruined tower dating back to Roman times. See p. 325.
- **Amarante:** Inland from Porto, Amarante sits on a tree-lined curve in the River Tâmega. Its Renaissance-style riverside church, built with Spanish and Italian influences out of soft golden local stone, is surrounded by townhouses rising up the hillside and spreading along the riverbank. It is home to a fine luxury hotel, a surprising museum of modern art, and famed cafes serving sweet almond and cinnamon-flavored pastries. See p. 361.
- **Marvão:** As dramatic locations go, this could hardly be better. Marvão is perched on a rocky crag rising 860 meters (2,800 ft.) out of the Alentejo plain. It stood as a frontier post for centuries, fought over by Celts and Romans, Muslims and Christians, Castilians and Portuguese. Inside its medieval battlements, the old whitewashed town has survived all those battles. Views are extraordinary, especially if you're there at dawn or sunset. See p. 265.
- **Porto Moniz:** This little red-roofed fishing village is located on a nub of land jutting out into the Atlantic on Madeira's northwestern tip. It is surrounded by precipitous mountain slopes rising directly out of the ocean. Narrow waterfalls cascade down them through lush semitropical vegetation. The views are amazing, but Porto Moniz's main attraction are the black lava rock basins lapped by the waves, which form one of the world's most beautiful swimming pools. See p. 435.
- **Miranda do Douro:** Located on the edge of a canyon formed by the River Douro where it marks Portugal's northeast frontier, Miranda has been a land that time forgot since 1762, when invading Spaniards blew up a big part of it and the authorities decamped farther from the border. Isolation has allowed the town to maintain its own unique language, Mirandese, and traditions like the war dance performed by local men wearing frilly skirts and striped woolen socks. There's a sturdy stone cathedral and cobbled streets lined with centuries-old homes. It's also famed for steak. See p. 406.
- **Piodão:** Huddled on a terraced hillside in a remote corner of the Açor mountains in the center of the country, homes here are made from dark,

almost black schist stone with slate roofs. In dramatic counterpoint is the little parish church, a wedding-cake confection in purest white with pale blue trim. At dusk, when the village glitters with yellow lights, it resembles a Neapolitan nativity scene. It's a great base for hiking the hills or sampling hearty highland dishes like goat slow-cooked in red wine. See p. 325.

- **Ponte de Lima:** Once a Roman outpost, Ponte de Lima lays claim to being the oldest village in Portugal. It's defined by the ancient stone bridge that arches over the slow-moving River Lima and connects the village to the slender tower of St. Anthony's Church on the west bank. Ponte de Lima is packed with historic mansions whose balconies overflow with summer flowers. It's set in the verdant hills of the Minho region and surrounded by baroque estates producing crisp *vinho verde* wines. See p. 382.
- **Mértola:** Clinging to a high ridge over the River Guadiana, this picturesque collection of white-painted houses surrounded by medieval walls was the capital of an Arab kingdom in the Middle Ages. Its parish church was a mosque with a multicolumned interior—a rare survivor of Islamic architecture in Portugal. Wandering its ancient streets, it's not hard to imagine its golden age as a cosmopolitan river port. The river provides swimming and kayaking opportunities, and local restaurants thrive on boar, hare, and other game hunted in the wild surroundings. See p. 269.

PORTUGAL'S best BEACHES

- **Porto Santo:** Madeira Island lacks beaches, but a 2-hour boat trip (or 15-minute flight) away is one of Portugal's best. The little island of Porto Santo boasts a 10km (6 mile) stretch of golden sand stretching around a bay of still blue water with views across the mountains of Madeira on the horizon. See p. 442.
- **Cabanas:** Cabanas is a little fishing village just outside the Algarve town of Tavira. After lunching in one of the great waterfront seafood joints, hop on one of the skiffs that skim across the blue lagoon to a sandbar island flanked with over 5km (3 miles) of soft yellow sand. See p. 258.
- **Praia da Marinha:** Coves of pale sand nestled beneath honeycomb cliffs, near the resort of Carvoeiro, this is one of the most iconic Algarve beaches. In summer, you won't have it to yourself, but its distance from the main resorts means it does not get as crowded as most along this stretch of coast. See p. 220.
- **Portinho da Arrábida:** This is the largest of a series of achingly beautiful coves cut into the Arrábida hills as they meet the sea west of Setúbal—a crescent moon of blond sand sandwiched between sapphire blue waters and the green hillsides. Expect traffic jams on the narrow access roads on summer weekends. See p. 183.

- **Guincho:** In the lee of Europe's westernmost point at Capo da Roca, this broad expanse of sand is the most dramatic of the beaches in the Cascais-Sintra area west of Lisbon. Its exposure to Atlantic breezes whipping around the cape means that except on rare calm days, it's better for surfers and wind sports rather than laying out on the sand. But the views are dramatic, and there are excellent restaurants along the coast road. See p. 156.
- **Supertubos:** Portugal's surfer beach *par excellence*. Although the waves here are not as big as the record-breaking rollers up the coast in Nazaré, this strand, just south of the fishing town of Peniche, is renowned for the regularity of its perfect tubular waves crashing on to the soft sand. "An amazing wave," according to Australian world champion surfer Mike Fanning, a frequent competitor at international competitions held here. See p. 206.
- **Quiaios:** Look north from the Serra da Boa Viagem hills above the resort of Figueira da Foz and Quiaios beach stretches as far as you can see—an endless strip of sand backed by dunes and pine forest. There's a small village at the southern end, and beyond that, solitude. Spain's *El País* newspaper called it the no. 1 beach in Portugal. Care can be needed with riptides; check with the lifeguard. See p. 288.
- **Moledo:** Portugal's northernmost beach has long been a favorite for the in-crowd from Porto. A vast sandy expanse, it curves down from the River Minho that forms the border with Spain. It is overlooked by the conical outline of Mount Santa Tecla over the frontier and a 15th-century fort on a small offshore island. As with other northern beaches, the water can be cold, the wind fresh, and the mornings shrouded in mist, but there is no denying the wild beauty of the location. See p. 395.

PORTUGAL'S best HOTELS

- **Belmond Reid's Palace** (Funchal): The grand old lady of Madeira hotels was built in 1890s and was once the favored retreat of Sir Winston Churchill. Tea and scones are still served on the terrace at 5pm as a reminder of the time when the British upper set wintered here, but Reid's has managed to shed a one-time fusty image without losing any of its period charm or superlative service standards. It's wonderfully located amid cliff-top gardens overlooking the Atlantic. See p. 418.
- **Fazenda Nova** (Tavira): The contrast with the concrete mega-resorts on some of the Algarve's more crowded stretches could hardly be greater. Set among almond and olive trees in the countryside above the pretty coastal town of Tavira, this country house, built in the 1830s, has been transformed into a chic boutique hideaway. There's a sheltered pool, a restaurant combining locally caught seafood with produce from the hotel garden, and a bar stocked with Portuguese wines. Guests can even chill to the owners' collection of over 1,000 vinyl records. See p. 259.

- **Herdade do Touril** (Zambujeira do Mar): Here's a chance to stay in a real Alentejo farmstead, just a stone's throw from the unspoiled beaches and hiking trails of the Costa Vicentina coastal park. The hotel is made up of a cluster of single-story buildings painted in traditional blue and white, grouped about the sun terrace and outdoor pool. As well as rooms, you can rent suites or whole houses with two or three rooms. Breakfast is served until noon, and the bar stays open to midnight. Relaxation guaranteed. See p. 286.
- **The Independente** (Lisbon): Lisbon has built a reputation for some of the world's hippest hostels, and this is one of the best: at the heart of the action in the Bairro Alto nightlife zone and with great views over the city. It has basic dorm bunks for as little as 11€ including breakfast—and this in a palatial, early-20th-century residence originally built for the Swiss ambassador! A couple of cool restaurants are in the building along with a rooftop bar. There are also some charming private suites, for those who can afford to pay for privacy. See p. 82.
- **Six Senses Douro Valley** (Lamego): Probably the most pampering you can get at any one place, this is the first European resort with the sensory overload approach of Asian luxury specialist Six Senses. It has acres of land among the Douro's riverside vineyards, a match of award-winning contemporary design with the charm of the original 19th-century mansion, great restaurants, and a superlative spa. See p. 369.
- **Memmo Alfama** (Lisbon): The Memmo is a luxury boutique hotel overlooking Lisbon's ancient Alfama neighborhood. In a city blessed with viewpoints, few can match those from the Memmo's brick-red rooftop infinity pool. Tucked away down a cul-de-sac lined with citrus trees, behind the 12th-century Cathedral, it blends hip, modern decor with ancient features like domed baker's ovens transformed into cozy sitting rooms. See p. 80.
- **Palácio de Seteais** (Sintra): The Dutch ambassador owned one of the most romantic palaces in Portugal, built in the 1780s on a forested hillside in Sintra. They say the name came later: "Sete ais" translates as "seven sighs," apparently uttered by Portuguese nobles forced to sign a humiliating treaty here after a 1807 defeat by Napoleon's invading armies. Any sighing you're likely to do today will be from pleasure—at the views, the lavish gardens, the gloriously restored neoclassical building, and the chance to plunge into the lifestyle of the old-world aristocracy. See p. 167.
- **Pousada de Évora, Lóios** (Évora): This hotel is part of the Pousada chain of inns, most set in grand historic buildings. It was conceived as a convent in the 1400s and stands adjacent to Évora's ancient Roman temple in the heart of the UNESCO World Heritage–protected city. Banish encroachments from the modern world as you dine under the vaulted ceiling of the cloisters, plunge into the courtyard pool, or slumber in a room that was once a medieval monk's cell, but has since moved a long way up the comfort ladder. See p. 280.

- **Vidago Palace** (Chaves): Of all Portugal's grand old spa hotels, this is the grandest. Built in 1910 on the orders of King Carlos I, who wanted a resort to rival the best of Europe, it oozes Belle Epoque glamour. Built over natural spring waters reputed for their curative properties since Roman times, it is surrounded by 100 hectares (250 acres) of forested parkland. Inside, expect expanses of marble, silk wall hangings, and monumental staircases, all tastefully restored when the hotel reopened in 2010. The gourmet restaurant and 18-hole golf course are bonuses. It's an hour's drive from Porto in the heart of Trás-os-Montes. See p. 401.
- **The Yeatman** (Porto): Emerging among the port wine lodges on the south bank of the River Douro, this luxury low-rise, wine-themed hotel ticks all the boxes: fabulous views of Porto and the river from just about every angle (including the bathrooms); a luxurious spa with wine-based treatments; huge, tastefully decorated balconied rooms; a wine list with over 1,000 choices; and last but by no means least, a gourmet restaurant that picked up its second Michelin star in 2017. See p. 345.

PORTUGAL'S best RESTAURANTS

- **Belcanto** (Lisbon): Lisbon's finest fine dining. The flagship of star chef José Avillez won its second Michelin star in 2014. Avillez brings a refined but irreverent approach to his cooking, which is revolutionary but firmly rooted in Portuguese traditions. His exquisite tasting menus can feature radical reworkings of classics like roast suckling pig, oxtail with chickpeas, or the country's Sunday lunch favorite—cozido (a one-pot of boiled meats and vegetables). The dining room is elegant and intimate, off a plaza facing the opera house. See p. 84.
- **Casa Vidal** (Aguada de Cima): The Bairrada wine region between Coimbra and Aveiro is filled with big, unfussy restaurants serving the local specialty: spit-roasted suckling pig. This is the best. They raise their own piglets, prepare a legendary peppery sauce, and have been serving crowds of hungry diners since 1964. Local opinion is split on whether red or white, still or sparkling wines are the best accompaniment. Whatever you chose, the meat will be divine. See p. 309.
- **Casa de Chá da Boa Nova** (Porto): First the location: surging out of rocks lapped by the Atlantic surf. Then the building: Built as a teahouse in the 1960s, this low-rise concrete-glass-and-wood construction is an early masterwork by architectural genius Álvaro Siza Vieira. Then the food, produced by star chef Rui Paula, whose "land and sea" menu combines crawfish with pork, oyster, and apple; wild rabbit with oat, cabbage, and mackerel. See p. 350.
- **Casa dos Passarinhos** (Lisbon): No visit to Portugal is complete without eating in a *tasca*. These are simple taverns, serving up hearty portions of traditional food to hungry workers. This is one of the best: just two simple dining rooms, which fill up quick. Garlicky bread mush with shrimp, deep-fried cuttlefish, and griddled steaks are among the specialties. See p. 90.

- **Estaminé** (Faro): One of Portugal's great gastronomic pleasures is sitting at a beachside restaurant watching the waves roll up to the shore while tucking into expertly prepared seafood that was swimming about beneath those same waves a few hours before. There are many swell places to do that in the Algarve, but Estaminé takes the concept a step further. It's located on a desert island, a short boat ride from the city of Faro, where there's nothing but sand, sea, and sky. Start on seafood specialties like cured belly tuna or razor clams, then settle down to a whole grilled bream, bass, or other fish as the main event. See p. 253.
- **Fialho** (Évora): The cooking of the Alentejo region is considered by many Portuguese to be the country's best. It's based on acorn-reared pork, free-range lamb, game in season, the finest olive oils, and organically grown produce. For more than 70 years this family-run restaurant has been a temple to the region's authentic cruise. The roast lamb is sublime, the rice with wild pigeon delectable, the sliced black pork heavenly. A national treasure (p. 282).
- **IBO** (Lisbon): Portugal's colonial empire is long gone, but its close ties with former outposts bring Brazilian, Goanese, Angolan, and other exotic cuisines in Lisbon and other big cities. This riverside place serves a sophisticated take on the cuisine of Mozambique, a fascinating mix of African, Asian, and European influences. Start with crab and mango salad, move on to fish in coconut and cilantro sauce with sweet potato and cassava, and finish with caramelized banana with sesame. See p. 87.
- **Ramiro** (Lisbon): Bright, noisy, and invariably crowded, Ramiro is monarch of the *marisqueiras*—specialist seafood restaurants. The idea is to take a succession of shellfish dishes: clams steamed with garlic and cilantro, whole crabs (you get a mallet to smash the claws), shrimp in various sizes, goose barnacles that must be wrestled from their leathery sheaths. It's traditional to follow up with a steak sandwich. Lines to get in got longer after a TV rave from Anthony Bourdain. See p. 88.
- **Café Santiago** (Porto): The *francesinha* is Porto's great gift to the sandwich world. A mountainous mix of meats wedged between two hunks of white bread, wrapped in cheese, baked, and served swimming in a piping-hot, spicy sauce. Just about every joint in town serves them. The queue outside will tell you this no-frills eatery produces one of the best. See p. 354.
- **O Sapo** (Penafiel): Before entering, loosen your belt. Better still, don't wear a belt. Portugal's north is famed for eating large, but this rustic place takes it all a step further. They'll start by loading your table with wooden platters filled with appetizers—smoked meats, cheeses, fried balls of salt cod, pigs'-ear salad, egg with cornbread, and so on. Just go with the flow, but remember to leave space for the mighty, meaty main courses. Help it down with the local red *vinho verde* served in china mugs. See p. 358.

PORTUGAL'S best PALACES & CASTLES

- **Palácio da Pena** (Sintra): An extraordinary 19th-century confection sitting atop the Sintra hills, this palace was built by King consort Ferdinand II, the German husband of Portugal's Queen Maria II. It boasts a potpourri of styles—Neo-Gothic, Moorish revival, imitation Renaissance, pastiches of Portugal's maritime-inspired Manueline—inspired by the romantic mountaintop fantasy castles of Bavaria. Painted in shocking reds and yellows, it looms over thick forests, a palace fit for fairytales. See p. 164.
- **Praça-forte de Elvas** (Elvas): As Portugal battled to regain its independence from Spain in the 1640s, the border town of Elvas held a key position on the road from Madrid to Lisbon. To fortify it, they brought in a Dutch military architect, who built the biggest fort of its type in the world. A massive series of defensive walls and ditches circle the pretty, whitewashed town. The fortifications and the aqueduct ensuring the inhabitants could get water even during a siege were declared a UNESCO World Heritage Site in 2012. See p. 275.
- **Casa de Mateus** (Vila Real): Familiar around the world to fans of the rosé wine that bears its name and image on the label, this is the most beautiful of the baroque manor houses scattered around the wine lands of northern Portugal. The reflecting pool out front perfectly duplicates the white-and-gray stone facade with its double staircase and decorative spires, partly the work of the great Italian architect Nicolau Nasoni in the 1740s. It's surrounded by delightful formal gardens. See p. 402.
- **Palácio de Mafra** (Mafra): This was originally supposed to be a convent for a dozen monks, but King João V decided he'd spend some of his Brazilian gold-mine riches expanding it. The result is a monster-sized mix of church and royal residence covering an area bigger than 7 football fields. Completed in 1755, its vast yellow-painted facade dominates the little town of Mafra, just north of Lisbon. The construction forms the backdrop of *Baltasar and Blimunda*, one of the best novels by Nobel Prize–winning author José Saramago. Inside, the royal apartments and old hospital are well worth visiting, but the real treasure is the rococo library lined with almost 40,000 books dating back to the 14th century. See p. 173.

PORTUGAL'S best MUSEUMS

- **Museu Calouste Gulbenkian** (Lisbon): If you go to one museum in Portugal, this should be it. Whatever your taste in art—from ancient Egyptian funeral masks to French Impressionist paintings, Persian carpets to Lalique jewelry—you're sure to find something interesting. The remarkable collection was amassed by Armenian oil magnate Calouste Gulbenkian (1869–1955), who found a home in neutral Portugal during World War II. The museum complex also includes concert halls and a separate modern art museum, all housed in discreet 1960s buildings integrated into shady gardens that are a peaceful getaway in the heart of the city. See p. 107.

- **Museu Nacional do Azulejo** (Lisbon): Wherever you go in Portugal you'll see *azulejos*—painted ceramic tiles used to decorate buildings inside and out, from ancient churches to modern metro stations. The best place to understand this thoroughly Portuguese art form is this museum situated in a 16th-century convent in Lisbon's riverside Madre de Deus neighborhood. The collection contains tiles dating back over 600 years. Highlights include a giant panel showing Lisbon before the great earthquake of 1755 and the convent church filled with tiles and gold leaf. See p. 104.
- **Serralves** (Porto): Porto's modern art museum is housed in a fine Art Deco villa and a purpose-built contemporary gallery built by local architect Álvaro Siza Vieira. It holds a huge collection of Portuguese and international art from the 20th and 21st centuries and hosts temporary exhibitions, serving as the most dynamic cultural center in the north. In 2016, the museum got a boost when it received over 80 works by Spanish artist Joan Miró. See p. 339.
- **Museu Nacional de Arte Antiga** (Lisbon): The country's best collection of Portuguese and international painting is housed in a 17th-century palace high on a cliff overlooking the River Tagus. Much of the collection was brought together from monasteries and noble homes after the civil war of the 1830s. Among the highlights: the nightmarish *Temptations of St. Anthony* by Hieronymus Bosch; Japanese screen paintings showing the arrival of Portuguese mariners in the 16th century; and Nuno Gonçalves' *Panels of St. Vincent*, depicting Lisbon society at the time of the Discoveries. The gardens at the back offer peaceful views over the river. See p. 108.
- **Museu Colecção Berardo** (Lisbon): In the depths of the bunker-like Centro Cultural de Belém is a ground-breaking collection of modern and contemporary art. It was put together by Joe Berardo, an emigrant from Madeira who made a fortune in South Africa. The museum covers the greats of 20th century art including Jackson Pollack, Roy Liechtenstein, and Giorgio de Chirico, along with cutting-edge artists of today. See p. 103.

PORTUGAL'S best CHURCHES & ABBEYS

- **Mosteiro dos Jerónimos** (Lisbon): Begun in 1502 in the riverside Belém district, this great monastery is the best example of the Manueline style developed in Portugal to combine late-Gothic and Renaissance architecture with motifs inspired by the great maritime voyages of discovery. Built from white limestone, the soaring nave of the main church building looks almost organic, like a coral-and-algae-crusted sea cave. Inside are the tombs of explorer Vasco da Gama and poets Luís de Camões and Fernando Pessoa. The cloister, decorated by fine Manueline stonework, is a delight. See p. 102.

- **Santa Maria de Alcobaça** (Alcobaça): Don't be fooled by the ornate baroque facade added in the 18th century. This church was founded in 1153 by Portugal's founding father, King Afonso Henriques. Inside, the slender, soaring nave is done in unadorned early-Gothic style, then newly imported from France by Cistercian monks. The church is the resting place of several medieval royals, among them King Pedro II and his murdered mistress Inês de Castro, whose tragic story has long inspired poets and musicians. Their extravagant tombs are treasures of Gothic stonework. See p. 194.
- **Igreja de São Francisco** (Porto): Porto's "Golden Church" doesn't look like much from its plain Gothic exterior. But inside it is a gilded grotto, shimmering from floor to ceiling with wood carvings coated in gold leaf, a technique known as *talha dourada* developed by Portuguese craftsmen in the 18th century when the precious metal was pouring in from Brazilian mines. The church dates back to 1244. Amid all the gold, the towering "Tree of Jesse" sculpture showing the family tree of Jesus is a standout. See p. 333.
- **Mosteiro da Batalha** (Batalha): In 1385, a Portuguese army defeated a much larger Spanish invasion force in a field south of Leiria, guaranteeing the country's independence for 200 years. To mark the victory, King João I, who led the troops, erected this masterpiece of the Flamboyant style of Gothic architecture close to the battlefield. Using local limestone that glows golden in the setting sun, a succession of architects brought in influences from France, England, and beyond to make a unique construction. Unfortunately, 20th-century planners were less gifted, placing a busy highway close to the main facade. See p. 210.
- **Convento de Cristo** (Tomar): Another World Heritage Site, this convent in the pretty little town of Tomar once served as headquarters for the Knights Templar, who held off a siege by Arab forces in 1190. Around that time, they built a circular church at the center of the convent, taking as their model the Dome of the Rock in Jerusalem. Inside, it is richly decorated with Gothic sculptures and paintings. The Templars were sent packing in the early 1300s, but successive Portuguese monarchs kept adding to the grandeur of the convent, particularly during the Discoveries period, adorning it with some of the best examples of Manueline stonework. See p. 266.

PORTUGAL IN CONTEXT

2

Portugal has always been shaped by the ocean. For centuries, the country turned its back on its often prickly Spanish neighbors and the rest of Europe to the east. It reached out instead to continents beyond the Atlantic. "Where the land ends and the sea begins" was how the revered poet Luís Vaz de Camões defined his homeland in the 16th century.

In Camões' day, Portuguese seafarers like Vasco da Gama and Ferdinand Magellan pushed back the boundaries of the known world, discovering routes to Africa, Asia, and America, laying the foundations for a global empire. Today's Portugal carries the legacy of that Age of Exploration, from the Brazilian gold that lines its churches to the diversity of the population, and the exotic touches that spice Portuguese cuisine.

The sea also provided an escape route. In hard times, millions of emigrants sailed for a better life, founding communities that today flourish as outposts of Portuguese culture, from Massachusetts to Macau, Paris to São Paulo.

Maritime expansion had a dark side. Up to the 1970s, the dictatorship in Lisbon fought to cling to its overseas colonies. The wars left Portugal cut off from the European mainstream, economically backward, and culturally isolated. Since a peaceful 1974 revolution restored democracy, the country has taken huge strides toward modernity. Portugal joined the European Union in 1986 and adopted the euro currency in 1999. Today, Lisbon is fast developing as a tech hub. Tourism is booming, thanks to Portugal's reputation as a safe, easy-on-the-wallet destination, plus the timeless advantages of living on Europe's southwestern seaboard—from the endless sun-kissed beaches to superlative seafood and cities brimming with heritage.

PORTUGAL TODAY

Late in 2015, the global tech community was shocked when the organizers of Web Summit—one of the world's most influential yearly geek gatherings, attracting over 7,000 CEOs—announced they were abandoning their Irish homeland to relocate to Lisbon.

Portugal's government had lobbied hard to secure the summit, offering a prime location beside the River Tagus, but the event's founder, Paddy Cosgrave, saw attractions. "There's just a great community spirit and real optimism about a better tomorrow," he told *The Financial Times*. "I saw it in the incubators I visited and in the bars where I went for drinks with young entrepreneurs and investors... The spirit is just let's work together and set aside past mistakes."

That optimism Cosgrave found stands in contrast to the gloom that had settled over much of Portugal since the country was hit by the international economic crisis in 2009. The shock triggered a long recession that cut short the progress Portugal had been making since the 1980s when it emerged from decades of dictatorship and years of post-revolutionary turmoil. From 2009 to 2013 the economy shrank by 8%. Unemployment hit record levels. Within the euro-zone, only Greece fared worse. Yet although there were demonstrations aplenty, Portugal remained peaceful, escaping the civil unrest endured by Greece. Tens of thousands of young Portuguese, often the best educated and most dynamic, moved abroad to seek opportunities. The media spoke of a "lost generation," but many returned, bringing new skills and experiences, giving Lisbon a renewed creative buzz.

Areas of the economy have bounced back. Textiles and shoe making, traditional industrial mainstays in the north, have re-emerged with a new focus on high-quality production. Portugal is now second only to Italy in terms of high-end footwear exports.

Tourism has boomed, thanks in part to security fears in rival Mediterranean destinations. In recent years, French visitors in particular have been leading demand. Many are coming to stay. Foreign homebuyers—with French and Chinese investors in the forefront—have led a real estate boom contributing to urban renewal in downtown Lisbon and Porto. The property frenzy is also generating concern as locals are pushed out and the spread of vacation rentals erodes the authentic character of historic neighborhoods.

The long recession has left scars. Recovery has been slow, unemployment remains high. Visitors to city centers or the main tourist resorts may see a thriving country, but there's widespread poverty in suburbs and rural areas.

Politically, Portugal took a turn to the left at the end of 2015, with the arrival of Socialist Prime Minister António Costa, who promised to roll back unpopular austerity policies introduced by his center-right predecessor. Costa relies on support in parliament from two far-left parties, but has pledged to respect commitments of fiscal responsibility and avoid a clash with euro-zone partners.

Portugal now looks toward Europe, but retains close economic, political, cultural, and personal ties with its former colonies. Brazilians make up the biggest immigrant community. Angola in 2014 was the biggest market outside Europe for Portuguese exports.

The long recession may have slowed economic progress, but the country is now firmly established as a modern European democracy unrecognizable from the poor, backward dictatorship of the early 1970s. Back then, under over four decades of authoritarian rule instituted by dictator António de Oliveira Salazar, Portuguese women were forbidden to travel without the permission of husbands or fathers, homosexuality was outlawed, and poor children left school illiterate with minimal education.

Today, women make up 34% of lawmakers (compared to 29% in Britain and 19% in the United States). The mainly Roman Catholic nation legalized same-sex marriage in 2010. Education is free and compulsory until the age of 18. The quality of Portugal's universities is gaining international kudos—the numbers of foreign students they attracted rose 76% in the five years up to 2016.

LOOKING BACK: HISTORY

ANCIENT BEGINNINGS Legend has it Lisbon was founded by the Greek hero Ulysses, somewhat off course as he voyaged home from the Trojan War.

It is sure that man and beasts have lived in Portugal for several millennia. Some of Europe's most spectacular dinosaur remains were unearthed at Lourinhã up the coast from Lisbon. Rock carvings in the Côa valley are among humanity's oldest known art. In the Iron Age, Celtic tribes settled and traded with visiting Mediterranean seafarers—Phoenicians, Greeks, and Carthaginians.

The Romans began muscling in around 200 B.C. as part of their struggle with Carthage for Mediterranean supremacy. They met tough resistance from the Lusitanians, a Celtic tribe whose leader, Viriato, is Portugal's oldest national hero. As usual, the Romans won, but they named their new province Lusitania after their defeated foes. For around 600 years, they built roads and cities, kept order, and eventually introduced Christianity.

INVASIONS FROM NORTH & SOUTH As Roman power waned, the Iberian Peninsula filled with Germanic folk. The Suevi founded a kingdom

DATELINE

- **22000–10000 B.C.** Paleolithic people create some of the world's earliest art with rock carvings of animals in the valley of the Côa River.
- **210 B.C.** Romans begin takeover of the Iberian Peninsula.
- **139 B.C.** Local Lusitanian tribes and their leader Viriato defeated by the Romans after 15 years of resistance.
- **27 B.C.** Emperor Augustus creates the province of Hispania Ulterior Lusitania comprising much of Portugal and western Spain.
- **A.D. 409** Germanic tribes begin invasion of Roman Iberia. The Visigoths gain control of Portugal.
- **711** Muslim warriors arrive in Iberia, conquering Portugal within 7 years.
- **868** County of Portugal created in today's Minho region by the Spanish kingdom of Asturias on land reconquered from the Muslims.
- **1018** Arab rulers in the Algarve declare their emirate independent of the Muslim Caliphate in southern Spain.

covering northern Portugal that lasted 150 years. They were ousted in 588 by the Visigoths, who built a Christian kingdom covering Spain and Portugal, and made Braga a major religious center.

In 711, Islamic warriors crossed from North Africa. They took less than a decade to conquer almost all of the peninsula and would remain for over 8 centuries. At times, Portugal formed part of powerful Caliphates based in Cordoba, Seville, or Marrakesh. At others, local emirs ran independent Muslim kingdoms like those in the Algarve, Lisbon, and Mértola. Arabic influences are still felt in Portugal's culture, cuisine, and language.

PORTUGAL IS BORN In the early days, resistance to Muslim rule was led by the Kingdom of Asturias in the high mountains of northern Spain. Toward the end of the 9th century, land between the Minho and Douro rivers was reconquered and given the name Portocale after a Roman-era town close to today's Porto.

Christian knights from across Europe traveled to join the fight. One was Henry of Burgundy, given the title Count of Portugal in 1092 by his father-in-law, one of the kings of León. When Henry died young, his son, Afonso Henriques, took the title, but since the boy was just 3 years old, his mother Teresa got to rule the country.

As he grew, Afonso became unhappy with his mother's politics and her love life, viewing her cozy relations with a leading Spanish nobleman a threat. The youngster led a rebellion by Portuguese nobles, defeated Teresa at a battle outside Guimarães, and in 1139 declared himself King Afonso I of Portugal.

Impressed by Afonso's prowess battling the Muslims and his enthusiastic church construction program, the Pope confirmed Portugal's status as an independent kingdom in 1179.

1139 Afonso Henriques is proclaimed the first king of Portugal after leading a rebellion against his mother and her allies in the Spanish kingdom of Leon.

1147 After a 4-month siege, Afonso I captures Lisbon from the Arabs with the aid of northern European crusaders.

1249 Afonso III completes the *Reconquista*, taking the Algarve from the Muslims.

1290 Portugal's first university formed in Coimbra.

1373 Portugal signs treaty with England forming the world's oldest surviving diplomatic alliance.

1383 King João I defeats Castilian invaders at the Battle of Aljubarrota, securing Portugal's independence.

1415 Henry the Navigator sets up a navigation school in Sagres. Portugal conquers Ceuta in North Africa, triggers era of overseas expansion. Madeira is discovered in 1419; the Azores in 1427.

1434 Sea captain Gil Eanes rounds Cape Bojador, opening up the coast of West Africa.

1484 Diogo Cão discovers the Congo River.

continues

THE RECONQUISTA With the aid of Northern European crusaders, Afonso expanded his kingdom southward. Lisbon was reconquered after a 4-month siege in 1147. Fighting ebbed and flowed, but Afonso Henriques' great-grandson, Afonso III, completed the Portuguese *reconquista* in 1249, driving the Muslims out of their last stronghold in Faro.

The danger now came from the east in the shape of the powerful Spanish kingdom of Castile. Clashes between Portugal and Castile were common even as both fought the Muslims. In 1385, Spanish king Juan I sent an invasion force of 30,000 to back his claim to the Portuguese throne. They were defeated at the Battle of Aljubarrota by much-outnumbered Portuguese forces in a struggle that preserved Portuguese independence and helped forge a national identity. Legend has it a baker-woman wielding heavy wooden bread trays joined the fray, whacking several Castilian knights. French cavalry backed the Spanish while English archers joined the defenders under the Anglo-Portuguese treaty of 1373—the world's oldest surviving diplomatic alliance. Victorious King João I built the magnificent Gothic monastery at Batalha, now a UNESCO World Heritage Site, to celebrate his win.

THE AGE OF DISCOVERY With its frontiers secured, Portugal started looking overseas. In 1415, João I opened the era of maritime expansion when he captured the city of Ceuta on the coast of North Africa. João's son, Henry, fought at the battle to win Ceuta from the Moroccans. He never voyaged farther, but would change the face of world history and be forever known as Henry the Navigator.

Henry gathered sailors and scholars on the wind-swept southwestern tip of Europe at Sagres to brainstorm on what may lay beyond. Using new navigational technology and more maneuverable boats, the Portuguese sent out probing voyages that discovered Madeira Island off the coast of Africa around 1420 and the mid-Atlantic Azores 8 years later.

1488	Bartolomeu Dias passes the Cape of Good Hope into the Indian Ocean.
1494	Portugal and Spain divide up the New World with the Treaty of Tordesillas.
1497	Manuel I orders expulsion of Portuguese Jews.
1497–98	Vasco da Gama's first voyage to India, opening up East-West trade.
1500	Pedro Álvares Cabral discovers Brazil; Corte-Real brothers sail to Newfoundland.
1506	Lisbon Massacre: hundreds murdered in anti-Jewish pogrom.
1510	Afonso de Albuquerque conquers Goa, starting Portuguese colonization in India.
1542	Inquisition installed in Portugal. It will execute hundreds accused of being Jews.
1542	Portuguese seafarers reach Japan.
1578	King Sebastião I killed in disastrous invasion of Morocco, leaving Portugal without an heir.
1581	Philip II of Spain proclaimed king of Portugal, ushering in 6 decades of Spanish rule.
1640	Portuguese nobles rebel, proclaim the Duke of Bragança as João IV; a 28-year war will restore independence.

PEDRO & INÊS: A MEDIEVAL love story

Centuries before Shakespeare gave us Romeo and Juliet, Portugal was gripped by its own tale of star-crossed lovers.

Seeking Spanish alliances, King Afonso IV in 1339 married off his son and heir, Pedro, to Constance, a Castilian princess. Nineteen-year-old Pedro promptly fell in love with one of his new wife's ladies-in-waiting, a noblewoman called Inês de Castro. They began a very public affair and Inês bore Pedro three children.

King Afonso was outraged, frightened of offending the Castilians and worried about the influence of Inês' ambitious brothers. He pleaded with Pedro to break it off, then banished Inês to the Santa Clara Monastery in Coimbra. When all that failed to break Pedro's passion, Afonso had Inês murdered. In Coimbra today, beneath the clear spring water that bubbles to the surface at the spot where she was decapitated, there's a red rock, supposedly forever stained by her blood.

Grieve-stricken, Pedro revolted against his father. He captured two of the killers and personally ripped out their hearts. Pedro became king when Afonso died in 1357 and announced that he'd secretly married Inês before her death. On the day of his coronation, Pedro ordered Inês' corpse removed from its tomb, dressed in a regal gown, and crowned queen beside him. Portugal's nobles lined up to kiss the hand of the woman slain two years before.

The story has inspired poets, painters, and musicians from Camões to Ezra Pound. Today, Pedro and Inês lie side by side in ornate tombs within the great medieval monastery at Alcobaça.

A breakthrough came in 1434, when captain Gil Eanes sailed around Cape Bojador, a remote Saharan promontory that had marked the limits of European knowledge of the African coast. Eanes showed the sea beyond was not boiling and monster-filled, as was believed. The way was opened to Africa and beyond.

1661 Princess Catarina da Bragança marries Charles II of England, gives him Mumbai and Tangiers as wedding presents, introduces the British to tea.

1697 The discovery of gold in southern Brazil makes João V Europe's richest monarch; he builds gilded palaces, churches.

1755 Earthquake destroys Lisbon, killing up to 50,000. Prime Minister Sebastião de Melo, Marquis of Pombal, leads reconstruction efforts.

1807 Napoleon invades; British troops under Duke of Wellington will finally send him back to France in 1814.

1822 Brazil declares independence.

1828–34 War of the Two Brothers between liberal Pedro IV and conservative Miguel I leaves Portugal further weakened.

1856 First railroad opens in Portugal, but the 19th century sees economic decline and political instability.

1908 Carlos I and his son Crown Prince Luís Filipe are assassinated.

1910 Republican revolution overturns the monarchy.

1916 Portugal enters World War I on the Allied side.

continues

In the years that followed, Portuguese navigators pushed down the West African coast. They sailed into the Gulf of Guinea. Henry died in 1460, but the exploration went on. Portuguese explorers were finding more and more of what they were looking for: gold, ivory, spices, and slaves. By 1482, Diogo Cão reached the mouth of the Congo River. In 1488, Bartolomeu Dias sailed past Africa's southern tip: He called it the Cape of Storms, but the name was quickly changed to Cape of Good Hope to encourage further voyages. That worked. Vasco da Gama traded and raided up the coast of east Africa. Then in 1498, he reached India. World trade would never be the same. Over the next 4 decades, Portuguese explorers moved into southeast Asia, up the coast of China, and eventually into Japan. Along the way they set up trading posts and colonies. Portugal grew rich by dominating east-west exchanges and forging the first global empire. But the Portuguese also destroyed cities reluctant to submit to their power and frequently massacred civilians.

There were setbacks. In the 1480s, King João II rejected repeated requests to finance the westward exploration plans of a Genovese seafarer called Christopher Columbus, who eventually claimed the New World for his Spanish sponsors. And King Manuel I took a dislike to veteran Portuguese sea dog Fernão de Magalhães. Piqued, he crossed the border with his plans to reach Asia by sailing west and ended up leading the Spanish fleet that became the first to sail around the world. Later historians called him Ferdinand Magellan.

The Portuguese also moved west. Six years after Spain and Portugal agreed to divide up the world with the 1492 Treaty of Tordesillas, Pedro Álvares Cabral discovered Brazil, which conveniently lies on the eastern Portuguese side of the dividing line.

A small arched building in the Algarve coastal town of Lagos has a grim past. It is reputed to be the site of Europe's oldest African slave market, first used in the early 15th century. Early Portuguese settlers in Brazil began using

1926	After years of political chaos, a military coup topples the Republic.
1932	António de Oliveira Salazar appointed prime minister, establishing a conservative dictatorship that will last over 4 decades.
1939–45	Portugal stays out of World War II. In France, diplomat Aristides de Sousa Mendes defies orders, saving thousands of Jews by issuing visas to neutral Portugal.
1961	Insurgent attacks in Angola start 14 years of colonial war in Portugal's African empire; Indian army drives Portugal out of Goa.
1974	Almost bloodless revolution led by junior army officers topples the dictatorship.
1975	Portugal grants independence to five African colonies; brings home up to a million refugees.
1976	After a power struggle with leftist radicals, General António Ramalho Eanes is elected president, steers Portugal toward pro-Western path.
1980	Center-right Prime Minister Francisco de Sá Carneiro is killed in mysterious air crash.
1986	Portugal joins the European Union.

captured natives as slaves, but as demands of sugar plantations and gold mines grew in the 17th and 18th centuries, more and more slaves were shipped from Africa. Slavery was abolished in Portugal itself in 1761, but it continued in its African colonies until 1869 and in Brazil until 1888, 66 years after the South American country's independence.

INDEPENDENCE LOST & RESTORED In 1578, Portugal overreached. King Sebastião I, an impetuous 24-year-old, invaded Morocco. He was last seen charging into enemy lines at the disastrous Battle of Alcácer Quibir, where a large slice of the Portuguese nobility was wiped out. Sebastião had neglected to father an heir before he set off. An elderly great-uncle briefly took over, but he was a cardinal known as Henry the Chaste, so when he died in 1580, Portugal was left without a monarch. King Philip II of Spain's army marched in, crushed local resistance, seized a fortune in Lisbon, and extinguished Portuguese independence for the next 60 years.

Iberian union made Philip ruler of the greatest empire the world had ever seen, controlling much of the Americas, a network of colonies in Asia and Africa, and European territories that included the Netherlands and half of Italy. Spanish rule strained Portugal's old alliance with England: The Spanish Armada sailed from Lisbon, and Sir Francis Drake raided the Portuguese coast.

By 1640, the Portuguese had had enough. While Spain was distracted fighting France in the 30 Years War, a group of nobles revolted and declared the Duke of Bragança to be King João IV. It took 28 years, but the Portuguese eventually won the War of Restoration. An obelisk in one of Lisbon's main plazas commemorates the victory.

Meanwhile a new enemy, the Dutch, had seized some of Portugal's overseas territories. Malacca and Ceylon (today's Sri Lanka) were lost. Faced with such threats, João IV strengthened Portugal's British alliance by marrying his

1987 Center-right Social Democratic Party under Prime Minister Aníbal Cavaco Silva wins electoral landslide.

1998 Millions flock to Lisbon for EXPO '98 World's Fair; economic growth peaks at over 7%.

1999 Portugal becomes founder member of euro currency bloc.

2004 Prime Minister José Manuel Barroso appointed President of the European Commission.

2011 Hit hard by euro-zone debt crisis, Portugal requests $86 billion IMF-EU bailout; prolonged recession, record unemployment.

2014 Banco Espírito Santo, Portugal's second-largest bank, collapses.

2015 Left wins narrow election victory; minority Socialist government takes power under Prime Minister António Costa, vows to roll back austerity.

2016 Cristiano Ronaldo leads Portugal to victory in Euro 2016 soccer championship, country goes wild; former Prime Minister António Guterres appointed U.N. Secretary General.

FOUR NAVIGATORS WHO CHANGED world maps

From 1415 to 1580, Portuguese explorers opened up the world, discovering new routes from Europe to Africa, Asia, and the Americas. They created a global empire and rewrote world maps.

Bartolomeo Dias (ca. 1450–1500) was 38 and from a family of navigators when he led an expedition of three boats down the coast of West Africa in 1487. He failed in his mission to find the mythical Christian kingdom of Prester John, but became the first European to sail around the southern tip of Africa into the Indian Ocean. Dias was killed in a shipwreck off the Cape of Good Hope in 1500 while serving with Pedro Alvares Cabral on the expedition that discovered Brazil.

Vasco da Gama (ca. 1460–1524) didn't discover India—wealthy Europeans had been spicing their food with its cinnamon, pepper, and nutmeg for centuries—but the trade was controlled by price-hiking Venetian, Turkish, and Arab middlemen. By discovering the sea route in 1498, da Gama opened up direct trade between Europe and Asia. His adventures are celebrated in Portugal's national epic, *Os Lusíadas*, by swashbuckling 16th-century poet Luís de Camões. The two men are buried near each other in Lisbon's Jerónimos monastery. Da Gama died of malaria in 1524 in Kochi on his third voyage to India. Europe's longest bridge, a city in western India, and a leading Brazilian soccer club bear his name.

Brazil was discovered by accident in 1500, when the fleet of 13 ships commanded by **Pedro Álvares Cabral** (ca. 1467–1520) sailed too far west while heading down the coast of Africa on the new route opened by da Gama. At least that's the official story. Some believe the Portuguese already knew about Brazil but kept it quiet until they had concluded the 1492 Treaty of Tordesillas with Spain to divide the world along a line halfway between Portugal's Cape Verde outpost and the newly discovered Spanish territories in the Caribbean. Brazil was clearly in the Portuguese sphere. Cabral didn't stay long, but sailed on to Africa and India, becoming the first man to visit four continents. In India, he started a war with the state of Kozhikode, but got away laden with valuable spices. His birthplace in the pretty village of Belmonte and tomb in Santarém are much visited by Brazilian travelers.

In 1519, **Ferdinand Magellan** (ca. 1480–1521) was a 39-year-old veteran of the Portuguese Discoveries. He'd served 8 years in India, fighting against Turks, Arabs, and Indian states. He played a key role in the capture of Malacca, a hub for Portuguese power, in southeast Asia. He picked up a wound at the siege of Azemmour in Morocco. Yet despite all this service, he managed to annoy King Manuel I. There were rumors he went AWOL, had rustled cattle, and engaged in shady deals with the Moroccans. Unable to get a ship in Lisbon, he went to Spain, where his stories of Spice Island riches convinced Emperor Charles V to send him on a mission to reach Asia by sailing west—avoiding the Portuguese-controlled eastern routes. Magellan led the fleet into the Pacific as far as the Philippines, where he was speared to death in battle with local warriors. What was left of the exhibition sailed on. Only one of the five ships made it back to Spain, the first to sail around the globe.

daughter Catherine of Bragança to King Charles II. Her dowry included Tangiers and Mumbai. Perhaps more significantly for the British, she introduced them to marmalade and the habit of drinking hot water flavored with a

PORTUGAL'S jewish heritage

In 1497, King Manuel I, the monarch behind the golden age of Portugal's Discoveries, married a Spanish princess, a political move designed to improve relations with the powerful neighbor. Spain's condition: Portugal had to get rid of its thriving Jewish community, as Spain had done 5 years before. Manuel agreed, ordering all Jews to convert to Catholicism or leave. Many fled, finding refuge in the Ottoman Empire, North Africa, France, and the Netherlands, where they built Amsterdam's splendid Portuguese Synagogue. Others stayed and accepted conversion, becoming so-called "New Christians."

They were still not safe. In 1506, a riot over Easter led to the murder of up to 2,000 *conversos* in what became known as the Lisbon Massacre. Manuel I executed some of the perpetrators, but 30 years later the state institutionalized persecution when it set up a Portuguese branch of the Inquisition, tasked with hunting down heretics—especially converts suspected of maintaining Jewish practices in secret. It ordered almost 1,200 burned at the stake over the next 2 centuries and was only abolished in 1821. Nevertheless, some crypto-Jews managed to cling to their faith. A community in the remote village of Belmonte practiced in secret into the 1980s. There is now a small but open community there with their own rabbi.

Jews began returning to a more tolerant Portugal in the 19th century. During World War II, neutral Portugal became a haven for many fleeing the Nazis. Although dictator António Oliveira Salazar tried to prevent Jewish refugees arriving in 1940 as Hitler's troops marched into France, the Portuguese consul in Bordeaux, Aristides de Sousa Mendes, defied orders and handed out thousands of visas, saving up to 30,000 lives. Salazar ruined his career and plunged his family into poverty, but Sousa Mendes is today regarded as a national hero.

President Mário Soares formally asked for forgiveness for past persecution in 1989. In 2015, Portugal's parliament passed a law offering citizenship to the descendants of Jews expelled from the country. Today there are small Jewish communities, mostly in Lisbon, Porto, and Madeira Island, but recent genetic studies suggest that up to 20% of Portugal's population may have Jewish ancestry.

new-fangled Asian herb they called tea. In return, the British named one of their American settlements in her honor: Queens.

Fortunately for the Portuguese, they managed to hang on to Brazil through these turbulent times. At the end of the 17th century, huge gold deposits were found inland from São Paulo. The gold rush made King João V the richest monarch in Europe. He used it to build the vast palace at Mafra and to line baroque churches up and down the country with glimmering gilt carvings.

DISASTER & DECLINE On All Saints' Day in 1755, churches were packed when Lisbon was struck by great earthquake. The tremor was followed by a tsunami and raging fire. Much of the city was destroyed. Up to 50,000 people are believed to have died. Reconstruction was led by Prime Minister Sebastião José de Carvalho e Melo, later Marquis of Pombal. He laid out Lisbon's downtown, or Baixa, in the grid pattern of sturdy, four-story buildings that remains today, although the Gothic ruins of the Carmo Convent were left overlooking the city as reminder of the quake's destructive force.

Pombal also battled to modernize the country. He curbed the powers of the Inquisition and expelled the Jesuit order. Foreign experts were brought in to expand industry and agriculture. Education and the military were reorganized.

Still, Portugal's days as a great power were already long gone when French troops marched in as part of Napoleon's grand design for European domination. The French met little resistance and the royal family fled to Rio de Janeiro. Harsh French rule, however, saw uprisings in Spain and Portugal. Eventually Portugal's old ally was able to land troops in support, and after a long campaign, the Duke of Wellington led a combined British and Portuguese army that drove Napoleon's forces back to France in 1814.

Portugal was much weakened. The decline was compounded when Brazil declared independence in 1822 and civil war broke out in the 1830s between the liberal King Pedro IV (also Emperor Pedro I of Brazil) and his conservative brother, Miguel I.

As Europe pushed ahead with industrialization in the 19th century, Portugal fell further behind, dogged by political instability and slipping into economic backwardness. Government debt mounted, pushing the state toward bankruptcy.

Unrest grew. In 1908, King Carlos I and his oldest son were assassinated in Lisbon's Praça do Comércio. Two years later, Lisbon erupted in revolution, the monarchy was overthrown, and the last king, Manuel II, left for exile.

The change of regime did little to ease Portugal's economic woes or political tensions. Over the next 16 years, there were no less than 49 governments. Portugal entered World War I in 1916 on the side of its old ally, Britain. Around 8,000 soldiers were killed in France and Africa. Instability continued until a military coup in 1926 put an end to the first Republic.

DICTATORSHIP & DEMOCRACY The junta appointed António de Oliveira Salazar as finance minister in 1928. He became the dominant figure in Portugal's 20th-century history, establishing a dictatorship that ruled with an iron hand for over 4 decades. Prime minister from 1932, Salazar constructed a Fascist-inspired regime, the *Estado Novo*, or New State. He brought some order to the economy and managed to keep Portugal neutral during World War II. Dissent was suppressed and censorship strict. A secret police force—the PIDE—spread fear; opponents were jailed or worse.

In 1961, the regime was shaken by an Indian invasion of Goa, Daman, and Diu, Portugal's last colonies in south Asia. That same year, pro-independence forces launched attacks in Angola, the start of war across Portugal's African empire. Salazar struck back, dispatching ever more conscripts to fight rebel movements in Angola, Mozambique, and Guinea-Bissau. Proportionally, Portugal suffered more casualties in the colonial wars than the U.S. in Vietnam. The fighting drained the economy and left Portugal internationally isolated. Hundreds of thousands of Portuguese emigrants fled poverty, oppression, and conscription, mostly to France, Switzerland, and Luxembourg.

Salazar suffered a stroke in 1968 and died 2 years later, but the regime limped on. On April 25, 1974, a group of war-weary officers staged a coup and the people of Lisbon rose up to support the troops. Flower sellers in Rossio square handed out spring blooms to the young soldiers and sailors, so the uprising was immortalized as the "Carnation Revolution." Censorship was lifted, exiles returned, and political prisoners were released to joyous scenes.

The revolutionaries, however, faced enormous difficulties. The wars were ended and independence hastily granted to the African colonies. Portugal then had to organize the evacuation and integration of a million refugees fleeing the new nations. Investors retreated as radical leftists ordered the nationalization of banks, industry, and farmland. For a while the country looked like it would veer toward communism.

Then, in 1976, the first presidential elections brought a moderate, General António Ramalho Eanes, to office. Socialist Party leader Mário Soares was elected prime minister the same year. Together they steered Portugal on a pro-Western course. It remained a loyal NATO ally and joined the European Union along with Spain in 1986. The previous year, Aníbal Cavaco Silva, leader of the center-right Social Democratic Party, won a landslide election on a pledge to free up the economy. The combined impact of EU membership and stable, business-friendly government led to an economic boom and rapid modernization. In 1999, Portugal handed Macau back to China, ending almost 600 years of overseas empire. Women's rights made giant strides. The successful hosting of the EXPO '98 World's Fair in Lisbon symbolized Portugal's emergence as a successful European democracy.

However, problems lay ahead. The rise of China and the EU's inclusion of new members from eastern Europe exposed the Portuguese economy to competition it was ill-equipped to handle. The global financial crisis of 2008 hit hard. As the economy tanked and debt soared, the government was forced in 2011 to seek a bailout from the EU and International Monetary Fund to stave off bankruptcy. In exchange for a 78€-billion rescue package, creditors demanded tough measures to bring state finances under control. The economy stabilized, but at a high cost in unemployment, cuts to public services, and increased poverty. After elections in November 2015, a new Socialist government was narrowly elected under Prime Minister António Costa, promising to ease up on austerity.

In July 2016, spirits received an enormous boost from the victory of Portugal's national soccer team in the European championships. The first major success for a soccer-crazy nation triggered country-wide celebrations.

ART & ARCHITECTURE

From prehistoric carvings to world-class contemporary buildings, Portugal is packed with art and architecture that reflect the country's history and unique style. A country the size of Maine, it has 14 UNESCO World Heritage Sites—four more than the entire United States.

ANCIENT BEGINNINGS Discovered in the 1990s and saved from destruction during a dam-building project, the outdoor rock carvings in the **Côa valley** form some of humanity's oldest art. The oldest of the enigmatic animal depictions date back to 22000 B.C. A state-of-the-art hilltop museum explains the site and arranges visits to the rocks.

Portugal is dotted with standing stones and prehistoric tombs. The most complete include the **Almendres Cromlech,** made up of circles of almost 100 menhirs near Évora that dates back to 6000 B.C., and the **Great Dolmen of Comenda da Igreja,** a Stone-Age burial site outside Montemor-o-Novo.

Northern Portugal contains some of Europe's best-preserved remains of fortified hilltop villages built by the ancient Celts. Those of **Citânia de Briteiros** near Guimarães and **Monte Mozinho** close to Penafiel are well worth a visit.

FROM ROMAN TO ROMANESQUE During 600 years of occupation, the Romans built cities, roads, and villas across the country. To get an idea of life in Roman Portugal, visit **Conímbriga,** 16km (10 miles) south of Coimbra, where the remains of a complete settlement have been excavated complete with baths, forum, theater, and mosaic-decorated private homes. Other Roman monuments include the 1st-century **Temple de Diana** in Évora, a bridge constructed during the reign of Emperor Trajan that's still used in **Chaves,** and the well-preserved remains of ancient Coimbra beneath the **Museu Machado de Castro.**

Few physical traces remain of the Germanic peoples who flowed in after the Romans, although the **Chapel of São Frutuoso** in Braga is of Visigoth origin. The pretty town of **Mertola** in the Alentejo region was briefly the capital of an Arab kingdom. Its mosque was converted into the parish church but still offers the best example of Islamic architecture in Portugal. Several medieval castles also bear witness to Portugal's Muslim past, notably that in **Silves** and the hilltop **Castelo dos Mouros** in Sintra.

As the *reconquista* gathered pace in the 10th century, churches in the European Romanesque style sprang up across northern Portugal. The cathedrals of Braga and Lisbon date from this time, but **Sé Velha** in Coimbra is where the Romanesque style is at its purest, with fewer later additions. The **Rates Monastery** near Póvoa de Varzim is one of the oldest Romanesque buildings. Others can be discovered along the **Romanesque Route** (*Rota do Românico*) linking over 50 churches and other monuments in the hills east of Porto. The granite **Domus Municipalis** (municipal house) in Bragança is a rare example of civic architecture to survive from the period.

Portugal's most remarkable Romanesque building forms the core of the **Convent of Christ** in Tomar. The circular 12th-century church was built by the Knights Templar who had their base here. They copied it from the ancient churches in Jerusalem that the knights had visited during the Crusades. The whole magnificent complex, which includes later medieval and renaissance additions, is a UNESCO World Heritage Site.

THE GOTHIC ERA The history of the Gothic style in Portugal is bookended by two fab monasteries, built just 25km (14 miles) apart. **Alcobaça Monastery** was built in the 12th century, its white stone arches following the pure, unadorned style imported from France by the Cistercian order of monks. Although the church's exterior was significantly modified in the baroque era, the interior remains a hugely atmospheric medieval monument. Constructed 2 centuries later to celebrate a famous victory over invading Spaniards, **Batalha Monastery** is a flamboyant example of the ornate late Gothic style, bristling with statues, spires, and richly decorated arches. Lit by the setting sun, its limestone facade glows golden. Both monasteries are now UNESCO Sites.

Between these two masterpieces, major Gothic churches were built all around the country; the **Church of São Francisco** in Porto, **Évora Cathedral,** and the ruined **Carmo** convent in Lisbon are among the best. However, **Santarém,** high on the north bank of the Tagus River, holds the title "capital of Gothic," thanks to the sheer number of medieval churches there.

PORTUGAL'S UNIQUE MANUELINE STYLE Named for King Manuel I, the monarch behind Portugal's era of Discoveries, the Manueline style is unique to Portugal. It combines elements of medieval Gothic and the new ideas of the Renaissance, but adds elements inspired by Portugal's adventures on the high seas. Maritime motives become an integral part of the architecture—shells, ropes, branches of coral, and navigational instruments, as well as exotic touches brought back from distant lands.

Best-known among the Manueline monuments are the iconic **Torre de Belém** fortress guarding the Tagus River in Lisbon's Belém neighborhood and the neighboring **Jerónimos Monastery,** a spectacular building containing the tombs of explorer Vasco da Gama, poets Luís de Camões and Fernando Pessoa, as well as King Manuel himself.

Other fine examples of the Manueline style can be found in Tomar's Convent of Christ, the **Royal Palace** in Sintra, and the **Monastery of Jesus** in Setúbal.

The Discoveries period also saw a flowering of Portuguese painting. The country most cherished art work is **Nuno Gonçalves**' giant *Panels of Saint Vincent*, which contains portraits of 60 people, a cross-section of 15th-century society, from nobility (including Henry the Navigator) to friars and fishermen. It alone justifies a visit to Lisbon's Museu Nacional de Arte Antiga.

A RICH handicraft tradition

Aside from high art, Portugal retains a wealth of regional handicraft traditions. The small town of **Arraiolos** in the Alentejo is famed for carpets, woven from local wool into designs that reflect the flowers of the region. Hand-painted pottery from **Coimbra** is refined and colorful, based on designs from the 15th and 16th centuries. Artists around **Barcelos** in the Minho have always produced ceramic figures: demons, saints, and the rooster, which has become a national symbol. Delicate golden filigree jewelry is a specialty of **Viana do Castelo.** **Madeira** is famed for lacework. Many countries produce decorated ceramic tiles, but in few are they so central to the folk art tradition as *azulejos* are to Portugal. They appear on buildings ranging from ancient churches to brand new subway stations. Even the sidewalks can be works of art. The *calçada portuguesa* technique uses small cubes of white and black limestone to make patterned pavements that are found around Lisbon and other Portuguese cities—Rossio square in the heart of the capital is one fine example.

Another renowned painter of the Discoveries period is **Grão Vasco,** best known for his sumptuous religious works. Many are displayed in the excellent Grão Vasco museum in his hometown of Viseu.

BAROQUE GOLD The drama and exuberance of the baroque style were embraced across the Catholic world in response to austere Protestant values. Nowhere was this truer than in Portugal and its empire, where the wealth pouring in from Brazilian gold fields in the 17th and 18th centuries fueled a spending spree on ornate churches and palaces.

Two specifically Portuguese art forms thrived in this period: *talha dourada*, wood carving gilded with gold leaf, and the glazed ceramic tiles known as *azulejos*. The combination of the intricately carved altars gleaming with gold and the soft blue and while tiles makes church interiors of this period uniquely beautiful. Wonderful examples can be found in the **São Roque** church in Lisbon, the church of **Santa Clara in** Porto, or the tiny church of **São Lourenço de Almancil** in the Algarve. Elsewhere, baroque architects demand an upward gaze: The 75-meter (246-ft.) tower of the **Clérigos** church is a symbol of the city of Porto, while Braga and Lamego both have hilltop churches reached by monumental stairways.

Secular art also thrived in the baroque era, including the **Queluz Royal Palace,** the **Palácio de Mateus** vila near Vila Real, and the splendid **Joanina Library** in Coimbra University. Putting all the others into shade, however, is the enormous **Mafra Palace,** built by King João V, north of Lisbon. It covers an area larger than seven football fields, filled with sumptuous ballrooms, churches, a hospital, and a library lined with 36,000 volumes. The 4 decades of construction feature prominently in *Baltasar and Blimunda*, one of the best novels by Nobel Prize–winner author José Saramago.

Portugal's greatest sculptor emerged during this period—**Joaquim Machado de Castro** (1731–1822), whose works grace many churches and plazas, including the statue of King Jose I on horseback in the center of Lisbon's Praça do Comércio.

RECONSTRUCTION & ROMANCE After the excesses of the baroque era, the Marquis of Pombal imposed his sober-minded architectural vision after the great earthquake of 1755. The prime minister ordered the rebuilding of Lisbon's **Baixa** district in an orderly grid pattern of solid, unadorned blocks. In the Algarve, an entire town, **Vila Real de Santo António,** was laid out in this Pombaline style.

Architecture in the 19th century looked backward. Ancient Athens inspired neoclassical buildings like Lisbon's **Dona Maria National Theater** or the **São Bento palace,** which houses the parliament. Other styles looked closer to home. The sumptuous **Arab Room** in Porto's Stock Exchange is a gilded Moorish fantasy. Nostalgia for the Age of Discovery saw the development of a neo-Manueline fashion represented by Lisbon's **Rossio station,** or the delightfully romantic **Buçaco Palace,** a royal residence that's now a luxury hotel surrounded by lush forest. The Romantic movement in Portuguese architecture reached its peak with the completion in 1854 of the mountaintop

Pena Palace in Sintra, a multicolored potpourri of styles devised by Ferdinand, the German prince married to Queen Maria II.

Industrialization was slow coming to Portugal, but the building of the railroads created a network of stations decorated with exquisitely painted *azulejo* tiles. The stations in Aveiro, the Douro wine town of **Pinhão,** and **São Bento** in Porto are among the prettiest. The railway also graced Porto with a magnificent iron bridge over the Douro. The **Maria Pia Bridge** (p. 342) was built in 1877 by a French engineer called Gustave Eiffel, who went on to build a certain tower in Paris. At the time, it was the world's longest single-arch bridge. Nine years later, a colleague of Eiffel's built an even longer span just next door: the double-decker **Dom Luís I Bridge**. Portugal's other great iron structure of the Industrial Age is the **Santa Justa Elevator,** a startling 13-meter (43-ft.) tower that offers vertical transportation between Lisbon's downtown and the chic shops of the Chiado district.

Despite political turmoil and economic decline, the arts flourished in the 19th century. Talented naturalist painters included **José Malhoa** (1855–1933), best known for his depictions of fado singers and boozers in Lisbon taverns, and **Columbano Bordalo Pinheiro** (1856–1929), arguably Portugal's greatest painter, whose impressionistic portraits captured intellectual life in the capital. Columbano's dandyish brother, **Rafael Bordalo Pinheiro** (1846–1905), a sculptor, created fantastical ceramic works that range from plates and bowls decorated with animal and plant motifs to comic figurines caricaturing figures of the day. His works remain hugely popular and are still produced in the factory he built in Caldas da Rainha.

20TH CENTURY The most influential figure in Portuguese modern art was **Amadeo de Souza Cardoso** (1887–1918), a daring figure who painted bold, bright canvases, flirting with cubism, futurism, and abstraction. Souza Cardoso was cut down young by the Spanish flu epidemic, but international interest in his work was revived in 2016 by a major exhibition in Paris.

PORTUGUESE ART'S armenian connection

Lisbon's art scene owes an inestimable debt to an Armenian-born philanthropist named Calouste Gulbenkian. One of the first to appreciate the potential of Middle East oil, Gulbenkian amassed a fortune in the early–20th century.

He settled in neutral Lisbon in 1942 to escape WWII. When he died 13 years later, Gulbenkian thanked his adopted homeland by leaving much of his wealth to a foundation based there to promote culture, education, and science. Located in a shady park, the Gulbenkian Foundation remains a driving force behind the arts. Its concert halls offer some of the city's best classical, jazz, and world music.

The Gulbenkian Museum is a must-see attraction housing the tycoon's wonderfully diverse collection—from ancient Egyptian statuary to French Impressionist masterpieces, fine Ming vases to exquisite Persian rugs. Its collection of Fabergé jewelry is dazzling. The Modern Art museum at the Gulbenkian showcases Portuguese and international works from the 20th and 21st centuries.

Other 20th-century giants in Portuguese art include **José de Almada Negreiros** (1889–1970), a non-conformist much influenced by the Italian futurist movement; and **Maria Helena Vieira da Silva** (1908–92) who worked mostly in Paris, where the French government made her the first woman to be awarded the Grand Prix National des Arts. Her abstract works recall Portuguese *azulejos*, endless libraries, and the winding alleys of Lisbon.

During the early years of the Salazar dictatorship, architecture was much influenced by the grandiose ideas emanating from Fascist Italy and Nazi Germany, although softened by a Portuguese touch recalling the country's medieval or maritime past. Modern extensions to **Coimbra University,** the **Monument to the Discoveries** jutting into the river at Belém, and the **Praça Francisco Sá Carneiro** in Lisbon showcase the *Estado Novo* style.

Later, the Porto School of Architecture produced a crop of designers whose cool, modernist buildings have won worldwide acclaim. **Álvaro Siza Vieira** (b. 1933) is the best known. His clean white cubic buildings grace cities around the world, including the Serralves contemporary art museum in Porto and the Portuguese Pavilion in Lisbon's Parque das Nações district. **Eduardo Souto de Moura** (b. 1952) is a fellow winner of the Pritzker Prize, considered architecture's "Nobel." The soccer stadium in Braga carved into the rock walls of a quarry is among his most distinctive works.

Contrasting with the geometric purity favored by the Porto School, Lisbon architect **Tomás Taveira** (b. 1938) made an eye-catching contribution to the capital's skyline in the early 1980s with his giant Amoreiras shopping and residential center, whose oddly shaped towers in pink, black, and silver are monuments to then-trendy postmodern style.

ART TODAY The arts scene today is thriving. Contemporary works are showcased in important new galleries like the **Berardo Museum** (see p. 103) in Lisbon's Belém district, the **Serralves** (p. 339) center in Porto, and the **MAAT** museum (p. 102) that opened in the fall of 2016.

Joana Vasconcelos (b. 1971) is perhaps the contemporary artist who has gained most international recognition, after three appearances at the Venice Biennale. She uses colorful textiles, crochet, and lacework to cover and distort familiar Portuguese objects, from ceramic shellfish to a Tagus riverboat.

Paula Rego (b. 1935) divides her time between London and Cascais, where there's a museum dedicated to her work designed by Pritzker Prize–winning architect Eduardo Souto de Moura. Her paintings often reflect a sinister, fairytale world populated by powerful, muscular women.

Lately, Lisbon has gained a reputation as a center of graffiti art, including towering works covering abandoned apartment blocks that greet visitors on the way into town along Av. Avenida Fontes Pereira de Melo. **Vhils** (b. 1983) is Portugal's most renowned urban artist. His haunting portraits carved into the side of buildings have sprung up around the world from San Diego to Sydney, Beijing to Bogota, as well as locations around Lisbon.

BOOKS

The ideal literary companion to a visit to Portugal is a guide by the country's only Nobel Literature Prize winner, José Saramago. In 1979, Saramago set out on a meandering drive from north to south seeking the soul of his homeland's history and culture. His ***Journey to Portugal*** is an intimate, highly personal portrait that reaches into the lives of the Portuguese people.

For an up-to-date survey, ***The Portuguese: A Modern History*** by The Associated Press Lisbon correspondent Barry Hatton looks at how history has shaped today's Portugal. The country's love of soccer, the significance of fado, and the importance of good eating are all included in this excellent introduction.

HISTORY

Before his death in 2012 at the age of 92, José Hermano Saraiva was Portugal's best-known historian, a familiar face to millions thanks to his TV series on the country's past. Saraiva's ***Portugal: A Companion History*** provides a sweeping saga of the land you're about to visit.

A Concise History of Portugal by David Birmingham is a readable short overview, while Malyn Newitt's ***Portugal in European and World History*** puts the story in the wider international context.

A wide range of books focuses on Portugal's Age of Discovery. ***Conquerors: How Portugal Forged the First Global Empire*** by Roger Crowley is a rip-roaring account of Portugal's expansion into the Indian Ocean, which isn't shy in portraying the brutality of the early colonial enterprise. Indian historian Sanjay Subrahmanyam's ***The Portuguese Empire in Asia*** presents an epic alternative to euro-centric views of the Discoveries.

For gripping accounts of great voyages, try ***The Last Crusade: The Epic Voyages of Vasco Da Gama*** by Nigel Cliff, ***or Over the Edge of the World: Magellan's Terrifying Circumnavigation of the World*** by Laurence Bergreen.

PORTUGUESE LITERATURE

The earliest poems in the Portuguese language emerged from the troubadours of the old kingdom of Galicia, one of the Christian states fighting Muslim rule in the Iberian Peninsula. The written language was refined in the Middle Ages by the chroniclers of the royal reigns. The first great Portuguese literature emerged in the 15th century, by playwright Gil Vicente, whose works range from moral tales with a maritime theme to bawdy comedies.

Born in 1524, Luís de Camões is the towering figure in Portuguese letters and considered one of the greats of world literature, alongside Shakespeare, Dante, and Cervantes. His epic poem ***Os Lusíadas*** is a heroic retelling of the voyages of discovery. A swashbuckling one-eyed veteran of Portugal's overseas adventures, Camões is a national hero whose death is commemorated on June 10 as the national holiday.

The Portuguese novel came of age in the 19th century and the greatest novelist of the age was José Maria de Eça de Queirós. A diplomat, his novels about Portuguese society blend biting satire with often dark tragedy dealing

FIVE ESSENTIAL portuguese reads

Five of the best by Portuguese authors:

The Crime of Father Amaro by José Maria de Eça de Queirós: Written in 1875, this tale of forbidden passion between a young priest and an innocent girl in the provincial city of Leiria still has the power to shock.

The Year of the Death of Ricardo Reis by José Saramago: This deeply atmospheric book set in dictatorship Lisbon during the 1930s evokes the mysterious world of poet Fernando Pessoa.

Os Lusíadas by Luís de Camões: Portugal's national epic was written in 1572 by the seafaring poet whose statue stares down on Lisbon's Chiado district. Inspired by Homer's Odyssey, Camões tells a heroic tale of Portugal's voyages of discovery through the eyes of Vasco da Gama, embellished by encounters with giants, seductive nymphs, and Greek gods.

The Book of Disquiet by Fernando Pessoa: This literary oddity has become a cult favorite. A meandering reflection on life and Lisbon, it is at turns funny and sad. Chosen as one of the 100 greatest books ever in a survey of world authors.

The Return by Dulce Maria Cardoso: Set in 1975, this new novel by one of Portugal's best current writers tells of the trauma of the *retornados*, the up to one million Portuguese who fled Angola and other newly independent African nations at the end of Portugal's colonial wars. Winner of a 2016 PEN Award for translated books.

with themes like incest, adultery, and clerical abuse. ***The Maias*** and ***The Crime of Father Amaro*** are the most powerful of his novels.

Poet Fernando Pessoa is a unique figure. Considered a founder of modernist literature, his writings are mystical and deeply philosophical, but struck a chord with his compatriots, who rate him second only to Camões among their literary greats. ***A Little Larger Than the Entire Universe: Selected Poems*** gives a selection of his works translated into English.

Among modern writers, José Saramago stands out as the Portuguese language's only winner of the Nobel Prize for Literature. A lifelong Communist who had sometimes a testy relationship with the authorities, he is widely revered. When he died in 2010, 20,000 attended his funeral. Saramago's novels like ***The Elephant's Journey*** and ***Baltasar and Blimunda*** delve into Portuguese history. ***Blindness*** and ***The Double*** are dark parables of modern life.

Younger writers carrying on that intellectual tradition include **José Luís Peixoto** and **Gonçalo M. Tavares;** both have novels translated into English.

FOREIGN FICTION SET IN PORTUGAL

Lisbon's curious position in World War II as a neutral port filled with refugees and spies has inspired many novels. The best is ***The Night in Lisbon*** by the German anti-Nazi writer Erich Maria Remarque, who was himself a refugee.

Italian author Antonio Tabucchi, a frequent Nobel Prize contender, had a long love affair with Portugal. His novel ***Pereira Declares*** is a story of intrigue set in 1930s Lisbon. Another classic with a Lisbon setting is ***Confessions of Felix Krull,*** about a visiting con artist by German Nobel winner Thomas Mann, who unfortunately died before writing the ending.

Recent books include ***Alentejo Blue,*** a series of tales set in the rural south by award-winning British writer Monica Ali; ***The Last Kabbalist of Lisbon,*** a best-seller by Richard Zimmer focusing on a Jewish family during the persecutions of the 16th century; and ***The High Mountains of Portugal,*** a whimsical tale of journeys to the remote Trás-os-Montes region by Canada's Yann Martel.

FOOD & DRINK

The recent international discovery of Portugal's healthy and delicious cuisine has triggered a sudden blooming of cookbooks and food guides. Manhattan-based culinary superstar George Mendes has penned a mouthwateringly beautiful tribute to the cooking of his homeland in ***My Portugal***. ***Food of Portugal*** by Jean Anderson is an excellent introduction for anybody wanting to cook up a taste of the country, while Maria de Lourdes Modesto's encyclopedic ***Traditional Portuguese Cooking*** is a sacred text in many Portuguese kitchens.

Combining recipes with travelogue are ***Eat Portugal*** by Célia Pedroso (co-author of this guide) and Lucy Pepper, and ***The Portuguese Travel Cookbook*** by food blogger Nelson Cavalheiro.

For the secrets of Portugal's most complex tipples, try Richard Mayson's ***Port and the Douro,*** and ***Madeira: The Mid-Atlantic Wine*** by Alex Liddell.

MUSIC

Portugal's most distinctive music is **fado,** the urban blues of Lisbon that comes close to encapsulating the nation's soul. Fado traditionally involves a singer, male or female, accompanied by two guitarists, one playing the familiar classical guitar, called a *viola* in Portuguese, the other plucking the unique, tear-shaped *guitarra Portuguesa*. With 12 steel strings, the Portuguese guitar can, in the right hands, produce an amazing range of sound.

The word "fado" means "fate." Although not all fado songs are melancholic, the music is deeply associated with *saudade*, an untranslatable word that implies longing for lost loves and distant homelands. It is a sentiment ingrained in the national character since the days when long sea voyages and successive waves of emigration carried the Portuguese to the far corners of the globe.

Fado has its roots in the bars and bordellos of Lisbon's docklands and the tightly packed old neighborhoods of Alfama and Mouraria. **Maria Severa,** the earliest fado great, was a renowned lady of the night in the early-19th-century Lisbon. The music's disreputable origins are summed up in the painting *O Fado* by José Malhoa, on show in Lisbon's Fado Museum.

Early in the 20th century, fado went mainstream. Although some maintained a bohemian edge, fado singers moved from backstreet bars to boulevard theaters, radio studios, and movie sets. Many *Casas de fado*—fado houses—became chic restaurants. The Salazar dictatorship sought to sanitize fado, censoring lyrics and seeking to promote conservative values though the music.

Towering above all this was **Amália Rodrigues,** fado's biggest name. From a poor background, she began singing as a teenager in the 1930s and became fado's first global star. She sang lyrics penned by the nation's greatest poets and popularized the song "April in Portugal," which became a hit for the likes of Louis Armstrong and Eartha Kitt.

Boosted by radio, cinema, and later TV, fado singers became household names. When Amália died in 1999, the government declared three days of national mourning. The media calculated the crowds who packed Lisbon streets for her funeral to be in the hundreds of thousands. The emotion shown for the diva's passing sparked a revival of interest in fado and thrust a new generation of singers into the limelight.

Young singers like **Mariza, Camané,** and **Ana Moura**—who has sung with the Rolling Stones—have gone on to international success. Suddenly fado is sexy again. Alongside the posh, sometimes stuffy fado houses, new hip venues have sprung up. Uninhibited new stars are experimenting, adding piano, bass, and saxophone to the traditional guitars, blending elements of jazz, tango, and bossa nova. Current sensations include **Carminho, Aldina Duarte,** guitarist **António Chainho** and the exuberant **Gisela João,** hailed by some as the best voice since Amália.

The university city of Coimbra (see p. 290) has its own distinctive form of fado. There, it's traditionally sung only by men and the songs tend to have a lighter, more romantic feel, dating back to the days when lovesick students would sing nocturnal serenades beneath the windows of their latest flames.

A number of Portuguese pop bands have used fado and other folk elements to create a modern sound rooted in tradition. The most successful is **Madredeus,** whose haunting sound has won them an international following.

Portugal's musical traditions go way beyond fado. From the powerful male-voice choirs formed by miners and farm workers in the southern Alentejo to the Celtic-tinged bagpipe music of the north, each region has a distinctive sound.

Singer-songwriters rooted in the folk tradition, but also taking in outside influences from French chanson to American protest songs, evolved in the 1960s and 1970s to produce a highly politicized sound in opposition to the long dictatorship. The major figure was **José "Zeca" Afonso,** whose songs range from biting political satire to lyrical evocations of the Portuguese countryside. When revolutionary soldiers seized the state radio station in the early hours of April 25, 1974, they played his banned song "Grândola, Vila Morena" over the airways as a signal to comrades to move to the next phase of the uprising that restored democracy. Zeca died in 1987, but other veterans of that era, like **Sérgio Godinho, Vitorino,** and **Júlio Pereira,** remain popular performers.

Portuguese jazz has its spiritual home in Lisbon's Hot Club de Portugal, an archetypal basement dive that's been bopping since the 1940s. Portuguese jazz musicians who have made international splashes include vocalist **Maria João** and pianist **Mário Laginha.**

Portugal's close ties with its former colonies mean that Lisbon nights echo with the sounds of Brazilian samba, Cape Verdean mournas, and Angola's sensual kizomba music. The riverside B.Leza club is a legendary venue for live African music. Over the past decade, **Buraka Som Sistema,** a group from Lisbon's northern suburbs, has found international success with its blend of techno beat and Angolan rhythms.

For classical music, the Lisbon-based **Gulbenkian Orchestra** is tops. In the north, Porto's Casa da Música is a major venue. Lisbon's gilded 18th-century São Carlos theater is the premier opera venue, while the modern Teatro Camões is home to the prestigious National Ballet Company.

A final word should go to **pimba,** a style scorned by city cool kids but wildly popular at rural festivals. It's strangely similar to Germany's Schlager music, involving singers belting out saucily suggestive up-tempo dance numbers backed by electric organ, guitar, and accordion. Performers tend to be curvaceous blondes or middle-aged guys flanked by scantily clad dancing girls.

FILM

The good news for film fans heading to Portugal is that theaters there run movies in the original language with subtitles, rather than dubbing them. That means English-speakers are free to enjoy the latest Anglophone flicks in a mega-mall multiplex, in Lisbon's cool *Cinemateca* movie museum, or at a number of intimate art house theaters in the capital.

Portugal's own movie industry was long dominated by one man, **Manoel de Oliveira,** who died in 2015 at the age of 106 as the world's oldest working director. Oliveira's often slow-moving and melancholic adaptations of literary works were loved by critics, less so by mass audiences. The most accessible of his movies is his first, *Aniki-Bóbó*, a tale of street urchins in 1940s Porto.

Two of the best recent films that have been hits with both critics and audiences have been *Os Maias*, **João Botelho's** adaptation of the great 19th-century novel, and *The Gilded Cage*, a heart-warming comedy about Portuguese emigrants in Paris, by the promising young actor/director **Ruben Alves.**

THE LAY OF THE LAND

3

Portugal is a roughly drawn rectangle on Europe's southwestern seaboard. It's about 550km (350 miles) from north to south, 200km (110 miles) from east to west. To the north and east it's bordered by Spain. On the south and west it's bathed by the Atlantic Ocean. There are two Atlantic island groups, Madeira lying off the coast of Morocco and the nine Azores islands, halfway to Boston.

As a general rule, the landscape north of the River Tagus is hilly and often rugged, while the south has softly rolling plains. Over 80% of Portugal's 10.5 million people live in districts bordering the ocean, while the interior is often scarcely populated.

Within that general picture, the regions vary greatly. The **Algarve** occupies the southern coastal strip. Separated from the rest of the country by low forested hills, it basks in a Mediterranean-type climate that facilitates the growth of orange, lemon, fig, and almond trees and draws tourists to its sheltered, south-facing beaches.

Above it lays the **Alentejo,** a region that covers a third of the country. Here the endless, sun-soaked grasslands bring to mind the African savannah, but with the baobabs replaced with umbrella pine, cork oak, and olive trees, and flocks of sheep or black pigs rooting around for acorns instead of herds of antelope. The Alentejo's whitewashed towns and villages are among the country's most beautiful, and the coast here is lined with wild surfing beaches. Even in the Alentejo there are occasional hill ranges, like the Serra de Grândola overlooking the coast or the Serra de São Mamede topped by the stunning fortified town of Marvão overlooking the Spanish border.

The River Tagus, known in Portugal as the Tejo, cuts the country in half. "Alentejo" means "beyond the Tagus." The river rises deep in Spain and reaches the Atlantic just downstream of Lisbon. East of the capital, the flat Tagus valley is characteristic of the **Ribatejo** region. This is cattle country. Local festivals feature bullfights and displays of horsemanship by *campinos*, the local cowboys, sporting red vests and green tasseled caps. **Estremadura** along the coast north of Lisbon has a gentle landscape filled with vineyards, apple and pear orchards, and hills topped with stubby white windmills. The hills of Sintra create a cool, lush microclimate that's resulted in the growth of thick rainforest. The Arrábida range south of Lisbon has Mediterranean weather and overlooks some of the country's best beaches.

The **Beiras** form a vast region covering the center of the country. While the coastal strip is cultivated and low lying, including the marshlands of the Aveiro lagoon and the Bairrada wine region, the interior is made up of austere landscapes of boulder-strewn plateaus and bare mountains. The country's highest peaks are in the Serra da Estrella, reaching almost 2,000m (6,500 ft.). The land here has an epic grandeur. Rough-hewn villages and the few cities preserve a hearty cuisine and age-old handicraft traditions. Cutting a green swathe through the region is the valley of the River Mondego, the longest wholly Portuguese river.

The far north is made up of two contrasting regions. To the northwest, the **Minho** is green, its hills covered with trellised vineyards and dissected by fast-flowing rivers. It's well populated, a center for the textile and footwear industries. Farther east lies remote **Trás-os-Montes,** a region whose name means "beyond the mountains." Here life can be harsh; locals sum up the climate as "nine months of winter, three months of hell." The high plains are bare and empty, but starkly beautiful. Girdling the north, the River Douro flows from the Spanish border to the Atlantic near Porto. Farthest east it forms the frontier and cuts a deep canyon where vultures and eagles soar. Downstream, its banks are cultivated to grow grapes, creating perhaps the world's most beautiful wine region.

Finally, the **Azores** islands are nine specks of grass-covered volcanic rock rising from the Atlantic, containing Portugal's highest mountain, the astounding volcano of Pico, and a unique variety of landscapes and culture. Subtropical **Madeira** enjoys a climate of year-round spring. Its mountainous interior and thick forests are a paradise for hikers.

WHEN TO GO

Summer is the most popular season, when it can seem that half of Europe is heading to Portugal's beaches. July and August are the hottest, most expensive, and most crowded months in the Algarve and other beach destinations. Although Atlantic breezes generally keep the coast relatively cool, if you are planning to tour in the interior, it can get seriously hot—topping 100°F (40°C). Humidity, however, is usually low. You get better deals if you go in September or June, when the weather is still good.

Portugal's climate is similar to California's. Lisbon is Europe's sunniest capital, and along the coast the country enjoys mild winters and warm summers. Average temperatures range from 77°F (25°C) in summer to about 58°F (14°C) in winter. Spring can be a great time to visit, when wildflowers paint Algarve cliff tops, Alentejo pastures, and northern hillsides with color. Temperatures are more extreme inland. Winters in the northern hills can be bitter, snowfall is common, and there is some (limited) skiing in the Serra da Estrela mountains. Winter can also bring delights. In February, groves of almond trees are covered in snow-white blossoms in Trás-os-Montes and parts of the Algarve. Cool but sunny winter days can be best for exploring the cities or playing a round of golf on one of the Algarve's many excellent courses.

Madeira has its own subtropical climate. It boasts of year-round springtime. When it rains on one side of the island, you can often escape to sunshine on the other side, with a short scenic drive over the mountainous interior.

Lisbon and Estoril enjoy 46°F (8°C) to 65°F (18°C) temperatures in winter and temperatures between 60°F (16°C) and 82°F (28°C) in summer.

Lisbon's Average Daytime Temperature (°F & °C) & Monthly Rainfall (Inches)

	JAN	FEB	MAR	APR	MAY	JUNE	JULY	AUG	SEPT	OCT	NOV	DEC
Temp. (°F)	57	59	63	67	71	77	81	82	79	72	63	58
Temp. (°C)	14	15	17	19	22	25	27	28	26	22	17	14
Rainfall	4.3	3.0	4.2	2.1	1.7	0.6	0.1	0.2	1.3	2.4	3.7	4.1

Public Holidays

New Year's Day (Jan 1); **Carnaval** (Feb or early Mar—dates vary); **Good Friday** (Mar or Apr—dates vary); **Freedom Day** (Apr 25); **Labor Day** (May 1); **Corpus Christi** (May or June—dates vary); **Portugal Day** (June 10); **Assumption** (Aug 15); **Republic Day** (Oct 5); **All Saints' Day** (Nov 1); **Restoration of Independence** (Dec 1); **Immaculate Conception** (Dec 8); **Christmas Day** (Dec 25). The **Feast of St. Anthony** (June 13) is a public holiday in Lisbon, and the **Feast of St. John the Baptist** (June 24) is a public holiday in Porto.

Events

Where Spain has its fiesta, Portugal has *festa*. There are countless traditional celebrations held up and down the country. Just about every village has a *festa* of some sort. Many have a religious origin, based on a pilgrimage (*romaria*) to honor a local saint. Others are feasts created around a prized local product. In the Algarve, for example, **Lagos** celebrates traditional almond, fig, and carob cakes in July; **Portimão** and **Olhão** hold two of the biggest food-based festivals at the height of the summer season in August, the former focused on sardines, the latter on shellfish. More modest is the Festival of Sweet Potatoes held in November in the pretty west coast town of **Aljezur.** The pattern is repeated up and down the country. Some such events are humble: where villagers carry a holy statue through the streets, attend a church service, and then follow up with a communal barbecue, performance by the local folklore group, and a wine-fueled *baile* (dance). Others go on for several days, attracting big-name performers and crowds of visitors.

The bigger festivals are concentrated in the summer, but there is always plenty going on in Portugal. Kicking off the year, Madeira's capital, Funchal, hosts one of Europe's most spectacular **New Year's Eve** parties, with the city streets strung with colored lights and a dazzling firework display over the bay. February sees **carnival** celebrations around the country. Many are rather less-glamorous imitations of Rio. Once again, Funchal's is the biggest: Madeira islanders claim their emigrants took the carnival tradition to Brazil. For a more authentic experience, head to northern villages like Podence in Trás-os-Montes or Lazarim, near Lamego, where young men still act out pagan traditions dressing in bizarre colored costumes, donning devilish masks, and chasing girls around the streets.

Easter is an altogether more solemn occasion, especially in the religious center of Braga, where **Holy Week** processions feature masked marchers and bejeweled floats along with fireworks, folk dancing, and torchlight parades. Students in Coimbra's ancient university will paint the city red in early May with the **Queima das Fitas** celebrations, when they mark the end of the school year by burning the colored ribbons worn to designate their faculties, then get down to nights of serious partying.

Early May also sees the **Festas das Cruzes,** in Barcelos, where since 1504, women dress in gold-adorned regional costumes as part of a procession over streets strewn with millions of flower petals. May 13 sees the start of the pilgrimage season in **Fátima,** where many Catholics believe the Virgin Mary appeared to shepherd children in 1917. Pope Francis was scheduled to attend the centenary of the apparitions in 2017. Pilgrims flock to the Fátima shrine all year round, but the main gatherings are on the 13th of every month between May and October.

Recently, Portugal has emerged as a popular venue for rock festivals, drawing the biggest international names. Highlights include **Nos Alive** and **Super Bock Super Rock,** held in July in Lisbon, and the **Nos Primavera Sound,** held in June in Porto. The **Rock in Rio** festival is held every other May in Lisbon; the next is in 2018. Recent performers have included Bruce Springsteen, the Rolling Stones, and Justin Timberlake.

Street parties to celebrate Lisbon's patron saint, **Santo António,** on June 12 and 13, are a joyous celebration. Neighborhoods compete to produce the best *marcha*, a musical promenade in costume down the Avenida da Liberdade, then head home to eat grilled sardines, drink red wine or sangria, and dance the night away in squares decked with fairy lights and paper decorations. Similar scenes are repeated in Porto when the second city honors **São João** on June 23 and 24. Portugal's biggest agricultural fair, the **Feira Nacional da Agricultura,** is held every June in Santarém, the heart of cattle country. Expect bullfights, displays of horsemanship, and opportunities to consume heaps of regional food.

Farther down the River Tagus, Vila Franca de Xira holds its **Festa do Colete Encarnado,** featuring Pamplona-style bull-running through the riverside streets, in early July. Portugal's bullfighting season reaches its height in the summer. There are weekly performances at Lisbon's exotic Campo Pequeno ring. Unlike in Spain, the bulls are not killed in Portuguese bullfighting, but the spectacle can be disturbing for animal lovers.

One of the most striking traditional events is the **Festa dos Tabuleiros,** held every 4 years in Tomar, which features a procession of young women in traditional costume balancing trays laden with 30 stacked loaves of bread, decorated with flowers and topped with crowns. The next is due in July 2019.

The Portuguese **soccer season** runs from August through May. Catching a *clássico* game between the top clubs—Benfica, Sporting Lisbon, or FC Porto—in a packed stadium of impassioned fans is a powerful experience showing just how deeply engrained the love of club is for most Portuguese.

September sees the **Romaria da Nossa Senhora** festival in Nazaré, Portugal's most famed fishing town, where a sacred statue is carried to the sea, followed by folk dancing, singing, and bullfights. A relatively recent tradition is the **Caixa Alfama** festival in September, where top fado singers perform in venues throughout Lisbon's Alfama neighborhood.

Horse lovers should head to Golegã in early November for the **Feira Nacional do Cavalo,** a celebration of all things equine, where the beautiful *Lusitano* breed holds pride of place. **Christmas** (*Natal*) is a family affair. Midnight masses fill churches up and down the country.

EATING & DRINKING

In her book *Invitation to Portugal,* Mary Jean Kempner gets to the heart of the Portuguese diet: "The best Portuguese food is provincial, indigenous, eccentric, and proud... It takes no sides, assumes no airs, makes no concessions or bows to Brillat-Savarin—and usually tastes wonderful."

DINING CUSTOMS Most Portuguese breakfast lightly: milky coffee with toast, fresh bread rolls with preserves, perhaps a pastry—variations on croissants are common, sometimes filled with ham and cheese, an innovation considered scandalous by the French.

Short shots of espresso, known here as *bica*, are ingested through the day, often accompanied by the sweet, sticky pastries on show in all cafes. In Lisbon, custard tarts (*pasteis de nata*) are the calorie shot of choice.

Lunch is often the main meal of the day, and working people fill restaurants throughout the week to tuck in. Portions in traditional restaurants are large. In all but the poshest places, it's completely acceptable to share a main course or ask for a half-portion (*meia-dose*). Aside from their printed menus, most restaurants offer dishes of the day (*pratos do dia*), which are usually a good bet, with market-fresh products at a good price.

Many people will take *lanche* in the afternoon—a light meal with tea or coffee. Dinner is usually eaten between 8pm and 9pm, although Spanish-style late-night dining is catching on. People drink wine with both lunch and dinner.

Waiters will usually bring you a selection of appetizers unbidden—they can range from a few olives or bread with a pot of sardine pâté to an array of cheeses, sausage, and seafood. Most of the time, you'll be charged a cover fee for what you eat (so say "no" if you don't want any of the appetizers).

CUISINE Portuguese cooking is one of Europe's best gourmet secrets. There's great regional variation, with a more Mediterranean feel to Algarve cuisine, heartier, meatier options as you go farther north and farther away from the coast.

The Portuguese are among the world's biggest fish eaters. The coastal waters produce a rich variety of seafood that is served super-fresh in markets and restaurants up and down the country. One of the country's great treats is enjoying fresh, charcoal-grilled fish—gilt-head bream (*dourada*) and bass (*robalo*) are the most popular species—with a splash of olive oil and lemon juice and a glass of chilled white wine in a beachside restaurant. Fish served this way is usually priced by weight on the menu.

Long considered the most humble of fish, sardines (*sardinhas*) are grilled in the streets during the summer season, bringing a pungent scent to the old neighborhoods of Lisbon and other cities. They are eaten by the boatload during Lisbon's Santo Antonio festival in June and are a particular specialty in the fishing ports of the Algarve. They are usually accompanied by roasted red bell peppers, green salad, and boiled potatoes drenched in olive oil, and best washed down with cold beer or red wine. Fresh sardines should only be eaten during the summer season, when they are at their fattest. After the weather turns cooler, sardines come from a can.

Another much-cherished fish dish is *caldeirada*, the Portuguese version of bouillabaisse, a fish stew enriched with tomatoes, bell peppers, and potatoes. Hake (*pescada*) is eaten "boiled with everything" (*cozida com todos*), meaning potatoes, carrots, green beans, and a boiled egg. In Madeira and the Algarve, tuna steaks (*bifes de atum*) are a specialty, pan-fried in olive oil with garlic and onions.

Despite the panoply of fresh local seafood, Portugal's favorite fish is cod caught in the waters of Norway or Iceland and preserved by drying and salting. *Bacalhau*, or salt cod, is as close to the Portuguese soul as soccer or fado music. It dates back to pre-refrigeration times, when salting enabled *bacalhau* to become a staple on long sea journeys or deep in the interior of the country. They say Portugal has more ways of serving *bacalhau* than there are days in the year. Popular versions include *bacalhau à brás*, a Lisbon treat with scrambled eggs, olives, and fries; *pastéis de bacalhau*, fish cakes often served with black-eyed peas; and *bacalhau com broa*, crumbled with cornbread.

Shellfish is generally excellent, best enjoyed in specialist restaurants called *marisqueiras*, which are often bright, busy places where customers slurp cilantro-and-garlic-steamed clams (*amêijoas à bulhão pato*) from their shells; smash crab claws with mallets to get at the flesh within; or prise shrimp from their shells with fingers sticky with spicy sauce. There's a tradition of finishing off a seafood feast with a steak sandwich, or *prego*. A classic shellfish main course is *arroz de marisco*, a pot of rice and seafood in broth flavored with garlic, cilantro, tomato, and just a touch of *piri-piri*—a fiery chili sauce of African origin that's a favorite condiment in Portugal.

Piri-piri is also used to spice up spit-roasted chicken, one of Portugal's most successful culinary exports, that's served in specialty restaurants known as *churrasqueiras*.

Portuguese pork is among some of the world's best. Black pigs roam semi-wild in the plains of the Alentejo region, feasting on the acorns that fall from the region's cork forests. The *porco preto* meat they produce is fabulous. The region's signature dish, *carne de porco à Alentejana*, combines red-pepper-marinated pork with clams. The black pigs also produce superlative hams (*presunto*) and an array of sausages, including paprika-spiced *chouriço*, cumin-flavored blood puddings (*morcela*), and soft, smoky *farinheiras*. All of these porky pleasures are combined in *cozido à portuguesa*, an artery-stopping one-pot that's become the national dish, and that can include hunks of beef, pigs' ears, chicken, cabbage, turnips, chick peas, carrots, potatoes, squash, and beans, as well as an array of spiced sausages.

Lamb (*borrego*) is another Alentejo speciality, served grilled, fried, or in hearty stews. Goat is more common in the center and north; a succulent meat, it usually comes in the form of roasted young kid (*cabrito assado*), although around Coimbra older goats or sheep are slow-stewed in red wine to make *chanfana*. Beef is good in the north; the *posta Mirandesa* is a succulent steak served in Trás-os-Montes, but the Atlantic island of Madeira also boasts a beefy signature dish in the shape of *espetada*, cubes of garlic-rubbed meat skewered on a laurel branch and roasted over hot coals.

The Portuguese have a weakness for offal. Tripe stewed with beans (*tripas à moda do Porto*) is Porto's favorite dish. Lisbon prefers liver sautéed in white wine (*iscas*). Pig's feet, stomachs, ears, and snouts will all find their way into hearty stews.

Soups are a common way of starting a meal. The most popular, especially in the north, is *caldo verde*, a green broth made from cabbage, sausage, potatoes, and olive oil. Typically southern, *açorda alentejana* is made from simmered bread, poached eggs, cilantro, and a ton of garlic. *Sopa da pedra* is a meal in itself from the Ribatejo region, combining meat, beans, sausage, and just about every conceivable ingredient except the stone (*pedra*) from which it gets its name.

Portuguese cheeses deserve to be better known internationally. The best is *queijo da serra:* Made from sheep's milk in the high central mountains, it is rich and creamy, fabulous on freshly baked rye bread. Similar but more delicate is *queijo de Azeitão* from the hills south of Lisbon. *Queijo de São Jorge* is a hard cow's milk cheese made in big wheels in the Azores islands. Soft, unaged white cheeses called *queijo fresco* are often served as an appetizer.

Fruit ripened in Portugal's Mediterranean climate is fabulous. Bananas and passion fruit from Madeira, pineapple from the Azores, cherries from the central mountains, juicy Rocha pears from the far west, and honey-sweet figs from the Algarve are just some of the treats. If your tooth is still sweeter, traditional Portuguese desserts promise calorific overload. Many are based on old convent recipes using eggs, almonds, and the cinnamon that explorers of the 15th century went to such great lengths to bring from the orient.

As with music, Portugal's ties with its former colonies have spiced up the local cuisine: Brazilian shrimp *moquecas*, curries from Goa, or Angolan chicken *muamba* are all exotic additions to Lisbon menus.

A COFFEE survival guide

From Brazil to East Timor, many of Portugal's former colonies happened to produce wonderful coffee (*café*), so coffee culture runs deep. The Portuguese imbibe inordinate amounts of the stuff in an array of styles. Here's what to order:

Bica: Thimble-sized shots of strong black espresso. Portugal's default option, if you ask for *café*, this is what you get.

Café cheio: As above, but slightly less strong, a full espresso cup.

Café pingado: A *bica* with a drop of milk.

Garoto: Espresso cup of half-coffee, half-milk.

Café duplo: A double espresso.

Abatanado: Large black coffee.

Galão: Weak milky coffee like a caffe latte, served in a tall glass.

Meia de leite: Big cup of half-milk, half-espresso, like a café au lait or flat white.

Café com cheirinho: Shot of black coffee tipped up with *aguadente* (firewater).

Recently, a new generation of younger chefs has been building on the country's traditional cuisine to forge modern adaptations of cherished additions and win international accolades. Leading the pack is **José Avillez,** whose Belcanto restaurant (p. 84) became Lisbon's first with two Michelin stars.

WINE For years, international interest in Portuguese wine (*vinho*) was largely limited to cheap-and-cheerful rosé and the complex Porto and Madeira fortified wines. In recent decades, however, the world has woken up to the full range of terrific tipples made under Portugal's unique blend of Atlantic and Mediterranean conditions.

Strong yet sophisticated reds produced from the beautiful terraced hillsides along the Douro or the rolling, sun-soaked Alentejo plains have drawn admiration from critics and drinkers around the world. Great wines are also produced in the valleys of the Dão, the coastal Bairrada region, and the flatlands flanking the Tejo River east of Lisbon. Tangy whites made from *arinto* grapes or sweet *Moscatel* dessert wines are made on the edge of Lisbon's suburbs. Fresh white wines known as *vinho verdes* from the verdant hills of the northwest make an excellent partner for seafood. Even the Algarve, whose wines were once mocked as good only for unsuspecting tourists, is now producing quality reds and whites.

Port remains the most alluring of Portugal's wines. It was invented in the age of sailing ships, when exporters added brandy to Douro wines to prevent them from spoiling during the long sea journey to England. Quality controls exist since at least the 17th century. Drier white ports are traditionally sipped as an aperitif before meals, the sweet red tawny and ruby ports are served with dessert or cheese, and rare vintage wines from selected years are saved for special occasions. Wines produced on the volcanic island of Madeira are similarly fortified and aged and also range from drier aperitifs to sweet dessert wines.

BEER & OTHER DRINKS The beer (*cerveja*) market in Portugal has long been a duel between Lisbon's *Sagres* and Porto's *Super Bock*, both refreshing lagers, best chilled. Lately, there's been a craft beer revolution with breweries such as *Sovina*, *Letra*, and *Dois Corvos* edging onto the scene with some tasty thirst-quenchers.

The wine industry has a long distillery tradition resulting in fiery liquors like *bagaço* and *bagaceira*, which are clear, powerful, and similar to Italian grappa, or barrel-aged *aguardente velha*, at its best a wonderfully warming after-dinner tipple that can rival French cognac.

Many regions have their own special drinks: *Poncha* is a potent mix of local rum and lemon from Madeira; *ginja* is a sweet cherry liqueur knocked back in hole-in-the-wall Lisbon bars; the Algarve has a firewater made from a forest fruit called *medronho; Licor Beirão* is an herby liqueur from the Beiras.

Mineral water is commonly drunk, bottled from springs around the country. Waiters will inevitably ask if you want it *com gas* (sparkling) or *sem gas* (still), *fresca* (cold) or *natural* (room temperature). The *Compal* range of fruit drinks can make a healthier alternative to international soda brands.

SUGGESTED PORTUGAL ITINERARIES

4

Portugal is a relatively compact country, and major road investments over the past few decades means fast highways have cut driving times, even to the most remote regions. Despite its size, there's a great variety of landscapes, from the rolling plains of the Alentejo to sun-kissed resorts along the coast and the rugged highlands of the north and center, where rough-hewn granite towns rise out of the hillsides.

Whether you race along the *autostradas*, prefer pottering along country roads, or discovering the country by rail, traveling around Portugal can be a delight. Driving from Lisbon, in less than 3 hours you can be bronzing on a beach in the Algarve or sipping port in a riverside bar overlooking Porto.

Yet it would be a mistake to spend your holiday rushing from point to point. Portugal is a land that lends itself to taking things easy. If you've got a week, spend time exploring Lisbon, the historic and happening capital that is the heart of the country's cultural life; take a relaxed ride out to nearby attractions, driving through forested hills or vine- and orchard-covered countryside to view World Heritage Sites within an hour or so of the city; chill on a beach, admire the view from a cliff-top lighthouse; or settle down to a seafood lunch.

If you've more time, or on a return trip, move north to the great city of Porto, or to smaller but culturally rich cities such as Braga or Guimarães, the beautiful wine regions of the Douro and Minho, or the wild landscapes of Peneda-Gerês National Park. Or go south, passing through the Alentejo's picturesque cities and villages, gastronomic temples, and landscapes redolent of African savannah before reaching the Algarve's beaches.

The following itineraries assume that you'll be traveling by car outside the main cities. You can do most of it by train or bus, but it will take longer to get from place to place. *Boa viagem!*

LISBON & AROUND IN 1 WEEK

This tour will give you time to get an impression of the capital, from its medieval heart to futurist new riverside districts, plus

Lisbon and Around & Northern Delights

delights in the surrounding area, reaching no less than six World Heritage Sites without spending more than an hour per day on the road.

Days 1, 2 & 3: Lisbon ★★★

Lisbon is the highlight of Portugal. As the capital and biggest city, it is packed with cultural attractions, great restaurants, and exciting nightlife. It has a fabulous river-mouth location and maintains timeless traditions and a unique maritime heritage while reaching out to the world as a dynamic, cosmopolitan metropolis.

DAY 1

9am: Start by getting your bearings. The best place to do that is from **Castelo de São Jorge (St. George's Castle;** p. 98). From the ramparts of this hilltop fortress you get stellar views over the city's neighborhoods. The castle is the cradle of the city and traces its roots back to Roman, Arab, and Crusader times. Spend an hour up there checking out the view, soaking up the history, and relaxing in the gardens.

10am: Next, head down to the **Alfama** (p. 68), a casbah-like ancient neighborhood tumbling down to the broad River Tagus. The warren of lanes is imbued with the plaintive sounds of **fado** music and the whiff of sardines on the grill. Take a couple of hours getting lost here, wandering in to baroque churches like the splendid **São Vicente de Fora** (p. 111), with its panels of *azulejo* tiles and rooftop views.

Noon: After admiring the view over Alfama's rooftops from **Portas do Sol** (p. 118) square, walk downhill following the tram line, pausing for a quick look at the **Sé,** Lisbon's fortress-like cathedral (p. 100) built in 1147, before reaching the downtown **Baixa** (p. 68) district. Rebuilt on a grid pattern after the devastation of a 1755 earthquake, this is the administrative and commercial heart of the city. Opening out onto the river is **Praça do Comércio** (p. 67), one of Europe's great city squares, surrounded by grand ministerial buildings linked by a triumphal archway. Running inland is **Rua Augusta** (p. 120), a pedestrianized shopping street built in the harmonious 18th-century Pombaline style. Pause to take a picture of the **Elevador de Santa Justa,** a 19th-century iron elevator whisking shoppers uptown. Grab **lunch** at one of the restaurants popular with locals in the parallel street, **Rua dos Correeiros.**

2pm: Nearby is the busy **Rossio** square (p. 120), the hub of the downtown bustle. From there, head uphill again to the **Chiado** district (p. 120), an uptown, upscale shopping area that's thrived since the 18th century, with its old-world stores, gilded theaters, and historic cafes, like **A Brasileira** (p. 135), serving up shots of coffee (or something stronger) to artists and poets since 1905. Walk there up **Rua do Carmo** and **Rua Garrett,** which are steep but have some of the best shops.

4pm: Hopefully, you'll be energized by that shot of coffee, so continue to climb. Head up **Rua da Misericórdia** to visit the **Igreja de São**

Roque church. Spend an hour inside admiring one the city's great baroque interiors and the attached museum.

5pm: Just behind the church is the **Miradouro de São Pedro de Alcântara,** a leafy viewpoint where you have another spectacular view of the city, this time looking across to the castle where you started the day. If you have the energy, walk uphill just a little bit farther to the **Jardim do Príncipe Real,** a garden surrounded by some of the city's trendiest boutiques, bars, and restaurants. The Arabesque architecture of the 19th-century **Embaixada** building may contain Europe's coolest shopping mall.

7pm: Drag your shopping bags into the **Pavilhão Chinês** bar for a cocktail among the extraordinary collection of vintage bric-a-brac before dinner.

DAY 2

10am: Start the day at the **Museu Nacional de Arte Antiga** (p. 108). You should spend a couple of hours here; it houses the country's best collection of old masters. Take coffee in the riverside garden and cafe.

Noon: Head along the river to the **Belém** district, a UNESCO World Heritage Site packed with monuments and museums. After lunch at one of the riverside restaurants near the **Monument to the Discoveries,** stroll along the river to the **Torre de Belém.** The white tower has guarded the entrance to the city since 1514 and is its most recognizable symbol. Skip the queues lined up to visit the less-than-overwhelming interior.

2pm: Walking past the vast stone buildings of the **Belém Cultural Center,** head now to the **Jerónimos Monastery** (p. 102), which dates to the early 1500s and is the most impressive church in the country, containing the tomb of explorer Vasco da Gama.

4pm: Time for refreshments. Next door to the monastery are the scrumptious, custard-filled tarts served at the **Pastéis de Belém** cafe (p. 103) dating from 1837. You can beat the crowds lining up for takeout by taking yours at a table inside with coffee or tea.

4:30pm: Finish your visit to Belém with a visit to the **National Coach Museum** (p. 104), featuring one of the world's greatest collections of Cinderella-style carriages.

DAY 3

10am: Time to get modern. After all that history, the **Parque das Nações** comes as a shock. Built to house the EXPO '98 World's Fair, it's a showcase of contemporary architecture spectacularly located on the broadest expanse of the River Tagus. The highlight here is the **Oceanário** (p. 114), arguably the world's paramount aquarium. A multistoried treasure trove devoted to ocean life, it features creatures from huge sharks circling the main tank to tiny iridescent jellyfish. You'll need a whole morning to visit the aquarium and to stroll among the modern architecture.

2pm: After lunch, head back into town to the **Calouste Gulbenkian Museum** (p. 107), an awe-inspiring collection of artwork—from 3,000-year-old Assyrian sculptures to French Impressionist masterpieces—all amassed by an Armenian oil magnate. The museum buildings are integrated into soothing landscaped gardens, and there's a separate modern art museum.

4pm: Up the hill from the Gulbenkian complex, the top of **Parque Eduardo VII** provides yet another stunning viewpoint over the city, from which the world's biggest Portuguese flag is flown. Walk down and you come to **Avenida da Liberdade,** the city's swankiest boulevard, over 1km (0.6 mile) of leafy walkways, grand buildings, and luxury brands.

Day 4: Sintra ★★★

9am: Head out to **Sintra** (p. 161). Packed with palaces, this little town in the thickly wooded hills west of Lisbon has been a retreat from the summer heat for the capital's elite for centuries.

11am: A hilltop fantasy built in the 19th-century Bavarian mode, **Palácio da Pena** (p. 164) was the dream of the German husband of Portugal's Queen Maria II. Views are amazing. Spend a couple of hours visiting the palace and strolling the romantic gardens.

1pm: The whole Sintra area is a World Heritage Site. After lunch in the town, drive west through the lush semitropical vegetation dotted with aristocratic abodes. Pass through the charming little wine village of **Colares** until you reach **Cabo da Roca** (p. 156), a blustery promontory that is Europe's most westerly point.

3pm: If the weather is good, nip down to the beach of **Praia da Adraga,** enclosed between soaring cliffs, to soak up some rays.

5pm: Return to Sintra via the **Parque e Palácio de Monserrate,** a fairy-tale Arabian-inspired palace surrounded by semitropical parkland that inspired Lord Byron and Hans Christian Andersen. Overnight in Sintra.

Day 5: Mafra ★★★, Óbidos ★★★, Alcobaça ★★★ & Nazaré ★★

10am: It's a 20-minute drive north from Sintra to **Mafra** (p. 173), home to the vast palace and monastery built by King João V, using riches acquired from an 18th-century Brazilian gold rush. The sheer scale of it is mind-boggling. You'll need a couple of hours to tour the inside, including the library, which holds 36,000 leather-bound books, some over 500 years old.

Noon: Next stop, **Óbidos** (p. 193), 40 minutes farther north through the vineyards and apple and pear orchards of Portugal's far west. Surrounded by high walls, this is one of the country's best-preserved medieval towns. It's filled with whitewashed houses, their doors and windows picked out in deep blue and yellow. Take lunch in the town.

3pm: From here, it's a short hop to the **Mosteiro de Alcobaça** (p. 202), founded in 1153 by Portugal's first king Afonso Henriques in the unadorned Gothic style newly imported from France. Entering the interior is like stepping into the Middle Ages. The little town of Alcobaça is also renowned for its brightly colored **chintz fabrics** and the heavenly treats based on centuries-old convent recipes sold by **Alcôa** pastry shop (p. 205).

6pm: Take an evening stroll around the cliff-top heights of **Nazaré** (p. 206), a picturesque fishing port 20 minutes to the west. Then finish the day with a hearty fish stew before overnighting in Nazaré.

Day 6: Batalha ★★★ & Tomar ★★★

9:30am: It's a 30-minute drive from Nazaré, the monastery at **Batalha** (p. 210), the first of two medieval UNESCO World Heritage Sites you'll visit today. Batalha is a tribute in golden stone to a Portuguese victory over invading Spaniards in 1385. It was the most luxurious and grandest monastery in all of Portugal, executed in a flamboyant Gothic style.

Noon: Another 40 minutes heading inland takes you to the pretty riverside town of **Tomar** (p. 265). After lunch in one of the restaurants in the pretty downtown, head up to the **Convento de Cristo** (p. 266), a fascinating complex of buildings dating back to the 12th century. It was once a stronghold of the Knights Templar. The architecture of the round church at the center was inspired by their crusading ventures to Jerusalem. Both Tomar and Batalha are World Heritage Sites. Spend the night in Tomar.

Day 7: Coimbra ★★★

9am: Leave early to make the hour-long drive through thick forests of eucalyptus to the romantic city of **Coimbra** (p. 290), where you'll spend the day.

10am: You'll need a couple of hours to visit Portugal's oldest **university,** dating back to 1290, including the ceremonial rooms, jail for unruly students, and the magnificent baroque **library.**

Noon: Wander down the narrow old street of the upper town, taking care descending steep **Rua Quebra Costas** (break back street), popping in for a look at the Romanesque **cathedral.** When you reach the busy **Baixa** commercial district, grab lunch at historic **Café de Santa Cruz.**

2pm: Move next door to the church bearing the same name as the café, then lose yourself in the maze of narrow streets making up the Baixa and enjoy an amble through the romantic gardens beside the **River Mondego.**

4pm: Uphill again, spend a couple of hours in one of Portugal's best provincial museums, the **Museu Machado de Castro** (p. 294). Be sure to explore the remains of the Roman city in the basement.

6pm: Catch an early-evening performance of Coimbra's own amorous version of **fado** music at **Fado ao Centro,** where they'll explain the music's significance and serve a glass of port at the end.

THE BEST OF PORTUGAL IN 2 WEEKS

You can return to Lisbon from Coimbra in a couple of hours but if you have time, head north. A second week will open up the delights of Porto and the Douro wine region.

Days 1–7

Follow the itinerary suggested above.

Days 8 & 9: Porto ★★★

Porto (p. 327) is an hour's drive from Coimbra. Both banks of the **River Douro** (p. 331) will keep you occupied on the first day.

DAY 8

10am: On the northern bank, the **Ribeira** district is Porto's most traditional neighborhood. Behind a row of high-fronted, brightly painted merchants' houses lining the quayside are a warren of alleys strung with washing, where you'll stumble on architectural landmarks like the gold-lined **São Francisco** church (p. 333) and the **Bolsa** (p. 334), or stock exchange, with its sumptuous **Arabian Salon** (p. 335). Afterward, grab lunch at one of the cool restaurants in **Largo de São Domingos.**

2pm: Walk up the pretty **Rua das Flores** shopping street. At the top, peek at the tiled hall of **São Bento** railway station, and then continue up the hill to the **Sé,** Porto's cathedral, where you'll want to look in at the richly decorated cloisters and admire the view from the patio out front. Then walk across the upper level of the double-decked **Dom Luís I bridge** (p. 342), whose mighty ironwork spans the Douro. Now you are in **Vila Nova de Gaia** (p. 331), home of port wine.

4pm: Take the **cable car** to the waterfront and admire the ***barco rabelo*** boats that once hauled wine barrels, moored in the Douro. Along the riverfront and rising up the bank are dozens of centuries-old warehouses where ports are blended, then left to age. Most **port lodges** offer **tasting tours.** Among the best are the 300-year-old **Taylor's** cellars up the hill.

DAY 9

9am: After that wine, it's time for coffee. The city of port has some fabulous old cafes. The most opulent is **Café Majestic** (p. 338), founded in 1921. After your caffeine shot, wander out onto **Rua Santa de Catarina** (p. 338), the main shopping street in Porto's uptown **Baixa** district (p. 336).

11am: Visit the **Bolhão market,** a colorful collection of stores selling the city's favored foodstuffs, and the traditional stores in the street around it. Lunch on Porto's famed *francesinha* sandwiches in a nearby cafe.

1pm: Continue your uptown tour, admiring **Avenida dos Aliados** (p. 332), the city's grandest boulevard, fronted with Belle Epoque buildings leading up to the tower of **City Hall**, the soaring **Clérigos** church tower (p. 339), and the intriguing **Lello bookstore** (p. 337).

2pm: Head to the leafy **Boavista district** (p. 332), where, among patrician villas, the **Serralves** (p. 339) cultural complex contains a cutting-edge modern art museum surrounded by parkland.

4pm: If the weather is fine, carry on to the coast to promenade along the oceanfront at **Foz** (p. 345) or swim on one of the suburb's sandy beaches.

8pm: Return to Boavista in the evening to catch a concert at the **Casa da Música** (p. 357).

Day 10: Braga ★★

10am: Make the 40-minute drive out to Portugal's spiritual capital, **Braga** (p. 383).

11am: Braga has been a center of Christianity since Roman times and is home to **Portugal's oldest cathedral** (p. 386), founded in 1070. After a visit, spend the rest of the morning exploring downtown around **Praça da República** and **Rua do Souto.** Be sure to get coffee at the iconic cafe **A Brasileira.**

2pm: After lunch, head up to the 18th-century church of **Bom Jesus do Monte** (p. 385) looming over the city at the summit of a 116-m (380-ft.) baroque staircase. The sanctuary is surrounded by gardens filled with statues, lakes, and grottoes.

4pm: Back in town, visit the **Museu dos Biscainhos** museum for a taste of the 18th century. The building has been preserved as a noble home, complete with ornamented ceilings and walls with panels of tiles and paintings. Spend the night in one of Braga's fine hotels.

Day 11: Ponte de Lima ★★ & Peneda-Gerês National Park ★★★

9am: Drive northeast through the green, vine-covered slopes of ***vinho verde*** wine country.

10am: Pull into the delightful wine town of **Ponte de Lima** (p. 382) with its medieval bridge arching over the River Lima.

Noon: You reach Portugal's most spectacular wilderness area, the **Peneda-Gerês National Park** (p. 392). Spend the rest of the day exploring Portugal's only national park, 700 sq. km (270 sq. miles) of rugged highland: boulder-strewn plateaus, mountains, forests of oak and pine, and valleys carved by fast-flowing rivers. Wolves, boar, and wild horses roam. The human geography is also fascinating. The area is studded with granite villages, where longhorn cattle, sheep, and goats are raised, and rural life can seem little touched by the 21st century. Sinister stone structures, looking like tombs raised on pillars, are everywhere: They are actually grain stores, known as *espigueiros*. The clusters of them around the villages of **Soajo** and **Lindoso** (p. 392) are striking. Fortunately, you can find 21st-century comforts in plenty of fine hotels and inns around the region.

Day 12: Guimarães ★★★

10am: Moving south again, head to **Guimarães** (p. 374), another of Portugal's World Heritage Site cities. It's also the cradle of the nation, birthplace of the first king, Afonso Henriques, in 1109, and Portugal's first capital. "Guimarães is Portugal, the rest is just what we conquered," locals like to say.

11am: The founding father's **hilltop castle** still looms over the city, along with a Renaissance-era **royal palace** (p. 378).

1pm: Head downtown for lunch, then explore the tangle of cobbled lanes and plazas—like **Largo da Oliveira** and **Largo do Tourel**—lined with centuries-old granite homes, often painted in bright tones, sporting wrought-iron balconies or glass-fronted verandas.

3pm: The arts scene got a boost when the city was made European Cultural Capital in 2012, and it remains vibrant, so try to catch the latest contemporary art show at **Centro Cultural Vila Flor.**

4pm: Guimarães is a center for Portugal's fashionable **footwear** industry, so leave some time to pick up a bargain in one of the city's outlets.

Days 13 & 14: The Douro Wine Region ★★★

For the final 2 days in the north, you'll be in the **Douro wine region** (p. 370), another UNESCO World Heritage Site.

DAY 13

9am: Drive south from Guimarães, stopping in the lovely riverside town of **Amarante** (p. 361) to check out the Renaissance church of **São Gonçalo.**

Noon: Continue the precipitous decline to the big river. At Mesão Frio you'll see the Douro winding its lazy way through a distinctive landscape of terraced hills covered with grapevines. Follow the winding riverbank road until the Douro port of **Peso da Régua** (p. 369), where you can have lunch and discover the secrets of winemaking at the **Museu do Douro** museum (p. 370).

3pm: Cross the bridge to the south bank and visit the town of **Lamego** (p. 366), with its remarkable mountaintop church, before overnighting in one of the wine estates or wine-themed hotels, where you can sample the nectars without having to worry about driving.

DAY 14

9am: Hopefully your head is clear in the morning, because you will start with a twisting drive along the **N-222** (p. 365) riverside road, which has been called the world's most scenic route. There are also plenty of wineries to visit along the way.

Noon: Make a short detour to visit the charming wine village of **Pinhão** (p. 364) before rejoining the N-222 as it climbs through the heart of the wine region—stopping to enjoy tastings at the estates you pass.

3pm: Vila Nova de Foz Côa (p. 372) is where you find the last World Heritage Site on the tour, with its **prehistoric rock carvings** (p. 372) that date back over 20,000 years. This is a chance to get up close and personal with some of humanity's earliest art, both at the riverside sites and in the excellent **museum** that's an architectural landmark in its own right.

SOUTHERN PORTUGAL FOR 2 WEEKS

An alternative to heading north out of Lisbon would be to discover the attractions of mainland Portugal's two southernmost regions, the Alentejo and the Algarve. They are very different. The **Alentejo**, taking up a third of the country, is mostly made up of rolling farmland broken up by occasional hill ranges. Amid vineyards, olive groves and forests of cork oak are some of the country's best-preserved historic towns and villages, painted white to reflect the sun which pushes summer temperatures over 40°C (100°F). The **Algarve** is separated from the rest of the country by a range of scrub-covered hills running east-west. It enjoys a Mediterranean-style climate where almond and citrus trees thrive. The beaches on the sheltered southern coast are among Portugal's biggest draws for visitors.

On this tour by car, we're assuming you'll want to spend some time chilling on those beaches, so we've have spaced out the sightseeing accordingly.

Days 1, 2 & 3

Follows the Lisbon schedule at the start of "Lisbon & Around in 1 Week," above.

Days 4 & 5: Tróia Peninsular ★★★ & Alcácer do Sal ★★

Heading out south out of Lisbon, you cross the red-painted **Ponte 25 de Abril** suspension bridge high above the River Tagus toward the outstretched arms of the **Cristo Rei** statue (p. 175) on the south bank. It's less than an hour to the handsome town of **Alcácer do Sal** on the banks of the River Sado. Whitewashed Alcácer is an ancient center for rice production. It's surmounted by a convent wrapped in a castle that's now a luxurious hotel overlooking the paddy fields. Spend a couple of hours there before joining the sun-worshipers on the fine **sandy beaches** 30 minutes farther west. The beaches curve south for almost 60km (40 miles) from the headland of **Tróia** to the fishing port of **Sines.** If you have the cash, bed down at the Tróia Design Hotel, the swankiest resort in the region, and a true paragon of design and service. It's become the "in" place for Lisbonites to escape for the weekend.

Days 6, 7 & 8: Lagos & the Western Algarve ★★★

To get to the Algarve, it will take you 2 hours down the A2 toll highway. Head to **Lagos** (p. 222), the best town in the western Algarve, which you'll make your base for the next 3 nights.

Day 6: Explore the town that was the center for Portugal's 15th-century voyages of discoveries. The old part lies within the walls that protected it from pirates. It retains its charm, although Lagos' popularity with a youthful surfer crowd means it's hopping on summer nights. Lagos is surrounded by **beaches,** quiet coves among honey-colored cliffs, curving dune-backed strands, and deep blue lagoons.

Day 7: Drive out to headland fortress of **Sagres** (p. 219), Europe's southwestern tip, where Prince Henry the Navigator established his headquarters for launching the discoveries. It is a wild atmospheric space. Try to be there for the spectacular sunsets. North of Sagres are some of Europe's best surf beaches.

Day 8: The western Algarve is your target. Drive inland through the orange groves to spend the morning in the former Moorish capital of **Silves** (p. 234) with its mighty medieval fortress. After lunch, head back to the coast. In the tiny cove of **Benagil** you can pick up a skiff that will

South for 2 Weeks of Culture & the Coast

take you to amazing **sea caves** carved into the sandstone and the beach at **Praia da Marinha,** arguably the most beautiful in Portugal.

Days 9 & 10: Tavira & the Eastern Algarve ★★★

Slow down and relax. The eastern Algarve, close to the border with Spain's Andalusia region, is known as the **Sotavento,** meaning "sheltered from the wind"—in contrast to the breezy west. Beaches here, many of them on long, sandbar islands, are tranquil with warmer water. **Tavira** (p. 258) is a sweet town, with patrician manor houses lining the banks of the Gilão River and streets filled with restaurants and cafes. There are plenty of good places to stay here, excellent for exploring the beaches. Be sure to take a boat tour in the marshy **Ria Formosa** nature reserve, a magnate for bird-watchers.

Day 11: Mértola ★★

Before leaving the Algarve coast, look in on **Vila Real de Santo António** (p. 260), a border town built after the 1755 earthquake, which is a rare example of 18th-century town planning. Then head north following the River Guadiana for about an hour to **Mértola** (p. 269), one of Portugal's most beautiful villages. Strung out on the crest of a ridge, its white houses and crenellated battlements are perfectly reflected in the river's still blue waters. This was once the capital of an Arab emirate and a busy medieval trading hub. Its parish church is one of the few in Portugal that still clearly shows the signs that it was once a mosque.

Days 12 & 13: Évora ★★★

It's a 2-hour drive north to **Évora,** the majestic capital of the Alentejo, a UNESCO World Heritage Site city. Take the slow road, winding your way through picturesque villages like **Serpa, Moura,** and **Monsaraz,** which occupies a spectacular location overlooking the **Alqueva** reservoir, western Europe's largest man-made lake.

Arriving in **Évora** in the late afternoon, spend your time moseying around its medieval, white-painted heart, admiring the medieval fortifications and 16th-century aqueduct before preparing to feast on Alentejo food in one of the city's excellent restaurants.

Next day, start out in the main square, the **Praça do Giraldo,** once a scene of executions and the horrors of the Inquisition, now an elegant focal point for city life and serious coffee drinking. Spend the rest of the morning visiting the 12th-century **cathedral**—being sure to admire the views from the roof—and the **Temple of Diana,** whose columns form one of the best-preserved Roman ruins in the Iberian Peninsula.

In the afternoon, visit the **Igreja de São Francisco,** which, besides being an impressive example of Portugal's "maritime discoveries-inspired" Manueline architecture, is best known for a chapel with walls made from human skulls and other bones.

Day 14: Elvas ★★★ & Marvão ★★★

For the final day, visit two very different frontier fortress towns. First **Elvas,** whose defenses, built during Portugal's war of independence from Spain in the 1640s, are the biggest of their type in the world. A giant complex of overlapping walls and ditches encircles the ancient white city on the old road leading to Lisbon from Madrid. It's also a World Heritage Site.

Just over an hour to the north, **Marvão** perches at the top of a spur of rock surging 860 meters (2,800 ft.) above the plain. It was fought over since ancient times due to its commanding position over the lands below. Inside its stone walls, the town of red-tiled, white-walled houses seems to grow out of the rocks. There's a special atmosphere, peaceful now, but it's easy to imagine as a battlefield between Celts and Romans, Christians and Moors, and Spanish invaders versus the British redcoats helping defend Portugal in the 1760s.

A WEEK IN LISBON WITH KIDS

Day 1

Lisbon is pretty much unique among European capitals in having summer-long sunshine, plus suburbs featuring broad sandy beaches and regular Atlantic rollers ideal for surfing. So rather than drag the kids around museums, get them enrolled in one of the city's many surf schools. That way they spend the mornings having fun in the waves, and you get to do cultural stuff undisturbed by the complaints of bored juniors, and you can all spend some quality time together in the afternoons.

Carcavelos Beach, just a 20-minute train ride from downtown, is ideal for beginners, but there are beaches within a short drive from Lisbon to suit all standards.

In the afternoon, it's time to discover what lies beneath the waves. The **Oceanário** (p. 114) is a delight for all ages, but children will marvel at its range of sea life. The aquarium also organizes special events such as concerts for young children, or sleepovers where kids (and parents) can spend the night next to the shark tank. You'll need at least a couple of hours to explore the Oceanário.

Day 2

After the morning at surf school, spend the afternoon on dry land. Take the kids to **Castelo de São Jorge** (**St. George's Castle;** p. 98) so they can admire the view, roam the ramparts, and imagine the colorful history of the Romans, Moors, and Crusaders who lived and battled there. Then head down the castle hill and up the next slope to the **Graça** neighborhood to catch **Eléctrico 28** (p. 70), the most iconic line of Lisbon's vintage yellow streetcars (*eléctricos*). It will likely be crowded with tourists, but remains a fun way to see the city as it rattles through the narrow lanes of the **Alfama** neighborhood, scoots through the grid pattern of **Baixa**'s streets, hauls up past the posh shops of **Chiado,** and finally terminates in front of the **Cemitério dos Prazeres,** Lisbon's largest cemetery. Few tourists venture here, but the great 19th-century necropolis, with its monumental family tombs, makes for an intriguingly spooky visit. Be sure to see the great pyramid built by Dom Pedro de Sousa Holstein, Duke de Palmela, believed to be Europe's biggest private mausoleum.

Day 3

In the afternoon head for the zoo. The **Jardim Zoológico de Lisboa** (p. 115) has been around for 132 years and contains over 2,000 animals from 300 different species. At least one you're unlikely to see anywhere else—the **Iberian lynx**—is the world's rarest cat, struggling to survive with the help of a conservation program in the wild lands of southern Spain and southeastern Portugal. The zoo has turned itself around after falling on hard times during the 1980s and is now a much-loved attraction for Portuguese schoolchildren who come to see the rare red pandas, dolphin show, or the "enchanted woods," where exotic birds fly in the open air.

Day 4

Take the train out to **Sintra** (p. 161). High up in the hills to the west of Lisbon, this was the summer retreat for the royal family and their aristocratic entourage. Among the thickly forested hills are fairytale palaces and secret gardens to explore. Make like 18th-century nobles and hire a

Lisbon with Kids

Benfica stadium **10**
Carcavelos beach **2**
Castelo de São Jorge **6**
Cemitério dos Prazeres **5**
Centro Colombo **11**
Jardim Zoológico de Lisboa **9**

Museu Nacional dos Coches **4**
Oceanário **7**
Pavilion of Knowledge-Ciência Viva **8**
Picadeiro Henrique Calado **3**
Sintra **1**

horse-drawn carriage to take you through the forests to the gates of the phantasmagorical **Palácio da Pena** (p. 164).

Day 5

Sport Lisboa e Benfica, better known simply as **Benfica,** is one of the world's great soccer clubs, twice European champions. In fact, it's believed to be the world's biggest club in terms of membership, with almost 160,000 paid-up fans. Catching a home game can be a tremendous experience, especially if they are playing against cross-town rivals Sporting or northern upstarts FC Porto. If you can't get to a match, you can still tour the **Estádio da Luz** stadium and visit its state-of-the-art **museum** dedicated to the club's 112-year history, in which its greatest player, Eusébio (1942–2014), plays a starring role.

Next door to the stadium is one of Europe's largest shopping malls, the **Centro Colombo,** offering 119,725 sq. meters (1.3 million sq. ft.) of retail therapy. There are 340 stores, 60 restaurants, 9 movie screens, and a bowling alley. It's all vaguely themed around the Portuguese era of Discoveries.

Day 6

Lisbon's coach museum, the **Museu Nacional dos Coches** (p. 104), has one of the world's greatest collections of historical carriages. It is Portugal's most visited museum and contains Cinderella-style carriages dating back to the 16th century. The oldest was used to bring King Filipe II from Madrid to Lisbon during the Spanish occupation, and the most exuberant is a gold-covered vehicle given as a gift to the Pope from a Portuguese king in 1715. It's housed in a new building that opened in 2015 in Lisbon's riverside **Belém** district.

Nearby in the **Picadeiro Henrique Calado** you can watch some 18th-century-style horsemanship. This arena is where the Portuguese School of Equestrian Arts holds its daily training and weekly performances, with horses and riders clad in period costumes to conjure up the displays they once put on to entertain the royal family. The **Lusitano** horses used in the performances are a unique Portuguese breed.

Day 7

Head back out to the riverside **Parque das Nações** district packed with modern architecture. Apart from the **Oceanário** (p. 114), kids will love the **Pavilion of Knowledge – Ciência Viva,** an interactive science museum, where they can engage in an array of experiments, including riding a bike on a tight rope. It's loads of fun. After that, take a ride in the cable cars that run high above the riverbank, giving a splendid view over Europe's longest bridge. Be warned: The area also contains another big shopping mall.

SETTLING INTO LISBON

5

Bathed in pure Atlantic light, crowned by the storybook St. Jorge's Castle and straddling seven hills, Lisbon is one of Europe's most visually striking capitals. Looks aside, the city will surely win you over with its genuine friendliness and blissfully laid-back pace. At once nostalgic and progressive, Lisbon's charm shines through in everyday life—listening to the mournful fado songs in the Moorish Alfama's alleys, indulging in custard tarts in gilded Art Nouveau patisseries and living it up at a Bairro Alto or Cais do Sodré street party.

THINGS TO DO Walk on the promenade along the river, from Praça do Comércio to Cais do Sodré, with a stop in the kiosk at sunset, overlooking the bridge and the estuary. Nothing says Lisbon like sipping a coffee or a drink while enjoying a panoramic view. Or a ride on century-old **tram 28,** which trundles past stately plazas and the Romanesque **Sé (cathedral**, p. 100). Jump off at hilltop **St Jorge's Castle** (p. 98) for a rampart stroll and views reaching to the Tagus River. Just steps away, the Moorish **Alfama** quarter's mazy lanes are full of laundry billowing, neighbors gossiping, and melancholic fado songs. Down by the river, take the 15 tram to Belém and visit **Jerónimos Monastery's** (p. 102) fantastically ornate Manueline cloisters that whisk you back to Portugal's Age of Discovery.

SHOPPING Leather gloves, Port and Madeira wine, tinned fish, buttons, vintage clothes and shoes—you'll find it all in the specialty stores lining **Pombaline Baixa, Cais do Sodré,** and **Chiado.** Compare purchases over a *bica* (espresso) inside Art Deco **Nicola** café (p. 120). Young Lisboetas combine bar crawling with late-night shopping in the **Bairro Alto,** where boutiques stock vintage fashion and the sassy collections of local designers. **Avenida da Liberdade** is Lisbon's catwalk of big-name designers; **Príncipe Real** and **Chiado** offer independent shops, like Embaixada and Storytailors.

DINING Arrive before the crowds at the famous **Pastéis de Belém** (p. 103) to devour crisp, cinnamon-dusted custard tarts hot from the oven. Lisboetas make the most of warm nights by dining alfresco on fresh fish in the Alfama's lantern-lit lanes and world flavors on pavement terraces in the buzzy Bairro Alto, Cais do

Lisbon

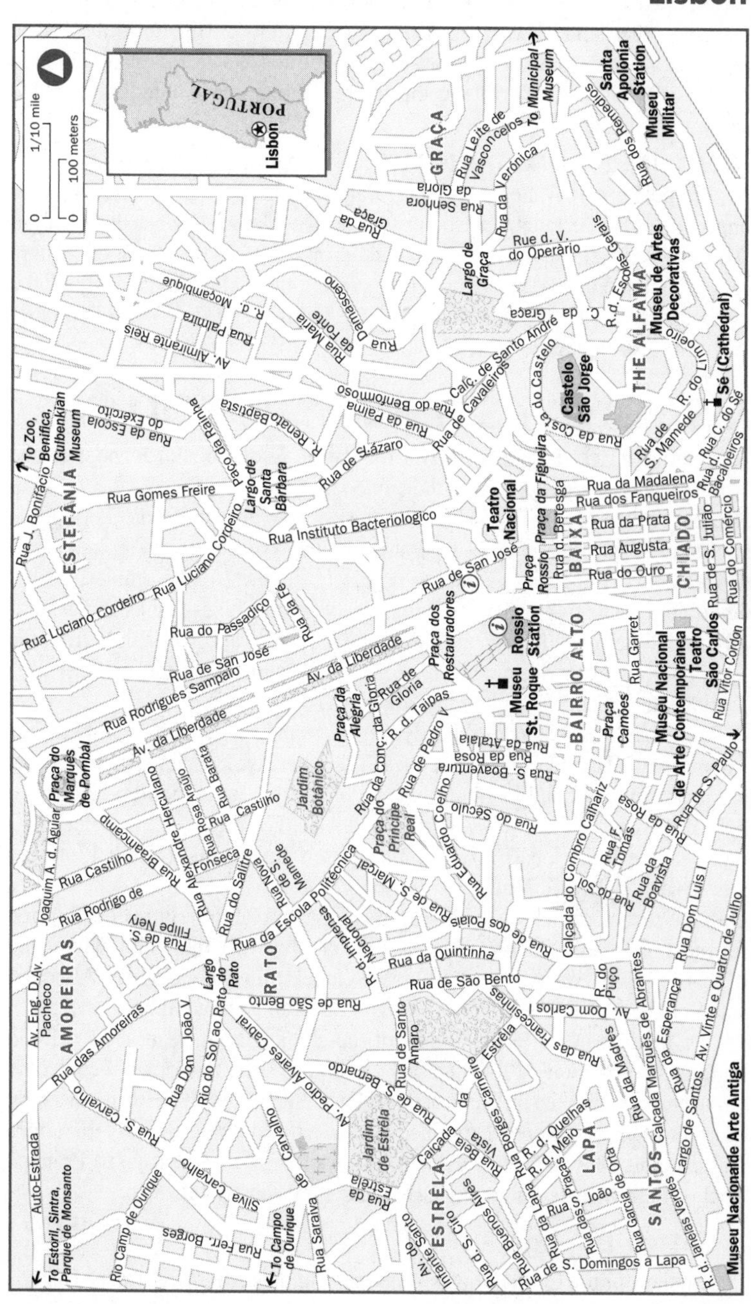

1/10 mile
100 meters
PORTUGAL
Lisbon
GRAÇA
To Municipal Museum
Santa Apolónia Station
Museu Militar
Rua dos Remédios
Rua Leite de Vasconcelos
Rua da Verónica
Rua da Senhora da Glória
Rua da Graça
Largo de Graça
Rue d. V. do Operário
R. d. Escolas Gerais
THE ALFAMA
Museu de Artes Decorativas
Sé (Cathedral)
R. do Limoeiro
Castelo São Jorge
Rua da Costa do Castelo
Calç. de Santo André
Rua de Cavaleiros
Rua do Benformoso
Rua da Palma
Rua de S. Lázaro
R. Renato Baptista
Rua Maria da Fonte
Rua Damasceno
R. d. Moçambique
Rua Palmira
Av. Almirante Reis
To Zoo, Benfica, Gulbenkian Museum
Rua da Escola do Exército
Paço da Rainha
Largo de Santa Bárbara
Rua Gomes Freire
ESTEFÂNIA
Rua J. Bonifácio
Rua Instituto Bacteriologico
Teatro Nacional
Praça da Figueira
Rua da Madalena
Rua dos Fanqueiros
Rua da Prata
Rua Augusta
Rua do Ouro
BAIXA
CHIADO
Rua d. Betesga
Praça Rossio
Rua de S. Julião
Rua do Comércio
Rua C. do Sé
Rua de S. Mamede
Rua de San José
Rua Luciano Cordeiro
Rua do Passadiço
Rua da Fé
Rua de San José
Rua Rodrigues Sampaio
Av. da Liberdade
Praça dos Restauradores
Rossio Station
Museu St. Roque
BAIRRO ALTO
Rua Garret
Museu Nacional de Arte Contemporânea
Teatro São Carlos
Rua Vítor Cordon
Praça Camões
Rua da Atalaia
Rua da Rosa
Rua S. Boaventura
Rua do Século
Rua de Pedro V
R. d. Taipas
Calç. da Glória
Praça da Alegria
Rua da Conç. da Glória
Jardim Botânico
Praça do Príncipe Real
Rua Eduardo Coelho
Calçada do Combro
Calhariz
Rua F. Tomás
Rua da Boavista
Rua do Sol
Rua de S. Paulo
To Rua Dom Luis I
Rua de Quatro de Julho
Rua de Poiais de S. Bento
Rua de S. Marçal
Rua da Escola Politécnica
R. d. Imprensa Nacional
Rua da Quintinha
Rua de São Bento
Praça do Marquês de Pombal
Rua A. d. Aguiar
Rua Braamcamp
Rua Castilho
Rua Alexandre Herculano
Rua Rosa Araújo
Rua Barata
Rua Fonseca
Rua do Salitre
Rua Nova de S. Mamede
Rua Rodrigo de
Joaquim
Rua de S. Filipe Nery
AMOREIRAS
RATO
Largo do Rato
Av. Eng. D. Av. Pacheco
Rua das Amoreiras
Rua Dom João V
Rio do Sol ao Rato
Rua Alvares Cabral
Rua de Santo Amaro
R. do Puço
Av. Dom Carlos I
Rua das Francesinhas
Rua das Madres
Calçada Marquês de Abrantes
Rua da Esperança
Av. Vinte e Quatro de Julho
Largo de Santos
SANTOS
Museu Nacional de Arte Antiga
R. d. Janelas Verdes
Rua de S. Domingos a Lapa
Rua Garcia de Orta
LAPA
Rua das Praças
Rua S. João
Rua da Lapa
R. d. Meio
R. d. Quelhas
Rua Borges Carneiro
Rua Buenos Aires
Rua Bela Vista
Estrêla
ESTRÊLA
Jardim de Estrêla
Calçada da Estrêla
Rua de S. Bernardo
Av. Pedro Alvares Cabral
Rua da Estrêla
Rua d. S. Ciro
Av. Infante Santo
To Campo de Ourique
Rua Saraiva de Carvalho
Silva Carvalho
Rua S. Carvalho
Rua Ferr. Borges
Rio Camp de Ourique
Auto-Estrada
To Estoril, Sintra, Parque de Monsanto

Sodré, Mouraria, or Campo de Ourique. The ornately tiled old school **Cervejaria Ramiro** (p. 88) pairs cold beers with the freshest seafood, like *amêijoas à Bulhão Pato* (clams with cilantro and garlic). Go to Chiado to the stylish Michelin-starred restaurant **Belcanto** (p. 84) by José Avillez, or party all night long if it's June and festivals to the saints are being celebrated with grilled sardines, wine, and music.

NIGHTLIFE & ENTERTAINMENT Toast the sunset at **Park** (p. 139), a bar set incongruously atop a parking garage that has the hippest scene in town and some of the best views. Lisbon's unrivaled hot spot is the bar-lined **Bairro Alto,** where revelers hit the street to chat, drink, and dance. The mood is more relaxed in the **Alfama,** where fado songs recalling lost love and destiny fill the atmospheric vaults of places like **Club de Fado** (p. 134) or **Parreirinha de Alfama** (less expensive, p. 135).

LISBON YESTERDAY & TODAY

In its golden age, Lisbon gained a reputation as the eighth wonder of the world. Travelers returning from the city boasted that its riches rivaled those of Venice. As one of the greatest maritime centers in history, the Portuguese capital imported exotic wares from the far-flung corners of its empire.

Treasures from Asia—including porcelain, luxurious silks, rubies, pearls, and other rare gems—arrived at Indian seaports on Chinese junks and eventually found their way to Lisbon. The abundance and variety of spices from the East, such as turmeric, ginger, pepper, cumin, cinnamon, and betel, rivaled even Keats's vision of "silken Samarkand."

From the Americas came red dyewood (brazilwood), coffee, gold, sugar cane, diamonds, and other gemstones. The extensive contact signaled a new era in world trade, and Lisbon sat at the center of a great maritime empire, a hub of commerce for Europe, Africa, and Asia. For more than a century Lisbon was the first global village, capital of an empire that included faraway places such as Brazil, Macao, or Goa.

In the second decade of the new millennium, and after a slumber that lasted for most of the 20th century, there is a new Lisbon awaiting you today. Some of that is good news and some of it isn't—at least for traditionalists. Although some medieval facades and old palaces have been restored, others have given way to modern office blocks; many of the city's Art Nouveau and Art Deco buildings, a mainstay of the cityscape, have also been torn down. Few iconic old trams are still seen on the streets, and they are gradually being replaced by buses or by newer, more streamlined, and much faster trams. Or by tram lines that do tours only, aimed at visitors, like the green ones that go to Príncipe Real or to the Castle (more expensive than they should be).

A Bit of Background

Phoenicians or the Carthaginians were the original settlers in Lisbon. Historians believe it's the oldest city in Europe, and although many of its layers were destroyed by the earthquake of 1755, the city still has an ancient feeling, especially in neighborhoods like Alfama, where the first settlements were found.

The Romans settled in Lisbon in about 205 B.C., later building a fortification on the site of what is now St. Jorge's Castle; they named the city Olisippo. The Visigoths captured the city in the 5th century A.D.; in 714, centuries of Moorish domination began. The first king of Portugal, Afonso Henríques, captured Lisbon from the Moors in 1147. But it wasn't until 1256 that Afonso III moved the capital here, deserting Coimbra, now the country's major university city.

The Great Earthquake occurred at 9:40am on All Saints' Day, November 1, 1755. "From Scotland to Asia Minor, people ran out of doors and looked at the sky, and fearfully waited. It was, of course, an earthquake," chronicled *Holiday* magazine. Tidal waves 15m (49 ft.) high swept over Algeciras, Spain. The shockwaves were felt all over Europe, up to Finland, and in northern Africa. Morocco was seriously hit and thousands died. Some 22 aftershocks followed. Roofs caved in; hospitals (with more than 1,000 patients), prisons, public buildings, royal palaces, aristocratic town houses, fishers' cottages, churches, and houses of prostitution—all were toppled. Overturned candles helped ignite a fire that consumed the once-proud capital in just 6 days, leaving it a gutted, charred shambles. Voltaire described the destruction in *Candide:* "The sea boiled up in the harbor and smashed the vessels lying at anchor. Whirlwinds of flame and ashes covered the streets and squares, houses collapsed, roofs were thrown onto foundations and the foundations crumbled." All told, around 90,000 inhabitants were crushed beneath the tumbling debris, drowned by the tsunami (12m/39 ft. high) or killed by the fire.

After the ashes settled, the Marquês de Pombal, the prime minister, ordered that the dead be buried and the city rebuilt at once. To accomplish that ambitious plan, the king gave him virtually dictatorial powers.

What Pombal ordered constructed was a city of wide, symmetrical boulevards leading into handsome squares dominated by fountains and statuary. Bordering these wide avenues would be black-and-white mosaic sidewalks, the most celebrated in Europe. Today, the mixture of old and "new" (post-earthquake) here is so harmonious that many consider Lisbon one of the most beautiful cities in Europe. Fountains abound; one, the *Samaritan,* dates from the 16th century. The boulevards flank new high-rise apartment houses, while in other quarters, laundry hanging from 18th-century houses flaps in the wind.

The Tagus, the river flowing through Lisbon, has been called the city's eternal lover—and in many ways it is the most vital part of the city. The port is still very important for the economy and container ships are part of the waterfront landscape.

Streets bear colorful names or designations relating to their uses over the ages, such as Rua do Açúcar (Street of Sugar), Pasteleiro (Baker Street), or Bacalhoeiros (cod fishermen). Praça do Comércio, the bull's-eye center of the Lisbon waterfront, is also known as Terreiro do Paço (Royal's Palace Square), in honor of the palace that stood here until it was destroyed by the earthquake.

Many who have never been to Lisbon know it well from watching World War II spy movies on TV. In the classic film *Casablanca,* Lisbon embodied the passage point to the Americas for refugees stranded in northern Africa. During the war, Lisbon, officially neutral, was a hotbed of intrigue, espionage and refugees. It was also a haven for thousands of refugees, including deposed royalty. From Graham Greene to Ian Fleming, many famous spies traveled to Lisbon. Fleming got the inspiration for his character James Bond, while visiting Casino Estoril, in the nearby beach resort of Estoril.

Lisbon Today

No longer the provincial town it was as recently as the 1970s, post-millennium Lisbon has blossomed into a cosmopolitan city often beset with construction pains. Many of its old structures that were falling apart have been restored, and renovation has started to attract private investment, particularly since tourism became such an important activity in the city after the difficult recession years and euro woes of 2011–14 (known as the "crisis"), in which austerity and recession forced many to leave the country. In the last 20 years, some of the formerly clogged streets of the Baixa have been turned into cobblestone pedestrian malls and new cultural centers have opened, including the Museum of Art and Architecture (see p. 102) in Belém.

Lisbon is growing and evolving, and the city is considerably more sophisticated than it once was, no doubt due, in part, to Portugal's joining the European Union (E.U.). Some 3 million people now live in the metropolitan area of Lisbon, but only 550,000 actually live in the city, due to expensive rents and a tight market for apartments (short-term rentals are growing). Textiles, shoes, clothing, china, techonology, and earthenware are among the leading industries in the region. But services like banking and tourism are driving the city's economy.

ORIENTATION

When to Visit

Consider an off-season visit, especially in the spring or fall, when the city enjoys glorious weather. The city isn't overrun with visitors then, and you can take in its attractions without being trampled or broiled (as you will be during the hot, humid months of July and August). November and December are also appealing as the city is quieter, but getting ready for the Christmas holidays.

Arriving

BY PLANE Foreign and domestic flights land at Lisbon's **Aeroporto de Lisboa** (www.ana-aeroportos.pt; © **21/841-35-00**), about 6.5km (4 miles) from the heart of the city.

An **AERO-BUS** runs between the airport and the Cais do Sodré train station every 20 minutes from 8am to 11pm. The fare is 3.15€. It makes 10 stops, including Praça dos Restauradores and Praça do Comércio. There's no charge for luggage, and you can use the same ticket to hop on and off as many of their buses as you like for the next 24 hours. This is also the most convenient way to get into the city; take the Metro and you'll have to switch trains (sometimes a few times).

Taxi passengers line up in a usually well-organized queue at the sidewalk in front of the airport, or you can call **Rádio Táxi** at © **21/811-90-00.** ***Tip:*** To avoid the line, exit through the departures rather than the arrivals exit and grab one of the taxis that is dropping off passengers. The average taxi fare from the airport to central Lisbon is 12€. Each piece of luggage is 1.60€ extra. **Uber** is also available, but there have been issues with their drivers picking up clients at the airport, due to taxi drivers' opposition. (Our advice: Take a taxi to avoid creating a confrontation.)

The **metro station** at the airport is part of the red line, connecting with central Lisbon in Alameda (green line), Saldanha (yellow line), or S. Sebastião (blue line) stations. A single journey costs 1.40€ plus 0.50€ for the reusable Viva Card.

BY TRAIN A smooth-running, modern train system connects Lisbon to all the towns and villages along the Portuguese coastal road. There's only one class of seat, and the rides are inexpensive and generally comfortable. You can board the train at the waterfront Cais do Sodré Station in Lisbon and head up the coast all the way to Cascais. For Sintra, you must go to the Estação do Rossio station, opening onto Praça de Dom Pedro IV, or the Rossio, where frequent connections can be made. The one-way fare from Lisbon to Cascais, Estoril, or Sintra is 3.40€ (www.cp.pt; © **21/261-30-00**).

Most international rail passengers (from Madrid and Paris, primarily) arrive at the **Estação da Santa Apolónia,** Avenida Infante Dom Henrique, the major terminal, by the Tagus near the Alfama district. Two daily trains make the 10-hour run from Madrid to Lisbon. Rail lines from northern and eastern Portugal also arrive at this station. But there are other busy stations connecting the city: Gare do Oriente, Entrecampos, Rossio, and Cais do Sodré.

Connected to the metro system and opened in time for EXPO '98, the **Gare de Oriente** at Parque das Nações is the hub for some long-distance and suburban trains, including service to such destinations as Porto, Coimbra, Minho, Faro, and the Douro. But if you have a choice, Santa Apolónia is much closer to the city center. At the **Entrecampos** station you can get on the train to the Algarve and also the suburban Fertagus train to the south bank. At the **Estação do Rossio,** between Praça dos Restauradores and Praça de Dom Pedro IV, you can get trains to Sintra. The Art Deco estação do **Cais do Sodré,** just beyond the south end of Rua Alecrim, west of Praça do Comércio, handles trains to Cascais and Estoril.

BY FERRY Long before the bridges across the Tagus were built, reliable ferryboats chugged across the river, connecting the left bank with the right. They still do, and have been rebuilt and remotorized so they're no longer noisy. Many Portuguese who live on the bank opposite Lisbon take the ferry to avoid the heavy bridge traffic during rush hour.

Most boats leave from Cais do Sodré, heading for Cacilhas. The trip is worth it for the scenic views alone. Ferries depart Lisbon throughout the day

One Card, Many Rides

For all modes of travel in Lisbon and in the surrounding areas, you can use the **Viva Viagem** card, bought at any ticket office or at the metro stations. This card allows you to travel on the ferry; suburban trains to Sintra, Cascais, or on the Fertagus line; in Carris buses and trams; and on the Metro. You pay less with the card than you would paying for individual rides. And it's relatively simple to use: You add credit to that card with the "zapping" system. Simply click the "zapping" option on machines in metro stations or ask for zapping at the counters in metro and train stations, the ferry terminal, Carris kiosks, and post offices. The card system is similar to London's Oyster card.

about every 10 to 20 minutes; trip time across the Tagus is 10 minutes. The ferry fare is 1.20€. There's a ferryboat from Belém to Trafaria (in the south bank, near Costa da Caparica) where you can take the car for more 4.70€, but it runs less often (www.transtejo.pt; ✆ **80/820-30-50**).

BY BUS Buses from all over Portugal arrive at the **Terminal Rodoviário de Sete Rios** (www.rede-expressos.pt; ✆ **21/358-14-72**). If your hotel is in Estoril or Cascais, you can take the Metro to Cais do Sodré and then the train. At least six buses a day leave for Lagos and Faro, in the Algarve, and nine buses head north every day to Porto. There are 14 daily buses to Coimbra, the university city to the north. One-way fare from Lagos to Lisbon is 20€.

BY CAR International motorists must arrive through Spain, the only nation connected to Portugal by road. The main roads are well maintained and there are many highways across the country. From Madrid, if you head west to north and central Portugal, the main road (N620) from Tordesillas goes southwest by way of Salamanca and Ciudad Rodrigo and reaches the Portuguese frontier at Fuentes de Onoro. If you head to Lisbon, drive toward Badajoz. As Portugal is part of the Schengen European treaty there are no border controls. See "Getting Around" below for info on car-rental agencies in the city.

Visitor Information

The main **tourist office** in Lisbon is at the Palácio da Foz, Praça dos Restauradores (www.visitportugal.com; ✆ **21/120-50-50**), at the Baixa end of Avenida da Liberdade. Open daily from 9am to 8pm (Metro: Restauradores), it sells the **Lisbon Card,** which provides transportation and entrance fees to museums and other attractions, plus discounts on admission to events and the chance to skip some queues. If you're planning to visit more than two museums or attractions, it's definitely worth buying as you'll save money in visits and transportation, and will get some line-jumping privileges. For adults, a 1-day pass costs 18.50€, a 2-day pass costs 31.50€, and a 3-day pass costs 39€. Children 5 to 11 pay 11.50€ for a 1-day pass, 17.50€ for a 2-day pass, and 20.50€ for a 3-day pass. Another tourist office is located in Praça do Comércio, 78-81 (www.visitlisboa.com; ✆ **91/051-78-86**). This tourist office is open daily from 9am to 7pm.

City Layout

MAIN STREETS & SQUARES Lisbon is the westernmost capital of continental Europe, spreading across more than seven hills, something you feel vividly in your muscles when walking in the city. Streets rise and fall across the hills, at times dwindling into mere alleyways, especially in old neighborhoods like Alfama, Castelo, Mouraria, or Bairro Alto.

Visitors are wise to start their Lisbon explorations in the **Praça do Comércio (Commerce Square).** It's one of the most perfectly planned squares in Europe, rivaled only by the Piazza dell'Unità d'Italia in Trieste, Italy, or San Marco square in Venice. Before the 1755 earthquake, Praça do Comércio was known as Terreiro do Paço, the Palace Grounds, because the king and his court lived in now-destroyed buildings on that site. The statue of bronze-green color is of José I, the king at the time of the earthquake. A deeply historic area, the stock exchange and government ministries once called this home, and in 1908 King Carlos I and his elder son, Luís Filipe, were fatally shot here by an assassin. The monarchy held on for another 2 years, but the House of Bragança effectively came to an end that day.

Heading north from Commerce Square, you enter the hustle and bustle of **Praça de Dom Pedro IV,** popularly known as the Rossio. The "drunken" undulation of the sidewalks, with their arabesques of black and white, is best seen from the top of the **Elevador de Santa Justa** (p. 99).

Opening onto the Rossio is the **Teatro Nacional de Dona Maria II,** a freestanding building whose facade has been preserved, after a fire destroyed most of the theater in 1964. The historical venue only opened again in 1978. If you arrive by train, you'll enter the **Estação do Rossio,** opposite the theater (its exuberant Manueline architecture is well worth seeing). Separating the Rossio from Avenida da Liberdade is **Praça dos Restauradores,** named in honor of the Restoration, when the Portuguese chose their own king and freed themselves of 60 years of Spanish rule. An obelisk commemorates the event.

Lisbon's main avenue is **Avenida da Liberdade (Avenue of Liberty).** Dating from 1880, this handsome thouroughfare is like a 1.5km-long (1-mile) park, with shade trees, gardens, and center walks for the promenading crowds. Flanking it are fine shops, luxury brands, coffeehouses, kiosks with sidewalk tables, bakeries, and hotels. At the top of the avenue is **Praça do Marquês de Pombal,** with a statue erected in honor of the 18th-century prime minister credited with Lisbon's reconstruction in the aftermath of the earthquake.

Proceeding north, you'll enter **Parque Eduardo VII,** named in honor of the son of Queen Victoria, who paid a state visit to Lisbon. In the park, which welcomes Lisbon's book fair (usually in May or June), is the **Estufa Fria** (p. 106), a captivating greenhouse.

FINDING AN ADDRESS Addresses consist of a street name followed by a number. Sometimes the floor of the building is given as well. For example, Av. Casal Ribeiro 18-3 means that the building is at number 18 and the address is on the third floor. ***Note:*** Finding an address in the old quarters of

Lisbon can be difficult because street numbering at times follows no predictable pattern (happily, this is just the case in that area of town).

Neighborhoods in Brief

Baixa A mix of shopping and business district, Baixa contains much Pombaline-style architecture. (The term refers to the prime minister who rebuilt Lisbon following the earthquake.) Many major Portuguese banks are headquartered here. And in recent years, hotels and restaurants opened here, too. Running south, the main street of Baixa separates Praça do Comércio from the Rossio. A triumphal arch leads from the square to **Rua Augusta,** a pedestrian street lined with many clothing stores, though the most interesting shops have closed. **MUDE** (p. 112), the Museum of Fashion and Design, is also located in this street. The two most important streets of Baixa were **Rua da Prata (Street of Silver)** and **Rua Áurea,** formerly called Rua do Ouro (Street of Gold). Some silversmiths and goldsmiths are still located on these streets, but most traditional shops have closed. For old-fashioned window shopping, walk to **Rua da Conceição,** a time-warp street where the old button shops are, as well as a modern wine shop.

Chiado If you head west from Baixa, you'll enter this shopping district. From its perch on a hill, it's traversed by **Rua Garrett,** named for the noted romantic writer Almeida Garrett (1799–1854). Many of the finest shops in the city, such as the Vista Alegre, a china and porcelain house, and the linen store Paris em Lisboa, are here. One coffeehouse in particular, **A Brasileira** (p. 135) has been a traditional gathering spot for the Portuguese literati since 1905 (you can take a photo sitting next to the statue of poet Fernando Pessoa outside). But don't miss **Bertrand Livreiros** (p. 125) considered by the Guinness Book of Records to be the oldest operating bookshop in the world since 1732, and a walk toward Largo de São Carlos where the opera house is.

Bairro Alto Continuing your ascent, you'll arrive at the Bairro Alto (Upper City). This sector, reached by trolley car 28, occupies one of the hills of Lisbon. Many of its buildings were left reasonably intact by the 1755 earthquake. Containing much of the charm and color of the Alfama, it's the location of some of the finest fado (meaning "fate" and describing a type of song that started here in Lisbon) clubs, as well as restaurants, bars, and original shops. It's one of Lisbon's favorite nightlife areas. Regrettably, many of the side streets at night are the haunts of drug dealers.

Santos Called the "design district," this waterfront district is one of the emerging new neighborhoods of Lisbon, attracting artists, designers, architects, and other creative people. Big development plans are underway to add a vast array of studios, restaurants, bars, designer outlets, and galleries. The area still has many 19th-century warehouses with wrought-iron balconies (they're being recycled for 21st-century use). The neighborhood of Bairro Alto lies next door, and locals go there for their nightlife, but Santos is beginning to develop its own after-dark diversions.

The Alfama East of Praça do Comércio lies the city's oldest district, the Alfama. Saved only in part from the devastation of the 1755 earthquake, the Alfama was the Moorish section of the capital. In the 20th century it used to be home, in some parts, to dockworkers, fishermen, and *varinas* (fishwives), but now gentrification and tourism is changing this traditional neighborhood. Overlooking the Alfama is **Castelo São Jorge** (p. 98), or St. George's Castle, a Visigothic fortification that was later used by the Romans. On the way to the Alfama, on Rua dos Bacalhoeiros, stands another landmark, the **Casa dos Bicos (House of the Pointed Stones),** an early-16th-century townhouse whose facade is studded with diamond-shaped stones. It now hosts the José Saramago Foundation. Saramago was a writer, awarded with the Nobel Prize for Literature. Be careful of muggers in parts of the Alfama at night.

Belém In the west, the neighborhood of Belém contains some of the finest monuments in Portugal, several built during the

Age of Discovery, near the point where the caravels set out to conquer new worlds. These include the **Mosteiro dos Jerónimos** (p. 102), a Manueline structure erected in the 16th century; and the **Museu Nacional dos Coches** (p. 104), the National Coach Museum, the finest of its kind in the world. Belém is Lisbon's museum district—it also contains the **Museu de Arte Popular,** the **Museu de Marinha** (p. 104), the **Museu Berardo** (p. 103, modern art), the **Museu de Electricidade,** and the newest **MAAT – Museum de Art, Arquitectura e Tecnologia** (p. 102) on the riverfront, an awe-inspiring structure by the British architect Amanda Levete.

Cacilhas On the south side of the Tagus, where puce-colored smoke billows from factory stacks, is the left-bank Cacilhas, a transport hub that has lost its canneries and shipyard industry. It's often visited by north-bank residents who come here for the seafood restaurants alongside the pedestrian street Cândido dos Reis or those on the pier to the right of the ferry, **Ponto Final** e **Atira-te ao Rio.** You can reach it by a ferryboat, popularly called *cacilheiros*, from Cais do Sodré.

The most dramatic way to cross the Tagus is on the **Ponte do 25 de Abril.** Completed in 1966, the bridge helped open Portugal south of the Tagus. The bridge is 2.2km (1⅓ miles) long, and its towers are 190m (623 ft.) high. The longest suspension bridge in Europe (it stretches for 16km/10 miles), **Ponte Vasco da Gama,** also spans the Tagus here. It's made areas from the north of the country and the southern Algarve, to the east across the Alentejo plain to southern Spain, more accessible. Standing guard on the left bank is a monumental statue of Jesus with arms outstretched, **Cristo Rei** (see p. 175).

GETTING AROUND

Central Lisbon is relatively compact. Because of heavy traffic, it is best explored by foot. That's virtually the only way to see such districts as the Alfama. However, when you venture farther afield, such as to Belém, you'll need to depend on public transportation like trams, which are inexpensive but often slow. Considering the hilly terrain, though, the tram system is a blessing.

As one Frommer's reader wrote, "In the 15 years since my last visit there, Lisbon has become one of the noisiest cities I've ever visited. Traffic is outrageous; driving is difficult because of the speed and the tendency of the natives to ride 6 inches from your rear bumper." Her description is, unfortunately, apt. The traffic is chaotic in some areas and the new tuk-tuks add more confusion to driving in the city.

By Public Transportation

CARRIS (www.carris.pt; ✆ **21/361-30-00**) operates the network of funiculars, trolleys, and buses in Lisbon. The company sells a 1-day pass for 6.15€. Passes (with Viva Card) are sold in CARRIS booths, open from 8am to 8pm daily, in most metro stations, news kiosks, and network train stations. A single ticket bought previous to boarding with your Viva Card costs 1.45€ and you can use it during 1 hour in Carris or metro. If you're using, for instance, a trolley and the metro on different days, it is worth charging your card with the *zapping* system (see p. 66). You can "top up" your Viva Card with 3€, 5€, or 10€ credit. This is the most economical and easiest way to travel around the city's public transport. You have to tap it in at turnstiles of metro and train stations or on special pads inside trams and buses. Be aware that if you don't have the Viva Card on the funiculars (Bica, Glória, or Lavra), the cost will be higher: 3.70€. On the trolley (like the popular 28 or 15), the price goes up to 2.90€, and on buses to 1.85€. If you run out of money on your card, add credit at metro stations or at kiosks with the symbol Carris.

METRO Lisbon's metro stations are designated by large M signs. A single ticket costs 1.40€, a day pass 6€, or you can use the Viva Card (see p. 66). The metro operates daily from 6:30am to 1am. For more information, go to www.metrolisboa.pt.

The Lisbon metro surprises most visitors with its impressive art collection. Paintings, glazed tiles, and sculptures in each station make it a veritable underground museum. Included are works by such famous Portuguese artists as Maria Keil and Maria Helena Vieira da Silva. Stations that display some of the finest art include Cais do Sodré, Baixa/Chiado, Campo Grande, and Marquês de Pombal. The red line stations, connecting with the airport, also have intriguing contemporary art.

BUS & TRAM Lisbon's buses and trams are among the cheapest in Europe. The *eléctricos* (trolley cars, or trams) make the steep run up to the Bairro Alto. Buses and *eléctricos* operate daily from 6am to 1am.

At the foot of the **Santa Justa Elevator,** on Rua Áurea (p. 99), there's a ticket office with maps tracing the zigzagging tram and bus routes.

The antediluvian *eléctricos,* much like San Francisco's cable cars, have become a major tourist attraction. Beginning in 1903, *eléctricos* replaced horse-drawn trams. The best ride for sightseers is *eléctrico* no. 28, which wends through the most history-rich part of Lisbon. If it is too crowded, the less touristy no. 25, from Corpo Santo (near Cais do Sodré) to Campo de Ourique, passes pretty São Paulo square, the Santos area, and the impressive domed Basílica da Estrela (at Praça Estrela). The no. 15 to Belém can also get overcrowded; when that happens take the train from Cais do Sodré to Belém but make sure it stops at that station, as some trains go direct to Cascais. Tram tickets are 2.85€.

FUNICULARS Lisbon has a trio of funiculars (www.carris.pt; ✆ **21/261-30-00**): the **Glória,** which goes from Praça dos Restauradores to Rua São Pedro de Alcântara; the **Bica,** from the Calçada do Combro to Rua da Boavista; and the **Lavra,** from the eastern side of Avenida da Liberdade to Campo Mártires da Pátria. A ticket on any of these costs 3.60€ but can be used twice.

By Taxi

Taxis in Lisbon tend to be inexpensive and are a popular means of transport for all but the most economy-minded tourists. They can be hailed on the street or at designated stands. The basic fare is 3.25€ for the first 153m (502 ft.), plus 20% from 10pm to 6am. After the initial amount you pay 0.47€ per each kilometer. The law allows drivers to tack on another 50% to your bill if your luggage weighs more than 66 pounds, but usually the luggage supplement is

1.60€. Portuguese tip about 10% of the modest fare. For a Rádio Táxi, call ✆ **21/811-90-00** (www.retalis.pt).

If you're staying in Estoril or Cascais, you'll probably find taxi connections from Lisbon prohibitively expensive. Far preferable is the train system (see p. 65).

Uber also works in Lisbon, though as we go to press, that company is being sued by the taxi associations (which are hoping to take Uber off the streets). Tuk-Tuks, the light 3-wheel vehicles, don't do taxi service. Instead, they give expensive tours of the city (we don't think they're worth the cost).

By Car

In congested Lisbon, driving is difficult. Theoretically, rush hours are Mon–Fri 8–10am and 5–7pm, but the traffic often lasts well beyond those hours. Parking is complicated and expensive. Our suggestion: Only rent a car if you're making excursions outside the capital. If you drive into Lisbon from another town or city, call ahead and ask at your hotel for the nearest garage or other place to park. Leave your vehicle there until you're ready to depart.

CAR RENTALS The major international car-rental companies are represented in Lisbon with kiosks at the airport and offices in the city center.

[FastFACTS] LISBON

See also "Fast Facts" on p. 454.

Babysitters Most first-class hotels can provide babysitters from lists the concierge keeps. At small establishments, the sitter is likely to be a relative of the proprietor. Babysitters charge between 15€ and 25€ per hour in Lisbon. Remember to request a babysitter early—no later than the morning if you're planning on going out that evening. Young people are often fluent in English, so it shouldn't be too difficult to find a sitter who can talk with your child.

Currency Exchange Currency-exchange booths at the Santa Apolónia station and at the airport are open 24 hours a day. But we suggest using ATMs instead, which offer better exchange rates. You'll find them throughout the central city.

Dentists The reception staff at most hotels maintains lists of local, usually English-speaking, dentists who are available for dental emergencies.

Drugstores **Farmácia Valmor,** Av. Visconde Valmor 60B (✆ **21/781-97-43**), is centrally located and well stocked. **Farmácia Largo do Rato,** Av. Pedro Álvares Cabral 1, is also central and is open 24 hours (✆ **21/386-30-44**).

Emergencies To summon the police or an ambulance, call ✆ **112.**

Hospitals At the **British Hospital,** Rua Saraiva de Carvalho 49 (✆ **21/394-31-00**), the telephone operator, staff, and doctors all speak English. You can also try **Infitravel,** a company that helps sick travelers find quality care from physicians and doctors who speak English (www.infitravel.com; ✆ **91/173-97-95**).

Internet Access Most restaurants, cafes, and hotels have free Wi-Fi (just ask for the password). Some public buildings, like the Time Out Market, also provide Wi-Fi at no cost.

Laundry For a self-service laundry, try **Lavatax,** Rua Francisco Sanches 65A (✆ **21/812-33-92**). Most hotels can also help you with laundry.

Lost Property For items lost on public transportation, inquire at **Secção de Achados da PSP,** Olivais Sul, Praça Cidade de Salazar Lote 180 (✆ **21/853-54-03**), which is open Monday to Friday 9am to 12:30pm and 1:30 to 5pm. If you're pickpocketed, there's a special police station in Palácio Foz, Restauradores, for tourists (✆ **21/342-16-23**) with officers who speak English.

Luggage Storage & Lockers These can be found at the **Estação da Santa Apolónia** (✆ **80/820-82-08**) by the river near the Alfama. **Cais do Sodré, Oriente,** and **Rossio** stations also have lockers.

Police Call ✆ **112.**

Safety Take precautions as you would in any big city. Pickpockets prey on tourists, aiming for wallets, purses, mobile phones, and cameras. Congested areas are particularly hazardous, especially the no. 28 tram. At night, avoid deserted streets or withdrawing money from ATMs in unpopulated areas.

Taxes Lisbon (and Cascais) imposes a 1€ city tax on hotel bills. The national value-added tax (VAT) applies to purchases and services (see "Taxes" under "Fast Facts," p. 461) and is included in the bill.

WHERE TO STAY

Lisbon has a wider range of accommodations than ever before. Unfortunately, as Lisbon's popularity grows, so do the prices.

Most visitors in Lisbon have to decide whether to stay in a hotel in the city proper or at a resort in the neighboring towns of Estoril and Cascais (see chapter 7). Since trains between the city and these beach resorts run about every 20 minutes, it's entirely possible to stay on the coast and still sightsee in Lisbon. But if you're primarily interested in seeing Lisbon's attractions, opting to stay in the city is a better bet. Also, the off season (Nov–Mar) is not ideal for a sea resort vacation. **A 1€ tax per night is added to all Lisbon hotel bills.**

In recent years, short-term rentals have become a favored option of travelers; check out such platforms as **Airbnb.com, Homeaway.com,** and **VRBO.com,** all of which offer apartments right in the city center for all budgets.

In the Center

EXPENSIVE

Four Seasons Hotel Ritz Lisbon ★★★ The 10-floor Ritz, opened in 1959 opposite the Lisbon's Eduardo VII Park, is now operated by Four Seasons. Its suites boast the finest decoration you'll see in any major Portuguese hotel: slender mahogany canopied beds with fringed swags, marquetry desks, satinwood dressing tables, and plush carpeting. Some of the soundproof, spacious, modern rooms have terraces opening onto the park; each boasts a marble bathroom. (***Tip:*** To get a view of the park, ask for an odd-numbered room.) The hotel is also known for its valuable art collection: You'll find works of important Portuguese artists such as Almada Negreiros, Lagoa Henriques, and Carlos Botelho, and the building is classified as a monument of national interest. On the rooftop there's a running track and a lovely restaurant, **Varanda.**

Rua Rodrigo de Fonseca 88. www.fourseasons.com. ✆ **800/819-5053** in the U.S., or 21/381-14-00. 282 units. 480€–685€ double; from 1,165€ suite. Free parking. Metro: Marquês de Pombal. Bus: 1, 2, 9, or 32. **Amenities:** Restaurant; bar; babysitting; concierge; exercise room; indoor heated pool; room service; spa. Free Wi-Fi.

Lisbon Accommodations

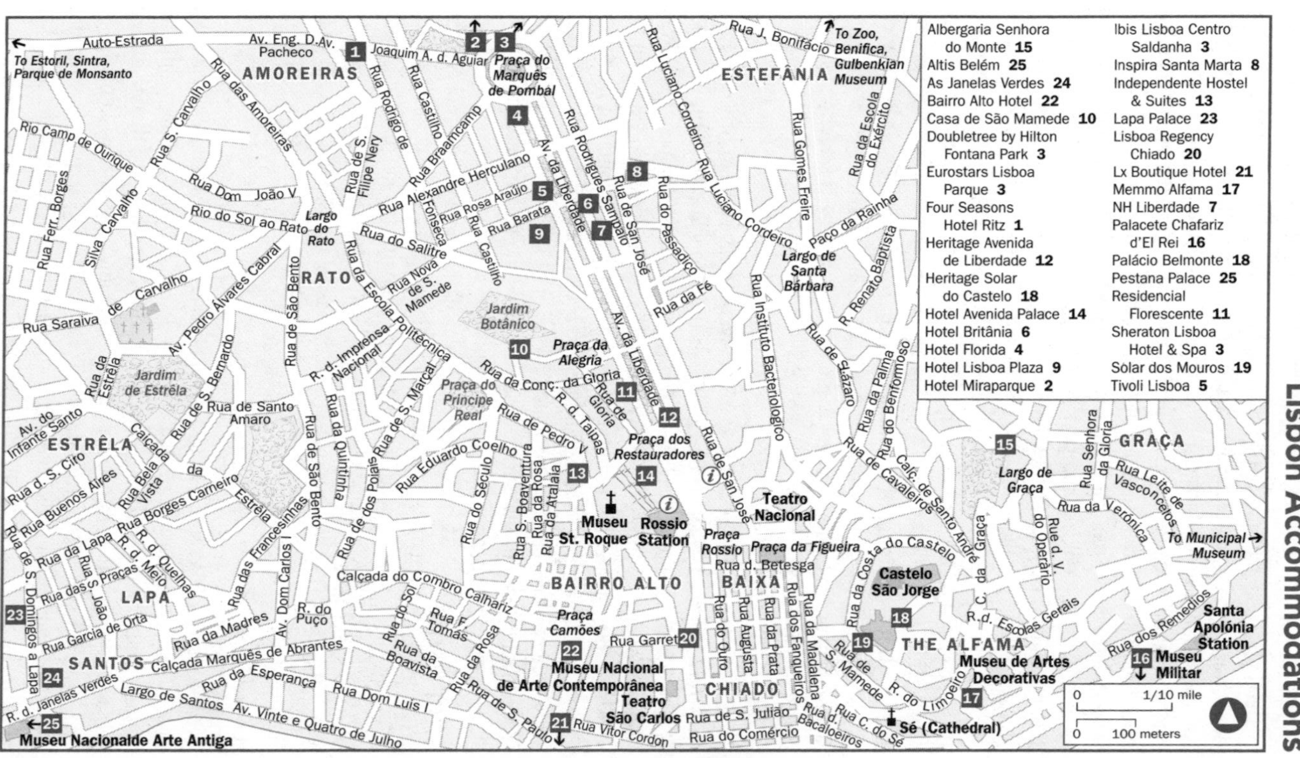

Heritage Avenida Liberdade Hotel ★★★ Right on the main street of Lisbon and set in a restored late-18th-century palace, this hotel strikes a perfect yin-yang balance between traditional and cool contemporary. The decor was created by noted architect and interior designer Miguel Câncio Martins (best known for his hipster Buddha Bar in Paris) and it is plush in both the public areas and the guest rooms. The former boasts original murals (by the lap pool) and curvy caramel- and honey-colored couches and armchairs in the lobby where guests enjoy a sumptuous included breakfast (custard tarts!) and free coffee, tea, cookies, and port 24 hours a day. Good-sized guest rooms feature restored Pombaline tiles and such original architectural details as high sloping ceilings (on the top floors) and floor-to-ceiling windows opening up to Juliet balconies. Their bedding is cloud-like (love the array of pillow types) and the furnishings dignified and comfy. We must also mention the staff, who are wonderfully accommodating. If you don't have the pleasure of staying here, do get a look at the exterior, a superb example of neoclassical Pombaline style.

Av. da Liberdade 28. www.heritage.pt. ✆ **21/340-40-40.** 42 units. 139€–340€ double. Children under 12 stay free in parent's room. Parking nearby 30€. Metro: Restauradores. **Amenities:** Bar; babysitting; concierge; exercise room; indoor heated pool; room service. Free Wi-Fi.

Hotel Avenida Palace ★★★ The Avenida Palace first opened in 1892 as a typical grand hotel in the European fin-de-siècle style. Full of atmosphere, the hotel hosted well-heeled refugees from the Spanish Civil War, undercover agents during World War II, and stars of screen and stage in the '50s and '60s. It later fell on hard times, but was given a complete facelift in 2009 that restored it to its full glamour. The neoclassical landmark is strategically located between Rossio square and the start of Avenida da Liberdade, close to all the city center attractions. The public rooms are glittering confections of gilt, crystal, and marble. An English-style bar in hardwood and worn leather is famed for its cocktails, and 5 o'clock tea with scones is served by white-coated waiters in the palatial main salon. Up the spectacular five-story stairwell, the rooms are decorated in light colors, with antique furnishings and old-master prints. A genuine classic in the heart of the city.

Rua 1 de Dezembro 123. www.hotelavenidapalace.pt. ✆ **21/321-81-00.** 82 units. 135€–450€ double; 198€–550€ junior suite. Rates include buffet breakfast. Free parking. Metro: Restauradores. Tram: 35. **Amenities:** Bar; babysitting; concierge; exercise room; room service. Free Wi-Fi.

Hotel Lisboa Plaza ★ Hotel Lisboa Plaza is a family-owned and -operated hotel where each guest is greeted with a welcome cup of port on arrival. The midsize guest rooms—with well-stocked marble bathrooms and double-glazed windows—are quite comfortable, with lots of flowered or striped upholstery and antique reproduction furnishings. Try for a unit in the rear, looking out over the botanical gardens. The hotel is located in a blessedly quiet area, but close to Av. Da Liberdade and Príncipe Real square.

Travessa do Salitre 7, Av. da Liberdade. www.heritage.pt. ✆ **21/321-82-18.** 106 units. 125€–385€ double; 270€–625€ suite. Children under 12 stay free in parent's room. Parking nearby 10€. Metro: Avenida. Bus: 1, 2, 36, or 44. **Amenities:** Restaurant; bar; babysitting; concierge; exercise room; room service; pets allowed. Free Wi-Fi.

Inspira Santa Marta ★★ "Green" is more than just a buzzword at this hotel—its power comes from 100% renewable sources. The restaurant serves organic produce and sustainable fish, and when it sells a bottle of water, the money goes to a charity that builds water pumps in Africa. But you don't just stay here to be a "do-gooder" (though that *is* a nice incentive): These are appealing digs. The design of the entire hotel was done with feng shui principles. Its lobby is a spectacular forest of slatted wood dappled with light. Harmony is evident in the guest rooms, which are decorated in subtle, relaxing colors (some, though, are quite small). The hotel's Open restaurant serves tasty Mediterranean food and has a certified gluten-free menu. Inspira is located on a backstreet behind Avenida da Liberdade.

Rua Santa Marta,48. www.inspirahotels.com. ✆ **30/880-69-95.** 331 units. 90€–230€ double; from 174€ suite. Parking 16€. Metro: Avenida. **Amenities:** Restaurant; bar; spa; exercise room; room service; sauna. Free Wi-Fi.

Lisboa Regency Chiado ★★ Opened in 2000, this hotel occupies several floors of an eight-story shopping center. It was designed by prestigious Portugal-born designer Siza Vieira, responsible for the reconstruction of Chiado, one of the most charming neighborhoods in central Lisbon, badly hurt by a fire in 1988. You'll register in a street-level lobby and then be ushered upstairs to one of the artfully minimalist bedrooms. The best of these have private terraces on a rooftop that blooms with bougainvillea vines and brightly colored wildflowers. The standard bedrooms are midsize, each with a well-organized bathroom. Of special note is the hotel's bar, a postmodern oasis of soaring vertical lines, copies of 18th-century antiques, and theatrical panoramas over the castle, Baixa and the river. It is one of the city's top rooftop bars.

Rua Nova do Almada, 114. www.lisboaregencychiado.com. ✆ **21/325-61-00.** 40 units. 129€–290€ double; 294€–400€ suite. Free parking. Metro: Baixa-Chiado. **Amenities:** Bar; airport transfers (30€); room service. Free Wi-Fi.

NH Liberdade ★ With its rooftop swimming pool and its chic black-and-cream motif (like the Heritage Avenida, it was designed by the Portuguese architect Miguel Martins), the NH Liberdade has become a hip address for travelers. The developers took a late-18th-century building and retained the facade and some original architectural features; otherwise, they created a hotel of contemporary comfort and extreme modernity. There are 83 stylish rooms, of which 25 are suites; some rooms have terraces with good city views. The hotel is conveniently located in the center of town in a sector that bridges the gap between the historic old town and the newer commercial sections of Lisbon.

Av. da Liberdade 180B. www.nh-hotels.com. ✆ **21/351-40-60.** 83 units.120€–180€ double; from 250€ suite. Parking 19€. Metro: Avenida. **Amenities:** Restaurant; bar; babysitting; concierge; access to nearby gym; outdoor pool; room service. Free Wi-Fi.

Olissipo Lapa Palace ★★★ Back in the 1880s, the Count of Valenças made his palatial home the glittering center of Lisbon's high society. The city's best artists were invited to decorate its grand salons and ballrooms, and a lush tropical garden was laid out where the in-crowd could stroll beside streams and waterfalls. Since 1992, the count's palace has been transformed into one of the capital's most luxurious hotels, favored by royalty, presidents, and movie stars. The 109 rooms are all individually decorated in keeping with the building's heritage, with themes ranging from rococo to Art Deco. The marble bathrooms are among the city's most elegant, often adorned with bas-reliefs. Each unit opens onto a balcony. The palace is located among the embassies and mansions of the upscale Lapa district on a hillside with broad views across the city and the River Tagus. The outside pool, set amid the tranquil greenery, is kept at a constant 25°C (77°F) from May through September, and there's a fully equipped spa, gym, and indoor pool center. The gourmet restaurant features five-star variations on Portuguese cuisine. All but about 20 of the rooms are in a modern six-story wing.

Rua do Pau da Bandeira 4. www.lapapalace.com. ✆ **21/394-94-94.** 109 units. 290€–675€ double; from 1,100€ suite. Rates include buffet breakfast. Free parking. Bus: 13 or 27. **Amenities:** 2 restaurants; bar; babysitting; children's center; concierge; exercise room; 2 pools (1 heated indoors); room service; spa. Free Wi-Fi.

Sheraton Lisboa Hotel & Spa ★★ Built in 1972 and regularly renovated, this deluxe hotel is sheltered in a 25-floor skyscraper lying at a traffic-clogged intersection a few blocks north of Praça do Marquês de Pombal. The impressive pink-marble lobby features chandeliers and fancy carpeting. Guest rooms are small to midsize for the most part, but have been given a trendy look with textured wallpaper, curvaceous lamps, and peekaboo glass walls into the bathroom (blinds can be drawn for modesty). The most desirable rooms are the ones with river and bridge views; some rooms can be noisy, so ask for a quiet one if you are a light sleeper. There's an outdoor pool on the roof and a good restaurant and bar on the 26th floor, with spectacular panoramic views.

Rua Latino Coelho 1. www.sheratonlisboa.com. ✆ **800/325-3535** in the U.S., or 21/312-00-00. 366 units. 125€–265€ double; from 415€ suite. Bus: 1, 36, 44, or 45. **Amenities:** Restaurant; 2 bars; babysitting; concierge; exercise room; outdoor pool; room service; spa. Free Wi-Fi. Deluxe rooms are the cheapest, parking fee of 19€ daily.

Tivoli Lisboa ★★ This grand Avenida da Liberdade landmark celebrated its 80th birthday in 2015. During World War II it was notorious as a haunt for spies. In the decades since, it's attracted visiting politicians, artists, and movie stars. The lobby oozes old-world elegance with marble columns and velvet armchairs in rich, deep tones. It's a preferred meeting spot for Lisbon's business elite before they head to lunch in the French brasserie on-site or the penthouse Terraço restaurant to enjoy five-star food served amidst spectacular views. Rooms are spacious and airy, overlooking the tree-lined avenue or the lush garden below. They are decorated in modern classic style with easy-on-the-eyes shades predominating. Superior rooms come equipped with Nespresso machines and iHome sound systems. Best of all: Its prices are not extravagant, considering the luxuries (a tennis court, pool, gym, etc.). The rooftop lounge bar attracts a crowd on summer nights and there's a small circular swimming pool surrounded by exotic foliage in the garden.

Av. da Liberdade 185. www.tivolihotels.com. ✆ **21/319-89-00.** 329 units. 200€–510€ double; from 372€ suite. Rates include continental breakfast. Garage 18€. Metro: Avenida. Bus: 1, 2, 9, or 32. **Amenities:** 2 restaurants; 2 bars; babysitting; concierge; exercise room; outdoor heated pool; room service; outdoor tennis court (lit). Wi-Fi (10€ per 24 hr.) free only for Discovery loyalty members or in the lobby.

MODERATE

As Janelas Verdes ★★ This 18th-century building was the former home of the great Portuguese novelist Eça de Queirós. Though the decor is modern, its traditional past has been respected by designer Graça Viterbo. The lounge evokes turn-of-the-20th-century Lisbon and the writer who once lived here. The latest renovation was in 2015, and it left guest rooms with handsome dark wood furnishings and very pretty, heavy, pastel drapes over the tall windows. Closet space is abundant. Other special features include a small but lovely garden where breakfast can be enjoyed, two honor bars, and a cozy top-floor library with a fireplace and terrace. The location is superb for exploring Madragoa, Lapa, and Santos and the riverfront. The Tejo room has the best view.

Rua das Janelas Verdes 47. www.asjanelasverdes.com. ✆ **21/396-81-43.** 29 units. 121€–295€ double; 225€–390€ triple. Parking 10€. Bus: 27, 40, 49, or 60. **Amenities:** Bar; babysitting; concierge; room service. Free Wi-Fi.

Doubletree by Hilton Fontana Park Hotel ★ Some will find the dark walls here restful, others may find them a little dreary—I think it all has to do with how much one likes ultra-contemporary decor. And while the all-black corridors with black doors can be confusing to navigate, the floor-to-ceiling windows in the rooms do brighten things up during the day (as do the wacky Philippe Starck, white Duravit bathtubs that twinkle with colorful lights). ***One warning:*** The walls could be thicker, so you may hear your neighbors. The inky black Bonsai Restaurant serves Japanese cuisine. DJ-spun music and *caipirinhas* lure visitors to the midnight-colored Fontana Bar. The hotel is in Saldanha, within walking distance of the Marquês de Pombal square.

Rua Engenheiro Vieira da Silva 2. www.fontanapark-hotel.com. ✆ **21/357-62-12.** 139 units. 87€–290€ double. Parking 20€. Metro: Parque. **Amenities:** Restaurant; bar; airport transfers (29€); room service. Free Wi-Fi.

EUSOSTARS Lisboa Parque ★ Location is the lure here: The Lisboa Parque is in the center of the city, but off a small street (the entrance can be hard to find), meaning it is wonderfully quiet. Other than that, you won't find much Portuguese character in this Spanish chain hotel. Nor are the on-site restaurant and cafe places you should eat. But for value, this makes the list—it is kept spic and span, the showers have good pressure, the mattresses are firm, and there are many terrific eateries nearby.

Largo de Andaluz 13 B. www.eurostarshotels.co.uk. ✆ **21/005-09-30.** 83 units. 60€–145€ double; 94€–192€ superior double. Parking 17€. Metro: Picoas. **Amenities:** Restaurant; bar; babysitting; concierge; exercise room; room service; sauna; fitness studio; business corner. Free Wi-Fi. Parking 18€ per 24 hr.

Hotel Britânia ★★ Designed in the 1940s by the well-known Portuguese architect Cassiano Branco, this boutique hotel is the only surviving original Art Deco hotel in Lisbon. Located about a block from Av. de Liberdade, its topnotch service has earned it a loyal clientele, as have the unusually large (for Lisbon) hotel rooms—the building once housed studio apartments. Happily, much of its original decor, including murals in the bar, the lavish use of marble, and the "porthole" windows and candelabra in the public lounge, are still intact. Yearly maintenance and upgrading have kept it looking good. Inside is also an old barber's shop now converted in a small museum.

Rua Rodrigues Sampaio 17. www.heritage.pt. ✆ **21/315-50-16.** 32 units. 123€–303€ double. Parking 15€. Metro: Avenida. Bus: 1, 2, 11, or 21. **Amenities:** Bar; concierge; room service. Free Wi-Fi.

Hotel Florida ★ Close to Marquês de Pombal, this hotel looks to California, not Florida, for inspiration. Life-size photos of *Sabrina* stars Humphrey Bogart and Audrey Hepburn stare back at you in the elevator. On some of the walls are famous American film quotations. Even the restaurant evokes a cinematic American diner from the '50s. Bedrooms are more generically modern but extend the movie kitsch, taking the names of Tinseltown stars like Robert De Niro and Jack Nicholson.

Rua Duque de Pamela 34. www.hotel-florida.pt. ✆ **21/357-61-45.** 72 units. 67€–229€ double; from 160€ junior suite. Rates include buffet breakfast. Metro: Marquês de Pombal. **Amenities:** Bar; concierge; room service. Free Wi-Fi.

INEXPENSIVE

Casa de São Mamede ★ Built in the 1758 as a private villa for the count of Coruche, this building was one of the first to use the wooden cage system inside the walls, a building technique adopted after the earthquake. Managed today by the Marquês family, it became a hotel back in 1945. Although renovated, the high-ceilinged rooms retain an aura of their original, slightly dowdy, somewhat frayed, charm. That being said, all units are quite clean and have private bathrooms with tub/shower combinations. Breakfast is served in a sunny second-floor dining room decorated with antique tiles. Service is friendly and attentive. The location is great for exploring Príncipe Real and the Bairro Alto but because it is right on the road, it can be a bit noisy.

Rua da Escola Politécnica 159. www.casadesaomamede.com. ✆ **21/396-31-66.** 28 units. 75€–110€ double; 140€ triple. Rates include breakfast. No parking available at the hotel. Bus: 22, 49, or 58. Metro: Rato. Free Wi-Fi.

Hotel Miraparque ★ Miraparque lies on a secluded, quiet street opposite Edward VII Park (some rooms offer views of its pretty greenery) and close to Marquês de Pombal roundabout. The small guest rooms haven't been called modern since the 1960s, but are kept quite tidy. So yes, the hotel is a little worn, but still recommendable because of its central location and low prices. The wood-paneled lounge, where the bar is, is endearingly vintage.

Av. Sidónio Pais 12. www.miraparque.com. ✆ **21/352-42-86.** 100 units. 60€–150€ double; 100€–180€ triple. Rates include buffet breakfast. Parking (in nearby lot) 15€.

Metro: Parque or Marquês de Pombal. Bus: 91. **Amenities:** Restaurant; bar; babysitting; room service. Free Wi-Fi.

LX Boutique Hotel ★★ This quirky hotel's motto is "five floors, five themes—one Lisbon." That means that each floor is dedicated to a particular aspect of the city. So, one covers the Tejo (Tagus) River with nautical artifacts and (naturally) has river views. Another floor is devoted to one of Lisbon's greatest poets, Fernando Pessoa (1888–1935), and yet another, "The Fado Floor," is filled with drawings and musical instruments evoking the sounds of fado. Bedrooms follow the themes of each floor. For instance, rooms on Pessoa floor have books and bookcase photos, the ones on Fado floor have photos of fado singers and instruments. But except for "superior rooms" and the Xplendid Suite (with a retracting glass roof and terrace), the digs here tend to be small. The on-site restaurant, Confraria, specializes in sushi; you can relax over a glass of port wine in the stylish bar. The hotel is in Cais do Sodré, convenient to Belém and the beaches of Estoril and Cascais, but also very close to one of the busiest nightlife streets in the city.

Rua do Alecrim 12. www.lxboutiquehotel.com. ✆ **21/347-43-94.** 45 units. 90€–145€ double; from 266€ suite. Metro: Cais do Sodré. **Amenities:** Restaurant; bar; concierge; room service. Free Wi-Fi.

Residêncial Florescente ★ Centrally located in the Baixa district, this is a solid budget choice in the city center… for now. Prices here are on the rise. On a bustling street, with many restaurants and theaters nearby, Florescente has a welcoming staff and no-frills bedrooms that are simply furnished—a bit like a roadside motel—but kept spotless. Some rooms have three beds, making the hotel especially suitable for families.

Rua das Portas de Santo Antão 99. www.residencialflorescente.com. ✆ **21/343-66-09.** 68 units. 55€–120€ double; 75€–140€ triple. Parking 15€. Metro: Rossio. Free Wi-Fi.

In the Alfama

EXPENSIVE

Heritage Solar Do Castelo ★ Set inside the walls of the formidable St. Jorge's Castle, this boutique hotel is reached only on foot. (The hotel has a golf car to pick up luggage from the castle gate.) Though the house is from the 18th century (on the site of the former royal palace), some of the medieval architecture remains, such as an old cistern that was part of the original palace. The bedrooms mix old elements such as original stone fortifications with contemporary fabrics and furnishings. Each room comes with a window overlooking a picture-perfect courtyard, a bonus for the romantic atmosphere, but the location, far from the city center, can be either a treat or a problem.

Rua das Cozinhas 2. www.solardocastelo.com. ✆ **21/880-60-50.** 14 units. 140€–350€ double. Parking not available at the hotel. Buses and trams stop far, taxi is better. **Amenities:** Bar; babysitting; concierge; room service. Free Wi-Fi.

Palacete Chafariz d'el Rei ★★★ Returning to his native Lisbon after striking it rich in Brazil, João Antonio Santos erected this stunning Art

Nouveau mansion at the turn of the 19th century. Painstakingly restored over the course of 2 years, today it's a fabulous hideway in the busy area close to the Alfama. Over the years, noted Barcelona architects, English filmmakers, and Berlin fashionistas have occupied the lavish suites, each of which comes with a Brazilian butler. Our favorite is the Suite Amaya, which is spacious and sensual, with vintage decorations, including embroidery work on the ceiling. Elaborate moldings, stained-glass windows, antiques, and for a contrast, cheeky works of contemporary art are found throughout, especially in the ground-floor public rooms. A special delight is the private terrace garden filled with flowering plants. Nonguests can come by for brunch or tea.

Chafariz del Rei 6, 1100-140 Lisboa. www.chafarizdelrei.com. ✆ **91/897-33-76.** 6 units. 280€–440€. Access is difficult, best to take a taxi or book a transfer with the hotel. **Amenities:** Breakfast room. Free Wi-Fi.

Palácio Belmonte ★★ There are hotels with history, and then there is the Palácio Belmonte. The Romans built one of the towers, and another two were erected over a thousand years ago when the Arabs ruled Lisbon. The noble palace chambers linking them together were constructed in the 15th century and once were home to the family of Pedro Álvares Cabral, the man credited, at least in this part of the world, with "discovering" Brazil. The current French owner has invested €26 million into turning the palace into an ultra-luxurious hotel with 10 suites. Each is unique, most have fabulous views, and all are furnished with comely antiques. There are bathrooms clad in rare gray marble with walk-in showers, sunken baths, and their own panoramic vistas. One tower-topping bedroom boasts 360-degree views high above the city, others have private terraces where you can take your organic, freshly prepared breakfast. A Michelin-starred chef is on hand to do the catering should you decide to dine in your suite. The walled garden is a haven of peace, complete with luxuriant vegetation, a swimming pool, and waterfall. Blue-and-white 17th-century tiles cover many walls, there are oriental carpets underfoot, and displays of contemporary art in the patio and the hotel's own gallery. It's a step away from the São Jorge Castle. So why only two stars from us? Although the atmosphere is fabulous, the service could be better (considering the rates).

Páteo Dom Fradique 14. www.palaciobelmonte.com. ✆ **21/881-66-00.** 11 suites. 450€–1.200€, minimum 2-night stay. Free parking. **Amenities:** Bar; outdoor pool; room service. Free Wi-Fi.

MODERATE

Memmo Alfama ★★★ Be sure to set your alarm and wake up early, as this hotel has the best sunrise views in the city, over the Alfama and to the river. It was the first boutique hotel in this historic district, cleverly crafted from the ruins of an old, abandoned building, and is an atmospheric place. A mural on the outside wall by famous street artist Vhils welcomes guests before they enter. Two brick-vaulted rooms (originally a wood-fire oven from a bakery) are now relaxing lounges with books and Eames-style chairs. Guest rooms aren't big, but they have a Scandinavian chicness to them (light woods, soft corners, white and beige everything) and have those spectacular views. We also must praise the breakfast, which tastes even better when taken on the rooftop terrace (just watch out for sneaky seagulls trying to steal pastries). In the afternoon and evening, the wine bar (where light meals and small plates are also served) and the pool are perfect to relax after a day of walking up and down the hills.

Travessa das Merceeiras. www.memmohotels.com/alfama. ✆ **21/049-56-60.** 42 units. 118€–250€ double. Parking not available at the hotel. Bus: 37. Tram: 28. **Amenities:** Bar; babysitting; concierge; room service; free guided tours through Alfama. Free Wi-Fi.

Solar dos Mouros ★★ This trendy small hotel occupies a tangerine-colored, steeply vertical antique building on a quiet street that runs parallel to the base of St. George's Castle. Rooms are straight out of *Architectural Digest*, each with at least one boldly abstract painting (some pieces are the work of the hotel's owner, Luis Memos), richly colored walls, contemporary wicker and wood furnishings, and hardwood floors. All are quite spacious, overlooking either the castle or the river, and open onto a starkly contemporary staircase. Breakfast is the only meal served, but the bar is nice for a sunset drink.

Rua Milagre de Santo António 6. www.solardosmouros.com. ✆ **21/885-49-40.** 12 units. 109€–320€ double. No parking available at the hotel. Tram: 28. **Amenities:** Bar; concierge; room service. Free Wi-Fi.

In the Bairro Alto

EXPENSIVE

Bairro Alto Hotel ★★★ With a location that's unmatched for its association with literary, historic, and Romantic-era Portugal, this 2005 reincarnation of Lisbon's oldest hotel sits within an ocher-colored six-story baroque building in the square (Praça Luís de Camões) that commemorates Portugal's most important literary patriarch. It debuted in 1845 when it was rebuilt from the rubble of Lisbon's earthquake (less than a century before) as the Hotel de l'Europe, then the capital's most visible hotel. A huge effort has been taken to blend the historic with the cutting edge here, from the ample use of thousands of feet of exotic hardwoods to the presence of all the electronic accessories that the post-millennium generation would expect. The triple glazing ensures that no noise from the noisy square bothers guests. Bedrooms and their furnishings are rich with references to Portugal's imperial past, yet updated with leather chairs and Ralph Lauren wallpaper. One drawback: Some rooms can be small. There's a sophisticated bar, a rooftop terrace with one of the best panoramas in the city, and a gem of a restaurant (p. 92). The hotel is being enlarged in 2017 and will offer more rooms and another restaurant soon.

Praça Luís de Camões 8. www.bairroaltohotel.com. ✆ **21/340-82-88.** 55 units. 205€–530€ double; 450€–650€ suites. Rates include buffet breakfast. Parking 21€. Metro: Baixa/Chiado. **Amenities:** Restaurant; bar; babysitting; concierge; exercise room; room service. Free Wi-Fi.

INEXPENSIVE

Independente Hostels and Suites ★★★ Known as one of the more stylish hostels in Lisbon (the owners define the aesthetic, oddly, as "bohemian and palatial"), this Art Deco mansion was the former residence of the Swiss embassador. Much of the old charm remains in the high and decorated ceilings and floors, and vintage details and furniture. The dorms are roomy and offer Scandinivian-looking wooden triple bunk beds. If you prefer privacy, book early—there are just four private suites (each with a balcony and panoramic views of the park and the viewpoint just opposite). Next to the Independent is an off-shoot, Independent Suites and Terrace, with private rooms (but no dorms) and the same friendly staff and trendy Northern-European looks. The new place has a hopping rooftop bar and restaurant, Insólito.

Rua S. Pedro de Alcântara 81. www.theindependente.pt. ✆ **21/347-80-69.** 4 suites and 19 rooms. Dorms: 10€–18€. 60€–125€ double without bathroom; 70€–165€ double with bathroom. No parking available at the hotel. Funicular: Elevador da Glória. Bus: 758. **Amenities:** Bar; restaurants; rooftop bar. Free Wi-Fi.

In the Graça District

MODERATE

Albergaria da Senhora do Monte ★★ This unique little hilltop hotel is perched near a belvedere (turret), the Miradouro Senhora do Monte, in a seldom visited part of the city. It has a memorable nighttime view of the city, the castle, and the Tagus as it sits on the highest hill of Lisbon. The intimate lounge evokes the feel of a living room in an upscale home and features large tufted sofas and oversize tables and lamps. Multilevel corridors lead to the fetching guest rooms, which reveal a decorator's touch with their gilt-edged door panels, grass-cloth walls, and tile bathrooms. All rooms have verandas.

Calçada do Monte 39. www.albergariasenhoradomonte.com. ✆ **21/886-60-02.** 28 units. 80€–145€ double; 120€–175€ suite. Rates include continental breakfast. Free parking nearby. Tram: 28. Bus: 12, 17, or 35. **Amenities:** Bar; babysitting; room service. Free Wi-Fi.

In Alto de Santo Amaro

EXPENSIVE

Pestana Palace ★★★ Set within a residential neighborhood known as Santo Amaro-Ajuda, about 5km (3 miles) west of the commercial core of Lisbon and about 1.5km (1 mile) north of the Alcântara Railway Station, this grand, imperial-looking hotel occupies a villa that was originally built in 1907 by a Portuguese mogul, Palácio Valle-Flor. The award-winning hotel's core is one of the best examples of Romantic Revival architecture in Portugal, combining at least four distinct architectural styles (including what the Portuguese refer to as *rocaille baroque* and Dona Maria revival) into one shimmering whole. It has been classified as a National Monument. The Pestana hotel chain added two rambling wings and state-of-the-art kitchens. Only four of the bedrooms—each a high-ceilinged suite—lie within the original villa. Most accommodations are elegantly modern, with hardwood trim, *trompe l'oeil* detailing, upholstered headboards, and hints of the Romantic Revivalism that permeates the hotel's original core. The luxury atmosphere is supported by a friendly and expert staff. The hotel offers its guests four-times-per-day shuttle service, without charge, to predesignated points in central Lisbon. The location is not close to central neighborhoods but is a good base for exploring Belém.

Rua Jau 54. www.pestana.com. ✆ **21/361-56-00.** 190 units. 220€–375€ double; 630€–3,000€ suite. Parking 17€. **Amenities:** Restaurant; bar; babysitting; concierge; exercise room; Jacuzzi; spa; heated indoor and outdoor pools; room service; sauna, business center; chapel. Free Wi-Fi.

At Parque Das Nações

EXPENSIVE

Tivoli Oriente ★ Set in an evolving residential and business neighborhood, the Tivoli Oriente features midsize guest rooms that are comfortably and traditionally furnished (though some renovated rooms boast a more modern decor). The room selection is wide ranging, from smaller single rooms to large suites. On the 16th floor is a gourmet restaurant offering a panoramic view over Lisbon and the Tagus River. The hotel is close to the Vasco de Gama shopping center and the airport. The Estação do Oriente, a major transportation hub for Lisbon, is just a 2-minute walk away.

Av. D. João II. www.tivolihotels.com. ✆ **21/891-51-00.** 279 units. 130€–330€ double; 415€ suite. Rates include buffet breakfast. Parking 13€. Metro: Oriente. Bus: 28. **Amenities:** 2 restaurants; bar; babysitting; concierge; exercise room; Jacuzzi; indoor heated pool; room service; sauna. Wi-Fi 15€ per day.

In Belém

EXPENSIVE

Altis Belém ★★ Opened in 2009, this marble-clad cube of modernist luxury is so close to the waterfront it feels like you're on a cruise liner floating down the River Tagus. It sits in the Belém district within sight of the iconic white tower, the UNESCO-rated Jerónimos Monastery, and the galleries and concert halls of the Centro Cultural de Belém. Despite all the history around it, the hotel is rigorously contemporary. The bar and lounge have clean black-and-white lines with liberal use of leather furniture and hardwood decks. Natural light is a big feature in the public and guest rooms, thanks to floor-to-ceiling windows opening out onto the water. All the rooms are spacious and airy with great views. Depending on their location, rooms come in a wide range of prices, from the relatively moderate to the very expensive. A top perk: the panorama from the rooftop pool. Downstairs, the Spa by Karin Herzog has 1,000 sq. meters (10,764 sq. ft.) where you can relax with a massage, sauna, or Turkish bath, or work out in the gym or dynamic pool. After burning up the calories, it's safe to treat yourself in the Michelin-starred Feitoria restaurant.

Doca do Bom Sucesso, Belém. www.altisbelemhotel.com. ✆ **21/040-02-00.** 50 units. 150€–570€ double; from 650€ suite. Bus: 28 or 43. **Amenities:** Restaurant; bar; concierge; exercise room; 2 pools (outdoor); room service. Free Wi-Fi.

WHERE TO EAT

The Lisboetas have always loved their food. In fact, the most frequent topic of conversation here is which eatery is now top of the heap.

Plenty of restaurants serve the usual fish and shellfish, but the cuisine goes beyond what you'll find in the rest of the country, with many erstwhile Portuguese colonials from Angola, Cape Verde, Brazil, Mozambique, and Goa owning restaurants in the capital. The menus in the best establishments remain on par with those of Europe's leading restaurants.

You needn't pay exorbitant prices for quality food, though. There is tasty fare to suit all budgets. For the best value, look for a daily special in a *tasca*, a no-frills restaurant with traditional food.

Lisboans tend to eat much later than most North American and British visitors, although not as late as their Spanish neighbors. Most go out to eat after 8:30pm, sometimes as late as 9pm. Some restaurants stay open very late.

You'll dine on a variety of local specialties including suckling pig, grilled fish, seafood, *petiscos*, and many rice dishes. Sandwiches are quite popular: *prego* (steak sandwich) and *bifana* (pork sandwich). And in summer there's nothing better than a plate of fresh grilled sardines with a grilled pepper salad or a tray of clams with garlic and cilantro, and a glass of vinho verde. Finally, Lisboetas love their cakes, especially *pastéis de nata* (custard tarts)—the best are at Pastéis de Belém café (p. 103), in Belém. Be prepared to order two, one is never enough!

In the Center

EXPENSIVE

Belcanto ★★★ CREATIVE PORTUGUESE Local chef José Avillez is at the helm of six superb restaurants in Lisbon. But the two-Michelin star Belcanto (the first in Lisbon to win this high rating) is the pinnacle of his genius, an exclusive room with just 10 tables that takes Portugese cuisine to new heights. Don't forgo the tasting menu; it will allow you to browse dishes that you might have tried in Lisbon before—like suckling pig or sea bass—that Avillez reimagines and elevates. Also not to be missed: the chocolate special, which plays with three different textures of the sweet to blissful effect. Note that the restaurant is formal, so dress accordingly. To get in you'll have to book far, far in advance, especially for dinner.

Largo de São Carlos,12, Chiado. www.belcanto.pt. ✆ **21/342-06-07.** Reservations required. Main courses 35€–45€; menu degustation 125 €–145€. Tues–Fri 1–4pm; Mon–Sat 8–11pm. Metro: Baixa/Chiado.

A Picnic in a "Green Lung"

Lisbon has many "green lungs" (public parks) where you can go with picnic fixings. Of these, the most appealing is the **Jardim Botânico,** Rua da Alegria, with its ornate iron benches and shrubs and trees from all parts of the world. But **Jardim da Estrela** is where you'll find more Lisboetas, a favorite for families. **Gulbenkian** (p. 107), next to the museum, has another relaxing and popular park.

Lisbon Restaurants

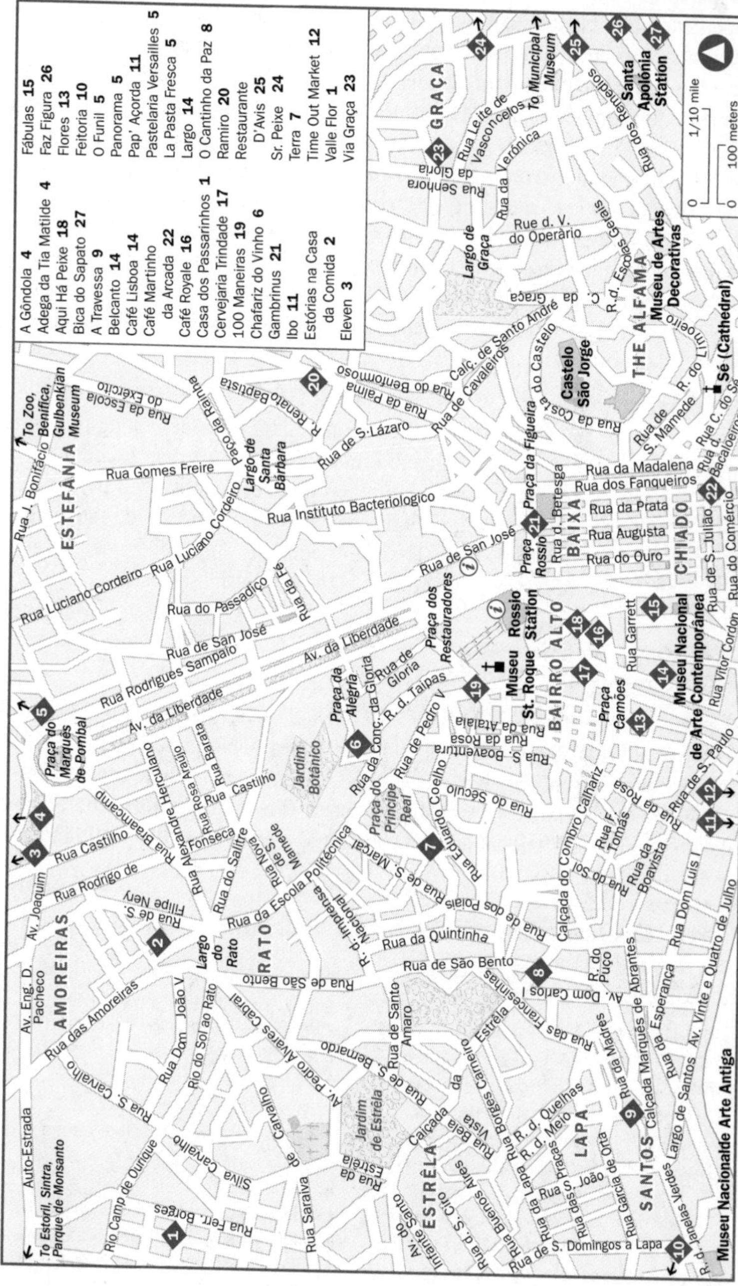

Restaurant	Map no.
A Gôndola	4
Adega da Tia Matilde	4
Aqui Há Peixe	18
Bica do Sapato	27
A Travessa	9
Belcanto	14
Café Lisboa	14
Café Martinho da Arcada	22
Café Royale	16
Casa dos Passarinhos	1
Cervejaria Trindade	17
100 Maneiras	19
Chafariz do Vinho	6
Gambrinus	21
Ibo	11
Estórias na Casa da Comida	2
Eleven	3
Fábulas	15
Faz Figura	26
Flores	13
Feitoria	10
O Funil	5
Panorama	5
Pap' Açorda	11
Pastelaria Versailles	5
La Pasta Fresca	5
Largo	14
O Cantinho da Paz	8
Ramiro	20
Restaurante D'Avis	25
Sr. Peixe	24
Terra	7
Time Out Market	12
Valle Flor	1
Via Graça	23

Eleven ★★ MEDITERRANEAN/MODERN PORTUGUESE Too many chefs spoil the broth, but 11 friends can work wonders when they decide to open a restaurant together—and hire the right chef. That man is Joachim Koerper, and he is an artist of the palate, putting together a seasonal, constantly changing menu that is sure to delight. Sea bass with beetroot and roasted lobster with butter beans are some recurring dishes. Meaty main courses range from raspberry-sauced duck from the French town of Challans to lamb in a lemon crust with a chestnut parfait. The restaurant itself makes the most of its scenic setting just above Parque Eduardo VII, next to the Amália Rodrigues Gardens, with floor-to-ceiling windows. And yes, the 11 owners named the place after themselves, sort of.

Rua Marquês de Fronteira. www.restauranteleven.com. ✆ **21/386-22-11.** Reservations required. Main courses 35€–59€; tasting menu 106€. Mon–Sat 12:30–3pm and 7:30–11pm. Metro: Parque.

Estórias na Casa da Comida ★ CONTEMPORARY PORTUGUESE Sometimes the old standbys lose their oomph. Not this one, a long-time fave with its charming walled garden and French Empire-style bar. It continues to dish out tasty fare. Chef Duarte Lourenço does especially well by salt cod with cornbread and olive oil, octopus in red wine, baby squid, and Iberian pork cheeks with clam polenta. The cellar contains an excellent selection of wines and the atmosphere is ideal for closing big business deals.

Travessa de Amoreiras 1 (close to Jardim de Las Amoreiras). www.casadacomida.pt. ✆ **21/388-53-76.** Reservations required. Main courses 19€–30€; menu degustation 45€; Mon–Sat 8–11pm. Metro: Rato.

Feitoria ★★★ CREATIVE PORTUGUESE Chef João Rodrigues is well aware of Portugal's colonial past: He assimilates Asian ingredients and cooking techniques from the areas visited by Golden Age Portuguese explorers, a technique that's earned him a Michelin star. Presentations are elaborate and flavors can be unusual, but always toothsome. Feitoria has two tasting menus

time out FOR A MARKET MEAL

Time Out magazine masterminded the transformation of the classic 19th-century Ribeira Market into a foodie wonderland in May 2014. They named it—surprise, surprise—the Time Out Market. Produce stands still take up about half of this massive, 19th-century covered market. The other half is chic chaos, with stalls from Michelin-starred chefs alongside stands from such classic restos as Manteigaria Silva or Garrafeira Nacional. That means a mix of price ranges and food types, everything from tinned octopus to gingery tuna tartar to warm beef sandwiches gussied up with shaved ham, melted cheese, and tangy barbecue sauce. The market has been a huge hit, getting some 2 millions visitors a year, so if you go for lunch or dinner, get there early to get a seat (either before 12:30pm or before 7:30pm) to make sure you get a seat.

Mercado da Ribeira, Av. 24 de Julho. www.timeoutmarket.com. ✆ **21/395-12-74.** Sun–Wed 10am to midnight, Thurs–Sat 10am–2am. Metro: Cais do Sodré.

that change twice a year. Our recommendation: Go for the epic Journey Menu, with such wonders as the squid, prawns, peanuts in algae broth, or a plating of sea bass, blue lobster, pumpkin, and borage (a Mediterranean herb).

Altis Belém Hotel & Spa, Doca do Bom Sucesso. www.restauranteleven.com. ✆ **21/040-02-00.** Reservations required. Tasting menu 85€–135€. Mon–Sat 7:30–11pm. Closed Jan 10–24. Best to take a taxi, as the 15 tram stops a bit far from the hotel.

Gambrinus ★ PORTUGUESE/SEAFOOD Gambrinus is resolutely old school, its menu unchanged for years and its dining room classically styled, with leather chairs under a beamed cathedral ceiling (I always try to nab the little table beside the fireplace at the raised end of the room). The restaurant is renowned for its seafood bisque, its lobster dishes, and the seafood *cataplana* (a traditional dish from the Algarve cooked in a copper pot). Those are all pricey, but you don't have to break the bank to dine here: Sitting at the counter (*barra*) the menu is affordable, featuring *petiscos* (a Portuguese type of tapas). Gambrinus is in the congested heart of the city, near the Rossio rail station, on a little square behind the National Theater.

Rua das Portas de Santo Antão 23. www.gambrinuslisboa.com. ✆ **21/342-14-66.** Reservations recommended. Main courses 22€–36€. Daily noon–1:30am. Metro: Restauradores or Rossio.

IBO ★ MOZAMBIQUE/PORTUGUESE At the Cais do Sodré docks, close to the ferry station, this restaurant opens onto an esplanade by the river. It's installed in an early-20th-century salt warehouse, which has been handsomely converted. Chef João Pedrosa runs the kitchen, offering up a delicious and spicy fusion of the food of Mozambique (where he has his roots) and Portuguese fare. So you might find yourself tucking into crispy Goan-style samosas or crab curry, both spicy and flavor-forward. Follow the chef's recommendations regarding the best wine pairings. For dessert, it has to be the inspired pumpkin confit in filo pastry with coconut ice cream.

Armazém A, Porta 2, Cais do Sodré. www.ibo-restaurante.pt. ✆ **21/342-36-11.** Reservations recommended. Main courses 17€–30€. Tues–Thurs 12:30–3.00pm and 7:30–11.00pm; Fri–Sat 12:30–3.00pm and 7:30pm–1am; Sun 12:30–3:30pm. Metro: Cais do Sodré.

100 Maneiras ★★ INTERNATIONAL Bosnian-born chef Ljubomir Stanisic is behind this restaurant, which translates as "100 ways of preparation." And those ways can be quite artful—on our last visit, our pieces of cod arrived at table hanging from clothespins. We can't guarantee you'll get that cod treatment; the chef is constantly changing the menu based on which ingredients are freshest at the city's Ribeira market. You might encounter a Brazilian rump steak, tender to the fork and full of flavor. Or an authentic Brazilian *feijoada* (bean stew). Not unexpectedly, there are Serbian dishes on the menu, too. 100 Maneiras is tucked away in a little section of Bairro Alto. The setting is intimate, the welcome warm.

Rua do Teixeira 35. www.restaurante100maneiras.com. ✆ **21/099-04-75.** Tasting menu 60€; 18€–28€. Daily 7:30pm–2am. Metro: Baixa-Chiado.

Panorama Restaurant ★★ INTERNATIONAL/PORTUGUESE The name doesn't lie: This restaurant and bar on the top of the 25-story Sheraton Lisboa Hotel & Spa is a celestial setting at night with the twinkling lights of Lisbon below. But you're not munching the views here, the food is topnotch, too, with such tantalizing dishes as dried fruits and fresh papaya salad sprinkled with sheep's-milk cheese, or filet of cod served in a savory ragout of fresh clams. Some of the chef's dessert concoctions are pure poetry, especially the Belgian chocolate fondant with ginger ice cream. The tasting menus are divided between northern and southern Portuguese cuisine.

Rua Latino Coelho 1. www.sheratonlisboa.com. ✆ **21/312-00-00.** Reservations required. Mains: 24€–32€. Tasting menus 55€–75€. Daily 7:30–11:30pm. Bus: 1, 36, 44, or 45.

MODERATE

Adega da Tia Matilde ★ PORTUGUESE We once overhead a Portuguese father here telling his son, "Food like this will make a man out of you." Indeed, it's a great place to sample the savory and hearty specialties of Ribatejo, including *cabrito assado* (roast mountain kid), *arroz de frango* (chicken with rice), *pato corado com arroz* (duck rice), and pungent *caldeirada* (fish stew). The Portuguese love this large, busy place in the Praça de Espanha area—foreign visitors are rare.

Rua da Beneficência 77. www.adegatiamatilde.com. ✆ **21/797-21-72.** Main courses 11€–28€. Mon–Sat noon–4pm; Mon–Fri 7:30–11pm. Metro: Praça d'Espanha. Bus: 31.

A Gôndola ★ PORTUGUESE/ITALIAN Although its decor isn't particularly inspired, the good food at A Gôndola—including some of the finest Italian specialties in town—makes the restaurant worth the trip out of the city center (you might also stop by after a visit to the nearby Gulbenkian Museum). We also think the prices are more than fair for the quality of the food. A meal might include Chaves ham with melon and figs, followed by filet of sole meunière or *bacalhau à brás* (salt cod with eggs and straw fries). Other choices are cannelloni Roman style or veal cutlet Milanese.

Av. de Berna 64. www.restaurantegondola.com. ✆ **21/797-04-26.** Reservations recommended. Main courses 13€–25€. Daily noon–3pm and 7:30–11pm. Metro: Praça de Espanha. Bus: 16, 26, 31, or 46.

Cervejaria Ramiro ★★★ PORTUGUESE Although it hasn't changed much since Anthony Bourdain made it famous on his TV show, the lines out the door betray that this is no longer just a local's *cervejaria* (beer joint with steaks and seafood). It was, of course, a Lisbon institution well before Bourdain came calling, for the consistent (high) quality of its food and friendly service. The atmosphere is quite lively, with the staff dashing between tables as diners hammer down crab legs, suck Algarve's tiger prawn heads, and mop up *amêijoas à bulhão pato* (clams with garlic, olive oil, and cilantro). I particularly like the the steak sandwich (the popular *prego*), also known as the "dessert." Make sure to ask the price of the big lobsters and crabs before you order as they are sold by the kilo, so your bill could skyrocket. This is also a good place to taste the *percebes* (gooseneck barnacles); it looks like dinosaur claws but is scrumptious, tasting like essence of the sea. ***Tip:*** To avoid lines, show up a bit earlier; that is, before 12:30 or 7:30 pm.

Av. Almirante Reis,1. www.cervejariaramiro.pt/. ✆ **21/885-10-24.** Main courses 10€–38€. Tues–Sun noon–1am. Closed some weeks in Aug. Metro: Praça d'Espanha: Intendente. Tram: 28.

La Pasta Fresca ★★ ITALIAN One of the leading Italian restaurants in Lisbon bets big and wins on freshly made pasta like eggplant *mezze lune* (ravioli with tomato sauce and salted ricotta), cuttlefish spaghetti with *cacciuco* (sauce made with squid, octopus, and cuttlefish), and carbonara with *guanciale* (pork cheek). All are cooked from scratch for each customer. The menu is proudly created by an Italian couple from Naples, Stefania Raiola and Giuseppe Godono, who fell in love with Lisbon and stayed to make the best *cannolo siciliano* (a dessert with *ricotta* and candied fruit) you can find in the city. The pastas are also available for takeout.

Av. 5 de Outubro, 186A. ✆ **21/796-09-97.** Main courses 12€–18€. Mon–Sat 12:30–11pm. Metro: Marquês de Pombal.

Martinho da Arcada ★★ PORTUGUESE In its way, the Martinho is one of the city's most famous restaurants, thanks to its age (it was established in 1782) and its association with Portugal's beloved poet Fernando Pessoa, whose photos hang on the wall, just above the table where he used to compose some of his most famous works. There are three distinct sections to this place—a cafe for drinks and sandwiches; an outdoor terrace, where the menu is less complete than what you'll find inside; and an old-world style inside dining room. Our recommendation goes to this last room, as it is rich with history. The menu here is also long and varied, but if you ask for what the kitchen is proudest of, a staff member will talk about the house-style cod (a thick "tenderloin" of salt cod served with twice-cooked onions and fried potatoes) or the filet steak served with coffee sauce and fresh vegetables. The fresh fish is another highlight and for the record, not as old as this historic place.

Praça do Comércio. ✆ **21/887-92-59.** Reservations recommended for dinner. Main courses 12€–22€. Mon–Sat 8am–11pm. Metro: Terreiro do Paço.

O FUNIL ★★ PORTUGUESE "The Funnel" does *cozinha Portuguesa* (Portuguese cuisine) so well and inexpensively that a line forms at the door most evenings. The menu offers an array of excellent choices, including roast goat, tiger shrimp in a picante sauce, and clams in wine sauce. The cod cakes with tomato rice are an excellent introduction to the love affair that the Portuguese have with this ocean dweller (in fact, they are the biggest consumers of this fish in the world). Or you could go for a meal of small dishes of *petiscos* (Portuguese-style tapas). The owners serve their own *vinho da casa* (house wine)—try the red Alijó.

Av. Elias Garcia 82A. www.ofunil.com. ✆ **21/796-60-07.** Reservations recommended. Main courses 13€–20€. Daily noon–3:30pm; Tues–Sat 7–10:30pm. Metro: Campo Pequeno. Bus: 1, 32, 36, 38, 44, or 45.

INEXPENSIVE

Casa dos Passarinhos ★ TRADITIONAL PORTUGUESE Solid comfort food at affordable prices—that's the promise of a *tascas* like this one, and it's a potent draw. Even more alluring: the idea of cooking for yourself. *Bife na pedra* (steak on the stone)—it comes raw for you to grill on a hot stone—is very popular here. It's smoky and smelly but also lots of fun. If you don't want to work for your supper, the octopus is recommended, as is the tuna steak and Iberian pork (called *secretos*). Arrive before 1pm or you'll have to wait, as that's when local workers arrive for lunch.

Rua Silva Carvalho 195. ✆ **21/388-23-46.** Mains: 8€–17€. Mon–Sat 12:30–3pm and 7:30–10:30pm. Bus: 758.

Cervejaria Trindade ★ PORTUGUESE In operation since 1836, this is the oldest *cervejaria* in Lisbon, owned by the brewers of Sagres beer. It was built on the foundations of the 13th-century Convento dos Frades Tinos, which was destroyed by the 1755 earthquake. Surrounded by walls tiled with Portuguese scenes, make your order a classic: *bife na frigideira* (steak with mustard sauce and a fried egg, served in a clay frying pan). Not into meat? Like all the *cervejarias*, Trindade has abundant shellfish options, though those in the know go for the *amêijoas* (clams) *à Trindade* and giant prawns.

Rua Nova de Trindade 20C. www.cervejariatrindade.pt. ✆ **21/342-35-06.** Main courses 12€–33€. Daily noon–2am. Metro: Baixa/Chiado.

Fábulas ★★ PORTUGUESE/INTERNATIONAL On gray winter days, Lisboetas flock to this converted brandy warehouse for brunch in its cozy cafe and restaurant. It's a refreshing oasis of informality, a stone-and-brick sanctuary in busy Chiado. Some rooms have vaulted ceilings and black and white 1920s movie star photos, as well as sewing-machines, always handy when you're travelling… But you're here to eat, of course, and you won't go wrong with the traditional Bacalhau à Brás (salt cod with eggs and straw fries) or the garlic prawns paired with a bottle of good organic wine.

Calçada de São Francisco 63. ✆ **21/353-87-80.** Main courses 11€–15€. Mon–Sun 11:30am–11:30pm. Metro: Baixa/Chiado.

Pap' Açorda ★ PORTUGUESE This beloved restaurant has left its traditional home in Bairro Alto and is now on the first floor of the Mercado da Ribeira. The menu is very similar to the original, and the food is still excellent, but somehow the charming old restaurant doesn't seem the same in its new clothes. It's still worth visiting, however, especially for the menu item that made its name: *açorda*, a traditional dish with bread, seafood, eggs, coriander, garlic, and olive oil. The *pastéis de massa tenra*, delicious savory pasties filled with meat, are also first rate. Finish with their famous chocolate mousse, thick and rich, and oh so good.

Av. 24 de Julho, 49, 1, Mercado da Ribeira. ✆ **21/346-48-11.** Reservations required. Main courses 16€–36€. Tues–Sat noon–2:30pm and 8–11:30pm. Metro: Cais do Sodré.

Pastelaria Versailles ★ CAFE/PASTRIES The most famous teahouse in Lisbon, Pastelaria Versailles is considered so iconic it has been declared part of the "national patrimony." When it opened in 1932, its specialty was *licungo*, the famed black tea of Mozambique; you can still order it, but nowadays English brands are more popular. (Ironic, as Portuguese historians claim that the the custom of tea-drinking was introduced to the English court by Catarina of Bragança after she married Charles II in 1662.) The decor is plush, with chandeliers, gilt mirrors, stained-glass windows, tall stucco ceilings, and black-and-white marble floors. For those with a sweet tooth, the cake window is a pure delight, from crispy custard tarts to fresh éclairs. But the cafe serves a wide range of food and drinks from beer and hot chocolate to codfish cakes and toasted ham-and-cheese sandwiches.

Av. da República 15A. www.pastelariaversailles.com. ✆ **21/354-63-40.** Sandwiches 3€; pastries 1€; daily specials 9.50€–22€. Daily 7:30am–10pm. Metro: Saldanha.

INEXPENSIVE

O Cantinho da Paz ★★ INDIAN This small restaurant honors the cuisine of Goa, which was a colony of Portugal until 1961. Curries are at the heart of the menu, and they draw discerning diners. Our favorite is shrimp curry flavored with coconut and laced with cream. Chili heads opt for the fiery vindalho made with lamb, fish, or pork; or the veal xacuti, succulent medallions of pork richly flavored with ginger and garlic. You'll also start to see how snack food in Portugal was deeply influenced by Goa when you try the crispy chicken or prawn samosas (*chamuças* in Portuguese).

Rua da Paz 4 (off Rua dos Poiais de São Bento). ✆ **21/396-96-98.** Reservations required. Main courses 10€–25€. Tues–Sat 12:30–2:30pm and 7:30–11pm. Tram: 28. Bus: 6 or 49.

Terra ★★ VEGETARIAN Even nonvegetarians will be enthralled with the rich flavors served by the kitchen here. In a restored 18th-century house with a private garden, patrons enjoy a daily changing buffet that features an array of curries, tempura dishes, burritos, and kebabs. Salads are a hallmark of Terra, and they take inspiratation from all of the continents, so you might find yourself chomping down on a Greek salad one day, a Waldorf salad the next. And after your healthy meal, we recommend treating yourself with dessert, especially the delectable chocolate brownie and a rice pudding based on a medieval recipe. The restaurant also serves the first kosher wines to be produced in Portugal in 500 years.

Rua da Palmeira 15. www.restauranteterra.pt. ✆ **70/710-81-08.** Reservations recommended Sat–Sun. Buffet 20€. Tues–Sun 12:30–3pm and 7:30–10:30pm. Bus: 758.

In the Chiado District

EXPENSIVE

Largo ★★ MEDITERRANEAN Formerly of the celebrated Buddha Bar in Paris, chef Miguel Castro e Silva creates meals with vigorous flavors in perfectly balanced dishes. This might mean a grilled sea bass in an orange fennel sauce, or sautéed squid with shrimp in a beurre blanc sauce. Meat is given the four-star treatment, too, like steak filet with sautéed foie gras in a wine sauce, or the delightful duck magret, sided by a truffled risotto. Starters might include a cold almond and fennel cream soup or smoked codfish in a pinenut vinaigrette. And the setting for the meal is just as special: The main restaurant was converted from the old convent of the Cloisters of the Church of the Martyrs, an elegant and now colorful space (with lettuce-green and fuschia walls), brick-vaulted ceilings, and modern chandeliers.

Rua Serpa Pinto 10A. www.largo.pt. ✆ **21/347-72-25.** Reservations required. Main courses 25€–30€. Mon–Fri 12:30–3pm; Sat 7:30pm–midnight. Metro: Baixa/Chiado.

MODERATE

Aqui Há Peixe ★★ SEAFOOD In Portuguese, the name of this stylish restaurant translates as "There is fish here"—and so there is, quite a lot of it, most of it caught off the coast only that night or in the early morning. The chef is a true "fish whisperer": Before opening this place, he had a restaurant in seaside Comporta for years, where he learned to coax out the natural taste of fish rather than burying it under heavy sauces. Begin with freshly shucked oysters or "duck clams," or perhaps a savory fish soup. The garlic prawns are a real delicacy, and the tuna steak sautéed with peppercorns wins a bravo. Vegetables accompanying the main dishes are always fresh and gathered that morning at the local market. Most in-the-know diners select a light *vinho verde* to go with their seafood.

Rua da Trindade 18A. ✆ **21/343-21-54.** www.aquihapeixe.pt. Reservations recommended. Main courses 14€–22€. Tues–Sun 7pm–2am. Metro: Baixa/Chiado.

Flores ★★ CREATIVE PORTUGUESE The groovy, 1960s-inspired decor—lots of orange, bulbous lamps—is just right for the groovy cooking of chef Bruno Rocha. He's a master of reinvention—just try his imaginative takes on salt cod, suckling pig, or seafood rice. And since the restaurant is part of a hotel, it also serves a mean breakfast.

In the Hotel Bairro Alto, Praça Luís de Camões 8. www.bairroaltohotel.com. ✆ **21/340-82-52.** Reservations recommended. Lunch main courses 12€–19€; dinner main courses 18€–28€. Daily noon–3pm and 7:30–10:30pm. Metro: Baixa/Chiado.

INEXPENSIVE

Café Lisboa ★★ PORTUGUESE One of the formal "showcase" salons within Lisbon's Opera House, originally built in 1765, was transformed into this restaurant by celeb chef José Avillez. Today it's the kind of airy, appealingly formal venue where sparkling wine might be served with steaks, and where you'll overhear diners relating the plot of a past opera performance. The staff will draw your attention to the similarities of this elegant small-scale venue with the neoclassicism of La Scala in Milan, and indeed, there's something Italian and rococo about the place, especially when the opera being rehearsed on the stage inside can be heard outside. It's the most traditional of Avillez's restaurants, but his imagination can still be seen here in such dishes as the octopus tartare, the garlic prawns, and the delicious fava beans with *chouriço.* Ask for the chef's special piri-piri oil.

Largo São Carlos. www.cafelisboa.pt. ✆ **21/346-80-82.** 9€–16€; main courses 15€–24€. Daily noon–midnight. Metro: Baixa/Chiado.

Royale Café ★★ INTERNATIONAL Tenderloin of deer topped with bacon and pears in a syrup of Porto, veal carpaccio with arugula, coriander-laced pesto, fresh artichokes with cheese from the Azores—these are just some of the unusual delights on offer here. The fare at Royale Café is of the 21st century, not the past. And the treats come at lunch as well as dinner, whether you go for the house salad (called Royale, a mixed-leaf bowl with arugula, mozzarella on cornbread, and strawberries and pesto); or some of the best sandwiches in Chiado, served on spelt bread, a wild wheat bread that existed in Europe before the agricultural revolution and still ground on millstones.

Largo Rafael Bordalo Pinheiro. www.royalecafe.com. ✆ **21/346-91-25.** Main courses 9€–14€. Mon–Sat 10am–midnight; Sun 10am–8pm. Metro: Baixa/Chiado.

In the Avenida District

MODERATE

Chafariz do Vinho ★★ PORTUGUESE/WINE Our favorite *enoteca* boasts not only one of the more varied and affordable wine *cartes* in Lisbon, but also features toothsome dishes, both in a tasting menu and a selection of tapas. The setting is also unique: an 18th-century stone-built aqueduct that once brought fresh water from the hills into Lisbon. The *enoteca* offers wines from relatively small, unknown producers, charging reasonable prices. Among the delectable tapas are smoked sausage with cabbage, smoked codfish with fresh grapes, or shrimp with mushrooms. The tasting menu pairs a different wine with every course, featuring such starters as carpaccio of octopus with "salsa verde" (an herb sauce) or dates with bacon, followed by goat cheese on toast or fresh pasta with spinach. For a main, you are likely to be served a platter of mixed smoked meats or a carpaccio of smoked duck followed by the fresh dessert of the day. Ask the helpful staff all you need to know about the Portuguese wines.

Chafariz da Mãe d'Água a Praça da Alegria. www.chafarizdovinho.com. ✆ **21/342-20-79.** Reservations recommended. Tasting menu 35€; tapas 3.50€–9€. Tues–Sun 6pm–2am. Metro: Avenida.

In the Graça District

MODERATE

Faz Figura ★ INTERNATIONAL/PORTUGUESE This is one of the most attractively decorated dining rooms in Lisbon—decked out in 19th-century style with pretty antique tiles and prints of city scenes—and the service is faultless. When reserving a table, ask to be seated on the veranda, overlooking the Tagus. The cuisine, including such specialties as *feijoada de marisco* (shellfish stew) and *cataplana* (a cooking pot) of fish and seafood, is generally very flavorful and occasionally spicy. But expect an expensive bill.

Rua do Paraíso 15B. www.fazfigura.com. ✆ **21/886-89-81.** Reservations recommended. Main courses 16€–32€. Mon–Fri 12:30–3pm and 7:30–11pm; Sat 7:30–11pm. Bus: 12, 39, or 46.

Via Graça ★ PORTUGUESE In the residential Graça district, a few blocks northeast of the fortifications surrounding Castelo de São Jorge, this restaurant boasts a panoramic view that encompasses the castelo and the Basilica da Estrela. Flickering candles and attentive service enhance the romantic setting. Dishes aren't inventive, but they're appealing to traditionalists who prefer hearty fare. Specialties of the house include such traditional Portuguese dishes as *pato assado com moscatel* (roast duck with wine from the region of Setúbal) and *linguado com recheio de camarão* (stuffed filet of sole served with shrimp).

Rua Damasceno Monteiro 9B. www.restauranteviagraca.com. ✆ **21/887-08-30.** Reservations recommended. Main courses 16€–30€. Mon–Fri 12:30–3pm and 7:30–11pm; Sat–Sun 7:30–11pm. Tram: 28.

INEXPENSIVE

Restaurant d'Avis ★ PORTUGUESE This simple but pleasing restaurant in East Lisbon was established in the late 1980s as a purveyor of the cuisine of Alentejo to cost-conscious diners. It serves regional dishes, such as roast pork with clams, roast baby goat, steaming bowls of *caldo verde* (a fortifying soup made from high-fiber greens and potatoes), and perfectly prepared fresh fish. Most start with the hearty bread soups that the southern region is famous for. Don't expect a luxurious setting or anything even vaguely formal—the rustic venue is deliberately unpretentious, and few members of the staff speak English.

Rua do Grilo 98. www.davis.com.pt. ✆ **21/868-13-54.** Main courses 7€–18€. Mon–Sat noon–4pm and 7:30–10:30pm. Bus: 18, 38, 39, 42, 59, or 105.

In Alto de Santo Amaro

Restaurant Valle Flor ★★ PORTUGUESE This is the most elegant hotel dining room in Lisbon, with a battalion of uniformed staff members and a physical setting that's revered as a national monument. It was designed as part of a cocoa mogul's private villa in 1907, and it contains a pair of dining rooms, each elaborately frescoed, gilded, and adorned with the finest Romantic Revival accessories of their day. Come here for an immersion in old-world glamour and protocol, and for a meal that will be impeccably presented and prepared. It might include such delicacies as baby snails nestled inside a potato shell; home-smoked Scottish salmon marinated in port with vermicelli and a lemon-flavored saffron sauce; a casserole of sea bass, turbot, and prawns in a white-wine sauce; or roasted quail stuffed with white sausage and sautéed turnip greens.

In the Pestana Carlton Palace Hotel, Rua Jau 54. www.pestana.com. ✆ **21/361-56-00.** Reservations recommended. Main courses 24€–35€; fixed-price menus 25€–29€. Daily 6:30–10:30am, 12:30–3pm, and 7–10:30pm. Tram: 15.

In Santa Apolónia

Bica do Sapato ★★ MODERN PORTUGUESE This hip restaurant has a retro-minimalist decor that's calculated to attract what a local commentator described as "the scene-savvy, design-obsessed jet set." Actor John Malkovich, along with four other partners (the most visible of whom is restaurant pro Fernando Fernandes), transformed what had been a boat factory into a three-part restaurant that packs in enthusiastic trend-setters virtually every night. A sushi bar is set one floor above ground level, and a "cafeteria" shares its space on street level with the establishment's gastronomic citadel, the restaurant, which is the place we heartily recommend above the other two. Its decor evokes the waiting lounge at a 1960s international airport, but the food takes brilliant liberties with traditional Portuguese cuisine. Stellar examples include seafood broth with grilled red prawns and Asian vegetables; codfish salad in olive oil, served with chickpea ice cream; and veal knuckle browned in olive oil, with garlic, sautéed potatoes, and bay leaves. The menu changes regularly but the quality is quite consistent.

Av. Infante Dom Henrique, Armazém (Warehouse) 8, Cais da Pedra à Bica do Sapato. www.bicadosapato.com. ✆ **21/881-03-20.** Reservations recommended. Main courses and platters 21€–32€ in restaurant; 9€–20€ in cafeteria; 6€–50€ in sushi bar. Restaurant Tues–Sun 12:30–2:30pm and 8–11:30pm, Mon 8–11:30pm; cafeteria Tues–Sun 12–3:30pm and 7:30pm–1am, Mon 5pm–1am; sushi bar Mon–Sat 7:30pm–1am. Bus: 9, 39, 46, 104, or 105. Metro: Santa Apolónia.

In Madragoa

A TRAVESSA ★ PORTUGUESE/BELGIAN Your taxi—the best way to reach the place—will deposit you within a warren of narrow, cobble-covered alleyways. The driver will then point you toward what was built in the 17th century as a convent, Convento das Bernardas, one the biggest in Madragoa neighborhood. Today, three of the convent's largest rooms, and part of its arcade-ringed courtyard, house this restaurant, in the heart of the Madragoa neighborhood. At least part of your meal might arrive unannounced from a communal platter wielded by the restaurant's congenial owner, António, who might dish a portion of duck-liver stew, or perhaps scrambled eggs with exotic black trumpet mushrooms, onto your plate as an *amuse-gueule* before your meal. John Dory in saffron sauce, as well as the fried mussels, are top picks on the menu. Other options include filet of wild boar in port-wine sauce, escalopes of foie gras with muscatel, and at least four different preparations of steak. If weather allows, eat in the courtyard.

Travessa do Convento das Bernardas 12. www.atravessa.com. ✆ **21/390-20-34.** Reservations recommended. Main courses 17€–29€. Mon–Fri 12:30–4pm and 8pm–midnight; Sat 8pm–midnight. Tram: 25 or táxi.

At Parque Das Nações

EXPENSIVE

Sr. Peixe ★ SEAFOOD This restaurant, "Mr. Fish" in English, lies in the Parque das Nações district at the northern tip of the site for EXPO '98, beyond the mammoth Pavilhão Atlântico. Most of the catch of the day, often from the port of Setúbal to the south of Lisbon, is charcoal grilled. Fish is generally sold by weight and can be quite expensive if you opt for the lobster or other shellfish dishes. You might begin with a fresh octopus salad or shrimp in garlic. The anchovies and sardines are cooked fresh. The chef also makes an excellent shellfish soup as a starter. A specialty is a simmering pot of *caldeirada,* a fish stew, or else lobster rice.

Rua da Pimenta, Parque das Nações. www.cidiarte.pt/senhorpeixe. ✆ **21/895-58-92.** Reservations required. Main courses 18€–28€. Tues–Sun noon–3:30pm and 7–10:30pm. Metro: Estação do Oriente.

6 EXPLORING LISBON

Too many visitors use Lisbon primarily as a base for exploring nearby sites and neglect the cultural gems tucked away in the Portuguese capital. Don't make that mistake. You need at least 5 days to do justice to the city and its environs.

Many of Lisbon's attractions remain relatively unknown, a blessing for travelers tired of fighting their way through overrun sights elsewhere in Europe.

SUGGESTED ITINERARIES

For more extended itineraries, not only of Lisbon, but Portugal itself, refer to chapter 4.

If You Have 1 Day

Take a stroll through the Alfama (see "Walking Tour 1" on p. 116), the most evocative district of Lisbon. Visit the 12th-century **Sé** (cathedral, p. 100), and take in a view of the city and the River Tagus from the **Miradouro Santa Luzia Belvedere** (p. 116)**.** Climb up to the **Castelo de São Jorge (St. George's Castle,** p. 98). Then, take a taxi or bus to Belém to see the **Mosteiro dos Jerónimos (Jerónimos Monastery)** and the **Torre de Belém.** While in Belém, walk on the riverfront, take in the **Discoveries Monument,** and be sure to try a *pastel de Belém* (custard tart).

If You Have 2 Days

On Day 2, head for **Sintra** (p. 161), the single most visited sight in the environs of Lisbon—Byron called it "glorious Eden." You can spend the day exploring the **Pena Palace** (p. 164) and at least one of the other palaces. Our recommendation goes to **Quinta da Regaleira** (p. 166), as it is so different from the Pena, with its masonic gardens, well, and grottoes. Return to Lisbon for a night at a **fado cafe.**

If You Have 3 Days

Yesterday and the day before were largely devoted to castles. Today you'll see the transportation the "palace set" used at the **National Coach Museum** (p. 104). For lunch, it's off to the innovative **Time Out Market** (p. 86). Set in half of the historic **Mercado da Ribeira,** this industrial-chic food court has stalls from many of the city's top chefs. Mix and match your way to a gourmet lunch. The afternoon is devoted to the **Museu Nacional de Arte Antiga** (p. 108, **National Museum of Ancient Art);** make sure to visit the garden and the viewpoint next to the museum. At day's end, have a sunset drink at the **Park** bar (p. 139) on the way to Chiado for dinner.

If You Have 4 Days

Take the metro to the **Oceanário** (see p. 114) in Parque das Nações—the largest such facility in Europe, this awe-inspiring aquarium is not just for children. Explore the newly revitalized riverfront neighborhood, grab lunch, and then head to the **Museu Calouste Gulbenkian** (p. 107), one of Europe's artistic treasure troves.

If You Have 5 Days

How to spend your last day? Ah, that's a tough one. There are so many wonders still to explore in Lisbon. You might devote a morning the ultra-contemporary art and architecture of **MAAT** (p. 102), or take in the 19th-century home of businessman Joe Berardo, today a museum filled with exquisite works of art and decorative arts (p. 103). If you've had enough of museums and historic sights, a shopping spree might be in order (see p. 123 for where to go). Or you could decide a beach day is in order, and whisk yourself off to the Estoril region (chapter 7). Toast the sunset on your last night with an aperitif in one of the bars in the Cais do Sodré area.

THE TOP ATTRACTIONS: THE ALFAMA, BELÉM & MUSEUMS

The Lisbon of bygone days lives on in the **Alfama ★★**, the most emblematic quarter of the city. The wall built by the Visigoths, and incorporated into some of the old houses, is a reminder of its ancient past. In east Lisbon, the Alfama was the Saracen sector centuries before its conquest by the Christians.

The devastating 1755 earthquake spared some of the buildings here, and, despite rampant gentrification, the Alfama has retained much of its original charm. You'll see narrow cobblestone streets, alleys, and small squares; cages of canaries; strings of garlic and pepper adorning old taverns; and fado restaurants. Houses are so close together that in many places it's impossible to stretch your arms wide. The poet Frederico de Brito dramatically expressed that proximity: "Your house is so close to mine! In the starry night's bliss, to exchange a tender kiss, our lips easily meet, high across the narrow street."

In June, the Alfama is overtaken by *arraiais*, neighborhood festivals for popular saints (Santo António, São João, and São Pedro), which means music, crowds, and lots of fish. The busiest night is on the 12nd, in honor of Santo António, when crowds flock to the small streets to eat barbecued sardines and drink wine, sangria, or *caipirinhas*. The massive human traffic jam gets intense.

Aristocrats once lived in the Alfama and a handful still do, but their memory is perpetuated by the noble coats of arms fading on the fronts of some 16th-century houses. The best-known aristocratic mansion is the one formerly occupied by the count of Arcos, the last viceroy of Brazil. Constructed in the 16th century and spared, in part, from the earthquake, it's on Largo da Salvador.

As you explore, you'll be rewarded with a parade of contrasting architectural styles, from a simple tile-roofed fishmongers' abodes to a festively decorated baroque church. One of the best views is from the belvedere of **Largo das Portas do Sol,** near the Museum of Decorative Art. It's a balcony opening onto the sea, overlooking the typical houses as they sweep down to the Tagus.

One of the oldest churches in Lisbon is **Santo Estêvão (St. Stephen),** on Largo de Santo Estêvão, originally constructed in the 13th century. The present marble structure dates from the 1700s. Also of medieval origin is the **Church of São Miguel (St. Michael),** on Largo de São Miguel, deep in the Alfama on a palm-tree-shaded square. Reconstructed after the 1755 earthquake, the interior is richly decorated with 18th-century gilt and trompe l'oeil walls.

Rua da Judiaria is another poignant reminder of the past. For ages, medieval Lisbon was a multicultural city with Jewish, Moorish, and Christian peoples living side by side. The Inquisition, in the 16th century, changed that, and drove out the Jews, who once lived on this particular street.

For specific routes through the Alfama, refer to the walking tour on p. 116. At night, the neighborhood is home to the city's best fado cafes (see p. 62).

Castelo de São Jorge ★★ CASTLE S. Jorge's Castle is considered the cradle of the city, and it *might* have been where the Portuguese capital began. Its occupation is believed to have predated the Romans. Beginning in the 5th century A.D., the site was a Visigothic fortification. It fell to the Saracens in the early 8th century. Many of the existing walls were erected during the centuries of Moorish domination. The Moors held power until 1147, the year Afonso Henríques chased them out and extended his kingdom south. Even before Lisbon became the capital of the newly emerging nation, the site was used as a royal palace.

For the finest **view ★★** of the Tagus and the Alfama, walk the esplanades and climb the ramparts of the old castle. The castle's name commemorates an Anglo-Portuguese pact dating from 1371, when King João I married Philippa of Lancaster (George is the patron saint of England). Portugal and England have been traditional allies in what is considered the oldest international alliance in the world, although their relationship was strained in 1961, when India, a member of the Commonwealth of Nations, seized the Portuguese overseas territories of Goa, Diu, and Damão.

Huddling close to the protection of the moated castle is a sector that appears almost medieval. At the entrance, visitors pause at the Castle Belvedere, one of the most splendid views of the city. It overlooks Alfama, the mountains of Monsanto and Sintra, Ponte do 25 de Abril, Praça do Comércio, the river, the

Up, Up & Away

Splendid views are the reward at the following two sites:

Santa Justa elevator platform (www.carris.pt; 9am–9pm; 5€ for entire ride, 1.50€ just up to viewing platform). This ornate concoction on Rua de Santa Justa was built in 1901. It goes from Rua Áurea, in the center of the shopping district near Rossio square, to the panoramic viewing platform that connects with Chiado. ***Tip:*** Walk up Rua do Carmo to Largo do Carmo to reach the platform, avoiding the line and the expensive ride.

Rooftop of Arco da Rua Augusta (9am–7pm; 2.50€ tickets). Right at the end of Rua Augusta, this lovely terrace boasts 360-degree views. To get there, you'll take the elevator and then climb some steps.

South Bank, and the tile roofs of the Portuguese capital. In the square stands a heroic statue—sword in one hand, shield in the other—of the first king, Afonso Henriques. The castle has different layers of history on display and while more fun for children, it is also interesting for adults, including the "Lisbon Through the Looking Glass – Camera Obscura."

Rua da Costa do Castelo. www.castelodesaojorge.pt. ✆ **21/880-06-20.** Admission 8.50€ adults, free for children under 10, family ticket 20€. Mar–Oct daily 9am–9pm; Nov–Feb daily 9am–6pm. Bus: 37. Tram: 12 or 28.

Igreja de Santo António ★ CHURCH St. Anthony (Santo António), an itinerant Franciscan monk who became the patron saint of Portugal, was born in 1195 in a house that once stood here near the Sé (cathedral). The 1755 earthquake destroyed the original church; Mateus Vicente de Oliveira was the author of the present building in 1812.

In the crypt, a guide will show you the spot where the saint was reputedly born. (He's buried in Padua, Italy.) The devout come to this little church to light candles under his picture. He's known as a protector of young brides and has a special connection with the children of Lisbon. To raise money to erect the altar at the church, the children of the Alfama built miniature altars with a representation of the patron saint. This is still a tradition. There's also the city hall's museum dedicated to Santo António next to the church, interesting to visit if you wish to learn more about his work, life, and travels.

Largo de Santo António de Sé. ✆ **21/886-91-45.** Church is free. Admission to the museum: 3€ adults, free for children. Museum: Tues–Sun 10am–1pm and 2–6pm. Bus: 37. Tram 28.

Museu de Artes Decorativas Portuguesas ★★ Here's a chance to find out how the other half lived in the 18th century. It is housed in an exquisite aristocratic abode and packed with four centuries' worth of Portuguese antiques collected by banker Ricardo do Espírito Santo Silva. It's laid out like a private home of the 1700s; visitors will be wowed by the collections of porcelain, crystal, silverware, and gilded furniture.

Largo das Portas do Sol, 2. www.fress.pt. ✆ **21/881–46-00.** Wed–Mon 10am–5pm. 4€ adults, 2€ students under 25 and the unemployed. Tram: 12E or 18E. Bus: 737.

Sé de Lisboa ★★ CATHEDRAL From the outside, Lisbon's severe cathedral looks more like a medieval fortress than a church. That may have been intentional: the new Catholic rulers purposely chose the site of the Moors' most important mosque for their first house of worship (construction started 3 years after the defeat of the Moors).

The building is a marriage of Romanesque and Gothic architecture, characterized by the twin towers flanking its entrance. The earthquakes of 1344 and 1755 damaged the structure, but didn't take it down (you can see evidence of the shaking in the bell towers and several other sections inside).

Beyond the rough exterior are many treasures, including the font where St. Anthony is said to have been christened in 1195 and the 14th-century Gothic chapel of Bartolomeu Joanes. Other items of interest are a crib by Machado de Castro (the 18th-century Portuguese sculptor responsible for the equestrian statue on Praça do Comércio), the 14th-century sarcophagus of Lopo Fernandes Pacheco, and the original nave and aisles.

A visit to the sacristy and cloister requires a guide, but is worth seeing. The cloister, built in the 14th century by King Dinis, is a serene space with a noted **Romanesque wrought-iron grill ★** and tombs with inscription stones. In the sacristy are marbles, relics, valuable images, and pieces of ecclesiastical treasure from the 15th and 16th centuries. Go in the morning when the stained-glass reflections on the floor evoke a Monet painting.

Largo da Sé. ✆ **21/886-67-52.** Admission: Cathedral free; cloister 2.50€. 9am–7pm; Cloister: winter 9am–5pm. Tram: 28. Bus: 37.

Belém ★★

At Belém, where the Tagus (*Tejo* in Portuguese) meets the sea, the Portuguese caravels (sailing ships) that charted the areas unknown to the Western world set out: Vasco da Gama to India, Álvares Cabral to Brazil and India, and Bartolomeu Dias to round the Cape of Good Hope. The district flourished as riches, especially spices, poured into Portugal. Great monuments, including the **Tower of Belém** and **Jerónimos Monastery,** were built and embellished in the Manueline style, named after the king Manuel.

In time, the royal family established a summer palace here and soon wealthy Lisboans followed, moving out of the city center and building town houses in Belém. For many years, this was a separate municipality, but eventually it was incorporated into Lisbon as a parish. Nowadays it's a magnet for visitors to its many museums, the Torre de Belém and the Monastery.

To reach the attractions previewed below, board tram no. 15 leaving from Praça do Comércio in the center of Lisbon (trip time: 15 min.). Bus no. 28 or 43 departs from Praça da Figueira, again taking 15 minutes. You can also take a suburban train leaving from Estação Cais do Sodré; it takes only 10 minutes, but make sure it stops in Belém (not all do). If you selected the tram or bus, get off at the stop marked Mosteiro dos Jerónimos, which is the next station after the stop called Belém. Once at the train station, cross the street and walk toward the main street where the Presidential Palace is. Then turn to the left side. You'll see the famous cafe Pastéis de Belém first. Mosteiro dos

Belém Attractions

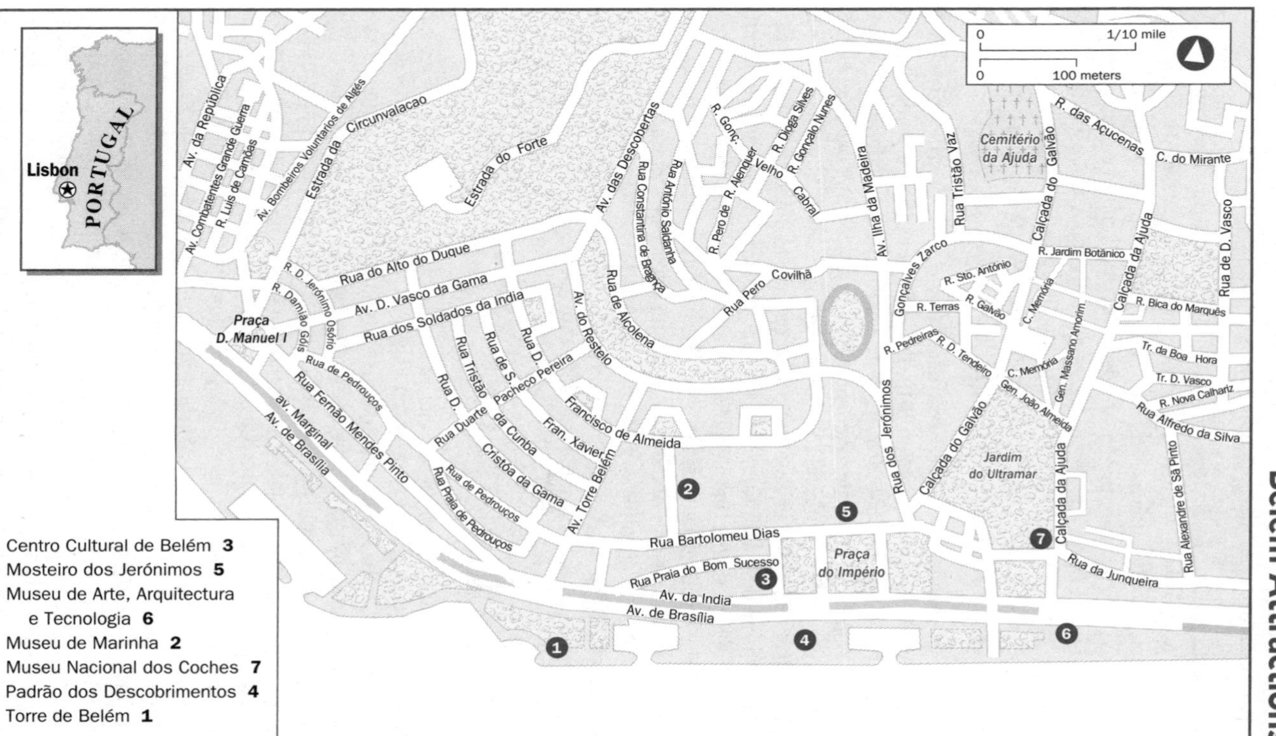

Jerónimos is a bit farther, on the right. The monument Padrão dos Descobrimentos, like a sailing ship, with statues of historical figures, fronts the water. It lies across the highway to your left (take the underpass).

Centro Cultural de Belém ★★ MULTIUSE SPACE This center functions as a concert hall, a temporary art museum, and a catchall venue. Events staged here, widely publicized in local newspapers, might include classical concerts and film festivals, theater, and dance. On weekends there are often free events and markets. An inexpensive cafeteria with a terrace, a restaurant, and a handful of shops are on the premises. The building was constructed in the early 1990s. The center is also the home of the Museu Colecção Berardo (see below).

Praça do Império. www.ccb.pt. ✆ **21/361-24-00.** Free admission. Daily 10am–7pm.

MAAT, Museum of Art, Architecture, and Technology ★★ MUSEUM Opened in October 2016, this ultra-contemporary museum (by Amanda Levete's London-based AL_A design firm) is an architectural game-changer, knitting together the river and city with a swooping panache. Locals delight in strolling atop its roof, and it set records for Lisbon museum attendance in its first week. Whether record crowds continue to come once the novelty wears off is an open question, however. The museum will be showcasing art, architecture, new media, and technology, in shows purposely built for the curvilinear interior space (I dare you to try and find a right angle here). So far, exhibitions have been less than scintillating, but with a space this unusual (one critic compared it to "an aquarium without fish"), it may take some time for the curators to find their stride. Also on view (always): the EDP Foundation Art Collection, including works from more than 250 Portuguese contemporary artists. The museum is next to the old Tejo Power Station (now the Electricity Museum).

Av. de Brasília, Central Tejo. www.maat.pt. ✆ **21/002-81-30.** Admission 5€ adults, 2.5€ students and seniors 65 and over; free for children and teenagers under 18. Wed–Mon 12am–8pm.

Mosteiro dos Jerónimos ★★★ RELIGIOUS SITE In an expansive mood, Manuel I, the Fortunate, ordered this monastery built to commemorate Vasco da Gama's voyage to India and to give thanks to the Virgin Mary for its success. Manueline, the style of architecture that bears the king's name, combines flamboyant Gothic and Moorish influences with elements of the nascent Renaissance. Prince Henry the Navigator originally built a small chapel dedicated to St. Mary on this spot. Today this former chapel is the Gothic and Renaissance **Igreja de Santa Maria ★★**, marked by a statue of Henry. The church is known for its richly carved stonework like the **network vaulting ★** over the nave and aisles and the carved retelling of the life of St. Jerome.

The west door of the church leads to the **Cloisters ★★★**, which represent the apex of Manueline art. The stone sculpture here is fantastically intricate. The two-story cloisters have groined vaulting on their ground level. The recessed upper floor is not as exuberant but is more delicate and lacelike in character. The monastery was founded in 1502, partially financed by the spice trade that grew following the discovery of the route to India. The 1755 earthquake damaged but didn't destroy the monastery. It has undergone extensive restoration, some of it ill-conceived.

The church encloses a trio of naves noted for their fragile-looking pillars. Some of the ceilings, like those in the monks' refectory, have a ribbed barrel vault. The "palm tree" in the sacristy is also exceptional.

Many of the greatest figures in Portuguese history are said to be entombed at the monastery; the most famous is Vasco da Gama. The romantic writer Alexandre Herculano (1800–54) is also buried at Jerónimos, as is the famed poet Fernando Pessoa.

Praça do Império. www.mosteirojeronimos.pt. ✆ **21/362-00-34.** Admission: Church free; cloisters 10€ adults, free for those under 12, better to buy the tickets online to avoid the lines. Those 65 and over pay 5€. May–Sept Tues–Sun 10am–6pm; Oct–Apr Tues–Sun 10am–5pm.

Museu Colecção Berardo ★★★ MUSEUM In the 1990s, Portugal got lucky. Madeira-born businessman Joe Berardo, after making a fortune in South African gold, decided the art works he'd purchased over the years should be thrown out to public view. Thus one of the world's greatest private collections of modern art found its way to the vast white halls of this museum embedded in the Belém Cultural Center.

The collection is divided into two parts. The first features sculpture and painting from 1900 to 1960 and is littered with works by Picasso, Miró, Warhol, and other acknowledged masters of 20th-century art. It also, surprisingly, has an exemplary collection of Art Deco furniture and decorative objects. The post-1960 section covers the latest movements of contemporary creativity from minimalism to Arte Povera and traumatic realism. There are 6-ft. robots made from flickering TV screens, a giant submarine suspended from the ceiling and filled with little wooden characters in a room playing African pop music, and a life-size plastic sheepdog by Jeff Koons. Berardo's collection is vast enough to also allow for regular temporary exhibitions; a recent one featured 100 years of advertising posters and autographed photos of stars like

BELÉM'S favorite SNACKS

"Heavenly" is an apt term to describe the justly famous custard cream tarts sold by **Pastéis de Belém,** Rua de Belém 84 (http://pasteisdebelem.pt; ✆ **21/363-74-23;** daily 8am to midnight July to September, 8am–11pm the rest of the year). When the monasteries were closed in 1834, the clergy had to make a living, so the monks from Jerónimos started selling these sweet pastries. The cafe Pastéis de Belém bought the recipe in 1837, creating a legion of followers firstly in Lisbon and Portugal, and worldwide since the 1980s. As they registered the name Pastéis de Belém, the others are now called *pastéis de nata.* With a crispy puff pastry, a slightly burnt top, and a gooey, soft custard center, the ones in Belém are quite unique. Legend has it that only four people know the secret recipe and those "master confectioners" handcraft them in a secret room. ***Tip:*** Don't be put off by the long lines: they're only for takeout. Instead, get a seat at a table inside and you'll be served immediately.

Laurence Olivier, Harry Belafonte, and Liberace, meaning you never know what's going to be on display at the time of your visit. The surprise of the museum: its unusual collection of Victorian and Edwardian chamber pots.

Praça do Império. www.museuberardo.pt. ✆ **21/361-28-78.** Free admission (except for special exhibits). Daily 10am–7pm.

Museu de Marinha (Maritime Museum) ★★ MUSEUM The Maritime Museum, one of the best in Europe, evokes the glory that characterized Portugal's domination of the high seas. Appropriately, it's installed in the west wing of the Mosteiro dos Jerónimos. These royal galleys re-create an age of opulence—dragons' heads drip with gilt, sea monsters coil with abandon. Assembling a large crew was no problem for kings and queens in those days. Queen Maria I ordered a magnificent galley built for the 1785 marriage of her son and successor, Crown Prince João, to the Spanish Princess Carlota Joaquina Bourbon. Eighty dummy oarsmen, elaborately attired in scarlet-and-mustard-colored waistcoats, represent the crew.

The museum contains hundreds of models of 15th- to 19th-century sailing ships, 20th-century warships, merchant marine vessels, fishing boats, river craft, and pleasure boats. In a section devoted to the East is a pearl-inlaid replica of a dragon boat used in maritime processions. A full range of Portuguese naval uniforms is on display, from one worn at a Mozambique military outpost in 1896 to a uniform worn as recently as 1961. In a special room is a model of the queen's stateroom on the royal yacht of Carlos, the Bragança king who was assassinated at Praça do Comércio in 1908. It was on this craft that his son Manuel II, his wife, and the queen mother Amélia escaped to Gibraltar following the collapse of the monarchy in 1910. The Maritime Museum also honors some early Portuguese aviators.

Praça do Império. http://ccm.marinha.pt. ✆ **21/362-00-19.** Admission 6.50€ adults, 3.20€ students and children ages 4–12, free for seniors 65 and over and children under 4. May–Sept Tues–Sun 10am–6pm; Oct–Apr Tues–Sun 10am–5pm; closed holidays.

Museu Nacional do Azulejo ★★ MUSEUM Azulejos are painted, glazed ceramic tiles that are an integral part of Portuguese culture, though this art form was originally brought here by the Arabs who ruled Lisbon from the 8th to the 12th centuries. Today the decorative tiles—mostly in blue and white—can be found covering the inside and outside of churches, palaces, simple homes, railway stations, and even private homes. Once you visit this museum you'll understand their significance. The permanent exhibition traces the history of tile painting in Portugal from its origins to designs by contemporary artists. The main building is itself an architectural gem; the convent church has rich baroque decoration where the blue of the tiles is matched by ornate gold-coated woodwork.

Rua da Madre de Deus 4, in Xabregas. ✆ **21/810-03-40.** Adults 5€, 2.5€ seniors over 65. Tues–Sun 10am–6pm. Bus: 718, 742, 794, or 759.

Museu Nacional dos Coches (National Coach Museum) ★★★ MUSEUM Every child who visits here must dream about hiding until midnight to find out if the gleaming gold carriages turn into pumpkins. This is one of Europe's finest collections of horse-drawn coaches and one of the most-visited museums in the country. It was founded in 1905 to showcase the carriages of the aristocracy and royal family. The oldest coach on exhibit carried King Phillip III of Spain on a visit to Lisbon in 1618. Others among the rococo contraptions were used by popes, nobles, and crowned heads from Portugal and around Europe, but there's no evidence any of them ever rushed a kitchen maid with a fairy godmother and two ugly sisters home from a ball. In 2015, the museum made a controversial move to a bigger (actually humongous) and less character-filled building. But even that transition hasn't dimmed the luster or this eyeful of a museum.

Praça de Afonso de Albuquerque. http://en.museudoscoches.pt. ✆ **21/361-08-50.** Admission 8€ (includes the museum and the royal academy), 4€ ages 14–25, free for children under 14. Tues–Sun 10am–6pm, last entrance at 5:30pm; closed on Jan 1, Easter Sunday, May 1, Dec 25. Bus: 28, 714, 727, 729, or 751. Tram: 15.

Padrão dos Descobrimentos ★ MONUMENT Like the prow of a caravel (ship) from the Age of Discovery, the Memorial to the Discoveries stands on the Tagus, looking ready to strike out across the Sea of Darkness. Notable explorers, chiefly Vasco da Gama, are immortalized in stone along the ramps, all led by Henry the Navigator.

The memorial was unveiled in 1960, and one of the stone figures is that of a kneeling Philippa of Lancaster, Henry's English mother—actually the only woman in the memorial. Other figures in the frieze symbolize the crusaders (represented by a man holding a flag with a cross), navigators, monks, cartographers, and cosmographers. At the top of the prow is the coat of arms of Portugal at the time of King Manuel. On the floor in front of the memorial lies a map of the world in multicolored marble, with the dates of the discoveries set in metal. It's worth taking the elevator to go to the terrace of the memorial to admire the river views to the bridge and Tower of Belém.

Praça da Boa Esperança, Av. de Brasília. www.padraodescobrimentos.pt. ✆ **21/303-19-50.** Admission: 4€. May–Sept Tues–Sun 10am–7pm; Oct–Feb Tues–Sun 10am–6pm.

Torre de Belém ★★ ARCHITECTURE The quadrangular Tower of Belém is a monument to Portugal's Age of Discovery. Erected between 1515 and 1520, the Manueline-style tower is Portugal's classic landmark and often serves as a symbol of the country. It stands on or near the spot where the caravels once set out across the sea.

Its architect, Francisco de Arruda, blended Gothic and Moorish elements, using such architectural details as twisting ropes carved of stone. The coat of arms of Manuel I rests above the loggia, and balconies grace three sides of the monument. Along the balustrade of the loggias, stone crosses represent the Portuguese crusaders.

The richness of the facade fades once you cross the drawbridge and enter the Renaissance-style doorway. Gothic severity reigns. A few antiques can be seen, including a 16th-century throne graced with finials and an inset paneled with pierced Gothic tracery. If you scale the steps leading to the ramparts,

secrets OF LISBON

The places below provide a view of Lisbon not often seen by the casual visitors passing through the city.

Ribeira ★★ While everyone knows Time Out Market (see p. 86), many will miss its attached fresh produce market Ribeira. Behind the Cais do Sodré train station, an enormous roof shelters a collection of stalls offering the produce used in Lisbon's fine restaurants. Women festively clad in voluminous aprons preside over the mounds of vegetables, fruit, and fish. As if on cue, vendors begin howling about the value of their wares, stopping only to pose for an occasional snapshot. There are also flower shops, butchers, and a grocery shop stocked with ingredients from the former colonies. In the summer one stall dedicates all its shelves to snails, something that the Lisboetas love.

Estufa Fria (The Greenhouse) ★★★ (http://estufafria.cm-lisboa.pt; ✆ **21/388-22-78;** 3€ entry) Against a background of streams and rocks, tropical plants grow in such profusion that the place resembles a rainforest. It's divided into three different areas: *estufa fria* (cold greenhouse), *estufa quente* (warm greenhouse), and *estufa doce* (sweet greenhouse, dedicated to cactus). The greenhouse is in the Parque Eduardo VII, named after Queen Victoria's son to commemorate his three trips to Lisbon. The greenhouse is open daily 9am to 5pm (winter) and 10am to 7pm (from the last Sunday of March until the last Sunday of October). Free for children under 6. Metro: Parque or Marquês de Pombal. Bus: 727, 732, 738, 744, 745, or 783.

Cemitério dos Ingleses (British Cemetery) ★ The British Cemetery lies up Rua da Estrela at one end of the Estrela Gardens. It's famous as the burial place of Henry Fielding, the novelist and dramatist best known for *Tom Jones.* Fielding went to Lisbon in 1754 to try to recover his health; his posthumous tract *Journal of a Voyage to Lisbon* tells the story of that trip. He reached Lisbon in August and died 2 months later. A monument honoring him was erected in 1830. This is the oldest cemetery in Lisbon. Open daily 8am to 2pm; ring the bell for entry. Bus: 9, 20, 727, or 738.

Jardim Botânico (Botanical Garden) ★ On Rua da Escola Politécnica 58, Principe Real (no phone; 2€ entry), near the Bairro Alto, this garden sprawls over 4 hectares (10 acres). Laid out in the

you'll be rewarded with a panorama of boats along the Tagus and pastel-washed, tile-roofed old villas in the hills beyond. But honestly, if you don't have much time, this beautiful jewel of the Manueline architecture is best from the outside, so don't worry if you don't visit its interiors.

Facing the Tower of Belém is a monument commemorating the first Portuguese to cross the South Atlantic by airplane. The date was March 30, 1922, and the flight took pilot Gago Coutinho and navigator Sacadura Cabral from Lisbon to Rio de Janeiro.

At the center of Praça do Império at Belém is the Fonte Luminosa (the Luminous Fountain). The patterns of the water jets, estimated at more than 70 original designs, make an evening show lasting nearly an hour.

Praça do Império, Av. de Brasília. www.torredebelem.pt. ✆ **21/362-00-34.** Admission 6€ adults, 3€ students ages 13–25; free for children under 12 and for seniors 65 and over; free for all Sun until 2pm. Oct–Apr Tues–Sun 10am–5pm; May–Sept Tues–Sun 10am–6pm.

mid–19th century, it was heralded a century ago as the best botanical garden in southern Europe. The garden is part of the Museum of Natural History and Science but can be visited separately. It's open daily from 9am to 7pm (till 6pm October–April). It's free to all Sunday until 2pm. Metro: Rato.

Jardim Botânico Tropical (Tropical Botanical Garden) ★★ Founded in 1912, this lovely garden is under the radar for most who visit Belém. It has more than 600 tropical species from the former Portuguese colonies—its original name was Colonial Garden—including a coffee plant from São Tomé and a small laurel forest from Madeira and the Azores. Most impressive: It has species that are considered extinct in their natural habitat, like Ginkgo biloba L e Eucommia ulmoides Oliv. It's on Largo dos Jerónimos (✆ **21/392-18-08;** 2€ entry), close to the Monastery and to the Pastéis de Belém cafe. It's open daily from 9am to 7pm (till 6pm October–March). Tram: 15 or 18. Bus: 714,727, or 728.

Aqueduto das Águas Livres (Águas Livres Aqueduct) ★★★ This magnificent work of engineering survived the earthquake of 1755. Part of the Museu da Água (Water Museum (✆ **21/810-02-15**), its construction was started in 1731 and it was the main supplier of water to the city of Lisbon until the 1960s. It is possible to walk across both walkways, known as *passeios dos arcos* (arches walkways), on the top of the aqueduct—the path is wide and flat and offers panoramic views. The distance between the main entrance in Campolide to the end of the path in Monsanto is about 1 kilometer (less than a mile). The aqueduct was also used as an access to the city rural people on a daily basis: washerwomen, market gardeners, men selling water, and many other tradespeople. Peek inside the tunnels where water used to flow. You can combine a visit here with another building of the museum, such as **Mãe d'Água,** Praça das Amoreiras, open Tuesday-Saturday, 10–5:30pm (Metro: Rato); admission is 3.00€) or **Patriarcal,** Praça do Príncipe Real, open only on Saturday 10-5:30pm (bus 758), 1.00€. Both have same info line: ✆ **21/810-02-15.** Entrance to the Aqueduct is in Calçada da Quintinha, 6 (in Campolide). Admission is 3.00€.Tuesday-Saturday, 10am to 5:30pm. Bus: 742, 751, or 758.

Two More Top Museums

Most major Lisbon museums are in Belém, but two major attractions are in the city proper: the National Art Gallery and the Gulbenkian Center for Arts and Culture.

Museu Calouste Gulbenkian ★★★ MUSEUM This is quite simply one of the world's greatest private art collections. Calouste Gulbenkian was an Armenian businessman who was among the first to comprehend the economic potential of Middle Eastern oil. He amassed a vast fortune and spent much of it on art. After his death in 1955, the collection was bequeathed to a foundation based in Lisbon, the city that gave him a haven during World War II.

Gulbenkian had discerning taste. The museum's collection is not huge, but it has at least one exquisite example from almost every era in the history of art—from gold-coated ancient Egyptian funeral masks to Impressionist treasures by Monet and Renoir. There are Turkish ceramics of the deepest Aegean blue; tempestuous Turner seascapes; salons filled with the furniture of French aristocracy; portraits by Rembrandt; illustrated medieval bibles; jade from the courts of Chinese emperors; Grecian urns; porcelain made in 13th-century Persia. The collection of jewelry by René Lalique is unsurpassed. It's all housed in a light-filled modernist low-rise that blends into landscaped gardens where, in summer, open-air concerts are held beside the ornamental lakes. As if the permanent collection wasn't enough, the museum also regularly hosts great temporary shows, like treasures of Czars brought over from the Kremlin or art from Spain's royal palaces. A must-see!

Av. de Berna 45. www.museu.gulbenkian.pt. ✆ **21/782-30-00.** Admission 10€; 50% off for seniors 65 and over, students, and teachers. Free on Sunday after 2pm. Wed–Mon 10am–6pm. Metro: Sebastião or Praça de Espanha. Bus: 716, 726, 731, 741, 746, or 756.

Museu Nacional de Arte Antiga ★★★ MUSEUM The National Museum of Ancient Art houses the country's greatest collection of paintings. It occupies two connected buildings—a 17th-century palace and an added edifice that was built on the site of the old Carmelite Convent of Santo Alberto. The convent's chapel was preserved and is a good example of the integration of ornamental arts, with gilded carved wood, glazed tiles, and sculpture of the 17th and 18th centuries. Amongst it all are some world-class masterpieces: Hieronymus Bosch's nightmarish vision of ***The Temptation of St. Anthony; The Saint Vincent Panels;*** Nuno Gonçalves' extraordinary depiction of Discovery-era Portuguese society; Francisco de Zurbarán's 12 larger-than-life portraits of the apostles; a wickedly seductive Salome by Lucas Cranach; and nanban screens from Japan showing the arrival of early Portuguese traders. Paintings from the 15th through the 19th centuries trace the development of Portuguese art.

The museum also exhibits a remarkable collection of gold- and silversmiths' works, both Portuguese and foreign. Among these is a cross from Alcobaça, the monstrance of Belém (constructed with the first gold brought from India by Vasco da Gama), and an exquisite set of 18th-century French silver tableware ordered by José I.

Diverse objects from Benin, India, Persia, China, and Japan were culled from the proceeds of Portuguese expansion overseas. Two excellent pairs of **screens ★★** depict the Portuguese relationship with Japan in the 17th century. Flemish tapestries, a rich assemblage of church vestments, Italian polychrome ceramics, and sculptures are also on display. There's a bar and a terrace garden with a view, perfect for a drink after the visit.

Rua das Janelas Verdes 95. www.museudearteantiga.pt. ✆ **21/391-28-00.** Admission 6€ adults, free for students and children under 12; 50% off for seniors 65 and over. Tues–Sun 10am–6pm. Bus: 713, 714, or 727. Tram: 25.

MORE ATTRACTIONS

The Bairro Alto ★★

Like the Alfama, the Bairro Alto (Upper City) preserves the characteristics of the Lisbon of yore. In location and population, it once was the heart of the city. Many of its buildings survived the 1755 earthquake. Today it is resoundingly colorful. From the windows and balconies, streamers of laundry hang out to dry, and canaries, parrots, parakeets, and other birds sing in their cages. Sadly, the *varinas* (fishmongers) and other vendors no longer sell from door to door, and bars and restaurants have replaced grocery shops or pharmacies. But women still lounge in doorways or lean on windowsills to watch the world go by.

Everything comes most alive at night, when the area lures visitors and natives with its restaurants, bars, fado cafes, dance clubs, and small eateries (called *tascas*)—so much so that the sidewalks are often elbow-to-elbow with partiers.

Originally called Vila Nova de Andrade, the neighborhood came into being in 1513 when the Andrade family bought part of the huge Santa Catarina and then sold the land as construction plots. Early buyers were carpenters, merchants, and ship caulkers. Some of them immediately resold their land to aristocrats, and little by little noble families moved to the quarter. The Jesuits followed, moving from their modest College of Mouraria to new headquarters at the Monastery of São Roque, where the *Misericórdia* (social assistance to the poor) of Lisbon is today. Fortunes reversed, as they do, and the Bairro Alto gradually became a working-class section once again, though some nobles kept their palaces there. It wasn't much affected by the earthquake in 1755, so it still holds a lot of older buildings, more than the nearby Chiado. At the end of the 19th century and throughout the 20th century the quarter was the domain of journalists—most of the big newspapers' plants were here. Nowadays only two survive. Writers, singers, and artists have been drawn here to live and work, attracted by the ambience and the good local cuisine. For the 19th century and much of the 20th, this was the red light district, something that would fade at the end of the 1980s.

Churches

"If you want to see all of the churches of Lisbon, you'd better be prepared to stay here for a few months," a guide once told us. True enough, the string of churches seems endless. What follows is a selection of the most intriguing ones.

Igreja de São Roque/Museu de São Roque ★★ CHURCH The Jesuits, who at one time were so powerful they virtually governed Portugal, founded St. Roque Church in the late 16th century. Beneath its painted wood ceiling, the church contains a celebrated chapel by Luigi Vanvitelli honoring John the Baptist. The chapel, ordered by the Bragança king João V in 1741, was assembled in Rome from such precious materials as alabaster and lapis

The Bairro Alto

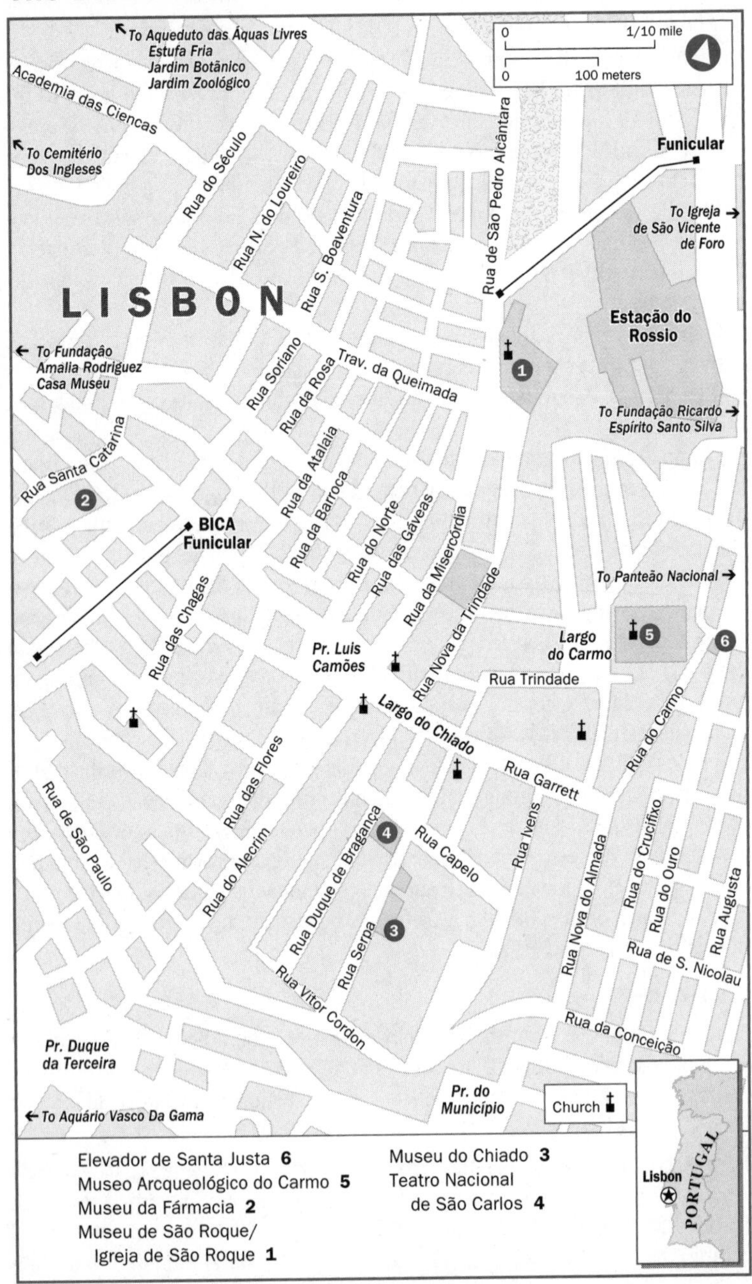

lazuli, and then dismantled, shipped to Lisbon, and reassembled. The marble mosaics look like a painting. You can also visit the sacristy, rich in paintings illustrating scenes from the lives of saints pertaining to the Society of Jesus.

The St. Roque Museum inside the church merits a visit chiefly for its collection of baroque silver. A pair of bronze-and-silver torch holders, weighing about 380 kilograms (838 lbs.) is among the most elaborate in Europe. The 18th-century gold embroidery is a rare treasure, as are the vestments. The paintings, mainly from the 16th century, include one of a double-chinned Catherine of Austria and another of the wedding ceremony of Manuel I. Look for a remarkable 15th-century Virgin (with Child) of the Plague and a polished 18th-century conch shell that served as a baptismal font.

Largo Trindade Coelho. www.museudesaoroque.com. ✆ **21/323-53-80.** Admission to the museum 2.50€ adults, free for children under 14 and seniors. Tues–Sun 10am–6pm (summer until 7pm); Mon 2–6pm. Metro: Baixa/Chiado. Bus: 758.

Igreja da São Vicente de Fora ★★★ CHURCH In this Renaissance church, the greatest names—and some forgotten wives—of the House of Bragança were laid to rest. It's the Bragança pantheon. Originally a 12th-century convent, the church was erected between 1582 and 1627. At that time, it lay outside the walls of Lisbon (hence the name St. Vincent Outside the Walls). On the morning of the 1755 earthquake, the cupola fell in.

The Braganças assumed power in 1640 and ruled until 1910, when the Portuguese monarchy collapsed and Manuel II and the queen mother, Amélia, fled to England. Manuel II died in 1932 and his body was returned to Portugal for burial. Amélia, the last queen of Portugal, died in 1951 and is entombed here, as are her husband, Carlos I (the painter king), and her son, Prince Luís Felipe; both were killed by an assassin at Praça do Comércio in 1908.

Aside from the royal tombs, the most important reason for visiting St. Vincent is to see its spectacular tiles, some of which illustrate the fables of La Fontaine. While we suspect that no one has officially counted them, their number is placed at 100,000. Look also for the curious ivory statue of Jesus, carved in the former Portuguese province of Goa in the 18th century.

Largo de São Vicente. ✆ **21/882-44-00.** Free admission. Mon–Sat 9am–6pm; Sun 9am–12:30pm and 3–5pm. Tram: 28. Bus: 712 or 728.

Panteão Nacional ★ CHURCH When a builder starts to work, the owner will often say, "Don't take as long as the workmen did on St. Engrácia." Construction on this Portuguese baroque church, Igreja de Santa Engrácia, began in 1682; though it resisted the 1755 earthquake, it wasn't completed until 1966, thus becoming a symbol of procrastination. The building, with its four square towers, is pristine but cold, and the state has fittingly turned it into a National Pantheon containing memorial tombs to heads of state.

Memorials honor Henry the Navigator; Luís Vaz de Camões, the country's greatest poet; Pedro Álvares Cabral, "discoverer" of Brazil; Afonso de Albuquerque, viceroy of India; Nuno Álvares Pereira, warrior and saint; and, of course, Vasco da Gama. Entombed in the National Pantheon are presidents of

Portugal and several writers. Also to be found are contemporary popular heroes such as the fado singer Amália and the football player Eusébio.

Ask the guards to take you to the terrace for a beautiful view of the river. A visit to the pantheon can be combined with a shopping trip to the flea market Feira da Ladra (walk down Campo de Santa Clara, heading toward the river).

Largo de Santa Clara. ✆ **21/885-48-20.** Admission 3€ adults, 1.50€ ages 15–25, free for children under 14; free for all Sun after 2pm. Tues–Sun 10am–5pm; closed holidays. Tram: 28.

Arts & Science

Fundação Amália Rodrigues Casa Museu ★ MUSEUM Fado diva Amália Rodriguez (1920–99) was a true phenomenon. Born in Lisbon into a large and very poor family, her musical expressions of *saudade* (nostalgia provoked by a sense of loss) are considered by many to be the laying bare of the Portuguese soul. After her death, which was considered a national tragedy, her body was buried with pomp and circumstance in the National Pantheon. In July 2001, her ocher-color town house was reconfigured as a museum to her life and accomplishments, and instantly became a pilgrimage site for fans. If you are one of them, you'll enjoy the multilingual (Portuguese, French, and English) guided tour of the premises, which includes videotapes of her performances. If not, this museum can be skipped.

Rua de São Bento 193. www.amaliarodrigues.pt. ✆ **21/397-18-96.** Admission 5€ per person, free for children under 5. Tues–Sun 10am–1pm and 2–6pm. Metro: Rato. Bus: 706, 749, or 774.

Fundação Ricardo do Espírito Santo Silva ★★ HISTORIC HOUSE Few other sites in Lisbon offer as comprehensive an overview of the 15th- to the 18th-century Portuguese aesthetic as this one. The setting is the 17th-century Azurara Palace, which was acquired in 1947 by the museum's namesake and benefactor. In 1953, his collection was bequeathed to a private foundation that, after his death, continued to amass hundreds of the country's finest antiques, art objects, silverware, porcelain, furniture, and paintings. These are proudly displayed over four floors of the stately looking building within a labyrinth of rooms and hallways that evoke 18th-century life in a hyper-upscale home. A bookstore and shop are on the premises. Besides the Decorative Arts Museum, the foundation has a school and workshop of decorative arts.

Largo das Portas do Sol 2. www.fress.pt. ✆ **21/881-46-00.** Admission 4€ adults, 2€ seniors, free for children under 12. Guided visits are 8€ and need to be booked. Tues–Sun 10am–5pm. Tram: 12 or 28. Bus: 37.

MUDE ★★ MUSEUM *Important note: As we go to press, this museum is closed for renovations; the description below is based on its original layout, so some details may change.* Icons of the 20th century form the nucleus of Lisbon's hip Museum of Design and Fashion. The ground-floor permanent exhibition holds a 1959 BMW "bubble car," the scarlet lips of a 1970s Bocca sofa, Dior dresses, post-modern '80s teapots, and hundreds of other landmark objects from last 100 years or so. There are temporary shows upstairs—they kicked off 2014 with a look at design successes by alumni of Lisbon University's architecture faculty. Opened in 2009, MUDE has contributed to Lisbon's growing reputation as one of Europe's coolest destinations. The museum is housed in the grandiose former headquarters of the Banco Nacional Ultramarino, the bank that financed Portugal's empire in Africa and Asia. A politically incorrect 1960s mosaic vaunting the benefits of colonization still dominates the lobby.

Rua Augusta 24. www.mude.pt. ✆ **21/888-61-17.** Free admission. Tues–Thurs and Sun 10am–8pm; Fri–Sat 10am–10pm. Metro: Rossio or Baixa/Chiado.

Museu Arqueológico do Carmo ★★ MUSEUM No other Lisbon museum so well conveys the sensation that you've wandered into a living relic and are now a witness to history. Here, the ruined nave of a Gothic church, originally built in 1389, stands in a state of partial collapse—a victim of damages wrought during the earthquake of 1755, when many parishioners died inside. Some backrooms contain a dusty collection of exhibits, such as historic *azulejos* (glazed tiles), but the star of the museum is the church itself. Unlike several nearby monuments, the church was not rebuilt but somehow survived despite further indignities inflicted upon it over the years, including vandalism by French soldiers (occupying Lisbon during the Napoleonic wars). To many Lisboans, it's the city's most evocative monument; it aggressively piques their sense of loss. In some seasons there are concerts and events set in the ruins. It's also very close to the Santa Justa platform and set in a lovely square.

Largo do Carmo. www.museuarqueologicodocarmo.pt. ✆ **21/346-04-73.** Admission 4€ adults, 3€ students and seniors, free for children under 14. Open Mon–Sat from Apr–Sept 10am–7pm; Oct–Mar 10am–6pm. Metro: Baixa/Chiado.

Museu da Farmácia ★★ MUSEUM Founded in 1996 and set in a former palace, this surprisingly compelling pharmacy museum covers more than 5,000 years of pharmaceutical history, from practices in ancient Egypt and Mesopatamia (c. 3600 B.C.) to modern techniques developed for the portable pharmacy kits used in the space shuttle Endeavour. Four pharmacies from the 18th to the 20th centuries have been reconstructed here, including a 19th-century Chinese drugstore brought intact from Portugal's former territory of Macao, off the coast of China. The building hosts a restaurant and bar with indoor/outdoor spaces (grab a seat facing Santa Catarina if you can), and yes, the pharmacy theme is kept going in the furnishings and flatware.

Rua Marechal Saldanha. ✆ **21/340-06-80.** Admission 5€ adults, 3.50€ students and seniors, free for children 2 and under. Mon–Fri 10am–6pm. Weekends only by booking. Metro: Baixa/Chiado. Tram: 28. Funicular: Bica.

Museu do Chiado ★ MUSEUM Housed in the former Convento de São Francisco, the Chiado Museum (also known as the Museum of Contemporary Art, or Museu Nacional de Arte Contemporânea) was designed by the French architect Jean-Michel Wilmotte. The permanent collection of post-1850 art and sculpture extends to 1950 and crosses the artistic bridge from Romanticism to Postnaturalism. Some excellent examples of modernism in Portugal are on display. The museum also houses changing contemporary exhibitions devoted to art, sculpture, photography, and mixed media. There's a new entrance and section in Rua Capelo, but it's not as interesting as the original building.

Rua Serpa Pinto 4. www.museuartecontemporanea.pt. ✆ **21/343-21-48.** Admission 4.50€ adults, 2.25€ students and seniors, free for children under 12. Tues–Sun 10am–6pm. Metro: Baixa-Chiado. Tram: 28.

Museu Militar ★ MUSEUM The Military Museum sits in front of the Santa Apolónia Station, not far from Terreiro do Paço and Castelo de São Jorge. Originally called the Artillery Museum, it was created in 1851 in the building of the Royal Arsenal, making it the oldest museum in the city. Today the facility exhibits not only arms, but also paintings, sculpture, tiles, and examples of architecture. Most importantly, the museum boasts one of the world's best collections of historic artillery. Bronze cannons include those weighing 20 tons and bearing Arabic inscriptions. Some iron pieces date from the 14th century. Light weapons, such as guns, pistols, and swords, are displayed in cases.

Largo do Museu de Artilharia. ✆ **21/884-25-69.** Admission 3€ adults, 1.50€ children 2–8, free for children under 2. Tues–Sun 10am–5pm; Sat–Sun closed btw. 12:30–3:30. Metro: Santa Apolónia. Bus: 709, 712, 728, or 735.

Oceanário de Lisboa ★★★ AQUARIUM This is the big one, the city's most popular indoor attraction. The largest aquarium in Europe, its centerpiece is a 180,000-cubic-ft. tank that is home to over 100 species, including sharks, rays, barracudas, shoals of tuna, sea horses, and the bizarre white-spotted guitar fish—a ray from off the coast of northern Australia that looks like a shark. The high-tech building has a themed tower on each of its four corners showcasing wildlife from the Atlantic, Indian, Antarctic, and Pacific oceans. In each of them, visitors begin above the surface, strolling among ice floes where penguins frolic or clambering through an equatorial mangrove above jewel-like tropical fish flitting among the roots of palm and coconut trees. As you descend deeper into the building, you'll see sea otters performing underwater gymnastics or discover the surprising beauty of fluorescent jellyfish and psychedelic-colored cuttlefish. At all levels, viewing panels two stories high allow you to gaze on the constantly changing spectacle of the global ocean-themed main tank. There are popular temporary exhibitions such as one on the life cycle of sea turtles, with special tanks for observing these endangered creatures. Opened in 1998 for the Lisbon World Exposition, the Oceanário also has a scientific role, helping to study and preserve marine life.

Esplanada d. Carlos I. www.oceanario.pt. ✆ **21/891-70-02.** Admission 15.30€ adults, 9.90€ students and children under 13 and seniors 65 and over. Family ticket costs 36€. Tickets can be bought online to avoid the high-season lines. Summer daily 10am–8pm; winter daily 10am–7pm. Metro: Estação do Oriente. Bus: 400 or 728. Pedestrians should turn right after leaving the metro station and go along Av. Dom João II, where you'll see a signpost directing you left and to the water for the attraction itself.

ESPECIALLY FOR KIDS

From the winding, narrow streets of Alfama to the "dragon ships" of the Maritime Museum at Belém, much of Lisbon evokes a movie set for kids. Each new day brings something new for kids to do—an aquarium, a zoo, a planetarium—it's all here.

Aquário Vasco da Gama ★ AQUARIUM The Vasco da Gama Aquarium, on N6 near Algés on the Cascais railway line, has been in operation since 1898. Live exhibits include the eared seals pavilion and a vast number of tanks that hold fish and other sea creatures from all over the world. A large portion of the exhibits consists of zoological material brought back from oceanographic expeditions by Carlos I. They include preserved marine invertebrates, water birds, fish, mammals, and some of the king's laboratory equipment. However, this old-school aquarium doesn't hold a candle to the Oceanário (see above), so go to that if you only have time to visit one.

Rua Direita do Dafundo. http://ccm.marinha.pt/pt/aquariovgama. ✆ **21/419-63-37.** Admission 5€ adults, 2.50€ children 7–17 and seniors 65 and over, free for children under 7. Daily 10am–6pm. Train: Algés. Tram: 15.

Pavilhão do Conhecimento-Ciência Viva ★★★ MUSEUM This wonderfully interactive science museum lets the little ones simulate an astronaut jump, try their hands at robotics, and try a number of gee-whiz experiments. The building was one of the highlights of EXPO '98. Its newest attraction is "DÓING," an interactive workshop inspired by the Tinkering Studio of the Exploratorium in San Francisco. The museum is located close to the Oceanário; it has a cafe.

Largo José Mariano Gago, Parque das Nações. www.pavconhecimento.pt. ✆ **21/891-71-00.** Admission 9€ adults, 6€ children 7–17 and seniors 65 and over, free for children under 2. Family ticket 20€. Daily 10am–6pm. Metro: Estação do Oriente. Bus: 400 or 728.

Jardim Zoológico de Lisboa ★★ ZOO With a collection of some 2,000 animals, this zoo occupies a flower-filled setting in the 26-hectare (64-acre) Park of Laranjeiras. It's about a 10-minute subway ride from the Rossio. It also has a small tram, a cable car, and a dolphin presentation. The reptile section has some rare species, and the zoo is part of an international conservation program.

Estrada de Benfica 58. www.zoo.pt. ✆ **21/723-29-00.** Admission 20.50€, 14.50€ children 3–11, free for children 2 and under. Daily 10am–8pm (Sept–Mar 10am–6pm). Metro: Jardim Zoológico. Bus: 715 or 758.

Planetário Calouste Gulbenkian ★ PLANETARIUM An annex of the Maritime Museum in Belém, the Calouste Gulbenkian Planetarium is open to the public all year, with astronomical shows throughout the day.

Praça do Império, Belém. http://ccm.marinha.pt/pt/planetario. ✆ **21/362-00-02.** Admission 5€ adults, 2.50€ children 10–18, free for seniors and children 6–9. Children under 4 not admitted. Tues–Sun 10am–6pm; Sat 1:45pm–4:30pm. Tram: 15. Bus: 714, 727, 729, or 751.

CITY STROLLS

Lisbon is a walker's delight; the city's principal neighborhoods abound with major sights and quiet glimpses into daily life.

WALKING TOUR 1: THE ALFAMA

START:	**Praça do Comércio.**
FINISH:	**Castelo de São Jorge.**
TIME:	**2 hours, more if you add sightseeing time.**
BEST TIMES:	**Any sunny day.**
WORST TIMES:	**Twilight or after dark.**

The streets of the Alfama are best traversed on foot, but at times you must walk up steep stone stairs. Very popular with tourists, it's also an area with amazing old architecture, allowing visitors the rare opportunity to wander back in time. ***Tip:*** Be careful, as the area does get pickpockets.

From Praça do Comércio, opening onto the water at the foot of Rua Augusta, which splits the center of midtown Lisbon, head east along Rua da Alfândega, which links Lower Baixa to the southern tier of the Alfama. When you reach the intersection with Rua de Madalena, head north, or left, to the Largo da Madalena. The square is dominated by:

1 Igreja de Madalena

This church dates from 1783 and incorporates the Manueline portico of a previous church that was built on this site.

Take Rua de Santa António da Sé, following the tram tracks to the small:

2 Igreja de Santo António

Opening onto Largo de Santo António de Sé, this church is from 1812 and was built over the beloved saint's alleged birthplace. For a full description, see p. 99.

A few steps higher, and to the immediate southeast, stands:

3 Sé de Lisboa

This is the cathedral of Lisbon, opening onto the tiny Largo da Sé. For a complete description, see p. 100.

Continuing east into the Alfama, go along Rua Augusto Rosa, which becomes Rua do Limoeiro. You'll soon be at:

4 Miradouro de Santa Luzia

This belvedere is one of the most famous in the Alfama and certainly the most romantic. From this viewpoint, you can look down over the jumble of antique houses as they seemingly pile into the Tagus River. Igreja de Santa Luzia, opens onto this square and had a cloister where the viewpoint now stands.

Walking Tour: The Alfama

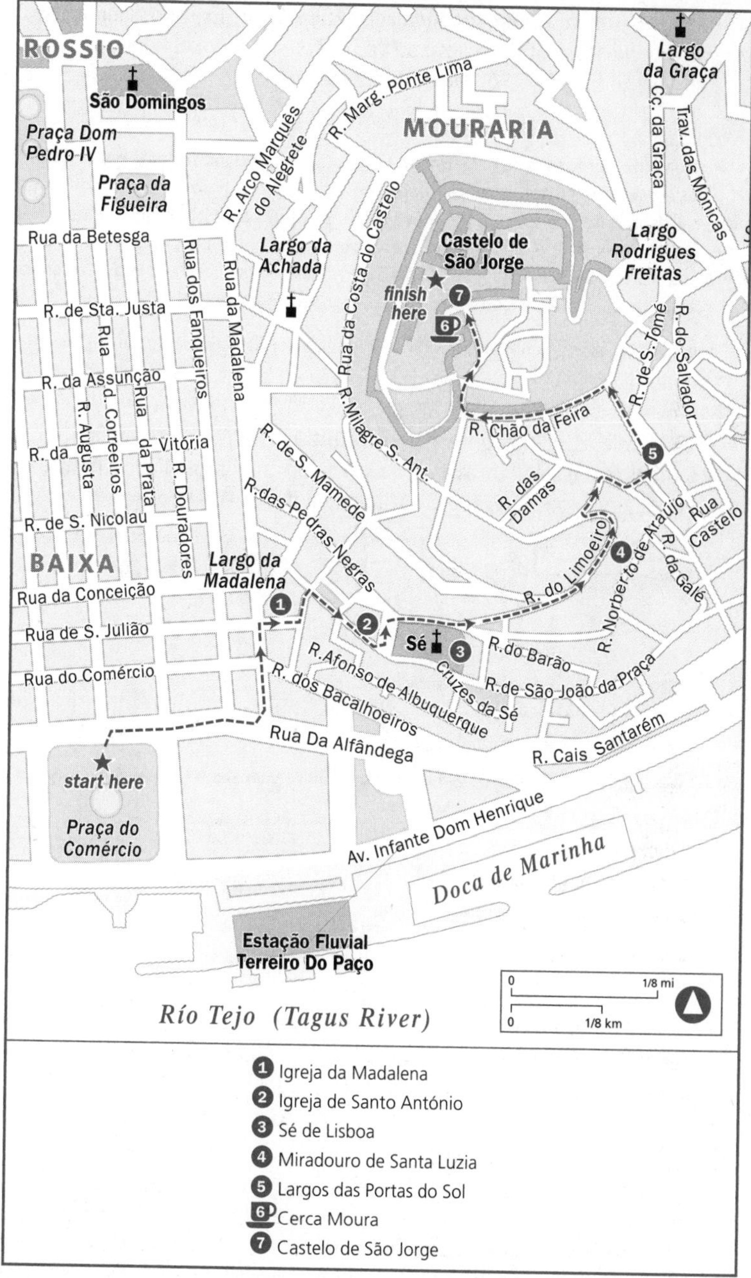

Continue northeast into the:

5 Largo das Portas do Sol

On this square stands the Fundação Ricardo do Espírito Santo Silva, a lovely museum of decorative art (p. 112) that you likely don't have time to visit in the course of this walking tour.

6 Take a Break

Near the Miradouro das Portas do Sol are several tiny **cafes** and **bars** with outside seating. Visitors from all over the world come here to order coffee and refreshments and take in the view of the shipping activity on the Tagus. These establishments are virtually the same, but we recommend **Cerca Moura,** Largo das Portas do Sol 4 (✆ **21/887-48-59**), which offers the finest menu of snacks and drinks in the area and affords a breathtaking view.

A short but steep climb from Largo das Portas do Sol via Travessa de Santa Luzia brings you to:

7 Castelo de São Jorge

The remains of this once grand fortification have been gussied up for tourists, but it's still the reason most visitors trek through the Alfama. The views alone are worth the effort to reach it. See p. 98 for more.

WALKING TOUR 2: BAIXA, THE CENTER & THE CHIADO

START:	**Praça do Comércio.**
FINISH:	**Elevador de Santa Justa.**
TIME:	**3 hours.**
BEST TIMES:	**Any sunny day except Sunday.**
WORST TIMES:	**Monday to Saturday from 7:30 to 9am and 5 to 7pm; Sunday, when shops are closed.**

The best place to begin this tour is:

1 Praça do Comércio (also known as Terreiro do Paço)

One of the most beautiful squares in Europe, it has been used as a parking lot and for government offices. Nowadays it's being put to better use with restaurants, cafes and bars, the Lisbon Welcome Centre, and exhibitions. The equestrian statue is of Dom José, the Portuguese king at the time of the earthquake, and there's a promenade connecting with Cais do Sodré.

Before you start walking, especially if it's a hot day, you might need to:

2 Take a Break

Café Martinho da Arcada, Praça do Comércio 3 (✆ **21/887-92-59**), has been the haunt of the literati since 1782, attracting such greats as the Portuguese poet Fernando Pessoa. The old restaurant has gone upscale, but it adjoins a

Walking Tour: Baixa, the Center & the Chiado

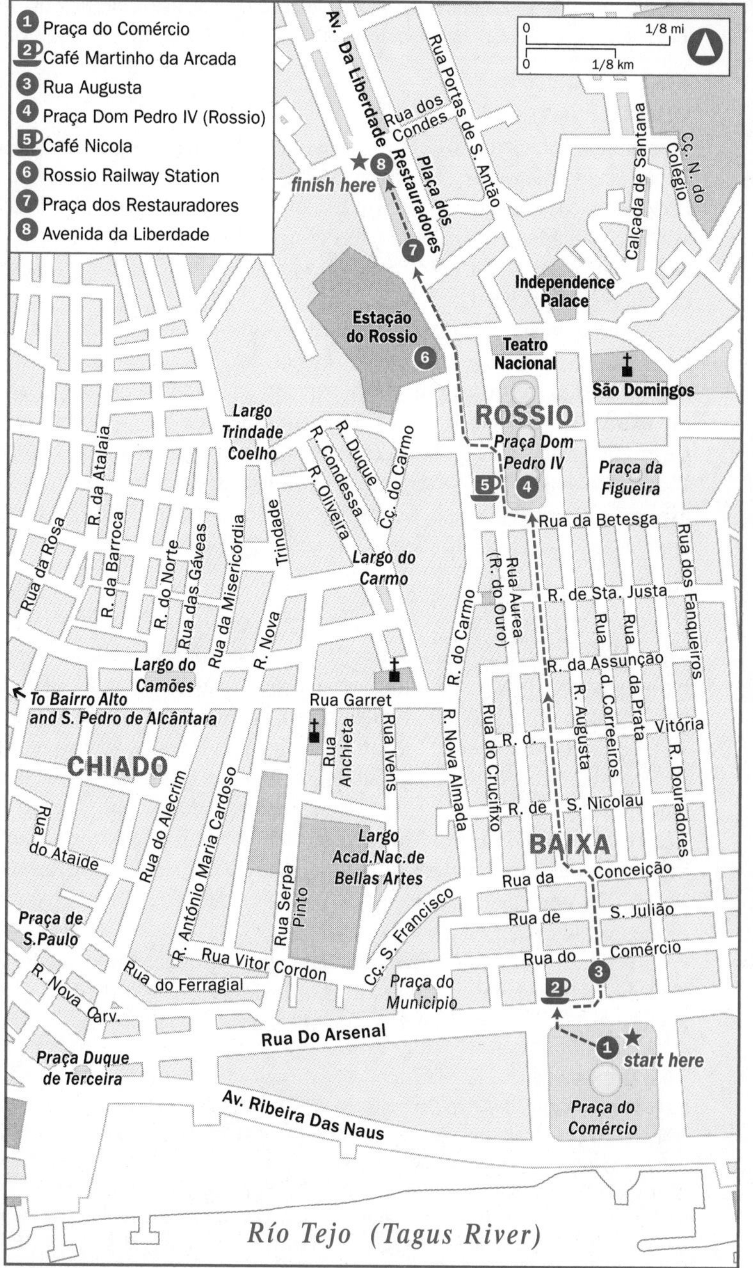

cafe. If you're here for lunch, go into the restaurant, ask for a traditional dish of fish and shellfish, called *cataplana,* or clam stew served in the style of the Algarve. If you're in a hurry, have a salt cod cake at the counter of the cafe, as locals do. It's open every day 8am to 10pm.

After dining, head north along:

3 Rua Augusta

This monumental street was one of Baixa's best-known shopping streets. Today, sadly, it's a mix of tourist traps and more authentic shoe shops (Lord, Arte), leather stores, embroidery outlets, and menswear like Pitta. We also like Macário, an old-style Portuguese deli. Many of the cross streets are closed to traffic, making window-shopping enjoyable. Be careful of pickpockets.

The western part of this grid of streets is known as the **Chiado.** It's the city's most sophisticated shopping district. In 1988, a devastating fire swept the area, destroying many shops, particularly those on the periphery of Rua Garrett and Rua do Carmo. But the area has bounced back. Head to Chiado, via Rua Nova do Almada, explore Rua Garrett (where Bertrand bookshop is). Alternatively, you can continue to walk uphill, exploring Bairro Alto and Igreja de São Roque up to Príncipe Real, enjoying the views of Miradouro São Pedro de Alcântara.

Largo do Carmo leads into the:

4 Rossio (formally called Praça de Dom Pedro IV)

The principal square of Baixa, the Rossio dates from the 1200s. During the Inquisition, it was the setting of many an *auto-da-fé*, and Lisboans turned out in droves to witness the torture and death of "infidels." This was the heart of Pombaline Lisbon as the marquês rebuilt it following the 1755 earthquake. Neoclassical buildings from the 1700s and 1800s line the square, which has an array of cafes and souvenir shops. The 1840 **Teatro Nacional de Dona Maria II** sits on the north side of the square, occupying the former Palace of the Inquisition. The statue on its facade is of Gil Vicente, the Shakespeare of Portugal, credited with the creation of the Portuguese theater.

Crowds cluster around two baroque fountains at either end of the Rossio. The bronze statue on a column is of Pedro IV, for whom the square is named. (He was also crowned emperor of Brazil as Pedro I.)

5 Take a Break

Café Nicola, Praça de Dom Pedro IV 18 (✆ **21/346-05-79**), dates from 1777. It gained fame as a gathering place of the Portuguese literati in the 18th and 19th centuries, including the poet Bocage, who is honored with a statue. The current handsome Art Deco interior dates from 1935. Pastries, endless cups of coffee, and meals can be consumed indoors or out, but inside is quieter and more charming. It's open Monday to Friday 8am to 10pm, Saturday and Sunday 9am to 11pm.

From the Rossio, proceed to the northwest corner of the square and walk onto the satellite square, Praça João da Câmara. If you continue north, you'll reach the:

6 Estação do Rossio

This is the city's main rail terminus. Built in mock Manueline style to resemble a lavishly adorned palace, it's one of the strangest architectural rail terminals in Europe. Trains from Sintra and East suburbs pull right into the heart of the city and leave from a platform that's an escalator ride above the street-level entrances. The bustling station abounds with varying businesses, including souvenir shops and currency-exchange offices.

7 Praça dos Restauradores

This square was named for the men who, in 1640, revolted against the Spanish reign. The event led to the reestablishment of Portugal's independence. An obelisk in the center of the square commemorates the uprising. The deep-red **Palácio Foz,** and the former **Eden Theatre** (a fascinating Art Deco building now converted to a hotel) are also on the square, as well as the old ice-cream shop.

8 Avenida da Liberdade

This is Lisbon's main thoroughfare, laid out in 1879. More than 90m (295 ft.) wide, the avenue runs north for 1.5km (1 mile), cutting through the heart of the city. It has long been hailed as the most splendid boulevard in Lisbon, although many of the Art Deco and Belle Epoque mansions that once lined it are gone. Its sidewalks are a black-and-white stone mosaic. This is the heart of Lisbon's high-end shopping, with most of the international brands concentrated here.

At this point, you can walk 1.5km (1 mile) along Avenida da Liberdade all the way to Praça do Marquês de Pombal, with its monument to the prime minister who rebuilt Lisbon after the earthquake. North of the square, you can stroll through Parque Eduardo VII and visit Estufa Fria.

ORGANIZED TOURS

Walking tours of Lisbon are offered by dynamic **Lisbon Walkers** (www.lisbonwalker.com; ✆ **21/886-18-40**). This company was one of the first to organize walking tours in the city. Their guides are very knowledgeable, and include art historians, architects, and journalists. Another well-regarded company is **Lisbon Explorer** (www.lisbonexplorer.com; ✆ **21/362-92-62**); it provides a range of walks in the city but also day trips to Évora or Sintra in comfortable vehicles. Their guides are scholars, licensed guides, art historians, and archeologists. In the city, their most intriguing tours are "Hidden Lisbon" and "Jewish Lisbon." If you're looking for a food tour, try **Culinary Backstreets** (http://culinarybackstreets.com/culinary-walks/lisbon). Disclaimer: The author is also a guide for this company, which offers a number of different routes where visitors learn about Lisbon's traditions and culture, eating and drinking as they go. The best of the river tours are offered by **Lisbon By Boat,** Av. Forças Armadas 95 (www.lisbonbyboat.com; ✆ **93/391-47-40**).

OUTDOOR & RECREATIONAL ACTIVITIES

Lisbon itself has very few sports facilities. Most outdoor activities, such as watersports, fishing, and scuba diving, take place on the Estoril coast, west of the city, or Costa da Caparica, on the south bank.

If you want to lie on the beach, you can take the train from Lisbon to Cascais; the main resorts there are Estoril and Cascais (see chapter 7).

FITNESS CENTERS Some hotels recommended in chapter 5 allow nonguests to use their health clubs for a fee. It's always best to call in advance. Outside of the hotels, a worthwhile fitness club is **Ginásio Keep Fit,** Av. João Crisóstomo 6 (✆ **21/793-15-36**; 18€ for one-time use; Mon–Fri 8am–10pm, Sat 10am–2pm). Bus no. 58. Metro: Saldanha.

GOLF The closest course to Lisbon (but not the best) is the **Lisbon Sports Club,** Casal da Carregueira, near Belas (www.lisbonclub.com; ✆ **21/431-00-77**). It's about a 25-minute drive from the center. A former playground of royalty, the **Golf Club** at Quinta de Penha Longa, Linhó, outside Sintra (www.penhalonga.com; ✆ **21/924-90-31**), is part of the Penha Longa Hotel Spa & Golf Resort. Ranked among the top 30 courses of continental Europe, the 18-hole, par-72 championship course was designed by Robert Trent Jones, Jr. The course opens onto panoramic views of the Atlantic and has been host to numerous international competitions, including the Portuguese Open. An adjacent course, the 9-hole, par-35 **Atlantic North Course** spreads around the core of the resort, often attracting late arrivals who want a round of golf before the sun sets. For the main course of 18 holes, greens fees range from 55€ to 120€. For the 9 holes, greens fees range from 15€ to 75€.

JOGGING With all the hills, jogging is challenging in Lisbon. That being said, daytime jogging in the Parque Eduardo VII is quite pleasant. Some joggers head for the Estádio Nacional (National Stadium), on the northwest outskirts of the city on the road to Estoril. A track worn smooth by joggers winds through pine woods. The easiest (read: flattest) areas are on the riverfront. We recommend jogging along the Tagus between Praça do Comércio, the Ponte do 25 de Abril (the major suspension bridge) and Belém, heading west as far as Algés. Another possibility (but likely to be congested) is the median strip of the main street of Lisbon, Avenida da Liberdade, from Praça do Marquês de Pombal toward Baixa.

TENNIS Public tennis courts are available at **Parque de Jogos 1 de Maio,** at Alvalade (www.inatel.pt; ✆ **21/845-34-70).** Farther away is **Club de Ténis do Estoril** in Estoril or the **Quinta da Marinha** in Cascais.

SPECTATOR SPORTS

SOCCER The Portuguese love football (known to Americans as soccer). Nothing—not even politics, boiled codfish, or fado—excites them more.

Lisbon has a trio of teams that play almost every Saturday or Sunday from the end of August to May. (You'll miss out if you visit in the summer.) Try to arrive at least an hour before the match is scheduled to begin; pregame entertainment ranges from marching bands to fireworks.

The best-known team is Benfica, which holds matches in northwest Lisbon at the new and gigantic **Estádio da Luz,** Avenida General Norton Matos (© **21/721-95-00;** Metro: Colégio Militar/Luz). The legendary Eusébio led this team to five European championship finals in the 1960s; a big statue of the footballer welcomes fans at the main entrance of this massive stadium (one of the largest in Europe). Red Store, in Rua Augusta (Baixa) sells Benfica tickets and merchandising.

The **Sporting Clube de Portugal** plays at the **Estádio do José Alvalade** (no phone), in the north of the city, near Campo Grande. The third team is Belém's **Belenenses,** which plays at the **Estádio do Restelo** (© **21/301-04-61**). The team might not be as good or nearly as famous as Benfica, but don't tell that to a loyal fan during the heat of the game. They also have the stadium with the best view to the river and are known by the nickname of "pastéis," as in the Pastéis de Belém, as the cafe is nearby.

Tickets vary in price depending on the event, ranging from 25€ to 80€. You can buy them on the day of the game at all three stadiums. However, when Benfica plays Sporting, tickets usually sell out; buy them in advance at the booth in Praça dos Restauradores or at the Red Store. Tickets also go fast when FC Porto, from the northern city of Porto, Lisbon's main rival, is in town to play Benfica or Sporting.

MUSIC Many open-air festivals take place in the city during summer. The most popular are **NOS Alive** in Passeio Marítimo de Algés, and **Rock in Rio** (every 2 years) in Parque da Bela Vista. Buy the tickets online in advance in https://ticketline.sapo.pt/ or in Lisbon at the Fnac Chiado ticket office.

LISBON SHOPPING

Portuguese handicrafts often exhibit exotic influences, in large part because of the artisans' versatility and their skill in absorbing other styles, especially those touched by Portugal's history as a seafaring nation. The best place to see their work is in Lisbon, where shopkeepers and their buyers hunt out unusual items from all over Portugal, including the Madeira Islands and the Azores.

SHOPPING AREAS Shops operate all over the city, but **Baixa,** in downtown Lisbon, is the major area for browsing. **Rua Áurea** (Street of Gold, the location of the major jewelry shops), **Rua da Prata** (Street of Silver), and **Rua Augusta** are Lisbon's three principal shopping streets. The Baixa shopping district lies between the Rossio and the River Tagus.

Rua Garrett, in the Chiado, is where you'll find many of the more upmarket shops. A major fire in 1988 destroyed many shops, but new ones have arisen.

Antiques lovers gravitate to **Rua Dom Pedro V** in the Bairro Alto. Other streets with antiques stores include Rua da Misericórdia, Rua de São Pedro de Alcântara, Rua da Escola Politécnica, Rua de São Bento, and Rua do Alecrim.

Shopping A to Z

Shops are open, in general, Monday through Friday from 9am to 1pm and from 3 to 7pm, and Saturday from 9am to 1pm. But some open daily, without the lunch break.

ANTIQUES

Along both sides of the narrow **Rua de São José,** close to Avenida da Liberdade, are shops stacked with antiques from all over the world. Antiques dealers from the U.S. and other countries come here to survey the wares. You'll find ornate spool and carved beds, high-back chairs, tables, wardrobes with ornate carvings, brass plaques, copper pans, silver candelabra, crystal sconces, chandeliers, and a wide selection of wooden figures, silver boxes, porcelain plates, and bowls. Don't, however, count on getting spectacular bargains.

Cavalo de Pau Antiguidades ★★ Set across the street from the Portuguese Parliament, on the street where fado diva Amália Rodriguez used to live, this is a genuinely charming store that's loaded with antiques from Portugal and art objects from around the globe. Look for elaborate baskets, sculptures, antique furniture, and gift items handcrafted in places such as Brazil, Indonesia, Mozambique, and France, with an articulate sales staff that's ready, willing, and able to describe the provenance of each piece. Rua de São Bento 164. www.cavalopau.pt. ✆ **21/396-66-05.** Tram: 28.

M. Murteira Antiguidades ★★ The artistic achievements of yesterday live on in this showcase of sculpture, paintings, and antiques that date back, in some cases, to the 1600s. Manuel Murteira Martins has pulled together this tasteful, well-chosen collection. This is one of the shopping highlights for those store-hopping in the Alfama district. Rua Augusto Rosa 19. ✆ **21/886-38-51.** Tram: 28.

The World of Vintage ★★ Lots of vintage furniture, objects, ceramics, and lamps. Some really quirky and fun stuff, like '60s and '70s neon signs, as well as colorful flea market–type collections. Rua de São Bento 291. ✆ **96/314-00-43.** Tram: 28.

ART GALLERIES

Chiado 8 Arte Contemporânea ★ Proud of its survival within an environment where some of its competitors have, during Portugal's economic woes, gone out of business, this gallery functions as a central exhibition point within the arts-conscious Chiado district. Within a warren of white, artfully illuminated exhibition spaces, you'll find a changing series of expositions by artists from Portugal and the rest of Europe. Largo do Chiado 8. www.culturgest.pt. ✆ **21/323-72-25.** Metro: Baixa/Chiado.

Galeria Jorge Shirley ★ This avant-garde gallery, one of Lisbon's most respected, lies close to Rua de São Bento. It was founded in 1999 in the city of Porto but moved to Lisbon in 2003 where it found immediate success. Its changing array of art is spread over two floors of open space. Emerging new artists, both Portuguese and foreign, are represented. Jorge Shirley has partnerships with galleries in Italy and Spain. Largo Hintze Ribeiro (à Rua S.Bento), 2 E/F. ✆ **21/386-84-97.** Metro: Rato.

Galeria 111 ★ Operated by Manuel and Arlete de Brito since 1964, Galeria 111 is one of Lisbon's major art galleries. The wide-ranging exhibitions of sculpture, painting, and graphics include work by leading contemporary Portuguese artists. The gallery also sells drawings, etchings, silk screens, lithographs, art books, and postcards. It's closed August 4 to September 4, Monday and Sundays. Campo Grande 113. www.111.pt. ✆ **21/797-74-18.** Metro: Entre Campus. Bus: 736, 738, or 788.

Galeria Yela ★ Set near the Four Seasons Hotel Ritz Lisbon, Galeria Yela prides itself on its cutting-edge expositions of emerging Iberian artists. Look for acrylics, drawings, and engravings, most of them innovative in their focus and inspiration. Rua Rodrigo de Fonseca 103B. ✆ **21/388-03-99.** Metro: Marquês de Pombal.

BASKETS & CERAMICS

Find Portuguese baskets and old ceramics at the **Feira da Ladra** (see "Markets," below). Also at **Pollux,** Rua dos Fanqueiros 276 (www.pollux.pt), a department store with all kinds of housewares.

BOOKS

Bertrand Livreiros ★★ Stop here for a selection of books ranging from the latest bestsellers to English-language magazines, travel guides, and maps of Lisbon and Portugal. At the entrance, look for the Guinness Book of Records plaque confirming this as the oldest bookshop in the world (founded in 1732). In the first room and corridor you can see posters telling the story of this Lisboan institution; it was a home away from home for many famous Portuguese writers and poets during the 18th and 19th centuries. Rua Garrett 73. www.bertrand.pt. ✆ **21/347-61-22.** Metro: Chiado.

Fabula Urbis ★ Many English-language editions on the art, literature, music, history, architecture, and gastronomy of Lisbon are found here in the historic Alfama district near the Cathedral and the Castle of St. George. The upper floor of the bookshop is used for monthly exhibitions of paintings and an occasional recital. Open daily 10:30am to 1:30pm and 3 to 8pm. Rua de Augusto Rosa 27. www.fabula-urbis.pt. ✆ **21/888-50-32.** Tram: 12 or 28. Bus: 37.

Tabacaria Mónaco ★★ This narrow *tabacaria* (magazine and tobacco shop) opened in 1893 and has kept its original Art Nouveau look. Tiles from Rafael Bordalo Pinheiro and an adobe painting by Rosendo Carvalheira adorn the impressive interior (a contrast with the simple exterior). You'll find a selection of international periodicals, guidebooks, and maps. Praça Dom Pedro IV 21. ✆ **21/346-81-91.** Metro: Rossio.

CANDLES

Caza das Vellas Loreto ★★ Two centuries ago, dozens of candle makers flourished within this neighborhood, close to the Praça Luís de Camões. Today, this is one of the very few candle makers still surviving within Portugal, and the only one in Lisbon. It's actually one the oldest shops in the city, originally from 1789. The smell of beeswax permeates the 18th-century setting, where customers don't proceed beyond a point of a few feet from the front door. Members of a polite staff will bring you samples of what's available. Depending on your tastes, candles contain the scent of fruit, apples, and entire bouquets of seasonal flowers. And chances are good that if a religious festival is scheduled for any time in the upcoming months, this shop will have a candle to commemorate the event. Photos are not allowed. Rua do Loreto 53–55. http://cazavellasloreto.com.pt. ✆ **21/046-88-02.** Metro: Baixa/Chiado. Tram: 28.

CHINA & GLASSWARE

JAO ★ This is one of the best shops in Lisbon for ceramics, displaying a choice selection from Vista Alegre (see below) as well as Atlantis glassware and the works of other Portuguese and continental manufacturers. If you don't see what you want, know that there is a large inventory warehouse at the rear of this two-floor outlet. Praça de Figueira 11C. ✆ **21/886-61-61.** Metro: Rossio.

Vista Alegre ★★ Founded in 1824, Vista Alegre turns out some of the finest porcelain dinner sets in the country, some of them limited editions. It also carries objets d'art for collectors, and a range of practical day-to-day tableware. The government presents Vista Alegre pieces to European heads of state when they visit. Largo do Chiado 23. www.vistaalegre.pt. ✆ **21/346-14-01.** Metro: Baixa/Chiado. Tram: 28.

CHOCOLATES

Bettina & Niccolò ★★★ This is a chocoholic's dream shop. There is no other place in Portugal like it. In 2008, it burst onto the scene, the creation of the Corallo family (owners of coffee plantations and cocoa fields on São Tomé and Príncipe, a former Portuguese colony in West Africa). The chocolates here are so pure, they don't need any milk. The sorbet (made with 100% chocolate, spring water, and sugar) is the star in the summer; in winter, the hot chocolate gets the most takers. Along with drinks are a range of chocolate truffles; coffee beans coated in chocolate; and chocolate-coated ginger, hazelnuts, orange peel, and salted caramel. The shop is small and there are only two tables with seats. Rua da Escola Politécnica 4. ✆ **21/386-21-58.** Metro: Rato. Bus: 758.

CRYSTAL

Depósito da Marinha Grande ★★ This simple, warehouse-like store offers glass items created in the century-old Marinha Grande factory. The merchandise includes traditional service glasses, dishes, water pitchers, and salt and pepper shakers, as well as modern colored glass. Other items include Atlantis crystal and Vista Alegre porcelain. Atlantis crystal from Marinha Grande is renowned in Portugal, and there are some good buys here. Another branch is down the road at Rua de São Bento 418–420 (✆ **21/396-30-96**).

Rua de São Bento 234–242. www.dmg.com.pt. ✆ **21/396-32-34.** Metro: Rato. Bus: 749 or 100.

DEPARTMENT STORES

El Corte Inglés ★★ If you're not planning to include Spain as a stop on your trip to Iberia, you can shop here, a major outlet for the largest department store chain in Spain. From fashion to handicrafts, you'll find a vast array of merchandise from across the Iberian Peninsula. Btw. avs. Antonio Augusto e Aguiar and Marquês de Fronteira e Sidónio Pais. www.elcorteingles.pt. ✆ **21/371-17-00.** Metro: São Sebastião.

EMBROIDERY

Madeira House ★★ As the name announces, they are specialists in the beautiful embroideries from the island of Madeira but have textiles, linens, and handicrafts from other parts of the country, too. Rua Augusta 131–133. www.madeira-house.com. ✆ **21/342-68-13.** Metro: Chiado. Tram: 28.

Príncipe Real Enxovais ★★ Príncipe Real sells linens elegant enough to grace the tables of monarchs and celebrities, including that of the late Princess Grace of Monaco and many other members of European royalty, Michael Douglas, and the Kennedys. Run by Victor Castro, son of the founder Cristina Castro, this store is one of the last that does artistic manual embroidery on order. Now in business for 90 years, it produces some of Europe's finest tablecloths and sheets in cotton, linen, and organdy. The owner-designer sells bed furnishings, too. The shop handles custom orders quickly and professionally. It employs skilled workers, who can execute a linen pattern to match a client's favorite porcelain. Rua da Escola Politécnica 12–14. www.principereal.com. ✆ **21/346-59-45.** Metro: Rato or Baixa/Chiado. Bus: 758.

Teresa Alecrim ★★ This store bears the name of the owner, who creates refined embroideries and traditional house linens. You'll see sheets, pillowcases, towels, and bedcovers in plain and patterned cotton, plus monogrammed damask cotton hand towels. Rua Nova do Almada, 76. www.teresaalecrim.com. ✆ **21/383-18-70.** Metro: Baixa/Chiado or Rossio.

FASHION

A Outra Face da Lua ★★ Owner Carla Belchior has an extraordinary eye for vintage and period clothing, and this is the best in the city. In fact, it is so good she often sells or rents wardrobe to film, TV, and theater people. Carla also creates her own original styles, if you're not into vintage, in addition to carrying rare wallpaper and tin toys. After shopping, you can relax on-site in the lovely little tearoom, which has a summer terrace for people-watching. Rua da Assunção 22. www.aoutrafacedalua.com. ✆ **21/886-34-30.** Metro: Rossio.

Camisaria Pitta ★★ In the Baixa district, this is Lisbon's oldest—and best—shirt maker for men. Superbly made shirts, they come in many colors and styles. The service is old school and the expert tailors here can also craft suits. Rua Augusta 195. ✆ **21/342-75-26.** Metro: Baixa-Chiado.

Laurenço e Santos ★ One of Lisbon's most prominent menswear stores, Laurenço e Santos is a place where a concierge at a grand hotel might refer a well-dressed guest who needs to augment his wardrobe with anything from a business suit to a golf outfit. Praça dos Restauradores 47. ✆ **21/346-25-70.** Metro: Restauradores.

Rita Salazar ★★ An internationally known name in fashion, Ana Salazar was one of the most trendy Portuguese designer of women's clothes. Her daughter Rita is following in her footsteps with a shop featuring the types of silky, flowy, very feminine styles her mother made famous (the shop sells other brands, plus some vintage clothes from her mother). Av. de Roma 16E. ✆ **21/848-67-99.** Metro: Roma.

Rosa e Teixeira ★★ This is another prominent Lisbon menswear store, with a variety of men's clothing and a tailor available for alterations. Although the quality of clothing here is on the same level as Laurenço e Santos, prices tend to be more reasonable. Av. da Liberdade 204. www.rosaeteixeira.pt/. ✆ **21/311-03-50.** Metro: Avenida or Marquês de Pombal.

Story Tailors ★★ If you're not afraid of ruffles, bold patterns, and unusual dress cuts, this is the store for you. Designers João Sanchez and Luís Branco craft women's clothing that is flirty, shapely, and will look nothing like anything you could ever find at Macy's. They have run this atelier since 2006 in a handsomely renovated 18th-century building. Calçada do Ferragial, 8-10. www.storytailors.pt. ✆ **21/343-23-06.** Metro: Baixa/Chiado or Cais do Sodré.

FOOD & WINE

A Carioca ★★ Millstones are still used in the big grinder at this 1930s-era, Art Deco coffee shop in the Bairro Alto district. We're in love with their Tavares blend (60% Arabica, 40% Robusta), but the aromatic and light São Tomé Monte, an Arabica from Ecuador and West Africa, is also pretty special. The shop also sells tea from the Azores and a variety of chocolates. Rua da Misericórdia, 9. ✆ **21/346-95-67.** Closed Sat (after 1 pm) and Sun.

Conserveira de Lisboa ★★ Seafood conserved in tins is a great delicacy in Portugal, and this is the top place to buy it—the packaging is handmade and handsome as it has been since this shop's founding in 1930. Most importantly, inside the tins is high-quality fish in olive oil—sardines, mackerel, horse mackerel, squid, octopus, and mussels. The type of fish varies by the season and there are several sauces; try the *picante* with hot chilis. You can bring these back to the U.S. and Canada with no problem. Rua dos Bacalhoeiros, 34. www.conserveiradelisboa.pt. ✆ **21/886-40-09.** Mon–Sat, 9am–7pm.

Garrafeira Nacional ★ In the Baixa district, this wine shop, founded in 1927, has one of the best selections of wine in Portugal. The shop is staffed by top professionals who will guide you to the right bottle, whether you're seeking out a special port, a Madeira, or some other Portuguese specialty. Rare whiskeys, cognacs, and other liquors you've never heard of are also on sale. The company has other shops (at Rua da Conceição and in Ribeira), but this has the best offerings. By the way, 2011 was an exceptional year for Portuguese wines. Rua de Santa Justa 18. www.garrafeiranacional.com. ✆ **21/887-90-80.** Metro: Rossio.

Loja das Conservas ★ More fish in a tin, this time from the National Association of Tinned Fish, meaning that a wider range of companies are available here than at Conserveira de Lisboa. Staff speak English and will help you choose. Rua do Arsenal 162. ✆ **91/118-12-10.** Metro: Cais do Sodré.

Manteigaria Silva ★★★ Dating from 1890 and still in the same family, this a must for lovers of cheese and ham, wine, olive oil, nuts, tinned fish, and salt cod. The owner, José Branco, sources cheese and ham from top producers, curing the meat in-house to guarantee quality. M.Silva has a new shop in Mercado da Ribeira, but the original has more variety and atmosphere. Rua Dom Antão de Almada 1 C/D. www.manteigariasilva.pt. ✆ **21/342-49-05.** Mon–Sat 9am–7pm.

Manuel Tavares Lda ★ This emporium of food and wine is one of the oldest stores in Lisbon, dating from 1860. Behind a traditional wood-framed shopfront, it has a superb collection of Portuguese wines, liquors, and brandies, and a well-stocked deli (though we prefer Manteigaria (above) for those items. It's easy to find on the smallest street in Lisbon. Rua da Betesga 1 A–B. www.manueltavares.com. ✆ **21/342-42-09.** Metro: Rossio.

GIFTS & SOUVENIRS

A Vida Portuguesa ★★ Retro-hip objects from the 1960s, '70s, and '80s exert a powerful iconic appeal to the Portuguese clientele who come here, but even outsiders will enjoy seeing the old-fashioned cosmetics (rice powders and unguents of the type in vogue before Salazar), weird kitchen tools, kitschy plastic models of Saint Anthony, and other items sold here. The store was established in 2006 by a journalist (Catarina Portas), and has been such a hit that it now has three other outlets, the biggest being in Intendente Square. Rua Anchieta 11. www.avidaportuguesa.com. ✆ **21/346-50-73.** Metro: Baixa/Chiado.

Empório Casa Bazar ★ In the Príncipe Real district, this is a vast emporium of flea-market kitsch, and as such, is one of the most amusing stores in Lisbon. Rua Dom Pedro V 65. ✆ **21/096-40-93.** Metro: Rato.

Luvaria Ulisses ★★★ Set in an Art Deco gem of a building in the Chiado, this is the last shop in Portugal that sells gloves, and only gloves, a tradition dating from 1925 when the store was founded. Although new styles have been introduced, the glove-making technique itself is decades old and all the goods are still handmade. The shop will even make gloves for you if your tastes veer to the exotic. Satin, wool, and all types of leather (lamb, calf, game, pig, even antelope) are available, as are every color in the rainbow, though simple black and brown are most popular. This unique shop is also known for its legendary small size. Rua da Carmo 87. www.luvariaulisses.com. ✆ **21/342-02-95.** Metro: Rossio.

HANDICRAFTS

A Arte da Terra ★★★ For that special gift or handicraft, this outlet, deep in the heart of the Alfama, is an ideal hunting ground. Since the shop's creation in 1996, it has been a showcase for some of the best crafts in the city. The owner travels Portugal to ferret out the creations of craftspeople working in all mediums: iron, wood, stone, sandstone, every kind of weaving and embroidery, plus hand-painted tiles and paintings. Standing alongside the Lisbon Cathedral, the shop is housed in a building that survived the 1755 earthquake. Rua Augusto Rosa 40. www.aartedaterra.pt. ✆ **21/274-59-75.** Tram: 28.

Loja dos Descobrimentos ★★ Exquisite hand-painted ceramics and tiles with designs that reflect different craft traditions across Portugal are the draw here, as is watching artisans do this work (in an atelier in the back). The store can ship purchases anywhere in the world. Loja dos Descobrimentos is in the Alfama, next to Casa dos Bicos, in a historic building from the 16th century. Rua dos Bacalhoeiros 12A. www.loja-descobrimentos.com. ✆ **21/886-55-63.** Bus: 737.

MARKETS

See also the Ribeira market in the "Secrets of Lisbon" box on p. 106.

Embaixada ★★★ Once an embassy (hence the name), this splendid 19th-century edifice, with its pillared arches, elaborate plasterwork, nude murals, and Moorish tiles, houses a small mall's worth of hipster lifestyle shops—think of it as "market 2.0." Adorable children's clothing, chic home goods, menswear, womenswear, shoes, and more are on sale, mostly from only-in-Lisbon small manufacturers. The shopping is lubricated by an excellent cocktail bar in the center of the space. Praca Principe Real, 26. www.embaixadalx.pt. ✆ **96/530-91-54.** Metro: Rato. Bus: 758.

Feira da Ladra ★★ Nearly everything you can imagine is for sale at this open-air street market, which competes with the flea markets of Madrid and Paris in terms of surprising finds. Vendors peddle their wares on Tuesday and Saturday mornings; for the finest pickings, go early. The market is about a 5-minute walk from the waterfront in the Alfama district or a short walk from the Estação Santa Apolónia metro stop. It's best to start your browsing at Campo de Santa Clara and then work your way up the hilly street, lined with portable stalls and individual displays. Note that haggling is expected here. As in any area with crowds, beware of pickpockets.

Mercado de Campo de Ourique ★★ This was the city's first concept market, opened in 2013. It integrates fine food and drink, restaurants, and vegetable stalls, but unlike the Time Out Market in Ribeira (see box, p. 86), here there's more interaction between the fresh produce stalls and the food kiosks and restaurants. And because it's much smaller, it's usually less busy and attracts more locals than tourists. It's in the Campo de Ourique neighborhood, a residential and vibrant part of the city, accessible via the scenic tram 28. Rua Coelho da Rocha. ✆ **21/386-62-95.** Sun–Thurs 10am–11pm, Fri–Sat 10–1am. Tram: 28.

SHOPPING CENTERS

Centro Colombo ★ In the Luz district, this vast complex is the biggest shopping center on the Iberian peninsula, a dazzling showcase of the capitalist system, with more than 420 stores. There's everything here from an indoor amusement park to a health club to a 10-screen multiplex, and many restaurants and cafes. Since it is always very busy, clerks tend not to be as friendly as those in the city center. Av. Lusíada. www.colombo.pt. ✆ **21/711-36-36.** Metro: Colégio Militar.

Centro Vasco da Gama ★ This modern shopping mall is hailed as the finest in Portugal, with 164 shops, 36 restaurants, a 10-screen movie theater, a health club, and a playground. Along with Portuguese-made products, you'll find a lot of designer labels in clothing, including Vuitton and Hugo Boss, selling at cheaper prices than you might find in other western European capitals. Shops keep unusually long hours, they're open daily 10am to midnight. Av. Dom João II within Parque das Nações. www.centrovascodagama.pt. ✆ **21/893-06-00.** Metro: Estação Oriente.

SILVER, GOLD & FILIGREE

W. A. Sarmento ★★★ At the foot of the Santa Justa elevator, W. A. Sarmento has been in the hands of the same family for well over a century. They are one of the most distinguished silver- and goldsmiths in Portugal, specializing in lacy filigree jewelry, including charm bracelets. The shop is a go-to place to buy treasured confirmation and graduation gifts, and its clientele includes aristocracy as well as movie stars and diplomats. Rua Áurea 251. ✆ **21/347-07-83** or 21/342-67-74. Metro: Rossio. Bus: 1, 21, 31, or 36.

TILES

Fábrica Sant'anna ★ This is oldest tile company in the country and in Europe, in business since 1716. This particular shop has been in Chiado for over 100 years and has dozens of lovely ceramics and tiles, with imperfections and differences that show they are all handmade. Famous folks order their tiles here, including former U.S. president Bill Clinton, who apparently ordered tiles with names of his pets. Rua do Alecrim 95. www.santanna.com.pt. ✆ **21/342-25-37.** Metro: Cais do Sodré or Baixa/Chiado.

Fábrica Viúva Lamego ★ Founded in 1879, this shop offers contemporary tiles—mostly reproductions of old Portuguese motifs—and pottery, including a wide selection of bird and animal motifs. When you reach the store, you'll know you're at the right place: Its facade is decorated with colorful glazed tiles. Largo do Intendente 25. www.viuvalamego.com. ✆ **21/885-24-08.** Metro: Intendente. Tram: 28. Bus: 8.

WOOL

Casa Bordados da Madeira ★★ Carries a wide selection of Nazaré-style fishermen's sweaters. Rua 1 de Dezembro 137; ✆ **21/342-14-47.**

Loja da Burel ★★★ In Chiado, sells a wide selection of Portuguese wool from the mountains of Serra da Estrela called *burel*, from scarves and backpacks to shoes and clothes, with original designs and high quality. On the ground floor you can see the loom. Rua Serpa Pinto, 15B; ✆ **21/245-69-10.**

LISBON AFTER DARK

The nostalgic sounds of fado, Portuguese "songs of sorrow," are at their best in Lisbon—the capital attracts the greatest *fadistas* (fado singers) in the world. Fado is high art in Portugal, so don't plan to carry on a private conversation during a show—it's bad form. Most of the authentic fado clubs are clustered in Bairro Alto, Mouraria, and in Alfama, between St. Jorge's Castle and the docks. If you're visiting the Alfama, have the taxi driver let you off at **Largo do Chafariz do Dentro,** a small plaza a block from the harbor, with the **Fado Museum** (free fado in its event schedule) on one side; in the Bairro Alto, get off at **Largo de São Roque.** Most of the places we recommend are only a short walk away.

In addition, the tourist office maintains a list of nightly events. Another helpful source is the **Agência de Bilhetes para Espectáculos Públicos,** in Praça dos Restauradores (www.bol.pt/Projecto/PontosVenda). It's open daily from 9am to 9:30pm and also sells tickets online.

Also check out copies of ***What's On in Lisbon*** (www.timeout.pt) available at most newsstands, and its online version. *Time Out,* a weekly magazine with entertainment listings. Your hotel concierge is a good bet for information, too, but we don't recommend booking through the concierge as there will likely be a hefty surcharge.

By the standards of the United States and Canada, "the party" in Lisbon begins late. Many bars don't even open until 11 or 12pm, and very few savvy young Portuguese would set foot in a club before 1am. The Bairro Alto, with some 150 restaurants and bars, is the most happening place after dark, followed by Cais do Sodré.

The Performing Arts

CLASSICAL MUSIC

Centro Cultural de Belém ★★ This center (p. 102), is a major venue for the presentation of concerts by international orchestras, top jazz artists, and other visiting musicians. Some of the best dance programs in Portugal are also presented here, along with top-of-the-line theatrical productions. Check the local newspapers upon your arrival in Lisbon to see if a featured presentation interests you. Praça do Império. www.ccb.pt. ✆ **21/361-24-44.** Tram: 15.

Museu Calouste Gulbenkian ★ From October to June, concerts, recitals, and occasionally ballet performances take place here; sometimes there are

FADO: THE MUSIC OF LOST love

The *saudade* (Portuguese for "longing" or "nostalgia") that infuses the country's literature is most evident in fado. The traditional songs express Portugal's sad, romantic mood. The traditional performers are women (*fadistas*), often accompanied by a guitar and a viola, but men also sing. Fado is included on UNESCO's Representative List of the Intangible Cultural Heritage of Humanity.

Experiencing the nostalgic sounds of fado is essential to comprehending the Portuguese soul. But while we like most of the old and new singers, you don't see many locals in fado places; we prefer to watch them in concert halls rather than the fado restaurants.

A rough translation of "fado" is "fate," from the Latin *fatum* (prophecy). Fado songs usually tell of unrequited love, jealousy, or a longing for days gone by. The music, as is often said, evokes a "life commanded by the Oracle, which nothing can change."

Fado became famous in the 19th century when Maria Severa, the beautiful daughter of a gypsy, took Lisbon by storm. She sang her way into the hearts of the people of Lisbon—especially the count of Vimioso, an outstanding bullfighter. Present-day *fadistas* wear a black-fringed shawl in her memory.

The most famous 20th-century exponent of fado was Amália Rodrigues, who was introduced to American audiences in the 1950s at the New York club La Vie en Rose and later at Carnegie Hall. Born into a simple Lisbon family, she was discovered while walking barefoot and selling flowers on the Lisbon docks near the Alfama. For many, she is the most famous Portuguese figure since Vasco da Gama. Swathed in black, sparing of gestures and excess ornamentation, Rodrigues almost single-handedly executed the transformation of fado into an international form of poetic expression.

also jazz concerts. Ticket prices vary according to the performance. Av. de Berna 45. www.museu.gulbenkian.pt. ✆ **21/782-30-00.** Metro: S.Sebastião. Bus: 718 or 726.

OPERA & BALLET

Teatro Nacional de São Carlos ★★★ This 18th-century theater attracts opera and ballet aficionados from across Europe, and top companies from around the world perform here. The season begins mid-September and extends through July. Rua Serpa Pinto 9. www.saocarlos.pt. ✆ **21/325-30-45.** Tickets 10€–100€. Box office Mon–Fri 1–7pm, Sat–Sun and holidays from 1pm to 30 min. after the show begins. Tram: 28. Metro: Baixa-Chiado.

THEATER

Teatro Nacional D. Maria II ★ Portugal's most famous and prestigious theater dates back to the mid-19th century. The season usually begins in the autumn and lasts through spring. It presents a repertoire of both Portuguese and foreign plays, with performances strictly in Portuguese. Praça de Dom Pedro IV. www.teatro-dmaria.pt. ✆ **21/325-08-00** or 21/325-08-35 for reservations. Tickets 7€–16€, half-price for students up to 25 years old and ages 65 and older with valid ID. Metro: Rossio. Bus: 2, 9, 39, 44, 45, or 91.

The Club & Music Scene

FADO CLUBS

At the clubs listed below, you often have to pay a minimum consumption charge (which can apply either to dinner or just drinks). The music begins between 9 and 10pm, but it's better to arrive after 11pm, which is when the top acts perform. Many clubs stay open until 3am; others stay open until dawn.

Adega Machado ★★★ Open since 1937, this is still one of the country's favorite fado clubs. Alternating with such modern-day *fadistas* as the critically acclaimed Marina Rosa are folk dancers in colorful costumes. Dinner service is a la carte; expect to spend between 25€ and 35€ for a complete meal. The dinner hour starts at 8pm, music begins at 9:15pm, and the doors don't close until 3am. It's open Tuesday through Sunday. Rua do Norte 91. www.adegamachado.web.pt. ✆ **21/322-46-40.** Cover (including 2 drinks) 16€. Bus: 758.

A Severa ★★ Although it's not quite as good as Adega Machado (see above), tasty food and the careful selection of *fadistas* make this a solid second choice if the other is fully booked. Every night, top male and female singers appear, accompanied by guitar and viola music, alternating with folk dancers. In a niche, you'll spot a statue honoring the club's namesake, Maria Severa, the legendary 19th-century *fadista.* As difficult or as unsettling as it might be to imagine, before Richard Nixon became U.S. president, he came here with his wife, Patricia, and led a conga-like line between tables. The kitchen specializes in Northern Portuguese cuisine; expect to spend at least 40€ per person for a meal with wine. Open Thursday to Tuesday noon to 3pm and 8pm to 3am. Rua das Gáveas 51. www.asevera.com. ✆ **21/346-12-04.** No cover. Bus: 20 or 24.

Café Luso ★ In a vaulted network of 17th-century stables, Luso is one of the most famous and enduring fado clubs of the Bairro Alto. Amália sang here. Despite a recent trend toward the touristy, it still exerts a folkloric appeal, as it has since the 1930s. The entertainment and regional food are presented most nights to some 160 patrons. There are three shows nightly: 8 to 9:15pm for the first show, 10:30pm to 12:15am for the second show, and 12:30 to 2am for the third show. A meal here will likely run 50€ per person. Travessa da Queimada 10. www.cafeluso.pt. ✆ **21/342-22-81.** Bus: 58.

Club de Fado ★★ In the heart of the Alfama near the cathedral, the finest guitar playing in Lisbon is heard, often as a backdrop to talented *fadista* voices. The atmosphere is traditional and romantic in a setting of columns, arches, and ogival ceilings. Both well-known performers and amateur artists entertain. You can order cocktails in the bar as well as a good selection of port wines, or else full meals in the restaurant, where main courses cost from 19€ to 25€. If you're not dining, the cost of the show is 7.50€. Open daily from 9pm to 2am. Rua S. João de Praça 92–94. www.clube-de-fado.com. ✆ **21/885-27-04.** Tram: 12 or 28. Bus: 37.

Museu do Fado ★ Some of the most outstanding *fadistas,* both male and female, perform most nights at this restaurant attached to the municipal **Museu do Fado.** If you're exploring the Alfama during the day, you can drop in for a visit to the museum, which pays homage to Portugal's most distinctive musical style through photographs, sheet music, musical instruments, listening stations, costumes, and trophies. The museum is open Tuesday to Sunday 10am to 6pm, charging 5€ for admission. Adjoining the museum is a restaurant serving regional food Tuesday to Sunday 7pm to 2am. Meals cost from 30€. Largo do Chafariz de Dentro 1. www.museudofado.pt. ✆ **21/882-34-70.** Bus: 728, 735, 745, 759, or 790.

Parreirinha da Alfama ★★ Every *fadista* worth her shawl seems to have sung at this old-time cafe, just a minute's walk from the docks of the Alfama. It's fado-only here, not folk dancing, and the place has survived more or less unchanged since its establishment in the early 1950s. In the first part of the program, *fadistas* get the popular songs out of the way and then settle into classic favorites. You can order a good regional dinner, although many visitors opt to come here just to drink. It's open daily from 8pm to 3am; music begins at 9:30pm. The atmosphere is a lot more convivial after around 10:30pm, when local stars (who include such luminaries and divas as Lina Maria) have warmed up the crowd a bit. Beco do Espírito Santo 1. ✆ **21/886-82-09.** Cover (credited toward drinks) 15€. Bus: 739 or 746.

Povo ★ In Cais do Sodré, this is a casual bar where you can grab a drink and listen to young, talented singers in the early hours, usually at 8 or 9pm. There are also meals and *petiscos* (small plates) if you're hungry. Check the calendar on their website. Rua Nova do Carvalho, 32–36. http://povolisboa.com/. ✆ **21/347-34-03.** Metro: Cais do Sodré.

COFFEEHOUSES & CAFES

To the Portuguese, the coffeehouse is an institution, a democratic parlor where they can drop in for their favorite libation, abandon their worries, relax, read the paper, write a letter, or chat with friends about tomorrow's football match.

The coffeehouse in Portugal, however, is now but a shadow of its former self. The older and more colorful places, filled with turn-of-the-20th-century charm, are rapidly yielding to chrome and plastic.

One of the oldest surviving coffeehouses in Lisbon, **A Brasileira** ★, Rua Garrett 120 (✆ **21/346-95-41;** Metro: Baixa/Chiado), is in the Chiado district. It has done virtually nothing to change its opulent if faded Art Nouveau decor (from 1905). Once a gathering place of Lisbon's poets and artists, now it's mostly busy with tourists due to expensive prices and not-so-nice service. Still, it's an evocative place. Sit inside at small tables on chairs made of tooled leather, amid mirrored walls and marble pilasters. A statue of the great Portuguese poet Fernando Pessoa sits on a chair amid the customers. Prices are a bit lower at the bar. Open daily from 8am to midnight. Cash only.

More interesting is **Versailles ★★★**, Av. da República 15A (✆ **21/354-63-40;** Metro: Saldanha), long known as the grande dame of Lisbon coffeehouses. It's also an ideal place for afternoon tea, in a faded but elegant 80-year-old setting of chandeliers, gilt mirrors, and high ceilings. As an old-fashioned and formal touch, immaculately attired waiters serve customers from silver-plated tea services. In addition to coffee and tea, the house specialty is hot chocolate. The homemade cakes and pastries are delectable. (They're baked on-site.) It's open daily from 7:30am to 10pm.

Port Wine Tasting

Lisbon Winery (www.lisbonwinery.com; ✆ **21/347-57-07**) is devoted exclusively to the drinking and enjoyment of Portuguese wine (including port and Madeira tastings) in all its glory and varieties. A tasting costs 10€ to 25€. Open Monday to Friday 11am to midnight; Saturday 2pm to midnight. It's located at Rua da Barroca, 9–13 (Metro: Baixa/Chiado; bus: 758).

On the street level of the Bairro Alto Hotel, the **Café Bar,** Praça Luís de Camões 8 (www.bairroaltohotel.com; ✆ **21/340-82-62;** Metro: Baixa-Chiado), sprawls across three floors with its hip minimalist decor. It is a gathering place of young Lisbon. Shared tables add to the conviviality as DJs spin the latest tunes. If you descend to the lower level, you'll find a lounge whose vaulted ceiling once sheltered alchemists mixing up brews from an age-old pharmacy.

DANCE CLUBS & LIVE MUSIC

Cabaret Maxime ★ Through its long history, Cabaret Maxime has been a brothel, a strip club, a gay disco, and even a luxury cabaret, drawing such clients as the King of Spain and many World War II spies. Today it's been turned into a concert venue and a first-rate bar. Open Thursday 10pm to 2am, and Friday and Saturday from 10pm to 4am. Praça da Alegria 58. ✆ **21/346-70-90.** Metro: Avenida.

Lux Frágil ★★★ Popular, free-form, and hip, this two-story warehouse contains a labyrinth of interconnected spaces, each of which is likely to feature a radically different scene from the one to the next. Set on the banks of the Tagus, a short walk from the Santa Apolónia railway station, it attracts counterculture hipsters, with theatrical lighting, deep sofas, cutting-edge music, and some highly unusual accessories—like an enormous chandelier composed entirely of steel wire and tampons. Expect this and other forms of offbeat humor, and an ambience that might remind you of a be-in from the 1960s. The upstairs bar, where a DJ spins records, is open daily from 10pm to 6am. The more manic, street-level dance floor is open Thursday to Saturday 1am to 7am. Entrance to both areas is free before midnight; after that, a 15€ cover applies, although there might be a doorman with a velvet rope/barrier keeping out rowdies on weekends. Av. Infante Don Henrique, Armazém (Warehouse) A, Cais da Pedra a Sta. Apolónia. www.luxfragil.com. ✆ **21/882-08-90.** Bus: 9, 39, or 46.

Musicbox Lisboa ★ New York is not the only city that never sleeps. Yes, most bars shut down at 2am, but that's when the Musicbox gets started as late-night owls pour into this joint under a bridge in the Cais do Sodré sector. Fashionistas, hustlers, PR reps, and various hipsters in their 20s and 30s frequent this cavernlike joint. DJs most often rule the night but occasionally live bands are brought in to entertain. Cover ranges from 8€ to 10€. Open from midnight to 6am daily. Rua Nova de Carvalho 24. www.musicboxlisboa.com. ✆ **21/347-31-88.** Cover 8€. Metro: Cais do Sodré.

Paradise Garage ★ A frequently reincarnated hot spot in Lisbon for live music is set within a battered early 20th-century building in the Alcantara district. It has witnessed the rise and fall of dozens of musical trends since its heyday in the 1970s; check online to find out what's on. A rock concert featuring a group from England or America might be the stars of the evening; other times you might find a theme night. Internationally known DJs are occasionally brought in to thrill the dancers. Gay nights are also a feature, and prices and times depend on what's playing. Rua João de Oliveira Miguéns 38–48. www.paradisegarage.pt. ✆ **21/324-34-00.** Tram: 15.

Silk ★★ If we had a date for a night in Lisbon with Madonna, we'd take her to this hot spot, all black and fuchsia, with a sexy sultriness. What you see going on in its deep plush couches would bring a blush to aging party boy Jack Nicholson. Adding to its luster: the incredible vista from the floor-to-ceiling windows and from the candlelit outdoor deck on the sixth floor. The DJ spins the tunes as chic young things sip Moët & Chandon or whatever. The club lies on the upper two floors of Espaço Chiado. Open Tuesday to Saturday 10pm to 4am. Rua da Misericórdia 14. www.silk-club.com. ✆ **21/780-34-70.**

JAZZ

Onda Jazz ★ The best jazz in Lisbon, often featuring artists from Africa, Latin America, and Asia, is presented in this Alfama dive. The cover can vary, but it's usually around 10€. Open Tuesday, Thursday, and Sunday 8pm to 2am; Friday and Saturday 8pm to 3am. Arco de Jesus 7. ✆ **21/888-32-42.** Tram: 28.

The Bar Scene

Bairru's Bodega ★ In a warm, inviting atmosphere, against a backdrop of Portuguese music, you sit at tables made from wine barrels. On offer: a wide array of Portuguese wines, which you can order by the bottle or by the glass, starting from 3.50€. The bartenders also enjoy introducing patrons to a number of exotic liqueurs, such as carob or lump loquat. Unlike other bars in the district, this bodega does not serve beer. Regional cheese and local hams and sausages accompany the tipples. Open Monday to Saturday 7pm to 2am. Rua da Barroca 3. ✆ **21/346-90-60.** Metro: Baixa/Chiado.

Bar Procópio ★ A longtime favorite of journalists, politicians, and foreign actors, the once-innovative Procópio has become a tried-and-true staple among Lisbon's watering holes. Guests sit on tufted red velvet, surrounded by stained and painted glass and ornate brass hardware. Mixed drinks cost 7€ and up; beer costs 3€ and up. ***One warning:*** It's hard to find. It lies just off Rua de João Penha, which is off the landmark Praça das Amoreiras, but in a hidden little alley. Open Monday to Friday 6pm to 3am, Saturday 9pm to 3am. Alto de São Francisco 21. www.barprocopio.com. ✆ **21/385-28-51.** Closed Aug 11–Sept 8. Metro: Rato. Bus: 9.

Bora-Bora ★ A Polynesian bar might seem out of place in Lisbon, but the theme draws packs of locals who are tired of a constant diet of Iberian folklore. As you might expect from an urban bar with a Hawaiian theme, Bora-Bora specializes in imaginative variations on fruity, flaming, and rum-laced drinks. The couches are comfortable and inviting, angled for views of the Polynesian art that lines the walls. Beer costs 4€; mixed drinks are 6€ and up. It's open Friday and Saturday from 9pm to 3:30am. Rua da Madalena 201. ✆ **21/887-20-43.** Metro: Rossio. Tram: 12 or 28.

Chapitô ★ Hidden away deep in the heart of the Alfama, right below the castle, is one of the drinking (or dining) secrets of Lisbon. The weathered building that contains was used, during its turbulent history, as a 17th-century prison and later as a state-sponsored school for the training of circus performers. The view is one of the most panoramic in the Alfama. You can drop in for a coffee or return later, taking a candlelit table to enjoy a limited but choice menu. Open Tuesday to Friday 7:30pm to 2am and Saturday and Sunday 10am to 2am. Rua Costa do Castelo 7, São Cristóvão. www.chapito.org. ✆ **21/886-73-34.** Tram: 28.

CINCO Lounge ★★ This is the hottest, chicest bar in all of Lisbon. Lying above the Bairro Alto, it features an array of dazzling cocktails—some 100 in all—using only the most expensive of liquors and the freshest of fruits. Feel like burning through your budget? Order the Black Amex, which costs 235€—it's a crystallized brown sugar cube dissolved in Hennessy VS Cognac and Cuvée du Centenaire Grand Marnier, spiked with Dom Perignon. The setting is elegant, with floor-to-ceiling windows, glass-topped tables, and the most flattering lighting in Lisbon. It's open daily from 5pm to 2am. Rua Ruben A. Leitão 17A. www.cincolounge.com. ✆ **21/342-40-33.** Metro: Rato.

Garrafeira Alfaia ★ This traditionally styled wine bar in the Bairro Alto is surrounded by a mélange of trendy shops, restaurants, bars, and houses where *fadistas* perform. It's a good place to spend the early part of the evening before going on to dinner, attracting a mixture of locals and visitors. You can sample an impressive collection of Portuguese wines and savory tapas (like *sericaia,* an airy, eggy soufflé served with the famous sugarplums of Elvas; charcuterie from the famous "black pigs" of Portugal; or a sheep's-milk cheese coagulated with cardoon thistle). Wines range from a chardonnay from the Alentejo region to some of the better vintages from the Upper Douro in the north. Glasses of wine cost between 3€ and 10€, with tapas priced from

6€ to 15€. Open daily 4pm to 1am. Rua do Diário de Noticias 125. www.garrafeiraalfaia.com. ✆ **21/343-30-79.** Bus: 58.

Panorama Bar ★ The Panorama Bar occupies the top floor of one of Portugal's tallest buildings, the 30-story Lisboa Sheraton. The view (day or night) is of the old and new cities of Lisbon, the mighty Tagus, and many of the towns on the river's far bank. The cosmopolitan decor incorporates chiseled stone and stained glass. You'll pay 8.50€ to 12€ for a whiskey and soda. Opening hours are Sunday to Wednesday noon to 2am; Thursday and Friday noon to 3am; Saturday 6pm to 3am; Sunday 6pm to 2am. In the Sheraton Lisboa Hotel & Spa, Rua Latino Coelho 1. www.sheratonlisboa.com. ✆ **21/312-00-00.** Metro: Picoas. Bus: 1, 2, 9, or 32.

Park ★★★ Possibly the hippest place to tipple in town is a rooftop bar set on a top of car park. Besides the wonderful view of the bridge and the river, the atmosphere is like that of a city garden. Caipirinhas and mojitos are the specialty, though you can order wine by the glass. ***Tip:*** Try to get a spot outside at sunset. Entrance is by the car park, up the elevator, and then upstairs from the top floor. It's open Tuesday to Saturday 12:30pm to 2am, and Sunday 12:30pm to 8pm. Calçada do Combro 58. ✆ **21/591-40-11.** Metro: Chiado. Tram: 28.

Pavilhão Chinês ★ The mother of all flea-market bars, this watering hole in the Bairro Alto contains a collection of kitsch that alone is worth the trek here. Replicas of everyone from Buddha to Popeye decorate the joint, along with bronze cupids, baubles and beads, and enough Victoriana to fill half the attics of London. It's a lively venue open Monday to Friday 6pm to 2am, and Saturday 9pm to 2am. Rua Dom Pedro V 89. ✆ **21/342-47-29.** Metro: Rato.

GAY & LESBIAN BARS & CLUBS

Although this ultra-Catholic country remains one of the most closeted in western Europe, many nightspots have sprung up in the Príncipe Real district. With each passing year, the gay presence in Lisbon becomes more visible.

Bar 106 ★ A short walk from the also-recommended Finalmente, this is a popular bar, rendezvous point, and watering hole for gay men, most of whom arrive here after 10pm. It has a simple, restrained decor and a busy bar area. It's open nightly from 9pm until 2am. Rua de São Marçal 106. ✆ **21/342-73-73.** Tram: 28. Bus: 100.

Finalmente Club ★ This is the dance club that many gay men in Lisbon end up at after an evening of drinking in other bars around the Bairro Alto. There's a hardworking, hard-drinking bar area; a crowded dance floor; lots of bodies of all shapes and sizes; and a small stage upon which drag shows allow local *artistes* to strut their stuff. A stringent security system requires that you ring a bell before an attendant will let you in. It's open daily from 1am to between 3 and 6am, depending on business. Rua da Palmeira 38. ✆ **21/347-99-23.** Cover 14€ includes first drink. Bus: 100.

Frágil ★ Don't expect a sign that indicates the location of this place: All you'll see are some blue neon lights and a vigilant doorman. Frágil devotes itself to counterculture music, gay men and women, and a scattering of heterosexuals who appreciate the scene. Technically, the place opens Tuesday to Saturday at 11:30pm, but don't expect a crowd until at least midnight—and a mob by around 2am. Closing is around 4am. Rua da Atalaia 126–128. ✆ **21/346-95-78.** Cover 10€. Bus: 58 or 100. Metro: Chiado.

Trumps ★ Known to local English-speaking wits as Tramps, it's positioned near (but not in) the Bairro Alto. Several bars are scattered throughout its two levels, along with an active dance floor and lots of cruising options within its shadowy corners. Lesbians make up about a quarter of the crowd. And in case you were wondering, Donald Trump has no stake in this joint. This place is open Friday and Saturday 11:45pm to 6am. Rua da Imprensa Nacional 104B. www.trumps.pt. ✆ **21/397-10-59.** Cover (credited toward drinks) 13€. Bus: 758.

ESTORIL, CASCAIS & SINTRA

7

Lured by Guincho (near the westernmost point in continental Europe), the Boca do Inferno (Mouth of Hell), and Lord Byron's "glorious Eden" at Sintra, many travelers spend much of their time in this region, just west of Lisbon. You could spend a complete day immersed in the wonders of the library at the monastery-palace of Mafra, dining in the pretty pink rococo palace at Queluz, or enjoying seafood at the Atlantic beach resort of Ericeira.

However, the main draw in the area is the Costa do Estoril. This string of beach resorts, with its sunny climate and gentle waves, attracts Lisboans, expats, and visitors. Estoril is so close to Lisbon that lodging there and darting in and out of the capital to see the sights is easy. An inexpensive train leaves from the Cais do Sodré station in Lisbon frequently throughout the day and evening; its run ends in Cascais. So why not stay one or two nights on the coast to really perfect your tan?

The region gained fame as a magnet for deposed royalty. Exiled kings, pretenders, marquesses from Italy, princesses from Russia, and baronesses from Germany—all came here to lick their wounds in the sun. Umberto II, the last king of Italy, forced into exile for life, chose Estoril. Other nobles who settled here include Don Juan, the count of Barcelona; his son, Don Juan Carlos, who was named successor by Franco; Joanna, the former queen of Bulgaria; and Carol II of Romania. Not long ago, Estoril was known as Costa dos Reis (Kings' Coast).

During World War II, the Estoril coast became a haven for many of the refugees who arrived in Lisbon fleeing the Nazis. Portugal was neutral and Lisbon became a hub for spies and diplomats (and the spies who spied on diplomats). Estoril, in particular, was a popular stomping ground for the Intel community on both sides—Ian Fleming, Graham Greene, and Kim Philby cruised the streets, the promenade, and the casino. It was actually this casino that inspired author Fleming when he penned *Casino Royale*.

Take a ride out on the train, even if you don't plan to stay here. You'll pass pastel-washed houses with red-tile roofs and facades of antique blue-and-white tiles; miles of modern apartment dwellings; rows of canna, pine, mimosa, and eucalyptus; and, in the background, green hills studded with villas and chalets. The train goes along the coast for most of this delightfully scenic ride.

Lisbon is the aerial gateway for the Costa do Estoril and Sintra. Once there, you can walk around or take public transportation.

ESTORIL: CHIC BEACH ★

13km (8 miles) S of Sintra; 24km (15 miles) W of Lisbon

This fashionable resort, with its beautiful beaches, has a long history as a home away from home for expats of all nationalities. Sometimes called the "Portuguese Riviera," this was the first vacation destination in the Lisbon area and is often credited as the first resort in Portugal. Today's Estoril was the creation of Fausto Figueiredo, who built the deluxe Palácio in 1930. The casino goes back to the beginning of the 20th century. During World War II, as Nazi troops advanced across Europe, many members of collapsing royal courts fled to Estoril to wait out the war in a neutral country. Nowadays, its neighbor Cascais is the main town.

Essentials

ARRIVING

BY TRAIN Trains leave from the waterfront Cais do Sodré station in Lisbon. The round-trip fare is 3€, and departures are every 20 minutes for the half-hour trip. Trains operate daily 5:30am to 1:30am. For info: www.cp.pt.

BY BUS Buses from Lisbon are impractical, considering the low cost and convenience of the frequent trains. But if you're coming to Estoril from Sintra, the bus is your best bet; about a dozen buses a day make the 1-hour run. The round-trip fare is 4€.

BY CAR From Lisbon, head west on Avenida Marginal (EN6), along the coast in one of the most scenic drives in Portugal. Driving time depends on traffic, which tends to be heavy at rush hour and heavy on summer weekends (it is also difficult to park in town then). It's lightest Monday to Friday 10am to 4pm. That being said, we think it's easier on the nerves to take the train and forget about driving along the coast.

VISITOR INFORMATION

Junta de Turismo da Costa do Estoril is no longer at Edifício Arcadas Parque (www.estorilcoast-tourism.com) but in Cascais instead, Praça 5 de Outubro.

It's open 9am to 6pm in winter, 9am to 8pm in summer.

Exploring Estoril

Parque Estoril, in the center of town, is a well-manicured green space of subtropical vegetation. The palm trees studding the grounds have prompted many

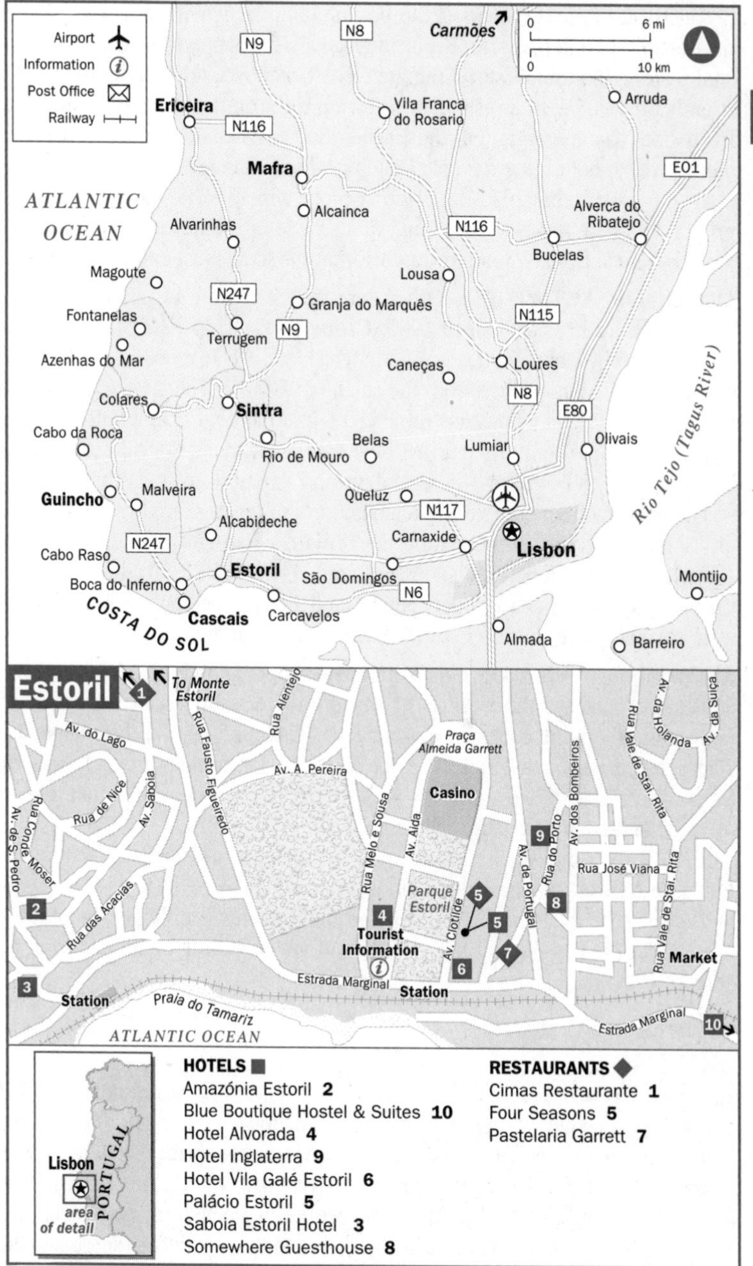

Airport
Information
Post Office
Railway
0 6 mi
0 10 km
ATLANTIC OCEAN
Ericeira
Mafra
Alcainca
Alvarinhas
Vila Franca do Rosario
Arruda
Carmões
Alverca do Ribatejo
Bucelas
Lousa
Magoute
Fontanelas
Azenhas do Mar
Granja do Marquês
Terrugem
Caneças
Loures
Colares
Sintra
Cabo da Roca
Belas
Rio de Mouro
Lumiar
Olivais
Rio Tejo (Tagus River)
Guincho
Malveira
Queluz
Alcabideche
Carnaxide
Lisbon
Cabo Raso
Boca do Inferno
Estoril
São Domingos
Montijo
Cascais
Carcavelos
Almada
Barreiro
COSTA DO SOL
N9
N8
N116
E01
N247
N115
N117
N6
E80
Estoril
To Monte Estoril
Av. do Lago
Rua Fausto Figueiredo
Rua Alentejo
Praça Almeida Garrett
Av. A. Pereira
Casino
Rua de Nice
Av. Saboia
Rua Conde Moser
Av. de S. Pedro
Rua Melo e Sousa
Av. Aida
Parque Estoril
Av. Clotilde
Av. de Portugal
Rua do Porto
Av. dos Bombeiros
Rua José Viana
Rua Vale de Stai. Rita
Av. da Holanda
Av. da Suiça
Rua das Acacias
Tourist Information
Estrada Marginal
Station
Praia do Tamariz
ATLANTIC OCEAN
Market
Lisbon
PORTUGAL
area of detail
HOTELS
Amazónia Estoril 2
Blue Boutique Hostel & Suites 10
Hotel Alvorada 4
Hotel Inglaterra 9
Hotel Vila Galé Estoril 6
Palácio Estoril 5
Saboia Estoril Hotel 3
Somewhere Guesthouse 8
RESTAURANTS
Cimas Restaurante 1
Four Seasons 5
Pastelaria Garrett 7

to call it "a corner of Africa." At the top of the park sits the casino, which offers gambling, international floor shows, dancing, and a restaurant.

Across the railroad tracks is the beach, Tamariz, where some of the most fashionable people in Europe sun themselves on peppermint-striped canvas chairs along the Praia Estoril Tamariz. The beach is sandy, unlike the pebbly strands of Nice. With a restaurant and club right on the sands, this stretch is lively both day and night. For those who don't like ocean swimming, Tamariz has a lovely pool (at the Reverse Beach & Pool Lounge).

To the east is São João do Estoril beach, which is backed by handsome private villas. If you enjoy walking, there's a long promenade connecting all these beaches, from S. João to Cascais, that the locals just call *paredão*.

OUTDOOR ACTIVITIES Other than the beach, the big activity here is golf. A fixture in Estoril since 1940, **Clube de Golf do Estoril,** Avenida da República (www.clubegolfestoril.com; ✆ **21/468-01-76**), lies in the foothills of Sintra, a 5-minute drive from the casino at Estoril. The course, one of the finest in Europe, has hosted a number of international championships. The club has a 9-hole course and an 18-hole course. Monday to Friday, nonmembers can play 18 holes for 80€ weekdays and 95€ on weekends.

The most modern complex of tennis courts in town, shared by most of the city's major resorts, is the **Clube de Ténis do Estoril,** Avenida Conde de Barcelona (www.clubedetenisdoestoril.com; ✆ **21/466-27-70**). It offers more than 20 courts, and charges between 9€ and 14€ per person per hour. Within a short walk of the Palácio Estoril, it's open daily from 9am until dusk.

SHOPPING Estoril does not abound with shopping options. Most dedicated consumers head for the markets of Lisbon, or for the Cascais center or the large-scale shopping center in Cascais (see "Cascais," later in this chapter), a 10-minute drive from Estoril. One exception, for foodies, the **Quinta do Saloio** (Av. Nice, 170), a grocery with excellent cheese, canned fish, wines, olive oil and other gourmet specialties.

In July and August, the resort sponsors an open-air handicrafts fair, the **Feira do Artesanato,** near the casino. It's worth a visit even if you're staying in Cascais. The fair runs nightly from around 5pm until midnight. In addition to regional food, stalls sell handicrafts and art, including ceramics, from all parts of Portugal.

Where to Stay

EXPENSIVE

Palácio Estoril ★★★ The Palácio is legendary as a retreat for exiled royalty and a center of espionage during World War II. At its 1930 debut, the Palácio received the honeymooning Japanese crown prince and his bride. Umberto, the deposed king of Italy, and Don Juan, the count of Barcelona, followed. During World War II, when people escaped from Nazi-occupied Europe with little more than a case of jewels and the clothes on their back, the hotel accepted diamonds, rubies, and gold instead of money. There's a gallery in the hotel documenting the celebrities and royals who have stayed there since the 1930s—including Graham Greene and Ian Fleming. The James Bond creator is said to have been inspired by Palácio's bar when spying was as effervescent as champagne, and vodka martinis were a favorite of the cosmopolitan guests of the hotel. Try one. Shaken, not stirred, of course.

The reception rooms are Pompeian, with sienna-colored marble pillars, bold bands of orange, and handmade carpets. The intimate salons are ideal for a tête-à-tête. The large guest rooms are traditional, with fine Regency-style furnishings, walk-in closets, and luxurious bathrooms with bidets and heated towel racks. Single rooms facing the rear are the smallest but also the quietest (and least expensive). The hotel opens onto the side of Estoril Park, which is capped by the casino. The beach is a short walk away but there's a large pool in the hotel, too good to miss. The same goes for the Banyan Tree Spa, with 14 massage treatment rooms and an indoor pool.

Rua Particular. www.palacioestorilhotel.com. ✆ **21/464-80-00.** 162 units. 150€–390€ double; from 270€–400€ junior suite. Free parking. **Amenities:** Restaurant; bar; babysitting; concierge; golf course nearby; outdoor and indoor pools; room service; spa; sauna; fitness center; animals admitted. Free Wi-Fi.

MODERATE

Amazónia Estoril ★ Partially because of its emphasis on golf (it's located about 2km from the Clube de Golf do Estoril course), this hillside hotel seems a lot like a corner of Scotland. Near the bar, there's a map of the golf course at St. Andrews, close to autographed photos of the many championship golfers who have stayed here. And, as you'll sometimes find in Scotland, guest rooms can be a bit musty. They're a mixed bag, with some perfectly fine, and others showing wear and tear (a chip here, a scuff there—they're not dirty, just in need of renovation). But the suites have a lovely perk: They are equipped with kitchenettes. ***One warning:*** The Wi-Fi here is erratic, so don't choose the Amazonia if connectivity is important to you.

Rua Eng. Álvaro Pedro Sousa, 175. www.amazoniahoteis.com. ✆ **21/468-04-24.** 32 units. 45€–196€ double; 135€–227€ suite. Rates include buffet breakfast. Free parking. **Amenities:** Restaurant; 2 bars; babysitting; outdoor pool; room service. Free Wi Fi.

Hotel Alvorada ★ This hotel, which opened its doors in 1969, provides simple, clean accommodations in a terrifically central location for a reasonable rate. The hotel stands opposite the casino and the Parque Estoril, just a 5-minute walk from the beach. It's recommended for its well-maintained but unstylish midsize guest rooms, each with its own balcony. The top-floor solarium offers a panoramic view of the sea. Only breakfast is served.

Rua de Lisboa 3, Estoril. www.hotelalvorada.com. ✆ **21/464-98-60.** 51 units. 50€–290€ double; 65€–330€ triple. Rates include buffet breakfast. Free parking. **Amenities:** Bar; babysitting; room service. Free Wi-Fi.

Hotel Inglaterra ★★ We're fans of this well-preserved historic gem, which boasts an idyllic location on a hilltop overlooking the coast. Around the turn of the 20th century, it was constructed as a private palace, but has been cleverly repositioned as a boutique hotel. The colonial look so typical of the country's hotels is missing here, however. In fact, you'd think that a grandchild of Salvador Dali had passed through, what with the kooky wallpapers, unusual art, and (in some places) lampshades that look like crinoline petticoats. It's a decor rich in whimsy and charm, and if you can snag one of the rooms with the private terraces overlooking the bay of Cascais (with all its expensive yachts) you've reached "hotel heaven." Many use the hotel as a romantic retreat, but it works for families, too—there's even a kiddie playground.

Rua do Porto 1. www.hotelinglaterra.com.pt. ✆ **21/468-44-61.** 55 units. 55€–250€ double; 110€–350€ suite. Free parking. **Amenities:** Restaurant; 2 bars; babysitting; bikes; children's center; concierge; exercise room; outdoor pool; room service. Free Wi-Fi.

INEXPENSIVE

Blue Boutique Hostel & Suites ★★ This property was chosen by Britain's *Guardian* newspaper as one of the smartest new hostels in Europe in 2015, and we think that assessment still holds. Set in a former family villa with a top location in Estoril, very close to the beach, it offers dorm rooms, private doubles, and suites (only the latter have private bathrooms). All types of rooms are cheery, with pops of bright colors (blue, pink, green), quality beds, wooden floors, and whitewashed walls. The public areas and gardens are particularly inviting, equipped with an abundance of seating, so guests can mingle in the sun. Other perks: use of a full kitchen, and the big screen TV and computers in the living room. The hostel is affiliated with a surf camp.

Av. Marginal, 6538. www.blueboutiquehostel.com. ✆ **21/466-30-06.** 17€–95€ dorms; 36€–48€ double rooms with shared bathroom; 59€–99€ suites with private bathroom. **Amenities:** Free parking; surf camp; 24-hr. reception. Free Wi-Fi.

Hotel Vila Galé Estoril ★★ Built in the late 1950s next door to the far more glamorous Palácio (see above), this hotel rises seven floors with walls of soaring glass. About half the rooms boast good-size balconies overlooking the water and the casino. Bedrooms are very pleasant and unusually roomy, featuring stylish modern stained-wood furniture and neatly kept bathrooms. Only a minute or so from the sea and the train station, it's in the center of Estoril's boutique district. Final perk: the friendly, helpful staff.

Av. Marginal, apt. 49. www.vilagale.pt. ✆ **21/464-84-00.** 75€–185€ double. Rates include buffet breakfast. Parking 7.50€. **Amenities:** Restaurant; 2 bars; babysitting; concierge; health club; Jacuzzi; golf course (nearby); outdoor pool; room service; sauna. Free Wi-Fi.

Saboia Estoril Hotel ★ Just a 500m (1,640-ft.) walk from the nearest good beach, this six-floor hotel dates from the 1970s and is set in a tranquil residential neighborhood of mainly 19th-century private villas. Since its opening, it has been renovated on an as-needed basis, which means that most of the bedrooms will be just fine, though occasionally you'll find chipping paint and other small issues. Guest rooms are small and decorated with standard motel-type furnishings (about half have balconies with sea views). All this being said, its prices are unusually reasonable for this area. Right next to the pool is a Jacuzzi and Turkish bath, and on-site is a small gym.

Rua Belmonte 1, Monte Estoril, 1km (less than 1 mile) west of town on the road to Cascais. www.hotelsaboia.com. ✆ **21/468-02-02.** 48 units. 50€–100€ double. Rates include buffet breakfast. Free parking. **Amenities:** Snack bar; babysitting; bikes; exercise room; outdoor pool. Free Wi-Fi.

Somewhere Guesthouse ★★ Another adorable former family villa, this is one of the best values in the region. Public areas are both homey and stylish, with quirky art and colorful furniture. In the bedrooms, the furniture is also modern but the colors have softer tones. The outdoor pool is sleek, like something out of a David Hockney painting, though it has no views (unfortunately). In the colder months there's a fireplace in the lounge, perfect for curling up with a good novel on one of the cozy sofas.

Rua Comandante Joaquim Nascimento Gourinho, 90. http://somewhere-estoril.com. ✆ **21/269-70-50.** 11 units. 45€–95€ per person. Rates include breakfast. **Amenities:** Free parking; 24-hr. reception; bar; dinner service. Free Wi-Fi.

Where to Dine

EXPENSIVE

Cimas Restaurante ★★ INTERNATIONAL/PORTUGUESE In Monte Estoril, just outside the center of Estoril, this restaurant is housed in the replica of an Elizabethan cottage. It's a historic site, but one that has nothing to do with Merry Olde England: The bar that opened here during World War II became a haven for spies. In time, it became the unofficial headquarters of opponents of the Franco regime in Spain. Novelists, journalists, politicians, and artists flocked here and some still do, drawn today by the impressive skills of the kitchen staff. Market-fresh ingredients and assertive flavors are the norm in such dishes as sea bass with clams, salt codfish casserole, monkfish on a spit with prawns and fresh squid, and lamb kidneys in a Madeira wine sauce. Save room for dessert: The crêpes suzette will make you wish you hadn't had a main course.

Av. Marginal, Monte Estoril. www.cimas.com.pt. ✆ **21/468-12-54.** Reservations recommended. Main courses 18€–38€. Mon–Sat 12:30–4pm and 7:30–11pm. Closed 2nd and 3rd week of Aug.

Four Seasons Grill Restaurant ★★★ INTERNATIONAL/PORTUGUESE This is one of the finest—and one of the most expensive—restaurants in Estoril. Other than the handful of intimate tables set on the upper mezzanine, the elaborately decorated tables cluster around a beautiful, but purely decorative, Iberian kitchen. The quiet, the candles, and the rich colors invite comparison to an elegant 19th-century Russian home. However, the discreet charm and polite manners of the well-trained staff are distinctively Portuguese.

The international cuisine is superb and, you guessed it, changes every season. For an appetizer, such delights as three-cheese crepes, lobster bisque, or chilled mussel soup are often on order. Of the mains we've tried, special recommendations go to the medallions of grouper with seaweed and salmon roe; a *parrillada* of lobster, shrimp, mussels, and clams for two; medallions of venison with chestnuts; and wild boar cutlets with pineapple.

In the Palácio Estoril, Rua do Parque. ✆ **21/464-80-00.** Reservations required. Main courses 24€–48€. Daily noon–3pm and 7:30–10:30pm.

MODERATE

Garrett ★★★ PORTUGUESE Inarguably one the best bakeries in the country, Garrett is famous for its *bolo-rei* (a Christmas cake). But year-round its cakes and desserts attract legions of fans and have done so since 1934. The savory *salgados* (snacks) are also topnotch and freshly made, making this a swell choice for lunch or dinner (a *very* early supper—it closes at 7pm). Our favorites are *rissóis de camarão* (shrimp-filled fritters) and the beef croquets. Combined with a salad they can be a delicious lunch. (***Tip:*** The snacks are more satisfying than the main dishes.) Before leaving, ask for some of the crunchy *pratas*—thin cookies made of egg-whites—to take with you for a late-night treat. The restaurant is set in a backstreet of Estoril, in front of the Palácio Hotel.

Av. de Nice, 54, Monte Estoril. ✆ **21/468-03-65.** Main courses 10€–24€. Wed–Mon 8–7pm. Closed 2nd and 3rd week of Aug.

Estoril After Dark

CLUBS & BARS The casino is the venue for the region's splashiest and most colorful weekend cabaret act, **Salão Preto e Prata,** in the Casino Estoril, Parque Estoril, Praça José Teodoro dos Santos (www.casino-estoril.pt; ✆ **21/466-77-00**). Expect leggy, feathered, and bejeweled dancers strutting around in billowing trains and bespangled bras. Food is served in the 700-seat theater or in the 150-seat satellite restaurant **Nobre Restaurant** (led by Portuguese chef Justa Nobre) or at the smaller **Zeno Lounge.** Shows are presented Saturday at 5pm and 9:30pm and again on Sunday at 5pm. Dinner, including access to the show, costs 56€ to 65€ per person. Fado and other live music can be seen at Lounge D. The cover charge is 21€ on both Saturday and Sunday.

GAMBLING An alcohol-stoked crawl through the upscale bars of such hotels as the Palácio is a classic way to experience the glamour of this pocket of Portugal. As is gambling at the **Casino Estoril,** in the Parque Estoril, Praça José Teodoro dos Santos (www.casino-estoril.pt; ✆ **21/466-77-00**). There's no cover charge for entrance into the section with the gaming tables (roulette, French banque, *chemin de fer,* blackjack, and craps); you can gamble to your heart's content every day between 3pm and 3am. You must, however, present a passport, driver's license, or other form of photo ID, and you must be 18 or over. A jacket is required. Entrance to the separate slot-machine room is also free but requires no ID. Built in the late 1950s, the casino rises from a formally landscaped garden on a hilltop near the town center. Glass walls enclose an inner courtyard with fountains and tiled paths.

CASCAIS ★★

6.5km (4 miles) W of Estoril; 61km (38 miles) W of Lisbon

Once known as a royal village because it enjoyed the patronage of Portugal's ruling family, it was here that King Carlos made sea swimming a fashionable activity. When the monarchy collapsed after the Revolution of 1910, the military replaced the royals, and by 1930s Cascais was best known as a fishing village that attracted artists and writers to its little cottages. The town's tie with the sea is old. If you speak Portuguese, chat up any of the local fishermen. They'll tell you that one of their own, Afonso Sanches, discovered America in 1482. Legend has it that Columbus learned of his accidental find, stole the secret, and enjoyed the subsequent acclaim.

To say Cascais is growing would be an understatement: It has exploded in construction. Apartment houses, new hotels, and the finest restaurants along the coast draw a never-ending stream of visitors.

However, the life of the simple fisherfolk goes on. Auctions, called *lotas*, of the latest catch still take place near the main square. In the small harbor, rainbow-colored fishing boats share space with the pleasure craft the international set dock here from early spring until autumn.

Essentials

ARRIVING

BY TRAIN The round-trip fare from Lisbon's Cais do Sodré to either Estoril (the second-to-last stop) or Cascais (the end of the line) costs 4.40€. Electric trains arrive from and depart from Lisbon at intervals of every 20 minutes. Service runs daily from 5:30am to 1:30am. For information in Lisbon, in Cascais, or Estoril, call © **70/721-02-20.**

BY BUS Buses from Lisbon are impractical, considering the low cost and convenience of the frequent trains. But if you're coming to Cascais from Sintra, the bus is your best bet; about a dozen buses a day make the 30-hour run. The round-trip fare is 7€.

BY CAR From Estoril (see "Estoril," earlier in this chapter), continue west along Route 6 for another 6.5km (4 miles).

VISITOR INFORMATION

The **Cascais Tourist Office** is at Praça 5 de Outubro, (www.visitcascais.com; © **91/203-42-14**). The tourist office is open Monday to Friday 9am to 6pm, Saturday and Sunday 9am to 8pm. In summer (June to September), it's open daily 9am to 8pm.

Exploring Cascais

Visitors, both foreign and domestic, clog the roads to Cascais in summer on the way to the beach (especially on weekends).

When you're not at the beach, the sprawling **Parque do Marechal Carmona** (daily 8:30am to 7:45pm summer and until 5:45pm winter) is a swell place to chill. At the southern tip of Cascais near the water, it boasts a shallow lake, a cafe, and a small zoo. Chairs and tables are set out under shade trees for picnics.

We also highly recommend popping into the **Igreja de Nossa Senhora da Assunção ★ (Church of Our Lady of the Assumption)**, which has a nave filled with the paintings by Josefa de Óbidos, a rare 17th-century female artist, and a celebrated one at that. The colors of the robes on her saints are still luminous today. Also worth seeing here: the hand-painted *azulejos* (tiles), which date from 1720 and 1748, and the handsome 16th-century altar. The church sits on Largo da Assunção (✆ **21/484-74-80**), a leafy square toward the western edge of town. It's open daily from 9am to 1pm and 5 to 8pm. Admission is free, although donations are gladly accepted.

These days the museum that attracts the most visitors is **Casa das Histórias Paula Rego ★★★** in Avenida da República, 300 (✆ **21/482-69-70**), which is dedicated to the works of this internationally acclaimed Portuguese artist. Dame Rego (b. 1935) has lived in London for many years (she was the first artist to get a residency from the National Gallery), but when it came time to choose a place for a permanent showcase of her works, she came home to Cascais. Some pieces by her late husband Victor Willing are showcased here as well, but the star attractions are her graphic, often surreal renderings of Portuguese folktales. The building, with its iconic pink towers, was designed by Souto Moura, winner of the Pritzker Award; it opened in 2009. Besides the permanent collection there are temporary exhibitions and events. The museum has a cafeteria and is open from Tuesday to Sunday, 10am to 6pm; admission is 3€.

Cascais' secondary (read: less popular) museums include the **Museu do Mar Rei D. Carlos (Museum of the Sea),** Rua Júlio Pereira de Mello (✆ **21/481-59-06**) which displays fishing artifacts, primarily equipment and model boats. Folkloric apparel worn by residents in the 1800s is also on display, as are historic photos of the town. The museum is open Tuesday to Sunday 10am to 5pm; on weekends it closes from 1 to 2pm; admission is free. The **Museu do Conde de Castro Guimarães,** Avenida Rei Humberto II de Itália, Estrada da Boca do Inferno (✆ **21/481-53-04**) occupies the former 19th-century home of a family whose last surviving member died in 1927. The museum offers a rare glimpse into life in the 18th and 19th centuries, with ceramics, antiques, artwork, silver ewers, samovars, and Indo-Portuguese embroidered shawls—you name it. It's on the grounds of the Parque do Marechal Carmona, and open Tuesday to Sunday 10am to 12:30pm and 2 to 5pm; admission is 3€ and free for children under 18 and seniors. Guided tours are on the hour between 10am and 5pm.

The most popular excursion outside Cascais is to **Boca do Inferno (Mouth of Hell) ★**. Thundering waves sweep in with such power that they've carved a wide hole resembling a mouth, or *boca*, into the cliffs. When the waves are high, a roar seems to emit from the gaping hole However, if you arrive when the sea is calm, you'll wonder why it's called a "cauldron." Take the highway toward Guincho and then turn left toward the sea.

OUTDOOR ACTIVITIES The best golf course is **Oitavos Dunes Quinta da Marinha** (www.quintadamarinha-oitavosgolfe.pt; ✆ **21/486-06-00**), 7km (4⅓ miles) west of Cascais, which evokes the golf courses of Scotland. Holes open onto distant views of the Atlantic and the Sintra mountain range. Designed by golf architect Arthur Hills, it is inside the Sintra-Cascais National Park. Greens fees are 65€ to 75€ in winter, rising to 130€ to 155€ in summer. Hours are daily 8am to 8pm. Also on-site: an equestrian center with some 230 horses and various indoor and outdoor riding arenas. A 30-minute ride goes for 25€; 1 hour costs 35€.

A second good golf course, **Clube de Golfe da Marinha,** Quinta da Marinha (© **21/486-01-00**) was carved out of sprawling woodlands of umbrella pines. The master himself, Robert Trent Jones, Sr., designed the 18 holes here, the showcase of an upscale residential resort complex that stretches over some 131 hectares (324 acres). Windblown dunes and sea-lashed outcroppings are part of the backdrop along its 6,120m (20,079 ft.). The 18th hole, facing a deep rocky gorge, is the most challenging. Greens fees from Monday to Sunday are 81€, or 40€ after 3:30pm.

SHOPPING As a prominent beachfront resort, Cascais offers lots of simple kiosks selling sunglasses and beachwear. The region's densest concentration of stores is nearby at the sprawling mall **Cascais Shopping,** Estrada Nacional 9, Estrada de Sintra (www.cascaishopping.pt), beside Hwy. 5A, on the road between Cascais and Sintra—you'll need a taxi or car to get there. Over two floors are more than 100 boutiques, with special emphasis on housewares, accessories, and clothing. In Cascais center there's also a smaller mall, **Cascais Villa,** Av. Dom Pedro I, Lote 1.

If you're in the mood for less overtly commercial settings, ignore the megamall. Wander instead through the warren of small ceramics shops that surround Cascais's church, or walk along the town's all-pedestrian walkway in the center, formerly Rua Direita, now Rua Frederico Arouca. Nearby is the most famous gelato shop in the region: **Santini ★★★** (Av.Valbom 28F). Founded in 1949, its flavors, especially the fruit ones, are out of this world. Old photos on the walls show visiting royals at the shop.

The most colorful shopping is at the markets, of which there are several. Head north of the center along Rua Mercado, off Avenida do 25 de Abril, and you'll find a good daily one. On Wednesday and Saturday mornings its devoted to goods from farmers in the neighboring region, on other days you'll find fish, fruit, baked goods, and other comestibles. Every Wednesday, the central **Jardim Visconde da Luz** turns into a sprawling market selling a mix of antiques and flea-market stuff. On Saturdays, handicrafts are sold here.

Galeria 50/50 ★★, at Rua Frederico Arouca 192A (© **21/486-17-16**), is an art gallery that also sells jewels, clothing, tiles, and accessories made by individual artists (many are quite lovely).

Casa da Guia (www.casadaguia.com; © **21/484-32-15**), on the road to Guincho, offers shopping with an ocean view, hosting a range of upscale boutiques and kiosks, as well as restaurants and cafes.

Where to Stay

EXPENSIVE

Albatroz ★★★ After many decades, this monument to aristocratic glamour still reigns as one of the most sought-after hotel reservations on the Costa do Estoril. Today, although confronted with stiff competition from newer hotels that are *almost* as charming, it continues to hold its reputation as a lodging for the quietly rich. Don't expect glitziness: The property is small-scale and restrained. Still its location is hard to beat: perched on the bay in Cascais, literally over the beach. Its centerpiece is a pair of interconnected beach houses, one of which was originally built in 1793 for the duke of Loulé and acquired during the 19th century as a holiday home for the Count and Countess de Foz. In the 20th century, it became an inn. In 1983, a series of additions and alterations eventually engulfed the villas, even though you can still see traces of the original architecture, especially in the foyer of the much-heralded restaurant. Today you'll find airy, open spaces, contemporary tilework, and low-slung furniture that's in keeping with its image as an upscale beach hotel. The hotel now also has a neighboring neo-Romantic villa, which was converted into a conference center with six extremely upscale suites. (We prefer guest rooms in the original hotel; they're less blandly conservative in their decor.)

Rua Frederico Arouca 100. www.albatrozhotels.com. ✆ **21/484-73-80.** 59 units. 170€–390€ double; 300€–580€ suite. Rates include buffet breakfast. Free parking. **Amenities:** Restaurant; bar; babysitting; concierge; outdoor pool; room service. Free Wi-Fi.

Farol Design Hotel ★★ The name doesn't lie. This "design hotel"—it's a member of that chain—is one of the most stylish along the coast, set in a handsomely converted 19th-century mansion. The building rises four stories, housing rooms with midsize to massive bedrooms. They have mostly monochromatic color schemes of either all-white (three of the rooms), or mostly red, mostly pink, or mostly dark gray. Furnishings are crafted from a handsome dark wood and are quite sophisticated, created by notable Portuguese designers. Bathrooms are blessed with hydromassage tubs (ah!). Final perk: You never have to leave here at night because a first-class restaurant serves international food, and two fashionable bars and a well-attended dance club entertain the young and beautiful. Sunset drinks at the terrace bar are a must.

Av. Rei Humberto II de Italia 7. www.farol.com.pt. ✆ **21/482-34-90.** 34 units. 125€–380€ double; 250€–480€ suite. Rates include buffet breakfast. Free parking. **Amenities:** Restaurant; bar; babysitting; outdoor pool; room service; sauna. Free Wi-Fi.

Hotel Cascais Miragem ★★ With its bedrooms opening onto the Atlantic, this sleek and inviting choice is located between Estoril and Cascais. Its array of bedrooms (average-size to spacious) are equipped with all the standard and even some luxurious features, like fine (and antiallergenic) linens and drapes, and a mixture of marble and wood for the furnishings and floors. Almost all have private terraces. The hotel does more than most to cater to families, with its children's pool, play area, kiddie menus, toys in the room, and even special excursions by prior arrangement. Its dining facilities serve a mixture of Portuguese dishes and international specialties. The staff is among the most gracious along the coast, and will be helpful arranging golf, excursions, restaurant reservations, you name it.

Av. Marginal 8554, www.cascaismirage.com. ✆ **21/006-06-00.** 192 units. 150€–260€ double; 550€–650€ suite. Children 11 and under stay free. Rates include buffet breakfast. Parking 12€. **Amenities:** 3 restaurants; 3 bars; babysitting; children's center; concierge; health club & spa; outdoor pool; room service. Free Wi-Fi.

Martinhal Cascais ★★★ The way to a traveling parent's heart? Give her a break from parenting… and treat her children like gold. Both happen at this uber-family friendly resort, a place that not only has a massive kid's club and several very different types of playgrounds and pools scattered around the resort, but a "baby concierge" who can set up sitters and supply you with all the gear your little one needs. All of this happens in a resort that's both elegant and indestructible—guest rooms and villas feature swank bedding on super-king-size beds (which can be split into two twins), fine woods for the furnishings, and plush carpeting… but no tempting tassles to pull or sculptures to send crashing down. Somehow they've made baby-proofing look sexy. While the kids are playing, the parents can be spa-ing in a topnotch facility, heading to the beach about 1km (less than 1 mile) away, or exploring the area.

Rua do Clube, Quinta da Marinha. www.martinhal.com/cascais/en/. ✆ **21/850-77-88.** 81 units. 165€–258€ double; more for villas. Free parking. **Amenities:** 3 restaurants; spa; 3 pools; room service; babysitting; kid's club; playgrounds. Free Wi-Fi.

MODERATE

Hotel Baía ★★ One of the most appealing things about this well-managed hotel is its location directly above the town's fishing port, adjacent to the town hall and within a short walk of deluxe hotels whose accommodations cost a whole lot more. Originally built in the 1960s, it has been extensively renovated, enlarged, and modernized. Today its five floors contain contemporary furnishings, with wooden panels and bright colors. Bedrooms are small but some have lovely views. The terrace bar is one of the liveliest spots to enjoy a drink in Costa do Estoril.

Av. Marginal. www.hotelbaia.com. ✆ **21/483-10-33.** 113 units. 70€–144€ double. Rates include buffet breakfast. Parking 10€. **Amenities:** 2 restaurants; bar; bikes; indoor heated pool. Free Wi-Fi.

Hotel Vila Galé Cascais ★ The balconied hotel, surrounded by palaces and the Parque da Gandarinha, offers simple but comfortable bedrooms with contemporary design, including 70 junior suites, each with a beehive-shaped balcony overlooking the sea or mountains. Junior suites (which comfortably house 2 adults and 2 children) and doubles with a sofa bed make this a choice of many families.

Rua Frei Nicolau de Oliveira, Parque da Gandarinha. www.vilagale.pt. ✆ **21/482-60-00.** 233 units. 70€–185€ double; 98€–287€ suite. Free parking. **Amenities:** Restaurant; 2 bars; babysitting; children's center; 2 outdoor pools; room service; sauna. Free Wi-Fi.

INEXPENSIVE

Casa da Pergola ★★★ Built in the 18th century, this graceful villa offers one of the most tranquil stays in Cascais. It was the childhood home of owner Patrícia Gonçalves, and today she still maintains it as if it were still her private domain. Her genteel staff proudly walk guests through the collection of antique furniture, and blue-and-white tiles that surround the elegant ground-floor parlor and second-floor sitting room. The accommodations are as handsomely decorated, with antiques, silky linens, and well-maintained bathrooms. Breakfast in the romantic garden is a highlight. Reserve well in advance.

Although it's technically closed in winter, the hotel will open during that time for any party that reserves five or more rooms. In the center of town, it stands in the midst of a flower-filled garden in a neighborhood blessed with lovely restaurants and shops. ***One warning:*** Children are not welcome here.

Av. Valbom 13. www.casadapergola-cascais-lisbon.com. ✆ **21/484-00-40.**10 units. 55€–150€ double. Rates include buffet breakfast. Free Wi-Fi. No credit cards. Parking (in nearby lot) 8€. Closed Dec 16–Feb 14.

Where to Dine

Cascais offers a good concentration of quality restaurants. Even if you're based in the capital, consider a trip to Cascais for seafood.

EXPENSIVE

Baía do Peixe ★★ PORTUGUESE/SEAFOOD This restaurant, located on the fishing bay, is one of the most sought after reservations in town by some of the coast's most discerning palates—locals and businesspeople often come here to show off their chic resort apparel at night. The decor features comfortable upholstered chairs set at nicely spaced tables with crisp white linens and crystal. The house specialty is *Rodízio de Peixe*, a sequence of different types of grilled fish brought to your table for a surprisingly affordable price. The chef's medallions of grouper with fresh shrimp is also excellent.

Av. D. Carlos 1–6. www.baiadopeixe.com. ✆ **21/486-51-57.** Reservations required. Main courses 13€–38€. *Rodizio* 15€. Tues–Sun 12:30–3pm and 7–10:30pm.

Restaurant Albatroz ★★★ INTERNATIONAL/PORTUGUESE The most famous hotel on the coast (see "Where to Stay," above) hosts one of the region's most beloved restaurants. Wide, wide windows offer a sweeping view of one of the most popular beaches in Cascais, genial service is a hallmark, and the room strikes just the right balance with its wicker and wood—this is a special-occasion place, yes, but one for holidaygoers, not deal-makers.

Most guests begin with an aperitif on the covered terrace. Next comes a parade of fine Portuguese and Continental specialties in the dining room: chestnut-and-mushroom soup, partridge stew, chateaubriand, or a savory version of stuffed sole with shellfish. Daily fresh-fish specials are served; two especially succulent offerings are monkfish with clams and the sea bass baked in sea salt.

In the Albatroz, Rua Frederico Arouca 100. ✆ **21/484-73-80.** Reservations required. Main courses 16€–30€. Tasting menu 30€. Daily 12:30–3pm and 7:30–10:30pm.

Restaurante Luzmar ★★★ PORTUGUESE An oldie but a goodie, this tavern-style eatery is anything but typical when it comes to the quality of its food or the deft touch of its chefs. Serving up an unusually wide variety of freshly caught seafood—spider crabs, monkfish, and octopus are just three favorites on the menu—it's important to note that all fishy mains are sold by the kilo, so prices can rise quickly. Be careful about getting too stuffed at the start of the meal: Diners are presented with an array of tempting appetizers and sometime overindulge. There is no more centrally located restaurant than this one, as it lies on the main street of town close to the beach. It is air-conditioned inside with breeze-cooled outdoor dining on its terrace.

Alameda dos Combatentes da Grande Guerra 104. ✆ **21/484-57-04.** www.luzmar.dcsa.pt. Reservations recommended. Main courses 18€–48€. Tues–Sun 12:30–4:30pm and 7pm–midnight.

Restaurante Visconde da Luz ★ PORTUGUESE/SEAFOOD A solid second-choice option if Luzmar is all booked up, this low-slung bungalow, with modernized Art Nouveau looks, is another seafood specialist. A meal might include fried sole, shellfish, pork with clams, seafood curry, or clams in garlic sauce, finished off with almond cake. Many choices are sold by the kilogram (2.2 lb.), a generous portion that can easily feed two… or three! Visconde da Luz is set at the edge of a park in the center of Cascais. The view encompasses rows of lime trees and towering sycamores where flocks of birds congregate at dusk (be warned if you're walking underneath).

In the Jardim Visconde da Luz. www.viscondedaluz.dcsa.pt. ✆ **21/484-74-10.** Reservations required. Main courses 16€–32€. Wed–Mon 12:30–4:30pm and 7pm–midnight.

MODERATE

Beira Mar Restaurante ★★ PORTUGUESE Cozy and crowded, with a terrace that spills onto a traffic-free plaza, this is one of the best restaurants in Cascais. Established in the 1950s with present management in place since 1973, it evokes a simple seafront tavern, except that the food and service are a lot better than that cliché might imply. Within sight of a well-scrubbed kitchen, you'll enjoy such menu items as a savory *sopa de marisco* (shellfish soup), filet of whitefish with shellfish rice, baked sea bass in a salt crust, or baked octopus with potatoes. In the season (summer) try the grilled sardines.

Rua das Flores 6. www.beiramarcascais.com. ✆ **21/482-73-80.** Reservations recommended. Main courses 15€–35€. Wed–Mon noon–4pm and 7pm–midnight.

INEXPENSIVE

B&B Restaurante ★★ PORTUGUESE No, the B&B in the name doesn't stand for bed-and-breakfast—rather for *bom* and *barato*, meaning good and cheap in Portuguese. The little eatery lives up to its name. One reader wrote that she would gladly have paid double for the meal she consumed here. The restaurant is run by an expat Frenchman who arrived in town some 30 years ago. The octopus always wins a rave from patrons; it's slowly cooked in the oven for about 2 hours before it's lightly grilled in olive oil and fresh herbs. For nonfish lovers, the steaks include the Brazilian *picanha*, a succulent beef cut. Pair it with a good Portuguese red wine from Alentejo.

Rua do Poço Novo. ✆ **21/482-06-86.** Reservations recommended. Main courses 12€–15€. No credit cards. Daily noon–3pm and 7–11pm.

Dom Manolo ★★ PORTUGUESE In the center of Cascais—in fact, on its main street—this Galician-operated restaurant is tops for grilled food. The kitchen dishes are reasonably priced, tasty, uncomplicated regional Portuguese fare. It attracts more local residents than foreign visitors. The perfectly cooked spit-roasted chicken, with french fries or a salad, is a favorite. Ask for extra piri-piri sauce if you like spicy food. Another good choices are the savory grilled sardines, but only during summer when they are in the season. For dessert, there's a velvety flan and crunchy almond tart.

Alameda dos Combatentes da Grande Guerra. ✆ **21/483-11-26.** Main courses 7€–18€. Daily 10am–11:30pm. Closed Jan.

Cascais After Dark

Baluarte Bar ★ Spacious, streamlined, and airy, this is the bar that many employees of local hotels and restaurants drop into when their workday is finished. It evokes the kind of hip, youth-oriented place that you might expect within the Bairro Alto of Lisbon, except that it occupies the street level of a condominium complex directly across the street from the town's most central beach, the Praia do Peixe. Although it's associated with a restaurant directly above it (Baía do Peixe), most clients come here just for a drink and a chat with their friends, and never actually climb the stairs for a meal. It's open daily from 4pm to 4am. Av. Don Carlos I, no. 6 (Marginal). ✆ **21/486-51-57**.

GUINCHO ★

6.5km (4 miles) N of Cascais; 9.5km (6 miles) N of Estoril

The word *guincho* is best translated as "caterwaul," the cry that swallows make while darting along the air currents over the wild sea. The swallows stay at Guincho year-round. Sometimes at night, the sea, driven into a frenzy, howls like a wailing banshee—and that, too, is *guincho.*

The area lies near the westernmost point on the European continent, known to the Portuguese as **Cabo da Roca ★**. The beaches are spacious and sandy, the sunshine is incandescent, and the nearby promontories, jutting into white-tipped Atlantic waves, are spectacular. Wooded hills back the windswept dunes; and to the east, the Serra de Sintra is silhouetted on the distant horizon.

Essentials

ARRIVING

BY BUS From the train station at Cascais, buses leave for the Praia do Guincho every hour. The trip takes 20 minutes.

BY CAR From Cascais, continue west along Route 247.

VISITOR INFORMATION

The nearest tourist office is in Cascais (p. 148).

Where to Stay

EXPENSIVE

Fortaleza do Guincho ★★★ This Relais & Châteaux hotel is one of the grandest and most prestigious properties in the region. It originated in the 17th-century within a few hundred feet of the westernmost point in Europe, when an army of stonecutters built one of the most forbidding fortresses along

TREACHEROUS BEACHES & seafood feasts

Praia do Guincho draws large beach crowds. However, the undertow is treacherous, so swim at your own risk and make sure to follow the lifeguards' recommendations (yellow and red flags mean no swimming).

Despite the danger, Praia do Guincho is popular with surfers and windsurfers. There's a surf school in Praia do Abano, **Moana Surf School** (http://moanasurf-school.com; ✆ **96/444-94-36**). Rates for private lessons start at 40€ for 1 hour or 130€ for 4 hours. This is also the beach with the popular **Bar do Guincho** (www.bardoguincho.pt; ✆ **21/487-16-83**), great for a snack or a full meal, except on Tuesday, when it's closed.

One of the primary reasons for coming to Guincho is to sample its seafood restaurants (see "Where to Dine," below). You can try the crayfish-size box-jaw lobsters known as *bruxas*, which in Portuguese means "sorcerer," "wizard," or "witch doctor." To eat like the Portuguese, you must also sample the goose-neck barnacles, called *percebes*. (Many foreign visitors fail to comprehend their appeal.) The fresh lobsters and crabs are cultivated in nearby shellfish beds, which are fascinating sights in themselves.

the coast. The twin towers that flank the vaguely Moorish facade still stand sentinel over a sun-bleached terrain of sand and rock.

The public rooms contain all the antique trappings of an aristocratic private home. In cold weather, a fire might blaze in a granite-framed fireplace, illuminating the thick carpets and the century-old furniture. Each small but luxuriously furnished guest room is behind a thick pine door heavily banded with iron under a vaulted stone ceiling. Most rooms overlook the savagely beautiful coastline. Some beds are set in alcoves. There are also three small but elegant suites, some with their own fireplace.

Estrada do Guincho. www.guinchotel.pt. ✆ **21/487-04-91.** 27 units. 130€–345€ double; 230€–415€ suite. Rates include buffet breakfast. Free parking. **Amenities:** Restaurant; bar; babysitting; bikes; room service. Free Wi-Fi.

MODERATE

Senhora da Guia ★★ After returning to their native Portugal following a sojourn in Brazil, the Ornelas family set their sights on restoring this former country villa of the Sagres brewery family to its former glory. Because of their efforts, it's now one of the loveliest hotels in the region. The 1970 house has thick walls, high ceilings, and elaborately crafted moldings that give the impression of a much older building. The elegant midsize guest rooms and suites contain reproductions of 18th-century Portuguese antiques, thick carpets, louvered shutters, and spacious modern bathrooms. The villa sits on a bluff above the sea, and the views are panoramic.

Estrada do Guincho. www.senhoradaguia.com. ✆ **21/486-92-39.** 41 units. 110€–245€ double; 280€–550€ suite. Rates include buffet breakfast. Free parking. **Amenities:** Restaurant; bar; airport transfers (60€); babysitting; bikes; exercise room; Jacuzzi; outdoor saltwater pool; room service; sauna. Free Wi-Fi.

Where to Dine

EXPENSIVE

Restaurant Fortaleza do Guincho ★★★ PORTUGUESE No other restaurant along the coast between Cascais and Guincho can compete with the sheer drama and majesty of this one. Set directly atop jagged rocks a few feet from the surf, it's part of what was once a military outpost for the Portuguese monarchs, built on this isolated site in the 17th century. In 2001, the restaurant was designated as a Relais & Châteaux establishment, thanks partly to its allegiance to the tenets of modern French cuisine. A disciple (Vincent Farges) of one of eastern France's most celebrated chefs (Antoine Westermann, owner of Buerehiesel, in Alsace) was installed as the hardworking director of the kitchens. Since then, the site has been acknowledged as the most gastronomically sophisticated in the region, with world-class cuisine and impeccable service. The chef now running the kitchen is Portuguese (a local from Cascais), Miguel Rocha Vieira. The restaurant has a Michelin star for his inspired work here. Menu items change with the seasons, but you'll likely encounter shellfish soup, cuttlefish, or black pig with a twist. If you can afford it, go for the tasting menu.

In the Fortaleza do Guincho hotel, Praia do Guincho. ✆ **21/487-04-91.** Reservations recommended. Main courses 30€–68€. Daily 12:30–3pm and 7–10:30pm.

MODERATE

Monte Mar ★★ PORTUGUESE/SEAFOOD One of the most appealing restaurants in the area occupies a seafront pavilion set above jagged rocks and a savagely beautiful landscape about 5km (3 miles) west of Cascais, beside the highway leading to Guincho. It contains two sun-flooded dining rooms separated by a busy, open kitchen. The entire structure is ringed with wide balconies. This has been a much-respected staple in Cascais for nearly a decade, thanks to an attentive staff and a policy of buying very fresh fish at least once (and usually twice) a day. Don't be fooled by what looks like a drainage ditch for storm water between the restaurant and the nearby sea. Beneath it are massive holding tanks that are likely to have contained some of the specialties that later appear at your table. If you're unsure of what to order, we recommend the sea bass or golden bream baked in a salt crust. Or, opt for the time-tested dish on which this place has built its reputation: deep-fried filets of hake served with tartar sauce and new potatoes or rice. Buttery and firm-fleshed, it's one of the most delicious—and artfully simple—dishes in the region. If you are in Lisbon, you'll recognize the name from the Mercado da Ribeira food court.

Oitavos, Estrada do Guincho. www.montemar.pt. ✆ **21/486-92-70.** Reservations recommended. Main courses 15€–55€. Tues–Sat noon–4pm and 7–11pm.

Porto de Santa Maria ★★★ PORTUGUESE/SEAFOOD Many drive out from Lisbon just to have a fish fest here. The genial staff serves every conceivable form of succulent shellfish, priced by the gram, as well as such house specialties as grilled sole. *Arroz de marisco* (shellfish rice) is the most popular specialty—and justifiably so—but don't miss the *percebes*, a pure taste of the sea. As in most restaurant, an appetizer will be put on your table that you pay for only if you eat it. Here it is rondelles of pungent and buttery sheep's-milk cheese. Don't resist! It's scrumptious.

Estrada do Guincho. www.portosantamaria.com. ✆ **21/487-10-36** or 21/487-02-40. Reservations recommended. Regular main courses 15€–33€. Tues–Sun 12:30–3:30pm and 7:30–10:30pm.

Restaurante Furnas do Guincho ★ PORTUGUESE/SEAFOOD In-the-know diners order the shellfish dishes here, as the fishing areas nearby produce some of the best catches along the coast. *Arroz de marisco* is a specialty, as well as the *cataplana* (a traditional pot that steams the food) with octopus and sweet potato. Service is efficient and most of the recipes are time-tested—meaning there's not a lot of experimentation here, but that doesn't matter much with food this fresh. The restaurant is on the road out of Cascais toward Guincho.

Estrada do Guincho (via Av. 25 de Abril). www.furnasdoguincho.pt. ✆ **21/486-92-43.** Reservations recommended. Main courses 15€–35€. Daily noon–4pm and 7:30–11pm.

QUELUZ

15km (9⅓ miles) NW of Lisbon

Queluz, only 20 minutes from Lisbon, makes a swell excursion from the capital or en route to Sintra. The Queluz Palace (see "Exploring the Palace," below), in its pink rococo glory, offers storybook Portuguese charm.

Essentials

ARRIVING

BY TRAIN From the Estação do Rossio in Lisbon, take the Sintra line to Queluz. Departures during the day are every 15 minutes. The trip takes 30 minutes. There are two train stations in town. Get off at Queluz-Massamá, as it is closer to the palace. A one-way ticket costs 1.50€. Call ✆ **80/820-82-08** for schedules. At Queluz, turn left and follow the signs for less than 1km (⅔ mile) to the palace. Or else take bus no. 101 or 103, both of which run in front of the palace.

BY CAR From Lisbon, head west along the express highway (A1), which becomes Route 249. Turn off at the exit for Queluz. It usually takes 20 minutes.

VISITOR INFORMATION

You can ask for information at the tourist office in Sintra (see below).

Where to Stay

Pousada D. Maria I ★★★ Uniquely located on the grounds of a palace, this is one of the gems of Portugal's network of pousadas. The building's function during the 17th century was to house the staff that maintained the Palace of Queluz, which rises in stately majesty across the road. The pousada

EXPLORING THE palace

Palácio Nacional de Queluz ★★ shimmers in the sunlight. It's a brilliant example of the rococo style in Portugal. Sadly, though, what you see is not original. Once the summer residence of King Pedro III, constructed between 1747 and 1787, it underwent two calamities. During the French invasions, the royal family fled to Brazil, bringing many of the palace's portable interior decorations with them. Then, in 1934, a fire destroyed a great deal of Queluz. Thankfully, tasteful and sensitive reconstruction has restored the lighthearted aura of the 18th century, and the work of original architect Mateus Vicente de Oliveira and French decorator-designer Jean-Baptiste Robillon (he was largely responsible for planning the garden and lakeside setting).

The gardens are especially lovely. Blossoming mauve petunias and red geraniums highlight the topiary effects, with closely trimmed vines and sculptured box hedges. Fountain pools on which lilies float are lined with blue tiles and reflect the muted facade, the statuary, and the finely cut balustrades.

Inside you can wander through the queen's dressing room, lined with painted panels depicting a children's romp; the Don Quixote Chamber (Dom Pedro was born here and returned from Brazil to die in the same bed); the Music Room, complete with a French *grande pianoforte* and an 18th-century English harpsichord; and the mirrored throne room adorned with crystal chandeliers. The Portuguese still hold state banquets here.

Festooning the palace are all the eclectic props of the rococo era. You'll see the inevitable chinoiserie panels from Macau, Florentine marbles from quarries that also supplied Michelangelo, Iberian and Flemish tapestries, Empire antiques, Delft indigo-blue ceramics, 18th-century Hepplewhite armchairs, Austrian porcelains, Rabat carpets, Portuguese Chippendale furnishings, and Brazilian jacaranda wood pieces—all of exquisite quality. When they visited Portugal, presidents Eisenhower, Carter, and Reagan stayed in the 30-chambered Pavilion of Dona Maria I, as did Elizabeth II and the Prince and Princess of Wales. These fabled chambers are said to have reverberated with the rantings of the grief-stricken monarch Maria I, who reputedly had to be strapped to her bed at times. Before becoming mentally ill, she was an intelligent, brave woman who did a great job as ruler of her country in a troubled time.

Largo do Palácio, 2745-191, Queluz. www.pnqueluz.imc-ip.pt. ✆ **21/434-38-60.** On the highway from Lisbon to Sintra, the palace is open Wed–Mon 9am–5pm. Closed on holidays. Admission 7€, free for children under 14.

is graced with an ornate clock tower that evokes an oversize ornament in the garden of a stately English home. In addition to the pousada's comfortable midsize guest rooms (high-ceilinged and severely dignified with fine beds and neatly kept bathrooms) and well-managed dining room, the premises contain touches of complicated Manueline stonework. The 17th-century theater holds occasional concerts.

Largo do Palácio, Queluz. www.pousadas.pt. ✆ **800/223-1356** for reservations in the U.S., or 21/435-61-58. 26 units. 88€–215€ double; 127€–230€ suite. Rates include buffet breakfast. Free parking. From Sintra, take Hwy. IC-19 and follow signs to Queluz. **Amenities:** Restaurant; bar; exercise room; room service. Free Wi-Fi in some rooms and public areas.

Where to Dine

Cozinha Velha (The Old Kitchen) ★★★ INTERNATIONAL/PORTUGUESE This was originally the kitchen of the palace, built in the grand style; it has since been converted into a colorful dining room favored by those seeking a gourmet dinner in a romantic setting.

The dining room is like a small chapel, with high stone arches, a free-standing fireplace, and marble columns. Along one side is a 6m (20-ft.) marble table laden with baskets of fruit and vases of flowers. You sit on ladder-back chairs surrounded by shiny copper, oil paintings, and torchieres. The innovative handling of regional ingredients pleases most diners, and the cooking uses spices, herbs, and textures well. We recommend the *petiscos*, such as the cod fritters or the tempura green beans, followed by a main course such as black grouper medallions with prawn béchamel, poached sole Cozinha Velha, fried goat with mashed turnip sprouts, or pepper steak with spinach mousse. For dessert, the classic choice here is the convent pastries—though non-Portuguese diners often find them too sweet.

In the Pousada D. Maria, Largo do Palácio. ✆ **21/435-02-32.** Reservations recommended. Main courses 18€–26€. Daily 12:30–3pm and 7:30–10pm.

SINTRA: BYRON'S "GLORIOUS EDEN" ★★★

29km (18 miles) NW of Lisbon

Writers have sung Sintra's praises ever since Portugal's national poet, Luís Vaz de Camões, proclaimed its glory in *Os Lusíadas* (The Lusiads). Lord Byron called it "glorious Eden" when he and John Cam Hobhouse included Sintra in their 1809 grand tour. English romantics thrilled to its description in Byron's autobiographical *Childe Harold's Pilgrimage.*

Picture a town on a hillside, with decaying birthday-cake villas covered with tiles coming loose in the damp mist. Luxuriant vegetation covers the town: camellias for melancholic romantics, ferns behind which lizards dart, pink and purple bougainvillea over garden trelliswork, red geraniums on wrought-iron balconies, eucalyptus branches fluttering in the wind, lemon groves, and honey-sweet mimosa scenting the air. But take heed—some who visit Sintra fall under its spell and stay forever.

Sintra is one of the oldest towns in Portugal. When crusaders captured it in 1147, they fought bitterly against the Moors firmly entrenched in their hilltop castle, the ruins of which remain today. Benefiting from a micro-climate, its humidity made way to a lush forest and vegetation. Sintra became a UNESCO World Heritage Site in 1995, the first in Europe chosen for its cultural landscape.

Essentials

ARRIVING

BY TRAIN Sintra is a 45-minute ride from the Estação do Rossio at the Rossio in Lisbon. A train leaves every 10 to 20 minutes. The round-trip fare is 3.80€. For info: www.cp.pt.

BY BUS The bus from Lisbon is not recommended because service is too slow. Visitors staying on the Costa do Estoril can make bus connections at Cascais or Estoril. The Sintra depot is on Avenida Dr. Miguel Bombarda, across from the main train station. Departures from in front of the Estoril rail station are every 45 minutes during the day. A one-way ticket costs 4€, and the trip takes 40 minutes. Eleven buses a day run between Sintra and Cascais. The journey takes 1 hour, and the round-trip fare is 4€. Once you're in Sintra, you can take bus no. 434, which traverses the tourist loop year-round, costing 4.50€ one-way. Departures are every half-hour during weekdays, more frequently as demand dictates on Saturday and Sunday. From the train station in the heart of Sintra, the bus goes up to Castelo dos Mouros and on to Pena Palace. A schedule is posted at the tourist information booth in the train station.

BY CAR From Lisbon, take the A5 and then exit to Sintra and follow the directions to Sintra to IC 19.

VISITOR INFORMATION

The tourist office, **Sintra Câmara Municipal,** is at Praça da República 23 (www.cm-sintra.pt; ✆ **21/923-11-57**). It's open daily 9am to 7pm from October to May, and daily 9am to 8pm from June to September.

SPECIAL EVENTS

From later May to early July, the **Sintra Festival** (www.festivaldesintra.pt; ✆ **21/910-71-17**) attracts many music lovers. The program consists entirely of a piano repertoire from the Romantic period, with the best interpreters from today's international music scene. The concerts, about eight in all, usually take place in the region's churches, palaces (Palácio da Vila, Palácio da Pena, and Palácio de Queluz), parks, and country estates. Each concert costs 15€ to 30€, depending on the event. The tourist office (see "Visitor Information," above) will furnish details.

Exploring Sintra

PALACES, CASTLES & CONVENTS

You can take an organized tour of Sintra out of Lisbon (or book one within Sintra itself), but this approach allows no time for personal discovery, a must in Sintra.

Horse-drawn carriages are available for rent between the town and Serra de Sintra. The 45-minute tour costs 30€ to 75€ for up to five passengers. It's well worth the price for an agreeable trip under the shady trees. The carriages start from and return to the large square in front of the National Palace of Sintra.

Sintra

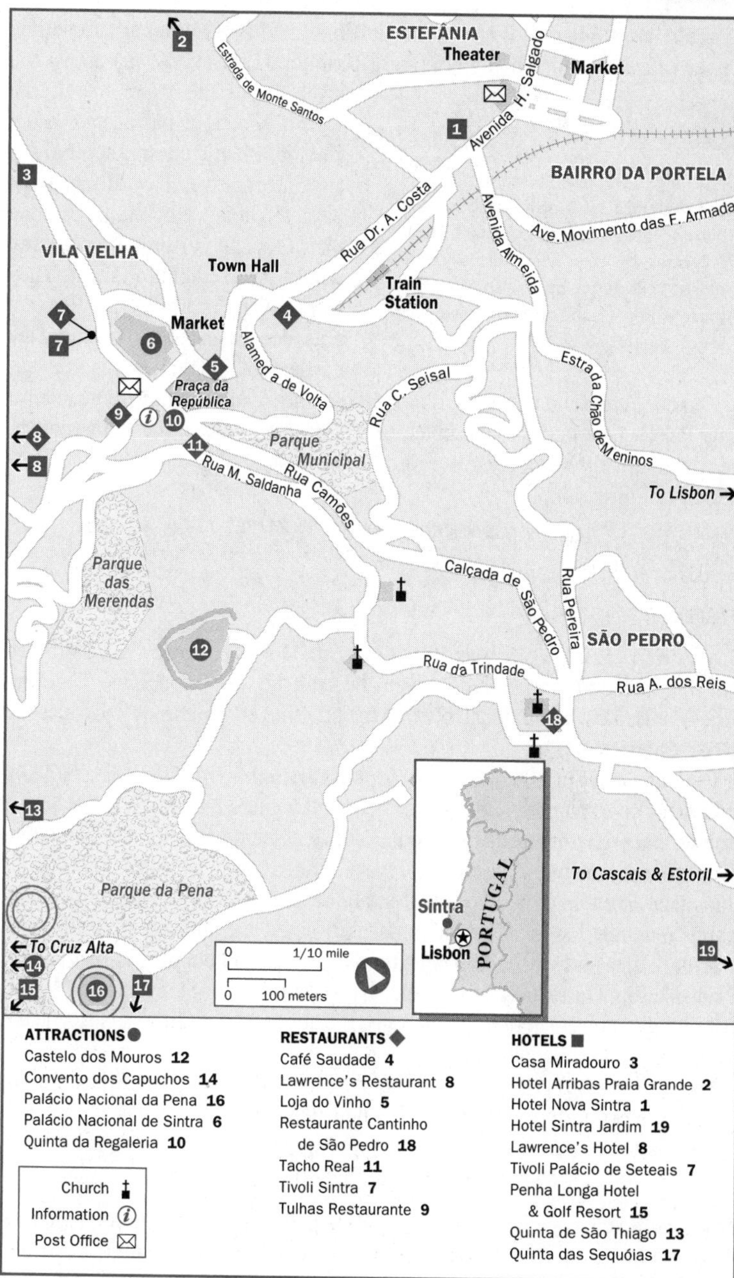
ESTEFÂNIA
Theater
Market
Estrada de Monte Santos
Avenida H. Salgado
BAIRRO DA PORTELA
Ave. Movimento das F. Armadas
Rua Dr. A. Costa
Avenida Almeida
VILA VELHA
Town Hall
Train Station
Market
Alameda de Volta
Praça da República
Rua C. Seisal
Estrada Chão de Meninos
Parque Municipal
Rua M. Saldanha
Rua Camões
To Lisbon
Parque das Merendas
Calçada de São Pedro
Rua Pereira
SÃO PEDRO
Rua da Trindade
Rua A. dos Reis
To Cascais & Estoril
Parque da Pena
To Cruz Alta
0 1/10 mile
0 100 meters
Sintra
Lisbon
PORTUGAL
ATTRACTIONS
Castelo dos Mouros 12
Convento dos Capuchos 14
Palácio Nacional da Pena 16
Palácio Nacional de Sintra 6
Quinta da Regaleria 10
Church
Information
Post Office
RESTAURANTS
Café Saudade 4
Lawrence's Restaurant 8
Loja do Vinho 5
Restaurante Cantinho de São Pedro 18
Tacho Real 11
Tivoli Sintra 7
Tulhas Restaurante 9
HOTELS
Casa Miradouro 3
Hotel Arribas Praia Grande 2
Hotel Nova Sintra 1
Hotel Sintra Jardim 19
Lawrence's Hotel 8
Tivoli Palácio de Seteais 7
Penha Longa Hotel & Golf Resort 15
Quinta de São Thiago 13
Quinta das Sequóias 17

If you arrive in Sintra by train, you'll have to either take a taxi to the sights or trek up the long, lush hill to the Pena Palace—a very long walk.

Castelo dos Mouros ★★ The Castle of the Moors was built sometime between the 8th and 9th centuries in a position 412m (1,352 ft.) above sea level. From the royal tower, the view of Sintra, its palace and castle, and the Atlantic coast is stunning—and informative. The Moors must have felt that, with the panoramic views this site afforded, no enemy would ever be able to take it. They were wrong. In 1147, Scandinavian crusaders besieged and captured the castle, not long after Lisbon was also taken. Ferdinand of Saxe-Coburg-Gotha, the royal consort responsible for Pena Palace (see below), attempted to restore the castle in the 19th century. He was relatively unsuccessful. From the parking area, a guide will send you in the right direction.

Crime Watch

Warning: Don't leave valuables in unguarded cars in Sintra, and beware of pickpockets and purse-snatchers. Not only does the town attract virtually every tourist in Portugal, but it also attracts those who prey on them. While violence is not generally a problem, theft is.

Calçada dos Clérigos. www.parquesdesintra.pt. ✆ **21/923-73-00.** Admission 6.50€ adults, 5€ seniors and children 6–17, free for children under 6 (small discount for booking ahead online). Oct 16–Mar Tues–Sun 10am–6pm; Apr–Oct 15 Tues–Sun 10am–6:30pm. From Pena Palace (10-min. walk), follow signs to the castelo.

Convento dos Capuchos ★★ In 1560, Dom Álvaro de Castro ordered that this unusually structured convent be built for the Capuchins. The construction used cork so extensively that the building is sometimes known as the cork monastery.

The convent is in a secluded area 7.3km (4½ miles) from Sintra. You walk up a moss-covered path and ring the bell, and a guide will come to show you around the miniature cells. Today the convent seems forlorn and forgotten. Even when it was in use, it probably wasn't noted for its liveliness. The Capuchins who lived here, perhaps eight in all, had a penchant for the most painstakingly detailed work. For example, they lined the monastery walls with cork-bark tiles and seashells. They also carved a chapel out of rock, using cork for insulation. Outside there's an altar fresco in honor of St. Francis of Assisi. In 1834, the monks suddenly abandoned the convent, most likely to escape the crowded, primitive conditions.

There's no bus service; if you're not driving, take a taxi from Sintra's main square. It's certainly worth seeing this unusual convent.

Estrada de Pena. www.parquesdesintra.pt. ✆ **21/923-73-00.** Admission 5€. Oct 16–Mar Tues–Sun 10am–6pm; Apr–Oct 15 Tues–Sun 10am–6:30pm.

Palácio Nacional da Pena ★★ Pena perches above Sintra on a plateau about 450m (1,476 ft.) above sea level. Part of the fun of visiting the castle is the ride up the verdant, winding road through the Parque das Merendas.

The inspiration behind this castle in the sky was Ferdinand of Saxe-Coburg-Gotha, the husband of Maria II. Ferdinand called on a fellow German, Baron

Eschwege, to help him build his fantasy. You can see a sculpture of the baron if you look out from the Pena toward a huge rock across the way. The palace's last royal occupant was Queen Amélia, who left in 1910, when it was clear that the monarchy in Portugal was ending. Having lost her husband and her soldier-son to an assassin 2 years before, she was determined not to lose her second son, Manuel II. Gathering her most precious possessions, she fled to Mafra, where her son waited. She did not see the Pena Palace again until 1945, when she returned to Portugal under much more favorable conditions. Pena has remained much as Amélia left it, making it a rare record of European royal life in the halcyon days preceding World War I.

In the early–16th century, King Manuel ordered a monastery for the Jerónimos monks built on these lofty grounds, and you can visit the preserved cloister and small oval chapel today.

Pena Park was designed and planted for more than 4 years, beginning in 1846. Ferdinand was the force behind the landscaping. He built one of the most spectacular parks in Portugal, known for the scope of its shrub and tree life. Admission to the park is included in the price of a ticket for entrance to the palace. A little carriage service inside the gate of the palace will take you up the steep hill to the palace for 2€ each way.

Estrada de Pena. www.parquesdesintra.pt. ✆ **21/910-53-40.** Admission 11.50€, 9€ children 6–17 and seniors, free for children 5 and under. Oct 16–Mar Tues–Sun 10am–6pm; Apr–Oct 15 Tues–Sun 10am–6:30pm.

Palácio Nacional de Sintra ★★★ A royal palace until 1910, the Sintra National Palace was last inhabited by Queen Maria Pia, the Italian grandmother of Manuel II, the last king of Portugal. Much of the palace was constructed in the days of the first Manuel, the Fortunate (b. 1469–d. 1521), making it the only palace in Portugal first established in the medieval era. Long before the arrival of the crusaders under Afonso Henríques, this was a summer palace of Moorish sultans. The original palace was torn down in 1863, and Moorish-style architecture was incorporated into latter-day versions.

The structure is now a conglomeration of styles, with Gothic and Manueline predominant. The glazed earthenware tiles lining many of the chambers are among the most beautiful in Portugal, but some of the chambers stand out for other reasons. The Swan Room was a favorite of João I, one of the founding kings of Portugal, father of Henry the Navigator; its swan-painted ceiling is exquisite. The Heraldic or Stag Room has a majestic domed wood coffered ceiling, and holds 72 coats of arms of the royal family and aristocratic Portuguese families—or once did. The Tavora family coat of arms was removed after they were accused of conspiring to dethrone Joseph I. The Room of the Sirens (or Mermaids) is a study in elegance. Tile-fronted stoves are in the Old Kitchen, where feasts were held in bygone days.

The palace is also rich in paintings and Iberian and Flemish tapestries, but many find it difficult to pull their eyes from the views: In most of the rooms, wide windows look out onto the sweep of the Sintra mountain range.

As you approach the palace, you can buy a ticket at the kiosk on your left. The palace opens onto the central town square. Outside, two conical chimney towers form the most distinctive landmark on the Sintra skyline. The walk from the train station at Sintra to the national palace takes about 10 minutes. After leaving the station, take a left and follow the road.

Largo da Rainha Dona Amélia. www.parquesdesintra.pt. ✆ **21/910-68-40.** Admission 8.50€ adults, 7€ ages 15–25, free for children under 14; free admission on Sun and some holidays. Thurs–Tues 9:30am–5:30pm.

Quinta da Regaleira ★★★ A UNESCO World Heritage Site, this quinta (manor house) in the old quarter was built at the turn of the 20th century. It incorporates architectural elements of the Gothic, Manueline, and Renaissance styles. When you tour the property, you'll see its antiques and artifacts, but, more interesting may be hearing about the owner, a Brazilian mining mogul who was obsessed with the Knights Templar and Freemasonry. Many of the elements in the house and garden are linked to those interests, including the bizarre 100-ft.-deep "initiation well" (an upside-down, underground tower). The building's turrets afford panoramic views.

Rua Visconde de Monserrate. www.regaleira.pt. ✆ **21/910-66-50.** Admission with tour guide 12€ adults, 8€ children 6–17, 3.50€ for children under 8; without tour guide 6€ adults. Daily 10:30am–5:30pm.

SHOPPING

History-rich Sintra has been a repository of salable Portuguese charm since the dawn of modern tourism. As you wander through its cobblestone streets and alleyways, you'll find many intriguing outlets for handmade folk art from the region and the rest of Portugal.

The best shops include **A Esquina,** Praça da República 20 (✆ **21/923-34-27**). It carries many hand-painted ceramics, some of which are reproductions of designs that originated between the 15th and 18th centuries. **Almorávida,** Rua Visconde de Monserrate 12–14 (✆ **21/924-05-39**), in front of Sintra Palace, sells Arraiolos carpets, lace, and intricately hammered copperware. A worthy antiques shop close to the town center, **Henrique Teixeira,** Rua Consigliéri Pedroso 2 (✆ **21/923-10-43**) specializes in sometimes dauntingly expensive furniture and accessories, including an exceptional collection of antique brass and bronze hardware. If you have the time to explore, head to the nearby **S. Pedro de Sintra** for its antiques shops, usually less expensive than Sintra.

Casa Branca, Rua Consigliéri Pedroso 12 (www.casabranca.gruposilva-carvalho.com; ✆ **21/923-05-28**), is *the* shop for linens. Recent clients have included former U.S. Secretary of State Madeleine Albright, who binge-shopped here for what we were told was more than 30,000€ worth of bed- and tableware. Inventories include the amazing embroideries from Madeira, the Azores, and the north of Portugal. Nightdresses and negligees, some of them with rich embroideries on silk or cotton, are particularly beautiful. **Violeta,** Rua das Padarias 19 (✆ **21/923-40-95**), also stocks hand-embroidered linen tablecloths, towels, sheets, and bedspreads, but isn't quite as dazzling.

Where to Stay

EXPENSIVE

Penha Longa Hotel & Golf Resort ★★★ This is the grandest resort in the Sintra area, especially for golfers, offering two world-class courses designed by Robert Trent Jones, Jr. Its recreational facilities beat the rest, too, thanks to its pools, tennis courts, and children's facilities. Before it became a grand hotel, the site was a retreat of royalty since the 14th century, and it still has a landmark monastery on the grounds. The present building is a graceful palazzo-style structure set among the rolling hills, clear lakes, and lush gardens of the southern tier of the Sintra mountains.

The elegant guest rooms have large marble bathrooms and private balconies opening onto panoramic views. Amenities run the gamut from Bulgari bath products and plush bathrobes to espresso coffee machines. Five gourmet restaurants and the best spa in the area are just part of its many attractions.

Estrada da Lagoa Azul-Malveira. www.penhalonga.com. ✆ **21/924-90-11.** 194 units. 160€–255€ double; 300€–1,500€ suite. Free parking. **Amenities:** 5 restaurants; 4 bars; babysitting; children's center; concierge; exercise room; 2 golf courses; 2 freshwater pools (indoor and outdoor); room service; spa; 4 outdoor tennis courts (lit). Free Wi-Fi.

Tivoli Palácio de Seteais ★★★ This is one of the most luxe palaces to stay in all of Portugal and advance reservations are a must. Seteais looks older than it is—a Dutch Gildemeester built it in the late 18th century. The fifth marquês de Marialva, who sponsored many receptions for the aristocrats of his day, later took over and restored the palace. Lord Byron worked on *Childe Harold's Pilgrimage* in the front garden before it became a hotel.

The hotel lies at the end of a long driveway; squint and it looks like the scenery from a ballet (it's *that* romantic looking). An arched entryway dominates the formal stone architecture. The palace is on the crest of a hill; most of its drawing rooms, galleries, and chambers overlook the formal terraces, flower garden, and vista toward the sea. A long hall and a staircase with white-and-gilt balustrades and columns lead to the lower-level dining room, drinking lounge, and garden terraces. The library and adjoining music room are furnished with period pieces and amazing chandeliers. The main drawing room contains antiques and a fine mural extending around the cove and onto the ceiling. The glamorous and spacious guest rooms are furnished with antiques and old style on the paintings on the walls. ***Tip:*** If you'd like to stay here but are appalled by the price, know that there are some smaller, less glitzy rooms that are quite reasonable in price. Ask. We'd also recommending dining and tippling elsewhere: The restaurant and bar need improvements in their offerings.

Rua Barbosa do Bocage 8, Seteais. www.tivolihotels.com. ✆ **21/923-32-00.** 30 units. 150€–680€ double. Rates include buffet breakfast. Free parking. **Amenities:** Restaurant; bar; babysitting; bikes; outdoor freshwater pool; room service; outdoor tennis court (lit). Free Wi-Fi.

MODERATE

Lawrence's Hotel ★★ Lawrence's Hotel boasts a pedigree that's older than that of any other hotel in Iberia. It originated in the 1760s, when an eccentric but formidable English innkeeper (Jane Lawrence) established the hotel. Its fortunes were assured in 1809, when Lord Byron stayed here for a 12-day visit and publicized the virtues of Sintra and the hotel in his writings. After millions of dollars of expenditures, the hotel is now one of the most desirable inns in Portugal. It occupies a low-slung yellow building a short walk uphill from the center of town, on the road that leads to the Pena Palace. Because of the sloping terrain on which it sits, you enter from the street onto the third floor of a six-story building with an elegant, completely unglitzy decor and the most recent in electronics and security devices. Bedrooms are airily furnished with tasteful replicas of 19th-century furniture in a spirit that emulates a discreetly upscale private home. Some units have private terraces. Enjoy some port wine in the cozy bar.

Rua Consigliéri Pedroso 38–40. www.lawrenceshotel.com. ✆ **21/910-55-00.** 16 units. 100€–174€ double; 190€–264€ suite. Rates include buffet breakfast. **Amenities:** Restaurant; bar; babysitting. Free Wi-Fi.

Quinta das Sequóias ★★ Standing on 16 hectares (40 acres) of wooded grounds, this beautiful 19th-century manor house lies less than 1km (⅔ mile) below the Tivoli Palácio de Seteais (see above). The manor house was originally built as a rural annex of a much larger palace (the Palácio do Relógio) in Sintra's center. The generally expansive rooms have high ceilings and formal 19th-century furniture. On the premises is a verdant English-style garden. Within a 16km (10-mile) walk from the main house are an archaeological dig, where Roman coins and artifacts from the Bronze Age have been unearthed, and bubbling springs whose pure waters were noted by historians during the 15th century.

Estrada de Montserrate, Casa da Tapada. ✆ **21/923-03-42.** 5 units. 130€–170€ double. Rates include buffet breakfast. Closed Oct 31–Mar 31. From Sintra, take the road signposted for Montserrat and then fork left at signpost for hotel. **Amenities:** Bar; outdoor pool; room service; sauna. Free Wi-Fi.

Quinta de São Thiago ★ Quinta de São Thiago is smaller and more intimate than Tivoli Palace, and certainly not as grand as Lawrence's Hotel, but like those two hotels, it too was visited by Byron. In many ways, it also offers a more authentic experience of what a quinta (manor house) looked like in another century. Reached by a rough road, it edges up the side of a mountain in a woodland setting. Its origins as a quinta go back to the 1500s, but it's now refurbished and decked out with well-maintained antiques (except for the plumbing; that's contemporary). Many of the units open onto views of the valley of Colares and the water beyond. The pool offers views of Monserrate and the Atlantic coastline.

In the finest British tradition, tea is offered in the parlor, which was transformed from the original kitchen. Dances are held in summer in the music room, as well as summertime buffets.

Estrada de Monserrate, 2710-610 Sintra. ✆ **21/923-29-23.** 9 units. 80€–115€ double; 130€–145€ suite. Rates include buffet breakfast. Free parking. **Amenities:** Bar; outdoor pool; outdoor tennis court. Free Wi-Fi.

INEXPENSIVE

Casa Miradouro ★★ At the edge of Sintra, this candy-striped house is a snug, cozy retreat. From its 1894 construction until 1987, it belonged to several generations of a family that included important figures in the Portuguese army. It's now a well-managed, attractively indulgent B&B. About .5km (1/3 mile) north of Sintra, it boasts a small garden, very few amenities other than the owner's genteel goodwill, and a facade that art historians have defined as Iberian chalet style. The excellently maintained rooms are most inviting, with provincial carpets, tile floors, and wrought-iron bedsteads. Views from upper-floor rooms include the Pena Palace and, on clear days, the faraway Atlantic.

Rua Sotto Mayor 55. www.casa-miradouro.com. ✆ **21/910-71-00.** 6 units. 85€–135€ double. Rates include buffet breakfast. Closed Jan 8–Feb 24. From the Tivoli Sintra (see above), take Rua Sotto Mayor for .4km (1/4 mile). **Amenities:** Bar; babysitting. Free Wi-Fi.

Hotel Arribas ★ One of Holtel Arribas' biggest assets is its location over the Atlantic-washed cliffs at the top of Praia Grande—it's one of the best beaches in the surroundings of Lisbon. If you don't want to walk to the beach, you can always use the hotel's saltwater swimming pool, spacious and safer for children, as currents here are strong and tricky. The panoramic restaurant serves good cuisine, featuring traditional Portuguese specialties. Rooms are well-maintained and good-sized, if lacking in character (think tile floors, mass-produced furnishings, and lot of beiges, with a bit of color here and there).

Praia Grande, Av. Alfredo Coelho, www.hotelarribas.com. ✆ **21/928-90-50.** 58 units. 60€–132€ double; 76€–176€ triple. **Amenities:** Restaurant; 2 bars; outdoor saltwater pool; room service.

Hotel Nova Sintra ★★ Rising like a private villa, this restored pension from 1875 stands in a satellite of Sintra known as Estefânia, right on the outskirts of town. When the little inn was restored and opened to receive guests, the 19th-century architectural features were maintained. The atmosphere is heavily laced with tradition, from the choice of furniture to the welcome. Umbrella-shaded tables and chairs are placed outside in fair weather.

Largo Afonso de Albuquerque 25, Estefânia. www.novasintra.com. ✆ **21/923-02-20.** 9 units. 70€–95€ double. **Amenities:** Restaurant; bar; babysitting; free parking. Free Wi-Fi.

Hotel Sintra Jardim ★ In São Pedro, a verdant suburb of Sintra, this 1850s stone house was commissioned by its former occupant, Viscount Tojal. Shortly after World War II, the German-born parents of the present owner, Susana Rosner Fragoso, bought the house and transformed it into a dignified *pensão* (boardinghouse). Surrounded by a spacious garden with venerable trees, the pastel-colored large rooms contain older but still comfortable furniture.

Travessa dos Avelares 12. ✆ **21/923-07-38.** 15 units. 60€–110€ double. Rates include buffet breakfast. From Sintra, take a bus marked SÃO PEDRO or MIRA-SINTRA. **Amenities:** Bar; outdoor pool; room service. Free Wi-Fi.

Where to Dine

MODERATE

Lawrence's Restaurant ★ INTERNATIONAL/PORTUGUESE The owners of this restaurant describe it as the main focus of the hotel that houses it, occupying more of their attention than the hotel itself. Outfitted in a tasteful interpretation of a late-19th-century decor, it has welcomed the most celebrated of diners—presidents, statesmen, diplomats, and actors—all of whom have appreciated the solidly tasty cuisine and graceful service. The menu changes frequently, but it's likely to include a sophisticated version of fish soup; black tagliolini with grilled octopus, squid ink, and fresh sweet basil; house-style codfish; and grilled filet of sea bass with a comfit of leeks. For a meaty meal, we like the roasted spit of both venison and white veal, and a roasted magret of duck served with Rösti potatoes and wild berry sauce.

In Lawrence's Hotel, Rua Consigliéri Pedroso 38–40. http://lawrenceshotel.com. ✆ **21/910-55-00.** Reservations recommended. Main courses 15€–28€. Daily 12:30–3pm and 7:30–10pm.

Restaurante Cantinho de São Pedro ★ FRENCH/PORTUGUESE Less than 2km (1¼ miles) southeast of Sintra, in São Pedro de Sintra, this is the place to chow down in this charming hillside village. It's right off the main square, Praça Dom Fernando II, where the *Feira da Sintra* (Sintra Fair) is staged every second and fourth Sunday of the month. Dating from the time of the Christian Reconquest, the fair is one of the oldest in the country. Best bet, as it's based on what's freshest at the market, will be the *pratos do dia* (daily specials), but if those don't entice, we can vouch for the velvety crepes stuffed with fresh lobster or the tender beefsteak in green-pepper sauce. For something very Portuguese, try the pork with clams in the style of Alentejo region.

Praça Dom Fernando II 18 (at Lojas do Picadeiro). www.cantinhosaopedro.com. ✆ **21/923-02-67.** Reservations recommended. Main courses 12€–20€. Daily noon–3pm and 7:30–10pm.

Tacho Real ★★ FRENCH/PORTUGUESE Yes, it's a hike to get to Tacho Real. It's set at the top of a steep flight of cobblestone steps and ramps that lead uphill (you'll huff-and-puff your way from the Praça da República below). But the reward is charm in abundance, from the kindly staff to this picture-perfect little tavern-style restaurant with its curved stone ceiling, white tablecloths, and flower-laden terrace. The kitchen deftly handles both fish and meat dishes; two popular house specialties are fish filet with shrimp sauce and rice, and filet steak with cream sauce and mushrooms. We're partial, however, to the bubbling fish stew and the sea bass with almonds. We know many Lisboans who come in from the city just to enjoy the well-prepared meals here.

Rua da Ferraria 4. ✆ **21/923-52-77.** Reservations recommended. Main courses 11€–30€. Thurs–Tues noon–3pm and 7:30–10:30pm.

Tivoli Sintra ★ INTERNATIONAL/PORTUGUESE Because this restaurant is within the concrete-and-glass walls of a hotel, many visitors might overlook the Tivoli Sintra as a dining spot. That would be a shame—it serves some of the finest food in town. The daily menu is likely to include such carefully crafted dishes as tournedos Rossini, fish soup, and filet of turbot with mushrooms and garlic. Staffed by a battalion of uniformed and friendly waiters, the room has a shimmering metallic ceiling, dark paneling, and floor-to-ceiling windows on one side.

Praça da República. ✆ **21/923-72-00.** Reservations recommended. Main courses 15€–29€. Daily 12:30–3pm and 7:30–10pm.

INEXPENSIVE

Café Saudade ★★★ CAFE Romance is in the air at the adorable cafe, with its hip flea-market decor and incredibly charming staff. It's the perfect spot for breakfast (try the "Saudade": condensed milk with two shots of espresso sided by a pastry), but lunch is pretty darn good, too. No, Saudade doesn't have ultra-gourmet fare, but the bread for the sandwiches will have been baked that morning and the salad ingredients likely plucked from the ground at the same time. The cafe, surprisingly, also has a smart wine list, making it the perfect place for a late-afternoon tipple after a long day of sightseeing. By the way, "Saudade" means a deep state of nostalgia, something we feel when writing about this lovely place.

Av. Miguel Bombarda, 6. http://saudade.pt. ✆ **21/242-88-04.** Main courses 6€–14€. Brunch: 16€. Daily 8:30–8pm.

Loja do Vinho ★★ CAFE/WINE BAR Set directly on the town's main square, this establishment combines aspects of both a restaurant and a wine shop. For your tipple, you can browse the extensive shelves with an inventory of wine and port from throughout the country. If you're hungry, you can sit at any of several low-slung tables and enjoy wine by the glass with some simple snacks. These might include a selection of Portuguese cheese, sausages, olives, or smoked ham. Overall, a visit here is a fine way to acquaint yourself with unusual Portuguese wines in a setting that evokes a medieval wine cellar.

Praça da República 3. ✆ **21/924-44-10.** Snacks, platters, and sandwiches 8€–21€. Daily 9am–10:30pm.

Tulhas Restaurant ★ PORTUGUESE Another budget gem, decorated with tiles and wood, and conveniently located between the tourism office and San Martin Church. Specialties of the house are codfish in cream sauce with potatoes, roasted lamb or duck with rice, and veal Madeira. Head here if you want well-prepared traditional meals, and aren't expecting creativity.

Gil Vicente 4. ✆ **21/923-23-78.** Main courses 10€–22€. Thurs–Tues noon–3:30pm and 7:30–10pm.

Sintra After Dark

Sintra is not a party town; at night it's a veritable ghost town and the most intriguing soirees are private. However, there is a genial bar in the center of town, where you might meet people from any country in Europe. It's called

Adega das Caves, Praça da República 2–10 (✆ **21/923-08-48**) and is a lunch restaurant that mellows into a likable bar and bodega after dark, specializing in beer and Portuguese wine. It's open every day until around 2am. A nearby competitor is the **Taverna dos Trovadores,** Largo D. Fernando II, São Pedro (www.taverna-trovadores.com; ✆ **21/923-35-48**), which lies in the center of the tiny hamlet of São Pedro, less than 2km (1¼ miles) south from the center of Sintra. Popular and convivial, it incorporates aspects of an old-fashioned *tasca* (tavern) with a modern singles bar, and features recorded and (on rare occasions) live music, a long drink list, and a cross section of residents from throughout the region.

ERICEIRA ★

21km (13 miles) NW of Sintra; 50km (31 miles) NW of Lisbon

This fishing port is nestled on the Atlantic shore. Whitewashed houses accented with pastel-painted corners and window frames line its narrow streets. To the east rise the mountains of Sintra.

The sea gives life to Ericeira, as it has for some 700 years. Fishermen still pluck their food from it. The beach lures streams of visitors every summer, giving a much-needed boost to the local economy. Along the coast, cliffside nurseries called *serrações* breed lobsters (these crustaceans are the house specialty at every restaurant in town).

In 1584, Mateus Álvares arrived in Ericeira from the Azores, claiming to be King Sebastião, who had reportedly been killed on the battlefields of North Africa. Álvares and about two dozen of his chief supporters were executed after their defeat by the soldiers of Philip II of Spain, but today he is regarded as the king of Ericeira. In October 1910, the fleeing Manuel II and his mother, Amélia, set sail from the Ericeira harbor to a life of exile in England.

The crescent-shaped, sandy **Praia do Sol,** the favorite beach of Portuguese and foreign visitors, attracts many travelers here. There are three other good beaches: **Ribeira Beach, North Beach,** and **St. Sebastian Beach.** All are suitable for swimming, unlike the beaches at Estoril and Cascais.

Essentials

ARRIVING

There is no direct rail service to Ericeira.

BY BUS **Mafrense buses** (www.mafrense.pt) from both Sintra and Lisbon serve Ericeira. One bus per hour leaves Lisbon's Campo Grande Station for the 1¼-hour trip. A one-way ticket costs 6.50€. From Sintra, there's one bus per hour. The trip takes 1 hour and costs 3.80€ one-way.

BY CAR From Sintra (p. 161), continue northwest along Route 247.

VISITOR INFORMATION

The **Ericeira Tourist Office** is at Rua Mendes Leal (✆ **26/186-31-22;** www.ericeira.net). It's open daily 9:30am to 7pm and Saturday 9:30am to 10pm.

Exploring the Area

Palácio Nacional de Mafra ★★★ This palace is a work of extraordinary discipline, grandeur, and majesty. At the peak of its 13-year construction, it reputedly employed 50,000; a small town was built just to house the workers. Its model was El Escorial, the Daedalian maze constructed by Philip II outside Madrid. Mafra's might not be as impressive or as labyrinthine, but the diversity of its contents is amazing. Its 880 rooms housed 300 friars who could look through 4,500 doorways and windows.

The summer residence of kings, Mafra, 40km (25 miles) northwest of Lisbon, was home to king João VI in 1805, when he decided to separate from queen Carlota Joaquina, who stayed in Queluz. Almost one century later his descendant Carlos I, the Bragança king assassinated at Praça do Comércio in 1908, made this his base for hunting trips. In one room he had chandeliers made out of antlers and upholstery of animal skins. His son, who ruled for 2 years as Manuel II, spent his last night on Portuguese soil at Mafra before fleeing to England with his mother, Amélia.

Two towers hold more than 110 chimes, made in Antwerp, Belgium, that can be heard for up to 24km (15 miles) when they're played at Sunday recital. The towers flank a basilica, capped by a dome that has been compared to that of St. Paul's in London. The church contains an assortment of chapels, 11 in all, expertly crafted with detailed jasper reredos, bas-reliefs, and marble statues from Italy. The monastery holds the pride of Mafra, a 40,000-volume library with tomes hundreds of years old—many gold-leafed. Viewed by some more favorably than the world-famous library at Coimbra, the room is a study in gilded light. The collection of elaborately decorated vestments in the Museum of Religious Art here is outstanding.

Terreiro D.João V. www.palaciomafra.pt/. ✆ **26/181-75-50.** Admission 6€ adults, 3€ seniors 65 and over and students 15–18, free for children under 15. Wed–Mon 10am–5:30pm. Bus: Mafrense bus from Lisbon.

Where to Stay

Casa Paco D'ilhas ★★★ Offering what it calls a "holistic leisure experience," this little guest house is a one-stop-shop for mind expansion. Most guests participate in the daily yoga sessions, still others come here to learn to kitesurf, stand-up paddleboard, and surf, and lately, mountain bikers have been staying here, too. Their digs are chicly rustic houses, each with a different setup—the smallest just has a double bedroom, the original 1869 house holds three bedrooms, and one house even has a dorm room for bigger groups. Each is awash in sunlight, with large windows, purposefully homemade looking (and often quite chic) wooden ceilings and furnishings, and exotic knickknacks here and there from across the globe. The owners are two Belgian surfers who fell in love with the waves here and have a real talent for hospitality: Along with daily breakfasts (included), they'll often throw in a curry dinner for guests. The resort is in a little hill town about a 10-minute walk from both the main town and the beach.

Estrada da Junceira, Paço de Ilhas. http://casapacodilhas.com. ✆ **21/910-55-00.** 14 units. 50€–85€ double, more for other configurations. Rates include breakfast. **Amenities:** 2 swimming pools; kitchens in some units; yoga classes; surf school; mountain bike rentals. Free Wi-Fi.

Hotel Vila Galé Ericeira ★★ Overlooking the beaches and the waters of the Atlantic, this is the westernmost hotel in continental Europe, and brings a bit of luxury to the center of town. An older structure, it was completely renovated and made both stylish and up-to-date recently, everything resting under a glistening green-tiled roof. The typical Portuguese glazed tiles have been used effectively throughout the building, both to adorn the walls and to cover the floors. Spiffy bedrooms, midsize and larger, have quality dark-wood furnishings and beds, and perky striped curtains and comforters. The magnet in summer is the alfresco bar, extending like the prow of a ship toward the sea.

Largo dos Navegantes, www.vilagale.pt. ✆ **26/186-99-00.** 202 units. 80€–169€ double. Free parking. **Amenities:** Restaurant; bar; babysitting; bikes; children's center; exercise room; 3 outdoor pools; room service; spa. Free Wi-Fi.

Where to Dine

Marisqueira César ★★ PORTUGUESE This is the port's best nonhotel-based restaurant and a favorite for locals. The kitchen takes full advantage of the ocean's riches (ask and they'll let you see the tanks of live crabs, lobsters, and other shellfish in the basement), but also brings in fresh meat. The spacious dining room faces the beach so as you eat you'll be able to watch the roiling Atlantic. The waves are quite dramatic here, especially in winter. For families, there's also a children's playground.

Estrada Nacional 247, km 49. ✆ **26/186-09-50.** Main courses 11€–35€. Tues–Sun noon–11pm.

SOUTH OF THE TAGUS

Historically cut off from Lisbon, the narrow isthmus south of the Tagus is wild and rugged as well as lush. In different places, this strip of land plummets toward the sea, stretches along miles of sandy beaches, and rolls through groves heavy with the odors of ripening oranges. With craggy cliffs and coves in the background, the crystalline Atlantic is ideal for swimming in Arrábida and Sesimbra, skin diving, surfing in Caparica, or fishing for swordfish and bass.

The construction of the Ponte 25 de Abril, in 1966, a long suspension bridge, made it possible to cross the Tagus in minutes by car or by train—though views are better taking the ferry from Cais do Sodré in Lisbon and docking in Cacilhas. Another bridge, around 18km (11 miles) long, Ponte Vasco da Gama, opened in 1998, and makes it possible to go south and to Alcochete directly from the airport area. Whichever crossing you prefer, good roads will allow you to head rapidly through Lisbon's suburbs and then reach more rural areas, namely the apex of the triangle once known as the region of the Three Castles: Sesimbra, Setúbal, and Palmela. It's also a region worth a detour if you're driving to Alentejo and the Algarve.

The land immediately south of the Tagus River is a highly populated suburban area. But drive further south you'll find the area retains vivid reminders of its past, reflected in its Moorish castle (Sesimbra), Roman ruins and roads (Tróia), Phoenician imprints (Alcácer do Sal), dinosaur footprints (Cabo Espichel), and Spanish fortresses (Setúbal). The region's proximity to Lisbon (Setúbal is only 40km/25 miles southeast of the capital) makes it perfect for a 1-day excursion.

ALMADA

The first city on the south bank near Lisbon is Almada. Its claim to fame is as the home of **Cristo-Rei** (Christ the King) statue. Inspired by the Christ Redeemer statue in Rio de Janeiro, it was built with donations from citizens across Portugal as a way of giving thanks that the country had been spared the horrors of World War II. It took more than a decade of fundraising to erect the monument, which opened in 1959. At the sanctuary you can follow the 14 stations of

South of the Tagus

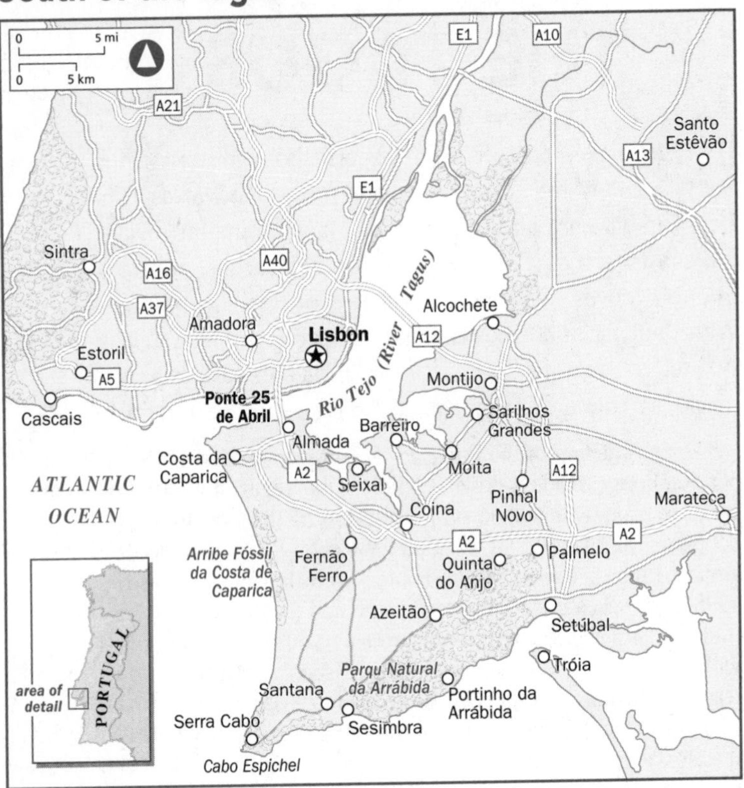

the Via Sacra. Built on a hill 104m (304 ft.) high, the statue of Christ towers 28m (92 ft.).

The sanctuary offers an impressive view of the bridge and of the city of Lisbon. For those not afraid of heights, the same view is even better from the bottom of the statue. There's an inside elevator that will take you as high as possible, opening onto an extremely windy terrace. (From Cacilhas there's an elevator, right of Cais do Ginjal, that will take you to the old center of Almada, and then you'll have to walk up to Cristo-Rei.) But the best way to go to the sanctuary is to take the ferry from Cais do Sodré to Cacilhas, and then the bus 101 in the bus terminal to Cristo-Rei.

The monument is open every day from 9:30am to 6pm (until 6:45 in the summer). Elevator: 4€; 2.50€ for seniors over 65.

If you're peckish after a visit, we have two restaurants to recommend: the innovative **Atira-te ao Rio,** Cais do Ginjal, 69-70 (www.atirateaorio.pt; ✆ **21/275-13-80,** closed Mon); and the more traditional **Ponto Final,** Cais do

Ginjal, 72 (✆ **93/686-90-31,** closed Tues). Both have enviable locations on the riverfront and both are expert in preparing seafood.

From these restaurants you can take the elevator Boca do Vento (1€), nearby, to the old Almada town, where you'll find **Casa da Cerca** (✆ **21/272-49-50;** Tues–Fri 10–5:30pm, Sat–Sun 1–5:30pm; free admission), a museum dedicated to contemporary art; if the current exhibit isn't all that interesting, wander through its lush gardens and enjoy the views.

From Cacilhas, you can reach also **Costa da Caparica** (bus 135 or 124), part of the Almada municipality, with its long stretch of sandy beaches, surf- and body-board schools, and fish restaurants. The Transpraia train runs to this area from June 1 to September 30. Schedules at www.transpraia.pt.

Essentials

If you take a ferry from Lisbon's Cais do Sodré to Cacilhas, you can catch a bus there for the beaches of Costa Caparica. The ferry from Belém to Trafaria goes closer to Caparica, but doesn't run often.

Otherwise, you can take a bus from Lisbon to the beaches at Caparica in about 45 minutes. There's also a convenient beach shuttle that runs from June to October only, departing from Praça da Figueira. In summer, a narrow-gauge railway runs for 8km (5 miles) along the Costa da Caparica, making 20 stops at beaches along the way.

AZEITÃO ★★

15km (9⅓ miles) NW of Setúbal; 25km (16 miles) SE of Lisbon

This sleepy village lies in the heart of quinta country. In its most meager manifestation, a quinta is a simple farmhouse surrounded by land. At its best, it's a mansion of great architectural style filled with art. Azeitão boasts some of the finest quintas in the country. The village makes a good base for trekkers, especially those who want to scale the limestone Serra de Arrábida, with eye-poppingly beautiful trails within the national park. For others, long walks through scented pinewoods, oak trees, or silvery olive groves will suffice (and are quite appropriate: *Azeite* is the Portuguese word for olive oil). To cap off your day, indulge in the renowned specialty of the region: soft and buttery *queijo de Azeitão* (sheep's-milk cheese). It is so unique it has a DOP certification; a local thistle flower is used to coagulate the milk in an ancient cheese tradition. Pair that with a bottle of local *Moscatel de Setúbal*—a fortified wine (like port or Madeira, the maker stops the fermentation process of the grapes by adding a spirit, thus keeping all the sugar). Finish up with *torta de Azeitão*, a luscious, soft sponge cake with an egg and cinnamon filling.

Azeitão is also home to one of the region's best ceramics companies: **São Simão Arte** (www.saosimaoarte.com; ✆ **21/218-31-35**). The factory outlet sells its products at prices that are somewhat less than in equivalent retail shops. You can also request a visit to see how the *azulejos* (tiles) are manually produced and painted by local artisans.

Essentials

ARRIVING

Azeitão is not well served by public transportation, making a car the best option. After crossing one of the bridges across the Tagus, continue south along the old road to Setúbal (N10) until you see the turnoff for the village of Azeitão. Otherwise take the Fertagus train from Lisbon (Entrecampos or Sete Rios station) to Coina and then a Sulfertagus bus to Azeitão. Tickets are 3.20€ to Coina (www.fertagus.pt) and must be validated before boarding.

Visiting a Quinta

Quinta da Bacalhôa ★★★ PALACE Manuel I reputedly introduced the concept of quintas in the early–16th century when he built the Quinta da Bacalhôa with the help of famed Tuscan architect Sansovino. Eventually, this quinta fell into disrepair and vandals carted off many of its decorations, specifically the antique tiles. An American woman, Orlena Scoville, bought the mansion in 1936 and worked for years to restore it to its original condition, renovating and recovering many of the tiles. Some architectural critics have suggested that it's the first example of the Renaissance in Portugal.

A ticket to the palace includes the Renaissance gardens, developed by the son of Afonso de Albuquerque, a former viceroy of India—his years of travel clearly influenced the gardening aesthetic. You'll see lots of sheared topiary and rigorously clipped boxwood hedges in serpentine patterns alongside a lake. The quinta's farmland, part of which is visible beyond the walls of the garden, is devoted to vineyards owned by **Bacalhôa Wines of Portugal.** Most plan visits that combine tours of the gardens and palace with tasting sessions at the winery; the two together take around 2 hours.

Bacalhôa Palace: Vila Fresca de Azeitão. ✆ **21/218-00-11.** Admission 4€ adults, free for children under 13. Mon–Sat 1–5pm. Winemaking museum: Estrada Nacional 10, Vila Nogueira de Azeitão. www.bacalhoa.pt. ✆ **21/219-80-60.** Admission 3€ adults, free for children under 13. Mon–Sun 9am–5pm (except palace, closed on Sundays). Combined visit costs 6€. Booking recommended.

José Maria da Fonseca ★ MUSEUM/WINERY The winery **José Maria da Fonseca,** and the 19th-century house that originally functioned as the Fonseca's family home, are 2km (1¼ miles) away from Quinta da Bacalhôa, in the center of the village of Azeitão. JMF was the first company to sell wine in bottles, the well-known Periquita. It's also one of the oldest wineries in Portugal, founded in 1834. A visit includes a tour of the on-site museums (tools, paintings, a bit of history) and the cellars, where you'll see massive mahogany vats of Periquita and oak barrels of moscatel, a dessert wine made from muscat grapes.

Casa Museu José Maria da Fonseca: Rua José Augusto Coelho, 11/13, Vila Nogueira de Azeitão. www.jmf.pt. ✆ **21/219-89-40.** Admission: 3€. Mon–Sun 10–7:30pm. Booking recommended.

Where to Stay & Dine

Hotel Club de Azeitão ★★ The setting is the lure at this converted 17th-century mansion, which is surrounded by lush gardens—palm trees, olive trees, cork trees, orange trees, and even vineyards—in the foothills of Arrábida Mountains. That means calm, peace, and lots of time to splash around in the pool or hit balls on the tennis court. The common rooms are evocative, still blessed with the original (and gorgeous) blue-and-white tiling and a roaring fireplace in winter. In fact, many guests get to know the lobby a little too well, as Wi-Fi doesn't work in the guest rooms. As for those rooms, they're crisply contemporary, if not brimming with character.

Quinta do Bom Pastor, Vila Fresca de Azeitão, Azeitão. www.turim-hotels.com/hotels/azeitao/hotel_club_de_azeitao. ✆ **21/219-85-90.** 46 rooms. 50€–100€ double. Rates include buffet breakfast. **Amenities:** Restaurant; bar; outdoor pool; room service; free parking. Free Wi-Fi in lobby.

Casa das Tortas ★ PORTUGUESE Founded in 1910 and looking exactly as it did back then, this is the place to come for the region's soft sponge cake with egg and cinnamon filling; you'll also find many of the wines produced by nearby wineries. In the summer, grab a table in the alfresco setting for a straightforward but tasty meal of grilled fish and meat. When it's colder, a small interior room opens for dining; go early as locals arrive to lunch around 1pm and you might not get a seat.

Praça da República, 37, Azeitão. ✆ **96/914-69-96.** Main courses 10€–16€; noon–3pm and 7:30–11:30pm. Closed Mon.

SESIMBRA ★★

26km (16 miles) SW of Setúbal; 43km (27 miles) S of Lisbon

Among the Portuguese, Sesimbra used to be a closely guarded secret. It was justifiably considered one of the most unspoiled fishing villages in the country. Today, signs of rapid growth are everywhere, with urban areas lining the hillsides. However, fishermen still go about the time-honored task of plucking their livelihood from the Atlantic. When the fleet comes in, the day's catch is auctioned at the harbor (Porto de Abrigo), which can be interesting to watch. Sesimbra is also a popular sport-fishing center.

Essentials

ARRIVING

BY TRAIN From Lisbon, the bus is a better choice. Rail passengers go to Setúbal by train and then have to double back on a bus to get to Sesimbra.

BY BUS Buses to Sesimbra (bus 207 or 206) leave regularly from Lisbon's Praça de Espanha (Metro: Praça de Espanha) and from Cacilhas (bus 203), across the Tagus from the center of Lisbon. The 1-hour trip costs 4.30€ or 3.85€. For information and schedules, call **Transportes Sul do Tejo** (www.tsuldotejo.pt; ✆ **21/112-62-00**).

BY CAR From Lisbon, cross the Ponte do 25 de Abril bridge and continue southwest on the A2 to Setúbal. At the junction of N378, head directly south into Sesimbra. There are car parks before reaching the center.

BY FERRY Take the ferry to Cacilhas from the Cais do Sodré wharf in Lisbon (Metro: Cais do Sodré). Then take a bus from Cacilhas.

VISITOR INFORMATION

The **tourist office** is in Fortaleza de Santiago, Rua da Fortaleza (www.visit.sesimbra.pt; ✆ **21/228-85-40**). June to September, hours are daily 9:30am to 8pm; October to May, it's open daily 9am to 12:30pm and 2 to 5:30pm.

SPECIAL EVENTS

Sesimbra has many fairs and festivals during which the town attracts a lot of visitors, making accommodations hard to come by unless reservations are made well in advance. Each year, in February or early March (dates vary), Sesimbra stages ***Cegadas,*** which are a series of street theater presentations during the wildly popular Carnival celebrations. But unless you speak Portuguese, it's more interesting for the casual visitor to attend the **Procissão da Senhor das Chagas** (a procession honoring the patron saint of the fishermen) celebrated every year on May 4. There's another festival on May 31 in honor of the fishermen, **Dia do Pescador,** with a parade of fishing boats. From June 10 to June 30, Sesimbra, like many towns and villages in Portugal, stages the annual **Festival of the Popular Saints,** which is an exciting event, even for non-Catholics. The town is gaily decorated with paper flowers, parades are staged, and live music, along with the smoky aroma of grilling sardines, drifts through the streets.

Exploring Sesimbra

The most intriguing sight in Sesimbra is the picturesque (and often photographed) **harbor ★**, which lies against the foot of a green cliff. It is still an important and bustling center for **fishing.** During summer it's fascinating to watch the town's fishermen use the ancient technique of *arte xávega*, in which they pull massive nets on to the shore and unroll them to get the fish, a process that was once accomplished with the help of oxen, but is now done mechanically. You'll see this spectacle at *Praia da Califórnia* (Monday, Thursday, and Saturday) and *Praia do Ouro* (Thursday, Friday, and Saturday) from 6 to 9am and 7 to 9pm.

The seas in this area are famous for their swordfish and scabbard-fish, and many local fishermen will take visitors out in their boats to try their own hand for a negotiated fee. Inquire at the tourist office (see "Visitor Information," above) about making arrangements.

Farther down the beach, beyond the boat-clogged harbor, the 17th-century **Fortress of St. Teodósio** (Forte S. Teodósio or Forte do Cavalo) was built to fortify the region against pirates. The site is not open to the public, but the walk to it is the town's most scenic, taking amblers along the beach and by the old port, with dramatic views of the sea on one side and colorful cliffs on the other.

A walk along the ruined battlements of the five-towered **Castle of Sesimbra** is also recommended. The 9th-century castle, originally a Moorish fortress, encloses a 12th-century church, the oldest in Sesimbra. For years it had an important role defending the coast, especially during Middle Ages. The site is open daily from 9am to 7pm and has a cafeteria. Admission is free.

From Sesimbra, you can head west to the headland of **Cabo Espichel,** with its arcaded pilgrim hospices dating from the 1700s. The baroque interior (gilded wood and sculpture) of a pilgrimage church, the **Santuário de Nossa Senhora do Cabo,** can be inspected daily between 9:30am to 1pm and 3 to 6pm. Admission is free. Later, walk to the edge of the cliffs behind the church for a panoramic view of the sea. Set at the southern end of the Arrábida Mountain chain, this pilgrimage site has been popular since the 13th century. The small chapel, **Ermida da Memória,** with blue-and-white tiles from the 18th century, is also worth a look-see. There's no guardrail, and it's a sheer drop of more than 100m (328 ft.) to the ocean waters, so be very careful.

Keep a sharp eye for the signs indicating the many dinosaur footprints discovered in the cliffs.

From Sesimbra, six buses a day make the 30-minute journey to this southwestern cape, but we recommend driving on your own, as waits for the next bus can be lengthy.

OUTDOOR ACTIVITIES Sesimbra's popularity stems from its position on a long, lovely sandy **beach.** The beach is overpopulated in summer, but the unpolluted and quiet water is ideal for swimming. If you don't mind hiking, there's a beautiful—and less crowded—beach, with a very difficult and hilly access called **Ribeiro do Cavalo** (ask locally for directions). It is easiest to get there by boat; take a snack and water as it has no facilities.

Boat rides and scuba diving are also available, as Sesimbra sea has quiet waters and rich underwater fauna. Ask at the tourist center.

SHOPPING **Avenida da Liberdade,** in the heart of town, is lined with all kinds of souvenir shops, selling cork articles, textiles, tinned fish, tackle, and fishing equipment. The ceramics outlet at Azeitão (see above) is just 15km (9⅓ miles) from the center of town, along the road to Setúbal.

Where to Stay

EXPENSIVE

SANA Sesimbra Hotel ★★★ Since hotels are basically places to sleep, we have to give the SANA Sesimbra extra points for the top quality of both their mattresses and bedding. You will slumber soundly here and you'll do so lulled by the sounds of the waves, as this modern, balconied hotel is right on the beach (make sure you get a room that faces the sands). While awake, you'll enjoy the nautical slant of the decor (lots of navy and white stripes), and the company of staff who are unusually helpful and friendly. In terms of facilities, this is one of the better-equipped hotels in the area, with a rooftop pool, restaurant, bar, exercise room, Jacuzzi, and sauna.

Av. 25 de Abril. www.sanasesimbrahotel.com. ✆ **21/228-90-00.** 100 units. 129€–160€ double. Rates include buffet breakfast. Parking 6€. **Amenities:** Restaurant; bar; babysitting; concierge; exercise room; Jacuzzi; outdoor pool; room service; sauna. Free Wi-Fi.

Sesimbra Hotel & Spa ★★ Luxe living and extensive facilities are what bring visitors to this resort. Set against the backdrop of the Arrábida Nature Reserve, the hotel opens right on the water, with all of its bedrooms boasting private balconies with sea views. Accommodations have a jaunty look, with aqua-and-white-striped headboards mirroring the aqua-striped curtains, and offsetting the rooms' light woods. If this weren't a hotel, it would be a Scandinavian yacht. At the on-site Aquarium Restaurant—one of the finest in the area—the catch of the day is unloaded each morning by local fishermen; by evening, it's on your plate. Guests also have vegetarian and

THE BEST BEACHES: WHERE THE locals SUN

The beaches along the Costa da Caparica, on the left bank of the Tagus, across from the center of Lisbon, are better and have more space than those along the more fashionable Estoril and Cascais. But due to easier transportation, foreigners still flock to the Costa do Sol, leaving much of the Costa da Caparica to locals.

The *costa*, on the west side of the Setúbal Peninsula, stretches for some 9km (5⅔ miles) and abounds with sandy beaches and coves. Rocky outcroppings and clear, placid lagoons characterize these strands. The farther you go from the little resort of Caparica, the more beautiful they become.

A narrow-gauge railway serves the coast, making 20 stops over 8km (5 miles). Each white-sand beach along the way has a different allure and distinct beach bars. In general, families of all age groups are attracted to the beaches along the first eight stops. Beginning at stop 9, gay visitors become more prominent. As you travel the greater length of Costa da Caparica, the beaches become less crowded, and in the final southern stretches, after Fonte da Telha, nudists are often seen.

To reach the beach strip by public transport, you can take a ferry from Lisbon to Cacilhas. They leave every 15 minutes from Cais do Sodré's Terminal Fluvial (Metro: Cais do Sodré). You then board a bus marked CAPARICA at the station next door to the ferry terminal. The trip to the beaches takes about 45 minutes. The narrow-gauge train runs from June to September, and the bus from Cacilhas stops at the rail terminus. You then have to walk to connect with the little train.

The Setúbal Peninsula has many other wonderful beaches. There are sandy and quiet ones at Sesimbra (see above), but they are likely to be overcrowded from June to August.

The most alluring beach strip is across the mouth of the Sado, at Tróia (p. 189), a major resort with some utterly charmless apartment complexes but also some new hotels. Ferries leave from Setúbal harbor every 45 minutes throughout the day. Trip time is 15 minutes. The ocean side of the promontory at Tróia is less filled with beach buffs and is less polluted. If you're not driving, make sure to take the passenger ferry , as it docks closer to the ocean side.

low-cal options on hand at the Mosaico Restaurant & Bar. Eat too much? You can work it off in the well-equipped gym. The spa here is first class, too. Our only disappointment? The bathrooms, which need updating.

Rua Navegador Rodrigues Soromenho. www.sesimbrahotelspa.com. ✆ **21/330-05-41.** 100 units. 75€–200€ double; 135€–400€ suite. Free parking. **Amenities:** 2 restaurants; 2 bars; children's center; exercise room; 2 freshwater pools (1 heated indoor); room service; spa. Free Wi-Fi.

MODERATE

Hotel do Mar ★ One of the most unusual beach-resort hotels south of the Tagus, Hotel do Mar spreads from a high cliff to the water below. The main lobby houses a glassed-in tropical-bird aviary, and the passageways are like art galleries, with contemporary paintings and ceramic plaques and sculpture. Alas, rooms aren't as comely, with mass-produced furnishings and little style. Still, this is a good place for families, thanks to its locale and all the entertainment facilities on-site.

Rua General Humberto Delgado 10. www.hoteldomar.pt. ✆ **21/228-83-00.** 168 units. 72€–210€ double; 245€–310€ junior suite; 515€–600€ suite. Rates include buffet breakfast. Free parking. **Amenities:** Restaurant; bar; Jacuzzi; 2 pools (1 heated indoor); room service; sauna; 2 outdoor tennis courts. Free Wi-Fi.

Where to Dine

Along with the suggested restaurant below, many of the simple, local restaurants offer up very tasty grub: grilled fish and shellfish plates featuring the local small shrimps. Dining is much cheaper here than in Lisbon.

Restaurante Ribamar ★★ INTERNATIONAL/PORTUGUESE A short stroll from the beach, with a view of the bay from most of the indoor and outdoor seating, Ribamar serves seafood fresh from local waters. The standout menu choice is the platter of mixed fish and shellfish for two. Other faves include clams flavored with cilantro and garlic, the seafood soup (a perennial winner at the annual fish festival in Lisbon), and the grilled black scabbard fish (*peixe-espada*) caught in local waters.

Av. dos Náufragos 29. www.ribamar.com.pt. ✆ **21/223-48-53.** Reservations recommended. Main courses 18€–26€. Daily noon–11pm.

PORTINHO DA ARRÁBIDA ★★

13km (8 miles) SW of Setúbal; 37km (23 miles) SE of Lisbon

The village of Portinho da Arrábida, a favorite with vacationing Lisbon families, is at the foot of the **Serra da Arrábida ★**. It is a lovely place, with a crystalline bay, but if you drive here in July and August, watch out. There's virtually no parking, and the road should be one-way but isn't—you can wait for hours to get back up the hill. In addition, the walk down and back could qualify you for the Olympics. Try to park on a wider road above the port, and then negotiate the hordes of summer visitors on foot. Or drive to Creiro, the beach next to Portinho, where there are a few parking lots.

During the rest of the year, Portinho is quite accessible. After a day on the beach, your best bet is to return to Sesimbra or to drive on to Setúbal or Azeitão for the night, though there are some short-term rental properties here.

Essentials

ARRIVING

BY BUS There is no bus service between Sesimbra and Portinho da Arrábida. In summer there's a bus connecting Setúbal with Praia da Figueirinha, but not with Portinho.

BY CAR From Sesimbra, continue along N379 toward Setúbal, forking right at the turnoff for Portinho da Arrábida. But first, see the warning about parking, above. Portinho makes a good lunch stop for motorists exploring the foothills of the Serra da Arrábida.

VISITOR INFORMATION

The nearest tourist office is at Setúbal (✆ **26/553-91-20**) or Sesimbra (✆ **21/228-85-40**), but neither offers much help to visitors to Portinho.

SETÚBAL ★

40km (25 miles) SE of Lisbon

On the right bank of the Sado River lies one of Portugal's largest and oldest cities, said to have been founded by Noah's grandson. Motorists often include it on their itineraries because of the exceptional inn, the **Pousada de Setúbal, São Filipe,** in a late-16th-century fort overlooking the sea (see "Where to Stay," below).

Setúbal, the center of Portugal's sardine industry and home to a delightful fish and vegetable market, is known for the local production of the most exquisite muscatel wine in the world. Orange groves, orchards, vineyards, and outstanding beaches such as the popular Praia da Figueirinha all lie near Setúbal. The white pyramidal mounds dotting the landscape are deposits of sea salt drying in the sun, another major commercial asset of this seaside community.

Many artists and writers have come from Setúbal, most notably the 18th-century Portuguese poet Manuel Maria Barbosa du Bocage, forerunner of the Romantics. A monument honors him at Praça do Bocage.

Essentials

ARRIVING

BY TRAIN The trip from Lisbon, with the Fertagus train service, takes 55 minutes; a one-way ticket costs 4.35€. For more information and schedules, call ✆ **70/712-71-27.**

BY BUS Buses from Lisbon arrive every hour or two, depending on the time of day. The trip takes an hour, and a one-way ticket costs 6.50€. For more information and schedules, go to www.rede-expressos.pt.

EXPLORING THE mountains

The limestone, whale-backed Serra da Arrábida stretches for about 36km (22 miles), beginning at Palmela and rolling to a dramatic end at Cabo Espichel on the Atlantic. The Portuguese government has wisely set aside 10,800 hectares (26,687 acres) as a sanctuary between Sesimbra and Setúbal to protect the area from developers and to safeguard the local scenery and architecture. The National Park of Arrábida has some spectacular trails and the Oceanographic Museum (near Portinho). Contact the park if you wish to know which trails are open (✆ **26/554-11-40**).

At times, the cliffs and bluffs are so high that it seems you have to peer through clouds to see the purple waters of the Atlantic below. More than 1,000 species of plant life have been recorded, including holm oaks, sweet bay, pines, laurel, juniper, cypress, araucaria, magnolia, lavender, myrtle, and pimpernels. Our favorite time to visit is in late March or the beginning of April (around Easter), when wildflowers—everything from coral-pink peonies to Spanish bluebells—cover the mountains.

Numerous sandy coves lie at the foot of the Serra da Arrábida's limestone cliffs. One of the finest beaches is **Praia de Galapos.** Another popular beach is **Praia de Figueirinha,** between Portinho da Arrábida and Setúbal, known for sport fishing, windsurfing, and sailing. The *serra* (mountain ridge) abounds with caves and grottoes. The best known is **Lapa de Santa Margarida,** of which Hans Christian Andersen wrote, "It is a veritable church hewn out of the living rock, with a fantastic vault, organ pipes, columns, and altars." On the top of the mountain there's the amazing **Convento da Arrábida,** home of Franciscans friars in the 16th century. Visits are for groups only and need to be booked (✆ **21/219-76-20**).

BY CAR After crossing one of the Tagus bridges from Lisbon, follow the signs to Setúbal along the express highway, A2, until you see the turnoff for Setúbal. The old road (N10) to Setúbal is much slower.

VISITOR INFORMATION

The **Setúbal Tourist Office** is at Travessa Frei Gaspar 10 (www.turismolisboavaledotejo.pt; ✆ **26/553-91-20**). The office is open June to September Monday to Saturday 9:30am to 7pm and Sunday 9:30am to 12:30pm. From October to May, hours are Monday to Saturday 9:30am to 6pm.

Exploring Setúbal

Ingreja de Jesús ★★ Possibly the earliest example of Manueline architecture (it was built in the late–15th century), its main chapel is of particular interest, thanks to the ornate decorations on the principal doorway and the twisting Arrábida marble columns. Diogo de Boitaca, who later went on to build Lisbon's Mosteiro dos Jerónimos (Jerónimos Monastery), was the architect, making this a particularly interesting site to tour for those who will see both of these structures. Hans Christian Andersen called the monument "one of the most beautiful small churches that I have ever seen." The church was extensively restored in 2015 and now absolutely gleams.

Praça Miguel Bombarda (off Av. do 22 de Dezembro). ✆ **26/553-78-90** or 26/552-41-50. Tickets: 2€, including audio guide. Free for children under 16 or adults over 65. Tues–Sat 9am–1pm and 1:30–5:30pm. Bus: 1, 4, 7, 10, or 12.

Museu de Setúbal ★ Adjoining the Igreja de Jesus, this unpretentious town museum houses some early-16th-century Portuguese paintings, as well as Spanish and Flemish works and contemporary art. The museum is also rich in antique *azulejos* (hand-painted tiles) and has a large antique coin collection, plus artifacts from archaeological digs in the area. Of special note: the collection of ecclesiastical gold and silver, especially a Gothic processional cross in crystal and gilt from the 15th century. If you have a free hour or so, this museum is well worth a visit.

Rua Balneário Paula Borba. ✆ **26/553-78-90.** Free admission. Tues–Sat 9am–noon and 1:30–5:30pm. Bus: 1, 4, 7, 10, or 12.

OUTDOOR ACTIVITIES

Today the once-lonely, rocky stretches of land between Lisbon and Setúbal are dotted with golf courses that are considered among the best in Europe.

One of Portugal's most acclaimed is the **Aroeira Clube de Golf ★★**, Herdade de Aroeira, Fonte da Telha, 2825 Monte de Caparica, Aroeira (www.aroeira.com; ✆ **21/297-91-00**). Designed as a 364-hectare (899-acre) "golf estate" in the early 1970s by the English architect Frank Pennink, it's a par-72, 6,040m (19,816-ft.) course. International golf magazines have hailed the layout as one of the most challenging on the continent. Low, rocky cliffs and a network of lakes separate the long, lush fairways and copses of pine trees from the surging Atlantic. Advance reservations are essential. Greens fees for 18 holes run 60€ to 90€, depending on the day and time. Golf clubs can be rented for 40€, and an electric cart costs 20€ for 18 holes. To reach the club from Lisbon (a 25km/16-mile ride, which takes about 35 min.), take one of the bridges over the Tagus. Drive south on the A2 (20 miles) and exit the highway at Costa da Caparica, the first after crossing the bridge. Then exit the IC20 and take the A33 to Charneca and exit at Aroeira. From Setúbal (a 40km/25-mile ride, which takes about 1 hr.), take the A2 to Lisbon and exit at Fogueteiro.

If the Aroeira course is booked, there are some good second choices. You can schedule a round at **Quinta do Perú Golf & Country Club,** Alameda da Serra 2, near the hamlet of Negreiros (www.golfquintadoperu.com; ✆ **21/213-43-20**). From Setúbal, take Estrada Nacional 10 for about 19km (12 miles), following signs to Lisbon. Reservations are required. Another option is the **Golfe do Montado** in the village of Montado (www.montadoresort.com; ✆ **26/570-81-50**). From Setúbal, drive 10km (6¼ miles) south along the Estrada Nacional, following signs to Alentejo and Algarve. Greens fees are comparable to those at the Aroeira, but professionals don't consider either of those newcomers as exciting.

SHOPPING Setúbal offers enough outlets for local handicrafts to keep any devoted shopper busy for at least a full afternoon. **Mercado do Livramento,**

the fresh produce market, is one of the best in the country. Open in the morning, it's a cornucopia of vegetables, fresh seafood, cheese, sausages, ham, and flowers. There's also an antique and flea market on the first and third Saturday of every month, between 9am and 6pm, in Avenida Luísa Todi. The biggest event, though, is Feira de Santiago, usually in the first week in August, involving concerts, handicrafts, and traditional food.

Fortuna (✆ **21/287-10-68**), a ceramics factory and technical school, dominates the hamlet of **Quinta do Anjo,** 6.5km (4 miles) northeast of Setúbal. To reach it, follow signs to Palmela.

Where to Stay

EXPENSIVE

Hotel do Sado Business & Nature ★★ The first allergy-friendly hotel in the country, the Hotel do Sado has special rooms for guests with respiratory allergies, and gluten- and lactose-free menus—a boon for many travelers. All of the spacious, airy accommodations open onto a small balcony, with swell views. The on-site restaurant is terrific (see "Where to Dine," below).

Rua Irene Lisboa 1 and 3. www.hoteldosado.com. ✆ **26/554-28-00.** 66 units. 60€–175€ double; 140€–300€ suite. Rates include buffet breakfast. Free parking. **Amenities:** Restaurant; bar; babysitting; bikes; room service; car rental. Free Wi-Fi.

Pousada de Setúbal, São Filipe ★★ This fortress-castle, built by Philip I (Philip II of Spain) on a hilltop overlooking the town and the harbor, dates from the 17th century. It's the work of Italian architect Philipe Terzi. The road leading to the pousada winds up a mountain and passes through a stone arch and past towers to the belvedere. The walls of the chapel and the public rooms contain tile *dados* depicting scenes from the life of São Filipe and the life of the Virgin Mary. They're dated 1736 and signed by Policarpo de Oliveira Bernardes.

Guest rooms that once housed soldiers and the governor have been tastefully furnished with antiques and reproductions of 16th- and 17th-century pieces. Guns and ammunition have given way to soft beds and ornate Portuguese-crafted headboards. The hotel is flooded with what seems like miles of plant-filled corridors.

If you're not driving, take a taxi from Setúbal—the walk is a long one.

Castelo de São Filipe. www.pousadas.pt. ✆ **26/555-00-70.** 16 units. 145€–240€ double; 190€–270€ suite. Rates include buffet breakfast. Free parking. **Amenities:** Restaurant; bar; bikes; room service; watersports equipment/rentals. Free Wi-Fi.

INEXPENSIVE

Luna Esperança Centro Hotel ★ A functional, clean hotel, we recommend it primarily for its location and pricing. In the center of Setúbal, it offers a view of the Sado River from many of its rooms. Appropriate for both business travelers and vacationers, it features midsize bedrooms that are simply but comfortably furnished and well maintained. There is no restaurant, but the hotel is within walking distance of many cafes, and a hearty buffet breakfast is served each morning.

Av. Luisa Todi 220. www.lunahoteis.com. ✆ **26/552-17-80.** 80 units. 62€ double; 119€ suite. **Amenities:** Lobby bar; room service. Free Wi-Fi.

Setúbalense Residencial ★ Another hotel that's recommended for its superb location, about a minute's walk north of Setúbal's central plaza, Largo da Misericórdia in this case. This family-run property is set in a restored three-story building that was erected 200 years ago as a substantial private home. The small rooms have high ceilings and streamlined modern furniture, including neatly kept bathrooms with tub/shower combos.

Rua Major Afonso Pala 17. www.setubalense.com. ✆ **26/552-57-90.** 24 units. 50€–60€ double. Rates include buffet breakfast. **Amenities:** Bar; room service.

Where to Dine

Casa Santiago Rei do Choco Frito ★★ PORTUGUESE The name of the restaurant translates as "king of choco frito" (deep-fried cuttlefish), which would sound pompous if it weren't true. This is the top place in Setubal to try this local specialty, which comes with a side of crispy fried potatoes. Pair a platter with the sparkling house wine, just as all of the Lisbon residents who flock here on vacation do. It's so busy that there's sometimes a line outside, so be sure to arrive early, before 1pm for lunch or 7:30pm at dinnertime.

Av. Luísa Todi 92. ✆ **26/522-16-88.** Main courses 7€–13€. Mon–Sat noon–10pm.

Hotel do Sado Business & Nature ★★ CONTINENTAL/PORTUGUESE This is the showcase restaurant of Setúbal's best hotel, a much-renovated 19th-century manor house (see above). The restaurant lies within a 5-minute drive from the city's core, on the hotel's uppermost (eighth) floor, and is directly accessible via a dramatically angular elevator whose shaft rises as a distinctly separate structure from the building's historic core. At the summit, wide-angled views extend outward in all directions, sweeping out over the surrounding coastline and the estuary of the Sado River. Many guests opt for selections from the menu's "daily fish market"—very fresh grilled fish. Other smart choices include codfish stuffed with local cheese, monkfish with coriander sauce, or fried lamb chops with potatoes and tomatoes.

Irene Lisboa 1-3. ✆ **26/554-28-00.** Reservations recommended. Main courses 11€–22€. Mon–Sat 12:30–3pm and 7:30–10:30pm.

Restaurante Carnes do Convento ★★★ PORTUGUESE If you need a break from fish, fish, and more fish, head to this carnivore's mecca. Beyond a superb version of Portugal's black pork, you'll also find succulent Brazilian beef here, wild boar, cook-your-own steak options (on hot rocks), and more. If the weather cooperates, grab a table outside on the square so you can gaze at the church while you dine.

Large de Jesus, 7. www.carnesdoconvento.com. ✆ **26/523-36-20.** Main courses 10€–25€. Daily noon–2:30pm and 7–11pm.

Tasca da Fatinha ★★ PORTUGUESE Right in the port area, facing the fishing boats, Tasca da Fatinha places only the freshest of fish on its charcoal grills. They are then cooked with deep pride and expertise. That may be why there's often a line outside: Locals and visitors alike can't get enough of their grilled red mullet, grilled sardines, and, for a group, seafood rice.

Av. José Mourinho 58. ✆ **26/523-28-00.** Main courses 7€–20€. Daily noon–10pm.

Setúbal After Dark

The densest concentration of nightlife options lies near the western terminus of Avenida Luisa Todi, the road leading west to a string of beaches. Another fun place to party is the seafront village of **Albarquel,** less than 2km (about 1¼ miles) west of Setúbal. Try the late-night eatery **Restaurant All-Barquel,** Praia de Albarquel (✆ **26/522-19-46**), which caters to night owls of all ages.

PENINSULA DE TRÓIA

20 min. from Setúbal by ferry

Tróia is a long, sandy peninsula across the River Sado estuary that is accessible by ferry from Setúbal. It is graced with many good sandy beaches and crystal-clear waters, which makes it a choice vacation spot for families. Its appeal had begun to wane around the turn of the millennium but now it's making a comeback, especially with the opening of the Tróia Design Hotel (see below).

Essentials

ARRIVING

BY FERRY From Setúbal, **Atlantic Ferries,** Doca do Comércio (✆ **26/523-51-01**), operates both car and passenger ferries to the peninsula every half-hour to the hour 24 hours a day. From the port of Setúbal, the cost is 2.50€ per person on the passenger ferry or 11€ per person in a car headed to Tróia.

BY CAR Because Tróia is a peninsula, it's possible to drive there along Route N251 to reach it, but the road is circuitous and not a very good one. The car ferry is better.

VISITOR INFORMATION

There is no tourist office, but you can call **Tróia Resort,** Tróia-Carvalhal at ✆ **26/510-55-00** during the day or look for information at **www.troiaresort.net**.

Exploring the Area

Cetóbriga, on the peninsula, contains ruins of a once-thriving Roman port. Excavations began in the mid–19th century. The city, dating from the 3rd and 4th centuries, shows traces of villas, bathing pools, a fresco-decorated temple, and a factory for the salt preservation of fish. Cetóbriga's ruins are about 2.5km (1½ miles) from the site of the present tourist development of Tróia, but are worth seeing only if you have time. Otherwise, the simple foundations of long-gone buildings are too minor to merit a special visit. They're open

Tuesday to Saturday from June to August and Easter and New Year's; Saturday only from September to May. More info about schedules and tickets: http://troiaresort.pt/en/ruinas-romanas.

One of the top attractions of the island is the **Tróia Golf Course** designed by Robert Trent Jones at Complexo Turistico de Tróia, Carvalhal (www.troiagolf.com; ✆ **26/549-41-12**). This is an 18-hole, 6,374m (20,912-ft.), par-72 course that features a pro shop, restaurant, and bar. The course lies close to the sea and has many obstacles in its setting of maritime pines, tropical flora, and plenty of sand. Beginning players often find it too difficult; even to more experienced golfers, it's a big challenge. The cost is 73€ on Saturday and Sunday, lowered to 61€ weekdays. A handicap certificate is required.

Another popular attraction, especially for families, is dolphin watching. A family of around 30 dolphins lives in the estuary of the River Sado and they play and perform when the boats approach. Though many boat companies make the excursion, we recommend **Vertigem Azul** (http://vertigemazul.com/pt; ✆ **91/698-29-07**), operated by Pedro Narra and Maria João, who know all the dolphins by their fins.

Where to Stay & Dine

Aqualuz Suite Hotel Apartamentos Tróia Mar & Rio ★ Don't be put off by the boring architecture, especially when compared with the striking Tróia Design Hotel (see below). Aqualuz is a good value, not only for its nightly rates and beachy location, but because this is an all-apartment complex, meaning guests can save a bit by cooking some meals. We think the top apartments are nicest, thanks to their views (to Arrábida, the estuary of the River Sado, and the Atlantic beach) though none are exciting to look at—think practical digs meant to take the wear and tear of lots of people tracking in sand. Aqualuz also has a kid's club, a spa, and a good restaurant, Azimute. One warning: The Wi-Fi in the rooms can be spotty.

Tróia-Carvalhal. www.shotels.pt/aqualuz. ✆ **26/549-90-00.** 365 units. 76€–170€ double; 250€–400€ suite. **Amenities:** 2 restaurants; 2 pools; bar; bikes; children's programs; concierge; exercise room; babysitting; spa, sauna. Free Wi-Fi.

Tróia Design Hotel ★★★ This is the most luxurious resort in this area of Portugal. The creation of a number of the country's leading designers and architects, the hotel overlooks the marina. The complex rises 14 floors, its undulating facade studded with balconies. A sleek contemporary design, the structure consists of glass, concrete, and chrome crossed with wood and lacquer.

It's a family favorite because accommodations can be rented as one-, two-, or three-bedroom apartment units, each with their own private Jacuzzi. Bedrooms are spacious and well furnished, and the hotel opens right onto a good beach. On the roof are two pools: one for kids, and a swellegant infinity pool only for adults. A children's center keeps kids between 3 and 12 years old happily occupied.

The on-site spa is the best in this part of Portugal, with four distinct areas of treatment. More than 70 different treatments are performed by qualified therapists. The **Salinas Brasserie** is a stylish place for seafood and other dishes, and the **B&G** is more sophisticated, with a more refined cuisine.

Marina de Tróia-Carvalhal. www.troiadesignhotel.com. ✆ **26/549-80-00.** 205 units. 199€–219€ double; 259€–438€ suite. **Amenities:** 2 restaurants; bar; bikes; children's programs; concierge; exercise room; golf course; room service; spa. Free Wi-Fi.

PALMELA ★★

8km (5 miles) N of Setúbal; 32km (20 miles) SE of Lisbon

The village of Palmela lies in the heart of wine country, in the foothills of the Arrábida Mountains. It's famous for its fortress, which offers one of the best views in Portugal from an elevation of 366m (1,201 ft.). From this vantage point, you can see over sienna-hued valleys and vineyards flush with grapes to the capital in the north and to the estuary of the Sado to the south.

Essentials

ARRIVING

Take the Fertagus train service to Palmela, from Sete Rios or Entrecampos; www.fertagus.pt.

BY CAR From Lisbon, cross the Ponte do 25 de Abril bridge and head south along A2. Exit at the cutoff marked PALMELA and go the center. From Setúbal, continue along A2 to the same exit.

VISITOR INFORMATION

The local tourist office (✆ **21/233-21-22**) is at the Pousada de Palmela, Castelo de Palmela (see below). The office is open in summer Monday to Friday 9:30am to 8:30pm; in winter, hours are Monday to Saturday 9am to 1pm and 2 to 5:30pm.

Exploring Palmela's Castle

Palmela is famous as the site of a 12th-century fortress built by Afonso Henríques, the first king of Portugal, who drove out the Moors and secured control of the fertile lands south of the Tagus. Into the medieval walls of this fortress the Portuguese government built the **Pousada de Palmela,** in the Castelo de Palmela (see description, below). Today, part of the castle/fortress's complex incorporates the pousada, with the remainder open for visits, without charge, to anyone who drops in. On the premises, what was originally built in the 15th century as a church (Igreja de Santiago) is now a museum dedicated to a changing array of temporary exhibitions related to the art, folklore, and history of the region. It's open without charge Tuesday to Sunday from 10am to noon and from 2 to 6pm. For more information about the fortress, the church, and its temporary exhibitions, or the dining and accommodations within the castle, contact the pousada (see below).

Where to Stay & Dine

Pousada de Palmela, Castelo de Palmela ★★★ This is one of the last remaining segments of the town's 12th-century Moorish castle. It was built as a monastery within the castle walls in 1482, on orders of João I, and dedicated to St. James (Santiago). Its use as a pousada kept it from falling into ruin, and the skillful, unobtrusive conversion preserved the classic look and feel of a cloister. On the crest of a hill, the pousada is traditional in design; a huge square building opens onto a large courtyard, and the lower-level arches have been glassed in and furnished with lounge chairs.

Most of the guest rooms have been opened up, enlarged, and brought glamorously up to date. They're furnished in Portuguese style with hand-carved pieces and fine fabrics and tapestries, and most of the rooms open onto nice views. There's plenty of space, high ceilings, mosaic clay floors, and a general atmosphere of being in an historical place. Near the dining room is a comfortable drawing room with a noteworthy washbasin that the monks once used for their ablutions.

On a clear day the view from the castle walls is incredible: You can spot Lisbon and the statue of Cristo-Rei. Dinner in the pousada's restaurant is a highlight; besides the lovely setting there's warm service and authentic regional cuisine, paired with great wines from the area. Start your meal with local Azeitão cheese.

Castelo de Palmela. www.pousadas.pt. ✆ **21/235-12-26.** 28 units. 99€–235€ double; from 134€ suite. Rates include buffet breakfast. Free parking. **Amenities:** Restaurant; bar; babysitting; bikes; room service. Free Wi-Fi.

OESTE & FÁTIMA

Stretching for almost 200km (almost 125 miles) along the coastline north from Lisbon is the Oeste, or West, region. The fine beaches here are largely untouched by mass tourism, but are much sought after by surfers from around Europe and beyond. Inland is a region of gentle hills, vineyards, and fruit trees, with a sprinkling of lovely towns as old as the Portuguese nation.

The region is, in many ways, the spiritual heart of Portugal. Towns like Óbidos and Nazaré retain a charm undiminished by the passing of time. Farther inland, the monumental medieval monasteries of Batalha and Alcobaça are UNESCO World Heritage Sites. The Catholic shrine at Fátima draws countless pilgrims to a site where the Virgin Mary is said to have appeared to three shepherd children during World War I. Restaurants along the coast are renowned for their fresh seafood. The region's apples and pears are exported around the world, but nowhere do they taste sweeter.

One practical note: Because public transportation here is sparse and unreliable, we highly recommend renting a car.

ÓBIDOS ★★

93km (58 miles) N of Lisbon; 7km (4⅓ miles) S of Caldas da Rainha

The poet king Dinis and his saintly wife, Isabel of Aragón, once passed by the walls of this medieval village and noted its beauty. The queen likened the village to a jewel-studded crown. Eager to please, Dinis made her a present of the village. He established a tradition: Instead of precious stones, Portuguese royal bridegrooms presented Óbidos to their brides.

Entered through a tile-coated gatehouse, the town is definitely a trip back in time. The **medieval city ★★** rises on a sugar-loaf hill above a valley of vineyards. Its golden towers, crenellated battlements, and ramparts (which afford views of the tranquil Valley of the Ria Arnóia, vineyards, tiny cottages, and cultivated fields) contrast with gleaming white houses and the rolling countryside, where windmills clack in the breeze. It's one of the best preserved medieval villages in Portugal because its development was halted centuries ago, thanks to the silting of its harbor.

It can be crowded in the high season (from April to October), and especially during the temporary events—like the Chocolate Festival (usually during March) and the Medieval Fair (in August), both of which attract many Portuguese visitors.

Essentials

ARRIVING

BY BUS You can take a connecting bus from Lisbon, but the train is easier. Buses leave from Campo Grande in Lisbon to Caldas da Rainha, and then to Óbidos. Trips take around 1 hour. The one-way fare is 8€. Tickets can be purchased on the bus. For information, go to http://rodoviariadooeste.pt.

BY CAR From Lisbon, the trip takes around 40 minutes. The best route is on Hwy. A8, as the road is well maintained and speedy.

VISITOR INFORMATION

You'll find the **Óbidos Tourist Office** on Porta da Vila (www.rt-oeste.pt; ✆ **26/295-92-31**). It's open May to September daily from 9:30am to 7:30pm, and October to April daily from 9:30am to 6pm.

Exploring the Town

In the Renaissance church **Igreja de Santa Maria,** blue-and-white *azulejos* (tiles) line its **interior** ★. Look for the Renaissance **tomb** ★ and the paintings of Josefa of Óbidos, a renowned female 17th-century artist. The church lies to the right of the post office in the central square. It's open daily 9:30am to 12:30pm and 4:30 to 7pm April to September, and 9:30am to 12:30pm and 2:30 to 6pm October to March. Admission is free.

The other major attraction in Óbidos is the **castle** ★★ (part of which is now a *pousada,* an elegant inn; see "Where to Stay," below). The castle suffered severe damage in the 1755 earthquake but was restored. It's one of Portugal's greatest medieval castles, with a host of Manueline architectural elements. In 1148, Dom Afonso Henríques and his troops, disguised, legend has it, as cherry trees, captured the castle from the Moors. The Moors were driven from the land, and Henríques went on to become the founding father of Portugal; he was proclaimed its first king.

The main entrance to Óbidos is a much-photographed gate, the narrow, zigzag **Porta da Vila.** You'll have to park outside in the parking lots and walk through the gate.

There's a notable—and surprising—attraction just about 10km (about 6 miles) south of Óbidos: **Buddha's Eden** ★★ (www.buddhaeden.com) in the town of Bombarral. The largest Asian garden in Europe, it was created in response to ISIS's destruction of the Bamiyan buddhas in Afghanistan. You'll see replicas of those buddhas and reproductions of statues from across Asia—from the terracotta warriors of China to many Japanese and Indian buddhas. These are alongside a koi pond, pagodas, works of modern art, and a winery (Quinto dos Loridos), where you can do wine tastings after your sightseeing. The grounds are open daily from 9am to 6pm; entry is 2.50€.

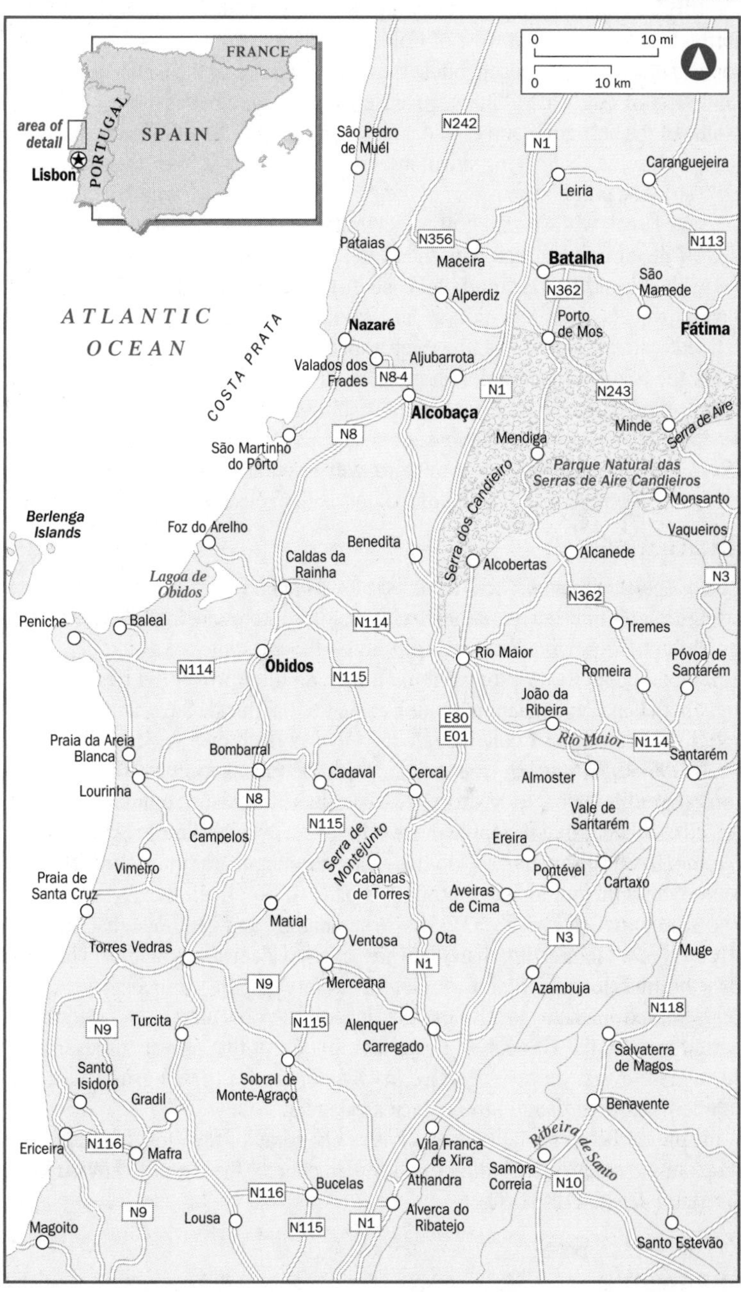

0
10 mi
0
10 km
FRANCE
SPAIN
PORTUGAL
area of detail
Lisbon
ATLANTIC OCEAN
COSTA PRATA
São Pedro de Muél
N242
N1
Caranguejeira
Leiria
Pataias
N356
Maceira
Batalha
N113
São Mamede
N362
Alperdiz
Porto de Mos
Fátima
Nazaré
Valados dos Frades
N8-4
Aljubarrota
N1
N243
Alcobaça
Minde
Serra de Aire
São Martinho do Pôrto
N8
Mendiga
Parque Natural das Serras de Aire Candieiros
Monsanto
Serra dos Candieiros
Berlenga Islands
Foz do Arelho
Benedita
Vaqueiros
Caldas da Rainha
Alcobertas
Alcanede
Lagoa de Óbidos
N3
N362
Peniche
Baleal
N114
Tremes
Óbidos
N114
Rio Maior
N115
Romeira
Póvoa de Santarém
João da Ribeira
E80
E01
Rio Maior
N114
Santarém
Praia da Areia Blanca
Bombarral
Lourinha
Cadaval
Cercal
Almoster
N8
Vale de Santarém
Campelos
N115
Serra de Montejunto
Ereira
Vimeiro
Pontével
Cartaxo
Praia de Santa Cruz
Cabanas de Torres
Aveiras de Cima
Matial
Ventosa
Ota
N3
Muge
Torres Vedras
N1
Merceana
Azambuja
N9
N118
Turcita
N115
Alenquer
N9
Carregado
Salvaterra de Magos
Santo Isidoro
Sobral de Monte-Agraço
Gradil
Benavente
Ribeira de Santo
Ericeira
N116
Mafra
Vila Franca de Xira
Samora Correia
Athandra
N10
Bucelas
N116
Alverca do Ribatejo
N9
Lousa
N115
N1
Magoito
Santo Estevão

Outdoor Activities

Ideal for general sunning and swimming is the beach at Lagoa de Óbidos, northwest of Óbidos and west of Caldas da Rainha. You can rent windsurfing boards and rigs on the beach, but surfers generally prefer the beach at Peniche, southwest of Lagoa de Óbidos, because the waves are better there.

One of the best golf courses in the region, **Praia d'el Rey Golf** is right on the coast with some challenging situations. Two rounds start at 89€ (www.praia-del-rey.com). The golf course is part of the Praia d'el Rey resort, which includes the Marriott Hotel, with special golf packages available for guests. Another option is **Golf do Vimeiro,** allied with the **Hotel Golf Mar,** at Torres Vedras (http://www.ohotelsandresorts.com/hotel/o-hotel-golf-mar; ✆ **26/198-08-00**), which towers over the cliff. The course has 9 holes, all relatively narrow and well defined by trees and shrubs; the river is an ever-present hazard. The first-class hotel, the best sports complex in the area, also offers tennis, three swimming pools (one heated), horseback riding, fishing, great views, access to several beaches, and a recommended restaurant, all for a reasonable price. Doubles are 45€ to 115€. The thermal spa of Vimeiro, with its curative waters, is close by. The course is 34km (21 miles) south of Óbidos, and greens fees are 25€ for 9 holes.

Shopping

Óbidos is one of the most active folkloric towns in Portugal; dozens of boutiques line the town's main street, **Rua Direita ★**. These stores are loaded with ceramics, embroideries, wine, and woodcarvings—though some are a bit touristy and lacking authenticity. Top buys in town include thick woven fabrics, regional rugs (both hand- and machine-made), raffia and handmade bags, and local lace.

Individual outlets of note include the **Oficina do Barro ★**, Rua Direita, 95 (✆ **26/295-92-31**), which is associated with the town's tourist office. It maintains a studio (open to visitors) that produces delicate ceramics—usually glazed in white—that resemble the texture of a woven basket. These are called *verguinha* and are native to Óbidos. This handicraft tradition almost disappeared, but Oficina do Barro brought it back to life. **Loja dos Arcos,** 35-37, Rua Direita (✆ **26/295-98-33**) sells wine, leather, and ceramics that are usually a bit more interesting than the wares at equivalent shops nearby. They sell also the traditional *ginjinha de Óbidos*, a very popular sour cherry liqueur that's served in many local bars. Get it with the chocolate cup—a tradition started here by the **Chocolate Festival,** a big event that attracts thousands of Portuguese every year (in March). In October there's the **Literary Festival,** another important date on the village's calendar.

In spite of being a small place, Óbidos has some of the most unique bookshops in the country, including one inside a church, the **Grande Livraria de Santiago** (✆ **26/210-31-80**).

Where to Stay

EXPENSIVE

Pousada de Óbidos, Castelo de Óbidos ★★★ This Manueline-trimmed stone palace is one of the most heavily booked in the country, so you should reserve rooms as far in advance as possible. It's also one of the most expensive *pousadas*, due to its history-rich location in the medieval castle. Rooms vary in size, but most of them are quite comfortable and well furnished with reproduction furniture inspired by the 16th and 17th centuries. Homemade quilts or fabrics cover the beds, and the bathrooms, a bit small, are covered with hand-painted *azulejos* (tiles). Some of the rooms are more than 700 years old and look it—in a charming way. Deep-set windows have tiny ledges from which you can look out onto the countryside— these were originally part of the watchtowers of the castle. If you prefer digs that are less austere, the *pousada* has more modern accommodation in Casa do Castelo, where some rooms have fireplaces and terraces. Public areas are full of antiques and references to Portuguese royalty. The cuisine and service are the finest in Óbidos.

Paço Real, Óbidos. www.pousadas.pt. ✆ **26/295-50-80.** 17 units. 129€–260€ double; from 180€–360€ suite. Rates include buffet breakfast. **Amenities:** Restaurant; bar; bikes; massage in room on request; free parking. Free Wi-Fi.

Praia d'El Rey Marriott Golf & Beach Resort ★★★ You'll find the most luxurious hotel in the area lying 16km (10 miles) west of Óbidos. The Praia d'El Rey opens onto a splendid sandy beach stretching for 4km (2½ miles). The resort hotel itself, with its 18-hole championship golf course, stands on 243 hectares (600 acres) of oceanfront property. Even in rainy weather, you can swim in the indoor pool, where columns evoke a Roman bath. The bedrooms, roomy and light, are the most cushy in the area, containing all those extras that make for a good stay, including bottled water, bathrobes, coffee/tea makers, and individual climate control. They all features private terraces or balconies opening onto ocean views or garden/golf views. Restaurant facilities range from a pool grill to alfresco dining on a terrace overlooking the ocean. The hotel was renovated in the first months of 2017, so everything should be spiffy and new when you arrive.

Av. D. Inês de Castro, 1, Amoreira. www.marriott.com/lisdr. ✆ **26/290-51-00.** 179 units. 104€–450€ double; 218€–1,000€ suite. **Amenities:** 3 restaurants; 4 bars; babysitting; bikes; children's center; concierge; 18-hole golf course; health club & spa; 2 freshwater pools (1 heated indoor); 7 outdoor tennis courts (lit); extensive watersports equipment/ rentals. Free parking. Free Wi-Fi.

MODERATE

Casa das Senhoras Rainhas ★★ Although it hardly ranks up there with the Pousada de Óbidos, this substantial but small inn is installed in a tiled-roof villa that was constructed to blend harmoniously with the antique architecture of Óbidos. It's located inside the walls, and the rooms are downright hip with a white, purple, and gray color scheme (it works) and top-quality beds. Seven of the rooms have a balcony. On-site is the popular Restaurant Cozinha das Rainhas (call ahead for reservations).

Rua Padre Nunes Tavares 6. www.senhorasrainhas.com. ✆ **26/295-53-60.** 10 units. 110€–169€ double; 175€–200€ suite. **Amenities:** Restaurant; bar; babysitting; bikes. Free Wi-Fi in lobby.

Casa d'Óbidos ★★ Atmospheric accommodations in the area right outside Óbidos are available in this carefully restored manor house dating from the 19th century. Standing in the midst of well-landscaped gardens, the house is furnished with antiques and tiles made by local artisans. Both the public and private rooms are exquisitely decorated, whether you stay in the main house or one of the cottages or private apartments on the grounds. The cottages are a good value for families and are equipped with kitchenettes. Breakfast is also provided to the cottages.

Quinta de S. José. www.casadobidos.com. ✆ **26/295-09-24.** 10 units. 70€–90€ double. Cottages 70€–175€. Extra bed 23€. **Amenities:** Outdoor pool; outdoor tennis court; free parking. Free Wi-Fi.

Casas de S. Thiago ★★ You get comfort and tranquillity in an intimate atmosphere at this manorial guesthouse situated inside the city walls, near the castle. Walls are covered with authentic Portuguese *azulejos*, and all the bedrooms have a fireplace and tiled private bathroom. Best of all: The personalized hospitality here makes you feel like you're staying in a private home. Bedrooms are small but have a cozy decor, including iron beds. Many guests spend as much time in the pleasant courtyard, where breakfast is served when the weather cooperates.

Largo de S. Tiago do Castelo. www.casas-sthiago.com. ✆/fax **26/295-95-87.** 8 units. 60€–95€ double. Rates include buffet breakfast. Free Wi-Fi.

Hotel Real d'Óbidos ★★ The present owners took over a property that dated from the 14th century and rebuilt it according to the original architectural plans, filling it with armor, swords, and other medieval bric-a-brac. Bedrooms vary widely: Some carry on the old-timey theme with beamed ceilings, four-poster beds, and heavy tapestries; others look like rooms in a hundred other Portuguese hotels (cheery, with white walls and neutral furnishings). Bathrooms are contemporary, tiled, and well maintained. The lounge has a huge fireplace, perfect for gray days; while the swimming pool allows guests to toast in the sun while contemplating the castle. A hearty buffet breakfast is part of the deal.

Rua D. João de Ornelas. www.hotelrealdobidos.com. ✆ **26/295-50-90.** 15 units. 105€–195€ double; 150€–230€ suite. Rates include buffet breakfast. **Amenities:** Restaurant; bar; babysitting; outdoor pool; room service; free parking. Free Wi-Fi.

The Literary Man-Óbidos Hotel ★★ For book lovers, this is the equivalent of a vacation in Disneyland. The hotel's extensive libraries display over 45,000 volumes… and the collection keeps growing. Most of the books are in English, but you'll find Portuguese, French, German, and Spanish titles, too, including many original editions. (Part of the collection is also for sale to help fund charity projects.) But not only are there books everywhere, this lodging does its best to set a mood conducive to curling up with a good mystery or romance. The renovated convent has a lot of charm, the bedrooms graced with iron beds below high ceilings, and decorated with recycled wood. Yes, rooms

THE beaches

Take your pick from the ribbonlike string of beaches that stretches almost continuously along the west coast. Some 240km (149 miles) of sand extend all the way to its northern edge, just south of the beach resort of **Figueira da Foz.**

Many of Oeste beaches are uncrowded and blessed with powdery sand bordering crystal-clear waters. Strong currents and waves make many of them excellent for surfing, but not so good for swimming. Make sure to go to a beach with a lifeguard and avoid those near the industrial areas—some of these are polluted. Look for beaches flying a blue banner, which indicates that the European Union has granted its seal of approval to the beach's hygiene and safety.

One of our favorites beaches is in the seaside village of **São Martinho do Porto,** 116km (72 miles) north of Lisbon and a short run south of overcrowded Nazaré. Nestled between pine-covered foothills and the ocean, its waters are calm and clear. Another swell strand, north of Nazaré, is at **São Pedro de Moel,** 135km (84 miles) north of Lisbon. It has a 63-room resort hotel, **Hotel Mar e Sol,** Av. da Liberdade 1 (www.hotel-maresol.com; ✆ **24/459-00-00**), where guests can take a room or a meal. Rooms range from 60€ to 95€ for a double, including breakfast. The chefs here serve an excellent regional cuisine for lunch and dinner, focused mainly on locally caught fish. Main courses cost 8€ to 20€.

Avid tanners will also want to seek out the town of **Peniche,** 92km (57 miles) north of Lisbon. This fishing port stands high on a peninsula, with wide, sandy beaches at the foot of rocky cliffs. When you tire of the beach, you can explore **Cabo Carvoeiro** on the peninsula, about 4.8km (3 miles) east of Peniche. It offers panoramic views of the surf smashing against the rock formations hundreds of feet below the road. Those with kids may want to head to the large waterpark complex, **Sportágua,** Avenida Monsenhor Bastos (www.sportagua.com; ✆ **26/278-91-25**), which has water slides and swimming pools for adults and separate ones for children, plus dining places. Admission is 12€ for adults, 10€ for children 6 to 10, and free for children under 5. Hours are daily 10am to 7pm from mid-July to mid-September.

Many of the area's most popular beaches, those with the most facilities, are visited for their sands, not for swimming. (They might not have blue flags, depending on conditions, when you visit.) These include **Foz do Arelho** and **Nazaré,** the latter famed for its giant waves**.** Other less frequented but good beaches are at **Pedrógão, Baleal, Consolação, Porto Novo,** and **Santa Cruz.** All are signposted from the highway. Finally, if you wish to stay somewhere exclusive and close to the beach, choose **Areias do Seixo** (www.areiasdoseixo.com), a stunning hotel. Its luxury bedrooms come with fireplaces, huge bathrooms, and terraces. It's close to Santa Cruz and Praia da Mexilhoeira and is a favorite for honeymooners. The friendly owners welcome guests every day with songs, snacks, and wine in the Circle of Fire at sunset. Rooms are from 265€.

can be small (they were often nuns' quarters originally), but most guests don't seem to mind—they're likely distracted by what they're reading.

Rua Dom João de Ornelas. www.theliteraryman.pt. ✆ **26/295-92-17.** 30 units. 77€–110€ double; 110€–130€ suite. Rates include buffet breakfast. **Amenities:** Restaurant; bar; room service; library; massages. Free Wi-Fi.

INEXPENSIVE

Albergaria Josefa d'Óbidos Hotel ★ This flower-bedecked inn lies outside the old town's fortifications, on a hillside that overlooks the main gate into Óbidos. The guest rooms range from small to midsize and are furnished mostly with modern furniture. Each unit comes with a tiny, neatly kept bathroom covered with hand-painted tiles. The restaurant, in the classic style of an old-fashioned Portuguese tavern, serves regional and international cuisine with an emphasis on fish. Main courses cost 10€ to 26€.

Rua Dom João de Ornelas. www.josefadobidos.com. ✆ **26/295-92-28.** 34 units. 50€–80€ double; 110€–150€ suite. Rates include buffet breakfast. **Amenities:** Restaurant; 2 bars; room service. Free Wi-Fi.

Albergaria Rainha Santa Isabel ★ On a narrow cobblestone street running through the center of town, this building, once a private home, is many centuries old. Blue, white, and yellow tiles cover the high-ceilinged lobby. The comfortable bar area is filled with leather sofas and Victorian-style chairs. An elevator runs to the simply furnished but immaculate guest rooms. Most guests deposit their luggage at the reception desk before parking for free on the square in front of the village church nearby.

Rua Direita, www.obidoshotel.com. ✆ **26/295-93-23.** 20 units. 40€–90€ double. Rates include buffet breakfast. **Amenities:** Bar; room service. Free Wi-Fi.

Where to Dine

MODERATE

Most visitors to Óbidos like to dine at Pousada de Óbidos, Castelo de Óbidos (see "Where to Stay," above). However, you get far better value, less formality, and more local color at one of the typical little restaurants inside or outside the city's walls.

Café/Restaurante 1 de Dezembro ★ PORTUGUESE This snack bar and restaurant is known for its reliable *pratos do día* (plates of the day), made with market-fresh ingredients, and thus much better at lunch time. You won't go wrong here with the Portuguese *cozido*, which is a thick meat and vegetable stew, or else *caldeirada*, a seafood stew. In summer, the grilled sardines are what to order. If you don't want a full sit-down meal, this is a reliable place to grab a quick bite.

Largo São Pedro 3. ✆ **26/295-92-98.** Main courses 10€–20€. Mon–Sat 8am–midnight.

Restaurante Alcaide ★★ REGIONAL PORTUGUESE A local favorite inside the city walls, this spot is known for its regional fare and good, inexpensive wines. Dishes that should tempt include an appetizer of clams with garlic and cilantro (*amêijoas à Bulhão Pato*), and mains like grouper filet gratin, baked salt cod with corn bread, or one of the meat specialties, such as escalopes of veal in a tangy port sauce.

Rua Direita 60. www.restaurantealcaide.com. ✆ **26/295-92-20.** Reservations recommended. Main courses 10€–22€. Thurs–Tues 12:30–3pm and 7:30–10pm.

A SIDE TRIP TO caldas da rainha

The rheumatic sister-queen of King Manuel, Leonor, discovered the therapeutic value of the springs here on a trip to Óbidos. The town has been a spa ever since.

Leonor returned to Caldas da Rainha again and again, and she constructed a hospital and an adjoining church. The chapel, **Nossa Senhora do Pópulo,** was built in the early–16th century in the Manueline style, then at its apex. The spa, which was particularly popular in the 19th century, lies some 95km (59 miles) north of Lisbon. People usually visit it after stopping at Óbidos, 6.5km (4 miles) away. It's worth the 30 minutes or so needed to explore the interior of the church: The walls are entirely covered in beautiful hand-painted *azulejos.* The outstanding artistic treasure of the church is a **triptych ★** of the Crucifixion, which lies above the triumphal arch of the temple.

Caldas da Rainha is also noted for its ceramics. Many roadside stands charge far lower prices than you'd pay in Lisbon. The best selections are in the showrooms of factories, notably **Secla,** Rua São João de Deus (www.secla.pt; ✆ **26/284-21-51**). But the most famous is **Bordallo Pinheiro,** Rua António Oliveira, 28 (http://pt.bordallopinheiro.com; ✆ **26/283-93-80**), a 19th-century company known for its traditional handmade ceramics in cabbage and other vegetable shapes, among other designs. On the first floor of the shop and showroom are the bargains, pieces with small (and often unnoticeable) flaws. The daily outdoor fruit market is famous for its variety and quality—some of the best fruit in Portugal is produced in the West region. You could graze at the market, or head for the restaurant **Raízes** (✆ **26/283-61-84**) inside the park, which puts out a toothsome spread of *petiscos* (small plates).

Tribeca ★★★ PORTUGUESE/INTERNATIONAL The name is as unexpected as the decor—a mix of French brasserie and Portuguese *cervejaria* (beer house)—but those in the know head to this unusually accomplished restaurant, for its kindly service and excellent cuisine. Any of the fish dishes here are worth trying, from Atlantic sea bass or sole, caught close by in the fishing port of Peniche, to the seafood pie (delicious!) or the lobster rice. The menu includes many meat dishes, too; top choices (we think) are the partridge pie or the black pig. The menu at lunchtime also includes burgers, salads, and light meals. The eatery is close to Serra d'el Rei and a 10-minute drive from Óbidos.

Avenida da Serrana,5, Serra d'El-Rei. www.tribeca-restaurante.com. ✆ **26/290-94-61.** Main courses 12€–42€. Open daily 12:30–2:30pm and 7:30–10:30pm, except Mon when it's closed for lunch.

ALCOBAÇA ★★

108km (67 miles) N of Lisbon; 16km (10 miles) NE of Caldas da Rainha

The main attraction in Alcobaça is its stately monastery. But the shopping is worthy, too—the nearby market is said to sell the best fruit in Portugal. (The peaches and the pears, grown in surrounding orchards originally planted by the Cistercian monks, are especially succulent.) Many market stalls also sell the blue-and-white pottery typical of Alcobaça.

Essentials

ARRIVING

BY BUS From Lisbon, four *expressos* depart each day for Alcobaça; the trip takes 2 hours and costs 11€ one-way. Buses are run by **Rede Expressos** (www.rede-expressos.pt; ✆ **70/722-33-44**).

BY CAR From Caldas da Rainha, continue northeast along N8 for 16km (10 miles).

VISITOR INFORMATION

The **Alcobaça Tourist Office** is in Rua 16 de Outubro, 7 (www.cm-alcobaca.pt; ✆ **26/258-23-77**). It's open May to July and September daily 10am to 1pm and 3 to 7pm; August daily 10am to 7pm; October to April daily 10am to 1pm and 2 to 6pm.

Exploring the Town

In the Middle Ages, the Cistercian **Mosteiro de Santa Maria (St. Mary Monastery)** ★★★ was one of the richest and most prestigious in Europe. Begun in 1178, it was founded to honor a vow made by Portugal's first king, Afonso Henríques, before he faced the Moors at Santarém. Alcobaça, at the confluence of the Alcoa and Baça rivers, was built to show his spiritual indebtedness to St. Bernard of Clairvaux, who inspired (some say goaded) many Crusaders into battle against the infidels.

Today, in spite of its baroque facade and latter-day overlay, the monastery is a monument to simplicity and majesty. Above the 98m-long (322-ft.) nave, quadripartite vaulting is supported on transverse arches. These rest on towering pillars and columns. The aisles, too, have stunning vertical lines and are practically as tall as the nave itself.

The transept shelters the **Gothic tombs** ★★ of two star-crossed lovers, the Romeo and Juliet of Portuguese history. Though damaged, their sarcophagi are the greatest pieces of sculpture from 14th-century Portugal. The artist is unknown.

The **Cloisters of Silence,** with their delicate arches, were favored by Dinis, the poet-king. He sparked a thriving literary colony at the monastery, where the monks were busily engaged in translating ecclesiastical writings.

Aside from the tombs and cloisters, the curiosity is the kitchen, through which a branch of the Alcoa River was routed. As in most Cistercian monasteries, the flowing brook was instrumental for sanitation purposes. Chroniclers have suggested that the friars fished for their dinner in the brook and later washed their dishes in it.

In the 18th-century **Salon of Kings** are niches with sculptures of some Portuguese rulers. The empty niches, left waiting for the rulers who were never sculptured, lend a melancholic air. The tiles in the room depict, in part, Afonso Henríques's triumph over the Moors.

OFF THE BEATEN PATH: nature in the raw

The area around Alcobaça contains two of the least discovered but most dramatic havens for nature in Portugal: a national park and an offshore island that's ideal for scuba diving.

Parque Natural das Serras de Aire e Candeeiros straddles the border between the Oeste and Ribatejo, almost halfway between Lisbon and Coimbra. Encompassing more than 30,000 hectares (74,132 acres) of moors and scrubland, the rocky landscape is sparsely settled. One small hamlet you will find here is **Minde,** where women weave the patchwork rugs that are well known in the region. Take along plenty of supplies (water, lunch, sunscreen, and so on) for a day's hike in the wilderness.

In this rocky landscape, farmers barely eke out a living. They gather local stones to build their shelters, and they get energy from windmills. If you'd rather drive than hike through the area, take N362, which runs for some 45km (28 miles) from Batalha in the north to Santarém in the south.

The other great area of natural beauty is **Berlenga Island ★★★**. A granite rock in the Atlantic, Berlenga is a nature preserve, so there are restrictions to the places you can visit. Eleven kilometers (6¾ miles) out in the ocean west of Peniche, a medieval fortress once stood guard over the Portuguese coastline from this island. Berlenga is the largest island in a little archipelago made up of three groups of rocky rises known as the Berlenga Grande, Farilhões, and Estelas.

The medieval fortress on Berlenga, **Forte de São João Batista,** was destroyed in 1666 when 28 Portuguese soldiers tried to withstand a force of 1,500 Spaniards, who bombarded it from 15 ships. Rebuilt toward the end of the 17th century, it now houses a hostel. You can take a stairway from the fortress to the lighthouse, stopping along the way to look over the panorama of the archipelago. A cobblestone walk from the top of the lighthouse site takes you down to a little bay with fishermen's cottages along a beach.

The **Furado Grande** is a long marine tunnel that leads to a creek walled in by the granite cliffs. Under the fortress is a cave the locals call the **blue grotto,** but its pool is really closer to emerald green. The clear waters of the grotto and the island itself make Berlenga a mecca for snorkelers and scuba divers. Local waters contain an array of fish, including bream, red mullet, and sea bass. If you don't snorkel, you can rent a small boat on the docks to visit the caves. To reach the island, head first for Peniche, 92km (57 miles) north of Lisbon. A ferry makes the trip to the island from the end of May to September 30. Visit www.viamar-berlenga.com for more info. A same-day round-trip ticket costs 20€. From September to June, one ferry a day leaves at 10am and returns at 6pm. ***A word of caution:*** This boat ride is rough. If you're prone to getting seasick, take the proper precautions—or skip this excursion.

The monastery (www.mosteiroalcobaca.pt; ✆ **26/250-51-20**) is located on Praça 25 de Abril and is open daily April to September from 9am to 7pm and October to March from 9am to 6pm. Admission costs 6€, plus 2€ for the sacristy; free for children under 12.

SHOPPING You'll find a dozen or so handicraft and ceramics shops lining the square in front of the monastery. The monument itself has a shop with replicas of artwork, plus books and regional products. We find the highest

ROOSTERS rising from the dead

Portugal's Atlantic melancholy, its majestic vistas, and its history's drama and occasional madness have all contributed to a rich body of legend, lore, and folklore. Some of these tales and myths were promoted as ideology that unified the country against the menace of neighboring Spain. Other tales were borrowed from Christian, Moorish, and—in some cases—Celtic mythology that permeated the land in prehistoric times.

In the 20th century, the Estado Novo propaganda (the fascist regime) made some legends part of the folklore and Portuguese symbols out of legends, like the rooster of Barcelos: The bird—although cooked and about to be served as the main course in a magistrate's dinner—crowed ecstatically to prove the innocence of a pilgrim wrongfully accused of theft.

Equally touching is the Legend of the Almond Blossoms, which dates from the 10th-century's Moorish occupation of the Algarve. A Viking maiden, captured as a child during battle, fell in love with the son of the local Caliph and married him. Despite their joy, only the sight of a field of almond trees, reminiscent of the snow of her native Norway, could keep her happy and healthy in her adopted Moorish home. In gratitude, the Caliph ordered the planting of thousands of almond trees. Today, residents of the Algarve recall this myth every January and February when the almond trees bloom.

Another legend involves Dom Fuas Ropinho, one of Portugal's founders and the subject of several poems by Camões. The devil, vengeful at the rare instance of facing a virtuous and incorruptible man, disguised himself as a stag during a hunt and led Dom Fuas to the edge of a steep rocky cliff. Only the image of the Virgin (which appeared suddenly in a blaze of light) caused the hunter to stop, only moments before he'd have been thrown by his horse over the rocks to his death. In 1182, Dom Fuas built, near the cliffs, a chapel to Our Lady of Nazaré. Rebuilt in the 1500s, it was visited by Vasco da Gama, who prayed there in thanks after discovering the sea route to India in 1498.

Finally, there is the Miracle of the Roses: The Aragonese Princess Isabella spent the bulk of her personal fortune to help the penniless nuns of Santa Clara. Her kind but thrifty husband, Dinis, was about to punish her severely for donating her final funds to the order but was stopped when the loaves of bread Isabella was carrying were miraculously transformed into roses. Since it was January, when roses were out of season, the king fell on his knees in thanks; to everyone's delight, Dinis massively increased her annual income so she could continue to make charitable gifts as she saw fit. Today, the sainted queen is the patron saint of Coimbra, with biannual torchlight processions held in her honor.

Other legends reflect the madness of some of the country's rulers and are in some cases historically true. In the 1300s, Prince Dom Pedro fell in love with one of his wife's ladies-in-waiting, a Spanish-born girl named Inês de Castro. Soon Inês was banished from the country. When Pedro's wife died, Inês returned to live openly with him. Fearing that Inês was fomenting a plot against the monarchy, a group of nobles (including Afonso IV, Pedro's father) arranged to have her killed. Pedro, upon finding her body, became insane. When he ascended the throne 2 years later, he had the hearts of Inês's murderers torn from their bodies, ordered that she be exhumed and dressed in royal clothes, and arranged for her coronation as queen of Portugal in the monastery of Alcobaca (see above). Part of the ceremony involved the obligatory kissing of the skeletal royal hand by all the nobles present. Today, the tomb of Inês that Pedro commissioned for Alcobaca is considered one of the most beautiful in Portugal.

quality goods at **A Casa, Artesanato e Garrafeira,** Praça 25 de Abril, 51–52 (✆ **26/259-01-20**), which sells antiques, ceramics, and regional wine, among other offerings. We're also partial to **Alcoa,** right in Praça 25 de Abril, 44 (www.pastelaria-alcoa.com; ✆ **26/259-74-74**), a bakery and cafe that uses centuries-old convent recipes. Expect lots of egg yolks, almonds, and sugar; don't skip their award-winning custard tarts.

Where to Stay

MODERATE

Challet da Fonte Nova ★★★ A majestic iron gate dating from the 19th century guards the entrance to this traditional chaletlike structure—the best accommodations in town. Once a private mansion, this is now a charming, graceful inn, consisting of three floors plus a basement that has been turned into a saloon with a pool table and bar. Bedrooms vary in dimensions, but all are elegant and comfortable, with swooping draperies, antiques (or antique reproductions), smooth wooden floors, and sometimes, wooden ceilings. The breakfast here is particularly good, as are the mattresses (though there's no breakfast in bed—sorry!).

Rua da Fonte Nova. www.challetfontenova.pt. ✆ **26/259-83-00.** 10 units. 70€ double; 145€ junior suite. Rates include buffet breakfast. **Amenities:** Bar; spa. Free parking. Free Wi-Fi.

INEXPENSIVE

Hotel D. Inês de Castro ★ This small hotel is strictly functional and of recent construction. It is, nonetheless, comfortable and convenient for an overnight stopover. Bedrooms are small and the decor is forgettable but in good condition. The location is convenient to explore Alcobaça and the monastery. A generous breakfast is served.

Rua Costa Veiga 44–48. www.hotel-inesdecastro.com. ✆ **26/258-23-55.** 37 units. 30€–100€. Free parking. Free Wi-Fi in public rooms.

Hotel Santa Maria ★ The most attractive modern hotel in town is ideally located in a quiet but central part of the historic city, on a sloping street just above the plaza in front of the monastery. Guest rooms are a bit cramped but cute, filled with polished paneling cut into geometrical shapes. They contain comfortable contemporary chairs and beds, and some have views and balconies over the monastery and square.

Rua Francisco Zagalo 20–22. www.hotelsantamaria.com.pt. ✆ **26/259-01-60.** 76 units. 39€–70€ double; 80€ suite. Rates include buffet breakfast. **Amenities:** Bar; room service; free parking. Free Wi-Fi in public areas.

Where to Dine

Trindade ★ PORTUGUESE Opening onto a side of the monastery fronting a tree-shaded square, Trindade has both full restaurant service and a snack bar. Your meal here is likely to include shellfish soup, fish rice, or the fresh fish of the day. Tender roast chicken is also available. The food is hearty and full of flavor, but get ready for a wait: The place is often overrun with international religious pilgrims and is a popular hangout for locals.

Praça do Dom Afonso Henriques 22. ✆ **26/258-23-97.** Main courses 10€–22€. Daily 9:30am–11pm (bar open until 2am). Closed 2 weeks in Oct or Nov.

NAZARÉ ★★

132km (82 miles) N of Lisbon; 13km (8 miles) NW of Alcobaça

The inhabitants of Portugal's most famous fishing village live in a tradition-bound world. The people remain insular, even as their village blossoms into a big summer resort and a surfing hot spot, especially since international media covered the giant waves at Praia do Norte.

Nazaré is best experienced in the off season; chances are you won't really get to see it in summer. You'll be too busy looking for a parking place (good luck) or elbowing your way onto the beach. The crowds that come to visit the "most picturesque fishing village in Portugal," coupled with widespread high-rise construction, have made people wonder what happened to the fishing village.

Essentials

ARRIVING

BY BUS Eight express buses per day arrive from Lisbon. The trip takes 2 hours and costs 11€ one-way. Buses are run by **Rede Expressos** (www.rede-expressos.pt; ✆ **70/722-33-44**) and depart from Sete Rios terminal in Lisbon.

BY CAR From Alcobaça (see above), continue northwest along N8-5 for about 13km (8 miles). From Lisbon, take Hwy. A-8.

VISITOR INFORMATION

The **Nazaré Tourist Office** is on Avenida Manuel Remígio (✆ **26/256-19-44**). It's open daily, but hours vary depending on the time of year, so you should call ahead.

Exploring the Village

Don't expect stunning architecture or historic sights—the big attractions in Nazaré are the people and their fabled boats and the stunning coast. The villagers' clothes are patchwork quilts of sun-faded colors. The rugged men don rough woolen shirts and trousers, patched in kaleidoscopic rainbow hues resembling tartan, as well as long woolen stocking caps, in the dangling ends of which they keep their prized possessions—a favorite pipe or a crucifix. Some women still wear embroidered, handmade blouses and pleated skirts of patched tartan woolens—the traditional costumes.

The fishing boats here are Phoenician in design: slender, elongated to face the waves, and boldly colored. Painted on the high, knifelike prows you'll often see crudely shaped eyes—eyes supposedly imbued with the magical power to search the deep for fish and to avert storms. Even so, the boats sport lanterns for the dangerous job of fishing after dark. During the gusty days of winter, or at high tide, the boats are hauled into a modern harbor about 10 minutes from the city's center. If you want to look at a boat, one of the locals will lead you—for a price.

Nazaré consists of two sections: the fishing quarter and the **Sítio ★**, the almost exclusively residential upper town. Near the beach you'll find handicraft shops, markets, restaurants, hotels, and boardinghouses. The main square opens directly onto the sea, and narrow streets lead to the smaller squares, evoking a medina in a Moorish village. At the farthest point from the cliff and square are the vegetable and fish markets, where auctions are held.

Jutting out over the sea, the promontory of the Sítio is a sheer drop to the ocean and the beach below. It's accessible by either a funicular or a steep cobblestone pathway. The Virgin Mary supposedly appeared here in 1182: A young horseback-riding nobleman, Dom Fuas Roupinho, was pursuing a wild deer near the precipice, which was shrouded in mist. The fog lifted suddenly to reveal the Virgin and the chasm below. In honor of this miracle, the nobleman built the **Chapel of Memory.** Today, near the spot, you can go inside the 18th-century structure honoring the event. The tiny chapel is known for its *azulejos*, or hand-painted tiles, that cover its facade, roof, and interior. Many of the tiles depict the legend of Dom Fuas Roupinho. A staircase leads down into a small crypt, and here, in a recess, is what is said to be the hoofprint left by Roupinho's horse as it came to a screeching halt at the edge of the cliff, saving its rider's life.

The **panoramic view ★★★** of Nazaré, the Atlantic coast and the impressive waves of **Praia do Norte,** is one of the great seascapes in this region. Praia do Norte is not recommended at all for swimming, just for watching the surfers attempt to ride the giant waves. It was here American surfer Garrett McNamara surfed the biggest wave ever, 30m (90 ft.) high, a new world record in 2011. The video and photos of a tiny man in a colossal wave that seemed to engulf the **Forte São Miguel Arcanjo** put Nazaré on the international map. Garrett even married his wife, Nicole, also American, in Nazaré in 2012, in the old lighthouse seen in the celebrated photos. On the edge of the promontory, this fortress from the late 16th century holds an exhibit about the spectacular waves caused by the underwater canyon, as well as an art gallery. But the view is the best feature and is totally breathtaking when the waves get bigger, usually in autumn/winter. Admission is 2€.

SHOPPING Few other towns in Portugal have so many shops—but so few that aren't disappointing. Perhaps it's the sheer volume of merchandise in the crammed boutiques, all featuring much the same wares. The residents of tourist-conscious Nazaré long ago lost their enthusiasm for their ubiquitous, rough-textured fisher's sweaters, which seem to spill over the shelves of virtually every boutique in town. The robust *varinas* (fishwives) of Nazaré have given up knitting in favor of more modern commercial pursuits, such as running snack bars, souvenir shops, and postcard kiosks. Most of the knitwear you'll see here is imported from less prosperous communities in Portugal's far north.

Where to Stay

Although Nazaré is one of the most popular destinations in Portugal, for some reason it has never had a first-rate hotel.

MODERATE

Hotel Miramar Sul ★★ You're paying for the views here, but what views they are! The hotel is situated at the top of the hill, and the vistas overlook the shimmering blue Atlantic and the beach from *almost* every bedroom, and from the lovely pool area. Bedrooms are pleasant, adorned with lightwood furnishings offset by cheery red throw blankets and drapes. All have a balcony. The on-site restaurant is first class, specializing in fish—try the local ocean sea bass—along with shellfish.

Caminho Real. www.hotelmiramar.pt. ✆ **26/255-00-00.** 62 units. 60€–156€ double. Free parking. **Amenities:** Restaurant; bar; babysitting; kid's room; exercise room; Jacuzzi; outdoor pool; room service; sauna. Free Wi-Fi.

Hotel Praia ★ The Praia (literally, "Beach") is decorated in a modern but uninspired style, with pops of bright orange and aqua blue here and there and lots of stainless steel and tan woods. It's about a 5-minute walk from the sandy beach where the fishing boats and bathing cabins are.

Av. Vieira Guimarães 39. www.hotelpraia.com. ✆ **26/256-14-23.** 40 units. 65€–160€ double; 90€–190€ junior suite. Rates include buffet breakfast. Parking 5€. **Amenities:** Restaurant; bar; concierge; exercise room; pets allowed; 2 pools (1 indoor); room service; sauna. Free Wi-Fi.

Mar Bravo ★★ Considerably improved in recent years and always beautifully situated (right off the beach), this place now has a clean-lined chic to it, though many rooms are the size of a postage stamp. The location on the main square right in front of the beach is convenient, but can be very busy in the summer months.

Praça Sousa Oliveira 70–71. www.marbravo.com. ✆ **26/256-91-60.** 16 units. 65€–150€ double. Rates include buffet breakfast. Free parking nearby. **Amenities:** 2 restaurants; bar; concierge; room service; pets allowed. Free Wi-Fi.

INEXPENSIVE

Hotel Da Nazaré ★ Located on a noisy street set back from the water, about a 3-minute walk from the promenade, Hotel Da Nazaré opens onto a tiny plaza. Many of the front guest rooms (all dated looking) have private balconies, some with sea views. The best features of this hotel are its fourth- and fifth-floor restaurant and bar. The dining room opens onto windowed walls peering out over the village housetops, the rugged cliffs, and the harbor.

Largo Afonso Zuquete. www.hoteldanazare.com. ✆ **26/256-90-30.** 52 units. 40€–90€ double; 95€–115€ suite. Rates include buffet breakfast. Free parking. **Amenities:** Restaurant; bar; room service. Free Wi-Fi.

Hotel Maré ★ A mixed bag, this hotel has a beach-friendly destination… that can be quite noisy (with street noises, plumbing noises, and din from room to room through the thin walls). The decor is contemporary and crisp-looking, but the beds are a hair too soft for most and the bathrooms are tremendously cramped. Still, for the price point it's a decent value, with a friendly staff and a good restaurant. ***Tip:*** The hotel's parking lot is uphill and a 5-minute walk from the property; don't waste 5€ per night to park there, as it's not convenient. You should be fine with street parking.

Rua Mouzinho de Albuquerque 8. www.hotelmare.pt. ✆ **26/255-01-80.** 36 units. 50€–111€ double. Parking nearby 5€. Free Wi-Fi.

Hotel Ribamar ★ This old-style restaurant-inn is right on the beach, and most of its small guest rooms open onto balconies. A twisting stairway in the rear leads to the rooms, each of which is individually decorated with carved wooden headboards, frilly linens, and flowered drapes. It's a bit like staying at your Portuguese grandma's home, though she'd likely serve a better breakfast. Still, the location is good, the rooms will charm many guests, and the staff go beyond the usual to make sure guests are happy.

Rua Gomes Freire 9. http://ribamar.pai.pt. ✆ **26/255-11-58.** 25 units. 40€–90€ double; 70€–130€ suite. Rates include continental breakfast. Parking 5€–10€. **Amenities:** Restaurant; bar. Free Wi-Fi.

Where to Dine

A Celeste ★★ PORTUGUESE This little restaurant is run by its cook and founder Celeste with humor, energy, and a love of all things "tubular." The restaurant is plastered with photos of the town's giant waves and surfing hero Garrett McNamara (there's even a dish named for him). McNamara has returned the favor, proclaiming that he loves the homemade food here and that Celeste is like a mother to him. We think you'll "feel the love" too, when you tuck into the surfer's favorite sesame seed salad and the grilled sea bass with *migas* (a side dish cooked with day-old cornbread, kale, and beans). Another specialty of this restaurant is *açorda de marisco*, a puréed bread dish with seafood—Celeste's unique version has the stew served inside hollowed-out bread. Save room for dessert: The rice pudding with cinnamon is a knockout.

Av. da República, 54. ✆ **26/255-16-95.** Regular main courses 10€–25€. Daily 12am–11pm.

Mar Bravo ★ PORTUGUESE One of the busiest restaurants in this bustling village, Mar Bravo is on the corner of the square overlooking the ocean. A complete, and consistently pleasing, meal here consists of soup followed by a fish or meat dish. For that main dish, best options are the classic bass caprice, the fish stew, seafood rice, and the grilled pork. Also usually good: the fresh fish of the day, which will be sold by the kilo to be grilled or baked in salt. Dessert might be a soufflé, fruit salad, or pudding. Upstairs is a second dining room with an ocean view.

Praça Sousa Oliveira, 71. www.marbravo.com. ✆ **26/256-91-60.** Reservations recommended. Regular main courses 12€–35€. Daily 12am–3:30pm and 7–10:30pm. From Nov–Feb, closed on Tues.

Taverna 8 a 80 ★★ TAPAS/MEDITERRANEAN Tired of fish and seafood dishes done in the traditional Portuguese way? Try this innovative tapas restaurant. Its original twists include mackerel wraps and shrimp with pineapple. Its wine list is also primo. For dessert, the Mojito ice cream is clearly a top choice. Many come by just for the gin cocktails, which can be sipped while watching the ocean.

Av. Manuel Remigio, Edifício Atlântico, Loja 8. ✆ **26/256-04-90.** Regular main courses 8€–18€. Wed–Mon 12am–11pm.

BATALHA

118km (73 miles) N of Lisbon

Batalha merits a visit for only one reason: to see the monastery. Most visitors choose to stay in Fátima or Nazaré, which have more hotels and restaurants, but we've included the best options for sleeping and eating in town below, in case you decide to linger.

Essentials

ARRIVING

BY BUS From Nazaré (see above), seven buses a day make the 1-hour trip to Batalha, with a change at Alcobaça; a one-way ticket costs 4.50€. From Lisbon, five *expresso* buses operate daily; the trip lasts 2 hours and costs 12€ one-way. More info at **Rede Expressos** (www.rede-expressos.pt; ✆ **70/722-33-44**).

BY CAR From Alcobaça (see earlier), continue northeast along N8 for about 20 minutes.

VISITOR INFORMATION

The **Batalha Tourist Office** is on Praça Mouzinho de Albuquerque (✆ **24/476-51-80**). If you're traveling by bus, the tourist office keeps detailed schedules of the best connections to surrounding towns. It's open daily from 10am to 1pm and 3 to 7pm. In August, it's open daily 10am to 7pm.

Visiting the Monastery

Mosteiro de Santa Maria da Vitória (or Mosteiro da Batalha) ★★★ In 1385, João I vowed on the plains of Aljubarrota that if his underequipped and outnumbered army defeated the invading Castilians, he would commemorate his spiritual indebtedness to the Virgin Mary. The result is the magnificent Monastery of the Virgin Mary, designed in Gothic and Manueline styles, known popularly as Mosteiro da Batalha, a mention to that battle with Castilians.

The **western porch** ★, ornamented by a tangled mass of Gothic sculpture of saints and other figures, sits beneath stained-glass windows of blue, mauve, and amber. The windows are exceptionally beautiful and are best enjoyed on a sunny day. Because the windows were damaged over the centuries, various artisans have replaced them in their original 16th-century Manueline detail.

In the **Founder's Chapel ★**, João I and his English queen, Philippa of Lancaster (daughter of John of Gaunt), lie in peaceful repose, their hands entwined on their stone effigies beneath an exquisite octagonal lantern. Prince Henry the Navigator's tomb is near that of his parents. His fame eclipsed theirs even though he never sat on the throne. The **Royal Cloisters ★★★** reveal the beginnings of the nautically oriented Manueline architecture.

The magnum opus of the monastery is the **Chapter House ★★**, a square chamber whose **vaulting ★★★** is an unparalleled example of the Gothic style, bare of supporting pillars.

Sentinels and the glow of an eternal flame guard the two tombs of Portugal's unknown soldiers from World War I. In one part of the quadrangle is the Unknown Soldiers Museum, which houses gifts to the fallen warriors from the people of Portugal and other countries. Beyond the crypt are the remains of the old wine cellars. You can visit the crypts daily from 9am to 5pm, but you might not want to unless you're a crypt aficionado. These consist of a series of dank and gloomy ancient tombs, but no notable treasures.

Stunning filigree designs ornament the coral-stone entrance to the seven unfinished **chapels ★★**. The *capelas*, under a "sky ceiling," are part of one of the finest examples of the Manueline style, a true stone extravaganza. Construction was abandoned so workers for Manuel I could help build his monastery at Belém. In Portuguese they are known as *capelas imperfeitas*—the unperfected chapels. The monastery has been part of the UNESCO World Heritage list since 1983 and is the most important example of Gothic architecture in Portugal.

Praça Mouzinho de Albuquerque. www.mosteirobatalha.pt. ✆ **24/476-54-97.** Admission 6€, free for children under 12; 50% discount for seniors over 65. Oct–Mar daily 9am–5:30pm; Apr–Sept daily 9am–6pm. There's free parking next to the monastery.

Where to Stay & Dine

MODERATE

Hotel Mestre Afonso Domingues ★ Standing right across the square from the monastery, this hotel allows guests to relax in well-kept modern comfort, if not great style. But the good-size rooms do have topnotch beds. Bathrooms are also spacious and have marble or tiled walls. The staff is helpful and friendly. And the restaurant here serves the finest cuisine in town, although that's no great compliment because Batalha is hardly a gourmet citadel. However, the location allows one to have a meal on the terrace contemplating the monument and all the history attached to it. The hotel name honors the master that started the construction of the monastery.

Largo do Mestre Afonso Domingues, 6. www.hotel.mestreafonsodomingues.pt. ✆ **24/476-52-60.** 21 units. 65€–100€ double; 100€–160€ suite. Rates include buffet breakfast. **Amenities:** Restaurant; bar; bikes; room service; free parking. Free Wi-Fi.

Hotel Villa Batalha ★★ Sleek lines, groovy wallpaper, sinewy lamps, and lots of polished steel announce that this is a hotel of today. It doesn't hurt that the interior space is flooded with natural light, and most bedrooms open onto private balconies overlooking the monastery (though the view is from a far greater distance than the hotel above). The on-site restaurant, Adega dos Frades, specializes in regional dishes, and does so exceedingly well. The hotel offers a good spa, complete with steam room, sauna, Jacuzzi, and indoor pool.

Rua Dom Duarte I, 248. www.hotelvillabatalha.com. ✆ **24/424-04-00.** 93 units. 81€–120€ double; from 110€ suite. **Amenities:** Restaurant; bar; bikes; concierge; golf course; indoor pool; room service; spa; outdoor tennis court (lit); free parking. Free Wi-Fi.

INEXPENSIVE

Hotel Casa do Outeiro ★★ If you get the right room here, you'll wake up in the morning to look out upon a view of the monastery itself from your own private terrace. If you don't, well, it's no great tragedy: This is a homelike and most welcoming little hotel. It is completely modern, with individually designed, midsize bedrooms that are both colorful and comfortable, with small private bathrooms. Breakfast is served by the pool. A great value in Batalha.

Largo Carvalho do Outeiro 4. www.casadoouteiro.com. ✆ **24/476-58-06.** 15 units. 54€–89€. **Amenities:** Children's center; exercise room; outdoor pool; free parking. Free Wi-Fi (in some).

FÁTIMA

142km (88 miles) N of Lisbon; 58km (36 miles) E of Nazaré

Fátima is a world-famous pilgrimage site because of reported sightings of the Virgin Mary in the early–20th century. The terrain around the village is wild, with an aura of barren desolation hanging over the countryside. However, when religious pilgrims flock to the town twice a year, in May and October, its desolation quickly turns to fervent drama. The year 2017 marked the 100th anniversary of the miracle.

Essentials

ARRIVING

BY BUS On bus schedules, Fátima is often listed as Cova da Iria, which leads to a lot of confusion. Cova da Iria is less than 1km (⅔ mile) from Fátima and is the focus of pilgrimages and the site of the alleged religious miracles. About three buses a day connect Fátima with Batalha. The trip takes 40 minutes and costs 4€ one-way. Many buses arrive from Lisbon. The 1½-hour trip costs 12€ one-way. For information and schedules, call **Rede Expressos** (✆ **70/722-33-44;** www.rede-expressos.pt), the departs are from Sete Rios terminal in Lisbon.

BY CAR From Batalha (see above), continue east along Route 356 for 15km (9⅓ miles).

VISITOR INFORMATION

The **tourist office** is on Avenida D. José Alves Correia da Silva (www.rt-leiria fatima.pt; ✆ **24/953-11-39**) and is open daily from 10am to 1pm and 2 to 5pm. On weekends and holidays it is open until 5:30pm.

THE ROLE OF THE church IN PORTUGAL

From its medieval origins, Portugal has been intricately bound in an allegiance to the Church. (The existence of the country itself in the early days of Afonso Henriques probably stemmed from a religion-based hatred of the Moors.) Although they were devout, the Portuguese monarchs never seemed as rabidly fanatical in their faith as their neighbors in Spain. Likewise, although Portugal endured an Inquisition, its purges never ran as deep or were quite as bloody as those of the Spaniards.

Today, although observant of Roman Catholic doctrine and reasonably devout, the country seems more interested in the melancholy passion of the fado and the fanfare of football (soccer) than in the passions of religion. Since the Industrial Revolution and the social unrest that accompanied it, Portugal has maintained an uncomfortable duality between its allegiance to the Roman Catholic Church and a general dislike for clerical directives coming from beyond their village or town. Nonetheless, applications to God tend to increase during times of trouble. Despite the influences of socialist politics and a general disillusionment, the Church continues to inspire great loyalty, especially in rural areas. In some villages, especially in the more devout northern sections, at least half of an entire village might be found in church on Sunday.

In rural areas, religion is closely associated with protection of fields, family, households, and domestic animals, and used as a kind of appeasement against the many ills that might potentially cause damage. Significantly, some of the most sought after rustic antiques in Portugal are traditional 19th-century ox yokes, lavishly carved from timbers into ornate depictions of Christian imagery, complete with crosses and symbols of fertility to bless and protect the oxen plowing the fields.

Today, despite tendencies within Portugal to both respect and condemn the Church, more than 85% of the people still profess to be Catholic. Faith is part of the popular saints festivals in June all over the country and particularly at Easter and Christmastime. But faith is probably seen the most in pilgrimages. Foremost among them is the shrine of Fátima (see below) that gathers huge crowds.

Exploring the Town

On May 13 and October 13, pilgrims overrun the town, causing the roads leading to Fátima to be choked with visitors. Many also approach on foot from all over the country. Once in Fátima, they camp out until daybreak. In the central square, which is larger than St. Peter's in Rome, a statue of the Madonna passes through the crowd between about 10am and 12:30pm. When it does, some 75,000 or more handkerchiefs flutter in the breeze.

Then as many as are able crowd in to visit a small, slanted-roof chapel known as the **Chapel of the Apparitions.** Inside stands a single white column marking the spot where a small holm oak once grew. An image of the Virgin Mary reputedly appeared over this oak on May 13, 1917, when she is said to have spoken to three shepherd children. That oak long ago disappeared, torn to pieces by souvenir collectors. The original chapel constructed here was dynamited on the night of March 6, 1922, by skeptics who suspected the church of staging the so-called miracle.

While World War I dragged on, three devout children—Lúcia de Jesus and her cousins, Jacinta and Francisco Marto—claimed that they saw the first appearance of "a lady" on the tableland of Cova da Iria. Her coming had been foreshadowed in 1916 by what they would later cite as "an angel of peace" who is said to have appeared before them.

Attempts were made to suppress their story, but it spread quickly. During the July appearance, the lady was reported to have revealed three secrets to them, one of which prefigured the coming of World War II; another was connected with Russia's "rejection of God." The final secret, a "sealed message" recorded by Lúcia, was opened by church officials in 1960, but the contents of that message were only recently published. According to the Vatican, it predicted that Pope John Paul II would be shot. Acting on orders from the Portuguese government, the mayor of a nearby town threw the children into jail and threatened them with torture, even death in burning oil. Still, they would not be intimidated and stuck to their story. The lady reportedly made six appearances between May and the final one on October 13, 1917, when the children were joined by an estimated 70,000 people who witnessed the famous Miracle of the Sun. The day had begun with pouring rain and driving winds. Observers from all over the world testified that at noon, "the sky opened up" and the sun seemed to spin out of its axis and hurtle toward the earth. Many at the site feared the Last Judgment was upon them. Others later reported that they thought the scorching sun was crashing into the earth and would consume it in flames. Many agreed that a major miracle of modern times had occurred. Only the children reported seeing Our Lady, however.

Both Francisco and Jacinta died in the influenza epidemic that swept Europe after World War I. Lúcia became a Carmelite nun in a convent in the university city of Coimbra. She returned to Fátima in 1967 to mark the 50th anniversary of the apparition, and the pope flew in from Rome. Later John Paul II also visited Fátima three times, and Pope Francis visited in May 2016.

A cold, pristine white basilica in the neoclassical style was erected at one end of the wide square. A new one was built in 2007 on the opposite side of the square, Basílica da Santíssima Trindade, with a more daring architecture and a circular shape. It's considered the fourth-biggest church in the world in capacity. If you want to go inside the temples, you might be stopped by a guard if you're not suitably dressed. Women should avoid shorts or short skirts and cover their shoulders (with a scarf or a cardigan, if you have a shirt with narrow straps). Men wearing shorts are also excluded.

NIGHTLIFE As you might expect of a destination for religious pilgrimages, Fátima is early to rise (in many cases, for morning Mass) and early to bed. Cafes in town tend to be locked tight after around 10pm, so religion-weary residents who want to escape drive 4km (3 miles) south of town along Estrada de Minde to the village of Boleiros. Here you'll find **Bar Truatilde** (www.truao.com; ✆ **24/952-15-42**), a music bar that is much more attuned to human frailties than the ecclesiastical monuments in the core. It has fado many nights and tipples every night.

SHOPPING Many of the souvenirs you'll find in Fátima are religious in nature; most are cheaply made and not worth purchasing. If you're interested in an evenhanded mixture of religious and secular articles, head for the town's biggest gift shop, **Centro Comercial Fátima (Fátima Shopping Center),** Estrada de Leiria (www.fatimashoppingcenter.com; ✆ **24/953-23-75**). The staggering inventory is piled to the ceiling. If you're looking for devotional statues or a less controversial example of regional porcelain, you'll find it here, 450m (1,476 ft.) from the town's main religious sanctuary.

Where to Stay

On major pilgrimage days, it's just about impossible to secure a room unless you've reserved months in advance. It's actually for the best if you stay outside Fátima and just visit it for the day using public transportation. There are also car parks, but traffic can be intense, especially in May and October.

INEXPENSIVE

Dom Gonçalo & Spa ★★ With an unbeatable location in the large garden at the entrance to town, only 365m (1,198 ft.) from the Sanctuary of Our Lady of Fátima, this contemporary but characterful hotel is among the town's finest. Rooms are oases of comfort, which chic brown and aqua throw pillows and comforters on the firm beds. The bathrooms are small but so cunningly well designed most don't mind. The indoor heated pool is a relaxing place to hang out after a day of touring.

Rua Jacinta Marto 100. www.hoteldg.com. ✆ **24/953-93-30.** 42 units. 55€–90€ double; 100€–150€ suite. Rates include buffet breakfast. **Amenities:** Restaurant; bar; babysitting; bikes; children's center; exercise room; indoor heated pool; room service; spa. Free Wi-Fi.

Hotel Lux Fátima ★ The rooms here are airy, with lots of light, modern furniture, wooden floors, and good desks. Prices are usually quite good, and we applaud the service here (topnotch). In fact, all is slightly better than it needs to be to stay full for a hotel as close as it is (about 100m/328 ft.) from the sanctuary.

Av. José Alves Correia da Silva Lote 2. http://fatima.luxhotels.pt/. ✆ **24/953-06-90.** 67 units. 50€–95€ double; 100€–155€ suite. Rates include buffet breakfast. **Amenities:** Restaurant; bar; room service; free parking. Free Wi-Fi.

Where to Dine

Grelha ★ GRILL/PORTUGUESE This is one of the best of the town's meager selection of nonhotel eateries. It's 275m (902 ft.) from the sanctuary at Fátima. Grelha offers regional specialties but is known for its grills, especially steaks and fish. Grilled codfish is an especially good choice as are the grilled beef medallions, followed by a lovely, house-made almond cake. In the cooler months, the fireplace is an attraction, and the bar is busy year-round.

Rua Jacinta Marto 78. ✆ **24/953-16-33.** Main courses 10€–25€. Fri–Wed noon–3pm and 7–10:30pm. Closed 2 weeks in Nov.

Tia Alice ★★ PORTUGUESE This simple, rustic restaurant offers copious portions of food inspired by the rural traditions of the region. It's become so well known that foodies from Lisbon and other cities come here just to try its scrumptious broad-bean soups, its roast lamb with rosemary and garlic, and its fried hake with green sauce. We also think the Portuguese sausage here is primo. The stone walls lend a cozy atmosphere to this other "sanctuary" in Fátima. Make sure to book far ahead as it is always very busy, especially on weekends.

Rua do Adro. ✆ **24/953-17-37.** Reservations required. Main courses 15€–25€. Tues–Sat noon–3pm and 7:30–10pm; Sun noon–6pm. Closed last 3 weeks of July.

THE ALGARVE

The maritime province of the Algarve, often called the Garden of Portugal, is the southwesternmost part of Europe. Its coastline stretches 160km (99 miles) from Henry the Navigator's Cape St. Vincent to the border town of Vila Real de Santo António, fronting once-hostile Spain. The varied coastline contains sluggish estuaries, sheltered lagoons, low-lying areas where clucking marsh hens nest, long sandy spits, and promontories jutting out into the white-capped aquamarine foam.

Called Al-Gharb ("the West") by the Moors, the land south of the *serras* (mountains) of Monchique and Caldeirão remains a spectacular anomaly that seems more like a transplanted section of the North African coastline than a piece of Europe. The temperature averages around 60°F (16°C) in winter and 74°F (25°C) in summer. The countryside abounds in vegetation: almonds, lemons, oranges, carobs, pomegranates, and figs.

The 1755 earthquake shook this region badly, as the epicenter was close. Entire communities were wiped out, first by the quake, and then by the tsunami; however, many Moorish and even Roman ruins remain. In the fret-cut chimneys, mosquelike cupolas, and cubist houses, a distinct Oriental flavor prevails. Phoenicians, Greeks, Romans, Visigoths, Moors, and Christians all touched this land.

Much of the historic flavor, however, is gone forever, swallowed by a sea of dreary high-rise apartment blocks surrounding most towns. Years ago, Portuguese officials, looking in horror at what happened to Spain's Costa del Sol, promised more limited and controlled development so that they wouldn't make "Spain's mistake." That promise has not been kept, especially in places like Albufeira, Armação de Pêra, Praia da Rocha, Quarteira, and even Vilamoura, where overdevelopment has ruined the natural beauty of much of the coastline.

Still, Algarvian beaches are some of the best in Portugal. Their quality has led to the tourist boom across the southern coastline, from high cliffs and rough waters to pristine pools with red rocks and sandy stretches where you can walk for miles without seeing anyone.

Starting in 1965, vast stretches of coastal terrain have been bulldozed, landscaped, irrigated, and reconfigured into golf courses. Many are associated with real-estate developments or major resorts, such as the 800-hectare (1,977-acre) Quinta do Lago, where

The Algarve

SPAIN
Rio Guadiana
Vila Real de Santo António
Monte Gordo
Castro Marim
A22
N122
N124
Rio de Foupanu
Rio de Odeleite
Golfo de Cádiz
Tavira
Ilha de Armona
N397
Ribeira de Alportel
Rio Vascão
Ribeira de Carreiras
São Brás de Alportel
Olhão
Cabo de Santa Maria
Barronco do Velho
Estói
Faro
N125
Ilha da Barreta
Loulé
Almancil
Quarteira
N2
N267
Serra do Caldeirão
N124
A22
Vilamoura
Albufeira
Ferreiras
São Bartolomeu de Messines
IP2
E01
IP1
IP1
São Marcos da Serra
Armação de Pêra
ATLANTIC OCEAN
Silves
Lagoa
A22
Carvoeiro
N266
Portimão
Praia da Rocha
Caldas de Monchique
Rio Mira
Odemira
Serra do Espinhaço de Cão
Lagos
Odeceixe
IC4
IC4
N125
Aljezur
PORTUGAL
Lisbon
area of detail
Carrapateira
N268
Vila do Bispo
Sagres
Ponta de Sagres
Cabo de São Vicente
0 6 mi
0 10 km

retirement villas nestle amid vegetation at the edges of the fairways. Most are open to qualified golfers.

Many fishing villages—now summer resorts—dot the Algarvian coast: Carvoeiro, Albufeira, Portimão, Quarteira, Olhão. The sea is the source of life, as it always has been. The village marketplaces sell esparto mats, copper, pottery, and almond and fig sweets, sometimes shaped like birds and fish. The flea markets are great places to "fish" for some antiques, especially ceramics and iron or copper goods. And surrender to the local's habits: There's no such thing as too much fish or shellfish. Or snails in the summer!

SAGRES: "THE END OF THE WORLD" ★

280km (174 miles) S of Lisbon; 34km (21 miles) W of Lagos; 114km (71 miles) W of Faro

At the extreme southwestern corner of Europe—once called *o fim do mundo* (the end of the world)—Sagres and Cape São Vicente are a rocky escarpment jutting into the Atlantic Ocean. From here, Henry the Navigator, the Infante of Sagres, launched Portugal and the rest of Europe on the seas of exploration. Contrary to popular belief, there was not a school of navigation here; rather, a center where navigators, cartographers, and scholars would meet and exchange ideas and knowledge.

Essentials

ARRIVING

BY BUS Ten EVA buses (www.eva-bus.com; ✆ **28/989-97-60**) in Lagos run hourly from Lagos to Sagres each day. The trip time is 1 hour, and a one-way ticket costs 3.90€. From Lisbon, there's a Rede Expressos bus (www.rede-expressos.pt; ✆ **70/722-33-44**) daily in the summer and one only at weekends for the rest of the year, costing 20€.

BY CAR From Lagos, drive west on Route 125 to Vila do Bispo, and then head south along Route 268 to Sagres.

Exploring Sagres

In the ancient world, the cape was the last explored point, although in time the Phoenicians pushed beyond it. Many mariners thought that when the sun sank beyond the cape, it plunged over the edge of the world.

Today, at the reconstructed site of Henry's windswept fortress on Europe's Land's End (named after the narrowing westernmost tip of Cornwall, England), you can see a huge stone compass dial. Henry supposedly used the "Rosa dos Ventos" in his naval studies at Sagres. Housed in the **Fortaleza de Sagres ★★**, Ponta de Sagres is a small museum that documents some of the area's history along with information on the flora and fauna of the area. It's open May to September daily 9:30am to 8pm, October to April 9:30am to 5:30pm. Admission is low, at just 3€ for adults, 1.50€ for ages 15 to 25, and free for children 12 and under. Not all go into the museum, but you'll be missing out if you don't take a cliff walk here (be careful, there's no guard-rail), and listen to the ear-splitting roar of the ocean hitting the stone. At a simple chapel, restored in 1960, sailors are said to have prayed for help before setting out into uncharted waters in small caravelles. You'll understand, in a visceral way, how very brave these men were when you stare into the swirling, powerful waves below. The chapel is closed to the public.

About 5km (3 miles) away is the promontory of **Cabo de São Vicente ★★**. It got its name because, according to legend, the body of St. Vincent arrived mysteriously here on a boat guided by ravens. A lighthouse, the second most powerful in Europe, beams illumination 100km (62 miles) across the ocean. To reach the cape, you can take a bus Monday through Friday, leaving from Rua Comandante Matoso near the tourist office. Trip time is 10 minutes, departures are at 11:15am and 2:25pm, and a one-way ticket costs 2€.

Outdoor Activities

BEACHES Many beaches fringe the peninsula; some attract nude bathers. Mareta, at the bottom of the road leading from the center of town toward the water, is the best and most popular. East of town is Tonel, also a good sandy beach. The beaches west of town, Praia da Baleeira and Praia do Martinhal, are better for windsurfing than for swimming.

FISHING Fishing is worthwhile (and legal) between October and January, although the quantity of fish has diminished in recent years. You can walk down to almost any beach and hire a local fisherman to take you out for a half-day; just about every large-scale hotel along the Algarve will arrange a fishing trip for you as well. Most fishing excursions are configured as half-day events, priced, with equipment included, at around 40€ per adult.

Where to Stay

MODERATE

Memmo Baleeira Hotel ★★ Named after the whaleboats (*baleeira*) whose mariners sailed to distant ports of the Atlantic, Memmo Baleeira Hotel occupies a 1960s-era complex that's angular, groovy, and perched on a low cliff above the jagged and rocky coastline of Sagres, above the fishing port, 50m (164 ft.) from a pleasant beach. The largest hotel on Sagres, and perhaps the most self-consciously "artful" in the calculated simplicity of its sun-flooded, mostly white interiors, it offers guest rooms with balconies and views over the open sea, the harbor, the gardens, or, at the cheapest level, a parking lot. The number of its rooms has nearly doubled in recent years; the older ones are quite small but still chicly furnished. The heated indoor pool and the spa are a boon on gray or windy days.

Sítio da Baleeira. www.memmohotels.com. ✆ **28/262-42-12.** 144 units. 85€–204€ double; 171€–290€ suite. Rates include buffet breakfast. Free parking. **Amenities:** Restaurant; bar; babysitting; bikes; children's center; exercise room; 2 freshwater pools (1 heated indoor); room service; spa; outdoor tennis court (lit); limited watersports equipment/rentals; kitchenette (in some). Free Wi-Fi.

Pousada de Sagres, Infante ★ Location is the lure here: Built in 1960, the white former government-owned tourist inn spreads along the edge of a cliff that projects rather daringly over the sea. Most guests are charmed by the rugged beauty of the rocky cliffs, the pounding surf, and the sense of the ocean's infinity. Happily, there are many outdoor spaces to enjoy the ocean air: The hotel boasts a long colonnade of arches with an extended stone terrace set with garden furniture, plus a second floor of accommodations with private balconies. Guest rooms are not as impressive (many could use a touch-up) but they are generally appealing, with wicker furnishings and excellent views. Ask for a west-facing room so that you can enjoy the sunset.

Ponta da Atalaia. www.pousadas.pt. ✆ **28/262-02-40.** 39 units. 72€–234€ double; 108€–250€ suite. Rates include buffet breakfast. Free parking. **Amenities:** Restaurant; bar; babysitting; outdoor freshwater pool; room service; outdoor tennis court (lit). Free Wi-Fi.

Romantik Villa Vivenda Felicidade ★★ As popular resorts along the Algarve become overcrowded in summer, more discerning visitors are finding hideaways in remote villages. Such a village is Salema, between Sagres and Lagos, where you'll find this lush villa lying along Route 125. Set in a pleasant garden, it features a swimming pool overlooking the ocean and a spa.

Urbanização Beach Villas, Lote M5, Budens. www.romantikvilla.com. ✆ **28/269-56-70.** 4 units. 80€–110€. No credit cards. Free parking. **Amenities:** Outdoor pool. Free Wi-Fi.

Where to Dine

Restaurante O Telheiro do Infante ★ SEAFOOD There may be a bit of a wait between ordering and dining here as everything is prepared fresh, unusual for a beachside joint. We always like to begin with the raw oysters followed by asparagus salad. *Peixe do dia*, or fresh catch of the day, can be grilled to your specifications, or sautéed and served in a butter sauce with vegetables. But the pork, from the Portuguese plains north of here, is also a good pick—it has a pleasant, sweet taste because the pigs are fed a diet of acorns. Some tables are placed outside so you can enjoy the view of the ocean.

Praia da Mareta. www.telheirodoinfante.com. ✆ **28/262-41-79.** Reservations recommended in summer but they are accepted only until 8pm. Main courses 15€–30€. Wed–Mon 10am–10pm.

Restaurante Retiro do Pescador ★★ SEAFOOD Informal, friendly, and simple looking, the food here is as good, if not better, as what you'll get in the town's fancier joints. As the name says, this is a "Fishermen Shelter," meaning it leads with perfectly grilled fish (and some charcoal-grilled meat for those who don't like the fruit of the sea). Our advice: Ask for the daily specials as what is freshest will change, though grilled sardines and horse mackerel are frequent offerings in summer. You also can't go wrong with clams cooked in a *cataplana* (a traditional Algarve copper pot that steams the food), fish soup, or *arroz de marisco* (seafood rice). Don't be afraid to try the *percebes* (gooseneck barnacles), likely caught just hours before in the rocky waters near Sagres.

Vale das Silvas. www.retiro-do-pescador.com. ✆ **28/262-44-38.** Main courses 9€–18€. Tues–Sun noon–3:30pm and 7–10:30pm.

Restaurante Vila Velha ★★ INTERNATIONAL In a rustic villa setting, this first-class restaurant's unusual menu wins many fans. Top dishes include stuffed quail in wine sauce, prawn curry, small pork filets with mango sauce, hake filets with scallops and hollandaise sauce, and tagliatelle with prawns and monkfish. Desserts are sumptuous, especially the homemade walnut ice cream with flambéed bananas and a chocolate sauce. Prepare yourself for a fine, if expensive, gastronomic evening.

Rua Patrão António Faustino. www.vilavelha-sagres.com. ✆ **28/262-47-88.** Reservations recommended. Main courses 28€–38€. Tues–Sun 6:30–10pm (until 10:30pm July 15–Sept 15).

Sagres After Dark

The best of the many nightspots in the town's historic core include the **Bar Dromedário,** Rua Comandante Matos (✆ **28/262-42-19**) and **A Rosa dos Ventos (Pink Wind) Bar,** Praça da República (www.rosadosventos.info; ✆ **28/262-44-80**). Folks from all over Europe talk, relax, and drink beer, wine, sangria, and cocktails (Brazilian caipirinhas are popular) in these buzzy, fun bars.

LAGOS ★★

34km (21 miles) E of Sagres; 69km (43 miles) W of Faro; 264km (164 miles) S of Lisbon; 13km (8 miles) W of Portimão

Lagos, known to the Lusitanians and Romans as Lacobriga and to the Moors as Zawaia, became a shipyard of caravels during the time of Henry the Navigator (he lived in Lagos, too). The Bay of Sagres was, at one point in its epic history, big enough to allow 407 warships to maneuver with ease. As a strategic port during the 15th and 16th centuries, Lagos was a busy place, with ships coming from Africa, Brazil, and India laden with all kinds of spices and goods. The connection with the maritime Discoveries has also a dark side: Lagos hosted the first slave market in Europe in 1444. A slavery and customs house (see below) illustrates the wrongs done during this period (Portugal traded more slaves than any other country in the 17th and 18th centuries); a museum is in the works as we go to press.

An ancient port city (historians traced its origins to the Carthaginians, three centuries before the birth of Christ), fishing is now secondary to the beaches and to the tourism attracted by the famed rock formations here (and in nearby Ponta da Piedade). In winter, the almond blossoms match the whitecaps on the water, and the weather is often warm enough for sunbathing. In town, a flea market sprawls through the narrow streets.

Less than 2km (1¼ miles) down the coast is the rocky headland of the **Ponta da Piedade (Point of Piety) ★★★**—awe-inspiring grottoes and caves.

We think this point is the most beautiful on the coast—the colorful cliffs and secret grottoes carved by the waves are as flamboyant as Manueline architecture in their way. Boat trips to the grottoes depart daily from the marina in Lagos.

Much of Lagos was razed in the 1755 earthquake, and it lost its position as the capital of the Algarve. Today, only the ruins of its fortifications remain. However, traces of the old city linger on the back streets.

Essentials

ARRIVING

BY TRAIN From Lisbon, take an Algarve-bound train to the junction at Tunes, where a change of trains will take you all the way to Lagos. Five trains a day arrive from Lisbon. The trip takes around 4½ hours and costs at least 23€ one-way. For more information and schedules, check www.cp.pt.

BY BUS Six buses a day make the run between Lisbon and Lagos (more run in the summer). The trip takes 4 hours and costs 20€ each way. Check Rede Expressos (www.rede-expressos.pt; ✆ **70/722-33-44**).

BY CAR If you're coming from Lisbon, after leaving Sines, take Route 120 southeast toward Lagos and follow the signs into the city. From Sagres, take N268 northeast to the junction with N125, which will lead you east to Lagos.

VISITOR INFORMATION

The **Lagos Tourist Office,** Praça Gil Eanes, Lagos (www.visitalgarve.pt; ✆ **28/276-30-31**) is open daily 9:30am to 1pm and 2 to 5:30pm.

Exploring the Town

Antigo Mercado de Escravos ★ HISTORIC SITE The Old Customs House stands as a painful reminder of the Age of Exploration. The arcaded slave market, the only one of its kind in Europe, looks peaceful today, but under its four Romanesque arches, captives were once sold to the highest bidders. The house opens onto the tranquil main square dominated by a statue of Henry the Navigator.

Praça do Infante Dom Henrique. Free admission.

Centro Ciência Viva de Lagos ★★★ MUSEUM Unlike the town's silly Discoveries Museum (a bunch of dusty wax figures you're charged 5€ to see), this educational center uses Portugal's seafaring history to promote an understanding of science. The stories of the Golden Age navigators are recounted (English available) and visitors can see and try the instruments that they used to plot daring trips across vast swatches of ocean. In one instance, visitors play a game to find the shortest maritime route to India. General scientific principles are also explored in a highly interactive manner. An excellent rainy day option for families.

Rua Dr. Faria e Silva, 34. ✆ **28/277-00-00.** Admission 3€ adults,; 1.5€ children under 17, students, and seniors 65 and older; free for children under 6. Tues–Sun 10am–6pm.

Igreja de Santo António ★★★ CHURCH The exquisitely lovely 18th-century Church of St. Anthony sits just off the waterfront. The altar is decorated with some of Portugal's most notable baroque **gilt carvings** ★, created with gold imported from Brazil. Begun in the 17th century, they were damaged in the earthquake but subsequently restored. What you see today represents the work of many artisans—each, at times, apparently pursuing a different theme, which makes this nonworking church even more interesting to tour.

Rua General Alberto Carlos Silveira. ✆ **28/276-23-01.** Admission 2€ adults, 1€ students and seniors 65 and older, free for children under 12. Tues–Sun 9:30am–12:30pm and 2–5pm.

Museu Municipal Dr. José Formosinho ★★ MUSEUM The Municipal Museum, next to, and part of, the Santo António church (above) contains a bewildering hodgepodge of (sometimes) intriguing and (sometimes) weird objects. These include replicas of the fret-cut chimneys of the Algarve, three-dimensional cork carvings, 16th-century vestments, ceramics, 17th-century embroidery, ecclesiastical sculpture, a painting gallery, weapons, minerals, and a numismatic collection. There's also a believe-it-or-not section displaying, among other oddities, an eight-legged calf. In the archaeological wing are neolithic artifacts, Roman mosaics found at Boca do Rio near Budens, fragments of statuary and columns, and other remains of antiquity from excavations along the Algarve.

Rua General Alberto Carlos Silveira. ✆ **28/276-23-01.** Admission 3.50€ adults, 1.50€ children 12–18 and seniors 65 and older, free for children under 12. Tues–Sun 10am–12:30pm and 2–5:30pm. Closed holidays.

Outdoor Activities

BEACHES Some of the region's loveliest beaches—including **Praia de Dona Ana** and **Praia do Camilo,** the most appealing—are near Lagos, south of the city. Follow signs to the Hotel Golfinho. If you go all the way to the southernmost point, Ponta da Piedade, you'll pass some pretty cove beaches set against a backdrop of rock formations. Steps are sometimes carved into the cliffs to make for easier access. Another good white-sand beach is at the 2.5km-long (1½-mile) **Meia Praia** (Half Beach), across the river from the center of town. It might be crowded in the summer, but its stretch of sand is so long that you'll find a quiet spot.

DIVING One of the Algarve's most highly recommended outlets for scuba diving is **Blue Ocean Divers,** Estrada de Porto de Mós (Motel Ancora; www.blue-ocean-divers.de; ✆ **96/466-56-67**), a fully licensed and insured scuba outfit. Its staff focuses on the coastline between Lagos and Sagres, site of numerous underwater caves and (mostly) 20th-century shipwrecks at depths of between 12m (39 ft.) and 35m (115 ft.) beneath the high-tide level. One dive with full equipment costs 50€; a PADI scuba course of 3 days and two dives costs 280€.

GOLF **Onyria Palmares Golf ★★★**, Meia Praia (www.onyriapalmares.com; ✆ **28/279-05-00**) was named best golf course in the country in 2016 by a major tourism trade magazine. Frank Pennink designed it in 1975 on land with many differences in altitude. Some fairways require driving a ball across railroad tracks, others small ravines, others around palm groves. Its landscaping suggests North Africa, partly because of its hundreds of palms and almond trees. The view from the 17th green is exceptionally dramatic. Par is 71. Greens fees are 77€ to 105€, depending on the season. The course lies on the eastern outskirts of Lagos, less than 1km (⅔ mile) from the center. To reach it from the heart of town, follow signs toward Meia Praia.

Santo António Golf ★★★ (formerly **Parque da Floresta**) in Budens (www.parquedafloresta.com; ✆ **28/269-00-54**) is one of the few important Algarvian courses west of Lagos. It's just inland from the fishing hamlet of Salema. Designed by the Spanish architect Pepe Gancedo, the par-72 course offers sweeping views; we find it to be more scenic and more challenging than the Palmares course, though critics of the course have decried its rough grading and rocky terrain. Some shots must be driven over vineyards, and others over ravines, creeks, and gardens. Greens fees are 35€ to 54€ for 9 holes, and 40€ to 87€ for 18 holes. To reach the course from the center of Lagos, drive about 15km (9⅓ miles) west, following road signs toward Sagres.

Go to www.visitgolfalgarve.com for more information on courses in the Algarve region.

Shopping

At **Terracota,** Praça Luís de Camões (✆ **28/276-33-74**), you'll find handsome pottery from Portugal and inlaid wood and artfully ornate brass and copper from Morocco, Tunisia, and artisans in other North African countries. The shop **Casa da Mãe,** Rua Jogo da Bola (✆ **96/83-69-732**) is excellent for gifts—everything from books and clothing to Portuguese design objects and ceramics. Shutterbugs will enjoy trolling the fresh **produce market** for good shots; there's also a **flea and antique market** on the first Sunday of every month at the car park of the Complexo Desportivo de Lagos (the sports center), from 8am to 2pm.

Where to Stay

EXPENSIVE

Romantik Hotel Vivenda Miranda ★★★ A real discovery, this small, Moorish-style hotel towers on a cliff overlooking the coast, 2.8km (1¾ miles) south of Lagos near the beach of Praia do Porto de Mós. Surrounded by exotic gardens and terraces, the inn opens onto the most panoramic views of any hotel in the area. Midsize to spacious bedrooms are very pretty, done up in warmly romantic colors with a handsome patterned headboard in one, a velvet armchair in another. This is the kind of hotel that would be ideal for a honeymoon, especially in the rooms with a terrace overlooking the ocean (some face the garden). The on-site restaurant is well above average (though service can be slow)—book a table on the terrace over the Porto de Mós beach. The spa has Neil's Yard Remedies, the first outside of England, exclusively made of organic skin care products. The hotel was fully renovated in spring 2017.

Porto de Mós. www.vivendamiranda.com. ✆ **28/276-32-22.** 28 units. 130€–240€ double; 140€–455€ suite. Rates include buffet breakfast. Free parking. **Amenities:** Restaurant; bar; babysitting; bikes; outdoor freshwater pool; room service; spa. Free Wi-Fi.

Tivoli Lagos ★ As solid as a castle from the exterior, Tivoli Lagos lies within its own ramparts and moats—okay, a swimming pool and a paddling pool. It's at the eastern side of the old town, a bit removed from the beach, and spreads over 1.2 hilltop hectares (3 acres) overlooking Lagos. Its lobby/lounge has a hacienda atmosphere, with white-plaster walls enlivened by sunny colors.

Rooms aren't as elegant; in fact, most are woefully outdated (we haven't seen TVs this bulky for a good decade!). Still, the Tivoli is worth a look for its many amenities, most notably the Duna Beach Club, on Meia Praia beach, which has a saltwater pool, a restaurant, and three tennis courts; guests have free membership during their stay. A private motorcoach makes regular trips to the beach club, 5 minutes from the hotel.

Rua António Crisógono dos Santos. www.tivolihotels.com. ✆ **28/279-00-79.** 324 units. 60€–184€ double; 120€–230€ suite. Rates include buffet breakfast. Free parking. **Amenities:** 2 restaurants; 2 bars; babysitting; bikes; children's center; health club & spa; 3 freshwater pools (1 heated indoor); room service; 3 outdoor tennis courts (lit); pets accepted. Wi-Fi free in lobby; in rooms, free for members with loyalty card.

MODERATE

Albergaria R Marina Rio ★★ Conveniently located in the center of town opposite the Lagos marina, the Albergaria boasts exceedingly pleasant midsize guest rooms, many of which open onto views of the sea. They feature top-quality bedding, lots of natural woods, and chic appointments (love the splashes of color). On the top floor is a sun terrace with pool overlooking the Bay of Lagos. In summer, a courtesy bus takes guests to the beaches and golfers to the course at Palmares. The only problem with staying here is that tour agents from Germany often book all the rooms en masse, so it can feel overcrowded in peak season.

Av. dos Descobrimentos (Apartado 388). www.marinario.com. ✆ **28/276-98-59.** 36 units. 58€–120€ double. Rates include buffet breakfast. Parking 10€. **Amenities:** Bar; babysitting; outdoor freshwater pool. Free Wi-Fi.

INEXPENSIVE

Casa da Moura ★★ The "House of the Moor Lady" was built originally in 1892 for a rich Lagos family and it retains its North African charm today. Lying inside the ramparts, a 5-minute walk from the center, the Casa imported most of its furnishings and raw materials from Morocco to match the architecture. That means hanging lanterns and elaborate rugs on the walls, wood-lined ceilings, stone and wooden floors, and wafty, sheer curtains. All accommodations have unique decorations and color schemes. For rent are two attractively furnished studios and six apartments. Breakfast is served on an open-air terrace overlooking the Atlantic. A character-rich place to stay.

Rua Cardeal Neto 10. www.casadamoura.com. ✆ **28/277-07-30.** 8 units. 42€–180€. Free parking. **Amenities:** Outdoor pool. Free Wi-Fi.

Where to Dine

EXPENSIVE

Rouxinol ★★ FUSION Set in a rustically charming former hunting lodge with (they say) the largest fireplace in the Algarve, "The Nightingale" is a primo special-occasion restaurant. The locale is lovely, and owner/chef Stefan has a special knack for making diners feel like VIPs. That skill was developed over many years—Stefan has operated restaurants in West Africa, Morocco, the Canary Islands, and the Caribbean, and he brings some of those flavors here (like the excellent piri-piri chicken). But most guests stick to the classic Portuguese fare, whether it is the freshly caught fish of the day, the shellfish stew, or the grilled Alentejo lamb, followed by a warm raspberry pie with ice cream. Food is served on an open-air terrace on balmy summer nights. The restaurant is located 42km (26 miles) from Lagos, near the town of Monchique.

Estrada de Monchique, Caldas de Monchique ✆ **28/291-39-75.** Reservations required. Main courses 10€–30€. Tues–Sun noon–9:30pm (until 10pm in summer). Closed Dec–Jan.

MODERATE

Reis ★ PORTUGUESE A simple place, yes, but Reis does very well by traditional Algarve food. The sole with almonds, the rice dishes, and the seafood *cataplanas* (steamed in a copper pot) are all well executed (and quite tasty). This is in addition, of course, to the ubiquitous grilled fish offerings. Reis was originally a small *tasca* back in 1949. It has a little terrace and, due to its popularity with locals, can be quite busy in the summertime.

Rua António Barbosa Viana, 21. ✆ **28/276-29-00.** Reservations recommended. Main courses 8€–25€. Daily noon–12 and 6–10:30pm. Closed Sun during winter; in the summer opens only for Sun dinner.

Restaurante D. Sebastião ★★ REGIONAL PORTUGUESE Too many stroll by this rustically decorated tavern on the main pedestrian street without a second glance, a shame because it serves some of the best, and most authentic, food in town. That means a varied menu of local treats like lip-smacking pork chops with figs, clams and shrimp grilled with savory spices, black pork cheeks with puréed sweet potato, and lobster plucked from a tank before being cooked and served. An excellent selection of local Portuguese wines accompany the tasty meal. In summer, outdoor dining is available.

Rua do 25 de Abril 20–22. www.restaurantedonsebastiao.com. ✆ **28/278-04-80.** Reservations recommended. Main courses 13€–28€. Daily noon–3pm and 7:30–10pm. Closed Dec 24–26 and Dec 31–Jan 2.

Lagos After Dark

You'll find hints of big-city life in Lagos and a devoted cadre of night owls. On Rua Cândido dos Reis are lots of hot spots, including **Inside Out Bar,** in the number 119 (no phone), with a fun staff and the largest *carte* of drinks in town. It usually stays open until 4am. Equally popular is the **Red Eye,** Rua Cândido dos Reis 63 (no phone), attracting a lot of Londoners and Aussies along with locals, who pile in here for the inexpensive drinks and the rock music. It stays open until 2am.

PORTIMÃO ★

18km (11 miles) E of Lagos; 61km (38 miles) W of Faro; 290km (180 miles) SE of Lisbon

Portimão is perfect if you want to explore a bustling fishing port rather than just lounge on a beach. Since the 1930s, **Praia da Rocha ★★**, 3km (1¾ miles) away, has snared sun-loving traffic. Today it's challenged by **Praia dos Três Irmãos,** but tourists still flock to Portimão in the summer.

The aroma of the noble Portuguese sardine permeates every street. Portimão used to be the leading fish-canning center in the Algarve. But it's no longer just canning; this town has become a hub for fine dining in recent years. Today, visitors stroll through its gardens and to its shops (especially noted for their pottery), drink wine in outdoor cafes, and roam down to the quays to see sardines roasting on braziers (there's a sardine festival every summer). Sadly, both Portimão and Praia da Rocha have been suffering of late from excessive development, so you'll see construction in many places.

Essentials

ARRIVING

BY TRAIN From Lisbon, there are five trains to Portimão (you'll have to leave and board another train in Tunes) and the price starts at 23.55€. From Lagos, trains on the Algarve Line run frequently throughout the day to Portimão. The trip takes 15 minutes and costs 1.50€. For information and schedules, go to www.cp.pt.

BY BUS From Lisbon, a bus from www.rede-expressos.pt makes the 3½-hour trip and costs 20€. A bus runs from the beach at Portimão, 3km (1¾ miles) away. For information and schedules, call © **28/989-97-60;** another source is www.eva-bus.com.

BY CAR The main highway across the southern coast, Route 125, makes a wide arch north on its eastern run to Portimão.

VISITOR INFORMATION

At Praia da Rocha, the **tourist office** (www.visitalgarve.pt; © **28/241-91-32**) is on Avenida Tomás Cabreira and is open daily 9am to 1pm and 2 to 6pm.

Exploring the Town

Although it lacks great monuments and museums, Portimão is worth exploring. High-rise buildings ring the area, but the core of the old town is somehow still intact.

Try to be in Portimão for lunch. Of course, you can dine at a restaurant, but it's even more fun to walk down to the harborside, where you can find a table at one of the low-cost eateries. The specialty is chargrilled sardines, which taste like nothing you get from a can. They make an inexpensive meal accompanied by chewy, freshly baked bread; a tomato salad; and a carafe of regional wine. If you're in town in August, stay for the **Sardine Festival** (dates vary), where the glory that is the Portuguese sardine is honored, lauded, and, finally, devoured.

If you'd like to go sightseeing, you can visit **Ferragudo,** a satellite of Portimão, 5km (3 miles) east and accessible by bridge. The beach area here is being developed rapidly but is great for children for its quiet waters. The picturesque fishing village is one the most photographed in the Algarve. The sandy beach lies to the south, and kiosks rent sailboards and sell seafood from a number of waterside restaurants. In the center you can see the ruins of the **Fort São João de Arade,** which was constructed to defend Portimão from English, Spanish, and Dutch raids. Stay in Ferragudo for some great fish in one of the many *tascas* around.

At Praia da Rocha, 3km (1¾ miles) south of Portimão, you can explore the ruins of the 16th-century **Fortaleza de Santa Catarina,** Avenida Tomás Cabreira, which was constructed for the same defensive purposes.

Outdoor Activities

BEACHES Most visitors head for the beach first thing in the morning. The favorite is **Praia da Rocha,** a creamy yellow strand that has long been the most popular seaside resort on the Algarve. English voyagers discovered the beauty of its rock formations around 1935. At the outbreak of World War II, there were only two small hotels and a few villas on the Red Coast, most built by wealthy Portuguese. Nowadays, Praia da Rocha is booming. At the end of the mussel-encrusted cliff, where the Arcade flows into the sea, lie the ruins of the **Fortress of Santa Catarina.** The location offers views of Portimão's satellite, Ferragudo, and of the bay.

Although **Praia dos Três Irmãos** is more expensive, you might want to visit its lovely beach, 5km (3 miles) southwest of Portimão, as well as its neighbor, **Prainha.** From Portimão's center, you can take a public bus; they run frequently throughout the day. The bus is marked PRAIA DOS TRÊS IRMÃOS. Departures are from the main bus terminal in Portimão, at Largo do Dique (✆ **28/989-97-60**).

Praia dos Três Irmãos has 15km (9⅓ miles) of burnished golden sand, interrupted only by an occasional crag riddled with arched passageways. This beach has been discovered by skin divers who explore its undersea grottoes and caves.

Nearby is the whitewashed fishing village of Alvor, where Portuguese and Moorish arts and traditions have mingled since the Arab occupation ended. Alvor was a favorite coastal haunt of João II, and now summer hordes descend on the long strip of sandy beach. The Ria de Alvor (the estuary) is protected due to diversity of its habitats and species. Alvor is accessible by public bus from Portimão's center.

GOLF **Penina ★★** (www.penina.com; ✆ **28/242-02-00**) is 5km (3 miles) west of the center of Portimão, farther west than many of the other great golf courses. Completed in 1966, it was one of the first courses in the Algarve and the universally acknowledged masterpiece of the British designer Sir Henry Cotton. It replaced a network of marshy rice paddies on level terrain that critics said was unsuited for anything except wetlands. The solution involved planting groves of eucalyptus (350,000 trees in all), which grew quickly in the muddy soil. Eventually they dried it out enough for the designer to bulldoze dozens of water traps and a labyrinth of fairways and greens. The course wraps around a luxury hotel (Penina Golf & Resort). You can play the main championship course (18 holes, par 73), and two 9-hole satellite courses, Academy and Resort. Greens fees for the 18-hole course are 83€ to 125€; for either of the 9-hole courses, they're 57€ to 83€. To reach it from the center of Portimão, follow signs to Lagos, turning off at the signpost for Penina Golf & Resort.

Visit www.visitgolfalgarve.com for more information on courses in the Algarve region.

Shopping

Fish, fruit, and vegetable markets are held every morning (except Sunday) until 2pm in the market building and open square. On the first Monday of every month, a gigantic daylong regional market shows off local artifacts, pottery, wicker, dried fruits, and more. Boutiques offering the Algarve's best selection of sweaters, porcelain, and pottery abound.

You'll find modern, Pan-European commercialism in this once-sleepy fishing village—most noticeably on such busy shopping streets as **Rua do Comércio, Rua São João de Deus,** and **Rua Vasco da Gama.** Goods include hand-knit sweaters, hand-painted porcelains, and tons of pottery from factories and individual artisans throughout Portugal, as well as some local copper goods.

Where to Stay

Hotels are limited in the center of Portimão, but Praia da Rocha has one of the largest concentrations on the Algarve. Praia dos Três Irmãos, though less developed, is the challenger to Praia da Rocha. In summer, don't even consider arriving at one of these beachfront establishments without a reservation.

CENTRAL PORTIMÃO

Inexpensive

Residencial Miradoiro ★ This B&B benefits from a central location on a quiet square opposite an ornate Manueline church. Its modern facade is banded with concrete balconies. A few of the no-frills guest rooms, which are rather small, have terraces. Furnishings are meager, but the beds are reasonably comfortable. All units have well-maintained bathrooms equipped with tub/shower combinations. Here you're likely to meet an array of European backpackers eager to converse and share travelers' tales. Motorists can usually find a parking space in the square just opposite the hotel.

Rua Machado Santos 13. ✆/fax **28/242-30-11.** 25 units. 30€–100€ double. Rates include buffet breakfast. Free parking; free Wi-Fi.

PRAIA DA ROCHA

Expensive

Hotel Algarve Casino ★★ With a vast staff at your beck and call, you'll be well provided for in this elongated block of rooms poised securely on the top ledge of a cliff. The midsize to spacious guest rooms have white walls, colored ceilings, intricate tile floors, mirrored entryways, indirect lighting, balconies with garden furniture, and marble bathrooms with separate tub/shower combinations. Some are vaguely Moorish in design, and many have terraces opening onto the sea. The Yachting, Oriental, Presidential, and Miradouro suites are decorative tours de force. The location, right on the beach, is excellent.

Av. Tomás Cabreira, Praia da Rocha. www.solverde.pt. ✆ **28/240-20-00.** 208 units. 71€–186€ double; 130€–410€ suite. Rates include buffet breakfast. Free parking. **Amenities:** 2 restaurants; 2 bars; babysitting; children's center; exercise room; Jacuzzi; 2 seawater pools (1 heated indoor); room service; sauna; 2 outdoor tennis courts (lit); limited watersports equipment/rentals. Free Wi-Fi.

Moderate

Júpiter Algarve ★★★ Hotel Júpiter occupies the most prominent street corner in this bustling summer resort. Boutiques fill the wraparound arcade, and guests relax, sometimes with drinks, on comfortable couches in the lobby. The midsize guest rooms are beauts: dazzling white walls and furnishings offset by dark-wood headboards, and brightly colored throw pillows and throw blankets. All have balconies with views of the river or the sea and better-than-usual art on the walls. A very usable and pleasant gym, plus a swank indoor pool, ups the appeal of this place. The hotel is just across from a wide beach. The bar offers a good selection of cocktails and live music.

Av. Tomás Cabreira, Praia da Rocha. www.hoteljupiter.com. ✆ **28/247-04-70.** 180 units. 43€–160€ double; 90€–300€ junior suite. Rates include buffet breakfast. **Amenities:** Restaurant; bar; babysitting; exercise room; outdoor freshwater heated pool; room service; spa. Free Wi-Fi.

Inexpensive

Residencial Sol ★ The location is noisy and the painted concrete facade of this establishment is somewhat bleak. In this case, however, appearances are deceiving. The small to midsize guest rooms offer some of the tidiest, least pretentious accommodations in town. Each unit is designed for two and contains a neatly kept bathroom. Think simple but cheaper than the norm and you'll be well pleased with your stay.

Av. Tomás Cabreira 10, Praia da Rocha. ✆ **28/242-40-71.** 30 units. 30€–65€ double. Rates include continental breakfast. Free parking. Closed Nov–Mar.

PRAIA DOS TRÊS IRMÃOS

Expensive

Penina Golf & Resort ★★ Located between Portimão and Lagos, this property was the first deluxe hotel to be built on the Algarve. Nowadays it has serious competition from the other luxury hotels, but fans of golf (see "Outdoor Activities," above) remain loyal to the Penina. It's a sporting mecca and stands near the Algarve's major casino. Besides the golf courses, the hotel has a private beach with its own snack bar and changing cabins, reached by a shuttle bus.

Guest rooms are a bit old-fashioned, and some are smaller than they should be at these rates, but they contain picture windows and honeycomb balconies with views of the course and pool, or vistas of the Monchique hills. The standard rooms are furnished pleasantly, combining traditional pieces with Portuguese provincial spool beds. The so-called attic rooms have the most charm, with French doors opening onto terraces. On the fourth floor are some duplexes, often preferred by families. The hotel celebrated 50 years in 2016 with some renovations—sadly, they have yet to improve the gym (too small) or better the food at the restaurants.

Estrada Nacional 125. www.penina.com. ✆ **28/242-02-00.** 196 units. 114€–192€ double; 267€–470€ junior suite. Rates include buffet breakfast. Free parking. **Amenities:** 5 restaurants; 3 bars; babysitting; bikes; children's programs; 3 golf courses; outdoor freshwater pool; room service; sauna; 6 outdoor tennis courts (lit); extensive watersports equipment/rentals. Free Wi-Fi.

Pestana Alvor Praia ★★★ This citadel of hedonism, built in 1968 and constantly renewed, has more joie de vivre than any other hotel on the Algarve. Its location, good-size guest rooms, decor, service, and food are ideal. "You'll feel as if you're loved the moment you walk in the door," one guest of the hotel told us. Poised regally on a landscaped crest, many of the guest and public rooms face the ocean, the gardens, and the free-form Olympic-size pool. Gentle walks and an elevator lead down the palisade to the sandy beach and the rugged rocks that rise out of the water.

Accommodations contain oversize beds, plenty of storage space, long desk-and-chest combinations, and well-designed bathrooms. All rooms have balconies, and most have sea views.

Praia dos Três Irmãos, Alvor. www.pestana.com. ✆ **28/240-09-00.** 195 units. 82€–350€ double; 140€–620€ suite. Rates include buffet breakfast. Free parking. **Amenities:** 2 restaurants; 2 bars; babysitting; bikes; health club; 3 saltwater pools (1 heated indoor); room service; sauna; 7 outdoor tennis courts (lit). Free Wi-Fi.

Where to Dine

If you're sightseeing in Portimão, you might want to seek out a restaurant here; otherwise, most people dine along the beaches, especially those at Praia da Rocha and Praia dos Três Irmãos. All the major hotels have at least one first-class restaurant. There's a wide selection catering to a range of budgets.

PRAIA DA ROCHA

Bamboo Garden ★★ CHINESE Bamboo Garden, which has a classic Asian decor, serves some of the best Chinese food on the coast. The large menu includes everything from squid chop suey to prawns with hot sauce. After deciding on a soup or an appetizer (try the spring roll), guests can select from various categories, including chicken, beef, squid, and prawns. Peking duck is the chef's specialty. This air-conditioned spot is a safe haven for reliable food when you've overdosed on Portuguese-style fish.

Avenida Tomás Cabreira Ed.Lj.1. ✆ **28/248-30-83.** Reservations recommended. Main courses 10€–18€. Daily 12:30–3pm and 6–11:30pm.

Safari ★ AFRICAN/PORTUGUESE Portugal's former colony of Angola is the inspiration here, and it does quite well by that cuisine. The fare includes steak, curries, and shrimp, and such dishes as swordfish steak in pepper sauce, charcoal-grilled fresh fish, and *bacalhau a Safari* (fried codfish with olive oil, garlic, and peppers, served with homemade potato chips). It's customary to begin with a bowl of toothsome fish soup. Ask for the homemade piri-piri (a spicy sauce) if you like your meals fiery. The building stands on a cliff overlooking the beach and has a glass-enclosed terrace. On summer weekends you might hear live Brazilian or African music.

Rua António Feu. ✆ **28/242-35-40.** Reservations recommended. Main courses 9€–21€. Daily noon–11pm (summer usually until midnight). Closed Dec.

PRAIA DOS TRÊS IRMÃOS

Restaurante Caniço ★★★ PORTUGUESE/MEDITERRANEAN Guests need to take an elevator down to this restaurant, as it is perched on the side of the cliffs of Prainha—an eye-popping, fabulous location. The most coveted reservations, not surprisingly, are at sunset. It's hard to compete with the views but the shellfish dishes do, like the *cataplana* and the seafood rice. They also do well by such simple comfort food as tomato with eggs or *xerém* (similar to polenta) with clams. If you just want to see the place and dine elsewhere, you can get an aperitif, truly *on the rocks* here, in the lively bar area.

Aldeamento da Prainha, Praia dos Três Irmãos. www.canicorestaurante.com. ✆ **28/245-85-03.** Reservations recommended. Main courses 14€–30€. Daily noon–5pm and 7–12pm. Closed btw. Nov and Mar.

Portimão After Dark

The town center has about a dozen *tascas* (taverns) and bodegas, as well as glossier after-dark venues in internationally minded Praia da Rocha. Many bars and pubs, as well as the resort's casino (see below), line Avenida Tomás Cabreira—perfect for a pub crawl. The most active and intriguing hangouts include **Farmer's Irish Bar,** Rua Engenheiro José Bívar Edifício Serra Mar-lj 10 (✆ **28/242-57-20**), which serves wine, beer, and cocktails. It's open daily from 10am to 4am. Danceaholics and devoted night owls appreciate the shenanigans at **Disco Pé de Vento,** Avenida Tomás Cabreira (no phone). It gets going after midnight every night in high season and remains open until the last person staggers off the next morning. The cover charge is 10€.

MONCHIQUE: ESCAPE TO THE cool mountains

The Monchique range of hills is the Algarve at its coolest and highest. The rocky peak of the range, some 900m (2,953 ft.) high, looks down on forested slopes and green valleys, burgeoning with orange groves, Indian corn, heather, mimosa, rosemary, oleander bushes, and cork-oak, chestnut, pine, and eucalyptus trees. Icy water springs from the volcanic rock that makes up the range, flowing down to the foothills.

The largest town in the borough, also named Monchique, lies on the east side of Mount Fóia, 26km (16 miles) north of Portimão. The town was once engaged in the manufacture of wooden casks and barrels and the making of oakum and rough cloth. The Manueline-style parish church, with its radiated door facing, dates from the 16th century. Colorful decorated tiles and carved woodwork grace the interior, along with a statue of Our Lady of the Immaculate Conception, an 18th-century work attributed to Machado de Castro. The convent of Nossa Senhora do Desterro is in ruins, but you can look at the curious tiled fountain and the impressive old magnolia tree on its grounds.

Caldas de Monchique was discovered in Roman days and turned into a spa. The waters, from springs in volcanic rock, are still considered good treatment for respiratory disorders, accompanied as they are by the clear air of the highlands. Nowadays Caldas is a resort with five stylish small hotels, a spa with invigorating Monchique waters, and restaurants. See www.monchiquetermas.com.

Nearly 13km (8 miles) from the town of Monchique, Alferce, nestled among trees and mountains, has traces of an ancient fortification. There's also an important handicraft center here. In the opposite direction, about 13km (8 miles) west of Monchique, is Fóia, the highest point in the Algarve. From here you have splendid views of the hills and the sea.

A small inn in the town of Monchique, the **Estalagem Abrigo da Montanha** (www.abrigodamontanha.com; ✆ **28/291-21-31**), is ensconced in a botanical garden. With all the blooming camellias, rhododendrons, mimosa, banana palms, and arbutus, plus the tinkling waterfalls, you'd never believe the hot Algarve coast was in the same province. The inn has 11 doubles and three suites. Rates are 60€ to 85€ for a double or 80€ to 105€ for a suite, including breakfast. On chilly evenings, guests gather before a fireplace in the lounge. The restaurant serves traditional mountain food, but also Algarve fare like razor-clam rice.

Casino Praia da Rocha ★ is on the glittering premises of the five-star Hotel Algarve Casino, Avenida Tomás Cabreira (✆ **28/240-20-00**). Its gaming tables and slot machines open every night at 4pm and shut down at 3am, or later if business warrants. Its entertainment highlight is the cabaret show, featuring lots of dancers in spangles and feathers, magicians, and a master of ceremonies telling not-very-subtle jokes. Dinner, served beginning at 8:30pm, precedes the show and costs around 45€. Formal dress required. Showtime is 11pm.

SILVES ★★★

6.5km (4 miles) N of Lagoa; 11km (6¾ miles) NE of Carvoeiro

Likely founded by the Romans during the period they ruled Lusitania, Silves has a character all its own. When you pass through its Moorish-inspired entrance, you'll quickly realize that Silves is unlike other Algarve towns. It lives in the past, recalling its heyday when it was known as Xelb, the name given by the Moors after they invaded the area in 713. Xelb was the seat of Muslim culture in the south and the capital of the Al-Gharb before it fell to the Christian Crusaders during the *Reconquista.*

Essentials

ARRIVING

BY TRAIN Trains from Faro serve the Silves train station, 1.8km (1 mile) from the center of the town. For information, see www.cp.pt.

BY CAR Coming east or west along Route 125, the main road traversing the Algarve, you arrive at the town of Lagoa (not to be confused with Lagos). From there, head north to Silves along Route 124.

VISITOR INFORMATION

The **tourist office** (www.visitalgarve.pt; ✆ **28/244-22-55**) is located on Estrada Nacional 124 and is open Monday to Friday 9:30am to 12:30pm and 2 to 5pm. There's also a Visitor Center for the Islamic Heritage of Silves in the central Praça do Município.

Exploring the Town

The red-sandstone **Castelo dos Mouros ★★★** (✆ **28/244-56-24**) likely dates to the 9th century, but as is so often true on the coast of Portugal, this spot was held by many nations—the Carthaginians, Greeks, Phoenicians, and Romans. What you'll mostly see today was built by the Moors. From the castle's ramparts you can look out on the saffron-colored, mossy tile roofs of the village houses and down the narrow cobblestone streets where roosters strut and scrappy dogs sleep peacefully in doorways. Inside the walls, the government has planted a flower garden with golden chrysanthemums and scarlet poinsettias. In the fortress, water rushes through a huge cistern and a deep well made of sandstone. The system of irrigation and water storage brought by the Moors was a sophisticated one, and the cistern originally supplied not only the castle but also the city. The site is open daily from 9am to 5pm (until 10:30pm in summer). Admission is 2.80€ and free for children 11 and under. A ticket of 3.90€ allows you to visit both the castle and the archeological museum.

The 13th-century former **Cathedral of Silves ★★★** (✆ **28/244-08-00**), on Rua de Sé, is another more-than-worthy stop. Built in the Gothic style using local red limestone, it is one of the most important examples of Gothic architecture in the Algarve. The aisles and nave are stunning in their simplicity. The flamboyant Gothic style of both the chancel and the transept dates from a later period. The cathedral might have been built on the place of the former mosque, but there's no clear evidence. Many of the tombs here are believed to be the graves of Crusaders who took the town in 1244. At one point King John was buried here (he died nearby in 1495), but his remains were ultimately moved to the Monastery of Batalha. His tomb slab remains, however, in the floor of the main chapel. It's open Monday to Friday from 9am to 5pm. Admission is free, but donations are welcome.

The best artifacts found in the area are on display at the **Museu Arqueologia ★**, Rua das Portas de Loulé (✆ **28/244-48-32**), a short walk from the Sé. The museum's major sight is an ancient Arab water cistern preserved as part of a 9m-deep (30-ft.) well. Admission is 2.10€ and 3.90€ for a ticket combined with the Castle. It's open daily from 10am to 5:30pm.

Outside the center of town, on the road to Enxerim, near an orange grove, a lonely open-air pavilion shelters a 15th-century stone lacework cross. This ecclesiastical artwork, **Cruz de Portugal,** is two-faced, depicting a *pietà* (the face of Christ is destroyed) on one side and the Crucifixion on the other. It has been declared a national monument of incalculable value and is quite lovely.

Where to Stay

Colina dos Mouros Hotel ★ On the outskirts of town, this modern inn at last provides a decent place to stay in Silves. Only a short walk from the historic core, the well-managed, immaculate hotel offers midsize-to-spacious bedrooms that are comfortable, though not inspired style-wise. You approach the hotel across a Roman bridge spanning the River Arade. Enveloped by gardens, the building opens onto views of the rooftops of Silves and its major monuments. Beaches are a short drive from the inn.

Pocinho Santo. www.colinahotels.com. ✆ **28/244-04-20.** 57 units. 38€–82€ double. Free parking. **Amenities:** Restaurant; 2 bars; bikes; buffet breakfast; outdoor freshwater pool. Free Wi-Fi in public areas.

Where to Dine

Marisqueira Rui ★ PORTUGUESE This regional restaurant, decorated with whitewashed walls and Algarvian handicrafts, draws more locals than visitors. The cooking is hearty, the way the townspeople like it. And why shouldn't they? The fish and shellfish are delivered fresh every morning from the coast down below. Our favorite dish here is the herbaceous kettle of shellfish rice. In the autumn the chef prepares appetizing game dishes, including partridge, wild boar, and Algarvian rabbit.

Rua Comendador Vilarim, 27. ✆ **28/244-26-82.** Main courses 10€–36€. Wed–Mon noon–2am (kitchen closes at 11 pm).

ALBUFEIRA

37km (23 miles) W of Faro; 325km (202 miles) SE of Lisbon

This cliff-side town, formerly a fishing village, is the busiest in the Algarve. At night, its long strip of bars are one giant party, mostly for the young Brits and Germans who come here en masse to guzzle beer and nuzzle each other. Massive tourism, sadly, means the town's genuine character was lost long ago, though there is a sliver of an old town left, with cobblestoned streets and authentic restaurants (alongside plenty of junky souvenir stores and more bars). The newer parts of town cater to those looking for the lazy life of sunshine, booze, and beaches. It's a popular formula: Albufeira is the largest resort in the region.

Essentials

ARRIVING

BY TRAIN Trains run between Albufeira and Faro (see "Faro," later in this chapter), which has good connections to Lisbon. For schedules, go to www.cp.pt. The train station lies 6.5km (4 miles) from the town's center. Buses from the station to the resort run every 30 minutes; the fare is 3.50€ one-way.

BY BUS Buses run between Albufeira and Faro every hour. Trip time is 1 hour and a one-way ticket costs 4.50€. For info, visit www.eva-bus.com.

BY CAR From east or west, take the main coastal route, N125. Albufeira also lies near the point where the express highway from the north, N264, feeds into the Algarve. The town is well signposted in all directions. Take Route 595 to reach Albufeira and the water.

VISITOR INFORMATION

The **Tourist Information Office** is at Rua do 5 de Outubro (www.visitalgarve.com; ✆ **28/958-52-79**). From July to September, hours are daily from 9am to 1pm and 2 to 6pm.

Exploring the Town

The big, bustling resort town rises above a sickle-shaped beach, with a rocky, grottoed bluff separating the strip used by sunbathers from the working beach, where brightly painted fishing boats are drawn up on the sand. Access to the beach is through a tunneled rock passageway. Unfortunately the "new" Albufeira was created solely for tourism, and signs and menus in English and touristy pubs with fish and chips are everywhere.

Families do enjoy the town, thanks in part to **Zoomarine,** N125, Guia (www.zoomarine.pt; ✆ **28/956-03-00**), 6.5km (4 miles) northwest of the center. It's a popular water park, with rides, swimming pools, gardens, and dolphin shows. Opening hours are March 1 to June 19 and September 3 to October 31 Tuesday to Sunday 10am to 6pm, and June 20 to September 2 Tuesday to Sunday 10am to 7:30pm. Admission is 29€ for adults and 20€ for children 10 and under and seniors over 65.

Outdoor Activities

BEACHES Some of the best beaches—but also the most crowded—are near Albufeira. They include **Falésia, Olhos d'Água,** and **Praia da Oura. Albufeira,** originally discovered by the British, is now the busiest resort on the Algarve. To avoid the crowds on Albufeira's main beaches, head west for 4km (2½ miles) on a local road to **São Rafael** and **Praia da Galé.** You might also go east to the beach at **Olhos d'Água.**

GOLF Many pros note that the extremely well-maintained **Pine Cliffs ★** course, Praia da Falésia 644 (www.pinecliffs.com; ✆ **28/950-01-00**), has the distinction of being relaxing without being boring. Opened in 1990, its fairways meander beside copper-colored cliffs that drop 75m (246 ft.) down to a sandy beach. Par is 33; it has only 9 holes scattered over a relatively compact area. The greens fees are 39€ to 49€ for Sheraton Algarve Hotel guests and 55€ to 69€ for nonguests. The course lies 6.5km (4 miles) west of Vilamoura and less than 5km (3 miles) east of Albufeira. To reach it from Albufeira, follow signs to the hamlet of Olhos d'Água, where more signs direct you to the Sheraton Algarve Hotel and Pine Cliffs.

Visit **algarvegolf.net** for more information on courses in the Algarve region.

Shopping

One of the busiest resorts along the Algarve, Albufeira maintains an almost alarming roster of seafront kiosks, many selling fun-in-the-sun products of dubious (or, at best, transient) value. The main shopping areas are along Rua do 5 de Outubro and Praça Duarte de Pacheco. An even denser collection of merchandise is on display in the town's largest shopping plaza, **Modelo Shopping Center,** Rua do Município, about .5km (⅓ mile) north of the town center. Most of the independently operated shops inside are open daily from 10am to 10pm. Although Albufeira produces limited amounts of ceramics, you'll find a wide selection of pottery and glazed terracotta from throughout Portugal at the **Casa Infante Dom Henrique House,** Rua Cândido dos Reis 30 (✆ **28/951-32-67**). Also look for woven baskets and woodcarvings.

Where to Stay

Though Albufeira has many accommodations, we prefer to stay outside the city itself. So below are both in-city options and a number within easy driving distance.

INEXPENSIVE

Flor de Laranja ★ For the cost of a hotel room, guests to this friendly complex get their own little apartment, complete with kitchenette. There are a variety of units, from studios to family-sized dwellings with two queen-size beds and a separate living room/kitchen, but all share the same homey vibe. No, they aren't fancy, but it's clear the owners care a lot, and so keep the property immaculate and add cozy touches like a flowered tablecloth here, a carved wooden headboard there. Around the two pools are four barbecue grills for guest use (the owners will sell you the wood). The complex is about a 15-minute drive from the center of Albufeira. ***One warning:*** The owner's cat is very friendly, so this isn't a place for those who are allergic.

Rua Samora Barros, Cerro da Piedade. http://flordelaranja.com. ✆ **91/979-80-58.** 8 units. 40€–65€ double. Free parking. **Amenities:** Kitchenettes; barbecue grills; restaurant next door; 2 pools. Free Wi-Fi.

Rocamar Beach Hotel ★ This cubistic hotel looks like a well-ordered assemblage of building blocks, or the partially excavated side of a stone quarry. Built in 1974, it was enlarged in 1991. It rises six stories above the tawny cliffs that slope down to one of the most inviting beaches on the Algarve. Many of its windows and all of its balconies benefit from the spectacular view (ask for a sea-view room). The hotel is a 5-minute walk from the town's attractions. Rooms are colorful and sunwashed, with contemporary furniture.

Largo Jacinto d'Ayet 7. www.rocamarhotels.com. ✆ **28/954-02-80.** 88 units. 45€–130€ double. Rates include buffet breakfast. Limited free parking on street. **Amenities:** Restaurant; bar; room service; outdoor pool; spa. Free Wi-Fi.

Where to Stay Nearby

AT SESMARIAS

São Rafael Suite Hotel ★★ This tranquil, all-suites hotel has unusually spacious digs, making it ideal for groups and families. Those types of guests also appreciate the resort's many facilities, including indoor and outdoor pools (one just for children), and its kid's club (summers only). The beachside hotel enjoys a garden setting, and its Relax Centre is well equipped with a Jacuzzi, sauna, Turkish bath, an indoor heated pool, and massage and treatment rooms. The helpful staff will also arrange many outdoor activities, including diving, snorkeling, sailing, windsurfing, water-skiing, and canoeing. The hotel operates both a buffet restaurant and a more gourmet a la carte dining room, and in season features lunch around the pool. Rates are all-inclusive. The hotel is 4km (2½ miles) west of the center of Albufeira.

Sesmarias. www.cshotelsandresorts.com. ✆ **28/954-03-30.** 101 units. 170€–355€ suite. **Amenities:** 3 restaurants; babysitting; bar; children's club; concierge; exercise room; 3 pools (1 indoor); room service. Free Wi-Fi in lobby.

PRAIA DE SANTA EULÁLIA

Grande Real Santa Eulália Resort & Hotel Spa ★★★ Luxury with a capital "L"—this is a hotel that pampers its guests, from the bend-over-backward service that all guests receive to the surprise bottle of champagne that's gifted to returning guests and those celebrating special events. Best of all, if you stroll out the back door you're right on a lovely sandy beach.

Guests have a choice of standard double rooms and posh apartment suites, with kitchenettes (including two- or three-bedroom suites). Windows in these accommodations open either onto the Atlantic or a well-landscaped garden. All are spacious and decorated in what we'd call "sunset" colors, with chic and quite bold patterns on many of the soft goods. The swankiest units contain a heated Jacuzzi on their private terraces.

The spa, with its range of treatments using sea water, is one of the best along the coast, with a team of hydrotherapists, beauticians, masseurs, and fitness trainers. The hotel is also one of the best on the Algarve for families with children, with a kiddie center with trained professionals and a small pools just for the little ones. The hotel is 4km (2½ miles) from the center of Albufeira.

Praia de Santa Eulália. www.granderealsantaeulaliahotel.com. ✆ **28/959-80-00.** 158 units. 90€–256€ double; 125€–435€ suite. Rates include buffet breakfast. Free parking. **Amenities:** 4 restaurants; 8 bars; babysitting; children's center; 4 freshwater pools (1 heated indoors); room service; spa; 2 outdoor tennis courts (lit). Free Wi-Fi.

PRAIA DA FALÉSIA

Falesia Hotel ★★ Downtown Albufeira is a short taxi ride away, but most guests don't seem to mind, thanks to the fun, fun, fun array of activities and amenities the Falesia provides for its guests. At the resort's heart is a lovely pool surrounded by even lovelier gardens, but that's just the start. The Falesia also has several lively bars and a restaurant, a spa with a Turkish bath, and a roster of kitschy entertainments, from pub quiz sessions to Adele-tribute shows. And when you retire to your room it will be a serene oasis, with a walk-in rainfall shower, a strong Wi-Fi signal, and looks that are more Scandinavian than Portuguese (lots of light wood and recessed lighting). The hotel is adults-only and gets many repeat guests, all of whom rave about the helpfulness of the staff. The beach is a short walk from the hotel.

Pinhal do Concelho, Praia da Falesia, Apartado 785, Albufeira. www.falesiahotel.com. ✆ **28/950-12-37.** 190 units. 50€–79€; from 79€ junior suite. Free parking. **Amenities:** Restaurant; 3 bars; concierge; exercise room; 2 pools (indoor and outdoor); tennis courts; room service; spa; free shuttles to the beach and to town. Free Wi-Fi.

Pine Cliffs Hotel, A Luxury Collections Resort ★★★ Laid out like an Algarve village, with no building rising higher than three floors, this property was designed to blend tastefully into its cliff-side oceanfront location—and so it does. Its wings ramble through a subtropical garden dotted with copses of the site's original pine trees; and buildings have wonderful Moorish touches, like rectangular windows with rounded tops and breezy open-air corridors. That aesthetic is continued in the guest rooms, all fully renovated in 2016. These have the traditional terracotta floors of the Algarve, many pieces of Portuguese decorative arts, curvaceous furnishings, and cloud-like beds. There's much to draw guests out of their rooms, including a top-notch spa, six swimming pools, a 9-hole golf course, nine restaurants and bars, and an elevator that leads down to a very private beach. Overall: a true "wow." The hotel is 8km (5 miles) east of Albufeira.

Praia da Falésia. www.pinecliffshotel.com/en. ✆ **800/325-3535** in the U.S., or 28/950-01-00. 215 units. 119€–439€ double; 195€–565€ suite. Rates include buffet breakfast. Free parking. **Amenities:** 9 restaurants; 5 bars; babysitting; bikes; children's center; concierge; golf course; health club & spa; 5 outdoor freshwater pools (1 heated); room service; 5 outdoor tennis courts (lit); extensive watersports equipment/rentals. Free Wi-Fi.

PRAIA DA GALÉ

Vila Galé Praia ★★ Like the even more glamorous hotel below, this is another winner positioned about 15km (9⅓ miles) west of Albufeira, an easy commute. In a room here, you're just 2 minutes from a good and spacious beach. The hotel mostly gets romantic couples, as the rooms are a bit small and not suitable for an extra bed. Most of the accommodations open onto balconies and are furnished with such amenities as bathrobes, ceiling fans, and blackout draperies. A Portuguese and international menu is served in the main restaurant or less formally in the bar lounge. The hotel emphasizes its spa and health facilities, with its mega-sized Jacuzzi and sauna, steam baths, special treatments, and massages; trainers even give yoga lessons. Courtesy buses take visitors into the center of Albufeira.

Praia da Galé. www.vilagale.com. ✆ **28/959-01-90.** 40 units. 85€–230€. Free parking. **Amenities:** Restaurant; bar; exercise room; 2 pools (outdoor); room service; spa. Free Wi-Fi.

Vila Joya ★★★ This is one the most elegant and intimate inns in the Algarve. The establishment lies 15km (9⅓ miles) west of Albufeira in a residential neighborhood dotted with other dwellings, but within the confines of its large gardens, visitors can easily imagine themselves in the open countryside. A footpath leads down to a pristine beach. All of the handsome accommodations—light filled, terracotta floors, fluffy beds—have a view of the sea and a private bathroom (some of which are tiled in traditional *azulejos*). Though the hotel is lovely, it's not as famous as its on-site restaurant, which made the 50 Best Restaurants in the World list in 2016 (a well-deserved nod to the artistry of Austrian chef Dieter Koschina). Guests get first dibs for restaurant reservations; on Thursdays the restaurant's celebrated eight-course gala dinner is served (the rest of the week, the tasting menu is six courses).

Estrada da Galé. www.vilajoya.com. ✆ **28/959-17-95.** 20 units. 325€–755€ double; from 620€ suite. Rates include breakfast. Free parking. **Amenities:** Restaurant; bar; babysitting; bikes; exercise room; golf course; Jacuzzi; outdoor heated pool; room service; sauna; spa; outdoor tennis court (lit). Free Wi-Fi. Closed Nov–beginning of Mar.

Where to Dine

The finest dining experience in the region (and one of the finest in all of Portugal) can be had at **Vila Joya** (see above). If you want to try and eat there, call months before your trip (reservations are difficult to come by) and save up—it's a pricey experience, but one that many feel is worth the outlay.

EXPENSIVE

O Cabaz da Praia ★★ (The Beach Basket) INTERNATIONAL/PORTUGUESE O Cabaz da Praia, or rather, "The Beach Basket," sits on a colorful little square near the Church of São Sebastião. In a former fisherman's cottage, the restaurant boasts a large, sheltered terrace with a view over the main Albufeira beach. So the setting can't be beat, but that's not the main reason you're here: The food is quite good, too. Main courses include such justifiable favorites as seafood rice, tuna in the Algarve style, monkfish with mango sauce, and beef filet with garlic and white-wine sauce, all served with a selection of fresh vegetables.

Praça Miguel Bombarda 7. http://cabazdapraia.blogspot.pt. ✆ **28/951-21-37.** Reservations recommended. Main courses 20€–28€. Daily noon–11pm.

MODERATE

A Casa do Avô ★★ PORTUGUESE Who doesn't love "all you can eat"? The Portuguese version of that is A Casa do Avô's *tasca* (tapas) table, part of the well-priced "Grandfather's Menu," which allows guests to graze on a selection of 30 enticing small bites, both hot and cold, at the start of a meal.

But be strategic! You'll want to save room for the main dishes—either fresh fish or an array of meats from Monchique, all prepared according to decades-old, traditional recipes. The welcome and looks of the place are also delightfully old-fashioned. The restaurant is located in the Vale de Parra, a scenic valley, near Guia, 6km (3¾ miles) west of Albufeira.

Sitio de Vale de Parra, outside Guia. www.restaurante-acasadoavo.com. ✆ **28/951-32-82.** Reservations recommended. Fixed-price menu 19.90€; main courses 15€–28€. May–Sept daily 12:30–3pm and 6:30–10pm; Oct–Apr Wed–Sun 12:30–3pm and Tues–Sun 6:30–10pm. Closed in Jan.

Churrasceria O Nosso Franguinho ★★★ PORTUGUESE No menu will be given when you arrive at this local's favorite. There's no reason: You're here to feast on the best piri-piri chicken you'll likely ever have... and that's all they serve. The dish, now considered a Portuguese classic, is actually based on peppers imported from Africa (from former colonies). Those peppers form the basis for a barbecue-style sauce that's slathered on the chicken before it's set atop a charcoal grill and cooked to juicy perfection. It comes sided with potato wedges. If you like your food fiery, ask to have the bird *picante* (with extra piri-piri, a spicy oil).

Estrada da Nora, Ferreiras. ✆ **28/957-23-03.** Main courses 7€–12€. Daily noon–3 pm and 7–10pm; Sun noon–3pm only. Closed in Jan.

Didi Cafe ★★ VEGAN Vegan fare isn't common in this region, which makes it all the more surprising to find a restaurant that not only serves it, but excels at animal-free fare. Didi's menu is small, but that's because everything served tastes like it has just been plucked from the ground, whether you go for mushroom in a pastry shell, a tropical salad, or tagliatelle. Siding the food is an array of freshly squeezed juices and smoothies. All is eaten in a very Zen little restaurant, with some of the kindliest waiters in the Algarve. Even dedicated meat-eaters will be enchanted by this place.

Travessa Cais Herculano 11. https://www.facebook.com/didicafealbufeira. ✆ **28/914-28-96.** Main courses 12€–25€. Mon–Sat 11am–11pm.

O Marinheiro ★★ PORTUGUESE/MEDITERRANEAN Ever since Monika and Joaquim Coelho came here around the turn of the millennium, they have been known for serving the best market-fresh cuisine in the area and seasonal ingredients. Besides the excellent fish and shellfish of the Algarve, a number of vegetarian dishes are always offered. The choice meat dish is filet of beef carpaccio—thin slices of filet of beef with pink peppercorns, virgin olive oil, and Parmesan cheese. A tantalizing selection of desserts is also available, including blackberry sorbet or a combination white-and-brown chocolate mousse. For those who enjoy dining alfresco, there's a shady garden terrace in summer and a temperature-controlled winter garden for the (slightly) chillier months. ***Note:*** This is a favorite for families, thanks to the patient staff, the children's menu, and the on-site playground.

Estrada da Praia da Coelha, Sesmarias. www.o-marinheiro.com. ✆ **28/959-23-50.** Reservations required. 18€–36€. Mar–Nov daily 6:30pm–midnight.

Albufeira After Dark

In this hard-drinking, fun-in-the-sun town, discovering a more laid-back bar can be difficult, especially if there are students or bachelors partying in town. So why not join in? To get rolling, you might begin at the **Fastnet Bar,** Rua Cândido dos Reis 10 (© **28/958-91-16**), where no one will object if you jump to your feet and begin to dance. From there you have many choices: The main street of Praia da Oura is the party neighborhood of Albufeira.

QUARTEIRA & VILAMOURA

23km (14 miles) W of Faro; 307km (191 miles) SE of Lisbon

This once-sleepy fishing village between Albufeira and Faro used to be visited by only a handful of artists. Now, with the invasion of sun-worshippers, the traditional way of life has been upset. A sea of high-rise buildings has swallowed Quarteira, and the town has become a bustling, overgrown resort. Its biggest attraction is BIG: one of the Algarve's longest beaches. In summer those sands are crowded with vacationing Portuguese and other Europeans.

Golfers who don't want to pay the high rates at Vale do Lobo or Vilamoura (both of which have 18-hole courses) can stay inexpensively in Quarteira (see "Where to Stay," below). The courses are only a 10-minute drive away, and Quarteira lies about 11km (6¾ miles) from the Faro airport.

The largest concentration of quality hotels and restaurants is not in Quarteira or even Praia de Quarteira, but in the satellite of Vilamoura. Buses run between Quarteira and Vilamoura frequently throughout the day.

At a central point on the Algarve coast, only 18km (11 miles) west of Faro airport, Vilamoura is an expansive land-development project. Although the remains of a Roman villa were discovered when builders were working on the local marina, the history of this new town is yet to be written—the museum and ruins of Cerro da Vila can be visited. There's a marina that can hold 1,000 pleasure boats. Vilamoura is now filled with "holiday villages" and apartment complexes, and becoming over-built. However, it's still more pleasant than some other beach areas.

Essentials

ARRIVING

BY BUS If you're dependent on public transportation, take a plane, bus, or train from Lisbon to Faro (see "Faro," later in this chapter), and then catch one of the buses that runs frequently between Faro and Quarteira. Contact EVA (www.eva-bus.com; © **28/989-97-60**) for schedules and information.

BY CAR From Albufeira, head east along Route 125; from Faro, go west on Route 125. Signposts point to the little secondary road that runs south to Quarteira, which is the center for exploring the more extensive tourist developments along Praia de Quarteira and Vilamoura.

VISITOR INFORMATION

The **tourist information office** in Quarteira is at Praça do Mar (www.visitalgarve.pt; ✆ **28/938-92-09**). It's open October to May Tuesday to Thursday from 9:30am to 5:30pm, and Friday and Monday 9:30am to 1pm and 2 to 5:30pm. June to September, it's open Tuesday to Thursday 9:30am to 7pm, and Friday to Monday 9:30am to 1pm and 2 to 5:30pm.

Outdoor Activities

Sports are the main attraction here. There are 18-hole golf courses, watersports, tennis courts, a riding center, and yachting. Shops and other tourist facilities, including restaurants and bars, also provide pleasant diversions.

BOATING Marinas have been tucked into virtually every navigable cove along the Algarve, and most contain a handful of sailboats or motorboats that can be rented, with or without a skipper, to qualified sailors. ***Note:*** Before you can rent, you must present accreditation or some certificate from a yacht club proving your seaworthiness.

Algariate operates a boat-charter business from the 100-berth Marina de Vilamoura, 8125 Quarteira (✆ **28/938-99-33**). Algariate was established in 1993 and is one of the largest yacht and motorboat charterers in the Algarve. Boats up to 14m (46 ft.) in length are available. Without a crew, they rent from 2,000€ per week, depending on size and season. Clients often use Vilamoura as a point of origin for visits to Madeira, North Africa, or the southern coast of Spain. If you prefer to have someone else worry about navigation, you can sail on the *Condor de Vilamoura* (✆ **28/931-40-70**), which departs from the Vilamoura Marina at least once a day, depending on business, for 3-hour cruises toward Albufeira. The cost is 40€ per person. A full-day cruise lasting about 7 hours costs from 55€, with lunch included.

We should also point out that such marketplace sites as **GetMyBoat.com** and **RentaBoat.com** allow users to charter vessels in the Algarve, often at a significant discount from the prices above. There are bare boats and ones with crews available, sometimes from individual owners (who only have one boat). As with any of these types of online marketplaces, do your due diligence before putting any money down.

GOLF **Vila Sol ★★★**, Alto do Semino, Vilamoura (www.pestanagolf.com/en/golf/vila-sol; ✆ **28/930-05-05**), has the best fairways and the boldest and most inventive contours of any golf course in the Algarve. Designed by the English architect Donald Steel, it opened in 1991 as part of a 147-hectare (363-acre) residential estate. Steel took great care in allowing the terrain's natural contours to determine the layout of the fairways and the impeccable greens. Vila Sol has twice played host to the Portuguese Open. Golfers especially praise the configuration of holes 6, 8, and 14, which incorporate ponds, creek beds, and pine groves in nerve-racking order. Par is 72. Greens fees start from 96€. From Quarteira, drive east for about 5km (3 miles), following signs to Estrada Nacional 125, and turn off where signs point to Vila Sol.

Vilamoura has three famous courses, each with its own clubhouse, managed and owned by the same investors. They're 4km (2½ miles) east of Quarteira and are carefully signposted from the center of town. Discounts on greens fees are offered to the guests of five nearby hotels according to a complicated, frequently changing system of hierarchies and commercial agreements.

The most famous and most sought-after of Vilamoura's trio of golf courses is the **Oceanico Old Course ★★**, sometimes referred to as Vilamoura I (www.oceanicogolf.com; ✆ **28/931-03-41**). Noted English architect Frank Pennink laid out the course in 1969, long before American tastes in golf influenced Portugal. In design, texture, and conception, it's the most English of southern Portugal's golf courses, and it's invariably cited for its beauty, lushness, and the maturity of its trees and shrubbery. Although some holes are almost annoyingly difficult (four of them are par 5), the course is among the most consistently crowded on the Algarve. Par is 73. Greens fees are 133€.

Adjacent to the Old Course are a pair of newer, less popular par-72 courses that nonetheless provide challenging golf for those who prefer different terrain. The first is the **Pinhal Golf Course,** also known as Vilamoura II (www.oceanicogolf.com; ✆ **28/931-03-90**), which opened in the early 1970s. It's noted for the challenging placement of its many copses of pine trees. Greens fees run 70€ to 120€, depending on the season and the time of day. Nearby is the most modern course, the **Laguna Golf Course,** or Vilamoura III (✆ **28/931-01-80**). Known for its labyrinth of water traps and lakes, it opened in the late 1980s. Greens fees are from 41€. Tee times during the midday heat are less expensive than those in the early morning.

Visit **www.algarvegolf.net** for more information on courses in the Algarve region.

TENNIS The English influence in southern Portugal is so strong that no self-respecting resort would be built without at least one tennis court. The **Vilamoura Ténis Academy,** 8125 Vilamoura (www.premier-sports.org; ✆ **28/932-41-23**), has 12. They're open to suitably dressed players for 16€ per hour. Hours are daily from 9:30am to 8pm. Tennis racquets and balls rent for 5€, and four tennis balls can be purchased for 7€.

Where to Stay

Praia de Quarteira is more genuine than sophisticated Vilamoura. You'll get better value in the former fishing town, but also bigger crowds.

PRAIA DE QUARTEIRA

Inexpensive

Conii Hostel & Suites Algarve ★★ A contemporary hostel with stylish dormitories and public areas, the Conii is aimed squarely at what's called the "flashpackers" (people who don't mind sharing rooms, but want those rooms to be chic). Recycled wood, whitewashed walls, and blue sofas and chairs give the place a northern European look. Along with dorms, there are private rooms with bathrooms for a small uptick in cost. This may well be the nicest hostel in the Algarve.

Rua Gago Coutinho, 24. www.coniihostel.com/en/. ✆ **93/26-88-30.** 15 units. 18€–28€ dormitory; 35€–100€ double. Rates include breakfast. **Amenities:** Bar; shared kitchen; self-service laundry. Free Wi-Fi.

Dom José Beach Hotel ★★ Hotel Dom José is sometimes completely booked, often by vacationers from Britain who consider its amenities considerably better than its government-assigned three-star status dictates. At its tallest point, the hotel has eight balconied stories; the outlying wings are shorter. The double rooms are small and plain but comfortably furnished and very clean. A low wall separates the pool and the cafe from the town's portside promenade and the beach. The public rooms fill every evening as guests enjoy drinks, live music, and the terrace sea view. In another corner of the ground floor, a lattice-covered room contains a wide-screen TV.

Av. Infante do Sagres 141–143. www.hoteldomjose.com. ✆ **28/931-02-10.** 154 units. 57€–170€ double. Rates include buffet breakfast. **Amenities:** Restaurant; 2 bars; babysitting; outdoor freshwater pool. Free Wi-Fi.

Hotel Zodiaco Hotel ★ This modern resortlike hotel, located only 400m (1,312 ft.) from Forte Novo Beach, is a good value choice. Its bedrooms, though lackluster, are well maintained and comfortable, with bright colors and wooden floors. Most of them are midsize. For those who want to lodge in the center of Quarteira itself at a reasonable rate, the Zodiaco is a good pick.

Fonte Santa. www.hotel-zodiaco.com. ✆ **28/938-14-20.** 60 units. 35€–120€ double. Rates include buffet breakfast. Free parking. **Amenities:** Restaurant; bar; babysitting; outdoor freshwater pool; room service; outdoor tennis court (lit). Free Wi-Fi.

VILAMOURA

Moderate

Dom Pedro Vilamoura Resort ★★ This 10-story hotel offers first-class comfort in the tourist whirl of Vilamoura. It's close to the casino and a short walk from the sands. The public rooms are sleekly styled. The midsize guest rooms are pleasantly furnished and carpeted, with private terraces, but the overall effect is uninspired. The house band provides nightly entertainment, the gym is well equipped, and there's a nice playground for the little ones. Deep-sea fishing and horseback riding can be arranged, and guests receive a 15 to 20% discount on greens fees at various area golf courses.

Rua Atlântico, Vilamoura. www.dompedro.com. ✆ **28/930-07-80.** 266 units. 75€–244€ double. Rates include buffet breakfast. Free parking. **Amenities:** 2 restaurants; 2 bars; babysitting; children's center; concierge; 3 freshwater pools (1 heated indoor); room service; spa; 3 outdoor tennis courts (lit). Free Wi-Fi. Closed btw. Nov–most of Feb.

Where to Dine

QUARTEIRA

Jacinto ★★★ PORTUGUESE This is one of the most popular *marisqueiras* (seafood places) in this part of the Algarve, not just among tourists but also with locals. They know that the very fresh fish being served comes from the excellent Quarteira market each morning. The monkfish rice and the octopus rice are the stars on the menu, served in portions that not even a sumo wrestler could finish (share plates!). Less often available, but excellent, are the local scarlet prawns (*carabineiros*)—if they're being offered, be sure to try them. If you can't reserve a table in advance, make sure to arrive early, before the locals, around 12:30 for lunch, 7:30 for dinner.

Av. Dr. Francisco Sá Carneiro, BL2. ✆ **28/930-18-87.** Reservations recommended. Main courses 14€–35€. Daily noon–3pm and 7–11pm. Closed Mon.

VILAMOURA

Willie's Restaurant ★★★ INTERNATIONAL Wilhelm Wurger is "Willie," and he's one of several master chefs making life tastier in the Algarve today (his major competition is Dieter Koschina of Vila Joya, p. 241, who has now won two Michelin stars; Willie is right behind with one). His cuisine is Pan-European and sinfully rich, with such offerings as homemade seafood ravioli in a vermouth cream sauce, saddle of monkfish in a mustard cream sauce with potato mousse, and tiger prawn curry over rice studded with raisins. Willie also has a sure hand with beef, which is well-aged and perfectly seared, so don't hesitate to order a steak if that's your preference. All is served in an opulent setting with fine crystal and silver, and fresh flowers. The restaurant is hidden away in an upscale residential area close to the Pinhal Golf Course.

Rua do Brasil, 7-B R/C. http://williesrestaurantevilamoura.pt/en. ✆ **28/938-08-49.** Reservations required. Main courses 25€–35€. Mon, Tues, Thurs–Sun 7–10pm. Closed Jan 10–Feb 4.

Quarteira After Dark

Much of the tourist expansion in this region has occurred outside the immediate confines of Quarteira, so you're likely to find only a handful of sleepy bodegas and *tascas* (taverns) inside the city limits. Most cater to locals and serve beer and wine.

Glossier diversions are the norm in the massive marina and tourist developments of nearby Vilamoura. Foremost among these is the **Casino Vilamoura** ★, Vilamoura, 8125 Quarteira (www.solverde.pt; ✆ **28/931-00-00**), one of the finest nightspots in the Algarve. Its most appealing feature is a gambling salon that offers roulette, blackjack, French banque, and baccarat. It's open every day from 3pm to 3am. To enter, you must present a passport or photo ID and pay 10€. A separate, less glamorous slot-machine salon at the casino, open daily from 4pm to 4am, doesn't charge admission.

Physically part of the casino, but with a separate entrance and separate staff, is Vilamoura's most action-oriented dance club, **Black Jack** (✆ **28/938-91-47**). Every clubber in the region comes to dance here. It's open Thursday, Friday, and Saturday 11pm to 6am. The casino and its facilities are open every night except December 24 and 25.

QUINTA DO LAGO & ALMANCIL

13km (8 miles) W of Faro; 306km (190 miles) SE of Lisbon

Almancil is a small market town with one of the most remarkable 18th-century churches in the country. **São Lourenço** church is covered with exquisite blue-and-white tiles inside telling the life of martyr São Lourenço. Entry is 2€ and it's open primarily in the afternoons. The town, however, is better known as a center for two of the most exclusive tourist developments along the Algarve. **Vale do Lobo** lies 6.5km (4 miles) southeast of Almancil, and **Quinta do Lago** is less than 10km (6¼ miles) southeast of town.

The name *Vale do Lobo* (Valley of the Wolf) suggests a forlorn spot, but in reality the vale is the site of a golf course designed by Henry Cotton, the British champion. It's west of Faro, about a 20-minute drive from the Faro airport. Some holes are by the sea, which results in many an anxious moment as shots hook out over the water. The property includes a 9-hole course, a 9-hole par-3 course, a putting green, and a driving range. The tennis center is among the best in Europe.

Quinta do Lago, one of the most elegant "tourist estates" on the Algarve, also has superb facilities. The pine-covered beachfront property has been a favored retreat of celebrities, from movie stars to European presidents. The resort's 27 superb holes of golf are also a potent lure. This is true luxury—at quite a price.

Essentials

ARRIVING

BY TRAIN Faro, the gateway to the eastern Algarve, makes the best transportation hub for Almancil and its resorts. Go to Faro by train (see p. 252) and then take a bus the rest of the way.

BY BUS Almancil is a major stop for buses to the western Algarve; about 17 a day run from Faro to Albufeira. Travel time is about 50 minutes. Whereas a taxi will cost around 40€ for up to four passengers, bus transit costs only around 5.50€ per person, with a stop at Almancil. For more information, visit www.eva-bus.com or call ✆ **28/989-97-60.**

BY CAR From Faro, head west along Route 125; from Albufeira or Portimão, continue east along Route 125.

VISITOR INFORMATION

Almancil's tourist office is at Av. 25 Abril 9 (✆ **28/939-26-59**). It's open Monday to Friday 9am to 12:30pm and 2 to 3:30pm.

Outdoor Activities

GOLF One of the most deceptive golf courses on the Algarve, **Pinheiros Altos ★★**, Quinta do Lago (www.pinheirosaltos.com; ✆ **28/935-99-00**), has contours that even professionals say are far more difficult than they appear at first glance. American architect Ronald Fream designed the 100 hectares (247 acres), which abut the wetland refuge of the Ria Formosa National Park.

Umbrella pines and dozens of small lakes dot the course. Par is 72. Greens fees are 50€ to 70€ for 9 holes and 95€ to 130€ for 18 holes. Pinheiros Altos lies about 5km (3 miles) south of Almancil. From Almancil, follow the signs to Quinta do Lago and Pinheiros Altos.

The namesake course of the massive development, **Quinta do Lago,** Quinta do Lago (www.quintadolago.com; ✆ **28/939-07-00**), consists now of three golf courses, the newest being Laranjal. Together they cover more than 240 hectares (593 acres) of sandy terrain that abuts the Rio Formosa Wildlife Sanctuary. Very few long drives here are over open water; instead, the fairways undulate through cork forests and groves of pine trees, sometimes with abrupt changes in elevation. Greens fees are 116€ to 144€, depending on the season. The courses are 6km (3¾ miles) south of Almancil. From Almancil, follow signs to Quinta do Lago.

Of the four golf courses at the massive Quinta do Lago development, the par-72 **San Lorenzo ★★** course, Quinta do Lago, Almancil (www.sanlorenzo golfcourse.com; ✆ **28/939-65-22**), is arguably the most challenging. San Lorenzo lies at the edge of the grassy wetlands of the Ria Formosa Nature Reserve. American golf designers William (Rocky) Roquemore and Joe Lee created it. The most panoramic hole is the 6th; the most frustrating is the 8th. Many long drives, especially those aimed at the 17th and 18th holes, soar over a saltwater lagoon. Greens fees are 95€for 9 holes and 190€ for 18 holes. From Almancil, drive 8km (5 miles) south, following signs to Quinta do Lago.

The **Vale do Lobo** course **★★**, Vale do Lobo, 8135 Almancil (www.valedolobo.com; ✆ **28/935-34-65**), technically isn't part of the Quinta do Lago complex. Because it was established in 1968 before any of its nearby competitors, it played an important role in launching southern Portugal's image as a golfer's mecca. Designed by the late British golfer Henry Cotton, it contains four distinct 9-hole segments. All four include runs that stretch over rocks and arid hills, often within view of olive and almond groves, the Atlantic, and the high-rise hotels of nearby Vilamoura and Quarteira. Some long shots require driving golf balls over two ravines, where variable winds and bunkers that have been called "ravenous" make things particularly difficult. The Royal Golf Course hosts the famous "hole 16," the most photographed in Europe, in a beautiful location by the sea. Greens fees, depending on the day of the week and other factors, range from 95€ to 190€ for 18 holes. From Almancil, drive 4km (2½ miles) south of town, following signs to Vale do Lobo.

Visit **www.algarvegolf.net** for more info on courses in the Algarve region.

Where to Stay

QUINTA DO LAGO

Hotel Quinta do Lago ★★★ A pocket of the high life since 1986, Hotel Quinta do Lago is a sprawling 800-hectare (1,977-acre) estate blessed with private plots beside the Ria Formosa estuary and national park. This means stunning views to Ria Formosa and a wonderfully serene locale, especially enticing for birders and other outdoorsy types who enjoy exploring the nature trails inside the estuary (the concierge can supply maps). The beach is attached to the resort via a long wooden bridge. The resort's riding center and 27-hole golf course are among the best in Europe. The indoor spaces are equally as special, and are kept at a human-scale: The estate's contemporary Mediterranean-style buildings rise three to six floors. Inside, classy, roomy guest rooms overlook a saltwater lake and feature modern comforts like thick carpeting, contemporary art, pillow-top mattresses, and lots of electrical outlets. Balconies open onto views of the estuary. And we'd be remiss if we didn't praise the restaurant, spa, and superb staff here.

Quinta do Lago. www.quintadolagohotel.com. ✆ **800/223-6800** in the U.S., or 28/935-03-50. 141 units. 180€–455€ double; 420€–2,350€ suite. Rates include buffet breakfast. Free parking. **Amenities:** 2 restaurants; bar; babysitting; bikes; children's center; exercise room; 2 freshwater heated pools (1 indoor); room service; spa; 2 outdoor tennis courts (lit). Free Wi-Fi.

Where to Dine

Casa do Campo ★★ PORTUGUESE/SEAFOOD An old and exceedingly charming Algarvian house, Casa do Campo offers its guests two options for dining: under the massive branches of the ancient fig tree out back or in front of a blazing fireplace in the winter months. These settings suit the cuisine, which has some creative options, like a pepper steak flambé that's prepared at your table, but mostly concentrates on such traditional favorites as fresh Atlantic sole on the grill or an Algarvian *cataplana* (steamed copper pot) of fresh fish and clams. Desserts, such as mango au gratin with an orange sabayon, are scrumptious. The paintings exhibited are from local painter Fonseca Martins.

Quinta do Lago, 8km south of Almancil. www.casadocampo-restaurante.com. ✆ **28/939-91-09.** Reservations required. Main courses 22€–30€. June–Sept Mon–Sat 7:30–10:30pm; off-season Mon–Sat 7–10pm.

Casa Velha ★★★ FRENCH Set on a hillside behind the massive Quinta do Lago resort, the excellent Casa Velha overlooks the resort's lake from the premises of a century-old farmhouse that has functioned as a restaurant since the early 1960s. But there's nothing old-fashioned about this place. Its decor, renovated in 2016, epitomizes discreet contemporary comfort (cushioned seats, muted colors). The food is even more cutting edge: Sculptural in its looks—really, each plate is prettier and more colorful than the next—it packs pleasurable punches of intense, often unusual flavor. This might mean a composed salad of chicken livers and gizzards with leeks and just the right touch of vinaigrette, or lobster infused with vanilla. The menu changes every few weeks, but if the breast of duck with 12 spices is available, get it. Catering for the luxury market of Quinta do Lago, the prices are dear.

Quinta do Lago. www.restaurante-casavelha.com. ✆ **28/939-49-83.** Reservations recommended. Main courses 18€–45€; fixed-price menus 76€–119€. Mon–Sat 7–10pm. Closed in winter until Feb 7.

Mr. Freddie's ★★ PORTUGUESE/INTERNATIONAL Everybody knows your name at Freddie's—or will by the end of the meal. This 15-year-old favorite is a place people return to over and over because the welcome here is genuinely warm. You'll feel that generosity of spirit on the plate, too. Not only are portions humongous (the starters are as big as mains are at other restaurants), but most dishes have a pleasing richness to them, whether you opt for the roast duck, the pepper steak, or our favorites: the filet of pork with apple slices and honey, or the grilled rack of lamb in a rosemary and mustard sauce. All platters are accompanied by garden-fresh vegetables.

Escanxinas–Estrada de Vale do Lobo. www.mrfreddies.net. ✆ **28/939-36-51.** Reservations recommended. Main courses 16€–23€. Mon–Sat 6–11pm. Closed Dec 25–Jan 1.

Restaurante Henrique Leis ★★★ FRENCH/INTERNATIONAL This is one of the region's most outstanding restaurants, Michelin starred and fully the equal of São Gabriel (see below). Named for its wizard of a chef, it serves food that is vivid and modern. The menu changes frequently, but may include fresh goose foie gras (prepared two different ways), scallop and langoustine supreme with a boletus sabayon, or an exquisite quail salad with foie gras and truffles from the Périgord region. Signature mains range from breast of Barbary duck with caramelized apples and passion fruit to lamb with a jelly of *xerém* (the traditional polenta of Algarve). The setting is as sophisticated as the food, making this the ideal "special occasion" restaurant.

Vale Formosa, 3km from Almancil. www.henriqueleis.com. ✆ **28/939-34-38.** Reservations required. Main courses 28€–46€; 6-course menu 76€. Mon–Sat 7–10pm in July and Aug; Tues-Sat 12:30–3pm and 7–10pm rest of the year. Closed Nov 15–Dec 25.

São Gabriel ★★★ PORTUGUESE/INTERNATIONAL Gourmets drive for miles around to sample the food and wine in this refined dining room and on the summer terrace. The actual dishes served depend on the time of year and the mood of the chef, Leonel Pereira, a son of the Algarve who honed his skills internationally. You might encounter lamb perfectly roasted in an old oven, tender duck flavored with port wine, or roasted veal cutlets with Swiss-style hash browns. The cuisine is remarkably well crafted, inspired by Algarve flavors, such as red mullet from Sagres, cured tuna, and carob (for dessert).

Estrada Vale do Lobo (directly southeast of Amancil). www.sao-gabriel.com. ✆ **28/939-45-21.** Reservations required. Main courses 25€–37€; tasting menu 80€. Tues–Sun 7–10:30pm, Sun noon–2:30pm and 7–10:30pm. Closed Nov–Feb 2.

FARO ★

258km (160 miles) SE of Setúbal; 309km (192 miles) SE of Lisbon

Once loved by the Romans and later by the Moors, Faro is the provincial capital of the Algarve. In this bustling little city of some 30,000 permanent residents, you can sit at a cafe, sample the wine, and watch yesterday and today collide as old men leading donkeys brush past German backpackers in shorts. Faro is a hodgepodge of life and activity: It has been rumbled, sacked, and "quaked" by everybody from Mother Nature to the Earl of Essex (Elizabeth I's favorite).

Since Afonso III drove out the Moors for the last time in 1266, Faro has been Portuguese. On its outskirts, an international airport brings in thousands of visitors every summer. The airport has done more than anything else to increase tourism not only to Faro, but also to the entire Algarve.

Most visitors use Faro only as an arrival point, rushing through en route to a beach resort. Those who stick around will enjoy the local color, exemplified by the tranquil fishing harbor. A great deal of antique charm is gone, however, thanks to the Earl of Essex, who sacked the town in 1596, and the 1755 earthquake. Remnants of medieval walls and some historic buildings stand in the Cidade Velha, or Old Town, which can be entered through the Arco da Vila, a gate from the 18th century.

Essentials

ARRIVING

BY PLANE Jet service makes it possible to reach Faro from Lisbon in 30 minutes. To get from the airport to the rail station, take the 16 bus from **Próximo** (www.proximo.pt) to Faro downtown. Once there you can connect with **EVA Buses** (www.eva-bus.com; ✆ **28/989-97-60**). Próximo runs many buses per day from the airport to the railway station, from 5:20am to 10:35pm, costing 2.22€.

BY TRAIN Trains arrive from Lisbon five times a day. The trip takes 4¾ hours and costs 20€. The train station is at Largo da Estação. This is the most strategic railway junction in the south of Portugal, thanks to its position astride lines that connect it to the north-south lines leading from Lisbon. For more information and schedules, visit www.cp.pt.

BY BUS There are five buses per day from Lisbon to Faro. The journey takes 3½ hours. The bus station is on Av. da República 5 (www.eva-bus.com; ✆ **28/989-97-60**); a one-way ticket costs 19.50€.

BY CAR From the west, Route 125 runs into Faro and beyond. From the Spanish border, pick up N125 west.

VISITOR INFORMATION

The **tourist office** is at Rua da Misericórdia 8–11 (✆ **28/980-36-04**) or at the airport (✆ **28/981-85-82**). It's open daily 9:30am to 5:30pm September to May, and 9:30am to 7pm June to August.

Exploring the Town

The most bizarre attraction in Faro is the **Capela dos Ossos** (Chapel of Bones). Enter through a courtyard from the rear of the **Igreja de Nossa Senhora do Monte do Carmo do Faro,** Largo do Carmo (✆ **28/982-44-90**). Erected in the 19th century, the chapel is completely lined with human skulls (an estimated 1,245) and bones. It's open daily 10am to 2pm and 3 to 5pm, 6pm in summer. Entrance is free to the church and 1€ to the chapel.

The church, built in 1713, contains a gilded baroque altar. Its facade is also baroque, with a bell tower rising from each side. Topping the belfries are gilded, mosquelike cupolas connected by a balustraded railing. The upper-level windows are latticed and framed with gold; statues stand in niches on either side of the main portal.

Other religious monuments include the old **Sé** (cathedral), on Largo da Sé (**© 28/989-83-00**). Built in the Gothic and Renaissance styles, it stands on a site originally occupied by a mosque. Although the cathedral has a Gothic tower, it's better known for its tiles, which date from the 17th and 18th centuries. The highlight is the Capela do Rosário, on the right. It contains the oldest and most beautiful tiles, along with sculptures of two Nubians bearing lamps and a red chinoiserie organ. Admission is free. The beautiful cloisters are the most idyllic spot in Faro. The cathedral is open daily from 10am to 5:30pm. Admission is 2€.

Igreja de São Francisco, Largo de São Francisco (**© 28/987-08-70**), is the other church of note. Its facade doesn't even begin to hint at the baroque richness inside. Panels of glazed earthenware tiles in milk-white and Dutch blue depict the life of the patron saint, St. Francis. One chapel is richly gilded. Hours are Monday through Friday from 8 to 9:30am and 5:30 to 7pm (but in the sleepy Algarve, you might sometimes find it closed).

If it's a rainy day, two minor museums might hold some interest. The municipal museum, or **Museu Municipal de Faro,** Largo Dom, Afonso III 14 (**© 28/989-74-19**), is in a former 16th-century convent, the Convento de Nossa Senhora da Assunção. Even if you aren't particularly interested in the changing exhibits, the two-story cloister is worth a visit. Many artifacts dating from the Roman settlement of the area are on display. Some of the Roman statues are from excavations at Milreu. The most important is the mosaic of various ocean gods, discovered buried in the city in 1926. The museum is open Tuesday to Sunday, 10am to 6pm (5pm on weekends). Admission is 2€ for adults, 1€ for those 13 to 26 years old, and free to those 12 and under.

The dockside **Museu Marítimo,** Rua Comunidade Lusíada (**© 28/989-49-90**), displays models of local fishing craft and of the boats that carried Vasco da Gama and his men to India in 1497. There are replicas of a boat the Portuguese used to sail up the Congo River in 1492 and of a vessel that bested the entire Turkish navy in 1717. It's open Monday to Friday 9am to noon and 2:30 to 4:30pm. Admission is 2€.

OUTDOOR ACTIVITIES Most visitors don't come to Faro to look at churches or museums, regardless of how interesting they are. Bus no. 16, leaving from the terminal, runs to **Praia de Faro;** the one-way fare is 1€. A bridge also connects the mainland and the beach, about 6km (3¾ miles) from the town center. At the shore, you can waterski, fish, or just rent a deck chair and umbrella and lounge in the sun. But this island can be too busy in the summer. The **Ilha Deserta ★★★** is a more serene option: It's really a desert island, with protected status and a sanctuary for birds. Besides the long sandy desert beach, there's a busier area with a wooden restaurant, **Estaminé,** the only building allowed in the island. The boat trip itself is great to see more of the Ria Formosa and the islands in the lagoon. For more info, visit http://ilha-deserta.com.

SHOPPING Most of the shopping outlets in Faro are on **Rua Santo António** or its neighbor, **Rua Francisco Gomes,** in the heart of town. Walk around the downtown in the pedestrian streets where some old shops still survive. Check out **J. Carminho,** Rua Santo António 29 (✆ **28/982-65-22**), a recommended outlet for handicrafts. If you're interested in wandering like a local resident amid stands and booths piled high with the produce of southern Portugal, consider a trek through the **Mercado de Faro,** Largo do Mercado, in the town center. It's open daily from 6:30am to 1:30pm.

Where to Stay

Eva Hotel ★ Eva dominates the harbor like a fortress, its eight stories taking up a full half of the side of that yacht-clogged anchorage. Most of the midsize guest rooms have an austere look to them, softened somewhat by sea views. The better rooms have large balconies and open onto the water. Eva's best features are its penthouse restaurant (perfect for a breakfast or dinner with a view) and rooftop pool, with sun terraces and a bar.

Av. da República 1. www.tdhotels.pt. ✆ **28/900-10-00.** 134 units. 75€–140€ double; 152€–221€ suite. Rates include buffet breakfast. Limited free parking available on street. **Amenities:** 2 restaurants; 3 bars; babysitting; concierge; exercise room; outdoor freshwater pool; room service; spa. Free Wi-Fi (3€ per 30 min. in the business center).

Hotel Sol Algarve ★ The Hotel Sol Algarve opened in 1999, but in 2006 it added a modern annex that greatly increased its room count—and the variety of room sizes. Long-story short: You could be put in a decently sized room, or get stuck in what should be a closet, all for the same rate (so ask to move if you're unhappy). The inn was created from an 1880s private dwelling that once belonged to a rich seafarer. When the present owner took over the premises, the building had deteriorated to the point that it had to be demolished. The reconstruction, however, honored the original architectural style—for instance, the iconic pineapple sculptures on the balconies have been preserved and copies of hand-painted tiles are displayed in glass cabinets in the foyer. Only a short walk from the historic core of Faro, the inn has both pluses (a friendly staff, breakfast on the roof terrace) and some minuses (dated-looking rooms foremost among them). Still it *is* well located and, usually, well priced.

Rua Infante Dom Henrique 62. www.hotelsolalgarve.com/en. ✆ **28/989-57-00.** 40 units. 45€–100€ double; 65€–135€ triple. Rates include continental breakfast. Parking 5€. **Amenities:** Bar; babysitting. Free Wi-Fi.

Stay Hotel Faro Centro ★ After a recent remodeling, this centrally located hotel looks more contemporary, with bright colors and such useful amenities as a kettle in each bedroom. It's still on the simple/plain side of the spectrum, but far more pleasant than it was pre-renovation. Some rooms have balconies, and all are well-maintained.

Rua de Portugal 17. www.stayhotels.pt. ✆ **28/989-80-80.** 60 units. 45€–95€ double; 84€–147€ suite. Parking 10€. **Amenities:** Bar; bikes; room service. Free Wi-Fi.

Where to Dine

Adega Nortenha ★ PORTUGUESE It's hardly a deluxe choice, but if you gravitate to simple yet well-prepared regional food, this little restaurant does the job. It's also one of the best value spots in town, which is why locals swear by it. Fresh tuna steak is a delicious choice, as is the roast lamb, which is perfumed with garlic. The service is friendly and efficient, and the restaurant is done up in typical Algarvian style—there's even a balcony that's great for people-watching on the street below.

Praça Ferreira de Almeida 25. ✆ **28/982-27-09.** Main courses 9€–25€. Daily noon–3pm and 7–10:30pm.

A Venda ★★★ INTERNATIONAL An adorable, knickknack-laden little place (with jam jars as candle holders and old oil paintings along the walls), A Venda is run by an equally adorable coterie of 20-somethings. Its name means "the chef decides," and that's how you should order. Ask your waiter which items are best that day, and then build a feast of tapas plates. We should note that the tapas (or *tascas*, as they say in Portugal) are larger than normal, but prices are so low, you're unlikely to overpay even if you do over-order. The menu changes nightly, but some recurring treats include goat cheese with almond pesto, fava bean croquettes topped with seitan, black beans with chorizo sausage, and spicy octopus. The menu contains an unusually large number of vegetarian-friendly options as well as gluten free dishes.

Rua Compromisso 60. ✆ **28/982-55-00.** Most dishes 3€–6€. Tues–Sat 12:30–4pm and 7pm–midnight.

Dois Irmãos ★ PORTUGUESE This popular bistro, founded in 1925, is in the group of the oldest restaurants still in business in the country. It offers a vibrant atmosphere and has many devotees. The menu is as modest as the establishment and its prices, but you get a good choice of fresh grilled fish and shellfish dishes. Clams in savory sauce are a justifiable favorite, and sole, squid, and cuttlefish are regularly featured—but, of course, everything depends on the catch of the day. Service is slow, but the breezy garden terrace feels really good on a hot summer day in Faro.

Largo do Terreiro do Bispo 20. ✆ **28/982-33-37.** Reservations recommended. Main courses 12€–26€. Daily noon–4pm and 6–11pm.

Tertúlia Algarvia ★★★ PORTUGUESE Opened in 2013 by a group of friends who wanted to preserve the Algarve's food traditions, Tertúlia is something of a "unicorn." By that I mean, it's one of those one-in-a-hundred places that has an ideal location and view (right on a lovely square in the historic part of town, in this case) that *actually* has excellent food. Though there's some fusion at play here, most of the fare is traditional, like mackerel filets with tomato and herb sauce, or the amazing *cataplanas*, their signature dish (copper pots that steam either octopus and sweet potato or other types of seafood). In addition to being a restaurant, Tertúlia offers cooking lessons, workshops, and seminars about the region's cuisine. Be sure to take a look at the ancient cistern the owners found on the premises and preserved.

Praça Afonso III 13-15. www.tertulia-algarvia.pt. ✆ **28/982-10-44.** Reservations recommended in summer. Main courses 9€–16€. Mon–Thurs noon–midnight, Fri–Sat noon–1am, Sun noon–11pm.

Faro After Dark

In the heart of town, adjacent to the Faro Hotel, Rua do Prior is chockablock with dozens of night cafes, pubs (English and otherwise), and dance clubs that rock from around 10:30pm until dawn. Head to this street anytime after sunset for insights into the hard-drinking, hard-driving nature of this hot southern town. Our favorite watering hole along this street is **CheSsenta Bar,** Rua do Prior 34 (✆ **91/874-58-37**), where the crowd is in their 20s and 30s, and downs one beer after another at 1.50€ a mug. It's open daily 9pm to 4am, with live music on the stage. Karaoke often rules the night at **O Conselheiro,** in the center of Rua Conselheiro Bívar (no phone). The best recorded music in town is played here by a DJ, and sometimes the bar converts to a dance floor. It too is open daily 10pm to 4am, and charges the same for beer. **O Castelo–Cidade Velha,** in Rua do Castelo, offers the best location for a sunset drink overlooking Ria Formosa and keeps it interesting through the night. Good cocktails and atmosphere can be found in **Columbus Bar,** right in Praça D. Francisco Gomes, open from noon to 4am.

Easy Excursions from Faro

Some of the most interesting towns in the Algarve surround the capital. Exploring any one takes a half-day.

Loulé ★★ This market town 15km (9⅓ miles) north of Faro lies in the heart of the Algarve's chimney district. If you think chimneys won't excite you, you haven't seen the ones here. The fret-cut plaster towers rise from many of the cottages and houses (and even the occasional doghouse).

Bus service is good during the day; about 40 buses arrive from various parts of the Algarve, mainly Faro. Five trains per day arrive from Faro at the Loulé rail station, about 5km (3 miles) from the center of town. There are bus connections to the center of town from the station, or you can take a taxi. In the end of June the central part of Loulé is closed to host the **MedFest,** a festival dedicated to world music of the Mediterranean regions.

The **Loulé Tourist Information Office** is on Avenida 25 de Abril (✆ **28/946-39-00**). It's open October to May Monday to Friday 9:30am to 5:30pm and Saturday 9:30am to 3:30pm.

Loulé and the villages around it are known for their handicrafts. They produce work in palm fronds and *esparto* (a type of grass), such as handbags, baskets, mats, and hats. Loulé artisans also make copper articles, bright harnesses, delicate wrought-iron pieces, clogs, cloth shoes and slippers, tinware, and pottery. Products are displayed in workshops at the foot of the walls of an old fortress and in other showrooms, particularly those along **Rua do 9 de Abril.**

In Loulé, you might want to visit the Gothic-style **Igreja de São Clemente, Matriz de Loulé,** or parish church, Largo do Matriz 19 (© **28/941-51-67**). It was given to the town in the late–13th century. It's open Monday to Friday 9 to 11am and Saturday 9am to 7pm. Admission is free, although donations are welcome.

The remains of the **Moorish castelo** are at Largo Dom Pedro I (no phone). The ruins house a historical museum and are open Monday to Friday 9am to 5:30pm and Saturday 10am to 2pm. Admission is 2€.

For meals, try the Portuguese cuisine at **O Avenida,** Av. José da Costa Mealha 13 (www.oavenidarestaurantept.com; © **28/946-21-06**), on the main street close to the traffic circle, the oldest restaurant in Loulé. The specialty is shellfish cooked *cataplana*-style. The restaurant is open Monday through Saturday from noon to 3:30pm and 7 to 10pm; it's closed for most of November. Meal prices start at 7€ to 15€. There's occasional live entertainment.

São Brás de Alportel ★★ Traveling north from Faro, you'll pass through groves of figs, almonds, and oranges, and through pinewoods where resin collects in wooden cups on the tree trunks. After 20km (12 miles) you'll come upon isolated São Brás de Alportel, one of the most charming and least-known spots on the Algarve. Far from the crowded beaches, this town attracts those in search of pure air, peace, and quiet. It's a bucolic setting filled with flowers pushing through nutmeg-colored soil. Northeast of Loulé, the whitewashed, tile-roofed town livens up only on market days. Like its neighbor, Faro, it's noted for its perforated plaster chimneys. The area at the foot of the Serra do Caldeirão has been described as one vast garden.

Olhão ★★ This is the Algarve's famous cubist town, long beloved by painters. In its heart, white blocks stacked one upon the other, with flat red-tile roofs and exterior stairways on the stark walls, evoke the casbahs of North Africa. The cubist buildings are found only at the core. The rest of Olhão has almost disappeared under the onslaught of modern commercialism.

While you're here, head to the fish market and the vegetable and fruit market, two big buildings full of fresh produce. The fish market, notably, has some species that aren't found anywhere else in the country. On Saturday mornings the farmers came to town to sell their produce, and the atmosphere, and what is on offer, is even better.

If you're here at lunchtime, go to one of the inexpensive markets along the waterfront. At **Casa de Pasto O Bote,** Av. do 5 de Outubro 122 (© **28/972-11-83**), you can select your food from trays of fresh fish. Your choice is then grilled to your specifications. Meal prices start at 10€. It's open Monday to Saturday noon to 3pm and 7 to 10pm. Another local choice, open for lunch only, is **Vai e Volta,** in Largo Do Grémio, 2 (© **96/80-27-525**) serving an all-you-can-eat fish festival for 11€ per person (with salads and side dishes).

If you are seduced by Olhão's many charms, the best place to stay is at one of the rental villas by **White Terraces,** perfect for groups of 4 or 6. They have renovated old Olhão traditional houses, keeping the terraces, Moorish chimneys, and whitewashed walls. Casa da Luz and Casa Barreta, in particular, have pools and terraces—they are just fabulous. For more info, visit www.whiteterraces.com. Alternatively, **O Convento,** set in a former convent, is the best place for couples and is run by the same team. Rates are 100€ to 120€. Visit www.conventoolhao.com for more info. Spring or autumn are quieter and usually lovely weather to explore the islands of **Armona** and **Culatra** (ferries depart from Olhão). Finally, to reach one of the most idyllic beaches on the Algarve, take a 25-minute motorboat ride to the **Ilha da Armona,** a nautical mile away. Ferries run year-round but are more frequent in summer; the round-trip fare is 7.50€. Olhão is 8km (5 miles) east of Faro.

Tavira ★★★ A gem 31km (19 miles) east of Faro, Tavira is approached through green fields studded with almond and carob trees. Tavira lies on the banks of the Ségua and Gilão rivers, which meet under a seven-arched Roman bridge. In the town square, palms and pepper trees rustle under the cool arches of the arcade. In spite of modern encroachments, Tavira is largely untouched by contemporary life, at least in its looks. Floridly decorated chimneys top many of the houses, some of which are graced with emerald-green tiles and wrought-iron balconies capped by finials. Fretwork adorns many doorways. The liveliest action centers are the market (now transformed with shops and restaurants) on the river esplanade and the little squares on the other side of the river, crossing the Roman bridge.

The **Tavira Tourist Office** is on Praça da República, 5 (✆ **28/132-25-11**). Tavira has frequent bus connections with Faro throughout the day. Climb the stepped street off Rua da Liberdade, and you can explore the battlemented walls of a **castle** once known to the Moors. From here you'll have the best view of the town's church spires; across the river delta, you can see the ocean. The castle is open daily from 9am to 5pm. Admission is free.

Once a tuna-fishing center, Tavira is cut off from the sea by an elongated spit of sand. The **Ilha de Tavira** begins west of Cacela and runs all the way past the fishing village of Fuzeta. On this sandbar, accessible by motorboat, are two beaches: the **Praia de Tavira** and the **Praia de Fuzeta.** Some people prefer the beach at the tiny village of Santa Luzia, about 3km (1¾ miles) from the heart of town.

If you're here for lunch, try the **Restaurante Imperial,** Rua José Pires Padinha 22 (✆ **28/132-23-06**). A small, air-conditioned place off the main square, it serves regional food—shellfish rice, garlic-flavored pork, roast chicken, pork with clams, and other Portuguese dishes—and good local wines. Leave room for their rich egg-and-almond dessert. Meals cost 9€ to 25€, including wine. Food is served daily from noon to 3:30pm and 7 to 11pm. Another swell option is the *tasca* **Zé da Bica** (Rua Almirante Cândido dos Reis, ✆ **96/87-62-059,** closed on Mondays), a locals' favorite, with excellent fish stews (*caldeiradas*), squid, and clam preparations (they are harvested nearby in the Ria Formosa). This simple but genuine restaurant has been discovered by Spaniards (the border is not far), who come here mostly on the weekends.

If you'd like to stay a while, consider checking into **Pousada de Tavira, Convento da Graça ★★**, Rua D. Paio Peres Correia (www.pousadas.pt; ✆ **28/132-90-40**), a 36-room hotel charging 130€ to 300€ for a double, 185€ to 438€ for a suite. Beginning in 1569, cloistered Augustinian nuns lived in the convent founded on this site. Today this historic building, with its Renaissance cloister and baroque central staircase, has been turned into one of the most colorful hotels in the Algarve. Many of the bedrooms have small balconies. The accommodations have all the "mod cons," and are soothingly done up in neutral colors with lots of wood (they're also larger than you'd expect rooms in a former nunnery to be). Archaeological traces of Islamic origin were discovered during the restoration, some of which are partially visible from the bar. The *pousada* has a good restaurant, a lively bar, 2 outdoor pools, and free Wi-Fi.

But the best place to stay not only in the Tavira area but in all of the eastern Algarve region is the awarded **Fazenda Nova Country House ★★★** (www.fazendanova.eu; ✆ **28/196-19-13**), a cozy luxury retreat in Estiramantens, Santo Estevão, inland west of Tavira. Once a rural family home, it has been renovated with care, keeping the original facade and Algarve character in the chimneys, terracotta floors, and colors. The lounge has a fireplace for colder days and lush gardens surround the terrace, where meals are served under a rosemary roof in warmer weather. Walks through the huge 10-hectare (25-acre) farm among olive trees, carob trees, and pomegranate and orange groves are sheer bliss. Guest rooms with private gardens cost 200€ to 295€ and have been beautifully decorated, mixing Algarve antiques and flea-market finds with handsome Asian furnishings and local terracotta floors. The hotel has free Wi-Fi, free parking, and owners who are keen to share tips about the best places to visit, including the great Fuzeta flea market (first Sunday of every month).

Estói ★★ A little village some 8km (5 miles) northeast of Faro, Estói is still mainly unspoiled by tourists. Buses run to the area from Faro.

The principal sight in Estói is the **Palácio do Visconde de Estói ★★**. The villa, with its salmon-pink baroque facade, has been described as a cross between Versailles and the water gardens of the Villa d'Este near Rome. It was built in the late–18th century for Francisco José de Moura Coutinho; José Francisco da Silva rescued it from near ruin between 1893 and 1909. A palm-lined walk leads to terraced gardens with orange trees along the balusters. Today, it has been turned into one of the charming *pousadas* of Portugal (Rua de São José, www.pousadas.pt; ✆ **25/882-17-51;** rates from 120€ to 280€ for a suite), one that can be surprisingly affordable. The entire aristocratic complex consists of 4 hectares (10 acres), including the old stables. A modern wing of first-class guest rooms has been installed, each room air-conditioned and comfortably furnished. Luxurious touches include an outdoor swimming pool and spa. Architecturally, many of the neo-baroque and neo-rococo features have been maintained, and the interior contains plaster ceilings, the finest in the Algarve. You can wander at leisure through the statue-studded gardens, which can also be enjoyed from a balcony from your room. Amenities include a restaurant, bar, and free Wi-Fi in public areas.

VILA REAL DE SANTO ANTÓNIO

314km (195 miles) SE of Lisbon; 85km (53 miles) E of Faro; 50km (31 miles) W of Huelva, Spain

Twenty years after the Marquês de Pombal rebuilt Lisbon, which had been destroyed in the great 1755 earthquake, he sent architects and builders to Vila Real de Santo António. They reestablished this frontier town on the bank opposite Spain in only 5 months. Pombal's motivation was jealousy of Spain. Much has changed, but **Praça de Pombal** remains. An obelisk stands in the center of the square, which is paved with inlays of black-and-white tiles radiating like the sun's rays and filled with orange trees. Separated from its Iberian neighbor by the Guadiana River, Vila Real de Santo António has a bridge between Portugal and Ayamonte, Spain.

Essentials

ARRIVING

BY TRAIN Most visitors from Lisbon take the train to Faro, then proceed by bus to Vila Real (see below).

BY BUS From Faro to Vila Real, buses run each day to the Vila Real bus station on Avenida da República. The trip takes 1¾ hours and cost 5.60€ one-way. For information and schedules, visit www.eva-bus.com.

BY FERRY In summer, ferries still run between Ayamonte, Spain, and Vila Real daily from 8:45am to 7pm. The fare is 1.90€ per passenger each way. Ferries depart from the station on Avenida da República; call ✆ **28/154-31-52** for more information.

VISITOR INFORMATION

The **tourist office** is on Avenida Infante D. Henrique, Monte Gordo (✆ **28/154-44-95**). It's open Monday to Friday 9am to 6pm October to April and Tuesday to Thursday 9:30am to 7pm, and Friday to Monday 9:30am to 5:30pm May to September.

Exploring the Town

Vila Real de Santo António is a superb example of 18th-century town planning, with the same grid and Pombaline architecture as Lisbon. A long esplanade, Avenida da República, follows the river, and from its northern extremity you can view the Spanish town across the way. Gaily painted horse-drawn carriages take visitors sightseeing past the shipyards and the lighthouse.

A 5km (3-mile) drive north on the road to Mértola (N122) leads to the gull-gray castle-fortress of **Castro Marim.** This formidable structure is a legacy of the border wars between Spain and Portugal. The ramparts and walls stand watch over the territory across the river. Afonso III, who expelled the Moors from this region, founded the original fortress, which was razed by the 1755 earthquake. Inside the walls are the ruins of the Igreja de São Tiago, dedicated to St. James. Nowadays, Castro Marim is also known for its salt pans and the artisanal salt and *flor de sal* (the first layer in the salt pans) of Salmarim (www.salmarim.com).

Southwest of Vila Real is the emerging resort of **Monte Gordo,** which has the second-greatest concentration of hotels in the eastern Algarve (after Faro). Monte Gordo, 4km (2½ miles) southwest of Vila Real at the mouth of the Guadiana River, is the last in a long line of Algarvian resorts. Its wide, steep beach, **Praia de Monte Gordo,** is one of the finest on Portugal's southern coast. This beach, backed by pine-studded lowlands, has the highest average water temperature in Portugal.

Sadly, what was once a sleepy little fishing village has succumbed to high-rises without any architectural interest.

Where to Stay

Hotel Apolo ★ This hotel on the western edge of town is a friendly place for a stopover on the Algarve, more than adequate for an overnight stay. Near the beach and the river, it attracts vacationers as well as travelers who don't want to travel over the Spain border at night. The hotel has a spacious marble-floored lobby leading to a large bar scattered with comfortable sofas and flooded with sunlight. Each small, simply furnished guest room has a private balcony and a good bathroom equipped with a tub/shower combination.

Av. dos Bombeiros Portugueses. www.apolo-hotel.com. ✆ **28/151-24-48.** 45 units. 55€–135€ double. Rates include buffet breakfast. Free parking. **Amenities:** Bar; bikes; outdoor freshwater pool. Free Wi-Fi.

Where to Dine

Casa Velha ★★ PORTUGUESE In the lovely coastal village of Cacela Velha (11km/7 miles from Vila Real Santo António) are some of the best places to gorge on clams and shellfish in the eastern Algarve. Our favorite is Casa Velha, a former small *tasca* now converted into a spacious restaurant with a terrace. The thing to get here is razor clams rice—just as soupy and runny as it should be. It attracts locals and many Spaniards from the neighboring villages. Go early (in summer they don't book tables) to get a seat. If you're tired of fish and shellfish by now, the grilled pork or beef, with a side of freshly made French fries, should hit the spot. Finish with a slice of almond or carob cake. And after lunch, walk toward the chapel square to enjoy the magnificent view of the Ria Formosa and the Atlantic, one of the best perspectives in the Algarve.

Sítio da Igreja, Cacela Velha. ✆ **28/195-22-97.** 9€–20€.Tues–Sun 12–3pm and 7–10pm.

Vistas ★★★ PORTUGUESE/ INTERNATIONAL Set in scenic Monte Rei Golf and Country Club (with short rental villas and one of the most praised 18-hole golf courses in the country), this is the type of restaurant that totally surprises diners. It's arguably one of best restaurants in the Algarve, led by award-winning chef Albano Lourenço (he had a Michelin star in his previous restaurant). Although he hasn't received a Michelin star here (yet), Albano's food is truly original and impeccably presented, from octopus *carpaccio* to eggs with tomato and samphire (a type of local vegetable that grows in salt water); to the rich pea soup with *alheira* (a Portuguese smoked sausage). Meals here are a feast of local ingredients married with international culinary techniques. In the warmer months, try to snag a terrace table (they have a view of the countryside and the golf courses of Monte Rei); in winter, the coveted seat in the dining room is right by the fireplace. The service follows a very high standard, and the sommelier is a genius (trust us!).

Sesmarias, Apartado 118. www.monte-rei.com. ✆ **28/195-09-50.** Tasting menu starts at 69€ (wines not included). Tues–Sat 7:30–10:30pm. Closed in Dec, reopens in Mar.

ALENTEJO & RIBATEJO

11

The adjoining regions of Alentejo and Ribatejo constitute the heartland of Portugal. Ribatejo is a land of bull-breeding pastures; Alentejo is a plain of vineyards, olive trees, and cork trees—and probably the most interesting culinary region in all the country.

Ribatejo is river country; the Tagus, coming from Spain, overflows its banks in winter. The region is famed for bluegrass, horses (including the famous Lusitano horse), and black bulls. Its most striking feature, however, is human: *campinos,* the region's sturdy horsemen, who also lead the bulls. Whether visiting the castle of the Templars, which rises smack in the middle of the Tagus at Almourol, or attending an exciting *festa brava*, you'll marvel at the passion of the people. Ribatejo's *fadistas* (fado singers) have long been noted for their remarkable intensity. Nowadays, Ribatejo is no longer an official region, but the people still call it by that name.

The cork-producing plains of Alentejo (which means "beyond the Tagus") make up the largest province in Portugal. It's so big that it was divided into the northern Alto Alentejo (the capital of which is Évora) and southern Baixo Alentejo (whose capital is Beja).

Locals in Alentejo insulate themselves in tiny-windowed, whitewashed houses—warm in the cold winters and cool during the scorching summers. This is the least populated of Portuguese regions, with seemingly endless fields of wheat. It's the world's largest producer of cork, whose trees can be stripped only once every 9 years.

In winter, the men make a dramatic sight, outfitted in characteristic long brown coats with two short-tiered capes, often with red-fox collars. Although dusty Alentejo is mostly a region of inland plains, it also has an Atlantic coast. It stretches from the mouth of the Sado River all the way to the border of the Algarve, just south of Zambujeira do Mar, in Odeceixe. This stretch of beach is the least crowded and least developed in Portugal. Towering rock cliffs punctuate much of the coastline south of Lisbon, interrupted by the occasional sandy cove and tranquil bay. Regrettably, there isn't much protection from the often-fierce waves and winds that rush in from the Atlantic; the waters are generally too chilly for swimming.

Driving is the best way to see the region—there are numerous towns to see and excursions to take from the major cities. Public transportation exists, but often you'll have a long, tiresome wait

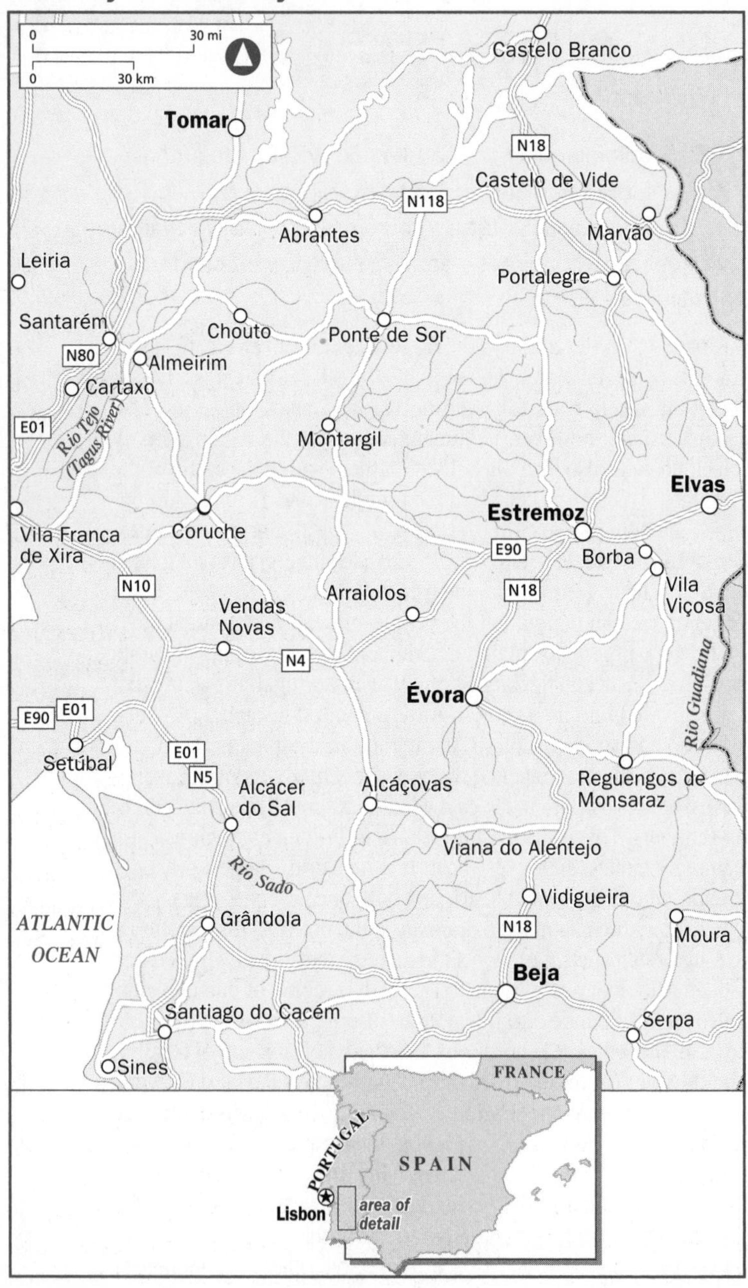
0
30 mi
0
30 km
Castelo Branco
Tomar
N18
Castelo de Vide
N118
Abrantes
Marvão
Leiria
Portalegre
Santarém
Chouto
Ponte de Sor
N80
Almeirim
Cartaxo
Rio Tejo
(Tagus River)
E01
Montargil
Elvas
Estremoz
Vila Franca
de Xira
Coruche
E90
Borba
Vila
Viçosa
N10
N18
Arraiolos
Vendas
Novas
N4
Rio Guadiana
Évora
E90
E01
Setúbal
E01
N5
Reguengos de
Monsaraz
Alcácer
do Sal
Alcáçovas
Viana do Alentejo
Rio Sado
Vidigueira
ATLANTIC
OCEAN
Grândola
N18
Moura
Beja
Santiago do Cacém
Serpa
Sines
FRANCE
PORTUGAL
SPAIN
Lisbon
area of
detail

between connections. Both regions lie virtually on Lisbon's doorstep—in fact, suburbs of the capital lie on their edges.

If you've just explored the Algarve (see chapter 10), you'll find Alentejo within striking distance. The best route to take into Alentejo from the south is IP-1 from Albufeira.

TOMAR ★★

65km (40 miles) N of Santarém; 137km (85 miles) NE of Lisbon

Divided by the Nabão River, historic Tomar was bound to the fate of the notorious quasi-religious order of the Knights Templar. In the 12th century, the powerful, wealthy monks established the beginnings of the Convento de Cristo on a tree-studded hill overlooking the town. Originally a monastery, it evolved into a kind of grand headquarters for the Templars. The knights, who swore a vow of chastity, had fought ferociously at Santarém against the Moors. As their military might grew, they built a massive walled castle at Tomar in 1160. The ruins—primarily the walls—can be seen today.

By 1314, the Templars had amassed both great riches and many enemies; the pope was urged to suppress their power. King Dinis allowed them to regroup their forces in Portugal under the new aegis of the Order of Christ in 1319. In the 15th century, Henry the Navigator became the most famous of the order's grand masters, using much of their money to subsidize his explorations.

It is a well-preserved historical town, crossed by the River Nabão, with a dynamic population. Every 4 years, Tomar hosts the **Festa dos Tabuleiros,** one of the biggest festivals in the country. Locals parade, with girls carrying the *tabuleiros*—a pile of bread, wheat sprigs, and flowers with the cross of Christ or a white dove symbolizing the Holy Spirit on top. There are around 30 breads on each pile making it very heavy to carry, and there's always a man standing by in case the *tabuleiro* falls. It's origins are in the Holy Spirit cult that goes back to the 14th century. But there's also an influence of pre-Christian harvest traditions related to bread and wheat. The next one is scheduled for 2019. Besides the main parade with the *tabuleiros*, there are a series of other popular events and games. The festival starts usually on Easter Sunday and the festivities last around 1 week, with the city totally covered in paper flowers.

Essentials

ARRIVING

BY TRAIN The train station (✆ **80/820-82-08**) is on Avenida Combatentes da Grande Guerra, at the southern edge of town. Five trains arrive daily from Lisbon (Santa Apolónia or Oriente); the trip takes less than 2 hours and costs 10€ one-way.

BY BUS The bus station is on Avenida Combatentes da Grande Guerra. For information, call the bus company, **Rede Expressos** (www.rede-expressos.pt; ✆ **70/722-33-44**). Four buses a day arrive from Lisbon (Sete Rios Terminal). The 1-hour, 45-minute trip costs 10€ one-way.

BY CAR From Santarém, continue northeast along Route 3 and then cut east at the junction of N110. When you reach Route 110, head north. To reach Santarém from Lisbon, go north on E1.

VISITOR INFORMATION

The **Tomar Tourist Office** is on Avenida Dr. Cândido Madureira (✆ **24/932-98-23**). It's open daily 9:30am to 12:30pm and 2 to 6pm.

Exploring the Town

Capela de Nossa Senhora da Conceição ★★ CHURCH On the way up the hill to see the monastery, you can stop off at this chapel, crowned by small cupolas and jutting out over the town. Reached through an avenue of trees, it was built in the Renaissance style in the mid–16th century and it's one of the best examples of this style in Portugal. The interior is a forest of white Corinthian pillars.

Btw. the old town and the Convento da Ordem de Cristo. ✆ **24/932-24-27.** Free admission. Daily 9am–6pm.

Convento da Ordem de Cristo ★★★ RELIGIOUS SITE From its inception in 1160, the Convent of the Order of Christ monastery experienced five centuries of inspired builders, including King Manuel. It also fell victim to destroyers, notably in 1810, when Napoleon's overzealous troops turned it into a barracks. What remains on the top of the hill is one of Portugal's most brilliant architectural accomplishments, showcasing differing architectural styles from Romanesque to Renaissance.

The portal of the Templars Church, in the Manueline style, depicts everything from leaves to chubby cherubs. Inside is an **octagonal church** ★★★ with eight columns, said to have been modeled after the Temple of the Holy Sepulchre in Jerusalem. The mosquelike effect links Christian and Muslim cultures, as in the Mezquita in Córdoba, Spain. The author Howard La Fay called it "a muted echo of Byzantium in scarlet and dull gold." The damage the French troops inflicted is very evident. On the other side, the church is in the Manueline style with rosettes. Throughout, you'll see the Templars insignia.

The monastery's eight cloisters embrace a variety of styles. The most notable, a two-tiered structure dating from the 16th century, exhibits perfect symmetry, the almost severe academic use of the classical form that distinguishes the Palladian school (if you've been to the Veneto in Italy, you'll recognize that style). This cloister is a Renaissance masterpiece, a major reason the site was inscribed on the UNESCO World Heritage list in 1982.

The monastery possesses some of the greatest Manueline stonework in Portugal. A fine example is the **west window** ★★★ of the chapter house. At first the forms emanating from the window might confuse you, but closer inspection reveals a meticulous symbolic and literal depiction of Portugal's sea lore and power. Knots and ropes, mariners and the tools of their craft, silken sails wafting in stone, and re-created coral seascapes—all are delicately interwoven in this *chef-d'oeuvre* of the whole movement. After the convent, visit the little Gothic church, **Santa Maria do Olival,** close by in town, where the Templar Knights were buried.

Atop a hill overlooking the old town. www.conventocristo.pt. ✆ **24/931-50-89.** Admission 6€ adults, 50% off for seniors 65 and over, free for children under 12. June–Sept daily 9am–6pm; Oct–May daily 9am–5pm.

Igreja de São João Baptista ★★ CHURCH In the heart of town is this 15th-century church, built by Manuel. It contains black-and-white diamond mosaics and a white-and-gold baroque altar; a chapel to the right is faced with antique tiles. In and around the church are the narrow cobblestone streets of Tomar, where shops sell dried codfish, and wrought-iron balconies are decorated with birdcages and flowerpots.

Praça da República. ✆ **24/932-24-27.** Free admission. Tues–Sun 10am–7pm.

Museu Luso-Hebraico ★★ MUSEUM This Portuguese-Hebrew museum lies in the heart of the old Jewish ghetto. The building was the Sinagoga de Tomar—the oldest Jewish house of worship in Portugal, dating from the mid-1400s. A Jewish community worshiped here until 1496, when the Catholic hierarchy ordered its members to convert or get out of town. In time, the synagogue assumed many roles: Christian chapel, prison, warehouse, even hayloft. Today it enjoys national monument status. Samuel Schwartz, a German who devoted part of his life to restoring it, bought the building in 1923. He donated it to the Portuguese state in 1939. In return, Schwartz and his wife were awarded citizenship and protection during World War II. The museum exhibits many 15th-century tombs with Hebrew inscriptions, along with Jewish artifacts donated from around the globe. An on-site excavation unearthed a mikvah, or ritual purification bath.

Rua Dr. Joaquim Jacinto 73. ✆ **24/932-98-14.** Free admission; donations accepted. Daily 10am–noon and 2–6pm (from Oct to May) and 3–7pm (from June to Sept).

Shopping

Shopkeepers in Tomar work hard to acquire premises on the town's main shopping thoroughfare, pedestrian Rua Serpa Pinto, an avenue known locally as *Corre Doura*, which refers to a medieval horse race that used to take place along this street in the 12th century. You'll find some folkloric goods, pottery, copperware, clothes, and wrought-iron goods, as well as cafes. It's a pretty street with the view of the convent on top and the Gothic church of S. João Baptista on one side.

Where to Stay

MODERATE

Estalagem de Santa Iria ★ Although not as swanky as Hotel dos Templários (see below), this charming inn offers good value and is like a grand country villa, filled with architectural and decorative touches from the region.

TRAVEL secrets OF THE PORTUGUESE PLAINS

Certain towns in the region—such as Évora—are on the main tourist circuit, but both Alentejo and Ribatejo have an abundance of charming small towns and villages that most non-Portuguese visitors miss. Our favorites:

Arraiolos Beautiful and small, it has a lovely *pousada* for those who'd like to stay overnight and is famed for its traditional tapestries.

Serpa Still languishing in the Middle Ages, Serpa is a walled town with defensive towers. It was incorporated into the kingdom of Portugal in 1295, after having belonged to the Infante of Serpa, Dom Fernando, brother of Dom Sancho II. Overlooking the vast Alentejo plain, Serpa is a town of narrow streets and latticed windows, famous for the sheep's-milk cheese that bears its name, pork sausage, olive oil, and sweets. Silvery olive trees surround the approaches to the town, and the whiteness of the buildings contrasts with the red-brown of the plains. The wild beauties of the River Guadiana, endless fields of grain, and cork-oak groves mark the landscape. In the town, you can see unique painted furniture, an archaeological museum, and several ancient churches. Serpa has become a lunch stop or rest stop for travelers on the way to and from Spain; many motorists spend the night at the hilltop *pousada*. Serpa is also home to one of the biggest solar-power plants in the European Union—the area is one of the sunniest in Europe.

Mação Not far from Tomar and Santarém, this village has an unusually relaxed pace of daily life. The region contains very important prehistoric sites; artifacts from them are displayed in the surprisingly compelling local museum (items mostly from the Paleolithic and Bronze ages).

Monsaraz The old fortified town of Monsaraz lies 51km (32 miles) east of Évora en route to Spain. It's a village of antique whitewashed houses, with cobblestone lanes and many reminders of the Moors who held out here until they were conquered in 1166. Some of the women still wear traditional garb: men's hats on shawl-covered heads and men's pants under their skirts. The custom derives from a need for protection from the sun. Monsaraz overlooks the Guadiana Valley, which forms the border between Spain and Portugal. The walled town can easily be visited from Évora in an afternoon. As you scale the ramparts, you're rewarded with a view over what looks like a cross between a bullring and a Greek theater. The highlight of a visit is the main street, Rua Direita. It contains the town's most distinguished architecture, wrought-iron grilles, balconies, and outside staircases. Nearby is the lake of **Alqueva,** a huge dam that supplies water to the region, mainly for farming. There are river cruises, and houseboats can be rented in Amieira Marina, http://amieiramarina.com, ✆ **93/429-94-70.** The company has also a restaurant close to the lake.

Borba On the way to Borba, you'll pass quarries filled with black, white, and multicolored deposits. In the village, marble reigns: Many cottages have marble door trimmings and facings, and the women kneel to scrub their doorways, a source of special pride. On Rua São Bartolomeu sits a church dedicated to São Bartolomeu. It displays a groined ceiling; walls lined with blue, white, and gold *azulejos* (decorative tiles); and an altar in black-and-white

Hallways with arches lead to the small to midsize guest rooms, which are furnished with regional artifacts, Portuguese tapestries, and wood furnishings. Decoration is simple, with plaster walls painted white. Families are fond of marble. The richly decorated ceiling is painted with four major medallions. Nearby are eight superb antique shops (surprising for such a small town) filled with intriguing items. Borba is also a big wine center, and you might want to sample the local brew at a cafe, or perhaps at the *pousada* at Elvas. There's a wine festival every year in November and the local winery, **Adega de Borba,** hosts wine tastings that can be booked in www.adegaborba.pt. If you can't drive after the wines, there's always a chance of staying in the lovely, antique-filled inn **Casa do Terreiro do Poço** (http://www.solaresdeportugal.pt/PT/solar.php?casaid=118).

Marvão This ancient walled hill town, close to Castelo de Vide, is well preserved and is visited chiefly for its spectacular views. Just less than 6.5km (4 miles) from the Spanish frontier, the once-fortified medieval stronghold retains a rich flavor of the Middle Ages. Those with limited time who can explore only one border town in Portugal should make it this one—it's that panoramic. You get to Marvão by following a road around the promontory on which the little town stands, past the Church of Our Lady of the Star, the curtain walls, watchtowers, and parapets. Arcaded passageways, balconied houses with wrought-iron grillwork and Manueline windows, and a number of churches can be seen along the hilly streets. The castle, built in the 13th century, stands at the western part of the rocky outcropping. From the parapet, you'll have a spectacular view of the surrounding country—all the way to the Spanish mountains in the east, and a vast sweep of Portuguese mountain ranges. In November there's a popular festival dedicated to the abundant chestnuts of the region.

Mértola The former capital of a small Moorish emirate (the Moors from Maghreb invaded the Peninsula in the 8th century), Mértola was an important port of the Guadiana River from Pheonician times forward. It has kept its character and its heritage. Its church, Nossa Senhora da Conceição, was a medieval mosque, but when it was transformed into a Christian house of worship, none of its original features were altered, which makes it fascinating to tour. The castle is also from the Islamic period. Take time to wander around and visit the museum of this *vila-museu* (a village museum), installed in different buildings in town. There's a biannual Islamic festival celebrating the town's history; the next is in May 2019. If you decide to spend the night here, stay in **Quinta do Vau** (no website, but bookable through a number of online travel agencies).

Mora Mora is now on the map for the **Fluviário,** an aquarium dedicated to the freshwater fish and otters of the country (children will enjoy its interactive exhibits). After the visit, relax in town with a *bifana* (pork sandwich) or a chicken pie from **Afonso,** this small town's main restaurant.

Lavre A whitewashed village Lavre has one of the best restaurants in the area, **Maçã** (https://www.facebook.com/restaurantemaca). It's worth heading here just to taste genuine Alentejo gastronomy. Many also visit the organic farm, **Herdade do Freixo do Meio,** in the neighborhood of Foros de Vale de Figueira, to learn about this type of agriculture and have lunch at its traditional long tables.

the inn because the staff provides extra beds for children 4 to 12 years at no extra cost. In business since the mid–20th century, the colonial-style, two-story inn lies in the center. Its on-site restaurant (traditional decor with prints and sculptures of the Tabuleiros festival) is a popular place with locals and visitors alike. The location is lovely, on a small island in the river.

Parque do Mouchão. www.estalagemsantairia.com. ✆ **24/931-33-26.** 14 units. 40€–65€ double; 70€–105€ suite. Rates include continental breakfast. Free parking. **Amenities:** Restaurant; bar. Free Wi-Fi.

Hotel dos Templários ★★ Five local businessmen created this hotel in 1967, but they would hardly recognize the place today. It looms over the small town, thanks to a 1994 expansion that made it the largest hotel in the district. Guest rooms are big, too, and quite agreeable, especially those in the new wing. Many open onto views of the Convent of Christ and to the river. All feature a perky decor with aqua-, orange-, and gray-striped coverlets, deep soaking tubs, and comfortable beds. The public areas, including the lounges and the terrace-view dining room, are also on the brink of grand. Best are the grounds: The hotel boasts wide sun terraces, extensive green spaces, and a greenhouse, as well as a spa and a large outdoor pool.

Largo Cândido dos Reis 1. www.hoteldostemplarios.pt. ✆ **24/931-01-00.** 177 units. 75€–132€ double; 135€–160€ suite. Rates include buffet breakfast. Free parking. **Amenities:** Restaurant; bar; babysitting; children's center; exercise room; 2 heated pools (1 indoor); room service; sauna; outdoor tennis court (lit). Free Wi-Fi.

INEXPENSIVE

Hotel Trovador ★ Rooms here are clean and comfortable, with conservatively patterned wallpaper, usable desks, and good beds, great for those traveling on a budget. Breakfast is the only meal served. The hotel is close to the bus station and the commercial center of town, in a neighborhood of drab apartment buildings.

Rua 10 d'Agosto. ✆ **24/932-25-67.** 30 units. 40€–70€ double. Rates include buffet breakfast. **Amenities:** Laundry; pets allowed. Free Wi-Fi.

A Place to Stay & Dine Nearby

Estalagem Lago Azul ★★ This country inn is an idyllic retreat by the water. The location is some 31km (9⅓ miles) southeast of Tomar, in the Castelo de Bode reservoir, on the banks of Zêzere River. Its terrace and pool provides a view of the lake of the dam, the important supplier of water to Lisbon. Guest rooms at the inn range from small to midsize, each attractively and comfortably furnished with wooden floors, leather sofas, tiled bathrooms, and large windows. The views can be of the blue lake that gives its name to the inn (these days looking more greenish) or of the mountains. The hotel staff will help you arrange canoeing and other water sports on the lake. The hotel also operates a traditional restaurant dedicated to Portuguese dishes.

Ferreira do Zêzere. www.estalagemlagoazul.com. ✆ **24/936-14-45.** 20 units. 60€–95€ double; 125€ suite. Rates include buffet breakfast. Free parking. **Amenities:** Restaurant; bar; exercise room; children's playground; nautical club; outdoor pool; outdoor tennis court (lit). Free Wi-Fi.

Where to Dine

Chico Elias ★★★ PORTUGUESE Foodies in the know make a special pilgrimage to try the creations of chef/owner Maria do Céu. To try her most famous dishes, you'll need to call in advance and request them. These include rabbit cooked in a pumpkin (it is delectable), fricassee of eel, slow-roasted kid, and roast cod with acorn-sweetened pork. Our favorite culinary lineup, however, is duck with figs, followed by snails with beans. But even the traditional peasant fare is elevated here, like *bacalhau* (dried codfish) with cornbread—it has garnered praise from the dozens of visiting journalists, diplomats, and politicians who have feasted here. For dessert, we'd recommend the glorious "drunken pears."

Rua Principal 70, Algarvias. ✆ **24/931-10-67.** Reservations required. Main courses 16€–32€. No credit cards. Wed–Mon noon–3:30pm and 6–10pm.

ESTREMOZ ★

46km (29 miles) NE of Évora; 174km (108 miles) E of Lisbon; 12km (7½ miles) W of Borba

Rising from the plain like a pyramid of salt set out to dry in the sun, fortified Estremoz is in the center of the marble-quarry region of Alentejo. Cottages and mansions alike use the abundant marble in their construction and trim.

Essentials

ARRIVING

BY BUS The bus station is at Avenida Rainha Santa Isabel. From Lisbon, there are at least six daily buses departing from Sete Rios terminal. Check **Rede Expressos** (www.rede-expressos.pt; ✆ **70/722-33-44**); the fare is 15.50€ one-way. Two buses arrive daily from Évora, 1 hour away; three buses a day arrive from Portalegre, 1½ hours away.

BY CAR From Évora (p. 276), head northeast along Route 18.

Exploring the Town

The center of Estremoz is the open quadrangle called the **Rossio Marquês de Pombal.** The **Town Hall,** with its twin bell towers, opens onto this square. It has a grand stairway whose walls are lined with antique blue-and-white tiles, depicting hunting, pastoral, and historical scenes.

In the 16th-century **Igreja de Santa Maria (Church of St. Mary),** you'll see pictures by Portuguese primitive painters. The church formed part of the ancient fortress. It is open Tuesday through Sunday from 9:30am to noon and 3 to 5pm. Admission is free.

Another church worth a stop is .6km (less than a half-mile) south of the town on the road to Bencatel. The **Igreja de Nossa Senhora dos Mártires (Church of Our Lady of the Martyrs)** has beautiful tiles and an entrance marked by a Manueline arch. Dating from 1844, the church has a nave apse modeled on the French Gothic style of architecture. Hours vary according to the season and demands on the church staff, but in most cases, it's open daily from 9am to 6pm. Admission is free, although donations are accepted.

Castelo da Rainha Santa Isabel ★★★ CASTLE From the ramparts of the Castle of Queen Saint Isabel, which dates from the 13th-century reign of Dinis, the plains of Alentejo spread out before you. Sitting on top of a hill, the route to the top is best covered by car. Drive to the top of the Upper Town and stop on Largo de Dom Dinis. The stones of the castle, the cradle of the town's past, were decaying so badly that the city leaders pressed for its restoration in 1970. It was turned into a luxurious *pousada* (see "Where to Stay," below), the best place in town to stay.

The castle's imposing, once-fortified tower, attached to a palace, dominates the central plaza. Dinis's wife, Isabella, died in the castle and was unofficially proclaimed a saint by her local followers. Also opening onto the marble-and-stone-paved Largo are two modest chapels and a church. Admission is free for all. Nonguests can visit Tuesday through Sunday 9am to 5pm.

Largo de Dom Dinis. No phone or website for sightseeing information. (See "Where to Stay," below, for hotel reservation information.)

Shopping

The town's most famous product is a type of traditional earthenware water jug. Known as a *moringue*, it has two spouts, one handle, and sometimes a decorative crest that's stamped into the wet clay before it's fired. At least half a dozen street merchants sell the jugs in the town's main square, **Rossio Marquês de Pombal**. Stylish reminders of Portugal's agrarian past, they're associated with love and marriage. (Housewives traditionally carried water in them to workers in the fields, though they were also used to store water at home.) Some are simple; others are glazed in bright colors. Either way the pottery in Alentejo and in Estremoz, in particular, is quite handsome.

In central Estremoz, handicraft shops sell hundreds of terracotta figurines, another of the town's specialties. Each represents an archetype from the Alentejo workforce, and the designs include artfully naive depictions of washerwomen, sausage makers, carpenters, priests, and broom makers. **Casa Galileu,** Rua Victor Cordon, 16 (✆ **26/832-31-30**) sells some of the region's other handicrafts, including metalwork, copper pots, woodcarvings, and weavings, as well as the colorful wooden furniture of the region, painted in bright colors. On Saturdays there's a flea market/antique market where you might snag a bargain, and a good outdoor farmer's market with the best cheese, vegetables, fruits, and the sausages in the region (like *chouriço*).

Where to Stay

EXPENSIVE

Pousada de Estremoz, Rainha Santa Isabel ★★★ This historic property is one of the best-known and most prominent *pousadas* of Portugal;

reserve well in advance. Set in the old castle, dominating the town and overlooking the battlements and the Estremoz plain, these are luxe digs; gold leaf, marble, velvet, and satin mingle with 17th- and 18th-century reproductions of furniture and decorations in the guest rooms and corridors. The accommodations range from former monks' cells to sumptuous suites with canopied beds. Ten rooms are in the very nice modern addition, as well (though we prefer the older lodgings). Dom Manuel received Vasco da Gama in the salon of this castle before the explorer left for India. In 1698, a terrible explosion and fire destroyed the royal residence, which then underwent several alterations. It became an armory, then a barracks, and then an industrial school. Its transformation into a castle-*pousada* (that used to be state-owned) has restored it as a historic monument without sacrificing comfort and style. Contact the reception to join a fishing trip or a wine tasting at a local cellar. The restaurant is also not to be missed (see below).

Largo de Dom Dinis. www.pousadas.pt. ✆ **26/833-20-75.** 29 units. 80€–180€ double; 120€–320€ suite. Rates include buffet or a la carte breakfast, according to season. Free parking. **Amenities:** Restaurant; bar; bikes; outdoor pool; room service. Free Wi-Fi.

MODERATE

Convento de São Paulo ★★★ The origins of this restored hotel actually go back to a convent from 1182, although the present buildings, of course, were built much later. Set on a huge, lush estate, some accommodations lie in the former convent's ancient cells; others are of more recent construction. Regardless of their date of origin, guest rooms are well scrubbed, comfortable, and dignified in their decor, with all-white walls, dark furniture, and in most cases, wrought-iron headboards. Some have fireplaces, others have wooden ceilings, and the floors are in clay mosaic. The collection of well-preserved blue-and-white tiles in the former convent is stunning, and is considered the biggest private collection in the country.

O Ermita, a handsome restaurant with restored 18th-century frescoes, is on-site. It makes use of many recipes passed down by the nuns, including the convent's famed egg and almond cakes. The hotel organizes cooking lessons around these treats. And if you eat too many, bikes are available free for guests to pump off some of the calories on the estate's trails.

A note on directions, as the hotel isn't in Estremoz: You'll drive 27km (17 miles) from Estremoz or 34km (21 miles) from Évora. Once in the town of Redondo, follow the signs to Aldeia da Serra for 10km (6¼ miles), where you'll come upon this charming inn.

Aldeia da Serra. www.hotelconventospaulo.com. ✆ **26/698-91-60.** 39 units. 70€–130€ double; 150€–210€ suite. Rates include breakfast. Free parking. **Amenities:** Restaurant; bar; room service. Free Wi-Fi in the rooms located in the old building and public areas.

Páteo dos Solares ★ This is a good alternative to the *pousada* (see above), if that's booked up. Though it's not quite in the same class, the *estalagem* does boast an atmosphere that evokes old Portugal. The manor house is pristine architecturally on its exterior, but inside is a chic boutique decor. That means guest rooms in symphonies of cream, beige, and taupe, with such contemporary twists as hydromassage tubs in some rooms. The hotel is set in well-kept gardens with an outdoor pool and tennis court, and is just a 10-minute walk from the town center. The on-site restaurant is known for its regional specialties.

Rua Brito Capelo, Largo do Castelo. www.pateosolares.com. ✆ **26/833-84-00.** 41 units. 69€–190€ double. Rates include buffet breakfast. **Amenities:** Restaurant; bar; babysitting; outdoor pool; room service; outdoor tennis court (lit). Free Wi-Fi.

Where to Dine

Mercearia Gadanha ★★★ PORTUGUESE Foodies travel from miles around to dine at this relative newcomer, a restaurant that rivals many of the most celebrated Lisbon gastronomic temples for its creative takes on traditional Portuguese cuisine. These might include *farinheira* with quail egg (that's egg with herbs and pork fat), lamb croquettes with mushroom aioli, or braised black pork cheeks. "Mercearia" means grocery shop, and so it is, at the front, meaning diners can take excellent treats with them for the road.

Largo Dragões de Olivença, 84A. ✆ **26/833-32-62.** Reservations recommended. Main courses 12€–20€. Daily 1–3pm and 7:30–10:30pm.

Pousada de Estremoz, Rainha Santa Isabel Restaurante ★★ PORTUGUESE You'll find all the regional specialties, expertly prepared, at this evocative, vaulted-ceiling eatery. These include the traditional tomato soup, an Alentejo classic, served along with another classic, fried pork flavored with fresh clams. The fried green beans and the wild local asparagus are a treat, in season, and incorporated into appetizers. Local trout filets are grilled with mint that's grown along the riverbanks. Meat dishes, such as grilled lamb cutlets flavored with fresh rosemary or lamb meatballs with cinnamon, are also uncommonly tasty, and pair perfectly with the red wines of the Alentejo.

Largo D. Diniz, Castelo de Estremoz. ✆ **26/833-20-75.** Reservations recommended. Main courses 12€–23€. Menu *pousada* 33€. Daily 1–3pm and 7:30–10:30pm.

ELVAS ★★

11km (6¾ miles) W of Badajoz, Spain; 223km (139 miles) E of Lisbon

The "city of plums," Elvas is characterized by narrow cobblestone streets (pedestrians have to duck into doorways to allow automobiles to inch by) and crenellated fortifications. The Moors held the town until 1226. Later, Spanish troops frequently besieged it. It finally fell in the 1801 War of the Oranges, which ended with a peace treaty signed at Badajoz. Elvas remained part of Portugal, but its neighbor, Olivença, became Spanish. The Elvas ramparts are an outstanding example of 17th-century fortifications, with gates, curtain walls, moats, bastions, and sloping banks around them.

Lining the steep, hilly streets are tightly packed gold- and oyster-colored cottages with tile roofs. Many of the house doors are just 1.5m (5 ft.) tall. In the tiny windows are numerous canary cages and flowering geraniums. The four-tier **Aqueduto da Amoreira,** built between 1498 and 1622, transports water into Elvas from about 8km (5 miles) southwest of the town.

Essentials

ARRIVING

BY BUS The bus station is at Praça 25 de Abril (© **26/862-28-75**). Seven buses per day make the 4-hour trip from Lisbon. The one-way fare is 18.50€. Many buses make the daily 2-hour trip from Évora. The one-way fare for that is 12.50€. From Badajoz, frequent buses run throughout the day. The ride takes 20 minutes.

BY CAR From Estremoz (p. 271), continue east toward Spain along Route 4.

VISITOR INFORMATION

The **Elvas Tourist Office** is on Praça da República (© **26/862-22-36**). It's open Monday to Friday 9am to 6pm (until 7pm in summer), Saturday and Sunday from 10am to 12:30pm and 2 to 5:30pm.

EXPLORING THE TOWN In **Praça Dom Sancho II** stands the **Sé** (cathedral). Under a cone-shaped dome, it's a forbidding, fortresslike building decorated with gargoyles, turrets, and a florid Manueline portal. The cathedral opens onto a black-and-white diamond square. Admission is free, and it is open daily from 10am to noon and 2 to 6pm. A short walk up the hill to the right of the cathedral leads to **Largo de Santa Clara** ★, a small plaza that holds an odd Manueline pillory with four wrought-iron dragon heads.

On the south side of Largo de Santa Clara is the **Igreja de Nossa Senhora de Consolação (Church of Our Lady of Consolation)** ★, a 16th-century octagonal Renaissance building with a cupola lined in 17th-century *azulejos* (tiles). It's open daily from 9am to 12:30pm and 2 to 5pm. Admission is free.

The **castelo** (castle), Praça da República, built by the Moors and strengthened by Christian rulers in the 14th and 16th centuries, offers a panoramic view of the town, its fortifications, and the surrounding countryside. It's open daily from 9:30am to 1pm and 2:30 to 5pm (until 5:30pm October 10 to April 1). Admission costs 1.50€. **Forte de Nossa Senhora da Graça** is another important fortification, with ramparts in the shape of a star. Like the castle, it played a key role in protecting the borders from attacks from Spain.

SHOPPING The abundant folklore of this small town might whet your appetite for souvenirs. Take a stroll along the town's best shopping streets, **Rua de Alcamim** and **Rua de Olivença,** where you'll find many rustic handicrafts from around the region.

Where to Stay

MODERATE

Estalagem Quinta de Santo António ★★ This once-private quinta, dating from 1668, now welcomes paying guests. This is one of the finest examples of Alentejo architecture in the region, and the property is enveloped by a beautiful garden. The interior was faithfully restored and decorated with antique furniture. The guest rooms are generally spacious and exceedingly comfortable, with well-maintained bathrooms. The on-site restaurant, A Quinta, is known locally for its superb cuisine of the Alentejo school. Activities on-site or nearby include horseback riding, biking, and motorboat rides.

Estrada de Barbacena, Apartado 206. www.qsahotel.com. ✆ **26/863-64-60.** 30 units. 50€–75€ double; 80€–150€ suite. Rates include buffet breakfast. 6.5km (4 miles) northeast of Elvas along Estrada de Portalegre. Free parking. **Amenities:** Restaurant; bar; babysitting; bikes; children's center; outdoor pool. Free Wi-Fi.

INEXPENSIVE

Hotel D. Luís Elvas ★ This well-established favorite is not only the largest hotel in Elvas, but one of the most affordable. It is the choice of most commercial travelers because of its conference rooms, but also a favorite with vacationers who enjoy its central location close to all the major monuments. It's right in front of the old and impressive aqueduct. The guest rooms are spread over four floors and are roomy, with comfortable furnishings, though some rooms show a bit of wear and tear. The hotel also operates a first-rate restaurant with a popular bar.

Av. de Badajoz-Estrada N4. www.hoteldluis-elvas.com. ✆ **26/863-67-90.** 90 units. 54€–115€ double. Rates include buffet breakfast. Free parking. **Amenities:** Restaurant; bar; outdoor pool; room service. Free Wi-Fi.

ÉVORA ★★★

102km (63 miles) SW of Badajoz, Spain; 155km (96 miles) E of Lisbon

The capital of Alto Alentejo, Évora, a designated UNESCO World Heritage Site, is often described as an open-air museum. Considering its size and location, it's also something of an architectural phenomenon. Its builders freely adapted whatever styles they desired, from Mudéjar to Manueline to Roman to rococo. Sixteenth- and 17th-century houses, many with tile patios, fill nearly every street. Cobblestones, labyrinthine streets, arcades, squares with bubbling fountains, whitewashed houses, and a profuse display of Moorish-inspired arches characterize the town.

Many conquerors passed through Évora. The Romans at the time of Julius Caesar knew the town as Liberalitas Julia. But its heyday was during the 16th-century reign of João III, when it became a capital for artists and academics; innovative artists, including the playwright Gil Vicente, congregated under the aegis of royalty.

Évora is a popular day trip from Lisbon, but it's a long trek, which

Special Events

Évora's major festival is the **Feira de São João,** a folkloric and musical extravaganza. All the handicrafts of the area, including fine ceramics, are on display; regional dances are presented; and hundreds of people from the Alentejo region come into the city. The event, which takes place over the last 10 days of June, celebrates the arrival of summer. The tourist office (see "Visitor Information," below) can supply more details.

doesn't leave enough time to enjoy the town. Because of its isolation amid some of the loveliest rural landscapes in Portugal, and because of the wealth of attractions within it, an overnight here is recommended. Arguably it's one of the most beautiful Portuguese cities, even if tourism masses have discovered it.

Essentials

ARRIVING

BY TRAIN Trains from Lisbon (Santa Apolónia) run five times a day. A one-way ticket costs 17.50€. For more info, visit www.cp.pt or call ✆ **70/721-02-20.**

BY BUS **Rede Expressos** (www.rede-expressos.pt; ✆ **70/722-33-44**) provides bus service for the area. Fifteen buses a day arrive from Lisbon; the trip takes 1 hour and 45 minutes and costs 12€ one-way. Three daily buses make the 5-hour trip from Faro, in the Algarve. The cost is 16€ one-way. Seven buses a day connect Beja with Évora; the trip takes 1¼ hours and costs 7.50€ one-way.

BY CAR From Beja (p. 283), continue north along Route 18.

VISITOR INFORMATION

The **Évora Tourist Information Office** is at Praça do Giraldo 73 (✆ **26/677-70-71**). It's open daily 9am to 6pm (7pm in summer).

Exploring the Town

Cromeleque dos Almendres ★★★ HISTORIC SITE The layers of history in this city are full of surprises. Like these prehistoric standing stones, 95 stones to be exact, gathered in a cork forest 9km (5½ miles) from Évora. Older than Stonehenge (7000 B.C.), the cromlech is part of a megalith past that encompasses 1,500 monuments in the region—the largest concentration in Europe. The stones were discovered by amateur archeologist Henrique Leonor Pina in 1963. Visiting the monument on your own (free access) is possible, but to better understand all the theories surrounding these monuments, we recommend a tour with **Ebora Megalithica** ★★★ (www.eboramegalithica.com; ✆ **96/480-83-37,** Monday to Saturday). The tour not only takes in the enclosure, but also one burial mound (Dolmen of Zambujeiro) and one standing stone (Menir of Almendres) and is usually led by young archeologist Mário Carvalho, who is passionate about history and is helping to protect this unique heritage. Objects removed from this monuments can be seen in **Évora Museum,** in front of the Roman Temple.

Igreja de Nossa Senhora de Graça ★ CHURCH The Church of Our Lady of Grace is notable chiefly for its baroque facade, with huge classical nudes over the pillars. Above each group of lazing stone giants is a sphere with a flame—pieces of sculpture often compared to works by Michelangelo. The church was built in Évora's heyday, during the reign of João III. Columns and large stone rosettes flank the central window shaft, and ponderous neoclassical columns support the lower level. The church can be viewed only from the outside.

Largo da Graça. No phone.

Igreja de São João Evangelista ★★ CHURCH This church deserves to be better known: Although it's one of Évora's undisputed gems, it's seemingly little visited. It contains a lovely collection of 18th-century tiles, and a guide will show you a macabre sight—an old cistern filled with neatly stacked bones removed from tombs. In the chapel's sacristy are some paintings, including a ghastly rendition of Africans slaughtering a Christian missionary. One highlight is a painting of a pope that has moving eyes and moving feet. You can also see part of the wall that once encircled Évora here. The Gothic-Mudéjar Church of St. John the Evangelist, facing the Temple of Diana and next door to the government-owned *pousada*, is connected to the palace built by the dukes of Cadaval.

Largo do Conde de Vila Flor. ✆ **26/673-00-30.** Admission 3€. Tues–Sun 10am–noon and 2–6pm.

Igreja Real de São Francisco ★★★ CHURCH The Church of St. Francis contains a chapel that's probably unlike any you've seen: The chancel walls and central pillars of the ghoulish 16th-century Capela dos Ossos (Chapel of Bones) are lined with human skulls and other parts of skeletons. Legend has it that the bones came either from soldiers who died in a big battle or from plague victims. Over the door is a sign that addresses visitors' own mortality: OUR BONES THAT STAY HERE ARE WAITING FOR YOURS! The church was built in the Gothic style with Manueline influences between 1460 and 1510.

Praça 1 de Maio. ✆ **26/670-45-21.** Admission 3€. Daily 9am–1pm and 2:30–6pm (until 5pm from Oct–May).

Roman Temple ★★ HISTORIC SITE The major monument in Évora is the Roman Temple (formerly wrongly known as Diana Temple), directly in front of the government-owned *pousada* (see "Where to Stay," below). Dating from the 1st or 2nd century A.D., it's a light, graceful structure with 14 granite Corinthian columns topped by marble capitals and a symbol of the city. Although it is said to have been dedicated to the goddess Diana, no one has actually proved it. The temple withstood the 1755 earthquake, and there's evidence that it was once used as a slaughterhouse. Walk through the garden for a view of the Roman aqueduct and the surrounding countryside.

Largo do Conde de Vila Flor. Free admission. Daily 24 hr.

Sé (Cathedral) ★★★ RELIGIOUS SITE The cathedral of Évora was built in the Roman-Gothic style between 1186 and 1204. The bulky structure was notably restored and redesigned over the centuries and is the biggest medieval cathedral in the country. Two square towers, both topped by cones, flank the stone facade; one is surrounded by satellite spires. The **interior ★★**

consists of a nave and two aisles. The 18th-century main altar, of pink, black, and white marble, is the finest in town. At the sculptured work *The Lady of Mothers*, young women pray for fertility.

The cathedral's museum houses treasures from the church, the most notable of which is a 13th-century Virgin carved out of ivory. It opens to reveal a collection of scenes from her life. A reliquary is studded with 1,426 precious stones, including sapphires, rubies, diamonds, and emeralds. The most valuable item is a piece of wood said to have come from the True Cross.

Largo Marquês de Marialva (Largo de Sé). ✆ **26/675-93-30.** Admission to cathedral 1.50€; to cloister 2.5€; to museum 5€ adults, free for children under 12. Daily 9am–noon and 2–4:30pm.

Universidade de Évora, Colégio Espírito Santo ★ UNIVERSITY
After Coimbra, this was the second university founded in Portugal. In 1559, during the town's cultural flowering, this university was constructed and placed under the tutelage of the Jesuits. It flourished until the Jesuit-hating Marquês de Pombal closed it in the 18th century. The compound wasn't used as a university again until 1973.

The most interesting building is the Colégio Espírito Santo. The double-tiered baroque main building here surrounds a large quadrangle. Marble pillars support the arches, and brazilwood makes up the ceilings. Blue-and-white tiles line the inner courtyard. Other *azulejos* (tiles) depict women, wild animals, angels, cherubs, and costumed men, and contrast with the austere elegance of the classrooms and the elongated refectory. Notice the balance in the renaissance facade of the west gate.

Largo do Colégio. www.uevora.pt. ✆ **26/674-08-00.** Free admission. Mon–Fri 8am–7pm (until 8pm in Aug and 1pm Oct–Dec with permission from the tourist office).

Shopping & Wine Tasting

The busiest shopping street in Évora is **Rua 5 de Outubro,** which leads from a point near the cathedral to the perimeter of the historic town. Along this street you'll find lots of gifts made locally from cork at **Montsobro** (from bags and purses to belts and aprons, it's #66 on the street). Nearby, at no.78, is **Teoartis,** a small gallery and shop dedicated to tiles and handicraft of all sorts, including furniture. The market in Praça 1 de Maio has handicraft, wines, cheeses, cakes, and leather gifts. For a sweet souvenir, the convent-recipe pastries at **Pastelaria Conventual Pão de Rala** (Rua de Cicioso no. 47) are downright heavenly.

Eye-opening (and eyelid-drooping) wine tastings are available at **Rota dos Vinhos do Alentejo** (the association of all the wineries) in Praça Joaquim António de Aguiar 20–21 (closed on Sunday). Alentejo wines are not as famous as the Douro wines, but you'll wonder why after tasting the scintillating reds and whites, usually blends of some indigenous grapes, available here. Occasionally you can find a single-grape wine, but that is not the tradition.

The winery **Ervideira** has a shop in Rua 5 de Outubro, 56, where you can simply taste the wines produced nearby, or schedule a visit to the winery between Évora and Reguengos de Monsaraz. Staff is friendly and knowledge. The most famous wine producer in Évora is **Cartuxa,** outside the city walls, around 1km (less than 1 mile) from the city, next to the Cartuxa Monastery. Visit the winery and taste the wines and the olive oil, booking ahead at www.cartuxa.pt or ✆ **26/674-83-83.**

Where to Stay

EXPENSIVE

Hotel M'AR De AR Aqueduto ★★★ Inside the old city walls and installed on the site of a palace and convent from the 16th century, this is the city's most coveted place to grab 40 winks. Though you may not want to close your eyes: From the original Sepulveda Palace that stood here, you can still see the lovely chapel, with its domed ceilings, and a cluster of post-Gothic Manueline windows studding the main facade.

Inside there's little of that old-fashioned feel; rooms have modular furniture, glass walls between the bedrooms and bathrooms (in many units) and floors of multicolored, shiny wooden slats. The most deluxe guest rooms are in the spa section and come equipped with treatments for couples who prefer the intimacy of their bedroom; showers in these units have a hydromassage tub as well as a deck terrace facing an orange grove.

A final reason to stay here: to patronize the on-site restaurant of award-winning chef António Nobre, author of *Portuguese Chefs, The Best Recipes*.

Rua Cândido dos Reis 72. www.mardearhotels.com. ✆ **26/674-07-00.** 64 units. 110€–160€ double; 207€–305€ suite. Free parking. **Amenities:** 2 restaurants; bar; bike rentals; children's programs; concierge; exercise room; outdoor pool; room service; spa. Free Wi-Fi.

Pousada de Évora, Lóios ★★★ The Pousada de Évora, Lóios, under UNESCO protection, occupies the Lóios Monastery, built in 1485 on the site of the old Évora Castle, which was destroyed during a riot in 1384. Official Inquisition reports were kept in the chapter room, which features 16th-century doorways in Moorish-Portuguese style. After the 1755 earthquake, extensive work was done to repair and preserve the structure. Over the years it was used as a telegraph station, a primary school, an army barracks, and offices. The 1965 opening of the *pousada* made possible the architectural restoration of the monastery. Its position in the center of Évora, between the cathedral and the ghostlike Roman Temple, is unrivaled.

The white-and-gold salon (once a private chapel) boasts an ornate Pompeii-style decor and frescoes, and is decorated with antique furnishings, handwoven draperies, crystal chandeliers and sconces, and painted medallion portraits. All the guest rooms are furnished in traditional style, with antique reproductions. Because the rooms used to be monks' cells, they are rather small, but they have been equipped with modern comforts. Family rooms are a little bigger and can accommodate an extra bed. Don't miss a meal in the cloister—the restaurant excels at executing local culinary traditions.

Largo Conde de Vila Flor. www.pousadas.pt. ✆ **26/673-00-70.** 32 units. 135€–175€ double; 190€–300€ suite. Rates include buffet breakfast. Free parking. **Amenities:** Restaurant; bar; outdoor pool; room service. Wi-Fi 12€ per 24 hr.

INEXPENSIVE

ADC Hotel (Albergaria do Calvário) ★★★ A former olive-processing plant, the ADC is about a 5-minute walk from the historic center. Next to the Convento do Calvário (a convent that's closed to the public), you'd never know this used to be a factory: The hotel is very attractive, with neoclassical and country rustic reproduction furnishings used extensively throughout. Breakfast is served in your room or on the Esplanade Terraces and is particularly good, offering organic foods (including the eggs, coffee, and tea) and a variety of fresh juices, breads, and pancakes, as well as seasonal offerings. The staff and owners are friendly and excel at helping guests plan a day's itinerary.

Travessa dos Lagares 3. http://adcevora.com/pt. ✆ **26/674-59-30.** 23 units. 90€–120€ double; 110€–133€ suite. Rates include buffet breakfast. Free parking. **Amenities:** Bar; bikes; room service; pets allowed. Free Wi-Fi in lobby).

Albergaria Solar de Monfalim ★ This 16th-century Renaissance palace will welcome you with its noble style as it has been doing since 1892, when it opened as a hotel. A stone staircase leads up to a plant-lined entrance decorated with tiles. Inside, the small to midsize guest rooms keep the original antique atmosphere, with whitewashed walls and iron beds. We especially like the terrace, where you can nurse a drink while peering through the cloisterlike mullioned veranda.

Largo da Misericórdia, 1. www.monfalimtur.pt. ✆ **26/675-00-00.** 26 units. 45€–95€ double. Rates include buffet breakfast. **Amenities:** Bar. Free Wi-Fi in public areas.

Hotel Riviera ★ This small inn sits beside the cobblestones of one of the most charming streets in town, about 2 blocks downhill from the cathedral. Designed as a private villa, it retains many handcrafted details from the original building, including stone window frames, ornate iron balustrades, and the blue-and-yellow tiles of its foyer. Its small guest rooms are quite comfortable, with good beds, but not all of them are tastefully decorated (think: mismatched furniture).

Rua do 5 de Outubro 49. www.riviera-evora.com. ✆ **26/673-72-10.** 21 units. 60€–90€ double. Rates include buffet breakfast. Parking nearby 10€. Free Wi-Fi.

Pensão Policarpo ★ Inside the city walls, this guesthouse is somewhat hostel-like, but for these prices we're not complaining. And its location, behind the cathedral, is one of the most tranquil in town. The property was once the private manor house of the Counts of Lousã, in the 17th century. On one side, the pension opens onto a panoramic view of the Alentejan plain; on the other, it fronts a tiny patio with a granite gateway. No two rooms are alike, but most of them lie under wooden beams and high ceilings and are furnished with hand-painted regional beds and tables, some a bit worn out. Room 101 is the most atmospheric, lined with *azulejos* and a massive wooden bed. Breakfast is taken in a room decorated with local art. Only half of the rooms are air-conditioned and contain private bathrooms.

Rua da Freiria de Baixo 16. www.pensaopolicarpo.com. ✆ **26/670-24-24.** 19 units (8 with bathroom). 29€–42€ double without bathroom; 48€–64€ double with bathroom. No credit cards. **Amenities:** Bar; bike rentals; children's programs (ages 3–12). Free Wi-Fi.

Where to Dine

Botequim da Mouraria ★★★ TRADITIONAL PORTUGUESE Once a locals' well-kept secret, this tiny restaurant, tucked away in the backstreets of Évora, is now known internationally. They don't accept reservations, so you'll have to go very early—noon for lunch or just after 6pm for dinner—as they only have nine seats. Run by a culinary wonder-couple, Domingos serves at the counter and chats warmly with guests, while Florbela, his wife, cooks inspired Alentejo food. Usually the husband recommends the daily specials, but be sure to try the starter of ham with figs or the Serpa cheese oven-baked with oregano. In a city with so many great restaurants, this one sits at the top of the heap.

Rua da Mouraria, 16. ✆ **26/674-67-75.** Main courses 11€–30€. Mon–Fri 12:30–3pm and 7–9:30pm. Closed Sat–Sun.

Guião ★ TRADITIONAL PORTUGUESE Guião is a regional tavern just off the main square, Praça do Giraldo. It's charmingly decorated with antique blue-and-white tiles. The family-run tavern offers local wines and Portuguese specialties, and its robust meals are filling. A typical bill of fare includes grilled seafood, black pig cheeks, and clams with Alentejo-style pork. The kitchen also prepares partridge in season.

Rua da República 81. ✆ **26/670-30-71.** Main courses 11€–17€. Tues–Sat noon–3:30pm and 7–10:30pm; Sun noon–3:30pm.

Restaurante Fialho ★★★ TRADITIONAL PORTUGUESE Fialho, which has flourished on this site since the end of World War II, is Évora's most famous restaurant and the most awarded. Its entrance is unprepossessing, but the interior is warmly decorated in the style of a Portuguese tavern. Although Évora is inland, Fialho serves excellent fish dishes like the *sopa de Cação* (a shark soup), along with such succulent fare as pork with baby clams and partridge stew. Share a main course, as portions are generous. The staff is particularly proud of the lavish array of local wines—the restaurant has one of the most comprehensive cellars in the district. And leave room for the dessert: Their small cheesecakes (*queijadas*), a speciality of Évora, made with *requeijão* (similar to ricotta), are heavenly. As it should be: The recipe comes from the convent. The air-conditioned restaurant seats 90.

Travessa dos Mascarenhas 14. www.restaurantefialho.com. ✆ **26/670-30-79.** Reservations recommended. Main courses 14€–30€. Tues–Sun 12:30–4pm and 7pm–midnight. Closed Sept 1–21 and Dec 24–31.

Évora After Dark

The town's historic core contains a few sleepy-looking bars, any of which might strike your fancy as part of an after-dark pub-crawl. The bar of the **Pousada de Évora, Lóios,** Largo Conde de Vila Flor (✆ **26/673-00-70**), is a dignified option for a drink in a historic setting. **Molhóbico – The Party House** (✆ **26/674-82-35** in Rua de Aviz, 91), is a popular spot for drinks and music.

BEJA ★

187km (116 miles) SE of Lisbon; 76km (47 miles) S of Évora

Julius Caesar founded Beja, which was once known as Pax Julia, around 48 B.C. The capital of Baixo Alentejo, the town rises like a pyramid above the surrounding fields of swaying wheat, olive trees, and vineyards.

Beja's fame rests on a literary story. In the mid–17th century, in the Convent of the Conceição, a young nun named Sóror Mariana Alcoforado is said to have fallen in love with a French military officer. The officer, identified as the chevalier de Chamilly, reputedly seduced her and then left Beja forever. The girl's outpouring of grief and anguish found literary release in *Lettres Portugaises,* published in Paris in 1669. The letters created a sensation and endured as an epistolary classic. In 1926, F. C. Green wrote *Who Was the Author of the Lettres Portugaises?,* claiming that their true writer was the Comte de Guilleragues. However, a modern Portuguese study has put forth evidence that the *Lettres Portugaises* were, in fact, written by a nun named Sister Alcoforado.

Essentials

ARRIVING

BY BUS Seven *expressos* (express buses) per day make the 3-hour run between Lisbon and Beja; the one-way fare is 14€. Seven buses a day come from Évora. The 1-hour trip costs 7.50€ one-way.

BY CAR From Albufeira in the Algarve, take IP-1 north to the junction with Route 263, which heads northeast into Beja.

VISITOR INFORMATION

The **Beja Tourist Office** is at Largo Dr. Lima Faleiro (✆ **28/431-19-13**) inside the castle. The office is open Monday to Saturday 9:30am to 12:30pm and 2 to 6pm.

Exploring the Town

Castelo de Beja ★ CASTLE Beja castle, which King Dinis built in the early–14th century on the ruins of a Roman fortress, crowns the town. Although some of its turreted walls have been restored, the defensive towers—save for a long marble keep—are gone. Traditionally the final stronghold in the castle's fortifications, the old keep appears to be battling the weather and gold fungi. The walls are overgrown with ivy, the final encroachment on its former glory. From the keep you can enjoy a view of the provincial capital and the outlying fields.

Largo Dr. Lima Faleiro. ✆ **28/431-19-13.** Free admission. Mon–Fri 9am–1pm and 2–5pm; From the center, walk along Rua de Aresta Branco, following signposts.

Museu Rainha D. Leonor ★★ MUSEUM The Queen Leonor Museum (founded in 1927–28) occupies three buildings on a broad plaza in the center of Beja: the Convento da Conceição and the churches of Santo Amaro and São Sebastião. The main building was a convent founded in 1459 by the parents of the Portuguese king Manuel. Favored by royal protection, it became one of the richest and most important convents of that time. The Convento da Conceição is famous throughout the world because of a single nun, Mariana Alcoforado. She is said to have written the *Lettres Portugaises,* love letters to the French chevalier de Chamilly, at the convent in the 17th century.

Some of the building's most important features are the surviving pieces of the ancient convent. They are the church, with its baroque decoration, and the cloister and chapter house, which exhibit one of the area's most impressive collections of 15th- to 18th-century Spanish and Portuguese tiles. Also on display are statuary and silverwork belonging to the convent and a good collection of Spanish, Portuguese, and Dutch paintings from the 15th to 18th centuries. The *Escudela de Pero de Faria*, a piece of 1541 Chinese porcelain, is especially unique. The first-floor permanent archaeological exhibition features artifacts from the Beja region.

The Santo Amaro church is one of the oldest churches of Beja and rests on what could be an early Christian foundation. It houses the most important Visigothic collection (from Beja and its surroundings) in Portugal.

The Church of São Sebastião is a small temple of no great architectural interest. It houses part of the museum's collection of architectural goods from Roman to modern times. It's not open to the public; access is by special request.

Largo da Conceição. www.museuregionaldebeja.pt. ✆ **28/432-33-51.** Admission 2€, 1€ students, free for children under 15. Entry to the Convento and the Museu Visigotico. Free on Sun. Tues–Sun 9:30am–12:30pm and 2–5:15pm.

Museu Visigótico ★ MUSEUM Right next to the Castelo, this small museum fills a 6th-century church with artifacts from the Visigoths, who once ruled these parts. You can see the collections, weapons, pottery, and tombstones in about half an hour.

Largo de Santo Amaro. ✆ **28/432-14-65.** 2€ tickets cover entry here and to the Convento. Tues–Sun 9:30am–12:30pm and 2–5pm.

Shopping

Beja is known for handicrafts, including charming hammered copper, in the form of serving dishes and home accessories, as well as the many forms of pottery and woodcarvings you might see in other parts of Alentejo. **Rua**

Capital João Francisco de Sousa, in the town center, is lined with all manner of shops.

Where to Stay

MODERATE

Pousada de Beja, São Francisco ★★★ This conversion of a 13th-century Franciscan monastery opened in the early 1990s and quickly filled a need for a good hotel in the historic heart of town. From the end of World War II until the 1980s, it had functioned as an army barracks and training camp. The architects attempted to retain some of the building's severe medieval lines, with limited success because of serious deterioration. Rooms are former monks' cells, but some are surprisingly spacious and all are attractively furnished, with solid old-style beds and excellent bathrooms. There's a garden on the premises with a modest chapel.

Largo Dom Nuno Álvarez Pereira. www.pousadas.pt. ✆ **28/431-35-80.** 35 units. 75€–143€ double; 128€–209€ suite. Rates include buffet breakfast. Free parking. **Amenities:** Restaurant; bar; outdoor pool; room service; outdoor tennis court (lit). Free Wi-Fi.

INEXPENSIVE

Hotel Melius ★★ This is the town's best-regarded independent hotel; it's a better choice than the nearby Residencial Santa Bárbara (see below), but not as good as the *pousada* (see above). Opened in 1995, it lies on the southern outskirts of town beside the main road to the Algarve. The four-story hotel provides amenities like a gym and sauna—unusual in this region. Midsize guest rooms, though bland and not particularly well decorated, are comfortable and well maintained, with good beds.

Av. Fialho Almeida, ✆ **28/431-30-80.** 60 units. 55€–70€ double; 80€–95€ suite. Rates include buffet breakfast. Parking 3€. **Amenities:** Bar; exercise room; room service; sauna. Free Wi-Fi.

Residencial Santa Bárbara ★ The Santa Bárbara is an oasis of affordability in a town that has few good-value accommodations. The hotel is a shiny-clean, well-kept bandbox building. It's small in scale, with only a whisper of a reception lobby and elevator, but it is in the historic neighborhood. The guest rooms are compact and plain but adequate. Some have a small balcony, and there's a fireplace in the lounge.

Rua de Mértola 56. www.residencialsantabarbara.pt. ✆ **28/431-22-80.** 26 units. 42€–60€ double. Rates include buffet breakfast. Parking 3€. **Amenities:** Bar; room service. Free Wi-Fi.

VILA NOVA DE MILFONTES

32km (20 miles) SW of Santiago do Cacém; 186km (116 miles) S of Lisbon

A good stopover in lower Alentejo as you're heading south to the Algarve is the little beach town of Vila Nova de Milfontes. At the wide mouth of the Mira River, the sleepy resort attracts visitors with the soft white-sand beaches that

time to walk: ZAMBUJEIRA DO MAR

Going south to the Algarve you'll find Zambujeira do Mar, another fishing village that attracts crowds to its lovely beaches. If you like walking, this is a good place to start, with the old Fishermen's Trail (*Rota Vicentina*). It's a beautiful hike on the cliffs of this protected coastal area (a huge national park from south of Setúbal to the Algarve), a stunning wild coast with few constructions on the site. The entire walk can take up to a week, so you'll want to stop at places like the **Herdade do Touril** (www.touril.pt; ✆ **28/395-00-80**) a lovely *monte*, the traditional houses in Alentejo with one floor and a plot of land. Touril is close to the Atlantic (Praia do Tonel is close by, with a difficult access but gorgeous views) and offers the perfect place to rest and relax after a day of hiking, with its peaceful countryside views. The house is part of a huge farm (365 hectares/902 acres).

Avoid Zambujeira in August, as the Sudoeste rock festival attracts crowds from all over the country. The ocean can be a bit rough in this area with strong currents, and some small beaches don't have lifeguards, so take precautions before heading into the water. For more info about the trail, visit http://en.rotavicentina.com.

line both sides of the river. Besides the beach and the water sports, there are no other attractions and nothing to do here but relax, or perhaps search for antiques.

The castle that once protected the area from Moroccan and Algerian pirates has been restored and is now an inn.

Essentials

ARRIVING

BY BUS Three express buses a day make the trip from Lisbon, but in summer they are much more frequent. It takes 3½ hours and costs 16.40€ one-way. For schedules, contact Rede Expressos (www.rede-expressos.pt; ✆ **70/722-33-44**).

BY CAR Chances are you'll drive south from the Setúbal (p. 184). Continue along N261 in the direction of Sines, and then follow N120-1 until you see the cutoff heading west in Vila Nova de Milfontes.

VISITOR INFORMATION

The **tourist office** is on Rua António Mantas (✆ **28/399-65-99**). It's open daily 10am to 1pm and 2 to 6pm.

Where to Stay

Casa dos Arcos ★ In the center of town and just a 5-minute walk from the beach is this simple yet comfortable guesthouse. The small to midsize guest rooms were modernized recently and feature neatly kept bathrooms. There is no grandeur or pretense here—the place provides an adequate stopover for the night, nothing more.

Rua do Cais. ✆ **28/399-62-64.** 25 units. 33€–75€ double. Rates include buffet breakfast. No credit cards. Free Wi-Fi.

Where to Dine

Restaurante Marisqueira O Pescador ★ PORTUGUESE/SEAFOOD O Moura, as it's known locally, is a classic *marisqueira* (seafood restaurant), serving up savory treats like monkfish with rice and kettles of *caldeirada,* a seafood stew. The place is air-conditioned, and the welcome is friendly. The owners, Mr. and Mrs. Moura, used to be fishmongers, and they know their product well. Don't expect much in the way of decor—people come here for the food, not the atmosphere.

Largo da Praça 18. ✆ **28/399-63-38.** Reservations recommended. Main courses 12€–24€. No credit cards. Daily noon–midnight. Closed 2 weeks in Oct or Nov.

Tasca do Celso ★★★ PORTUGUESE/SEAFOOD An even better place for celebrating the love for fish and shellfish in this blessed part of the country, Tasco do Celso is an institution in this former fishing village (now a beach resort). Simple charcoal-grilled fish reaches sublime taste heights, as does the clams with garlic and cilantro (*bulhão pato*) and the prawns with garlic. If you like spicy food, dose it all with the restaurant's homemade piri-piri sauce.

Rua dos Aviadores. ✆ **28/399-67-53.** Reservations recommended. Main courses 13€–27€. No credit cards. Daily noon–midnight.

COIMBRA & THE BEIRAS

12

The three historic provinces making up the Beiras are often overlooked by travelers heading to the northern wine lands, Algarve beaches, or Lisbon's cool city attractions. That is a mistake. The Beiras comprise spectacular mountain landscapes, historic cities, picturesque villages, unspoiled beaches, and restaurants serving some of the country's most enticing culinary delights.

Among the urban attractions, pride of place goes to the historic university city of Coimbra. The region's de facto capital sits on a bend in the slow-moving River Mondego. At its heart is the 13th-century university, with its wonderful baroque library. Almost 25,000 students ensure that the city's UNESCO World Heritage old town is no sleepy historical backwater. The narrow alleys and plazas are packed with taverns and restaurants serenaded by students' own version of fado music. Crammed with museums and monuments, Coimbra makes a great base for exploring the region. On its doorstep are the ruins of the Roman town of Conimbriga, the medieval riverside fortress at Montemor-o-Velho, and verdant Penacova, a jumping-off point for kayaking trips down the Mondego.

Figueira da Foz is the main resort on Portugal's **Costa da Prata** (Silver Coast), which stretches up to Porto. The famed town draws sun devotees to its broad wedge of pale sand—Europe's widest urban beach. In the grid of streets behind a high-rise seafront, are charming Art Deco buildings recalling the boom days of the 1920s and 1930s. Seekers of solitude can find unspoiled beaches like the 30km (19-mile) stretch of unbroken sand stretching north from **Praia de Quiaios.** Inland from here, the **Bairrada** wine region is renowned for Portugal's best sparkling wines among an array of excellent reds and whites. It's also home to some of the country's most atmospheric old spa hotels and one of its gastronomic treasures *leitão à Bairrada* (roast suckling pig).

The coastal city of **Aveiro** is Portugal's "Venice," crisscrossed by a network of canals leading out into its vast, mysterious, marshy lagoon. A tour in one of the colorful high-prowed *moliceiro* boats is a must.

Beyond the coastal strip, the two inland provinces of **Beira Alta** (Upper Beira) and **Beira Baixa** (Lower Beira) form a land of spartan beauty. Empty highlands are strewn with giant boulders and the

Coimbra & the Beiras

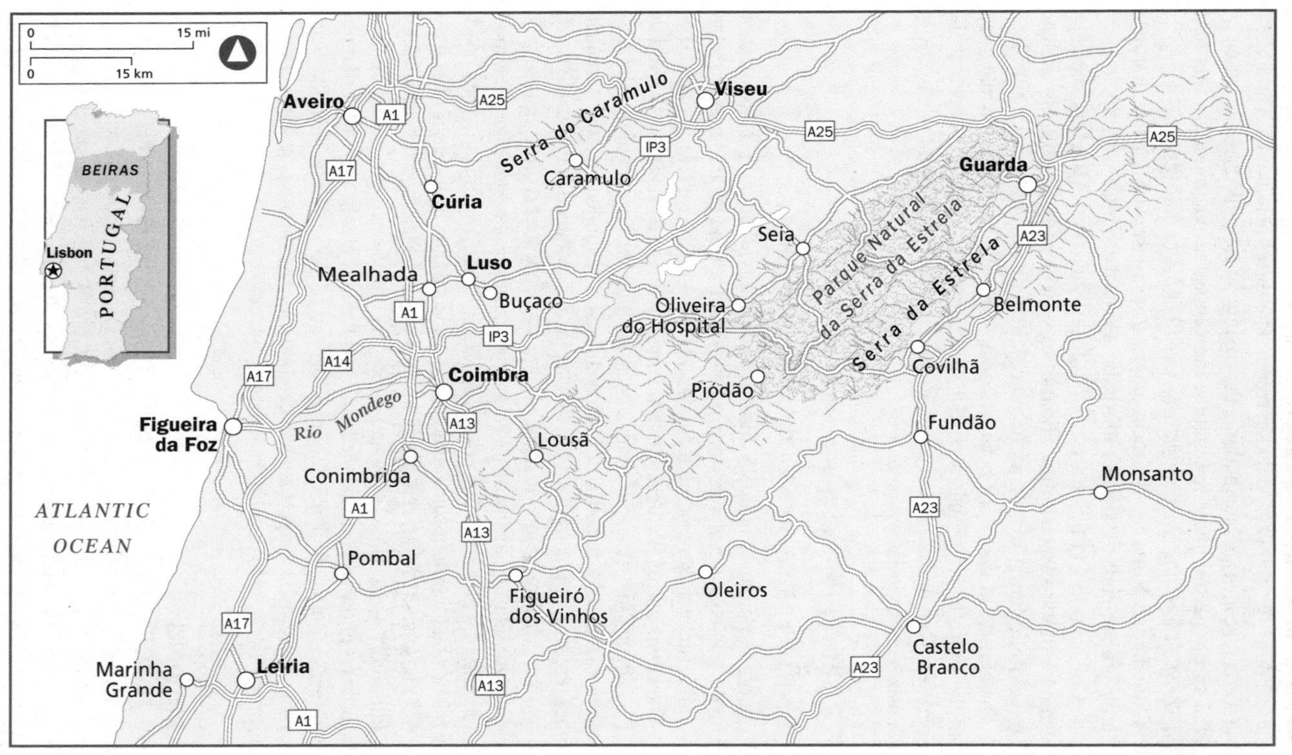

occasional rock-hewn village. They rise to peaks of almost 2,000 meters (6,562 ft.) in the **Serra da Estrela.** Mainland Portugal's highest mountain range boasts the country's only ski resort. The pistes may not be world class, but the landscapes are breathtaking, the creamy ewes'-milk cheeses crafted by local shepherds are to die for, and the indigenous Estrela mountain dog (*cão da Serra da Estrela*) is a shaggy, bear-sized bundle of cuteness.

Guarda and **Viseu** are the main cities of the Beira Alta, clustered around sturdy granite-built medieval cathedrals. Along the border with Spain are a string of historic fortified towns and villages, including **Almeida,** sheltered within a vast star-shaped fortress; **Belmonte,** with its unique Jewish history; and **Monsanto,** offering vast views from homes encrusted into a rocky hillside.

The climate of the interior can be harsh. Summers are hot and winters icy, but the Beira Baixa reveals a gentler side in spring, when the slopes of the **Serra da Gardunha** around **Fundão** are coated with the pink blossoms of countless cherry trees.

COIMBRA ★★★

118km (73 miles) S of Porto; 198km (123 miles) N of Lisbon

Coimbra is perhaps Portugal's most romantic city, thanks to its association with the tragic medieval love story of Pedro and Inês and the tradition of guitar-wielding students serenading their sweethearts with alfresco **fado** tunes.

The city is one of Portugal's oldest. It briefly served as capital in the Middle Ages, when King Afonso Henriques was pushing the borders of his kingdom southward. Its old cathedral, the Sé Velha, is a reminder of those turbulent times, constructed more like a fort than a place of worship, a defendable haven in case of Muslim counterattack. Coimbra's narrow streets are crammed with museums and monuments, from Roman granaries to baroque churches, most important of which is the university, founded in 1290. The old university buildings surround a hilltop square, including a spectacular 18th-century library.

All those students make Coimbra a lively place. Male and female students traditionally wear black suits and capes decorated with the colors of their faculties: yellow ribbons for medicine, red for law, etc. In early May, the ribbons are ceremonially burned to mark the end of the academic year, the spark for one of Europe's biggest student celebrations: the Queima das Fitas, a week of processions, fado concerts, and booze-fueled parties.

Essentials

ARRIVING

BY TRAIN Coimbra has two train stations: **Coimbra-A,** in the city center, and **Estação Coimbra-B,** 2km (1½ miles) north of downtown. Mainline trains from Lisbon and Porto stop at Coimbra-B, where you can change to a local shuttle train for the 4-minute trip to Coimbra A. Over 20 trains run daily to Coimbra from Lisbon's Oriente station, from 6:09am to 10:09pm. On the fastest Alfa-Pendular trains, the journey takes just over 1 hour 30 minutes. A second-class one-way ticket costs 22.80€. From Porto's Companhã station,

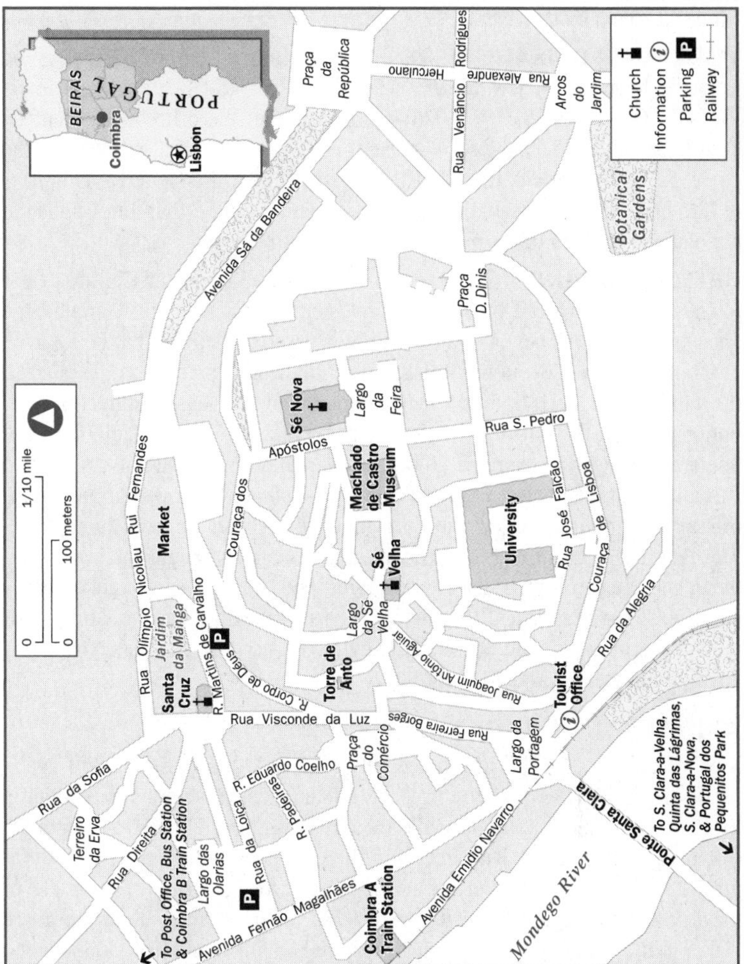

the journey to Coimbra takes around 1 hour and costs 16.70€. For tickets and information from the CP rail company: www.cp.com; © **77/210-22-20.**

BY BUS Buses leave from Lisbon roughly every 30 minutes for the 2½-hour trip to Coimbra, from 6:15am to just after midnight. Tickets cost 14.50€. From Porto, it's 12.50€ for the 1½-hour journey. Coimbra's **bus station** is on Avenida Fernão de Magalhães. For tickets and information at the Rede Expressos national bus company: www.rede-expressos.pt; © **70/722-33-44.**

BY CAR From Lisbon, it should take about 2 hours north on the A1 express highway. From Porto, it takes just over 1 hour heading south on the same road. If your hotel does not have a car park, driving and parking in the city center can be a challenge. It is sometimes possible to find free parking in side streets up by the modern part of the university. If not, there are a number of paying car parks down by the river.

VISITOR INFORMATION The main **Coimbra Tourist Office** is on Largo da Portagem (www.turismo-centro.pt; ✆ **23/948-81-20;** summer hours Mon–Fri 9am–8pm, Sat–Sun 9am–6pm, in winter the office opens half an hour later on weekends, closes between 12:30 and 1:30pm, and closes for the day at 5:30pm). The city tourist office website (http://turismodecoimbra.pt) is in dire need of an overhaul, but more information can be found in English at the national tourism department (www.visitcentro.com).

GETTING AROUND The narrow, often car-free streets of Coimbra's old town are best explored by foot. In fact, getting lost in a stroll around the ancient warren of lanes is one of the city's great pleasures. That being said, climbing from the downtown **Baixa** district to the university and other sites in the uphill **Alta** neighborhood can be tough on the legs. Public transport options include the safe and efficient bus network. As well as regular buses, it operates an **elevator** from the colorful food market up to the university from 7:30am to 9pm, and electric **buses** called *pantufinhas* that run a hop-on, hop-off service through the historic districts once or twice an hour in daytime. Tickets offering unlimited travel on all services can be bought for 3.50€ from the ticket office in front of the elevator. Single-journey tickets bought on buses are 1.60€. **Taxis** are plentiful and inexpensive. A trip from the Coimbra-A railway station to the old university should cost less than 5€. The central reservation number is: ✆ **23/949-90-90.**

Exploring Coimbra

Most of Coimbra's sights are shared between the **Alta** upper town, Portugal's academic center where the country's oldest and most prestigious **university** is located; and the **Baixa,** traditionally the city's commercial heart, although the stores along the elegant **Rua Ferreira Borges** and the maze of narrow shopping streets have suffered from the opening in recent years of a couple of mega malls on the outskirts. It's also worth taking a stroll along the green banks of the **Mondego River,** which inspired countless student fado singers, and crossing the river to visit the monasteries of the **Santa Clara** district.

Universidade de Coimbra ★★★ HISTORIC SITE Most visitors' first impression of the ancient university is something of a shock. Instead of buildings reflecting the medieval origins of this venerable house of learning, they are confronted with a row of very 20th-century monolithic faculty blocks constructed during the Salazar dictatorship and reflecting the Fascist-inspired architectural tastes of the time. Things change when you step through the 17th-century **Porta Férrea** (iron gate) leading to the university's inner core.

Inside is a harmonious quadrangle surrounded on three sides by the facades of buildings dating back to the 15th century, when the university was installed in what was a royal palace.

Grabbing the eye is a cloistered arcade, the **Via Latina** and the baroque clock tower, which has become a symbol of the city despite the unkind nickname, ***a cabra*** (the she-goat), given to it by generations of students called back to class by the tolling of its bell. Up the double staircase, where there may be a guitar-strumming student wrapped in the traditional black cape, you enter a series of ornate halls that for centuries have hosted grand royal and academic events. Most splendid is the **Sala Grande dos Actos** (Ceremonial Hall) decorated with red-damask walls, blue-and-white *azulejos* (tiles), and an intricately painted ceiling. Kings of Portugal once held court here. Their stern-faced portraits look down on the chamber where solemn ceremonies, such as formal opening of the school year and the handing out of doctoral awards, are still held.

Other highlights of the university tour include the **University Chapel**, its interior a blaze of blue-and-yellow *azulejos*, gold-covered altars, marble columns, and a glorious baroque organ. In contrast is the grim **Academic Prison.** Its cells, with their thick stone walls and iron-barred doorways, were used to punish badly behaved students from 1593 until 1834. The university's star attraction is the **Biblioteca Joanina,** one of Europe's great historic libraries. Named after its founder, King João V, who used the vast riches of newly discovered Brazilian gold mines to embellish the country with baroque monuments, the early-18th-century library contains over 300,000 books. Some are over 500 years old, including early accounts of the Portuguese Discoveries. You'll find volumes of historic or artistic import, opened and put on display in glass cabinets on the library's lower floor.

There are three high-ceilinged salons walled by two-story tiers of lacquer-decorated oak bookshelves. Pale jade-and-lemon-colored marble floors complement the gilded woodwork. Chinese-inspired patterns are painted on emerald, red, and gold lacquer work. The library tables are built of ebony and lustrous rosewood, imported from the former Portuguese colonies in India and Brazil. The overall effect is sumptuous.

Tickets can be bought at the store of the university's modern library building to the right of the Porta Férrea. There is a somewhat bewildering variety of ticket options for visiting different parts of the university. To see the main sights, a combined ticket allowing unguided access to the ceremonial chambers, chapel, and library costs 10€ for adults, 8€ for seniors 65 and over, and students under 26; it's free for children under 12. For a bit more you can customize, adding the 18th-century Physics Laboratory and Natural History collection (4€ more), or the tower (an extra 1€). Guided tours start at 12.5€. Due to limited space, the library door is opened every 20 minutes to let in a maximum of 60 people at a time.

Largo Porta Férrea. www.uc.pt. ✆ **23/985-98-00.** Mar 16–Oct 31 daily 9am–7:30pm; Nov 1–Mar 14 daily 9:30am–1pm, 2–5:30pm. Closed Dec. 24–25 and Jan. 1. Closed Jan. 31 at 4pm and May 8 at 1pm for the Queima das Fitas Parade to mark the end of the school year.

Sé Velha ★★ CHURCH Of Coimbra's two cathedrals, this is the older and most interesting one. Its fortress-like construction—plain stone with crenellated battlements and arrow-slit windows—is a reminder of the days when the Mondego was a front line in battles between Christians and Muslims for control of the Iberian Peninsula. Founded in 1170 by Portugal's founder king, Afonso Henriques, it is considered Portugal's best-preserved Romanesque cathedral. But inside, in the wide, atmospheric space beneath great barrel-arched roof, you'll see the lingering Islamic influence on Portuguese art (in the years of the *Reconquista*) on the plant and animal carvings at the tops of the columns and the geometric ceramic tile patterns. Look around and still *another* influence intrudes: Contrasting with the Romanesque simplicity, the main chapel is filled with a soaring flamboyant Gothic **retable** carved by Flemish artists in the 15 century with gilded sculptures telling the story of Christ. Sé Velha is conveniently located on the way down from the university to the Baixa district and it's surrounded by cafes, bars, and restaurants.

Largo Sé Velha. http://sevelha-coimbra.org. ✆ **23/982-52-73.** Free admission (requested donation of 2.50€). Mon–Sat 10am–6pm; Sun and religious holidays 1–6pm. Visits not permitted during services.

Museu Nacional de Machado de Castro ★★★ MUSEUM Even if it were empty, this museum would be worth a visit for the stunning historic building alone. Housed in a palace that was home to the city's bishops in Renaissance times, the upper floors contain an award-winning modern extension completed in 2012, including a cool cafe offering a panoramic view over the city. In the basement are the ruins of Coimbra's ancient Roman forum, where visitors can take a subterranean stroll through 1st-century warehouses and market stores. Comprised within is one of Portugal's best art collections. The focus is on medieval painting and sculptures, with masterpieces such as the Passion of Christ by Flemish artist Quentin Matsys, a golden chalice dating from the 12th century, and the haunting Last Supper, a monumental series of saintly sculptures shaped by Philippe Hodart in the 1530s. The 2012 renovation has created magnificently airy spaces to display such works at their best.

Largo Dr José Rodrigues. http://www.museumachadocastro.pt. ✆ **23/985-30-70.** 6€ adults, 3€ students and seniors 65 and over, free for children under 12. Wed–Sun 10am–6pm; Tues 2–6pm; closed Mon.

Mosteiro da Santa Cruz ★★ CHURCH The fabulous white-stone entrance of the Holy Cross Monastery looks out over **Praça 8 de Maio,** one of Coimbra's prettiest downtown plazas lined with little stores selling everything from handcrafted guitars to fine wines. The church dates back to the earliest days of the Portuguese kingdom in the 12th century, but the swirling white additions to the facade were built in 1507, a masterpiece of the Manueline, that uniquely Portuguese architectural style inspired by the age of maritime discoveries (ropes, sea plants, and ornate decorations that recall Indian temples—they're all in the mix). Inside is the **Gothic tomb** of Portugal's first king, Afonso Henriques, his feet resting on a lion. His son, Portugal's second King Sancho I, lies nearby. The rich decoration includes a **pulpit** carved by

Frenchman Jean de Rouen, and **choir stalls** that preserve, in carved configurations, the symbolism, mythology, and historic import of Portuguese exploration. With its twisted columns and 13th-century tombs, the two-tiered Gothic-Manueline **cloister** is impressive. All in all the church is a heady architectural cocktail of Gothic, Manueline, and Renaissance styles.

St. Anthony of Padua lived in the monastery as a young Franciscan friar in the 12th century. A century later, the church was the scene of the gruesome denouement of the Inês de Castro story, when King Pedro I had the body of his murdered lover dug up and crowned queen beside him (see p. 19).

Attached to the church is one of Portugal's nicest historic cafes. The **Café Santa Cruz,** opened in 1923, was built into an abandoned wing of the monastery in a monumental neo-Manueline style (splendid arched ceiling and stained-glass windows) that reflects its holy neighbor. It is one of the best places in town to hear **fado,** with regular free concerts at 6pm and 10pm (✆ **23/983-36-17** for dates.

Praça do 8 de Maio. ✆ **23/985-10-90.** Free admission. Mon–Fri 9am–5pm, Sat 9am–noon and 2–5pm; Sun 4–5:30pm.

Baixa ★★ NEIGHBORHOOD This downtown district was for centuries Coimbra's commercial heart. In recent years some of the life has been sucked out due to the construction of out-of-center shopping malls, particularly the giant **Forum Coimbra.** Nevertheless, the neighborhood retains great charm. It's also fighting back, with trendy new shops opening alongside traditional stores that give the narrow streets a souk-like buzz. The area's main drag is the elegant, boutique-lined **Rua Ferreira Borges,** now pedestrianized to provide a pleasant stroll between the Praça 8 de Maio and another cafe-lined plaza, the riverside Largo da Portagem. The **Café Briosa,** established in 1955, may just be the best place to try the Coimbra region's sinfully tasty pastries, like the *pasteis de Tentúgal* (cigar-shaped filo-pastry tubes with a cinnamon-scented filling) or the *pasteis de Santa Clara* (pastries filled with almond paste). Between Ferreira Borges and the river, the Baixa fragments into a maze of narrow alleys filled with quirky stores, where you can buy everything from a jersey of the local soccer club, Académica, to agricultural implements. At **Praça do Comércio,** the lanes broaden out into an elongated plaza surrounded by the narrow white facades of town houses reaching seven stories high. At the northern end of the plaza is the **Igreja de São Tiago,** one of the city's oldest churches, its earliest parts dating back to the 10th century. It's open Mon–Fri, 10am–5pm. Its Romanesque interior is gloomy and atmospheric.

Arco e Torre de Almedina ★ MONUMENT The arch and tower of Almedina form the gateway into the upper town, or Alto, leading to steps and lanes that clamber up toward the university. The Gothic arch and medieval tower form an imposing entry point into what was the Arab medina before the city fell to the Portuguese in 1064. Beyond, the sharply rising **Rua Quebra Costas** is Coimbra's most emblematic street. Its name, "back break street," references the difficulty in climbing up with a heavy load and the dangers of slipping on the steep stairs. Nowadays, it's lined with bars and shops, and is one of the best places to pick up a souvenir. At the top, close to the university and the museum, is the **Sé Nova,** or New Cathedral, once the home of the Jesuit order. Its rather austere Mannerist style inspired Portuguese colonial church builders from Brazil to India. Admission is free. It's open Mon–Sat 9am–6:30pm and Sun 10am–2pm.

Convento de Santa Clara-a-Nova ★ CHURCH On the left bank of the Mondego, on a hill with commanding views over the city, is the New Convent of St. Clara. Its gold-covered baroque interior is one of the best examples of *talho dourado*, the Portuguese art form that involves covering intricate carved woodwork in gold leaf. It surrounds a **silver casket** holding the remains of St. Elizabeth of Aragon, a 13th-century queen of Portugal revered for her work helping the poor and her peacemaking efforts between Spain and Portugal. There's a small museum dedicated to the saint and a peaceful double-decked renaissance cloister. In 2016, plans were announced to turn adjoining buildings once used as military barracks into a luxury hotel.

Alto de Santa Clara. ✆ **23/944-16-74.** 3€. Daily 9am–5pm.

Convento de Santa Clara-a-Velha ★ CHURCH The original Santa Clara convent was built down the hill on the riverbank by St. Elizabeth herself, when she lived with nuns of the Poor Clare after the death of her husband King Diniz in 1325. Unfortunately, the site was prone to flooding, and the fine Gothic structure was gradually swamped by mud, hence the building of the new convent up the hill, where the saint's remains were taken in the 17th century. The convent has undergone extensive restoration work to clear it of centuries of ooze, which, it turned out, had done an effective job of preserving much of the ruin's medieval decoration. It's also used as a site for summer concerts and outdoor theater productions.

Rua das Parreiras. ✆ **23/980-11-60.** 4€. Tues–Sun 10am–7pm.

Especially for Kids

Portugal dos Pequenitos ★ AMUSEMENT PARK "Portugal for the Little Ones" is a retro theme park built in the 1940s and dear to the heart of generations of Portuguese. Children can feel like Gulliver strolling through this Lilliputian world made up of miniature reconstructions of Portugal's main monuments and traditional homes from around the country. Since it was built in colonial times, there are also Indian temples, Chinese palaces, and African villages, surrounded by tropical vegetation. If all that wasn't sufficiently high on the kitsch quota, in 2013, the park got a new addition: a **Barbie Museum,** with over 300 of the diminutive beauties.

Just over the bridge from downtown in Largo Rossio de Santa Clara. www.portugaldospequenitos.pt. ✆ **23/980-11-70.** Admission 9.5€ adults, 5.95€ children and seniors. Jan–Feb and Oct–Dec daily 10am–5pm; Mar–May and Sept 16–Oct 15 daily 10am–7pm; June–Sept 15 daily 9am–8pm.

Museu da Ciência ★ MUSEUM Up on university hill, the charmingly eccentric Science Museum combines collections of gemstones, stuffed animals, and mockups of 18th-century chemistry labs with state-of-the-art interactive exhibits to fire up young imaginations. Nominated for a European Museum of the Year Award when it opened in 2006, it is housed in a graceful old neoclassical palace.

Situated in Largo Marquês de Pombal, next to the Sé Nova. www.museudaciencia.org. ✆ **23/985-43-50.** Admission 4€ adults, 2€ students, teachers, and seniors. Tue–Sun 10am–6pm.

Parque Biológico da Serra da Lousã ★ ZOO A stroll through forested slopes takes you to enclosures containing animals who live, or once lived, in the Portuguese interior. There are deer, foxes, boar, lynx, wolves, and bears on show. The park also has a handicraft store and an excellent restaurant, the **Museu da Chanfana,** which rather incongruously serves some of the animals you've just seen in the park (the best dish on the menu: chanfana, which is aged goat slow-cooked in red wine, a local specialty).

Outside the hilltown of Miranda do Corvo, half an hour outside Coimbra. ✆ **23/953-84-44.** Entry 6€ adults, 4€ children. 10am–6pm in winter, 9am–7pm in summer.

For some open-air fun right in the city, head to the Parque Verde Mondego (Avenida Emídio Navarro, free, open 24 hours), a cool riverside park that opened in 2004. It contains bike paths, a skate park, playgrounds, a swimming pool, and waterfront cafes, with bikes, canoes, and pedaloes to rent. Leading architects have designed the exhibition halls, and a footbridge spans the river named after the tragic lovers Pedro and Inês.

Older children will enjoy an adventurous kayak trip down the Mondego from the pretty upriver town of Penacova to Coimbra. The longest established company offering the service is O Pioneiro do Mondego (www.opioneirodomondego.com; ✆ **23/947-83-85**). Cost is 22.50€ for adults, less for students and groups, transport from Coimbra included), founded by a Belgian couple in 1988. They offer two trips from Penacova, one 18km (11 miles) lasting 3 to 4 hours to Torre de Mondego, the other a full 25km (15 miles) into Coimbra itself. For most of the trip the current pushes you through the thickly forested banks, but there are a couple of modest rapids to get the adrenalin going and a sandy beach where you can picnic or take a dip.

Where to Stay

EXPENSIVE

Hotel Quinta das Lágrimas ★★★ The most luxurious place in town, the "Estate of Tears" gets its name from the medieval love story of Pedro and Inês de Castro. She was murdered on the quinta's grounds and it's said her tears were transformed into a pure, fresh stream of water that still bubbles forth in the garden. The red color of the rocks is reputedly stains from her spilled blood. The building traces its roots back almost 700 years; guests have included the Duke of Wellington, an emperor of Brazil, and various kings of Portugal. Today's visitors can choose between romantic rooms in the old building reflecting the palatial 18th-century style, or the cool, contemporary new spa wing, which offers individual Jacuzzis and views over the lush tropical gardens. It's a 15-minute walk to the city center.

Rua António Augusto Gonçalves. www.quintadaslagrimas.pt. ✆ **23/980-23-80.** 57 units. 100€–260€ double, including breakfast. Free parking. **Amenities:** Restaurant; bar; room service; babysitting; exercise room; 9-hole golf course; 2 pools (1 heated indoor); spa. Free Wi-Fi.

MODERATE

Hotel Astória ★★ A Coimbra landmark dating back to the 1920s, in a mixture of Belle Epoque, Art Nouveau, and Art Deco styles, the wedge-shaped building is a exuberant collection of cupolas, balconies, and wrought-iron balustrade arches. The location is swell, in the heart of the city looking out over the river. As for the rooms: "faded grandeur" are the words that come to mind. The Astoria may not have all the "mod cons," but the rooms are comfortable, with high ceilings, windows looking out over the Mondego or the old city, and period furnishings. The reception and bar are a step back to the Jazz Age. Perfect for those seeking old-world elegance, even if it's a bit creaky.

Av. Emídio Navarro 21. www.themahotels.pt. ✆ **23/985-30-20.** 62 units. 55€–156€ double, including breakfast. No parking. **Amenities:** Bar; babysitting; concierge; room service. Free Wi-Fi.

Hotel Oslo ★★ It might not look much from the outside, but beyond the drab, 1960s exterior, this is an excellent, mid-price downtown option. The quirky, 1960s decor mixes Nordic-style design with lots of pale pine with traditional Portuguese textiles and Coimbra ceramics. The rooftop bar—and several of the upper-floor rooms—offer some of the best views of the city. Although windows are double-paned to keep out the street noise, it might be better to ask for room at the back if you're a light sleeper. The superior rooms are perhaps a better choice for a small extra price. They have floor-to-ceiling windows and private verandas. Free valet parking is another plus.

Av. Fernão de Magalhães 25. www.hoteloslo-coimbra.pt. ✆ **23/982-90-71.** 36 units. 65€–165€ double, including breakfast. Free valet parking. **Amenities:** Bar; sun terrace; family rooms; bikes; room service. Free Wi-Fi.

Palácio da Lousã ★★ This beautifully restored aristocratic 18th-century residence is in Lousã, a small town up in the hills about a half-hour drive from Coimbra. Its soft pastel furnishings recall the time when it was built by one of the region's grandest families. Rooms are divided between the palace and a modern new wing. During the Napoleonic wars, the palace was the scene of a famous incident, when the French general occupying the palace fled so fast from a surprise British attack that the Duke of Wellington was able to sit in the dining room and enjoy the meal prepared for his foe. The restaurant today retains great period charm and serves such delights as duck basted in the local Beirão liquor.

Rua Viscondessa do Espinhal, Lousã. www.palaciodalousa.com. ✆ **23/999-08-00.** 46 units. 50€–130€ double, including breakfast. Free parking. **Amenities:** Outdoor pool; terrace; garden; bar; restaurant; children's play area; games room. Free Wi-Fi.

Pousada de Condeixa ★★ Part of the Pousada chain of luxury inns, this hotel in the small town of Condeixa, 16km (10 miles) southwest of Coimbra, is a perfect base for visiting the nearby Roman ruins of **Conímbriga.** It's housed in a noble manor house with red roof tiles dating back to the 16th century, although much restored prior to its opening in 1993. The furnishings feature many antiques, and rooms are spacious with tiled bathrooms. There are extensive gardens and an outdoor pool that's perfect for cooling off after a day of sightseeing.

Rua Francisco Lemos, 3–5, Condeixa-a-Nova. www.pousadadecondeixa-coimbra.com. ✆ **23/994-40-25.** 43 units. 95€–120€ double, including breakfast. Free parking. **Amenities:** Outdoor pool; garden; restaurant; bar; children's play area; babysitting. Free Wi-Fi.

Tivoli Coimbra ★ The well-established Tivoli group has built a deserved reputation for discreet quality and service. The Coimbra hotel is no exception—it's functional and comfortable, although perhaps lacking a bit in charm. The midsize rooms are light and airy, with tasteful patterned wallpapers, spacious desks, and widescreen TVs. Some rooms offer views over the city, others overlook the small garden behind the hotel. It's a pleasant 10-minute walk to the heart of downtown.

Rua João Machado 4–5. www.tivolihotels.com. ✆ **23/985-83-00.** 100 units. 77€–132€, including breakfast. Parking 8€ per day. **Amenities:** Restaurant; bar; room service; babysitting. Free Wi-Fi.

Tryp Coimbra ★ This is a functional modern hotel in a quiet residential area near the University Hospital but out of the center—it's a 30-minute walk to the old university. All of the midsize guest rooms are completely soundproof, and tastefully and comfortably furnished. Light wood furniture predominates, and beige and brown accents are used nicely. The atmosphere is so uncluttered that the hotel almost appears Japanese in its simplicity. It's comfortable and businesslike, if lacking in local color. The Japanese theme is echoed in the well-reputed restaurant, which serves sushi as well as modern-Portuguese cuisine. It has bikes that guests can use for free if they leave a deposit.

Av. Armando Gonçalves 20. www1.melia.com. ✆ **23/948-08-00.** 133 units. 55€–107€ double, including breakfast. Parking 7.50€ per day. **Amenities:** Restaurants; bar; loaner bikes. Free Wi-Fi.

Vila Galé Coimbra ★★ Portugal's Vila Galé group is best known for its seaside hotels, and this ultra-modern hotel has the air of a beach resort in the city center. The L-shaped, white-stone-and-glass four-story building is wrapped around the wide, riverside outdoor pool. When the weather is cooler, there's an indoor pool, spa, and fitness center. Rooms are spacious, with about half offering views over the pool and the Mondego, although some guests complain that the railway line running between the pool and the river spoils the vista. It's a 10-minute walk to downtown.

Rua Abel Dias Urbano, 20. www.vilagale.com. ✆ **23/924-00-00.** 229 units. 107€–135€, including breakfast. Parking 7.50€ per day. **Amenities:** 2 restaurants; bar; family rooms; pools; spa; sauna; Turkish bath; gym. Free Wi-Fi.

INEXPENSIVE

Casa Pombal ★ Tucked away in a winding hillside alley close to the university, Casa Pombal is a completely unpretentious guest house run by a Dutch lady, with simple, clean rooms, with just a touch of kitschy hominess. It feels a bit like the house of a kindly aunt you'd love to visit. There's a Dutch-style breakfast (cheese, ham, eggs) or vegetarian options that you can take either in a room decorated with gorgeous dark-blue Portuguese tiles, or on a cute, flower-filled patio out back. The cheaper rooms have shared bathrooms. Charming, with very helpful staff, but with few amenities, and parking can be tricky.

Rua das Flores 18. http://casapombal.com. ✆ **23/983-51-75.** 9 units. 37€–65€ double, including breakfast. **Amenities:** Terraces. Free Wi-Fi.

Serenata Hostel ★★ Taking its name from the moonlight serenades sung by Coimbra's wandering fado singers, this is the city's premier hostel. Located in an early-20th-century town house that once served as a maternity hospital and a music school, today it's a vibrant meeting place for travelers, offering both private rooms and dorms for up to 10 people, with bunk beds and private lockers. The private rooms and suites are of the standard of a good boutique hotel, although some have shared bathrooms. The location couldn't be more central, right next to the medieval Sé Velha cathedral. Decor is stylishly shabby-chic, with many of the building's original features maintained. Walls are decorated with large-scale line drawings of Portuguese cultural figures and handwritten poetry quotations. This place can be noisy, and not just from serenading singers.

Largo da Sé Velha, 21/23. www.serenatahostel.com. ✆ **23/985-31-30.** 18 units. 39€–55€ double; 15€–18€ dormitory bed. Rates include breakfast. **Amenities:** Bar; dining room; kitchen; reading room. Free Wi-Fi.

Where to Dine

EXPENSIVE

Arcadas ★★★ MODERN PORTUGUESE Coimbra isn't overflowing with fine dining options, but the swish restaurant at the Hotel Quinta das Lágrimas is one of Portugal's foremost gourmet experiences. Chef Vítor Dias, who took over in 2015 at just 35, uses fresh, seasonal produce, with many of his fruits, vegetables, and herbs grown organically in the hotel garden. The menu changes with the seasons, but typical dishes include duck with wild berries and orange gnocchi, or mixed fish in lobster sauce with samphire. Desserts include pineapple petals with pink pepper, coconut, and *pão-de-ló*, a local sponge cake. Dias's dishes are a visual delight, combining forms, textures, and colors to make each plate a work of art. The restaurant is located in the old palace stables, its arched windows overlooking a lush, tropical garden. There's a terrific selection of wines, with a focus on the Dão and Bairrada regions just north of Coimbra.

Rua António Augusto Gonçalves. www.quintadaslagrimas.pt. ✆ **23/980-23-80.** Main courses 32€–34€; fixed-price menus 60€–95€. Daily 7:30–10pm.

MODERATE

Casa do Bragal ★★ PORTUGUESE A refined yet relaxed place serving traditional Portuguese food with a modern touch. The dining room is decorated with striking paintings by the owner, featuring portraits of Portuguese divas like *fadista* Mariza or *Pulp Fiction* star Maria de Medeiros. There are always seasonal variations, but roast kid is the signature dish, served with roast potatoes, rice cooked with the goat's offal, and broccoli raab. Fish options include filets of John Dory with roe and rice, or salt cod cooked with onions and vintage port. Located east of the city center in a leafy residential suburb, it's well worth making the trip out, especially for those with a sweet tooth—the buffet of traditional desserts is legendary. There's an attractive terrace for a pre-dinner aperitif.

Urbanização de Tamonte – Rua Damião de Gois. ✆ **91/810-39-88.** Main courses 11€–30€. Wed–Sun 12:20–2:30pm, Tues–Sat 7:30–10:30pm.

O Trovador ★ PORTUGUESE A romantic place in the city's heart just in front of the old cathedral, "the Troubadour" offers the chance to eat traditional Portuguese food in refined surroundings and listen to some of Coimbra's best guitarists and fado singers. There are *azulejos*, vintage photos of the city and its illustrious inhabitants on the walls; and white-shirted waiters providing old-fashioned good service. The *chanfana à Senhor da Serra*, an emblematic dish from the hills above Coimbra involving goat slow-cooked in red wine, is excellent here.

Largo Sé Velha, 15. www.restaurantetrovador.com. ✆ **23/982-54-75.** Mains 9€–14€. Mon–Sat noon–3pm and 7–10pm.

Solar do Bacalhau ★ PORTUGUESE This used to be an Italian restaurant. When it reverted to serving traditional Portuguese food in 2014, they kept the wood-fired oven and still serve pizza. However, salt cod or *bacalhau* is the main attraction. This Portuguese staple is served fried with onions, peppers, and tomato sauce, baked in the traditional Coimbra style with smoked ham and crumbled cornbread, and a number of other ways. Perhaps the most challenging dish for outsiders is *arroz de línguas de bacalhau*, a creamy, risotto-like mix of rice and salted cod tongues. There's also a range of fresh fish and meat dishes, with a focus on beef. Downtown Coimbra's biggest restaurant, this bustling place spreads over two floors and around a central, glass-roofed atrium. The decor is a mix of modern and rustic, with wooden floors, stone walls, and antiques.

Rua da Sota, 12. www.solardobacalhau.pt. ✆ **23/909-89-90.** Main courses 7€–14€. Daily noon–3pm, 7pm–midnight.

INEXPENSIVE

Fangas Mercearia & Bar ★ PETISCOS The Portuguese equivalent of Spain's tapas are *petiscos*, and this friendly, trendy place amid the narrow streets leading up the university is the place to sample them. Bright colors dominate, with a stylized cityscape painting on one wall, bold stripes on another. There's a vast range of snacks and light meals to share—tinned tuna with oregano, marinated mussels, grilled blood sausage, partridge paté—best washed down with a glass of sangria or something from the extensive Portuguese wine list. You can also drop in for a coffee or tea with one of their delicious sweets, like apple pie with *queijo da serra* (sheep's cheese).

Rua Fernandes Tomás 45/9. www.fangas.pt. ✆ **93/409-36-36.** Snacks from 4€–15€. Daily noon–4pm and 7pm–12:30am.

Nacional ★★ PORTUGUESE Off the beaten track on a side street on the northern edge of the Baixa, this place was a renowned billiards hall before it was turned into a spacious, second-floor restaurant in 1977. Now it's an institution where generations of families, office workers, and groups of friends come to enjoy home-style Portuguese comfort food. There's modern art on the bare stone walls, but also a feeling little has changed here for years. A selection of regular specials is offered each day of the week. Friday, for example, offers *cozido à Portuguesa* (mixed boiled meats, traditional smoked sausages, boiled vegetables, and rice); *pato assado à Ribatejana* (roast duck, giblets in rice, and smoked sausages); or *bacalhau à Vila Nova* (fried salt cod with mayonnaise and mashed potatoes). Old school, but delicious. A half-portion (*meia dose*) will satisfy all but the most gargantuan appetites.

Rua Mário Pais, 12. www.en.restaurantenacional.pt. ✆ **23/982-94-20.** Mains 6.50€–8.50€ (half-portions). Mon–Sat noon–3pm and 7–midnight.

Zé Manuel dos Ossos ★★ PORTUGUESE As a student town for centuries, Coimbra is filled with backstreet taverns serving hearty, cut-price cooking. This is perhaps the most famous, serving up the likes of roast baby goat (*cabrito asado no forno*), bean stew with wild boar (*feijoada de javali*), or ribs with beans and rice (*ossos com arroz de feijão*). It's tiny, cramped, and you'll probably have to stand in line to get in because they don't take reservations. But a meal squashed in beneath the hundreds of messages of appreciation stuck to the walls by grateful students—along with other oddities like a bespectacled stuffed boar's head and an alligator hanging from the ceiling—will undoubtedly be a memorable occasion. A half-portion (*meia dose*) will normally more than suffice for one hungry person.

Beco do Forno, 12. ✆ **23/982-37-90.** Mains 5€–8€ (half-portion). Mon–Sat noon–3pm and Mon–Fri 7:30–10pm.

Shopping

Along **Rua Ferreira Borges,** up the steep **Rua Quebra Costas** and through the warren of lanes making up the **Baixa,** there's a plethora of small stores selling potential souvenirs, from CDs of Coimbra fado to handmade conserves, colored wool blankets from the hills, or hammered copper work. The most authentic buy in Coimbra is **pottery,** handpainted in colorful, centuries-old designs (clay plates, pitchers, vases, boxes, and much more). Tradition patterns feature birds, animals, and flowers, which clearly show the Arabic influence on Portuguese artwork of the time. **Casa de Artesanato da Sé Velha,** Largo Sé Velha, 1 (✆ **23/983-61-19**) has a huge pottery selection.

While much of the work is actually produced in and around Condeixa, just to the south of Coimbra, you can watch artist **Carlos Tómas** at work and buy some of his creations at Largo Sé Velha, 4 (© **23/981-29-45**).

Coimbra After Dark

The city's large student population guarantees an active, sometimes raucous nightlife. You'll find plenty of **bars** around **Largo Sé Velha,** packed with students, professors, and locals who drink, gossip, and discuss politics. **Bar Quebra Costas,** on Escadas de Quebra Costas, 45/49 (© **23/984-11-74**) is one of the oldest and most popular spots. There are also several late-night hangouts around Praça da República that are popular with students. Quirky **Aqui Base Tango** (Rua Venâncio Rodrigues 8; http://aquibasetango.com; © **23/982-16-90;** closed Mon) may be the most interesting. Housed in a pink-painted former police station, it has fab cocktails and eclectic music ranging from bossa nova to indie rock that spills over from the retro interior into a cool garden.

For late-night **fado,** head for **À Capella,** Rua Corpo de Deus (www.acapella.com.pt; © **23/983-39-85**), which was turned into a cafe from a chapel constructed back in 1364. Open daily 4pm–3am, it offers nightly performances starting from 9:30pm. An earlier alternative is **Fado ao Centro,** Rua de Quebra Costas 7 (www.fadoaocentro.com; © **91/323-67-25**). It provides a great introduction to the music, with daily 6pm performances from top-class musicians lasting 50 minutes. They'll also explain the often mysterious world of fado and are happy to chat after the show over a glass of port that's included in 10€ entry fee. The atmospheric **Café Santa Cruz** (Praça 8 de Maio; www.cafesantacruz.com; (© **23/983-36-17**) also has daily free fado performances at 10pm and occasional shows at 6pm.

Movie fans can visit the multiple screens in the **Alma** shopping mall, Rua General Humberto Delgado (© **23/979-80-90**) or the **Fórum Coimbra** mall (© **70/724-63-62**). For a more intimate experience, try the University theater at **Teatro Académico de Gil Vicente,** Praça da República, www.tagv.pt, © **23/985-56-36,** which also hosts regular concerts and plays as well as movies.

Side Trips Around Coimbra

One of Europe's great Roman archeological finds, **Conímbriga ★★**, is 16km (10 miles) southwest of Coimbra. A stroll around the ruins will give you a taste of everyday life in Rome's Lusitania province from the time of Emperor Augustus in the 1st century A.D. There's a forum, a theater, thermal baths, and the later addition of a Christian basilica, but the private houses are the most fascinating, giving a real insight into domestic life from the 1st to 3rd centuries. The homes have colonnaded courtyards, fountain-filled gardens, and magnificent mosaics showing scenes of hunting and mythology, or geometric patterns in blood red, mustard, gray, sienna, and yellow. An on-site museum shows the development of the site from Celtic village to thriving provincial town until its destruction by Germanic invaders in the 5th century.

The ruins are open daily 9am–8pm (until 6pm in winter), Tues–Sun. Admission is 4.50€ (www.conimbriga.pt; ✆ **23/994-11-77).**

For travelers without a car, buses leave every half-hour weekdays from the Coimbra bus terminal to the little town of Condeixa, which is just a 1.8km (1-mile) walk or short taxi trip to the Roman site. If you fancy lunch, the charming main square in Condeixa has a number of restaurants specializing in roast kid (cabrito asado). **O Regional do Cabrito** is a safe bet, Praça da República, 14 (✆ **23/994-49-33).**

If you have a car, winding roads through hills to the east of Coimbra provide a chance to get in touch with a hidden side of Portugal, where culinary, cultural, and handicraft traditions run deep. In the **Serra da Lousã ★** and **Serra do Açor ★** hills, the **Aldeias do Xisto** initiative is an attempt to inject new life into highland villages that were suffering from desertification as younger people moved to the cities. Twenty-seven villages constructed from the dark local schist stones are included, many hosting shops that sell local crafts including basketwork, woolen blankets, honey, and liquors. They also organize hiking, cross-country biking, kayaking, and other outdoor activities. For more information, go to http://aldeiasdoxisto.pt (✆ **27/564-77-00**).

The website also lists rural restaurants and accommodations, ranging from rustic home stays to luxury hotels.

One of the most imposing of the small towns in the hills is **Penela ★**, a half-hour drive south from Coimbra. Its heart is a cluster of whitewashed homes sheltering beneath the imposing medieval **castle,** another reminder of the days of *reconquista*, when it formed part of a network of defenses against Muslim counterattacks. Admission is free. It's open daily 9am–7pm (until 9pm Apr–Sept). Sheep and goats roaming the hillsides here are used to make ***queijo de Rabaçal,*** mild cheeses tasting of wild herbs that come in hockey-puck-size rounds. Along the main street in the village of Rabaçal you can buy from cafes, stores, and private homes of small producers.

While the Mondego upriver from Coimbra winds through forested hills, once it's through the city, the river broadens out and flows gently to the Atlantic through marshes, rice paddies, and salt flats. Dominating the flat landscape is the imposing **castle** of **Montemor-o-Velho ★**, 28km (17 miles) west of Coimbra on the road to the ocean. This was another bastion in the medieval fight for control of Portugal, captured from the Moors in 1064. The fortress was expanded over the years and its current form dates mostly from the 14th century. There's a gem of a Romanesque church within its walls, and a modern teahouse (*casa de chá*) built into the ruins of the *Paço das Infantas* (Princesses' Palace).

A prized specialty in the watery lands around Montemor is duck served roasted (*pato assado*) or with rice (*arroz de pato*). One of the best places to try such delights is **Casa Arménio ★★** in the village of **Tentúgal,** on Rua Mourão between Coimbra and Montemor (meals around 15€, ✆ **23/995-11-75**). This rustic restaurant located in an old aristocratic manor house is a temple to regional cuisine. The staff are friendly, but this is very much a local favorite with little preparation for international visitors, but the food is divine. Finish off with some of the almond-egg-cinnamon confections that have their origins in the nearby convent and are now favorite sweet treats around the country. There are also a number of good cafes serving *pasteis de Tentúgal* and other wonderful regional pastries: Bustling **Pousadinha ★★,** Estrada Nacional 111 (✆ **23/995-11-58**), is perhaps the best.

FIGUEIRA DA FOZ ★

140km (90 miles) S of Porto; 200km (125 miles) N of Lisbon; 50km (30 miles) W of Coimbra

With Europe's largest urban **beach,** 2.5km (1.6 miles) long and 600m (2,000 ft.) at its widest, Figueira has been attracting sunseekers since the 19th century, and remains a popular vacation destination of Portuguese families and Spaniards, who race down the highway to hit the sand here every summer.

These days, the beach is backed by a jumble of steel, glass, and concrete high-rises, which give it something of mini Copacabana feel. However, some remnants of the more elegant Belle Epoque and Art Deco constructions of the resort's golden age can be found in streets behind the waterfront, particularly in the **Bairro Novo** district, just inland from the Mondego.

Figueira in summer is a busy, happening place, with its **casino** hosting big-name concerts. The size of the beach means there's always space for the colorful, candy-striped beach huts and tents. Sunsets are amazing.

Anyone seeking a quieter time can head over the **Serra da Boa Viagem,** a mountainous, forest-covered headland to the wild and wonderful **Praia de Quiaios** beach, or a string of popular surfing spots south of the Mondego River.

Essentials

ARRIVING

BY TRAIN Trains arrive at Largo da Estação (✆ **80/820-82-08**) near the river. Sixteen trains per day arrive from Coimbra. The trip lasts just over 1 hour. One-way tickets are 2.30€.

BY BUS The bus station, **Terminal Rodoviário,** is next door at Avenida Saraiva de Carvalho – Largo da Estação (✆ **70/722-33-44**). Four buses a day arrive from Lisbon; the trip takes around 3 hours and costs 16€ one-way. The Moises bus company (✆ **23/982-82-63**) runs buses from Coimbra to Figueira for 4.30€. There are nine trips per day during the week, five on Saturdays and two on Sundays, and the journey takes around 1 hour and 30 minutes one-way.

BY CAR From Lisbon, it's a 2-hour drive up the A8 and A17 toll highways.

VISITOR INFORMATION

The **Figueira da Foz Tourist Office** is on Avenida do 25 de Abril (www.visitcentrodeportugal.com.pt/figueira-da-foz; ✆ **23/342-26-10**) and is open daily 9:30am–1pm and 2–5:30pm.

Exploring Figueira da Foz

Figueira is easily explored on foot. A good place to start is the **Forte de Santa Catarina** fortress perched at the mouth of the Mondego. Built in the 17th century to ward off pirates, it now houses a seafood restaurant and offers a fine view over the beach and the curving, cafe-laden Av. 25 de Abril running along the waterfront. A good place for a break is the **Geladaria Emanha Avenida ★**, Av. 25 de Abril, ✆ **23/342-65-67,** which has been serving handmade ice cream for generations. Open in summer from 10am–2am, in winter 1pm–midnight.

Most visitors don't come to Figueira to look at museums, but there are a couple of good ones. In a country famed for its own ceramic tiles, the **Casa do Paço ★**, Largo Prof. Vítor Guerra 4 (www.cm-figfoz.pt/index.php/onde-ir/casa-paco, ✆ **23/343-01-03,** Tues–Sat 10am–5pm, admission 2.45€ adult, 1.20€ children and seniors) contains one of the world's greatest collections of 18th-century **Delft tiles** from the Netherlands, numbering almost 7,000, depicting landscapes, ships, and warriors with gaudy plumage, among other things. Nobody is quite sure how they got here, but local legend has it they were recovered from a Dutch frigate wrecked off the beach in 1706. The collection is housed in a neoclassical palace fronted by a bougainvillea-rich garden. It was the center of Figueira's social life in the 19th century when royalty attended balls there.

Up the hill, the **Museu Municipal Santos Rocha ★**, Rua Calouste Gulbenkian (✆ **23/340-28-40)** is a low-rise modern building housing an eclectic collection ranging from medieval sculpture to historic firearms, perhaps the most interesting of which relate to Portugal's colonial past, with artifacts from Africa, South America, and Asia. There's an abundance of Indo-Portuguese furniture resulting from a fusion of styles in the colonial days of the 17th century. In summer it's open Tues–Fri, 9:30am–6pm, weekends 2–7pm. In winter it's closed all day Sun and weekdays from 5pm. Admission is 2€ for adults.

OUTDOOR ACTIVITIES Figueira's main attraction is the beach. The main urban beach, known as **Praia da Claridade ★★**, has a Sahara-like vastness. It can take 5 minutes to reach the ocean along the wooden boardwalks that run toward it from the promenade. The beach has soccer fields, volleyball pitches, and cycle paths. At the northern end, the beach narrows as it approaches the **Buarcos ★** neighborhood, once a fishing village, which has many cafes and restaurants and a cozier feel than the main Figueira strip. The strand here has some rocky coves and is popular with windsurfers.

For solitude, take a ride over the towering **Serra da Boa Viagem ★** hills that reach the Atlantic at the **Cabo Mondego** promontory. The views over the city and the wilder coast to the north are spectacular, especially at sunset. Unfortunately, the site is scarred by an abandoned cement works; however, it is not visible from many of the viewpoints and there are plans to recover the land. Beyond the cape, the great **Praia de Quiaios ★★★** stretches away to the horizon, backed by dunes and pine forest. There is a small settlement with a couple of restaurants and a small hotel, but for mile after mile, there is just beach. It is one of Portugal's best beaches, but be aware that tides and waves on the west coast can be dangerous. Don't swim if there's a red flag flying. If in doubt, ask the lifeguard stationed near the beach restaurant through the summer season.

South of the Mondego, there's a string of excellent beaches, too, which are very popular with surfers from around Europe. The fine white sand and regular waves of **Praia do Cabedelo ★★** are a particular favorite.

Where to Stay

Eurostars Oasis Plaza ★★★ Opened in 2014, the futuristic 15-story building was inspired by the curving forms of a classic cruise liner, its prow pointing toward the ocean. A flagship of the Spanish Eurostars group, it provides state-of-the-art comfort. The suites are a spacious 50 sq. meters (540 sq. ft.) with balconies and sea views. Furnishings are in soft earth colors. The beach is just across the avenue, but you may not want to tear yourself from the top floor indoor pool with its wide Atlantic views.

Avenida do Brasil. www.eurostarsoasisplaza.com. ✆ **23/320-00-10.** 166 units. 85€–260€ double with breakfast. Parking 10€ per day. **Amenities:** 3 bars; 2 restaurants; indoor pool; gym; room service. Free Wi-Fi.

Mercure Figueira da Foz ★★ This renovated 1950s-era hotel, on the seafront promenade overlooking the ocean, has an undeniable retro charm. An architectural landmark, it could do with a bit of freshening up, but has a primo seafront location, is close to the casino, and next door to the Figueira Beach Club pool complex. The interior is a world of marble and glass, with some cute vintage Portuguese tapestries in the lobby. Most rooms have ocean views and balconies.

Av. do 25 de Abril 22. www.accorhotels.com. ✆ **23/340-39-00.** 102 units. 75€–175€ double with breakfast. **Amenities:** Restaurant; bar; room service. Free Wi-Fi.

Paintshop Hostel ★ Probably not the place to go if you want a quiet break, this is a hip, fun place for the surf-and-party crowd. We're talking budget accommodations and a cool vibe, plus bike, board, and wetsuit hire. There are funky private rooms for couples and discount dorms for groups. The English owners organize regular BBQ and pizza nights, and there's a hip bar and patio out back for hanging out and making friends. It's closed from mid-October through April. Located in a typical Figueira town house down a side street a short walk from the beach and the station.

Rua da Clemencia, 9. www.paintshophostel.com. ✆ **23/343-66-33.** 8 units. 45€–50€ double, 18€–20€ dormitory beds, breakfast included. **Amenities:** Bar; bike rental. Free Wi-Fi.

Sweet Atlantic ★★ Great views and pampering are the trademarks of this ultra-modern tower overlooking the beach. The building's blue-glass facade dominates much of Figueira's beachfront skyline. As the sun sets over the Atlantic the building turns the color of burnished copper. On-site restaurant choices range from modern Portuguese to Japanese. Most rooms open onto water views. Bathrooms are stocked with Sundari beauty products. Studio suites offer balconies and a separate living room, plus small kitchenettes. The spa is perhaps the most complete and relaxing in town.

Av. 25 de 3 Abril 21. www.sweethotels.pt. ✆ **23/340-89-00.** 68 units. 82€–210€ double, including breakfast. **Amenities:** Restaurant; bar; spa; babysitting; room service. Free Wi-Fi.

Universal Boutique Hotel ★★ A salmon-colored four-story town house in the quaint Bairro Novo neighborhood on a side street, a block from the beach, Universal was recently renovated and oozes low-key glamour. Its style is softly contemporary with antique touches, like the patrician portraits in the stylish first-floor bar. Some rooms are on the small side, and those under the sloping attic roof mean guests have to watch bumping their heads, but they are romantic, with pastel colors and soft lights. A cozy contrast to the big beachfront options.

Rua Miguel Bombarda 50. ✆ **23/309-01-10.** 29 units. 57€–175€ double. Breakfast 10€ per person. **Amenities:** Bar; babysitting; bike hire. Free Wi-Fi.

Where to Eat

Casa Havanesa ★ PETISCOS Open since 1885, this place has been a tobacco store (hence the name—"house of Havana"), grocery, drugstore, bookshop, and photographer's studio. It's always been a meeting place, part of the city's fabric in the heart of the Bairro Novo. Today, Casa Havanesa overflows with a jumble of books, wine crates, sardine cans, and artifacts that recall past days. You can pop in for coffee, a drink (their gin selection is legendary), *petiscos* (Portugal's answer to tapas), a full meal, attend a book launch, or dance the night away. Food choices range from scrambled eggs with spiced sausage to dogfish stew or salt-cod hamburgers. There's a fine outdoor terrace overlooking a pedestrian street.

Rua Cândido dos Reis 89. ✆ **96/455-54-61.** Mains 15€–25€, *petiscos* from 1.95€. Officially daily 5pm–4am, but in summer often open from lunch or even earlier, and in winter open later.

Marégrafo ★ SEAFOOD They actually do a range of steaks, but seafood is the main attraction of this simple and relaxed old house in the fishermen's district of Buarcos. The fish dishes vary depending on the catch, but can include fried anchovies, grilled tuna belly, and cod-tongue rice. You can also choose seafood *petiscos* from a vast selection that includes fried eels or roe salad. The interior is decorated with blue-and-white tiles, wine bottles, and vintage newspaper cuttings, but you may prefer to sit outside in a sunny square overlooking the Atlantic.

Largo Maria Jarra, 2. ✆ **23/343-31-50.** Mains 10€–15€. Wed–Mon noon–2am.

O Peleiro ★★ PORTUGUESE Perhaps because their restaurants are so dependent on the tourist trade, Figueira locals tend to be a bit sniffy about eateries in town. However, they flock to this place in the village of Paião, 10km (6¼ miles) south over the Mondego bridge. It's a classic rustic Portuguese place: terracotta floors, *azulejos* on the wall, dark-wood furnishings in a barnlike building that used to be a tannery—the leopard skin on the wall is a clue to its former use. Specialties include *sopa da pedra* (a rich soup of beans, smoked sausage, and vegetables), *cabrito asado* (roast kid), and *espetadas* (grilled skewers of meat or fish).

Largo Alvideiro 5, Paião. ✆ **23/394-01-20.** Mains 14€–22€. Mon–Sat noon–4pm and 7pm–midnight.

Shopping & Nightlife

The Mondego estuary south and east of Figueira is a strange, watery landscape made up of salt pans—shallow rectangular pools where the summer sun evaporates seawater, leaving behind pure, white **sea salt.** Bags of the stuff are sold around town in various grades that can make a taste-enhancing souvenir. The best is *flor de sal*, the first layer taken from the surface, great on salads. Others include salts flavored with herbs and spices. A number of stores in town sell it, including at the **Mercado Municipal,** Passeio Infante Dom Henrique, Figueira's handsome covered market where locals have been going to stock up on food since 1892. Recently renovated, it's a wonderful place to buy fresh fish or fruit and vegetables or to just soak up the bustling atmosphere. The market is open in summer daily from 7am–7pm and in winter from Mon–Sat, 7am–4pm. Some of the salt producers also sell their products directly to visitors, should you head out to the little salt museum **Nucleo Museologico**

LITTLE piggies

Strung out along the old Lisbon to Porto highway, **Mealhada** is not one of Portugal's most beautiful towns. It is, however, the center of one of the country's gastronomic treasures: ***leitão da Bairrada*** ★★★. Vegetarians should look away now. *Leitão* is suckling pig, a piglet in the first weeks of life still fed on its mother's milk. Here they are dispatched on an industrial scale. It's estimated 3,000 are eaten every day in the restaurants of Mealhada and the surrounding Bairrada region. Many of the factory-sized eateries in the town raise and slaughter their own animals. They are basted in a garlic-and-black-pepper sauce, then spit-roasted in wood-fired ovens until the skin is crisp and golden, the flesh pink and oh-so-tender. It's usually served with freshly fried potato chips, salad, and slices of orange, and washed down with excellent **Bairrada wines.** Some prefer to serve either white or red sparkling wine (*espumante*); others insist a hearty red is best. Locals are passionate defenders of their favorite among the over 30 *leitão* restaurants along the N1 road. **Pedro dos Leitões** (✆ **23/120-99-50**), set up in 1949, is best known, with space for 430 diners. Its neighbor and competitor, **A Meta dos Leitões** (✆ **23/120-95-40**) is of similar dimensions. Across the road, **Rei dos Leitões** (✆ **23/120-20-93**) is more upmarket. There are those, however, who say the very best *leitão* can be had a few miles to the north at **Casa Vidal** (✆ **23/466-63-53**) in the village of Agueda de Cima.

do Sal, Armazéns de Lavos, Salina Municipal do Corredor da Cobra (✆ **23/ 340-28-40;** summer Wed–Sun 10:30am–12:30pm, 2:30–6:30pm, in winter from Thurs–Sun, 10:30am–12:30pm, 2:30–4:30pm; 1€ adults, children and seniors free); or hike the salt pans walking route, where you might spot pink flamingos among the pyramids of fresh salt.

From the outside, **Casino Figueira,** Rua Dr. Calado 1 (www.casinofigueira.pt; ✆ **23/340-84-00;** free admission; daily 4pm–4am, 4pm–3am Sun–Thurs in winter) is a city-block-size cube of glass. Inside, the gilt-painted domed ceiling of its grand salon recalls a colorful history dating back to the 1880s. The casino is the focus of Figueira nightlife, featuring nightly shows, dancing, a nightclub, and gambling salons, and hosts regular big-name concerts. Games of chance include blackjack, roulette, poker, and slot machines. The live show begins at 11pm.

BUÇACO ★★

30km (29 miles) N of Coimbra; 230km (145 miles) N of Lisbon

The **Mata Nacional do Buçaco** is a magical place of tranquil beauty: a small range of hills covered with exotic forest planted by monks in the 17th century using seeds and saplings sent by far-flung missionary brothers. Amid the lush greenery is the **Bussaco Palace Hotel,** a fairytale fantasy built as a royal retreat in the dying days of the Portuguese monarchy, now an atmospheric hotel. The nearest town is the quaint spa center of **Luso,** which together with its nearby rival **Curia** provides an excellent opportunity to relax amid the hot springs and old-world atmosphere.

Essentials

ARRIVING

There are five **buses** a day from Coimbra to Buçaco on weekdays, two on Saturdays. One-way tickets cost 3.85€. **Trains** from Coimbra to Luso run three times a day and cost 2.60€. A taxi from Coimbra should cost around 30€. By car it takes about 40 minutes from Coimbra.

VISITOR INFORMATION

Luso Tourist Office is on Rua Emídio Navarro 136 (✆ **23/193-91-33;** summer 9:30am–1pm, 2:30–6pm; winter 9am–12:30pm, 2–5:30pm).

Exploring the Area

The Buçaco (you may also see it spelled Bussaco) hills have been a hideaway for hermits and monks since at least the 7th century. In 1628, the humble order of barefoot Carmelites embarked on their program of forestation around their isolated monastery. To native species they added eucalyptus, Chilean pine, Mexican cedars, monkey puzzle trees, and giant ferns. The natural beauty of the place earned such renown that the pope threatened to excommunicate anyone caught destroying trees.

There are trails through the **Mata Nacional** ★★ (national forest), leading past panoramic viewpoints, ruined chapels, and springs bubbling with cool water.

The climb up to the 550m (1,804-ft.) high point at **Cruz Alta** is one of the best ways to savor Buçaco. Pass through the vegetation and hermitages, and you are rewarded with a fabulous view from the summit.

Entry is free if you walk or bike up from Luso, although you will be charged 5€ for bringing a car into the park. A foundation runs the park and its office next to the hotel can provide information on trails and organized guided visits (www.fmb.pt; ✆ **23/193-70-00**). The park is open 8am–8pm in summer and 8am–6pm from Oct–Apr.

Near the Palace Hotel (see below) are the remains of the **Santa Cruz do Buçaco** convent, which houses some intriguing religious paintings and venerated statues. There's also a **small military museum** (✆ **23/193-93-10,** Tues–Sun 10am–12:30pm and 2–5pm, admission 2€) recalling the events of 1810, when the peace of the forest was shaken by a major battle between Anglo-Portuguese forces led by Duke of Wellington and a French army commanded by Marshal André Massena, one of Napoleon's most trusted generals. Wellington slept in the convent the night after his victory.

At the beginning of the 20th century, King Carlos I built a hunting lodge over the ruins of the convent. It's a palatial structure, now the **Bussaco Palace Hotel ★★★,** with twisted columns and towers topped by navigational spheres—an exuberant architectural tribute to the Age of Discoveries (in the style known as neo-Manueline). It's also heavily influenced by the medieval romanticism of Carlos's German grandfather, recalling the fairytale mountaintop castles of Bavaria. The king didn't have long to enjoy it. He was assassinated, along with his son, Crown Prince Filipe, in 1908. After the fall of the monarchy 2 years later, it was turned into a very special place to stay (see below). Even if you are not staying overnight, it is well worth popping in for a peek at the amazing decor.

Just outside the walls of the forest park is the little spa town of **Luso ★**. Bottled water bearing the Luso brand is sold all over Portugal, and visitors come here to stroll the shady avenues, admire the turn-of-the-century villas, and fill up bottles from the springs.

For a more serious taking of the water, the spa center **Termas do Luso ★**, Rua Álvaro Castelões 9 (www.termasdoluso.com; ✆ **23/193-79-10;** Jul–Sept Sun–Fri 9am–1pm and 2–7pm; Sat 10am–1pm and 2–8pm; Oct–Jun Mon–Fri 10am–1pm, 2–6pm, Sat 10am–1pm, and 2–7pm) offers treatments from everything from skin conditions to kidney stones. You can go just for pampering, with the full range of massages, facials, and body treatments. A 130-minute detox wrap and massage costs 145€. There's a splendid 1930s hotel linked to the spa, with an Olympic-sized pool (see below).

Down the hill, about 20 minutes' drive to the northwest, is a rival spa town, **Cúria ★**, which maintains a decidedly 1920s feel with its gardens, lakes, and grand old hotels. The lemon-and-white late-19th-century building of the **Termas da Curia ★** spa center (www. termasdacuria.com; ✆ **23/151-98-00**) also offers a range of wellness and medicinal treatments.

Where to Stay

Bussaco Palace Hotel ★★★ A national treasure. In 2017, the Bussaco palace celebrated 100 years since the former royal retreat was turned into one of the country's foremost hotels. It may be showing its age in places, and service and furnishing can be a tad creaky, but the shortfalls will be forgotten among the splendor of the architecture, decoration that includes splendid *azulejos*, paintings by some of Portugal's best 19th-century artists, colonnaded verandas, monumental staircases, gloriously lit dining room, and more. Outside there are formal gardens and pools where swans glide by, all surrounded by the tropical majesty of the Buçaco forest. For a really special occasion, try the royal suite decked out in a sumptuous Louis XVI style, complete with 1920s marble bathroom.

Mata do Buçaco. www.themahotels.pt. ✆ **23/193-79-70.** 62 units. 92€–223€ double; royal suite from 552€. Rates include breakfast. Free parking. **Amenities:** Restaurant; bar; babysitting; concierge; room service. Wi-Fi free in public areas.

Cúria Palace ★★ There's a definite "Grand Budapest" air about this splendid palace, recently restored to its original 1920s glory. The Art Deco gem is under the same management as the Bussaco Palace (above) and it exudes glamour. You expect to see flappers dancing the Charleston here. Spacious rooms with a mix of understated modern and antique furnishings look out on swans gliding by on ornamental ponds and a swimming pool inspired by the Golden Age of ocean liners (alas, it needs freshening up). Everywhere, there's marble, wrought-iron work, and dark polished woodwork. A trip back to an age of elegance. There's a fine spa and a golf course nearby.

Rua Pinheiro Manso. www.curiapalace.com. ✆ **23/151-03-00.** 100 units. 69€–160€ double, including breakfast. Free parking. **Amenities:** Restaurant; bar; babysitting; exercise room; 2 pools (1 heated indoor); room service; spa; tennis; garden. Wi-Fi free in public areas.

Grande Hotel de Luso ★★ Built in 1940, the Grande Hotel is a prime example of Portugal's take on the Art Deco style. Its lemon-yellow exterior makes a pretty counterpoint to the glistening blue of its Olympic-size outdoor pool, the green forest surrounds, and purple bougainvillea in the gardens. There's also an indoor pool and a private tunnel, which means guests have an easy stroll to the next-door thermal center. While the lobby maintains a vintage air with its flowing Art Deco curves, the rooms have been modernized and decorated in a familiar beige-and-dove-gray contemporary style.

Rua Dr. José Cid de Oliveira. www.hoteluso.com. ✆ **23/193-79-37.** 132 units. 72€–132€ double, including breakfast. Free nearby parking. **Amenities:** Restaurant; bar; babysitting; bikes; children's center; 2 pools; room service; spa; squash; tennis courts; billiards. Free Wi-Fi.

Quinta de Lograssol ★ An alternative to all the grand old hotels, this boutique, family-run establishment opened in 2012 in a converted 19th-century farmhouse. It's 5km (3 miles) from Buçaco. There are six spacious rooms located in the pastel yellow main building and a modern extension. Simple

ART WITH wine

The **Aliança Underground Museum ★★** (www.alianca.pt, ✆ **23/473-20-45**) is an extraordinary fusion of winery and art museum in the small town of **Sangalhos,** in the heart of the Bairrada wine region between Coimbra and Aveiro. In its cool, dark subterranean caverns you file past great wooden barrels filled with ripening brandy or countless thousands of backlit bottles of maturing sparkling wine. In amongst them are wonderfully diverse collections of **African art,** ranging from 500-year-old Nigerian phalluses to contemporary works by Zimbabwe's leading sculptors. There are glistening Brazilian mineral samples, fossils dating back 20 million years, and a definitive selection of Portuguese ceramic art over the centuries. It's all the brainchild of self-made millionaire and art connoisseur **Joe Berardo,** whose magnificent modern art acquisitions form the heart of one of Lisbon's most sought-after museums. Berardo invested in the venerable Aliança vineyards and used its vast cellars to showcase his collections. Visits are by guided tour only and can be booked on the website or by phone. Tours last 1 hour and 30 minutes, and run daily at 10am, 11:30am, 2:30pm, and 4pm. The price is 3€. Wine tastings are also available.

Many of the other wineries in the Bairrada region offer visits, where you can follow the production process, sample and buy wines, and sometimes enjoy a meal. **Quinta do Encontro ★**, Rua de São Lourencinho, São Lourenço do Bairro, Anadia (www.quintadoencontro.pt, ✆ **23/152-71-55**) is one of the most striking. Its curved wooden facade resembles a giant barrel emerging from the vine-covered fields. As well as tastings and tours, there is an excellent restaurant that serves modernized regional cuisine.

decor makes the most of the house's original wood floors, ceilings, and other features. There's a shaded porch looking out over the gardens and pool. The cozy lounge decorated with family artifacts around an old-fashioned fireplace is a big favorite with guests.

Rua Joaquim Luís Alves de Melo, Lograssol. www.quintadelogressol.pt. ✆ **23/193-91-45.** 6 units. 70€–90€ including breakfast. No credit cards. Free parking. **Amenities:** Outdoor pool; garden. Wi-Fi free in public areas.

Where to Dine

João Vaz ★★ FRENCH/PORTUGUESE The restaurant of the Bussaco Palace Hotel was once a royal dining room, and it is a glorious setting for any meal. The Moorish-inspired ceiling glistens with countless small lights, ornate horseshoe-shaped windows look out on a romantic terrace and the forest beyond, and walls are lined with epic paintings by João Vaz, a 19th-century artist. The cooking is rooted in classic French and regional Portuguese cuisine. Notable dishes include salt cod slow-cooked in local olive oil with celery purée and sautéed cabbage, or duck in Calvados sauce. The wine cellar is legendary, with vintages dating back to the 1940s. A unique fine-dining experience.

Mata do Buçaco. www.themahotels.pt. ✆ **23/193-79-70.** Main courses 23€–26.50€. Daily 1–3pm and 8–10pm.

AVEIRO ★

250km (160 miles) N of Lisbon; 80km (50 miles) S of Porto

Inevitably, Aveiro gets called the "**Venice of Portugal.**" The city is criss-crossed with canals, flowing between colorful, high-gabled houses and traversed by humpbacked bridges. Narrow boats called ***moliceiros*** glide along the waterways, their high bows brightly painted with images ranging from the religious to the risqué.

Although its roots are ancient, Aveiro boomed in the 19th and 20th centuries, thanks in part to its role in the cod trade. Its rich architectural heritage of **Belle Epoque** and **Art Nouveau buildings** bear witness to this prosperous age.

The center can easily be explored on foot (or from a tour in a *moliceiro*), but it's worth getting out of town to explore its vast and mysterious lagoon, the **Ria de Aveiro ★★**, now mostly a nature reserve; its fine beaches, particularly the resort suburb of **Costa Nova ★** with its distinctive candy-striped houses; and the historic **Vista Alegre ★** fine porcelain factory in Ílhavo.

Aveiro cuisine is centered on eels from the lagoon, the salt cod ships once brought to its harbor from Norway and Greenland, and sweet eggy treats called *oves moles*.

Essentials

ARRIVING

BY TRAIN The **rail station** is at Largo da Estação (✆ **70/721-02-20**). Fast Alfa Pendular trains run 10 times a day from Lisbon, making the trip in just over 2 hours. Tickets cost 26.30€. From Porto, the trip takes 30 minutes and costs 14.20€.

BY BUS **Rede Expressos** (www.rede-expressos.pt; ✆ **70/722-33-44**) runs six buses a day from Lisbon to Aveiro. The trip takes 3 to 4 hours and costs 16.50€.

BY CAR The drive north from Lisbon takes about 2 hours and 30 minutes either along the A1 toll highway via Coimbra, or the more westerly route along the A8 and A17 highways, which tend to have less traffic.

VISITOR INFORMATION

The **Aveiro Tourist Office,** Rua João Mendonça 8 (www.turismodocentro.pt; ✆ **23/442-07-60;** open summer Mon–Fri 9am to 8pm, weekends 9am–6pm; winter Mon–Fri 9am–6pm, weekends 9:30am–1pm and 2–5:30pm).

Exploring Aveiro

The best introduction to Aveiro is a ***moliceiro*** **boat tour ★★** along the canals. Looking a bit like mini-Viking long boats or pimped gondolas, the *moliceiros'* high, pointed bows and sterns are painted with colorful design themes, ranging from saints to soccer stars to lewd jokes. The boats were originally used to collect seaweed from the lagoon, which used for fertilizer. Nowadays, they ferry tourists around town, past wharfs lined with brightly painted fishermen's cottages or Art Nouveau mansions covered in shining *azulejos*. You can book an excursion at the tourist office or online from a number of companies like **Viva a Ria** (www.vivaaria.com; ✆ **96/900-86-87**) or **Aveitour** (www.aveitour.com; ✆ **23/409-75-73**). Tours start from 8€ per person for trips of up to 40 minutes around the city; you also have the option of spending a whole day exploring the wide, watery spaces of the lagoon.

A short walk from the double bridge over the main canal is the **Museu de Aveiro ★★**, Parque de Santa Joana (✆ **23/442-32-97;** Tues–Sun 10am–6pm; 4€ for adults, free for children and seniors), housed in a 15th-century convent. The museum centerpiece is the **Igreja de Jesus** church decorated with golden woodwork and blue *azulejos*, it's an exquisite example of the Portuguese baroque style. Amongst it all is a masterpiece, the **tomb of St. Joana,** a Portuguese princess who retired to the convent in 1472. Her remains are housed in a grand confection of multicolored Italian marble. An enigmatic **portrait** of the rosy-cheeked young princess by an unknown 15th-century artist is one of Portugal's most cherished artworks.

Some of Aveiro's prettiest **Art Nouveau** buildings are around the canal-side Rossio gardens; one splendid sky-blue town house fronted with white-stone carvings of eagles and floral columns was recently converted into a little museum dedicated to the style. The **Museu Arte Nova ★**, Rua Barbosa de Magalhães, 9–11 (✆ **23/440-64-85;** Tues–Fri 9:30am–12:30pm and 2–6pm; weekends 2–6pm; 2€ adults, includes entry to two other small museums on the city's history and salt industry) also contains a charming period **teahouse** that makes a hip alternative to the more traditional cafes serving the artery-clogging local specialty: *oves moles.* It turns into a cocktail-fueled bar and cultural space in the evenings. The tearoom opens at 9:30am and stays open until 2am, later on weekends.

About 6km (4 miles) south of central Aveiro, the town of **Ílhavo** has a pair of worthwhile museums bearing witness to the area's industrial heritage. The **Museu Marítimo de Ílhavo ★★**, Avenida Dr. Rocha Madahil (www.museumaritimo.cm-ilhavo.pt; ✆ **23/432-99-90;** Tues–Sat 10am–6pm, from Mar–Sept also Sundays 2–6pm; 5€ adults, 2.5€ children and seniors) focuses on cod fishing. It gives an insight into the centrality of *bacalhau* to the Portuguese psyche and to the tough life of the fishermen who sailed out for months at a time to the coasts of Canada and Greenland, braving north Atlantic storms to bring back the salt fish that became a national stable. There's even an **aquarium** filled with live cod.

Nearby is the factory settlement of **Vista Alegre ★★**, which has been producing fine porcelain for almost 200 years, gathering past and present European royalty among its fans. Britain's Elizabeth II has a personalized set of tableware. By the standards of the time, the early-19th-century Vista Alegre factory was known as an enlightened place, providing decent housing, a school, a chapel, and a theater for its workers. They can be visited today, along with the working factory, a **museum** tracing the history of the brand and a factory outlet shop to pick up a bargain souvenir. You can even attend a pottery or painting workshop to try your hand at producing some of the delicate porcelain, although you may struggle to match some of the top modern artists the factory now contracts to produce special pieces. The **Vista Alegre Museum** (http://vistaalegre.com; ✆ **23/432-06-00**), is open daily 10:30am–7pm. Admission is 6€ adults and 3€ children, students, and seniors.

OUTDOOR ACTIVITIES

Aveiro's flat, watery landscape makes cycling a treat. City Hall has a free public bike sharing scheme called **BUGA** that allows bikes to be picked up from and dropped off at a number of stands around the city between 9am and 6pm.

Biking is one way to explore the vast expanse of the **Ria de Aveiro ★★** lagoon, one of Europe's largest costal marshlands and a magnet for birdwatchers. A number of the companies organizing *moliceiro* boat tours in the city also offer longer trips into the lagoon. Half-day or full day tours by **Sentir Aveiro** (www.sentiraveiro.com; ✆ **91/008-59-37**) can include visits to boat builders and an eel cannery; from 45€. A new lagoon attraction is a chance to bathe in **salt pans,** which give a "Dead Sea"–like floating experience in the heavily salted water. Visitors can also enjoy the health benefits of a salt-infused mud bath or massage. The pools and spa are run by **Cale do Oiro** (www.caledooiro.com; ✆ **91/566-14-80**) daily from 10am–7pm.

Beyond the lagoon, there are some excellent beaches north and south of Aveiro. **Costa Nova ★** is a family spot best known for its beach shacks painted in bold stripes of white with red, blue, or yellow. Much wilder is **Praia de São Jacinto ★★** in a protected nature reserve, its dunes are beloved by seekers of seclusion, its waves favored by surfers. The **A Peixaria ★** restaurant (Rua Mestre Jorge Pestana; ✆ **23/433-11-65**) in the nearby lagoon town of São Jacinto is famed for fish, fried or grilled. Farther south, **Praia de Mira ★** is another surfers' favorite, where fishermen have only recently swapped oxen for tractors to haul their nets ashore.

Where to Stay

Hotel Aveiro Palace ★ With its rows of arches and monumental facade, this has been a landmark in the heart of the city since it opened in 1937. Recently extensively remodeled, it practically has the waters of the main canal lapping against its front door. The modernization work has left the rooms without any historical charm, but they are light and comfortable. Most have canal views, but the downside of its central location means nights can be noisy on the streets outside. There's a treat in the breakfast room, with walls covered with 1930s painted tiles uncovered during the restoration work. The collection of black-and-white photos also point to the hotel's status as part of the fabric of the city.

Rua de Viana do Castelo, 4. www.hotelaveiropalace.com. ✆ **23/442-18-85.** 48 units. 65€–91€ double, including breakfast. Parking 5€ per day. Free Wi-Fi.

Hotel Moliceiro ★ Graced with a central location overlooking the canal-side Rossio gardens, the exterior is a cubist block partly covered with modern *azulejos*. Inside is more attractive. Superior and deluxe rooms enjoy views over the canal or lagoon, and individual designs that range from Chinese- or Moroccan-style exotica to bold black-and-white motifs inspired by Coco Chanel's Paris, to soft, summery mint-green pastel shades. The standard rooms are more modest, but feature original artworks and a restrained modern design where dark-wood hues predominate. A sophisticated downtown choice.

Rua Barbosa de Magalhães. www.hotelmoliceiro.pt. ✆ **23/437-74-00.** 49 units. 99€–160€ double, including breakfast. No parking. **Amenities:** Bar; bike rental. Free Wi-Fi.

Montebelo Vista Alegre Ílhavo Hotel ★★★ Opening in late 2015, this is the first five-star hotel around the lagoon, a spectacular fusion of old and new that incorporates the palatial former home of the Vista Alegre factory owners and a low-rise modern block filled with white light. In the new wing, the rigorous modernism of the rooms is softened by whimsical touches that reflect the links with the porcelain manufacture: painted plates on the walls and cobalt-blue flowers painted on the sink in the state-of-the-art bathrooms. A sweeping spiral staircase leads to the palace wing, where the decor reflects its patrician heritage. The restaurant is first-class, focused on bacalau dishes. There's a big outdoor pool and a fine spa center. The hotel looks out over the lagoon, and offers tours and workshops to expand guests' understanding of Vista Alegre's world-renowned porcelain.

Lugar da Vista Alegre Ílhavo. www.hotelbontebelovistaalegre.pt. ✆ **23/424-16-30.** 82 units. 100€–185€ double, including breakfast. Free parking. **Amenities:** Indoor and outdoor pools; spa; fitness center; restaurant; bar; babysitting; room service; garden. Free Wi-Fi.

Pousada Ria ★★ It's hard to get any closer to the immensity of the Aveiro lagoon than a stay here. Built in the 1960s right on the shore, it can seem from the balcony rooms or the panoramic bar that the hotel is floating over the waters. The Pousada chain is a guarantee of quality, although sometimes things do need a little refreshing. The public rooms have a delightful retro feel, with many original features and furnishings. Sunny pastel colors in the rooms are enhanced by the natural light that floods in. This is a great location for exploring the lagoon or visiting the beaches. Downtown Aveiro is a 30-minute drive around the lagoon, but a ferry cuts the journey in half and is more fun. The lagoon-side pool is a plus.

Bico do Muranzel, Torreira-Murtosa. www.pousadas.pt. ✆ **23/486-01-80.** 19 units. 60€–198€ double, including breakfast. Free parking. **Amenities:** Restaurant; bar; babysitting; outdoor pool; room service; garden. Free Wi-Fi.

Where to Dine

Mercado do Peixe ★ SEAFOOD The fish can hardly be fresher at this restaurant on the second floor of Aveiro's covered market, where the catch of the day is shipped in for sale in the stalls downstairs. The dining area is a glass-fronted space incorporated into the iron frame of the 19th-century building. It looks out onto the canal and down into the market. The menu varies daily with the catch, but there's usually expertly grilled bass (*robalo*), brill (*rodovalho*), and a shoal of other creatures that were swimming in the Atlantic a couple of hours before landing on your plate. There's also the typical Aveiro selection of eel (*enguia*) and salt-cod (*bacalhau*) dishes, along with steaks for confirmed carnivores.

Largo da Praça do Peixe 1. http://mercadopeixeaveiro.pt. ✆ **23/424-19-28.** Mains 9€–18€. Tues–Sat noon–3pm and 7:30–11pm; Sun noon–3pm.

O Telheiro ★ PORTUGUESE For more than 30 years this no-nonsense place has been serving excellent regional cuisine to crowds of appreciative locals and visitors. The layout is labyrinthine with a succession of noisy rooms filled with families tucking in. Specialties include *caldeirada de enguias* (eel stew), *polvo à lagareiro* (roast octopus), and *cabrito assado* (roast kid). They'll bring a vast selection of appetizers, which is good because when it's busy, the mains may take awhile.

Largo da Praça do Peixe 20. ✆ **23/442-51-91.** Regular main courses 9€–16.50€. Tues–Sun noon–3:30pm and 7–11:15pm.

Salpoente ★★ MODERN PORTUGUESE Behind the bright-red wooden boards of an old salt warehouse is this exciting restaurant, run by young chef Duarte Eira. His kitchen team builds on Aveiro's history as a center of the cod and salt trade with the aim of producing the best *bacalhau* in the world. Dishes include salt-cod steak braised in olive oil with soft-shell crab; seafood rice and algae mayo; or, for real hardcore *bacalhau* enthusiasts, roe, tongues, and cheeks of *bacalhau* in a parsley-infused cream. For those not seduced by

A WALK ON THE wild side

A new attraction in the region, the **Passadiços do Paiva** ★★ is a series of walkways winding for 8.7km (5.5 miles) though the wild, untouched hills of the **Paiva river valley**—a UNESCO-recognized geo-park. This is a bracing outdoor adventure. The paths run along wooden walkways that include steep climbs, plunging descents, and a narrow rope bridge stretched over a gorge. A hike back and forward along the full length of the walk is not for the faint-hearted, but it is possible to walk just a part of it or to catch a taxi back to the start. There are picnic spots along the route. You can start at either end. Setting out from the Areinho end means you get the hardest climb over early, but ending there means you can cool off with a plunge from the **river beach.** Tickets cost just 1€, but you need to book in advance: online (http://passadicosdopaiva.pt), by phone (✆ **25/694-02-58**), or at the tourism office at Rua Abel Botelho, 4, in **Arouca,** the nearest town to the walkways, an hour's drive northeast from Aveiro. If you show up without a reservation, you may get in, but there will be a supplementary charge and a risk of being turned away because numbers are limited. Open daily Nov–Mar 9am–7pm, Apr–Aug 7:30am–8pm, and Sep–Oct 9am–8:30pm. The walkways were damaged by a forest fire in the summer of 2016, but quickly reopened.

the delights of the fish the Portuguese call their "loyal friend," there are tasty dishes of other fresh fish, meat, and vegetarian alternatives.

Canal de São Roque, 82. http://salpoente.pt. ✆ **23/438-26-74.** Mains 19€–38€. Daily 12:30–3pm and 7:30–10:30pm.

VISEU ★

290km (180 miles) NE of Lisbon, 128km (79 miles) SE of Porto

Handsome granite houses, cobbled streets, graceful churches, leafy public gardens, and a collection of some of the country's best Renaissance art make this bustling provincial capital a great base for exploring the rugged highlands of the Beira Alta region.

Viseu is full of history. A cave nearby was the hideout of Viriato, legendary leader of the Lusitanian resistance to the Romans. It's also a lively place, perfect for sampling hearty highland cuisine and wines produced in the valleys of the Dão region to the east, which include some of the country's most subtle tipples.

The city is also renowned for handicrafts, most notably its distinctive black clay pottery.

Essentials

GETTING THERE

Trains don't run to Viseu. The nearest rail station is at **Nelas,** about 20km (15 miles) south. There are three direct trains from Lisbon. The journey lasts just over 3 hours, and second-class tickets cost 19.70€. Call the national rail information line (✆ **70/721-02-20**) for more information. **Bus** is a much easier option. Rede Nacional de Expressos has departures from Lisbon more or less every 3 hours; the journey lasts just over 3½ hours and costs 18.50€ (www.rede-expressos.pt; ✆ **70/722-33-44**). **By car,** take the A1 highway to Coimbra then the IP3 expressway, where some care should be taken as it twists through the hills. The drive takes around 3 hours.

VISITOR INFORMATION

The tourist office is next to the cathedral in Adro Sé (www.turismodocentro.pt; ✆ **23/242-09-50**). Hours vary throughout the year.

Exploring Viseu

The place to start is **Adro da Sé,** one of the most harmonious squares in Portugal, where the severe bare-stone facade of this cathedral faces the airy white baroque front of the Igreja da Misericórdia.

The hilltop **Sé ★**, or Cathedral, at Largo da Sé (daily 9am–noon and 2–7pm, free admission) dates back to the 12th century, but has been much modified over the centuries. The fabulous interior features just about every architectural style, from Romanesque columns to a splendid Manueline ceiling made of knotted stone ropes and a cloister that is one of the earliest Renaissance buildings in Portugal.

THE high mountains OF PORTUGAL

The **Serra da Estrella ★★★** is Portugal's highest, wildest, and most spectacular mountain range. Over 1,000 sq. kilometers (380 sq. miles), it is protected as a nature park filled with bald, rounded summits; crystalline lakes; craggy peaks; plunging waterfalls; and boulder-strewn plateaus. At just under 2,000m (6,600 ft.), the mountain of **Torre** is the highest point of mainland Portugal, although Pico in the Azores is higher. With its marvelous scenery and wealth of traditional culture, a trip to the high Serra can be an invigorating counterpoint to the beaches or historic cities.

The climate here can be bracing. In summer it can get hot, although at times visitors driving up from the heat of the lowlands are caught by icy winds on the summits. Spring provides a carpet of wildflowers, while turning leaves can make fall a delight. Winter snowfall can mean crowds heading for the modest ski slopes—the only ones in Portugal.

Heading up from Coimbra, the gateway to the park is the town of **Seia,** which has a visitor center providing a good introduction to the mountains and tips on hiking trails, the **Centro de Interpretação da Serra da Estrela,** Rua Visconde de Molelos (✆ **23/832-03-00**), and a quirky museum dedicated to bread production housed in traditional stone buildings. The **Museu do Pão** complex also contains a shop selling local products, a cafe with great views, and a popular buffet restaurant serving local dishes. Heading up toward Torre, the road winds into **Sabugueiro,** a picturesque place of rough-hewn stone houses, that is Portugal's highest village. It's a good place to see the unique **Estrela mountain dog,** a gentle giant of a canine traditionally used to deter wolves from getting too close to the flocks of sheep kept on the high pastures. The puppies are irresistibly cute. Sabugueiro is also packed with stores selling mountain treats like bread baked in the communal oven, smoked ham, juniper firewater (*zimbro*), and most of all, the soft, creamy ***Queijo da Serra,*** the king of Portuguese cheeses, made from local ewes' milk. Local aficionados will tell you it's best when runny enough to be served with a spoon.

Between the Sé and the Misericórdia church is the **Museu de Grão Vasco ★★,** Adro da Sé (✆ **23/242-20-49;** Tues 2–6pm and Wed–Sun 10am–6pm; admission 4€, free for children under 12), housed in the severe gray stone former bishop's palace. This houses one of Portugal's best art collections, showcasing the work of Vasco Fernandes, known as "Grão" (great) Vasco, who was born here in 1475 and grew to become the country's finest Renaissance painter. His hometown museum has the most complete collection of his work, including the masterly *St. Peter Enthroned* and *La Pontecôte*, in which lancelike tongues of fire hurtle toward the saints, some devout, others apathetic. There's also an intriguing collection of sculpture from the 13th to the 18th centuries, with a stunning **Throne of Grace** from the 1300s. The rest of the collection ranges from 14-century religious regalia to Portuguese modern art.

A walk **through the old city ★★** of Viseu reveals ancient walls, handsome mansions, and quirky traditional stores. Just south of the cathedral, **Praça Dom Duarte** is surrounded by fine stone houses and overlooked by the

Torre itself can be bit of a disappointment, with its crowded ski slopes in season and some bland souvenir shops, although the views are rewarding and the white spheres of abandoned NATO radar posts add a surreal touch.

Down the slope heading north, **Manteigas** is the main town in the park and makes a fine base for visiting some of the Serra's best attractions, like the rocky, unspoiled peaks at **Penhas Douradas,** the wild beauty of the **Zêzere Glacial Valley,** or **Vale do Rossim,** where the lake has one of the best inland beaches in Portugal. Soft wool blankets and sweaters are sold all over the serra, but the **Burel Factory,** Amieiros Verdes, ✆ **92/654-20-95**, in Manteigas has given the handicraft a modern take, making fashionable clothes, furnishings, and accessories from the wool as well as more traditional items.

Farther north, the serra is even less populated. Watch out for golden eagles, peregrine falcons, and other birds of prey enjoying the solitude. There is, however, a scattering of pretty villages, like **Linhares da Beira,** clustered around its castle. To the south are the bigger towns of **Covilhã** and **Fundão,** where in spring the hillsides are covered in pink cherry blossoms.

The mountains are dotted with some excellent hotels for a get-away-from-it-all stay. Among the best is **Casa das Penhas Douradas ★★**, (www.casadaspenhasdouradas.pt; ✆ **96/338-40-26;** doubles with breakfast 130€–170€), which combines a remote highland location with cool 1950s furnishings, mountain views, a warming spa, and a roaring fire in the restaurant serving modern Portuguese cooking based on seasonal local products. Another sure choice is the **Pousada da Serra da Estrela ★★** (www.pousadas.pt; ✆ **21/040-76-60;** doubles with breakfast 70€–179€) located 1,200m (4,000 ft.) up in an imposing former sanatorium building converted into a luxurious hotel, complete with spectacular views, spa, and restaurant serving a choice of traditional and contemporary cuisine. In 2016, a five-star spa resort, the **Aqua Village ★★** in Caldas de São Paulo (www.aquavillage.pt; ✆ **23/824-90-40**), brought an advanced level of pampering to the western slopes of the serra.

Passeio dos Cônegos, or cannons' walk, a covered passage along old defensive walls. **Rua Direita** and Rua Formosa are long pedestrian streets lined with shops and restaurants. If you need a pit stop, pull into **Pastelaria Horta,** R. Formosa 22, a cafe and pastry shop that's been serving up local sweet specialties since 1873.

The narrow lanes of the old town eventually open up to the east to a broad tree-shaded plaza officially called **Praça da República,** but known to the locals who come to stroll or sit out at the sidewalk cafes as Rossio. If you can't find that ideal Viseu souvenir amid the old town stores, take a short walk to the **Casa da Ribeira,** Largo Nossa Senhora da Conceição, (✆ **23/242-97-61**), a restored water mill on the banks of the River Paiva which serves as an exhibition space and sales point for many of the region's best artisans.

Where to Stay

Casa da Sé ★★ This boutique option overlooks one of Viseu's most atmospheric squares, right beside the cathedral. The owners aim to blend

21st-century comfort with 18th-century charm. The building is filled with antiques and period furnishings. Rooms are named after historical Viseu characters and are individually decorated. There are guitars in one room bearing the name of renowned fado player Augusto Hilário, and regal velvet drapes in the King Duarte suite. The bonus is that if you like the furnishings, you can take them home: Many of the antiques are for sale.

Rua Augusta Cruz, 12. http://site.casadase.net. ✆ **23/246-80-32.** 12 units. 67€–121€ double, including breakfast. Free public parking nearby. **Amenities:** Bar; gourmet store. Free Wi-Fi.

Palácio dos Melos ★★ Nestled among the monuments of the old town, this former palace has been modernized into a boutique hotel full of charm and grace. It's built into the city walls, next to one of the ancient seven gateways that lead into the city's heart. Spacious, well-designed guest rooms are either in the main building or in a wing alongside. Those in the older building are more atmospheric, with warm navy or crimson fabrics. The esplanade makes a great spot for drinks with a view. Lack of parking can be a problem.

Rua Chão Mestre 4. www.hotelpalaciodosmelos.pt. ✆ **23/243-92-90.** 27 units. 62€–123€ double, including breakfast. No parking. **Amenities:** Restaurant; bar; room service; garden. Free Wi-Fi.

Pousada de Viseu ★★ This former hospital from 1842 was completely restored and turned into a lovely first-class hotel in 2009 by the famed architect Gonçalo Byrne. Guest rooms are furnished with sleek, contemporary pieces. Guests seeking more luxury can book one of the spacious suites with great views. The splendid neoclassical facade is topped by statues representing faith, hope, and charity. There's a spacious atrium bar, a huge swimming pool in the garden, and a soothing spa. The *pousada* also has a fine first-rate restaurant specializing in local products, like tender veal from the nearby Lafões region.

Rua do Hospital. www.pousadas.pt. ✆ **23/245-73-20.** 84 units. 60€–126€ double, including breakfast. Free parking. **Amenities:** Restaurant; bar; exercise room; 2 pools (indoor and outdoor); room service; spa; massage; garden. Free Wi-Fi.

Where to Dine

Muralha da Sé ★ PORTUGUESE There's an upmarket take on regional cooking in this noble house hewn from local stone in the cathedral square. The dining room is spacious and classically stylish with white linen table covers. Dishes are attractively presented on fine porcelain crockery. Grilled local veal, slow-cooked goat, and salt cod baked with olive oil and skin-on potatoes are among the specialties. On summer evenings, the outdoor terrace offers a romantic view of the cathedral. Prices are above average, but you can ask for a *meia-dose* (half-portion) that will satisfy most appetites.

Adro da Sé. www.muralhadase.pt. ✆ **23/243-77-77.** Mains 16€–25€. Mon–Sat 12:30–3:30pm and 7:30–11pm, Sun 12:30–3:30pm.

O Cortiço ★★ PORTUGUESE Open since the 1960s, this is a place of pilgrimage for lovers of Portugal's traditional cooking. A plain stone house in the heart of the old town, with bare granite walls and rustic furnishing, it is uncompromisingly dedicated to preserving the cuisine of Viseu and its surrounding villages. Signature dishes include rabbit in red wine and butter-fried octopus. A selection of smoked sausage and blood sausage fried up as an appetizer is most recommended. There's an excellent selection of local Dão wines. Game dishes are served in season.

Rua de Augusto Hilário, 45. www.restaurantecortico.com. ✆ **23/241-61-27.** Mains 10€–25€. Wed–Mon noon–3:30pm and 7–11pm.

GUARDA ★

325km (200 miles) NE of Lisbon; 200km (125 miles) SE of Porto

Squatting on a hilltop guarding the main road into Portugal from northern Europe, Guarda is known as the city of five "f's." While everybody can agree with "fria" (cold), "forte" (strong), "farta" (well-fed), and "fiel" (loyal—thanks to its resistance to Spanish invaders), there is some dispute if the final adjective is "formosa" (beautiful) or "feia" (ugly). The answer is in the eye of the beholder. Guarda today is surrounded by modern, high-rise suburbs, but its medieval core, clustered around the chunky **Gothic cathedral,** is certainly worth a visit.

Essentials

GETTING THERE

There are four direct **trains** from Lisbon to Guarda with journey times of just over 4 hours. Second-class one-way tickets cost 20.70€, although the evening international train heading to Madrid is more expensive. There are five daily **buses** run by the Rede Expressos company from Lisbon; journey times are about 4 hours and the cost is 18€. By **car,** the trip from Lisbon takes just over 3 hours along the A1 and A23 toll highways. Porto is 2 hours away on the A1 and A25. For travelers heading to Lisbon from northern Europe on the E80 international road through Spain, Guarda will be the first Portuguese city they meet.

VISITOR INFORMATION

Guarda's tourism office is in Praça Luís de Camões (✆ **27/120-55-30;** Mon–Fri 9am–7pm; Sat–Sun 9am–1pm and 2–7pm).

Exploring Guarda

Guarda has its detractors, but there is no doubt that the heart of this hilltop city founded in 1190 has a robust, if austere, charm. The high point of Portugal's highest city is the **Sé** (cathedral), Praça Luís de Camões (✆ **27/121-12-31;** open June–Sept 10am–1pm and 3–6:30pm; Oct–May 9am–12:30pm and 2–5:30pm; admission 1€, 2€ to visit roof terrace). The roof offers a viewpoint for looking down on the white-painted, red-roofed granite houses on the town and the surrounding rocky landscape. Built in bare local stone in 1390, its rugged, fortresslike outline is an appropriate symbol for this border city. The soaring interior combines Gothic and Manueline styles in a nave leading up to a magnificent altarpiece carved in limestone by the Renaissance master Jean de Rouen.

The cathedral opens onto the old town's central plaza, the triangular **Praça Luís de Camões,** which is surrounded by sturdy stone houses, some featuring arcades and balconies that show the Castilian influence on the local architecture. Within the old city walls is an atmospheric warren of narrow stone lanes winding between traditional stores, cafes, and restaurants.

One area of special interest is the **Judaria,** or Jewish quarter, a thriving area until Jews were forced to convert or flee in 1497. Some of the houses still bear crosses scratched into doorways as a sign of the inhabitants' (at least outward) conversion to Christianity. It's located behind the **Igreja São Vicente,** which together with the **Igreja de Misericórdia,** represents the best of baroque church architecture in the city.

More of the city's history is told in the **Museu da Guarda,** Rua General Alves Roçadas, 30 (✆ **27/121-34-60;** Tues–Sun 10am–6pm; admission 3€ adults). Housed in a 17th-century bishop's palace, its exhibits range from prehistoric archeological finds to contemporary art.

Where to Stay

Hotel Santos ★ A clean, simple, low-cost option, this granite-hewn hotel is built into the medieval walls, next to the Torre dos Ferreiros defensive tower. The massive stone fortifications are a feature in the lobby. The rooms are a little dated, but comfortable; some on the upper floors offer a view over the rooftops to the cathedral, which is particularly atmospheric at night. There's a hearty breakfast.

Rua Tenente Valadim, 14. www.hotelsantos.pt. ✆ **27/120-54-00.** 3 units. 46€ double, including breakfast. No parking. **Amenities:** Terrace; bar. Free Wi-Fi.

Solar de Alarcão ★ In a city not overflowing with accommodations, this guesthouse, located in a noble stone mansion built in 1686, is the best old-town option. The location next to the cathedral is perfect, and the guesthouse, with its covered arcade, patio, and magnolia-shaded garden, is a gem. Inside there are period furnishings that tread a thin line between charmingly antique and old-fashioned kitsch, but the welcome is warm. It's not the place for travelers expecting "mod cons" and luxurious fittings, but parking is easy, there's a hearty fire in the hearth to keep out the winter cold, and a fine breakfast is served in the tearoom.

Rua D. Miguel de Alarcao, 25. www.solardealarcao.pt. ✆ **96/232-71-77.** 3 units. 55€–75€ double, including breakfast. Free parking. **Amenities:** Garden; terrace; games room; billiards; bar. Free Wi-Fi in public areas.

VILLAGES OF THE beira interior

The rocky inland highlands of the Beira region are peppered with **historic small towns and villages ★★★**. Constructed with blocks of naked local stones, they often appear to grow organically out of the landscape. With their stark beauty, fascinating stories, and glimpses of unique rural lifestyles, the villages have a timeless attraction. Lately, however, the opening of several excellent hotels in restored buildings have given new life to remote areas and ensure that travelers can visit them in comfort. There's an excellent online guide to many of the villages at www.aldeiashistoricasdeportugal.com.

One of the most intriguing places is **Belmonte ★★**, where a Jewish community survived by pretending to be Catholic through the dark years of the Inquisition. It continued to practice in secret until the 1990s, when contacts with the Israeli embassy and Jewish community in Lisbon led them to come out. Today, there's a synagogue and a **Jewish Museum,** open Tues–Fri 9:30am–12:30pm and 2–6pm. The stone village sheltering beneath its medieval castle also holds special attraction for visitors from Brazil. Pedro Álvares Cabral, the first European to land there, was born in Belmonte in 1467. **The Pousada Convento de Belmonte ★★** (www.conventodebelmonte.pt; ✆ **27/591-03-00**) offers luxurious accommodations in a 16th-century convent overlooking the village, with award-winning cuisine produced by its Brazilian-born chef. Rates are 85€–153€ double.

Farther south, **Monsanto ★★** has been known since the 1930s as the "most Portuguese" village. It is a stunning location, with cobbled streets and houses fused with the boulders clinging to its hillside site. Climb the winding paths above it for stunning **views** of the sand-colored village and the endless plain stretching away toward Spain to the east. There are a number of cozy homestay options in the village; among the best are **Casa Tia Piedade** (www.casadatiapiedade.com; ✆ **96/691-05-99**) and **Taverna Lusitana** (http://tavernalusitana.com; ✆ **27/731-40-09**).

Arrive at dusk and the lights of **Piodão ★★**, glittering on the forested slope, look for all the world like a real, life-size Neapolitan crèche. Cut off from major routes, Piodão has a story linked to bandits and fugitives. Its cluster of homes are made from black-and-rust schist rock, their dark forms offset by the wedding-cake fantasy of the white painted parish church. Come in summer and there's a cooling pool built into the village stream, as well as Alpine-style, good value accommodations at the **Inatel Piodão** hotel (www.inatel.pt; ✆ **23/573-01-00** on the opposite slope.

Other wonderful Beira village locations include **Almeida,** behind the mighty walls of its star-shaped fortress; **Idanha-a-Velha,** with roots dating back to Roman and Visigoth times; and **Sortelha,** which contains mysterious rock-carved tombs and a restaurant, **Dom Sancho** (✆ **27/138-82-67**), renowned for game, within its medieval battlements.

Where to Dine

Belo Horizonte ★★ PORTUGUESE Serving up muscular Beira Alto cuisine since 1963, this is an old-town institution—dark-wood furnishings, white linen table coverings, bare granite walls. Specialties include a creamy, garlicy salt-cod dish inspired by the Count of Guarda, and mixed grilled meats served with rice and beans. There's an excellent selection of local smoked sausages and Portuguese wines. In the hunting season through fall and winter, the rice with hare (*arroz de lebre*) and stewed boar (*guisado de javali*) attract fans from across the border in Spain.

Largo Sao Vicente 2. ✆ **27/121-14-54.** Mains 7.50€–15€. Tues–Sun noon–midnight.

Dom Garfo ★ MODERN PORTUGUESE This island of fine dining is a surprise in a modern neighborhood down the hill from the old city. Chef Dona Olímpia has divided her menu between modern takes on regional dishes and her own creative inventions, which include dishes like salt cod and shrimp "strudel" and toasted escalopes of foie-gras with apple, chestnuts, and balsamic. The three dining rooms share a sophisticated modern design, with bold colors and outsize vintage photos of cute kids and Jazz Age lovers.

Bairro 25 de Abril, 10. www.domgarfo.net. ✆ **27/121-10-77.** Mains 12€–28€. Daily noon–3:30pm and 7–10:30pm.

PORTO & THE DOURO

Roughly translated, Rio Douro means "river of gold." The name is appropriate—when the setting sun catches its waters they glow with the color of burnished bullion. The name may also refer to the riches that the river's banks have brought to Portugal through the wine trade; in particular, the export of its legendary fortified ports.

13

From its source deep in the Spanish heartlands, the Douro winds westward 900km (560 miles) toward its meeting with Atlantic just beyond the city of Porto. For a while, it serves as the border between Spain and Portugal, carving a deep canyon through wild and remote country. For the 322km (200 miles) when it's exclusively Portuguese, the Douro Valley provides some of the country's most beautiful scenery. It contains three very different UNESCO World Heritage Sites: the historic but vibrant city of Porto, mysterious prehistoric artworks at Foz Côa, and vine-covered slopes that form what many view as the world's most-beautiful wine region.

PORTO ★★★

320km (200 miles) N of Lisbon; 566km (350 miles) W of Madrid, Spain

Porto is Portugal's second city, a major commercial center and capital of the industrious northern region. Its inhabitants like to repeat an old saying: "Braga prays, Coimbra sings, Lisbon has fun, and Porto works." Yet like other energetic second-cities—from Manchester to Milan, Mumbai to Shanghai—Porto has developed a reputation for playing as hard as it works.

In recent years, the city has taken off as a center of the arts, fashion, and nightlife. The expansion of its airport to take direct flights from North America and low-cost hops from dozens of European cities has opened it up to tourism. Atmospheric but rundown old neighborhoods are getting a facelift. Swish accommodation options are springing up across the city. Hip new restaurants and bars rival those in the capital. Modern architectural landmarks and cultural hubs like Rem Koolhaas' 2005 Casa da Música or the Serralves art center designed by hometown boy Álvaro Siza Vieira, are internationally renowned. In late 2016, Serralves became the permanent home of a major collection of works by the Spanish surrealist master Joan Miró after a public outcry prevented their sale abroad, and

2017 saw the opening of a fancy new gourmet market in the 100-year-old, *azulejo*-clad São Bento railway station. Also in 2017, Vogue opened the first western European branches of its super-chic cafe chain in Porto and Berlin, much to the chagrin of the Lisbonites.

Despite all this activity, Porto keeps its timeless charm. The windows overlooking narrow streets of the riverside Ribeira district are still hung with washing out to dry; restaurants serve gargantuan plates of beans and tripe; and across the river, in the wine lodges of Vila Nova de Gaia, countless oak barrels still hold their hoard of silently maturing port wine.

Essentials

ARRIVING

BY PLANE Portugal's **TAP** (www.flytap.com) airline runs direct flights twice a week from Newark Airport to Porto's **Aeroporto Francisco de Sá Carneiro.** The trip takes about 8 hours. Canada's **Air Transat** (www.airtransat.com) also runs weekly flights from both Toronto and Montreal. Porto is connected to over 60 European destinations, from Amsterdam to Valencia, mostly by low-cost airlines, with Ireland's **Ryanair** (www.ryanair.com) offering the most choice. There are three to five daily flights from London and two or three from Paris. Among airlines operating between Lisbon and Porto, TAP offers 18 daily shuttle flights, from 24€ each way.

It's easy to get from the airport into town. The clean, efficient subway system, the **Metro,** covers the 11km (7 miles) to the Bolhão station in the center in less than 30 minutes. Take the E line with the violet color code. You can buy an Andante ticket from machines at the airport for 2.45€. Keep it and charge it up for subsequent trips around town for 1.20€ per trip. You have to validate the ticket by swiping it at the machines at approaches to platforms. Buses 601, 602, or the 3M night bus run from the arrivals lounge into town. You can buy tickets onboard for 1.85€. Taxis normally cost 20€ to 30€ from the airport to the city center.

BY TRAIN Coming from Lisbon, the train is a quick, comfortable alternative to flying. The journey on the fastest **Alfa Pendular** express trains takes 2 hours and 35 minutes from Lisbon's Oriente station to Porto's **Campanhã** station, and costs 30.30€ for a second-class one-way ticket. If you choose to take the 4-minute shuttle train from Campanhã into the more central **São Bento** station, the price is included in the ticket. You can also take the metro from Campanhã. The **CP** railway company (www.cp.pt; ✆ **70/721-02-20**) runs a dozen Alfa Pendular trains daily from Lisbon to Porto, stopping at Coimbra and Aveiro. There are also slower Intercity (IC) trains.

BY BUS The **Rede Expressos** bus company (www.rede-expressos.pt; ✆ **70/722-33-44**) runs around 20 trips at day from Lisbon to Porto. The trip takes around 3½ hours and costs 20€ one-way. The **bus station** is central, at Rua Alexandre Herculano, 366. If you're coming from outside Portugal, the **Eurolines** bus company operates routes to Porto from a number of destinations. From Madrid the trip takes just over 9 hours and costs around 40€.

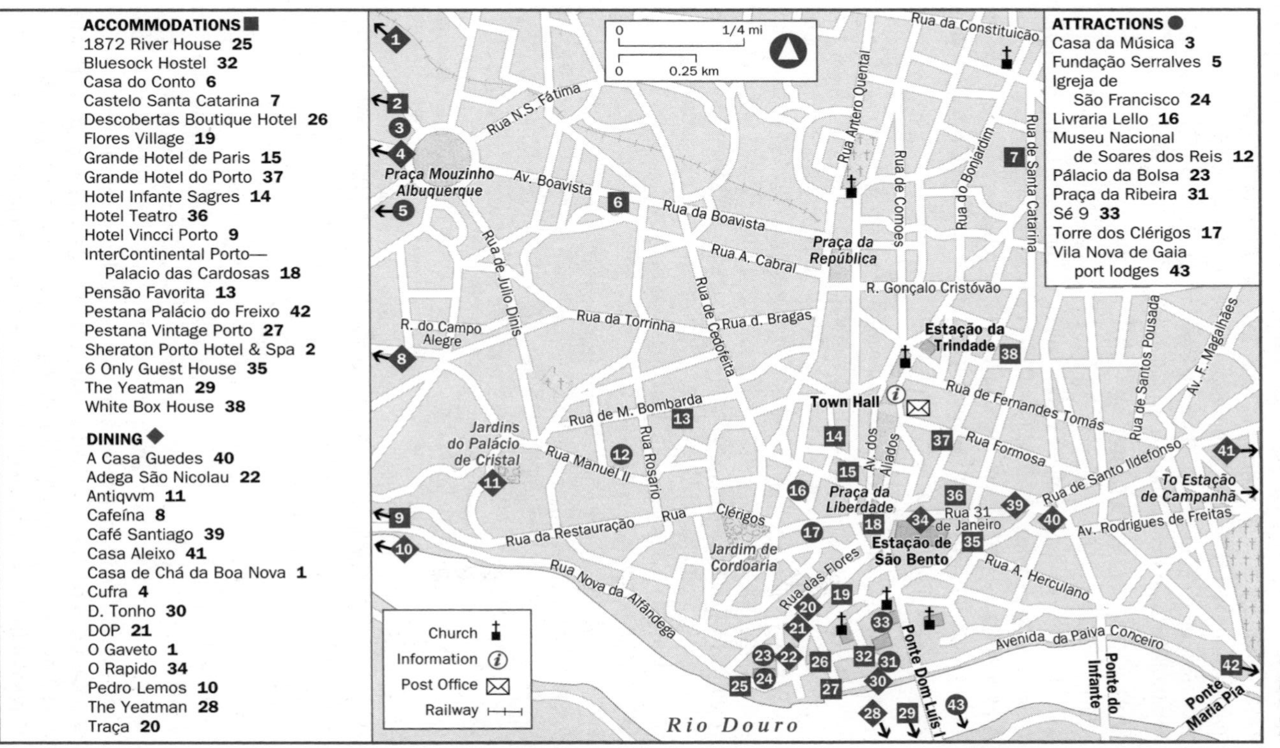
ACCOMMODATIONS
1872 River House 25
Bluesock Hostel 32
Casa do Conto 6
Castelo Santa Catarina 7
Descobertas Boutique Hotel 26
Flores Village 19
Grande Hotel de Paris 15
Grande Hotel do Porto 37
Hotel Infante Sagres 14
Hotel Teatro 36
Hotel Vincci Porto 9
InterContinental Porto—
Palacio das Cardosas 18
Pensão Favorita 13
Pestana Palácio do Freixo 42
Pestana Vintage Porto 27
Sheraton Porto Hotel & Spa 2
6 Only Guest House 35
The Yeatman 29
White Box House 38
DINING
A Casa Guedes 40
Adega São Nicolau 22
Antiqvvm 11
Cafeína 8
Café Santiago 39
Casa Aleixo 41
Casa de Chá da Boa Nova 1
Cufra 4
D. Tonho 30
DOP 21
O Gaveto 1
O Rapido 34
Pedro Lemos 10
The Yeatman 28
Traça 20
ATTRACTIONS
Casa da Música 3
Fundação Serralves 5
Igreja de
São Francisco 24
Livraria Lello 16
Museu Nacional
de Soares dos Reis 12
Pálacio da Bolsa 23
Praça da Ribeira 31
Sé 9 33
Torre dos Clérigos 17
Vila Nova de Gaia
port lodges 43
0 1/4 mi
0 0.25 km
Rua da Constituição
Rua N.S. Fátima
Praça Mouzinho Albuquerque
Av. Boavista
Rua da Boavista
Rua Antero Quental
Rua de Comoes
Rua do Bonjardim
Rua de Santa Catarina
Praça da República
Rua A. Cabral
R. Gonçalo Cristóvão
Rua de Julio Dinis
R. do Campo Alegre
Rua da Torrinha
Rua de Cedofeita
Rua d. Bragas
Estação da Trindade
Rua de Santos Pousada
Av. F. Magalhães
Town Hall
Rua de Fernandes Tomás
Rua de M. Bombarda
Av. dos Aliados
Rua Formosa
Jardins do Palácio de Cristal
Rua Manuel II
Rua Rosario
Rua de Santo Ildefonso
To Estação de Campanhã
Praça da Liberdade
Rua 31 de Janeiro
Av. Rodrigues de Freitas
Rua Clérigos
Rua da Restauração
Jardim de Cordoaria
Estação de São Bento
Rua A. Herculano
Rua das Flores
Rua Nova da Alfândega
Avenida da Paiva Conceiro
Ponte do Infante
Ponte Dom Luís I
Ponte Maria Pia
Rio Douro
Church
Information
Post Office
Railway

BY CAR The trip up the A1 toll highway from Lisbon takes around 3 hours. If you are driving from elsewhere in Europe, it is just over 7 hours from the Spanish-French border crossing at Irun. Take the E80/AP-1 highway to Burgos, then the A-231 to León. From there, turn south on the A-66 to Benavente, then west on A-52 to Verín, before crossing into Portugal at Chaves and driving into Porto on the A27 and A7.

VISITOR INFORMATION

The main **tourist office** is close to city hall in Rua do Clube Fenianos, 25. The tourist board runs an excellent website, packed with information in English (www.portoturismo.pt; ✆ **22/339-34-72**; open Nov–Apr daily 9am–7pm, and May–Oct 9am–8pm). There are smaller tourist offices and stands near the cathedral, in the Ribeira neighborhood, the airport, and Campanhã station.

Getting Around

Porto's historic center is compact, and **walking** around the winding alleys of Ribeira or bustling thoroughfares of the Baixa is one on the city's great pleasures. Be warned, however, that the steepness of the streets leading up from the riverside can be hard on the calves. An alternative is the **Guindais funicular,** dating back to 1891, which hauls passengers from Ribeira to the uptown Batalha district in 2 minutes, offering great views of the Dom Luís I bridge along the way. It runs daily from 8am to 8pm, later during the summer. Tickets can be bought on-site for 2.50€. Offering even better views is the **Teleférico de Gaia** (www.gaiacablecar.com; ✆ **22/374-14-40**), a cable car linking the port wine lodges of Vila Nova de Gaia to the cliff-top upper deck of the Dom Luís I bridge. Opened in 2011, it's become a major attraction in its own right (as well as a way to save on shoe leather). It runs from 10am to 6pm, although that's extended to 8pm in the high season, from late April to late September. One-way tickets are 5€ adults, half-price for children.

For traveling farther afield, Porto's subway system, the **Metro,** is quick, clean, and efficient. There are five lines designated by letter and color. For example, line E is the purple line, running from the airport to the Estádio do Dragão, soccer stadium, home of two-time European champion FC Porto. As well as serving the city center, lines run up the coast to the seaport of Matosinhos and as far as the beaches at Vila do Conde and Póvoa de Varzim. To get the most from a short stay, buy an **Andante Tour** ticket, which allows unlimited travel on all metro lines, city buses, and suburban trains. A 24-hour ticket costs 7€, 72 hours costs 15€. Alternatively, you can buy an **Andante Azul** ticket, which costs 60 cents, but then needs to be charged up with the number of rides you want to make. The zoning system controlling the prices is rather complicated. A Z2 trip in the center costs 1.25€, but if you charge 10 to your ticket, you get one free. You'll need to charge 1.85€ to your ticket for a Z4 trip out of the central zone to the airport. The metro operates from 6–1am.

Whatever type of ticket you buy, you'll need to validate it each time you travel by swiping it against one of the electronic machines on the way to the platforms. For more information, **Metro de Porto** has a well-explained English-language website: http://en.metrodoporto.pt.

Andante tickets are valid on the extensive **bus** network. You can also buy individual tickets on buses for 1.85€. Porto's buses offer free onboard Wi-Fi. There are also three **historic streetcar** (*eléctrico*) lines. Line 1 runs along the north bank of the Douro from Praça São Francisco, in the heart of the old city, to the Passeio Alegre in the seaside suburb of Foz; Line 18 runs from the riverside **Museu do Carro Eléctrico** to the *azulejo*-covered Carmo church; and Line 22 takes a circular route around the city center, connecting with the funicular stop in Batalha. Tickets can be bought from the streetcar drivers for 2.50€. The **STCP** bus company's English website is www.stcp.pt.

Another transport option is to buy a **Porto Card** from one of the city tourist offices or online (www.visitporto.travel). It offers free access to 11 museums and discounts on a number of others, plus restaurants, wine cellars, stores, and more. You can get one with free public transport included, or in a pedestrian version. Those offering free transport range from 13€ for 24 hours to 33€ for 4 days.

Taxis are available 24 hours a day; they are plentiful and relatively cheap. It's usually easy to hail one on the street or from stands around the city. You can also phone or book online from centrals such as **Táxis Invicta** (www.taxisinvicta.com; ✆ **22/507-64-00**) or **Radiotáxis** (www.radiotaxis.pt; ✆ **22/507-39-00**). The around 5km (3-mile) trip from Campanhã station to Praça da Batalha should cost less than 6€. Portugal's taxi drivers have been engaged in a campaign of protests demanding a ban on app-based services such as **Uber** (http://uberportugal.pt) and **Cabify** (https://cabify.com), but both still operate in Porto. **Tuk tuks** are a Southeast Asian import that have taken off recently in the narrow streets of Portuguese cities. They can be hired in the street or through companies such as **Tuktour Porto** (www.tuktourporto.com; ✆ **91/723-26-61**), which offers a number of tour options.

With its steep hills and cobbled streets, Porto is challenging for **cyclists.** But there a number of bike paths, notably the 5km (3-mile) ride along the river and Atlantic coast at Foz. There are several companies where you can rent bikes and get info on routes, such as **Porto Rent a Bike** (www.portorentabike.com; ✆ **22/202-23-75**), whose prices start at 6€ for 2 hours.

City Layout

The best place to grasp the lay of the land in Porto is from the **Miradouro do Mosteiro da Serra do Pilar** on the south bank of the **River Douro.** The broad, cliff-top terrace gives a panoramic view over the city. Technically it isn't actually in Porto. This side of the river is **Vila Nova de Gaia,** a separate city, but effectively a suburb of Porto. To the west, you see the overlapping jumble of red-tiled roofs over the **port wine lodges** that are Gaia's main attraction.

The way back to Porto proper lies across the vertigo-inducing upper span of **Dom Luís I bridge.** Below is the tightly packed **Ribeira** district, Porto's most characteristic neighborhood. Behind the colorful facades of riverside merchant houses is a maze of narrow streets where kids kick soccer balls while their grandmas string out the washing from window to window on the upper floors. Beyond Ribeira, other medieval neighborhoods cling to hillsides rising up from the river, like **Sé, Miragaia, Barredo,** and **São Nicolau,** where among the tangle of lanes you'll find hip bars, timeless old stores, and churches filled with gold-covered wood carvings. Many of Porto's once run-down central neighborhoods are undergoing a regeneration, thanks in part to the surge in tourism.

At the top of the hill is Porto's commercial center, oddly called the **Baxia,** which means "low." The main drag is **Avenida dos Aliados,** a stately avenue laid out in 1916, lined with grandiose hotels and banks and topped by the imposing **City Hall.** The area's main shopping street is the pedestrianized **Rua de Santa Catarina.** The whole area is a dynamic mix of wonderful old cafes, historic shops, and trendy new boutiques. Landmarks include the soaring baroque tower of the **Clérigos** church, the tile-covered **São Bento** railway station, and the **Bolhão** covered market.

Outside the center, the posh western district of **Boavista** has leafy boulevards, modernist villas, spacious parks, and two top cultural attractions: the **Serralves** art center and the **Casa da Musíca** concert hall, both icons of modern architecture. Beyond Boavista is the seaside suburb of **Foz,** boasting some of Portugal's best urban beaches. Up the coast, **Matosinhos** and **Leça de Palmeira** are no-nonsense seaports, renowned for their fab fish restaurants. At the northern extremity of the Porto metro system are the coastal towns of **Vila do Conde** and **Póvoa da Vazim,** where historic centers lay beside fine sandy beaches.

[FastFACTS] PORTO

ATMS/Banks Approximately 2,000 ATMs are scattered around the Porto metropolitan area; most offer multilingual services. There's a concentration of banks around the Avenida dos Aliados in the Baixa area and the Rotunda da Boavista to the west. Banks are open usually open from 8:30am to 3pm, although smaller branches may shut down for lunch. There are currency-exchange counters in Porto airport, but you'll generally get a better rate at an ATM (there are also several ATMs at the airport).

Consulates Neither the United States nor Canada maintains consulates in Porto. In emergencies, contact the embassies in Lisbon (see "Fast Facts" in chapter 16). The United Kingdom closed its physical consulate in 2013 but maintains an honorary consul; those requiring assistance should call ✆ **80/820-35-37.** A number of countries from Brazil to Sweden do maintain full or honorary consulates in the city; a full list with contacts can be found on the website of the tourism board: www.visitporto.travel.

Drugstores Pharmacies are normally open Monday to Friday 9am to 7pm, and Saturdays 9am to 1pm. However, they take turns staying open later and on Sundays, serving as *farmácias de serviço*. They will be listed on a notice posted in the windows of all pharmacies and on the website: www.farmaciasdeservico.net, which is in Portuguese only, but quite straightforward since you only have to click on the name of towns and districts to get a list. There's a limited number of pharmacies open 24/7, including **Farmácia Barreiros,** Rua Serpa Pinto, 12 (www.farmaciabarreiros.com; ✆ **22/834-91-50**) and **Farmácia Avenida,** Rua Primeiro de Janeiro, 20, close to the big hotels in Boavista (http://farmacia-avenida.com; ✆ **22/600-88-88**).

Emergencies Use the **112** European emergency number for police, firefighters, and ambulances. Porto's **Tourism Police,** with English-speaking officers, are based next to the tourist office at Rua Clube dos Fenianos 11 (✆ **22/208-18-33**), open daily 8am to midnight. The regular police, known as the **PSP,** are based at Largo 1 de Dezembro (✆ **22/209-20-00**).

Hospital The two major state health service hospitals are **Hospital de Santo António,** Largo Prof. Abel Salazar (✆ **22/207-75-00**), in the city center, and **Centro Hospitalar de São João**, north of downtown in Alameda Prof. Hernâni Monteiro (✆ **22/551-21-00**). Although both have English-speaking staff, there are a number of private hospitals that are better prepared for handling international patients, including **CUF Porto,** Estrada da Circunvalação, 14341, toward Foz (www.saudecuf.pt/en/porto-hospital; ✆ **22/003-90-00**), and **Lusíadas Porto,** Avenida da Boavista 171 (www.lusiadas.pt; ✆ **21/770-40-40**). The **Prelada** clinic, Rua João Andresen 76 (www.dentista.com.pt; ✆ **22/832-80-31**) offers 24-hour emergency dental treatment and has an English-speaking staff.

Internet Access Porto is a wired-up city. You'll get free Wi-Fi in most hotels, on buses and taxis, at free hotspots around the city in places like the Casa da Musica or public libraries, and in many restaurants and cafes.

Post Office The postal company is called **CTT.** Its main Porto post office is at Praça General Humberto Delgado (✆ **70/726-26-26**). It sells stamps Mon–Fri 8am–9pm and Sat 9am–6pm. There is a post office at the airport open Mon–Fri 8:30am–9pm, weekends 9am–12:30pm and 2–5pm.

Safety Porto is generally a safe city. Violent crime against strangers is rare. However, pickpocketing is a problem, particularly in crowded tourist areas and on public transport, so keep an eye on your wallets, cameras, and purses.

Exploring the City

RIBEIRA

Igreja de São Francisco ★★★ CHURCH From the outside this church, built between 1383 and 1410, looks like a rather plain and ungainly appendix to the adjoining Stock Exchange. Inside, it's astonishing, like a cave lined with gold. That's because the baroque woodwork, installed in the 17th and 18th centuries, is dripping with some 100kg to 600kg (220 to 1,300 pounds) of the stuff, which is used to gild cherubs, rose garlands, fruit cornucopia, and frenzied animals. Soaring overhead are wide-ribbed marble arches that seem to fade and blend mysteriously with the gray granite columns and floors. The church is considered the high point of ***talha dourada,*** Portugal's unique style of wood carvings gilded by the product of an 18th-century Brazilian gold rush. Amongst it all is the towering **Tree of Jesse,** an impossibly ornate carving purporting to show Christ's descent from the kings of Judah. In complete contrast are the spooky **catacombs** below, which contain sober, barrel-arched cellars lined with family burial vaults and a mass grave filled with thousands of skeletons into which you can peer, if you dare.

Rua do Infante Dom Henrique. ✆ **22/206-21-25.** Admission (including church and museum) 4.50€. Daily Nov–Feb 9am–7:30pm; Mar–June and Oct 9am–7pm; Jul–Sept 9am–8pm. Metro: São Bento.

PERUSING the port

Port is one of the world's great wines. But unlike burgundy, bordeaux, or chianti, it isn't a table wine meant to be quaffed over a meal. Port is made by fortifying regular wine (mostly red, sometimes white) with *aguardente*, or brandy. The result is a warm, silkily intense sweet wine. Traditionally, ports are taken after dinner with cheese, chocolatey desserts, or a good cigar.

The variety of port types can be confusing; they range from cheap and cheerful whites often used as mixers to wonderfully complex vintages that can be stored for generations and cost a fortune.

TYPES

Dry whites are the lightest ports, made with white grapes. They are usually served as an aperitif—great with toasted almonds or smoked ham—and are also used to make cocktails. They are popular in Portugal as a summer refresher mixed with tonic, on ice with a slice of lemon.

Beside the grape types, it's the aging process that makes the different styles of port. They break down into those aged in wooden barrels and those that age mostly in the bottle. **Rubys** are the entry-level red ports. As the name indicates, they have a gemlike reddish hue, fruity flavor, and are usually drunk young, after just a couple of years of barrel aging. They go well with blue cheese and red-fruit desserts.

Tawny ports are darker, richer blends. Kept longer under oak, sometimes for decades, they develop the sticky sweetness of dried figs or dates. They are great with caramelized fruits, chocolate, or mature hard cheeses. **Colheitas** are tawnys made from grapes harvested in a single year and matured for at least 7 years in the barrel.

Vintage ports are the top of the range. They are only made in particularly good years and spend just 2 years in the barrel before being left to age for at least 10 years in their bottles. The best are left for several decades, even centuries, and can cost thousands of dollars. They are sipped on their own like a fine cognac, or sublime with dark chocolate or Stilton cheese. **Single quinta vintages** are produced with grapes from a single estate, or quinta, rather than the traditional blending of several made in the port lodges by the riverside in Vila Nova de Gaia. **Late-bottled vintage,** or LBV, is a style developed since the 1970s. It uses grapes from a single exceptional year's harvest like a vintage, but the wine is kept in barrels longer, for 4 or 5 years, and is usually ready to drink rather than be kept in the bottle. Unlike true vintages, LBV can also be poured straight from the bottle, rather than needing to be decanted to remove the natural sediment and allow the wine to "breathe."

HISTORY

Legend has it that port wine took off due to a 17th-century war between England and France. Cut off from their traditional supplies of bordeaux, the Brits increased imports from Portugal and found that adding small amounts of brandy helped the wines weather the long sea journey from Porto. From there, the technique of fortifying the wine developed, leading to port's special character. Rules over where and how true port wine should be produced were first laid down in 1757 by the Marquis of Pombal, the statesman

Palácio da Bolsa ★★ MONUMENT In the mid–19th century, Porto business leaders decided to build a stock exchange so ornate it would earn the instant credibility of investors throughout Europe. This grand building is the result. Although the long neoclassical facade may look a little dull, the interior is an extravaganza of marble, crystal, and tropical woodwork. The grand

who oversaw the rebuilding of Lisbon after the great earthquake of 1755. The historic role played by the British producing and shipping port is still reflected in leading names today, like Croft, Cockburn's, and Taylor's, although shippers from Germany and the Low Countries also took up the trade.

TASTING

The best way to plunge into the flavors and history of port is to visit one of the **historic port lodges ★★★** on the south bank of the Douro, in **Vila Nova de Gaia.** Over a dozen of these old red-tiled warehouses spread back from the quayside, offering tours and tastings. They also keep a few of the narrow, flat-bottomed sailing boats known as ***barcos rabelos*** moored in the river, although they are no longer used to ship barrels of wine down from the vineyards of the upper Douro.

Among the best port lodge experiences, **Graham's** 1890 lodge up the hill in Rua Rei Ramiro (www.grahams-port.com; ✆ **22/377-64-84**) holds over 2,000 *pipas* (oak casks) within its cool granite caves. Its tasting rooms and award-winning restaurant offer wonderful views over the Douro and the river beyond. The basic tour and a tasting of three wines starts at 12€, but there are several options up to 100€ to sip on rare vintages in the club-like private tasting room. Visits only with advance booking. It's open Apr–Oct 9:30am–5:30pm; Nov–Mar 9:30–5pm.

A visit to the **Caves Ferreira,** Av. Ramos Pinto, 70 (http://eng.sograpevinhos.com; ✆ **22/374-61-06**) is a chance to discover a Portuguese-run port house dating back to 1751. As well as the cellars and tasting rooms, there's a museum behind the whitewashed walls of the warehouses. It's dominated by the story of **Dona Antónia Ferreira,** a legendary figure who battled to preserve the quality of the wines at a time when the region was hit by an attack of the vine-destroying phylloxera blight. Among the vintage bottles stored here are some from 1815, believed to be the oldest in the world. Tastings are held under a splendid wooden ceiling in the lodge shop, or the tile-decorated *sala dos azulejos.* Tours start from 6€, with a tasting of two wines.

Not a port lodge, but one of the most enjoyable places along the quay to try port is the **Espaço Porto Cruz,** Largo Miguel Bombarda, 23 (www.myportocruz.com; ✆ **22/092-54-01**) an exhibition, multimedia, and leisure space opened in 2012 by the French-owned Cruz label. Occupying an 18th-century riverside building, it's a flashy combination of old and new, with neon mixing with *azulejos* to brighten up the nighttime facade. Inside there are art shows, films, and digital displays tracing the story of port; a tasting room; restaurant run by star chef Miguel Castro e Silva; and a rooftop bar ideal for sipping cocktails while gazing over the river at the twinkling lights of Porto on the far bank. Tasting options include port pairings with cheese or chocolate, and prices range from 7.5€ to 45€ depending on the number and quality of the wines you sip on. The wine shop is open from Tues–Sun 11am–7pm.

Be aware that while most of the port lodges have shops where you can buy the wines you've tried, the prices are not necessarily cheaper than in stores in town.

chambers and reception rooms borrow decorative elements from ancient Rome, Renaissance Italy, and the court of Versailles. The most extraordinary of its architectural artifices is the **Salão Árabe ★★★** (Arabian salon), a glittering, gold-covered Moorish confection that looks like a Hollywood set for *One Thousand and One Nights*. Oval in shape, it is adorned with arabesques, carved woodwork, and stained-glass windows, all evocative of the Alhambra in Grenada. It's used for formal civic events and the occasional free classical music concert—catch one if you can. Other highlights include the domed **Hall of Nations,** which once housed the trading floor, and a clubby, upmarket restaurant called O Comercial.

Rua Ferreira Borges. www.palaciodabolsa.pt. ✆ **22/339-90-90.** Admission by guided tour only. Tour lasts around 45 min and is available in English. 8€ adults, 4.5€ students and seniors, free for children under 12. Daily Nov–Mar 9am–12:30pm and 2–5:30pm; Apr–Oct 9am–6pm. Metro: São Bento.

Praça da Ribeira ★★ PLAZA Porto's riverside district opens out onto the Douro here, looking across to the wine lodges of Gaia and the curving double-decker ironwork of the Dom Luis I bridge. To the east, the lanes of the Ribeira neighborhood run behind the row of narrow-fronted medieval town houses. To the west are gray stone aches of grander buildings constructed during an 18th-century remodeling. Everywhere, the facades are enlivened with yellow, red, and white paintwork or blue *azulejos*. The northern side is occupied by a three-story-high fountain built in the 1780s. Today, the square is filled with cafe terraces and is a hub of Porto's tourism, but it's not hard to imagine the noisy fish trading and bustling quayside commerce that for centuries took place here.

Metro: São Bento.

Sé ★★ CHURCH Porto's cathedral dates back to the 12th century and much of its form is in the original Romanesque style of the early Middle Ages. Fronted by two towers and a rose window, its squat outline in pale gray stone cuts a brooding figure on the city skyline. Inside there is a purity in its curved barrel-arched nave. Many of the chapels have baroque additions, notably the altarpiece fashioned entirely of silver in the **Chapel of the Holy Sacrament** (the work is so elaborate that the whole piece gives the illusion of constant movement). King João I married the English princess Philippa of Lancaster here in 1387, sealing the world's oldest diplomatic alliance. The cathedral is at its most charming in the **cloister,** where giant panels of *azulejos* depicting biblical scenes coat the walls between vaulted Gothic arches. Also notable is the **Casa do Cabido,** above the cloister, which features more *azulejos* and a sumptuous painted ceiling.

Terreiro da Sé. ✆ **22/205-90-28.** Admission to Sé free; cloister 3€. Mon–Sat 9am–12:15pm and 2:30–5:30pm, Sun 2:30–5:30pm. Stays open an hour later June–Sept. Metro: São Bento.

BAIXA

Avenida dos Aliados ★★ STREET Porto's grandest avenue celebrated its centenary in 2016. Named in honor of Portugal's World War I allies, the Avendia dos Aliados is Porto's living room, the place where locals come for a Sunday stroll, or to celebrate—on New Year's, during the Saint John's day parties in mid-June, or when FC Porto secures another soccer success. The boulevard runs from the dashing horseback statue of **King Pedro IV** (aka Emperor Pedro I of Brazil) uphill for 300 meters (330 yards) to the great tower of the mid-20th-century **City Hall.** Along the way it's lined with grand Belle Epoque buildings housing banks, insurance companies, hotels, and fancy stores. The little **statue** of a flat-capped fellow shouting the Portuguese equivalent of "read all about it" is a reminder that in years gone by newspapers once had their offices here. Another cherished statue is ***Juventude*** (Youth) made by local sculptor Henrique Moreira in 1929, and known affectionately as *a menina nua* (the naked girl). Opinion is divided over the city council's decision not to replant the gardens that ran down the center of the thoroughfare and were ripped up during work on the city subway in the early 2000s. Instead, Porto's two Pritzker Prize–winning architects, **Álvaro Siza Vieira** and **Eduardo Souto de Moura,** joined forces to design an open space of granite flagstones flanking a rectangular **pool** that reflects the surrounding buildings. Two places worth visiting along the Avenida are the **Guarany Café,** dating back to 1933 at No. 85/89 (www.cafeguarany.com; ✆ **22/332-12-72**; open daily 9am–midnight), and the Art Deco **Culturgest** art center (✆ **22/209-81-16**; open Mon–Sat 12:30–6:30pm) on the other side at No. 104. Metro: Aliados.

Livraria Lello ★★ HISTORIC STORE A contender for the world's most beautiful bookshop, this store, opened in 1906, is simply amazing. A slender Gothic Revival front decorated with Art Nouveau paintings representing art and science adorns the outside. Inside are twisting, interlocking wooden staircases, carved balconies and balustrades, stained-glass skylights, richly painted ceilings, and layer upon layer of dark wood bookshelves. It's more a temple to literature than a mere store. Lello is no frozen museum piece, however—it remains a dynamic cultural hub, hosting readings, book launches, and art events. Unfortunately, the store is a victim of its own success. Crowds wanting to get in mean there are often long lines. To limit numbers, the owners have introduced a 3€ fee, which you can reclaim against purchases.

Rua das Carmelitas 144. www.livrarialello.pt. ✆ **22/200-20-37.** Daily 10am–7:30pm. Metro: São Bento.

Museu Nacional de Soares dos Reis ★ MUSEUM Recently renovated, Portugal's oldest public art museum (founded in 1833) retains a pleasingly old-fashioned feel. Housed in a grand 18th-century palace, it was once the residence of the royal family when they sojourned in the north. Its eclectic collection contains artifacts ranging from Visigoth jewelry to Japanese screen paintings depicting the disembarkation of Portuguese merchants in the 1600s. The museum is best known for housing the north's widest collection of Portuguese painting and sculpture. The naturalist portrayals of Portuguese life by painters Henrique Pousão (1859–87) and António Silva Porto (1850–93) are particularly striking. Pride of place, however, goes to sculptor António Soares dos Reis (1847–89) for whom this museum is named. His statue in pure white Carrera marble, ***O Desterrado*** ★★ (The Exile), is a melancholic masterpiece.

potter IN PORTO

Was **Harry Potter** made in Porto? The answer is a mystery, but it is certain that Scottish author **J. K. Rowling,** creator of the world's most famous boy wizard, spent almost 2 years living in the city in the early 1990s while she was working on the manuscript of what would become the first Potter novel.

She taught English and was briefly married to a Portuguese journalist. They say Rowling jotted down key chapters of *Harry Potter and the Philosopher's Stone* while sipping coffee at the marble tables of the 1920s **Cafe Majestic,** where she was a regular customer. The marvelous **Lello bookshop** is said to have inspired Flourish and Blotts, the fictional store where junior sorcerers browsed for volumes of spells. Lello's seemingly endless staircase is supposedly the model for the moving stairs of Hogwarts School.

The school uniforms of Hogwarts bear an uncanny resemblance to the traditional black suits and capes worn by Portuguese university students. One story says that Rowling got the idea for Gryffindor house from the **Fonte dos Leões** fountain, featuring four winged lions cast in bronze, just up the hill from Lello.

Some say the broomsticks used in the game of Quidditch may just have entered the writer's imagination at the **Escovaria de Belomonte,** a 90-year-old store selling a baffling array of handmade brooms and brushes. The sinister wizard Salazar Slytherin could have been named for Portugal's long-lasting dictator, **António de Oliveira Salazar.**

How much of this is urban legend is not clear. Rowling certainly frequented the Majestic and the Lello, but doesn't talk much about her years in Porto, which were economically and emotionally tough. Potter, however, has been good for the city, as fans seek out the sorcerer's roots. Thousands besieged Lello when the bookshop organized a late-night launch of the latest volume, *Harry Potter and The Cursed Child*, in the summer of 2016. Enterprising guides offer tours of Harry-related haunts around the city; for details, visit www.withlocals.com.

There's a charming formal garden in the back overlooked by a cafeteria serving tasty light meals.

Rua de Dom Manuel II. www.museusoaresdosreis.pt. ✆ **22/339-37-70.** Admission 5€, 2.50€ seniors and students, free for children under 12. Tues–Sun 10am–6pm. Metro: Aliados.

Rua de Santa Catarina ★★ STREET Porto's main shopping drag is a bustling 1.5km (almost 1 mile) long. Most of it is pedestrian-only and covered with artful black-and-white paving stones. Shopaholics can find almost anything along Santa Catarina or the side streets running off it. There are big-name European brands like Zara, H&M, or FNAC alongside venerable family stores selling everything from freshly baked bread to upmarket leather goods. Among the landmarks are the **Majestic Café** at No. 112 (www.cafemajestic.com; ✆ **22/200-38-87**), the chicest place for a *cimbalino* (as the people of Porto call a shot of espresso) since 1921. It's filled with gilt-framed mirrors, marble-topped tables, and smiling plasterwork cherubs, and serves divine *rabanadas*—Porto's take on French toast. Continuing the old-world charm is the **Grande Hotel do Porto** at No. 197. There are two stylish **Art Nouveau**

corner shops guarding the southern entrance to the street beneath the *azulejo*-clad **Church of Saint Ildefonso,** and a modern shopping mall with a colorful facade at No. 312. The greatest gem on the street, however, is the **Capela das Almas,** at No. 428, a tiny church covered with tiles with such an intensity of blue they rival the summer sky. The church is from the 18th century, but although painted in the baroque style of that time, the tiles were actually added in 1929.

Metro: Bolhão.

Torre dos Clérigos ★★ LANDMARK What the Eiffel Tower is to Paris or the Empire State Building is to New York, this is to Porto: a 76m (250-ft.) church tower looming over the city center that's a cherished icon to the people of Porto. It was designed in 1754 by Italian architect Nicolau Nasoni, who left his baroque mark all over Porto and is buried in the handsome church attached to the tower. The richly decorated granite landmark was the tallest building in Portugal when it was built and still dominates the skyline. Views from the top are breathtaking—if you have any breath left after climbing the 225 steps spiraling up to the top.

Rua São Filipe De Nery. ✆ **22/200-17-29.** Admission including the tower and exhibitions in the church 3€, free for children under 10. Daily 9am–8:30pm. At times, it is possible to climb the tour at night with pre-arranged visits that can also include wine and chocolate tasting in the church. Metro: São Bento.

BOAVISTA

Serralves ★★★ MUSEUM You get three attractions in one with a visit to Porto's premier modern art venue out in the leafy Boavista district. On-site is a splendid 1930s villa in blushing pink, the best Art Deco home in Portugal (the art collection used to be housed here). Behind it is an 18-hectare (44-acre) handsomely landscaped park featuring over 200 species of native and exotic plants. The centerpiece, the Museum of Contemporary Art, which opened in 1999, is a masterpiece of modern architecture by native son Álvaro Siza Vieira. His use of diagonal white planes rising and falling at odd angles creates startling and constantly changing contrasts between sunlight and shadow, open sky, and the surrounding lawns.

Serralves has become the most dynamic cultural hub in the north, perhaps in the whole country (by some counts it is the most visited museum in the nation). As well as a permanent collection of over 4,000 works by Portuguese and international artists, it hosts regular temporary exhibitions, concerts, and a 4-day arts festival, **Serralves em Festa,** every June. In 2016, the museum received 84 works by the Spanish artist Joan Miró, which are now integrated into the permanent collection. There is a restaurant and teahouse with a verdant terrace, plus shops selling art books and Portuguese design items.

Rua Don João de Castro 210. www.serralves.pt. ✆ **80/820-05-43.** Admission to the museum and park 10€ adults, 5€ students and seniors, children under 12 free. Park only 5€ adults. Oct–Mar Tues–Fri 10am–6pm, Sat–Sun 10am–7pm; Apr–Sept Tues–Fri 10am–7pm, Sat–Sun 10am–8pm. Bus: 201, 203, 502, or 504.

WALKING TOUR: THE HEART OF PORTO

START: **Cais da Ribeira.**

FINISH: **Mosteiro da Serra do Pilar.**

TIME: **2 hours.**

BEST TIMES: **Afternoon (or morning, heading in the other direction).**

Begin your tour in the heart of the old town, at:

1 Cais da Ribeira

If you've lunched on Porto's signature dish of tripe and beans in one of the riverside neighborhood's restaurants—**Dom Tonho** or **Adega São Nicolau** would be a good choice—you'll now be ready to walk off the calories. Start by admiring the view along the river, then set the round, whitewashed church high on a cliff on the opposite bank as your eventual target.

Head along the river to Praça da Ribeira, then carry on along Cais da Estiva, admiring the facades of the high merchant houses behind the granite wall to your right, onto Largo do Terreiro. Then carry on up the pedestrianized Rua Alfândega.

2 Casa do Infante

At No. 10 is this solid stone house built in the 14th century and supposedly the place where Henry the Navigator was born in 1394. It was once the customs house and now holds exhibitions about the Portuguese Discoveries and the history of Porto (✆ **22/206-04-35;** admission 2.20€, free on weekends; Tues–Sun 10am–12:30pm and 2–5pm).

At the top of the road you'll find the gently sloping lawns of the Jardim do Infante. Your next destinations are on the left.

3 Igreja de São Francisco

The plain stone Gothic rear of the church that you see from the gardens will not prepare you for the glittering interior of Porto's "**golden church.**" If you visit one church in Porto, this is the one (see p. 333).

Just next door.

4 Palácio de Bolsa

This massive neoclassical building with its sober gray stone facade once housed the Stock Exchange. Grab a tour of its opulent interior, especially the fairytale **Arabian Salon** (see p. 335).

Continue up Rua de Ferreira Borges until you reach No. 27.

5 Port and Douro Wines Institute

The understated, cream-colored two-story building facing you is where the port wine trade—recently valued at a cool 175 million euros—is regulated. Inside you can get a guided tour, do some tasting of your own, and discover more about how this nectar is produced (www.ivdp.pt; ✆ **22/207-16-69;** admission 5€; Mon–Fri 11am–7pm).

Walking Tour: Porto

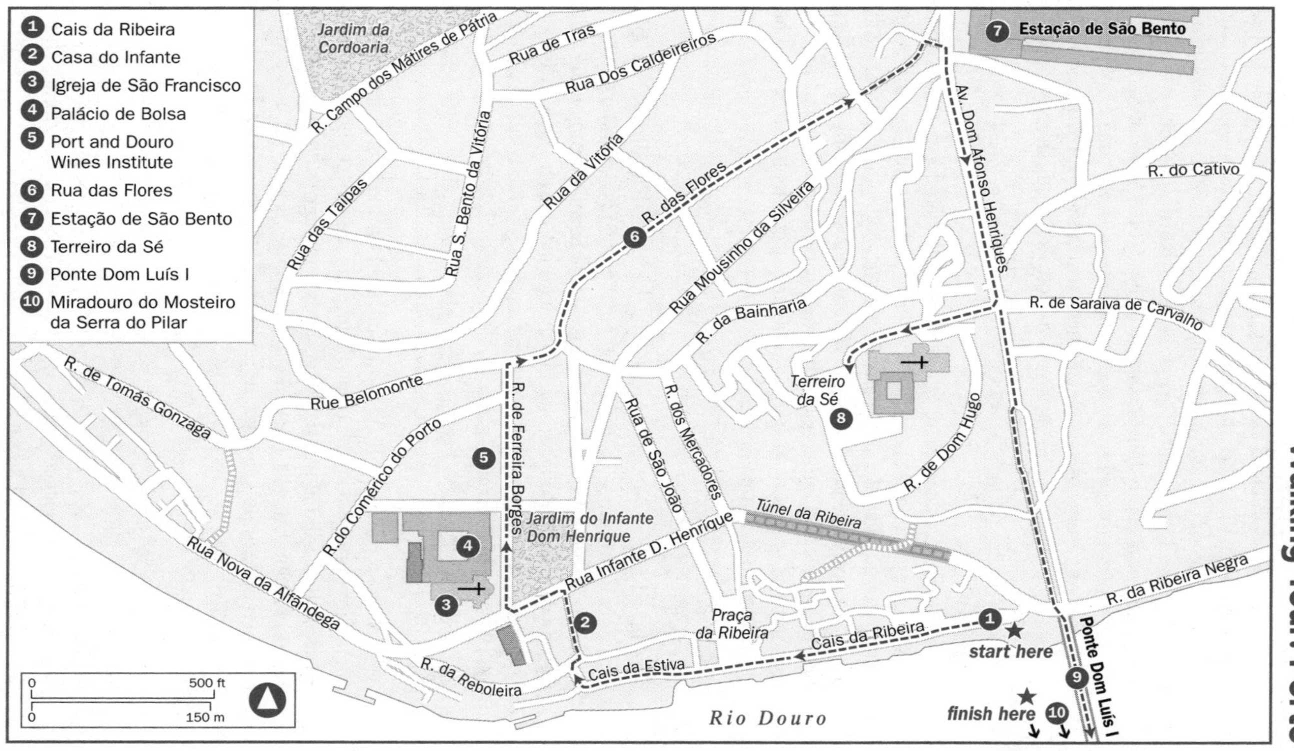

At the top of the hill, turn right onto Largo São Domingos.

6 Rua das Flores

For some, the "street of flowers" is Porto's prettiest. Cars have been banned since 2014, and it rises in a lazy curve between rows of centuries-old houses decorated with wrought-iron balconies. You'll pass monuments like the 16th-century **Igreja da Misericórdia** church or the **Casa dos Maias,** an aristocratic mansion in need of a makeover. It is the eclectic mix of stores old and modern that make Flores such a fascinating thoroughfare, from artisan chocolatiers and trendy restaurants to Art Nouveau jewelers and the purveyors of Porto's famed luxury soaps.

When you reach the top of the street, look straight ahead across the little square.

7 Estação de São Bento

Facing you across the square at the top of Rua das Flores, this is Portugal's grandest railroad station. It was built at the beginning of the 20th century in imitation of the Parisian Beaux-Arts style. Inside, however, the decor is purely Portuguese, with **20,000 tiles** painted by artist **Jorge Colaço** and formed into monumental wall panels depicting the history of transport and scenes of medieval daring-do. A gourmet market food hall opened in the station in 2017.

Now you have a steep climb up Av. Dom Afonso Henriques toward the cathedral.

8 Terreiro da Sé

This broad square almost surrounding the **cathedral** provides a great view over the rooftops of Porto's old neighborhoods, and offers a chance to admire the stone Romanesque facade of the Sé and the adjoining white **Episcopal Palace** designed by Italian baroque master Nicolau Nasoni. The impressive-looking pillory in the square is actually a fake, built in the 1940s to 18th-century plans.

Behind the cathedral, take Av. Vimara Peres north toward the river.

9 Ponte Dom Luís I

After a short walk you'll find yourself high on the upper deck of this mighty iron bridge with the Douro below and the city at your feet. When it was built in 1886, it was the longest bridge of its type in the world. The engineer behind it was Frenchman **Théophile Seyrig,** an associate of **Gustave Eiffel** of tower fame. Eiffel himself built the **Maria Pia Bridge** just a bit farther upstream, in 1877, which was also a world record-breaker at the time.

Once you cross the bridge, follow the streetcar tracks past the Jardim do Morro gardens, then take a sharp right up the Rampa do Infante Santo.

10 Miradouro do Mosteiro da Serra do Pilar

You have now reached your destination. The unusual round church behind you is worth a visit for its cloister, dome and exhibitions on northern Portuguese heritage. There is history here, too. During the Portuguese Civil War in the 1830s, Liberal forces fought a heroic defense to prevent

Conservative troops from taking Porto. The real reason for the climb, however, is the breathtaking **view** over the Douro and the city beyond. If you've timed it right, you'll arrive as the sun goes down and the lights of Porto start to twinkle against the purple sky. After that, head back down to Ribeira's bars or the wine lodges of Gaia for a well-deserved thirst-quencher.

Where to Stay

EXPENSIVE

1872 River House ★★ A pink-painted town house perched over the Douro on the old quayside where sailing ships used to moor to unload their cargoes of salt cod, this is now a fancy boutique B&B in the atmospheric Ribeira district. It is cozy, family-run, and best for guests seeking an up-close immersion into Porto life, rather than an amenity-heavy hotel experience. Half of the eight rooms look out right onto the Douro (offering views over to the wine lodges), and a few have balconies. The decor is in natural stone, wood, and *azulejos*. One room has a bed emerging from a huge stone fireplace. There's a comfortable lounge for relaxing and gazing out along the river. Breakfasts are a copious blend of fresh orange juice, cappuccinos, breads, pastries, fruit, and eggs made to order. It's served as late as you like it.

Rua do Infante D. Henrique, 133. www.1872riverhouse.com. ✆ **96/117-27-05.** 8 units. 145€–220€ double, including breakfast. Parking nearby 18€ per day. **Amenities:** Bike rental; bar. Free Wi-Fi.

Flores Village ★★ Behind the *azulejo*-covered facade of an 18th-century, five-story building (on the delightful Rua das Flores, see. p. 357) lies a different type of accommodation. Besides regular rooms, the hotel has suites and self-catering apartments for up to eight people, making it ideal for families. Opened in 2014, rooms cluster around a sunny urban garden. Many have huge windows and balconies over the street that look across to the towers of the cathedral on the opposite hilltop. Common areas include salons with baroque ceiling paintings and tasteful furnishings, and an exceptional spa with a Roman-style bath sunk among the foundations.

Rua das Flores, 139. www.floresvillage.com. ✆ **22/201-34-78.** 33 units. 108€–202€ double; apartments up to 457€. Parking in nearby public car park 20€ per day. **Amenities:** Bar; spa; indoor pool; bike rental; gym; garden. Free Wi-Fi.

Hotel Infante Sagres ★★ For decades this was the default option for downtown luxury in Porto, built in 1951 as the domain of cigar-chomping, port-swilling stalwarts of the wine trade and barons of northern Portugal's textile and furniture trade. Guests have included Bob Dylan, the Dali Lama, and British royalty. It still comes loaded with old-world elegance: wrought-iron balconies, plush oriental carpets, stained-glass windows, and genuine antique furnishings. Rooms are comfortable with heavy drapes, vintage prints, and marble-sheathed bathrooms. Yet of late, the old place was starting to look a little tired. The new owners (the same company that owns the Yeatman; see listing below) have started renovating the place, so hopefully it will be restored to its former glory.

Praça Filipa de Lencastre 62. www.hotelinfantesagres.pt. ✆ **22/339-85-00.** 70 units. 135€–260€ double, including breakfast. Nearby parking 18€ per day. **Amenities:** Restaurant; bar; spa; gift shop; babysitting. Free Wi-Fi.

InterContinental Porto—Palacio das Cardosas ★★ Once a convent, then the manorial abode of a business magnate grown rich in Brazil, this 18th-century neoclassical building is a Porto landmark. It lies at the foot of Avenida dos Aliados, Porto's equivalent of New York's Times Square. Opened in 2011 as a hotel, it's just as swellegant as you'd expect, its lobby lined with marble and crystal. There's an English library–styled bar off to the right, a century-old silversmith among the row of stores off to the left, and a floral scent in the air produced by Porto's famed Castelbel fragrance maker. Rooms are spacious but cozy, and many feature floor-to-ceiling windows overlooking the avenue. Breakfast is served in a light-filled salon opening onto a courtyard at the back, and dinner can be taken in the street-level Astoria restaurant, one of the city's best.

Praca da Liberdade, 25. www.ihg.com. ✆ **22/003-56-00.** 105 units. 182€–485€ double, including breakfast. Valet parking in nearby public car park 29€ per day. **Amenities:** Restaurant; bar; babysitting; fitness room; spa; bike rental. Free Wi-Fi.

Pestana Palácio do Freixo ★★★ Only the 18th-century formal garden and its gently trickling fountain separate this magnificent baroque palace from the River Douro. The location and the main building are spectacular. It was built around 1750 by Nicolau Nasoni, the architect behind Porto's landmark Clérigos tower, and is protected as a national monument. Inside, the chapel, lounge, and restaurant are decorated with airy murals, high windows, and gilded columns. Monumental fresh flower arrangements add to the "wow factor." The spacious rooms are located next to the main building in a 19th-century flour mill that underwent a remarkable renovation ahead of the hotel's opening in 2009. Standard rooms overlook the lush garden at the back, others look out over the river. Completing the picture is an excellent restaurant serving a number of classic Porto dishes, a luxurious spa, and a riverside outdoor pool. It is a bit out of the city center, but that means peace and quiet, and there is a free shuttle into town three times a day.

Estrada Nacional 108. www.pestana.com. ✆ **22/531-10-00.** 87 units. 153€–340€ double, including breakfast. Free parking. **Amenities:** Indoor and outdoor pools; spa; garden; terrace; fitness center; restaurants; bar. Free Wi-Fi.

Pestana Vintage Porto ★★ This hip option is smack in the center of the Ribeira district and comprises two blocks of buildings, some dating back over 400 years. The main edifice is a distinctive yellow landmark where Praça da Ribeira meets the river. Within its granite walls, the atmosphere is zesty and youthful. There's quirky art in the lobby, cool retro furniture, and a riverside bar where you can down a white port with tonic and chew on ceviche. No corners are cut with comfort in the rooms, where stylish modern design

PORTO by the sea

As if all the history, wine, and culture were not enough, Porto boasts some of Portugal's best urban beaches. If the traffic's moving, a little over 20 minutes by bus will whisk you from Avenida das Aliados to the soft sand and rolling Atlantic surf of the beach resort of **Foz do Douro.** Foz features fine seaside promenades; a string of beaches broken up by rocky outcrops; and plenty of good shops, cafes, and restaurants amid Porto's most sought-after real estate.

We particularly like **Bonaparte,** Av do Brasil, 130 (✆ **22/618-84-04;** open daily 5pm–2pm), a delightfully cluttered seafront bar serving snacks and a range of beers since 1975. Among the beaches, **Praia Homem do Leme** is many people's favorite, with shaded lawns and a couple of good beach bars.

Follow the coast a bit farther up and you reach **Matosinhos,** a fishing port that draws crowds from Porto, just 30 minutes away by metro, to its cluster of ***marisqueiras*** (seafood restaurants) around Rua Roberto Ivens. Matosinhos and neighboring **Leça da Palmeira** are also a draw for modern architecture enthusiasts, featuring works by hometown boy **Álvaro Siza Vieira** (b. 1933), including the **Piscinas de Marés** swimming complex on Leça beach and the **Casa de Chá** (teahouse) rising out of the rocks on **Boa Nova beach,** now a fancy restaurant.

A new architectural landmark sprung up on the Matosinhos harborfront in 2015, the spiraling white **Leixões cruise terminal,** and a major new exhibition space, the **Casa da Arquitetura,** are due to open in 2017.

Farther north, the Porto metro's red line extends up to the historic seaside town of **Vila do Conde,** which features a quaint medieval center, monumental convent overlooking the River Ave, and some of the best beaches in the north, notably **Praia de Mindelo** and **Praia de Moreiró.**

To the south just downriver from Vila Nova de Gaia is the pleasant fishing village of **Afurada** and a string of fine sandy beaches leading down to **Espinho.** Among the best, **Praia do Senho da Pedra** is easily reachable by suburban train to the Miramar stop; it features a little white chapel on the rocks as a counterpoint to the vast expanse of sand. **Praia de São Pedro da Maceda,** backed by dunes and pine forest, is good for seekers of solitude, although care is needed with the rip currents.

complements the building's original features. The award-winning restaurant specializes in beef.

Praça de Ribeira 1. www.pestana.com. ✆ **22/340-23-00.** 103 units. 135€–352€ double, including breakfast. Parking in nearby public car park 22€ per day. **Amenities:** Restaurant; bar; bike rental. Free Wi-Fi.

The Yeatman ★★★ This place really has it all: a Michelin-two-star restaurant serving some of the country's finest haute cuisine, a fabulous spa, super-comfortable rooms, and, most of all, views. From its hillside location above Gaia's wine lodges, the Yeatman has Porto laid before it. You can admire the skyline not just from your balcony, but also from your bathtub; not just from the restaurant and terrace bar, but also from the indoor and outdoor pools. The Jacuzzi with a view has become a popular spot for wedding proposals. Opened in 2010, the hotel is built in the style of a pastel-painted colonial villa. Owned by one of the old port shipping firms, it is dedicated to wine, with the decor of each room inspired by famed vineyards. The spa offers Caudalie wine therapy scrubs and massages. The wine cellar contains over 1,000 bottles, including vintage ports dating back to the 1850s.

Rua do Choupelo, Vila Nova de Gaia. www.the-yeatman-hotel.com. ✆ **22/013-31-00.** 83 units. 215€–350€ double, including breakfast. Parking 16€ per day. **Amenities:** Restaurants; bar; indoor and outdoor pools; spa; garden; sun deck; fitness center; cycle hire; children's playground; babysitting. Free Wi-Fi.

MODERATE

Casa do Conto ★ The name of this B&B means "the house of stories," and it has quite a story of its own. In 2009, a couple of weeks before it was due to open as a meticulously restored 19th-century town house B&B, fire swept through the building, destroying the interior. The architect owners pressed ahead, but now beyond the tile-covered facade there's nothing old timey about the place. Its hip looks are minimalist and contemporary, with large rooms spun off from a raw concrete staircase. Each guest room is individually designed: white and bare cement gray are the dominant colors, enlivened by bright splashes—a gold-framed mirror, mustard leather sofa, blue sky shining through the skylight, or broad bedroom windows. It can feel a bit like living in a rather austere art installation, but the welcome is warm and there's a cute garden out back. It's located close to the Casa da Musica and the up-and-coming Cedofeita neighborhood.

Rua da Boavista, 703. http://casadoconto.com. ✆ **22/206-03-40.** 6 units. 98€–160€ double, including breakfast. Rates include buffet breakfast. Parking available nearby 10€ per day, reservation needed. **Amenities:** Babysitting; bike hire; lounge; garden. Free Wi-Fi.

Descobertas Boutique Hotel ★★ Passersby often wander into the lobby of this hotel tucked away in a Ribeira back street, thinking it's an upscale, exotic antique shop. It's packed with Indian silk slippers, African fabrics, Chinese ceramics, cushions sown from tea or coffee sacks, and other items that recall destinations reached by Portuguese explorers. *Descobertas* means "Discoveries," and each floor is dedicated to a particular country, from Cape Verde to Macau. The building once housed a trade association, and you'll see that early-20th-century industrial heritage in the massive stone walls, iron pillars, and exposed wood beams. Guests with a sweet tooth will love breakfast.

Rua Fonte Taurina 14-22. www.descobertasboutiquehotel.com. ✆ **22/201-14-73.** 18 units. 99€–154€ double, including breakfast. Public car park nearby 20€ per day. **Amenities:** Babysitting. Free Wi-Fi.

Grande Hotel do Porto ★ Centrally located on Rua de Santa Catarina, the pedestrianized shopping street, the GHP is a Porto institution. Opened in 1880, the hotel has played host to royalty, aristocracy, and artists over the decades. You may recognize it when you walk in: Its Victorian interiors were used as a backdrop in movies by the acclaimed Porto-born director Manoel de Oliveira. Throughout, the GHP is warm and welcoming, with dark chintz wall coverings, hardwood paneling, velvet furnishings, and gilt-framed landscape paintings. Rooms are a pleasing mix of period and modern, including works by contemporary Portuguese artists and photographers. The on-site restaurant, named after one-time guest Emperor Pedro II of Brazil, is renowned for its Sunday brunch. There is also a small gym and wellness room offering a selection of massages. The only disappointment? Some of the standard rooms are on the small side.

Rua de Santa Catarina 197. www.grandehotelporto.com. ✆ **22/207-66-90.** 94 units. 64€–108€ double, including breakfast. Parking 11€ per day. **Amenities:** Restaurant; bar; wellness room; gym; rooftop terrace; babysitting. Free Wi-Fi.

Hotel Teatro ★★ Unleash your inner drama queen. The Hotel Teatro was built on the site of an 1850s playhouse, and its decor is an homage to the bohemian glamour of the site's past. Lighting is low and dramatic. The decor comes in tones of gold, copper, and chestnut. Racks of flamboyant theatrical costumes decorate the lobby, and guest rooms are sultry and decadent, with expansive soft beds, standalone baths, and wall-to-wall mirrors. Food options are a delight as well, thanks to Chef Arnaldo Azevedo, whose Palco restaurant has been in the limelight; it's one of the best gourmet options in town. Located in a modern, glass-fronted building in the heart of the Baixa neighborhood, Hotel Teatro is a member of the international Design Hotel collection.

Rua Sá da Bandeira, 84. www.hotelteatro.pt. ✆ **22/040-96-20.** 74 units. 99€–229€ double, including breakfast. Parking 14€ per day with reservation. **Amenities:** Restaurant; bar; massage; fitness center. Free Wi-Fi.

Hotel Vincci Porto ★★ If the thought of sleeping in a fish market doesn't sound appealing, think again. All right, this is not a *working* fish market, but traders once haggled over catches of hake and bass in this iconic 1930s building. Its cool Art Deco lines make it a lovely alternative to older-styled hotels downtown. The high-ceilinged, glass-fronted lobby, in particular, is a light-filled jewel. Sip a *porto-tónico* in the bar and you can imagine yourself on a Jazz Age cruise liner. The **33 Alameda** restaurant is another Art Deco beaut, featuring onyx columns and vertical lighting, not to mention an excellent modern take on Mediterranean cooking. As for the digs: Guest rooms and baths are large and handsomely color-coordinated. Some offer river views. The historic tram line stops just outside to whisk guests downtown.

Alameda Basílio Teles, 29. http://en.vincciporto.com. ✆ **22/043-96-20.** 95 units. 104€–246€ double, including breakfast. Parking 10€ per day with reservation. **Amenities:** Restaurant; bar. Free Wi-Fi.

Sheraton Porto Hotel & Spa ★ Here rooms are spacious, light-filled, and decorated in refined chocolate and white. Furnishings are contemporary and stylish. Live music is a nightly feature in the New Yorker Bar. Guests in the club rooms enjoy a rooftop terrace with a panoramic view. The hotel spa, with its adjacent juice bar, is among the finest in the city. Located in the leafy Boavista neighborhood, it's near to the Casa da Musica and Serralves park.

Rua de Tenente Valadim 146. www.sheratonporto.com. ✆ **22/040-40-00.** 266 units. 125€–250€ double, including breakfast. Parking 9€. **Amenities:** Restaurant; 2 bars; babysitting; health club & spa; indoor heated pool; terrace. Free Wi-Fi.

INEXPENSIVE

Bluesock Hostel ★ Spain's Carris hotel chain chose Porto for its first venture into the back-backer market, with this upscale hostel that opened in the summer of 2016. Occupying a traditional blue-tiled town house on the street leading out of Ribeira toward the Baixa, it offers a range of accommodations from cool modern suites with private bathrooms to dorms for up to 13 people with extra-wide bunks and locker space for luggage. Dorms are either mixed or women only. All can access chill-out lounges, computer rooms, and a bar, each with playful furniture set among raw stone walls, wooden beams, and the great arched basement ceiling.

Rua de São João, 40. www.bluesockhostels.com. ✆ **22/766-41-71.** 27 units. 64€–99€ double, dorm beds 15€–25€. No parking. **Amenities:** Bar; lounge. Free Wi-Fi.

Castelo Santa Catarina ★ A definite oddity. Built in 1887 as a textile baron's folly, it looks uncannily like a pimped version of Lisbon's Torre de Belém, with turrets, battlements, and arched windows. The "castle" is set in a private compound surrounded by pine and palm trees. Beyond the tile-covered exterior is an eccentric Victorian labyrinth of halls and stairways filled with painted ceilings, stained glass, and rosewood furniture. The rooms are rather more restrained, although the plumbing fixtures are designed with a florid Art Nouveau flair. There's a modern wing across the courtyard garden with a more contemporary feel. It's located in a residential neighborhood about 20 minutes' walk, or a short metro trip, to the town center. Free parking is a plus.

Rua de Santa Catarina 1347. www.castelosantacatarina.com.pt. ✆ **22/509-55-99.** 25 units. 56€–85€ double, including breakfast. Free parking. **Amenities:** Bar; garden; terrace. Free Wi-Fi.

Grande Hotel de Paris ★ Porto's oldest hotel was opened in 1877, a couple of steps away from the Avenida dos Aliados. Early guests in what was for years a French-owned establishment included the great novelist José Maria Eça de Queirós and the artist Rafael Bordalo Pinheiro. The decor in the rooms is a bit fusty, but this is still a solid budget option—it oozes old-world charm and is right in the city center. A real treat is the magnificent Belle Epoque salon where an equally impressive breakfast is served, including the likes of "English-style bacon" and Porto's cinnamon- and port-wine–infused French toast. In summer, breakfast is served under striped awnings in the garden, an unexpected haven of tranquility in the heart of the city. There's a small museum featuring old telephones, gramophones, and newspaper clippings from the hotel's golden days. ***Tip:*** Book early to get the best rates.

Rua da Fábrica, 27/29. www.hotelparis.pt. ✆ **22/207-31-40.** 45 units. 56€–162€ double, including breakfast. Public car park nearby, 12€ per day, reservation needed. **Amenities:** Bar; garden; terrace; bike rental. Free Wi-Fi.

Pensão Favorita ★★ An arty guest house in the core of Porto's trendy gallery and design district, the Favorita's decor is the handiwork of famed French designer Sam Baron. Rooms in the main town-house building are large and mostly white, but with colorful Portuguese touches, like cushions covered with traditional chintz fabrics from Alcobaça. Those in the newer red-brick garden extension are smaller, but have the advantage of a patio opening out into the lush, peaceful green space. There's a friendly welcome and families are catered to with roomy suites. The veranda is the perfect place to sip a glass of port or one of the Portuguese craft beers on offer.

Rua Miguel Bombarda, 267. www.pensaofavorita.pt. ✆ **22/013-41-57.** 12 units. 70€–90€ double, including breakfast. Public car park nearby, 15.50€ per day. **Amenities:** Bar; garden; terrace; bike rental; babysitting. Free Wi-Fi.

6 Only Guest House ★★ When it opened in 2009, this cool, charming, and affordable B&B had just six rooms, hence the name. Since then, owners Pedro and Mariana have expanded into the house next door, and now there are also six suites. They insist this is not a hotel but a meeting place where visitors can really get to know the city. The colorful rooms are decorated with natural finishes in wood, cork, cotton, and linen. Most of the units have high French windows and some feature balconies. There's a spacious breakfast room that opens out onto the patio garden. Expect to start the day with warm bread, croissants, and homemade pumpkin jam. It's a short walk to São Bento station and the shops of Rua de Santa Catarina.

Rua Duque de Loulé, 97. www.6only.pt. ✆ **92/688-51-87.** 12 units. 70€–85€ double, including breakfast. Public car park nearby, 9€ per day, reservation needed. **Amenities:** Bar; garden; terrace. Free Wi-Fi.

White Box House ★ Amid the shopping throng of Rua de Santa Catarina, this is a restored early-20th-century three-story town house with just six rooms. Its atmosphere is intimate and cozy; its prime perk is the shared kitchen and dining room for guests, plus a lounge with floor-to-ceiling windows over the pedestrian street below. Out back, the sunny garden is an urban oasis. Rooms are simply but comfortably furnished with soft duvets, throws in pale earthy colors, polished hardwood floors, and sink-into leather armchairs.

Rua de Santa Catarina 575. www.the-white-box.pt. ✆ **91/100-85-85.** 6 units. 62€–92€ double, including breakfast. No parking. **Amenities:** Garden; kitchen. Free Wi-Fi.

Where to Eat

The people of Porto are known across Portugal as *tripeiros*, or "tripe eaters." The nickname comes from the city's signature dish, *tripas à moda do Porto*, a hearty stew that includes butter beans, calves' feet, pigs' ears, and paprika-spiced chouriço sausage along with tripe—the chewy white lining of a cow's stomach.

Legend has it the city became hooked on offal after its patriotic citizens handed over all their meat to Prince Henry the Navigator in the 15th century to feed his army on its way to invade Morocco, leaving just the offcuts.

Lately Porto has undergone a culinary revolution. You can still find plenty of great traditional joints serving monster portions of *tripas* and other old favorites, like deep-fried octopus or wonderful *francesinha* sandwiches, but a new generation of innovative chefs is updating traditional north-Portuguese cooking to make Porto a hot destination for gourmet travelers.

EXPENSIVE

Antiqvvm ★★ MODERN PORTUGUESE Take an 18th-century manor house surrounded by a romantic park with splendid views over the Douro. Add a hugely talented chef with a track record of picking up Michelin stars, and you have Antiqvvm. Opened in 2015, it quickly established itself as one of Porto's fine-dining favorites. Vitor Matos proposes art-on-a-plate tasting menus that open with scallop and champagne ravioli with oyster, ginger, and cauliflower sauce, and finish with a dessert that brings in pumpkin, beets, tomatoes, and pistachios. Mains include something Matos calls "Portugal on a plate," which combines pigs' cheek in Douro wine sauce with bone marrow, smoked sausage, couscous, and fava beans. The dining room's row of arched stone windows overlook a formal garden located like a balcony over the river. The house upstairs holds a museum dedicated to Romanticism.

Rua de Entre-Quintas 220. http://antiqvvm.pt. ✆ **22/600-04-45.** Reservations recommended. Mains 18€–30€, tasting menus 100€. Tues–Sat noon–midnight, Sun noon–3pm. Bus: 200, 201, 207, 208, 302, 501, or 507.

Casa de Chá da Boa Nova ★★★ MODERN PORTUGUESE Here you are eating in a national monument, a low-lying concrete-and-glass building that seems to merge with the rocks tumbling down to the Atlantic. It's an early masterpiece by Porto's great modernist architect, Álvaro Siza Vieira. His "teahouse," which opened in 1963, had fallen on hard times, but reopened in 2014 in the hands of chef Rui Paula, the man behind Porto's DOP restaurant (below) and the riverside DOC up the Douro. Paula has created a menu equal to the architecture and the setting. Amid Siza Vieira's wood-lined interior, looking out over the surf, diners can tuck into exquisitely presented dishes like line-caught Atlantic hake served with goose barnacles; wild rabbit with oats, cabbage, and mackerel; or wagyu beef with wild mushrooms. A truly special dining experience out in the seaside suburb of Leça da Palmeira.

Av. da Liberdade, Leça da Palmeira. http://ruipaula.com. ✆ **22/994-00-66.** Reservations recommended. Tasting menus 85€–120€. Mon 7:30–11pm, Tues–Sat 12:30–3pm and 7:30–11pm. Bus: 507, or take the metro to Mercado do Matosinhos and grab a cab.

DOP ★★ MODERN PORTUGUESE Chef Rui Paula is a star of new Portuguese cooking, and this is a classy fine-dining option in the city center. The restaurant is in the stately Palácio das Artes building, which once held the Porto branch of the national bank. Four big French windows open onto the pretty Largo São Domingos square. Inside, the cream and soft browns of the decor have a Nordic simplicity. Paula says he's searching for "food with history" based on traditional mainstays of Portuguese cuisine. Dishes like sea bass and lobster in creamy rice, or preserved partridge with chestnuts, even his unique version of *tripas à moda do Porto*, are presented like works of art and sided with a superb wine selection. There are two tasting menus, one closely rooted in north Portuguese traditions, the other inspired by the sea.

Palácio das Artes, Largo de São Domingos. www.ruipaula.com. ✆ **22/201-43-13.** Reservations required. Mains 19€–23€, tasting menus 65€–75€. Mon 7:30–11pm, Tues–Sat 12:30–3pm and 7:30–11pm. Metro: São Bento.

Pedro Lemos ★★★ MODERN PORTUGUESE Amid a tangle of narrow residential streets behind the seafront at Foz is a little stone house that many believe holds the most extraordinary modern restaurant in Porto, if not the country. Chef Pedro Lemos won his first Michelin star shortly after opening in 2014. Menus are of three, five, or seven courses. What's on them depends on what the fishing boats have brought in that morning, or what's in season in Lemos's vegetable garden, but they will include treats like pigeon with foie gras and fennel, and sea bass with turnips and chestnuts. All is served in two intimate dining rooms decorated in warm gold and blue, and a rooftop terrace looking toward the mouth of the Douro.

Rua do Padre Luís Cabral 974. www.pedrolemos.net. ✆ **22/011-59-86.** Reservations required. Tasting menus 55€–90€. Tues–Sun 12:30–3pm and 7:30–11pm. Bus: 202.

The Yeatman ★★★ MODERN PORTUGUESE If they were serving soggy hotdogs, you'd want to come to this restaurant for the view alone. Fortunately, the kitchen is run by Ricardo Costa, one of Portugal's most talented young chefs and holder of two Michelin stars since 2017. His tasting menus are a never-ending parade of superlative minidishes—crab ceviche with avocado and black-beer foam; suckling pig with caramelized scallions, chanterelle mushrooms, and Azores cheese; and tangerine cream with lime, meringue, and mascarpone ice cream were just a few delights we had on a recent visit. The wines chosen to accompany each dish come from the hotel's selection of more than 1,000 tipples, with an emphasis on port and the Douro. Service is an impeccable blend of knowledge, warmth, and efficiency. The expansive dining room is bright, light, and decorated with murals of tropical landscapes. Then there's that view. Watching the sun fade to gold over the river and the lights of Porto twinkling in the twilight is unforgettable.

Rua do Choupelo, Vila Nova de Gaia. www.the-yeatman-hotel.com. ✆ **22/013-31-00.** Reservations recommended. Tasting menus 100€–145€. Mon–Fri 7:30–10pm, Sat–Sun 12:30–3pm and 7:30–10pm. Metro: General Torres.

MODERATE

Adega São Nicolau ★★ PORTUGUESE This Ribeira joint is where many of Porto's top chefs go when they want to eat good, home-style Porto cooking. Of course, its location in a charming Ribeira alleyway makes it popular with tourists, too, but the cuisine is authentic and the service friendly. Behind an unprepossessing exterior is a low, dramatically lit dining room with a curved wood ceiling. Fried octopus (*filetes de polvo*) is a signature dish, but it's also good for tripe, grilled fish, and unusual dishes like oxtail stew, or chicken slow-cooked in red wine.

Rua de São Nicolau 1. ✆ **22/200-82-32.** Reservations recommended. Main courses 9.5€–16€. Mon–Sat noon–3pm and 7:30–11pm. Metro: Tram 1 or Metro São Bento.

Cafeína ★ PORTUGUESE/FRENCH For 20 years this relaxed, cosmopolitan place has been serving good food a block from the sea out in the beach resort of Foz. Inside the tile-covered villa, there's background jazz, soft lighting, and discreet service. The food is a mix of classic French and Portuguese,

MARKET forces

Porto's **Bolhão ★★** market, Rua Formosa (open Mon–Fri 7am–5pm, Sat 7am–1pm), has seen better times. Many of the stalls in the iconic 1850s double-deck structure are dusty and abandoned. Competition from supermarkets means the partly open-air landmark no longer exudes the bustle of old. Still, there are enough vendors and loyal customers left to make a visit here a must for visitors who want to glimpse the soul, or at least the stomach, of Porto.

In the heart of the city, decorated with colorful vintage-tile advertising panels, it features greengrocers and florists with a riot of color, fishmongers with a gleaming catch-of-the-day selection and rock-hard planks of salted cod, bakers selling chunky cornbread loaves, bucket-loads of olives, butchers hawking smoked pigs' heads and rings of blood sausage, snack bars, and handicraft stalls.

The city council has been talking about renovating Bolhão for decades. There were plans to begin work in 2017, leading to a temporary relocation of the stallholders to a nearby shopping mall, but after so many delays, *tripeiros* are taking a seeing-is-believing approach.

Elsewhere, the **Mercado de Bom Sucesso,** Praça Bom Sucesso, 74-90, out toward Boavista has already had a makeover. In its 1952 building, traditional stallholders now stand alongside fancy food shops and gourmet snack bars. Show cooking, art exhibitions, and concerts are held here. The traditional part of the market is open Mon–Sat 9am–8pm, while the hip new part runs all week 10am–11pm, staying open until midnight on Fridays and Saturdays.

Out on the coast, the cute little market in **Foz,** Praça Dom Luís I, 44, and the excellent covered market in a 1940s building in the fishing town of **Matosinhos,** Rua Álvaro Castelões, also blend old and new. The regular supply of fresh raw material has made the **sushi bar** at the Matosinhos market much sought after.

Porto also hosts a number of regular open-air markets, which can make for some offbeat browsing. There's a **handicraft market** held every Saturday from 10am–6pm in and around Praça Parada Leitão. In summer, it also runs on Thursdays and Fridays. Perhaps the most colorful is the **Feira dos Passarinhos,** or bird market, which sells birds and pet-related items in the streets of the riverside Fontainhas neighborhood on Sunday mornings.

with some Italian touches. Portugal's cherished salt cod comes with a garlic-infused aioli mayonnaise from the south of France. There's coq au vin and a renowned tournedos Wellington steak. Save some space for the spiced walnut cake with cinnamon ice cream.

Rua do Padrão 100. http://www.cafeina.pt. ✆ **22/610-80-59.** Reservations recommended. Main courses 17€–19€. Daily 12:30–midnight. Bus: 200, 202, or 203.

Casa Aleixo ★ PORTUGUESE Pretty much the epitome of a traditional Porto eatery, Casa Aleixo is made up of a couple of long, low, cavelike dining rooms with walls of bare stone decorated with fading photos of illustrious diners. The place echoes with the chatter of regulars and foreigners who have hiked out to the off-the-beaten-track neighborhood near Campanhã station lured by a legendary version of a Porto classic—deep-fried filets of octopus served with octopus risotto (*filetes de polvo com arroz de polvo*). If octopus isn't your thing, their *tripas* is justly famed, and there's a mean steak made from a tasty breed of north Portuguese cattle (*posta de vitela Maronesa*). The typical northern desserts include *aletria* made from pasta, milk, and cinnamon.

Rua da Estação, 216. ✆ **22/537-04-62.** Mains 13€–19€. Daily noon–10pm. Metro: Campanhã.

Don Tonho ★ PORTUGUESE Its popularity with tourists can mean that locals get a bit disdainful about this riverside place that's been serving upmarket classic north Portuguese food since 1992. However, if you want to eat Porto classics in an historic Ribeira setting with a view over the Douro, it's hard to beat. Set in an old *bacalhau* warehouse whose arched stone walls date back 400 years, its terrace and window seats look out over the river in the shadow of the Dom Luís bridge. The guestbook includes signatures by presidents, pop stars, and Nobel Prize winners—Fidel Castro and the Rolling Stones are both in there. Porto-style tripe, several salt-cod dishes, and veal in red wine are all classics. There's a remarkable wine list.

Cais de Ribeira 13–15. www.dtonho.com. ✆ **22/200-43-07.** Reservations required. Main courses 12€–22€. Sun–Thurs 12:30–3pm and 7:30pm–midnight, Fri–Sat 12:30–3pm and 6:30pm–2am. Tram: 1 or Metro São Bento.

O Gaveto ★★★ SEAFOOD/PORTUGUESE The cluster of *marisqueiras*, or seafood restaurants, in the center of the seaside suburb of Matosinhos are a magnet for fish-favoring foodies from around Portugal. Seemingly little changed since it opened in the 1970s, this place features a bar—where locals snack perched on stools, hemmed in by glass tanks filled with crab and lobster—and a dining room out back that's a favorite with the Porto wine trade. The menu features a long list of ultra-fresh shellfish—from cat-sized rock lobsters (*lagosta*) to gnarled goose barnacles (*perceves*)—by the kilo; catch-of-the-day fish waiting to be slapped on the grill; and regular dishes of the day from the Porto cookbook. Sundays feature *bacalhau à Zé do Pipo* (salt cod baked with a mayonnaise crust); Mondays and Saturdays, there's a formidable *tripas à moda do Porto*. Also look out for seasonal dishes like shad (*savel*).

Rua Roberto Ivens, 826, Matosinhos. www.ogaveto.com. ✆ **22/937-87-96.** Mains 13€–20€. Daily 12:30pm–1:30am. Metro: Matosinhos Sul.

Traça ★★ PORTUGUESE/GAME Largo São Domingos has established itself as the epicenter of Porto's culinary renovation, and since 2011, this corner restaurant located in a former drugstore is one reason why. The design is functional, maintaining elements of the 19th-century shop with the walls divided between white tiles and dark wood panels. Antlers mounted on one wall point to a menu where game is a major factor. In season expect to find delights like wild partridge stewed with shallots and peas, or loin of venison with liver and wild mushrooms. There are fish, salad, and vegetarian options, but this is a seriously carnivorous hangout.

Largo São Domingos 88. www.restaurantetraca.com. ✆ **22/208-10-65.** Reservations recommended. Mains 12.50€–19.50€. Mon–Thurs noon–3pm and 7–11:30pm, Fri noon–3pm and 7pm–1am, Sat 12:30–4:30pm and 7pm–1am, Sun 12:30–4:30pm and 7–11:30pm. Metro: São Bento.

INEXPENSIVE

A Casa Guedes ★★ PORTUGUESE If the *francesinha* has a rival in the hearts of Porto's snackers, then it is the roast pork sandwiches (*sandes de pernil*) produced in this retro hole-in-the-wall near the São Lázaro gardens. The meat is tender, marinated in a secret sauce served with the roasting juice in a fist-size bread roll. There's a luxury version that comes with an added dose of creamy *queijo da serra* sheep's cheese. The accompaniment of choice is a glass of cold *vinho verde* (the crisp white wine of northwest Portugal) or a dark beer. There are a number of alternatives where the rolls are filled with smoked sausage or ham. Eat at the bar, in the street, or on the little sidewalk terrace in summer.

Praça dos Poveiros 130. ✆ **22/200-28-74.** Main courses 2.90€–9€. No credit cards. Mon–Sat 8:30am–10pm. Metro: Bolhão.

Café Santiago ★★★ SANDWICHES Porto's cherished *francesinha* is one of the world's great sandwiches. You take two thick slices of white bread, fill them with mortadella, chipolata, smoked sausages, steak, ham, and cheese. After toasting, it's wrapped in more cheese, baked, and then served hot, doused in a spicy sauce that every cafe in Porto will tell you is a state secret. The line waiting outside under this unpretentious cafe's neon sign is a clue that many consider this the best place on the planet to eat one. The sauce's special flavor apparently comes from being made in the same pan every day for decades. You can get them with or without fries, and you can add a fried egg on top. As for the name—*francesinha* translates to "little French girl"—the story goes that a Porto waiter, who returned from a spell working in France, invented the sandwich in the 1950s and named it because the sauce was as piquant as his memories of Parisian mademoiselles. Best with a cold beer.

Rua Passos Manuel, 226. http://caferestaurantesantiago.com.pt. ✆ **22/205-57-97.** Mains 3.50€–9.50€. Mon–Sat 11am–11pm. Metro: Bolhão.

Cufra ★ PORTUGUESE A Porto institution since its opening in 1974. The decor looks little changed, with wood-paneled walls, leather-wrapped bench seats, and white table covers. Serving from noon until way into the night, it's a snack bar, beer hall, seafood joint, and purveyor of traditional Porto food for generations. The *francesinhas* are renowned—they even do a special version with added shrimp—but the array of dishes is enormous, from hamburgers to boiled fish head; tripe to a famed mixed seafood grill (*parrilhada*). Steaks are a late-night favorite. It's located on a main road out in the Boavista neighborhood. Expect it to be crowded and noisy, especially when there's a soccer game on the big TV screens.

Av. da Boavista 2504. www.cufra.pt. ✆ **22/617-27-15.** Main courses 10€–20€. Tues–Sun noon–2am. Bus: 201, 203, or 502.

O Rapido ★★ PORTUGUESE This unassuming little place, tucked on a side road behind São Bento station, serves up the finest *tripas à moda do Porto*. Served in steaming pots, topped with slices of sausage, this is the real deal. The place takes its name from the fast trains that once pulled into São

Bento from Lisbon. Other options include T-bone steaks from cattle raised in the highlands around the little town of Arouca (*costeletas de vitela Arouquesa*), or salt cod with eggs and potatoes (*bacalhau à Gomes de Sá*). The decor was recently renovated and now features bold oversized photos of Porto scenes. There's an extensive wine list. Check the daily specials for bargain options.

Rua da Madeira, 194. ✆ **22/205-48-47.** Main courses 7€–9.50€. Mon–Sat noon–10pm. Metro: São Bento.

Shopping

Shopping in Porto is an exciting mix of top European brands, cutting-edge local design, and timeless stores little changed in generations offering authentic and original souvenirs.

The most vital Porto shopping street is the pedestrianized promenade of **Rua de Santa Catarina ★★**, running north for 1.5km (almost 1 mile) from Praça da Batalha. There's a great range of shops here, from Art Nouveau jewelers to the multicolored, modern **ViaCatarina ★** shopping mall filled with international names. As examples of the diversity: The **Loja da Casa Verde ★** at No. 678 (✆ **22/093-74-44**) was set up by a group of architects to promote Portuguese-designed objects, from jewelry to lighting and toys; you can dress as a 1940s pinup or heavy-metal warrior at **Oblivion Alternative Wear ★** (www.oblivionshop.net; ✆ **22/201-16-09**) at No. 356; or you can splash out for a top-of-the-range Swiss watch at **Marcolino ★** (http://www.marcolino.pt; ✆ **22/200-16-06**), jewelers since 1926, at No. 84.

Streets running off Santa Catarina are full of intriguing traditional stores, particularly those around **Bolhão market ★★**. Among them are **Casa dos Linhos ★**, Rua de Fernandes Tomás, 660 (✆ **22/200-00-44**), which specializes in linen goods, like the colorful, embroidered *bordados dos namorados* typical of northern Portugal; and its big sister, the **Armazém dos Linhos ★★**, Rua de Passos Manuel 15 (http://armazemdoslinhos.myshopify.com; ✆ **22/200-47-50**), selling a dazzling array of traditional textiles since 1905; the **Pérola do Bolhão ★★★**, Rua Formosa, 279 (✆ **22/200-40-09**), a grocery founded in 1917; or its rival, the **Favorita do Bolhão ★★**, Rua de Fernandes Tomás 783 (✆ **22/200-16-24**), little changed since 1934; and the **Casa Januário ★★**, Rua do Bonjardim, 352 (www.casajanuario.pt; ✆ **22/332-01-53**), a wine shop and grocery, where you're assailed by the aroma of freshly ground coffee. Casa Januário has been in the same family since 1926. For something completely different, the **FC Porto Store,** Rua Sá da Bandeira, 270 (www.fcporto.pt; ✆ **22/508-33-53**) is packed with merchandise of the European Champions' League–winning soccer club.

Wine, of course, makes an excellent gift from Porto. Besides picking up a bottle or two after tastings in the **Gaia wine lodges,** there are some top-notch wine stores in town. One of the best is **Touriga ★**, Rua da Fábrica 32 (✆ **22/510-84-35**) just off Avenida dos Aliados, which specializes in ports and other wines from the north and central Portugal and organizes regular tastings. It ships internationally, should you buy more than you can carry on the plane.

Another quality traditional product from Porto and its surroundings is **Filigree jewelry ★★★**, in which fine strands of gold or silver are stretched and twisted into delicates shapes. Hearts and crosses are typical, but a range of necklaces and earrings are also made from *filigrana*. Women in Viana do Castelo wear layer upon layer of filigree necklaces over traditional costumes on special occasions, but lately stars such as actress Sharon Stone and Portuguese supermodel Sara Sampaio have also been spotted wearing them as accessories. Jewelers around Porto sell them, but quality varies. Among the best are the upmarket **Eleuterio ★★** (www.eleuteriojewels.com; ✆ **25/394-91-00**) brand founded in 1925 in Braga and available from the even older **Machado ★★** store, Rua 31 de Janeiro, 200 (www.machadojoalheiro.com; ✆ **21/154-39-40**) and other fine jewelers. Bringing a contemporary touch to the tradition is **PURA Filigrana ★** (✆ **92/917-74-87**), whose store is in the Bom Sucesso market, Praça Bom Sucesso. At **O Cantaro ★**, Rua Lada, 50 (www.ocantaro.com; ✆ **22/332-06-70**) in the Ribeira district, you can watch the jewelry being crafted.

For a one-stop shop for all your Portuguese traditional goods, head to the Porto branch of **Vida Portuguesa ★★★,** Rua Galeria de Paris, 20 (www.avidaportuguesa.com; ✆ **22/202-21-05**). Located in the shadow of the Clérigos tower on the first floor of a splendid 19th-century department store, this vast, light-filled space is packed with woolen blankets from the Alentejo, Algarve sea salt, tins of Azores tuna, ceramic swallows based on 100-year-old designs, handmade scented soaps from around Porto, and even Renova's revolutionary black toilet paper. It's hard to think of a distinctive Portuguese product you can't get here. Nearby are a couple of branches of Porto's **Marques Soares** department store, Rua das Carmelitas, 80-104 and 130-136 (www.marquessoares.pt; ✆ **22/204-22-00**), founded in 1964 and selling a huge range of international and Portuguese fashion brands, including must-have locally made shoes by **Fly London** (www.flylondon.com) and **Luís Onofre** (https://luisonofre.com).

Two of Porto's hippest shopping streets are **Rua do Almada** and **Rua Miguel Bombarda.** Running parallel to Avenida dos Aliados, Rua do Almada has a cool urban feel with places like vintage furnishings and design store **Casa Almada ★** at No. 544 and 311 (www.casaalmada.com; ✆ **91/989-30-40**); **Louie Louie,** a vintage record emporium at No. 37 (www.louielouie.biz; ✆ **22/201-03-84**); and **Chua ★** designer kids' wear at No. 348 (www.chua.pt; ✆ **91/376-00-85**). Don't forget **Arcádia ★★**, chocolate maker since 1933 at No. 63 (www.arcadia.pt; ✆ **22/200-15-18**). Their port-filled chocolate bites are hard to resist. Rua Miguel Bombarda is the heart of Porto's art district, lined with galleries, designer and vintage clothes shops, and a fair sprinkling of cool cafes. Many of the most interesting stores are located in the **Centro Commercial Bombarda,** a mini-shopping mall at No. 285. Try to check out one of the street's "**simultaneous opening**" nights, when the galleries all launch new exhibitions and customers stroll around to view them all. Check with the tourist board for dates.

The **Boavista** and **Aviz** neighborhoods have Porto's poshest shopping. The **Wrong Weather** store, Av. da Boavista, 754 (www.wrongweather.net; ✆ **22/605-39-29**) has an uber-trendy collection of international menswear, including Comme Des Garçons, Maison Margiela, and Kenzo. Other upscale fashionista haunts in the neighborhood include **Ltd Edition** ★, Rua Pedro Homem de Melo, 38 (www.ltd-edition.pt; ✆ **22/616-15-79**) and **Fashion Clinic** ★, Av. da Boavista, 4167 (www. fashionclinic.com; ✆ **22/610-30-59**).

More down to earth, one of the nicest places to shop is **Rua das Flores,** which winds downhill from São Bento station. It's lined with little stores, cafes, and restaurants. Among the most interesting are **Flores Creative Concept Store** ★ at No. 270 (✆ **22/200-48-51**), selling modern and traditional Portuguese design; a hip deli, **Mercearia das Flores** ★ at No. 110 (www.mercearia dasflores.com; ✆ **22/208-32-32**), offering regional food products from cheese and sausage to canned sardines; and **Livraria Chamine da Mota** ★★ at No. 18 (✆ **22/200-53-80**), a bookworm's delight with a four-floor maze of rare, antiquarian, and secondhand books.

One easy-to-pack Porto gift is **soap** ★★. The city has a soap-making tradition dating back over 100 years, with classic brands like **Portus Cales, Castelbel** (www.castelbel.com), and **Ach. Brito.** The oldest, **Claus Porto** (https://clausporto.com), makes luxurious products endorsed by stars such as Oprah Winfrey. It opened a flagship at No. 22 Rua das Flores ★★ in 2016. Porto's soap makers have branched out to make sweetly scented candles, perfumes, and ambient fragrances with aromas of citrus, mimosa, and other aromatic delights designed to bring back memories of Portugal.

Porto After Dark

Porto is currently a hotspot on the European nightlife scene. Hipsters jet in on low-cost flights to throng its happening bars and clubs on weekends. If you want to dance to dawn, the options are unlimited. If your idea of a night out is a nightcap after a concert of top-class classic music or a couple of hours listening to cool jazz, Porto also has that covered.

One venue offers all those options under one roof. The **Casa da Música** ★★★, Av. da Boavista 604–610 (www.casadamusica.com; ✆ **22/012-02-20**) is an architectural landmark built by Dutchman Rem Koolhaas, a giant irregular rhombus in glass and white concrete that seems to balance precariously over the surrounding avenues. Its array of auditoria large and small, multimedia studios, bars, and restaurants hosts a huge variety of events. In a typical week you can listen to an acclaimed Russian violinist play baroque concertos, be serenaded by fado over dinner in the rooftop restaurant, catch a show by an upcoming local singer-songwriter, hear Hayden played by the symphony orchestra, chill with a U.S. jazz star or visiting Spanish guitar virtuoso, or strut your stuff on the dance floor to the rhythm of top international DJs.

Other venues include the **Rivoli** theater ★★, Praça D. João I (www.teatro municipaldoporto.pt; ✆ **22/339-22-01**), a legendary place in the Portuguese rock world that hosts classical, jazz, and pop concerts, as well as plays and

revealing THE ROMANESQUE

Portugal's northwestern corner was the nation's birthplace: first as an outpost of a Spanish mountain kingdom resisting Muslim rule, and then, after 1139, as an independent nation. Just east of Porto and south of the country's first capital in Guimarães, the valleys of the Sousa and Tâmega rivers are full of monuments from that early medieval era. Almost 60 of them are linked by the **Romanesque Route ★★** (www.rotadoromanico.com; ✆ **25/581-07-06**).

The route includes bridges arched over leafy streams and stern stone fortresses, but most of all, churches. They include the 10th-century Benedictine monastery of **Santa Maria de Pombeiro ★**, Pombeiro de Ribavizela, Felgueiras (✆ **25/581-07-06;** Wed–Sun 10am–6pm; entry 1€) and the **Salvador de Paço de Sousa ★** monastery, Largo do Mosteiro, Paço de Sousa (✆ **91/811-64-88;** open on request; admission free) outside Penafiel. Built in golden-tinged sandstone in the 13th century, it contains the tomb of an early national hero, Egas Moniz, tutor to the first king, Afonso Henriques.

Nearby is an even older monument, the **Castro de Monte Mozinho ★★**, Lugar de Vila, Oldrões, Penafiel (www.museudepenafiel.com; ✆ **25/571-27-60;** visitor center open daily 2–5:30pm, closed weekends Nov–Mar, but access to the site remains open all day and is free), a hill fort built by Celtic people at the time of the Roman occupation. The ruins are remarkably well preserved.

Solar Egas Moniz ★★, Rua dos Monges Beneditinos, 158, Paço de Sousa (www.solaregasmoniz.com; ✆ **25/575-42-49;** double rooms 89€–149€) is a swell base for exploring the route and the wider region. In this sweet and chic family-run hotel in a restored manor house, the charm of the individually decorated rooms is matched by the warmth of the welcome.

It's perhaps best to fast for a couple of days before dining at **O Sapo ★★★**, Lugar da Estrada, Irivo, Penafiel (✆ **25/575-23-26;** mains 11€–14€), a big, boisterous, belt-busting place that easily fills its 150 places on weekends with hungry locals and fans driving out from Porto to gorge on the seemingly endless plates of appetizers that land on the table—from smoked meats to fried octopus, or fresh fried eggs on cornbread—followed by roast meats or fish served with local wines. A classic.

dance. The **Coliseu ★★**, Rua Passos Manuel, 137 (www.coliseu.pt; ✆ **22/339-49-40**) holds shows by big names in Portuguese and international music, like American rockers the Pixies, fado star Cuca Roseta, and Russia's Classical Ballet performing "The Nutcracker." Porto's grandest theater is the **Teatro Nacional São João ★★**, Praça da Batalha (www.tnsj.pt; ✆ **22/340-19-00**). It has a dynamic repertoire of classic and modern plays, often with English subtitles, as well as regular opera performances.

Jazz fans should head for the **Sala Porta Jazz ★**, Avenida dos Aliados, 168 (https://portajazz.com; ✆ **91/419-99-13**), which holds regular sessions most weekend nights and also organizes open-air shows on summer evenings in the Palácio de Cristal gardens; or the intimate **Hot Five Jazz & Blues Club ★**, Largo Actor Dias, 51 (http://hotfive.pt; ✆ **93/432-85-83**).

Unlike most other European countries, cinemas in Portugal mostly show **movies** in the original language, with subtitles in Portuguese, which makes

Porto & the Douro

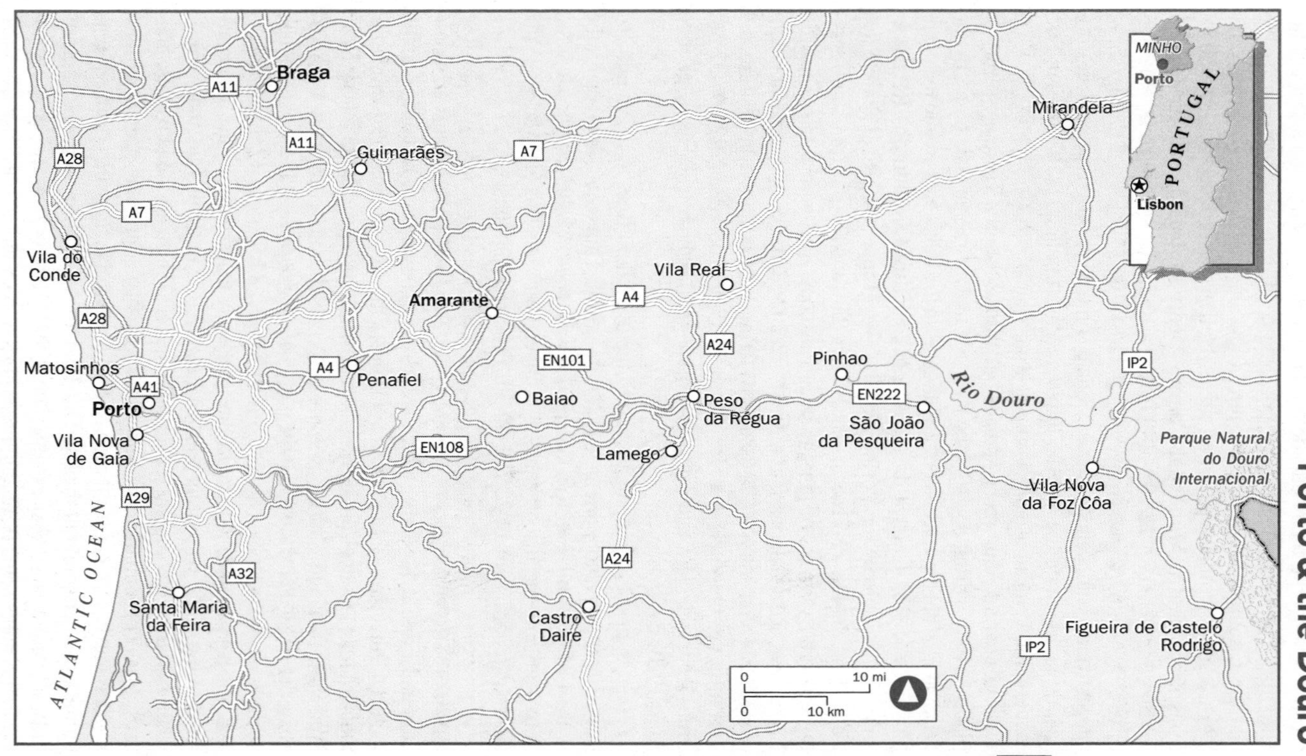

things easier for English-speaking film fans. The big movie theaters are mostly in shopping malls outside the city center. Among the closest are the **Cinemas Nos Alameda Shop e Spot,** Rua dos Campeões Europeus, 28-198 and the **Cinemas Nos GaiaShopping** (both on http://cinemas.nos.pt; ✆ **16 996**). A more intimate space that mixes Hollywood products with art house films is the **Teatro Municipal Campo Alegre ★**, Rua das Estrelas (http://medeiafilmes.com; ✆ **22/606-30-00**). The **Fundação Serralves ★**, Rua Serralves, 997 (http://www.serralves.pt; ✆ **22/618-00-57**) also has a program of alternative and independent films. Updates on theater programs across Portugal can be found on the website http://cinecartaz.publico.pt. It's only in Portuguese, but you can usually work out what's on where.

Porto's bar and club scene spreads out around the city. There are plenty of places to have a drink down by the riverside in Ribeira and Gaia or out by the beach in Foz, but the epicenter of nightlight is in the Baixa area around the parallel streets of **Rua Galeria de Paris ★★**, and **Rua Cândido dos Reis ★★**. Among the in places for a drink are **The Gin House ★★**, Rua Cândido dos Reis, 70 (✆ **96/476-49-71;** Sun–Thurs 7pm–2am and Fri–Sat 7pm–4am) serving over 160 varieties of gin and countless cocktail combinations; **Casa do Livro ★★**, Rua Galerias Paris, 85 (✆ **22/202-51-01;** Sun–Thurs 9pm–3am and Fri–Sat 9pm–4am), a laid-back watering hole in an old bookstore; and **Era uma vez em Paris ★★**, R. Galeria de Paris, 106-108 (✆ **22/208-37-56;** Mon–Wed 3pm–2am and Thurs–Sat 3pm–4am), which takes its inspiration from 1920s cabarets.

When things start jumping, hot clubs include **Plano B ★**, Rua Cândido dos Reis, 30 (http://planobporto.net; ✆ **22/201-25-00;** Thurs–Sat 10pm–6am); the funky **Café au Lait ★★**, Rua Galeria de Paris, 46 (✆ **22/205-20-16;** Mon–Sat 2pm–4am); or the discotheque-in-a-tunnel **Gare ★**, Rua da Madeira, 182 (www.gareporto.com; ✆ **22/202-60-30;** Fri–Sat 11pm–6am).

Gay Porto's favorite hangouts include **Café Lusitano ★★**, Rua de José Falcão 137 (www.cafelusitano.com; ✆ **22/201-10-67;** Wed–Thurs 9:30pm–2am and Fri–Sat 10–4am), which serves as a cocktail bar, restaurant, and a dancehall that really heats up at weekends. Other gay nightspots include the industrial-chic **Conceição 35 ★**, Rua da Conceição 35 (✆ **22/093-80-34;** Sun–Wed 9pm–2am and Thurs–Sat 9pm–4am), which transforms from a gin and tapas bar into a dance club; and the party palace **Zoom ★**, Rua Passos Manuel, 40 (http://zoomporto.wixsite.com; ✆ **91/835-32-82;** Fri–Sat 12:30am–6am).

If you happen to be in Porto in June, be aware that practically the whole city turns into a giant, wild night-spot on June 23, the **noite de São João ★★★**, when *tripeiros* celebrate their patron Saint John. There are street parties, bonfires, mass consumption of *caldo verde* (cabbage soup), and grilled sardines washed down with beer and red wine. A spectacular fireworks display lights up the Douro around midnight and the festivities from Ribeira to Foz carry on into the wee hours. Also in June, the **Nos Primavera Sound ★★** festival annually brings some of the biggest names in rock and pop to Porto for three nights of open-air music.

AMARANTE ★★

60m (37 miles) E of Porto; 368km (229 miles) N of Lisbon

Nestled in a willow-lined curve of the River Tâmega, Amarante's renaissance buildings, art history, and reputation for delectable pastries make it one of the most attractive small towns in Portugal.

ARRIVING

BY BUS The Rodonorte company (http://www.rodonorte.pt; ✆ **25/934-07-10**) runs up to 15 buses a day from Porto's Rua Ateneu Comercial do Porto, 19, to Amarante. The journey lasts 50 minutes and costs 7.90€. There is no rail service.

BY CAR Amarante is a 40-minute drive from Porto on the A4 autostrada.

VISITOR INFORMATION

The **Tourist Office** is at Largo Councilor Antonio Candido (www.cm-amarante.pt; ✆ **25/542-02-46**). It's open June–Sept daily 9am–7pm and Oct–May daily 9am–6pm.

Exploring Amarante

Amarante clusters photogenically around a high arched bridge over the Tâmega, which spills down from Spain through the surrounding hills on its way to meet the Douro. There is a succession of balconied, red-tiled houses rising up from the main square dominated by the Renaissance church of **São Gonçalo ★★**, Praça da República (✆ **25/543-74-25;** Mon–Sat 8am–7pm and Sun 8am-8pm; free). Built in the soft brown local granite, the church's main facade has a distinctly un-Portuguese feel. It was mostly built during the Spanish occupation in the late-16th-century and the three-tiered entrance has a Castilian grandiosity (oddly, the tiled dome and arcaded gallery carrying the statues of four kings is distinctly Italianate). Inside, the gold-covered baroque woodwork is more typically Portuguese. The church holds the tomb of Saint Gonçalo, a 12th-century monk, who has become the patron of spinsters on the lookout for a husband and the focus of fertility rituals with their roots in pagan times. Legend has it that unmarried women who pull three times on the rope belt worn by a wooden statue of the saint in the church's sacristy will find a husband. To ensure that the marriage is fecund, they're also supposed to eat a larger-than-life pastry that's decidedly phallic in form, known as a *doce de São Gonçalo*.

Thankfully for those with a sweet tooth, Amarante has other confectionary delights that are much more palatable. Just across the river is the **Confeitaria da Ponte ★★★**, Rua 31 de Janeiro, 186 (http://confeitariadaponte.pt; ✆ **25/543-20-34;** daily 8:30am–8pm), which is widely considered to produce some of the country's best traditional pastries. Opened in 1930, it specializes in regional cakes and those based on centuries-old recipes from nuns in the convents of northern Portugal. Rich in almonds, cinnamon, and eggs, they carry evocative names like bacon from heaven (*toucinho do céu*), angels' cheeks (*papos de anjo*), or little kisses of love (*beijinhos de amor*). There's also a tearoom with a terrace overlooking the river where you can sample them, accompanied, if you like, with a glass from their selection of port wines.

The graceful **Ponte de São Gonçalo ★** bridge that links the two halves of the town was built in 1790 after the 13th-century original was washed away in flooding. Constructed in the same golden stone as the church it leads to, the bridge has three arches and is decorated with a pair of baroque spires. The bridge also has historical significance as the site of the heroic battle in 1809 when a small Portuguese force, aided by a few British soldiers and the townsfolk, held back a much larger contingent of Napoleon's invading French army for 14 days. Eventually the French broke through and pillaged the town in revenge. Signs of the battle can still be seen with the marks left by shell fragments in the church and ecclesiastical robes ripped by bayonets in the church sacristy.

After Saint Gonçalo, Amarante's most famous son is Amadeo de Souza-Cardoso (1887–1918), arguably Portugal's greatest modern painter—"the best-kept secret in modern art," according to the Grand Palais gallery in Paris, which held a major exhibition dedicated to his work in 2016. Located in an old Dominican monastery linked to the church is the **Museu Municipal Amadeo de Souza-Cardoso ★★**, Alameda Teixeira de Pascoaes (www.amadeosouza-cardoso.pt; ✆ **25/542-02-72;** open Tues–Sun Oct–May 9:30am-noon and 2–5pm, June–Sept 10am–noon and 2–5:30pm; admission is 1€ adults, 0.50€ students and seniors, children under 15 free). Besides a collection of works by Souza-Cardoso, whose style absorbed influences from Cubism and Expressionism and Portuguese folk art, this small-town museum has a surprisingly wide selection of modern and contemporary works, mostly by Portuguese artists, and holds regular temporary exhibitions. Among the oddest works on show are a couple of oversize male and female demons sculptured in wood, supposedly copies of medieval originals shipped in from Indian trading posts and destroyed by the pillaging French. They, too, are linked to ancient fertility cults, as you might be able to guess from their prominent physical attributes.

Spreading out from the bridge are a number of pretty streets like **Rua 5 de Outubro** and **Rua 31 de Janeiro,** lined with centuries-old town houses where the white-painted facades contrast with naked stone window frames and corner posts. There are plenty of little stores selling woolen blankets from the hills and other handicrafts. It's also worth walking up the hill to the little round **Igreja de São Domingos** church, which has great views over the town and the river. Inside, there's a golden baroque altar and a museum of religious art. After all the sightseeing, a great place to relax is the **Café-Bar São Gonçalo ★**, Praça da República, 8 (✆ **25/543-27-07**, daily 7am–2am) a center of the town's social life since the 1930s, which retains its original decor, plus a life-size statue of local poet Teixeira de Pascoaes (1877–1952), who was a regular customer.

VINHO VERDE by the douro

Although the Douro is best known for port and big red wines, the region just east of Porto and the slopes running down to the river from Amarante are cultivated to produce ***Vinho Verde,*** "green wine," Portugal's fresh, mostly white tipples that are one of the country's most distinctive products.

The region is a delight to drive, with roads that twist up and down the valleys through forests and vineyards, curving suddenly to open up to vistas of the slow-moving Douro way below, or reveal the baroque tower of a whitewashed hilltop church.

Wine estates in this verdant area are also a pleasure to visit. Most organize tours and tastings, but may require booking in advance.

Among the most impressive is the **Quinta da Aveleda,** Rua da Aveleda, 2, Penafiel (www.aveledaportugal.pt; ✆ **25/571-82-00**), where you can wander through lush, tropical gardens surrounding the aristocratic family home and cellars where casks of fabulous **Adega Velha** brandy ripen, as well as tour the vineyards and taste their *vinho verdes.* Reservation are needed.

At **Quinta de Covela,** São Tomé de Covelas, Baião (http://www.covela.pt; ✆ **25/488-62-98**), you can sample highly rated *vinhos verdes* alongside other whites and reds in a stone manor dating back to the 1500s that once belonged to film director Manoel de Oliveira (1908–2015). The views down the valley to the Douro are heavenly. Booking is required.

The **Casa de Tormes,** Caminho de Jacinto, Santa Cruz do Douro (www.feq.pt; ✆ **25/488-21-20;** Tues–Sun 9:30am–12:30pm and 2:30–4:30pm; admission 5€ adults, 3.50€ students and seniors) offers the chance to mix wine with culture. The house once belonged to the writer José Maria de Eça de Queirós (1845–1900) and has been preserved as a museum. Fans like to walk up the hillside to the house from the pretty little railway station of Aregos on the banks of the Douro, a climb immortalized in his novel *The City and the Mountains.* The foundation that runs the museum and the vineyard has a restaurant where you can lunch on regional cuisine, and a cozy, rustically furnished guesthouse offering double rooms from 40€.

There are plenty of other excellent places to eat and sleep in the region. Among the accommodations, the **Casas de Pousadouro,** Caminho dos Moinhos, Laranjal – Santa Cruz do Douro (www.casasdepousadouro.com; ✆ **91/329-66-04)** is a standout, offering five restored and beautifully furnished rural stone houses on the banks of the Douro, from 120€. Nearby are two luxury spa hotels also spectacularly located above the river: the **Douro Palace,** Lugar do Carrapatelo, Santa Cruz do Douro (www.douropalace.com; ✆ **25-488-00-00;** double from 90€), and the **Douro Royal Valley,** Portela do Rio Pala, Ribadouro (www.douroroyal.com; ✆ **25/507-09-00;** double from 135€).

Hearty rustic restaurants abound. Locals drive for miles to the remote highland village of Almofrela to tuck into the lamb or chunks of young beef roasted in the wood-fired ovens of the **Tasquinha de Fumo,** Rua de Almofrela (✆ **25/554-11-20**). Similar hearty cuisine can be found at the **Residencial Borges,** Rua de Camões, 4, Baião (www.residencialborges.com; ✆ **25/554-13-22**) and the **Casa do Almocreve,** Rua da Serração, Portela do Gôve (www.casadoalmocreve.pt; ✆ **25/555-12-26**). Both also have guest rooms, which might be a good idea after trying local specialties such as *bazulaque,* a rich stew made from lambs' offal and blood.

BOATS, trains & automobiles

Between Porto and the Spanish border, the **Douro** flows through some of the world's most beautiful wine country. Hill after hill and valley after valley are covered with terraced vineyards overlooking the big river and its fast-flowing tributaries like the Côa, Tua, Sabor, and Corgo. Dotted among the scenery are the wineries. Many are located in centuries-old manor houses emerging from the greenery as specks of white paintwork and pale gray granite.

There are many options for exploring this UNESCO World Heritage–rated landscape, but a **boat trip ★★★** gets up close and personal with the river. They range from cheap and cheerful day trips from Porto with lunch on board and a scenic rail journey back, to romantic sailing tours or cabin-ship cruises lasting several days with side journeys to Lisbon or into Spain.

Among day-trip operators, **Rota do Douro** (www.rotadodouro.pt; ✆ **22/375-90-42;** starting from 60€) is popular with locals. Their basic cruise starts early, from 7:45am at the quayside in Vila Nova de Gaia. You get breakfast and lunch on board, a slow trip upriver, then a couple of hours in Régua to visit the Museum do Douro (see p. 370) before heading back by train. They also offer other trips heading farther up the Douro to **Pinhão** or **Barca D'Alva** through some of the most dramatic scenery. Other local day-trip operators include **PortoDouro** (www.portodouro.com; ✆ **22/938-99-33**) and **Cruzeiros Douro** (www.cruzeiros-douro.pt; ✆ **22/010-80-22**).

For **longer trips,** international companies such as AmaWaterways, CroisiEurope, Scenic Cruises, Viking River Cruises, and Uniworld Boutique River Cruises offer voyages for a week or more on the Douro, including during the September grape harvest. Vessels often feature a pool on top so that passengers can take advantage of the usually sunny climate.

Cruises including trips to vineyards and towns along the route, meals, and live fado music on board start from around $1,000 a week, but can run over $8,000 depending on services and season. Some companies offer add-on excursions to Lisbon or cities in Spain such as Madrid or the university city of Salamanca. The main local operator is Porto-based **Douro Azul** (www.douroazul.com; ✆ **22/340-25-00**), which has a fleet operating on a variety of routes up and down the river. Its unique attraction is the **Spirit of Chartwell,** a luxury barge fitted with artifacts from Pullman carriages and vintage liners. It was used to waft Britain's Queen Elizabeth II down the Thames on her Diamond Jubilee in 2011 before being sold to the Portuguese company.

Hiring your own boat is also possible. Douro Azul and a number of smaller specialized companies have crewed vessels for hire. One of the best is **Douro à Vela**

Where to Eat & Stay

Casa de Calçada ★★★ A member of the prestigious Relais & Chateaux group, Casa de Calçada is a five-story mansion in lemon-yellow tones dating back to the 1600s. Its location is a romantic one, beside the Tâmega looking across to the historic heart of Amarante. All but the cheapest rooms have views of the city, and several have balconies. Furnishings are plush and in a classical style, with velvet armchairs, damask drapes, soft lighting, and huge vases of fresh flowers. There's a spacious garden and outdoor swimming pool, spa, and nearby golf course. In the on-site Largo do Paço restaurant, holder of (www.douraavela.pt; ✆ **91/855-60-45**), which offers trips from 2 hours to 3 days on its sailing yacht or a 60-year-old river launch. Their cruises take in some of the most beautiful stretches upstream from Régua. Among the most popular is the 4-hour sunset dinner cruise, with catering by the award-winning DOC restaurant; 290€ for two. **Pipadouro** (www.pipadouro.pt; ✆ **93/919-62-62**) seeks to create a refined 1950s ambience with its "gentlemen's vintage boats" operating out of Pinhão. One once transported admirals in Britain's Royal Navy.

If you'd rather stay on dry land, there are **rail trips** ★★★ along the line that dip down to the Douro soon after leaving Porto and cling to the bank for over 3 hours before terminating at Pocinho, up near the Spanish border. The trip costs 13.15€. It also stops at several pretty, *azulejo*-decorated stations serving the wine towns and villages along the line. The **CP** rail company (www.cp.pt; ✆ **70/721-02-20**) also runs special day trips between June and October in historic carriages pulled by a **1925 steam engine** with local musicians and port tastings on board. Prices start at 37.50€ adults, children 17€. Then there's the **Presidential train** (www.thepresidentialtrain.com; ✆ **91/572-53-00**). Built in 1890 to carry heads of state, it's been beautifully restored and in 2016 started hauling lucky passengers on spring and fall runs along the Douro line. The 9-hour trip includes wine tastings at a top-class quinta and lunch served on board by Michelin-stared chefs. Details of the 2017 program were still being finalized as we went to press, but in 2016 the trip was priced at 350€ per person.

Get a car and you can discover the road proved scientifically to be the world's best drive. The **N-222** ★★★ sweeping along the south bank of the Douro between Régua and Pinhão beat the likes of California's Highway 1 and Australia's Great Ocean Road in tests to evaluate the thrill factor of the world's scenic routes, carried out in 2015 by a race-track designer, quantum physicist, and roller-coaster builder organized by rental company Avis. It is, however, just one of the dramatic drives around the Douro. The climb from Pinhão to the winery-packed village of **Provesende** is another. Given the twisting tracks, however, it's doubly important that drivers avoid the temptations on offer in vineyards along the way.

If you'd rather discover the Douro under your own steam, **We Love Small Hotels** (www.welovesmallhotels.com; ✆ **21/099-18-99**) organizes walking and cycling tours among the vineyards and historic sites, as well as self-drive trips, with overnight stops in some of the region's most charming accommodations, like the scrumptious **Vintage House** (www.vintagehousehotel; ✆ **25/473-02-30**) overlooking the Douro in Pinhão.

a Michelin star chef André Silva plates food almost too pretty to eat, with creations like cod and clams with trout roe, pak choi, and cilantro; or lamb with artichokes, morel mushrooms, and pistachios in red wine sauce.

Largo do Paço, 6. www.casadacalcada.com. ✆ **25/541-08-30.** 30 units. 168€–327€. Free parking. **Amenities:** Restaurant; bars; outdoor pool (June 1–Sept 15); spa; golf (nearby); bike hire. Free Wi-Fi.

Hotel Monverde ★★★ For a full-immersion experience in *vinho verde* culture, this is the place. Located in the Quinta da Lixa estate, the hotel is dedicated to all things enological. Your room will look out over the vines, you can get a massage with grape skins and vine leaves in the spa, or sip the estate's wines with your creamy monkfish rice or marinated pork with corn and wild mushrooms in the gourmet restaurant. You can even join in the seasonal work of the vineyard, including crushing grapes by foot during the late summer harvest, or get a master class in wine tasting. It's all in a modern architectural unit that uses natural local stone and wood to produce a contemporary but cozy environment complete with cotton duvets and a blazing fireplace for cooler evenings. It's a 20-minute drive north from Amarante.

Quinta de Sanguinhedo, Castanheiro Redondo, Telões. www.monverde.pt. ✆ **25/514-31-00.** 30 units. 110€–200€ double, including breakfast. Free parking. **Amenities:** Restaurants; bar; babysitting; exercise room; spa; children's play area; garden. Free Wi-Fi.

LAMEGO ★★

130km (70 miles) E of Porto; 350km (220 miles) N of Lisbon

Set back from the south bank of the Douro, this is another charming small town in the heart of wine country. Highlights include a marvelous hilltop church, an exceptional museum, and mouthwatering ham pies.

Essentials

ARRIVING

BY BUS **Rede Expressos** has two to five daily buses from Lisbon. The journey lasts 5 hours and costs 19.50€. From Porto there's only one direct bus, leaving at 5:15pm on weekdays. The trip lasts 2 hours and costs 11€. Others require a change in Vila Real or Viseu.

BY TRAIN There is no rail link to Lamego, but you can take the **scenic train** that runs along the Douro from Porto to Régua. From there it's a 15-minute bus trip to Lamego.

BY CAR It takes just over 3 hours to get there from Lisbon. Take the A1 autostrada north. Switch to IP3 at Coimbra, then take exit 9 in Viseu to join the A24. From Porto, the fastest way is to take the A4 east to Vila Real, then head south on the A24. It takes about 1 hour and 20 minutes.

VISITOR INFORMATION

The **tourist office** is at Rua Regimento de Infantaria, 9 (✆ **25/409-90-00**). It's open in summer 10am–7:30pm; in winter 10am–12:30pm and 2–6pm.

Exploring Lamego

However you arrive in Lamego, it's hard to avoid the **Santuário de Nossa Senhora dos Remédios ★★★**, Monte de Santo Estevão (✆ **25/461-43-92;** open May–Sept 7:30am–8pm, Oct–Apr 7:30am–6pm). The twin-towered rococo church looms over the city from its hilltop perch, linked to downtown by a monumental 686-step **staircase** that zigzags up to the summit in a cascade of blue tiles, baroque spires, fountains, and statues surrounded by greenery. It is an exceptional sight. At night, it's bathed in golden light. Work on the church started in 1750 on the site of a ruined 14th-century pilgrim's chapel, but it wasn't finished until 1905. The interior is a riot of gold-covered woodwork and *azulejos* under a carved ceiling in sky-blue and white. If you can't face the walk up the stairs, there's a road that snakes up through the forested hillside to the back of the church with parking at the top. Every year in early September, **pilgrimages** to the summit draw thousands to follow a procession behind sacred statues of the Virgin Mary carried on ox-drawn carts or the shoulders of devotees. One of the biggest religious festivals in Portugal, it's accompanied by 2 weeks of street parties, concerts, and fireworks.

Down in the city, many of Lamego's main sites are concentrated at the end of a broad tree-lined avenue, **Avenida Visconde Guedes Teixeira,** that leads toward the stairway. At No. 31, the **Pastelaria Scala ★** (✆ **25/461-26-99;** open Thurs–Tues 8am–8pm), makes a good place for a break. Its dark wood-lined interior conjures up a distinct 1950s feel, and it's usually packed with locals lining up to buy ***bôlas de Lamego***—thin slices of pie that can be filled with tuna, sardines, salt cod, or pork marinated in red wine, but most typically the famed local ham.

At the northern end of the avenue is the **Museu de Lamego ★★**, Largo de Camões (www.museudelamego.pt; ✆ **25/460-02-30;** open 10am–6pm; admission 3€ adults, 1.5€ students and seniors), one of Portugal's best regional museums. Housed in the former bishops' palace built in the 1700s, it holds an array of treasures including a series of five paintings by the Renaissance master **Grão Vasco** (1475–1542) depicting Biblical scenes, including a charming depiction of the creation of animals. There's a series of huge **Flemish tapestries** from the 16th century, enchanting multicolored tiles from the 17th century, and rare medieval sculptures. It also organizes regular cultural events, from open-air movie showings to exhibitions of photography and contemporary art.

Across the square from the museum is the **Sé ★**, Lamego's cathedral, Largo da Sé (✆ **25/461-21-47;** open 8am–1pm, 3–7pm; free admission). It was founded in 1159, but of the original building, ordered by Portugal's founding king Afonso Henriques, only the stubby, square bell tower remains. Most of the church is late-medieval Gothic in style. Beyond the great granite arches of the main door is a dramatic arched ceiling coated with **brightly colored frescos** showing Old Testament scenes. They were painted in 1738 by Nicolau Nasoni, the Italian architect who put the baroque into Porto's skyline. The graceful, double-level Renaissance cloister enclosing a tranquil garden is also worth a visit.

The oldest part of the city curves uphill toward the medieval castle along streets full of charm, like **Rua de Olaria** and **Rua do Castelo.** Busy **Praça do Comércio** is lined with handsome town houses fronted by high windows and wrought-iron balconies. The **Castle ★**, Rua do Castelo (✆ **25/409-80-90;** open Tues–Sun 10am–6pm; free admission) was fought over by Muslims and Christians in the 10th and 11th centuries. On misty nights, they say, the battlements are haunted by the spirit of a Moorish princess slain by her father for eloping with a Christian knight. The walls offer great views, and a recently opened **medieval water tank** in the basement holds a multimedia exhibition on the history of the city.

If you have time, pop into the nearby church of **Santa Maria de Almacave,** Rua das Cortes (✆ **25/461-24-60;** open 7am–noon and 4–7pm; free admission). Built in the 12th century in the Romanesque style, it's one of the oldest buildings in Lamego and is where Afonso Henriques held the first *cortes*, or parliament, of Portuguese nobles in 1143 after declaring independence from Spanish overlords. The interior is modest but has some pretty *azulejos*. Visitors staying into the evening should catch a show at the **Teatro Ribeiro Conceição,** Largo Camões (www.teatroribeiroconceicao.pt; ✆ **25/460-00-70**), which has regular concerts and movie showings. The building was constructed as a hospital in the 1720s. After a fire destroyed the interior, it was converted into an elegant, three-tiered theater in the 1920s.

A pleasant hour-long walk from downtown (or a 10-minute drive) is the **Capela de São Pedro de Balsemão** ★ on a little unnamed lane beside the stream running north out of town (www.culturanorte.pt; ✆ **25/460-02-30;** open Tues–Sun 10am–1pm and 2–8pm; free admission). This is reputed to be one of the oldest churches in Portugal, dating back to the 6th century. Although the outside was transformed in the 1700s, the interior is a fascinating mix of Visigoth and Romanesque with some unusual Islam-influenced touches. There's a splendid medieval tomb containing the remains of the bishop of Porto.

Farther afield, the pretty village of **Ucanha** ★, a 15-minute drive south of Lamego, is worth a visit for the imposing medieval tower protecting its stone bridge and the **Caves da Murganheira,** a sparkling-wine producer with its cellar carved deep into the rock, Abadia Velha, Ucanha (www.murganheira.com; ✆ **25/467-01-85;** open Mon–Fri 9am–5:30pm; visits by appointment only).

Where to Eat & Stay

Hotel options in the town center are limited. You're better off staying in one of the resorts or wine estate hotels in nearby villages and down the valley by the Douro.

Casa de Santo António de Britiande ★★ A lovingly restored 16th-century manor house, once the retreat of Franciscan friars, the hotel stands surrounded by 5 hectares (12 acres) of gardens planted with flowers, vines, and fruit trees. Beside the pool is a blaze of lavender. The owners have counted 26 species of wild birds here. Inside the thick stone walls the house is softly lit with coach lamps. Antique-style furnishings include big wooden beds with embroidered cotton covers and splashes of color provided by traditional Portuguese fabrics. You can sample still and sparkling wines grown on the owners' estates, accompanied by homemade delicacies: Lamego ham pies, smoked hams and sausages, or a full meal of local treats featuring meats roasted in the wood-fired oven. It's a 5-minute drive from downtown Lamego.

Largo de S. Sebastião, Britiande. www.casasantoantoniobritiande.com. ✆ **25/469-93-46.** 6 units. 100€–120€ double, including breakfast. Free parking. **Amenities:** Restaurant (prior booking needed); bike rental; outdoor pool; garden; shop. No children. Free Wi-Fi.

Quinta da Pacheca Wine House Hotel ★★ After driving through vineyards enclosed by a bend in the Douro, you enter though a noble stone gate and drive up to the house down an alley shaded by plane trees. The main building is an 18th-century manor at the center of the wine estate. With your stay you get a wine tasting and a tour, taking in the great oak barrels stored in the winery, but you will want to try more in the award-winning restaurant. The smallest rooms are 28 sq. meters (92 sq. ft.) and all come decorated in an uncluttered mix of old and new, with antique prints and natural colors. Some have balconies and four-poster beds. At harvest time guests are welcome to help get in the grapes and to roll up their pants to crush them underfoot. Otherwise, there are plentiful walk and bike-ride opportunities. It's 15 minutes from Lamego by car.

Rua do Relógio do Sol, 261, Cambres. www.quintadapacheca.com. ✆ **25/433-12-29.** 15 units. 110€–195€ double, including breakfast. Free parking. **Amenities:** Restaurant; bike rental; winery; garden; shop; babysitting. Free Wi-Fi.

Six Senses Douro Valley ★★★ Simply stunning. In 2015, Asia's super-luxurious Six Senses group chose a 19th-century manor overlooking the Douro for its first European resort. The result is a vast estate where landscape gardens blend into terraced vineyards; soothing Thai spa treatments can be followed up with tastings from the range of over 750 wines; and the panache of its blend of Portuguese heritage with contemporary design rivals the wizardry of its chefs crafting exquisite updates of regional cuisine. Save space for the pumpkin roll with creamy cheese and cinnamon ice cream. The outdoor pools are set in 8 hectares (20 acres) of land. Huge rooms offer views over the river or vineyards. It's a 20-minute drive north from downtown Lamego.

Quinta de Vale Abraão, Samodães. www.sixsenses.com. ✆ **25/466-06-00.** 57 units. 310€–640€ double, including breakfast. Free parking. **Amenities:** Restaurants; bars; bike rental; indoor and outdoor pools; garden; terrace; spa; games room; fitness center; tennis courts; babysitting. Free Wi-Fi.

PESO DA RÉGUA ★

120km (75 miles) E of Porto; 360km (225 miles) N of Lisbon

Peso da Régua, or simply Régua, is the main river port in the wine region, the place where raw wine used to be floated downstream in sailing boats to be turned into port. It is still a busy transport hub today, with bridges spanning the Douro. Despite a dramatic location and riverside promenades, it's not the prettiest town, but it is the center of the wine trade with a fine museum, some excellent restaurants, and wineries galore in the surrounding hills.

Essentials

ARRIVING

BY TRAIN The trip along the Douro-hugging railroad from Porto is a treat. It lasts just less than 2 hours and costs 9.60€. There are eight daily direct trains from Porto's Campanhã station. Four more are slightly longer and slightly cheaper, involving a change in Caide before the line dips down toward the river.

KINGS OF THE quintas

There are over 200 quintas, or wine estates, sprinkled around the Douro wine region. Their owners include multinational beverage industry giants and powerful dynastic producers, but many are small, family-run wineries who have been working the land for generations. Until a few decades ago, production was dominated by port, with raw wines shipped down to Porto to be blended and fortified. Since the 1990s, the region has become increasingly recognized for its DOC table wines, both red and white, winning international kudos for drinks that rival the best of Bordeaux or Chianti.

A **visit to a quinta ★★★** is a must. Most are open to visitors with offers that range from tastings and tours to meals and overnight accommodations, even a chance to join the harvest and press the grapes. It's usually best to call in advance to book a visit, although if they aren't too busy, wineries may welcome visitors who simply show up. Here are some offering the best visitor experiences:

Quinta das Carvalhas, Ervedosa do Douro (www.realcompanhiavelha.pt; ✆ **25/473-80-50**). This emblematic estate dates back to 1759 and belongs to the Real Campanhã Velha (Old Royal Company) set up around the same time to regulate port production. Dramatically set on the steep, terraced hills of the Douro's south bank, it produces great table wines, extra-virgin olive oil, and famed ports. The store and tasting rooms are open daily 10am–1pm and 2–7pm in spring and summer, 2–6pm in fall and winter. Walking tours, guided visits by bus or foot, and harvest participation are all available with booking.

Quinta do Bomfim, Pinhão (www.symington.com; ✆ **25/473-03-70**). Not only does this produce Dow's ports regularly judged to be among the world's best wines (Wine Spectator gave the 2007 vintage a record 100 score), but it'salso just a 5-minute walk from Pinhão railway station and quayside, making it an easy visit for travelers without a car. The main

BY BOAT Régua is major stop for river cruises, with many lines starting, ending, or stopping off here.

BY BUS **Rodonorte** (www.rodonorte.pt; ✆ **25/934-07-10**) has four daily buses from Porto, with a change in Vila Real. The trip costs 10€ and lasts 2½ hours.

BY CAR It's 3½ hours from Lisbon. Take the A1 north to Coimbra, turn onto the IP3, then take the A24 in Viseu. From Porto it's 1 hour and 15 minutes along the A4 east to Vila Real, then south on the A24.

VISITOR INFORMATION

The **tourist office** is at Rua da Ferreirinha (✆ **25/431-28-46**), open Mon–Sat 9am–12:30pm and 2–8pm.

Exploring Régua

Whether you arrive by train or boat, it's a short walk to the **Museu do Douro,** Rua Marquês de Pombal (www.museudodouro.pt; ✆ **25/431-01-90,** open daily 10am–5:30pm; admission 6€ adults; 3€ seniors and students—although they will have to pay 5€ if they want the glass of port offered free with lodge, with its cellars containing giant vats and barrels, dates back to 1896. There's a museum and tasting room overlooking the river. It's owned by the Anglo-Portuguese Symington family, who have been in the Douro wine business for 14 generations. Open Apr–Oct 10:30am–7pm, Nov–Mar 9:30am–5:30pm. Guided tours and picnics on request.

Quinta do Pôpa, EN 222, Adorigo (www.quintadopopa.com; ✆ **91/665-34-42**). This small family winery has one of the best views and warmest welcomes of any along the Douro. It also has a heartwarming story of an emigrant returning to fulfill his father's dream of owning a vineyard in the Douro, where he'd toiled for years as a laborer on the estates of others. Today, the third generation produces wines that are a tribute to the grandfather nicknamed "Pôpa"—a crested bird. The youthful team invites visitors to taste, tour, or lunch at the winery. Their picnics are particularly renowned. Open Tues–Sat 10am–5pm.

Quinta do Portal, EN 323 Celeirós, Sabrosa (www.quintadoportal.com; ✆ **25/993-70-00**). The cellars here were built by the great Porto architect Álvaro Siza Vieira in 2008 and form one of the most striking buildings in the region: amber-colored blocks coated in places by cork and slate for natural insulation. Inside it's a vast, temperature-controlled bunker lined with silently aging port barrels. You can linger in the estate's older buildings, converted into a sophisticated boutique hotel (double rooms 100€–120€, including breakfast) and a renowned restaurant that serves dishes, like baked salt cod with rosemary and olive oil, paired with the estate wines. Cellars are open from 10am–5:30pm; guided tours with tasting are 7.50€.

For more details on quintas and Douro wine production, check out www.dourowinetourism.com, which has wide range of information. Specialists in wine tours include **Wine Tourism Portugal** (www.winetourismportugal.com; ✆ **22/610-20-75**).

full-price admission at the end of the visit). This riverside museum, opened in 2008, is Régua's main attraction. Don't be put off by the largely Portuguese-only website, the museum itself offers a modern, multimedia explanation of wine production, history, and traditions of the region. It's housed in a 19th-century building built as the headquarters of the agency that regulated the port trade, and spills over into a modern extension.

The collection includes paintings of Douro landscapes, antique wine-making equipment, and vintage advertising posters. There are also regular temporary exhibitions that can range from historic photographs of work in the vineyards to contemporary art.

There's also a wine bar overlooking the river, a restaurant serving excellent value regional dishes (roast pork with chestnuts, trout stuffed with bacon), and a shop where you can stock up on wine or local handicrafts.

Where to Stay

Quinta do Vallado ★★ One of the oldest and most famous of the Douro's wine estates, this quinta, a 10-minute drive from the center of Régua,

STONE-AGE graffiti

The wild and beautiful **Côa River** valley was due to be drowned by a dam project in the 1980s. But before construction began, archeologists poking around in the verdant banks where the Côa runs into the Douro made a startling discovery: Rocks scattered about the valley were covered in images. Thousands of carvings of deer, goats, horses, and horned aurochs (ancestors of modern cattle) were etched into the stone. It turned out to be some of the world's oldest graffiti, dating back over 20,000 years.

After a campaign, work on the dam was abandoned and the valley is now a UNESCO World Heritage Site. Nobody really knows why prehistoric people over millennia kept coming to this spot to carve their images. Everything that is known about the engravings is explained in a striking new museum rising out of a nearby hilltop. The **Museu do Côa ★★★**, Rua do Museu, Vila Nova de Foz Côa (www.arte-coa.pt; ✆ **27/976-82-60;** open Mar 1–Oct 19 9am–5:30pm, Oct 20–Feb 29 9am–12:30pm and 2–5:30pm; admission 5€, seniors 2.5€, children under 10 free) is itself an architectural treasure, with an excellent restaurant and stunning views over the Douro landscape.

The rock carvings in the **Parque Arqueológico do Vale do Côa ★★★** can be visited on a guided tour arranged by the museum. They will take you by jeep into the valley and escort you on foot to see the rocks. Prices are 10€ for adults. There are also nighttime visits. Special arrangements can be made for disabled visitors. It is difficult not to be awed in the presence of some of humanity's earliest art, although, it has to be said, some visitors are underwhelmed when they actually see the carvings. They can be hard to visualize given that the artists scratched over their own or other's work. Guides refer to one particularly contorted site of overlapping scratches as "spaghetti rock."

If you need R&R after clambering over the rocks, the **Longroiva Hotel Rural ★★**, Lugar do Rossio, Longroiva (http://hoteldelongroiva.com; ✆ **27/914-90-20;** double rooms with breakfast 75€–120€) is the place. A 10-minute drive south of the Stone Age site, this crimson tile-covered 18th-century building was constructed over hot springs used since Roman times. The hotel, which opened in 2015 with a striking modern wing, offers stylishly comfortable rooms, a spa featuring a heated outdoor pool, and an excellent restaurant serving regional cooking.

There are also plenty of vineyards to visit amid the vine-covered hillsides around here. The best known near Foz Côa is the **Quinta de Ervamoira** (www.ramospinto.pt; ✆ **27/975-92-29;** visits by appointment), which is located in the archeological park and was saved from flooding by the discovery of the rock carvings. It is part of the Ramos Pinto port company and was the setting of a romantic French novel. Visits can include tastings, lunch, a tour of the estate's small museum, and a trip to the rock-carving sites.

celebrated its tricentenary in 2016. It produces some of the region's best wines—both ports and table wines—and is still run by the descendants of Dona Antónia Ferreira, a legendary figure in the story of port. In 2005, they opened their first rooms in the 18th-century manor, and added a modern extension in local schist stone that blends into the surrounding wine terraces. The views across the vine-covered hillsides are breathtaking, although slightly marred by the highway. There's a relaxing garden containing a pool with a view. Both the 21st-century and 18th-centrury rooms are tastefully furnished with natural materials and understated colors, and come with complimentary fruit and wine. Included with the room are visits to the winery, tastings, bikes, and fishing gear—in case you fancy trying to lift a trout from the Rio Corgo, which flows past on its way to the Douro.

Vilarinho dos Freires. www.quintadovallado.com. ✆ **25/431-80-81.** 13 units. 100€–180€ double, including breakfast. Free parking. **Amenities:** Restaurant; bar; babysitting; massage; outdoor pool; bikes; fishing; garden; library. Free Wi-Fi.

Where to Eat

Castas e Pratos ★ PORTUGUESE The name means "grapes and plates," and that just about sums up this modern place in a converted railway warehouse brimming with industrial chic. There's a well-stocked wine bar and store showcasing Douro products on the ground floor, and a light-filled dining room under the rafters upstairs. The kitchen serves up prettily presented food rooted in regional products like marinated shad with pepper salad or venison with chestnuts and squash.

Avenida José Vasques Osório. www.castasepratos.com. ✆ **92/720-00-10.** Main courses 20€–30€. Daily 10:30am–11pm.

DOC ★★ MODERN PORTUGUESE With a fabulous location right on the south bank of the Douro, 10 minutes upstream from Régua, this upscale modern restaurant is part of the culinary empire of stellar Porto chef Rui Paula. With the river lapping up against the glass walls, sit back, relax, and let his tasting menus take you on culinary tour of the region's finest products, from mountain-raised beef to the purest Trás-os-Montes olive oil, all presented in contemporary art-on-a-plate style.

Estrada Nacional 222, Folgosa. http://ruipaula.com. ✆ **25/485-81-23.** Main courses 20€–30€, tasting menus 60€–90€. Daily 12:30am–3:30pm and 7:30–11pm.

O Maleiro ★ PORTUGUESE This is an archetypal local Douro restaurant: shoulder-to-shoulder diners, noisy, brightly lit, with the ambition since 1975 to fill customers with unpretentious, hearty regional cooking. There are *azulejos* on the wall, soccer on the TV, and plates filled with baked cod and roasted-in-their-skins potatoes dripping with garlic and olive oil, or slow-roasted young goat. Don't come for a romantic dinner, but it's great for a slice of Douro life.

Rua dos Camilos 108. ✆ **25/431-36-84.** Main courses 7€–16€. Mon–Sat 11:30am–10pm.

THE MINHO & TRÁS-OS-MONTES

14

Portugal's two northernmost provinces present a contrast. The Minho, occupying the northwest, is a lush, green region where rivers rush to the Atlantic coast through hillsides covered with trellised vines producing famed *vinho verde*, white wines. It is a center of Portugal's fashion and footwear industries where ancient cities like Braga, Guimarães, and Viana do Castelo have developed thriving cultural scenes. The Minho is the birthplace of the Portuguese nation, a region where Celtic hill forts, churches built by Germanic settlers after the Romans retreated, medieval fortresses, and baroque mansions bear witness to a long, rich history.

To the east, between the River Douro and the Spanish border, Trás-os-Montes is a wild, otherwordly place. Its name means "beyond the mountains," and for centuries it was a remote place, cut off from the rest of the country by the highland ranges to the south and west. Although fast highways have brought it within easy reach of Lisbon and Porto, the region still has a distinct identity. The landscape is a rugged mix of high plateaus and rounded peaks. Population is sparse and there are few major cities, but in roughhewn hamlets rural traditions linger on, like winter festivals, where villagers don masks and weird costumes rooted in pagan lore; play Celtic bagpipe music; and speak Mirandese, a language spoken only in Portugal's far northeastern corner.

What both regions share is a hearty cuisine, rich handicraft heritage, spectacular natural landscapes, and a reputation for hospitality combined with some wonderful places to stay—from palaces and restored convents to country-chic home-stay cottages, even grainsilos made into a boutique hotel.

GUIMARÃES ★★★

55km (35 miles) NE of Porto; 365km (225 miles) N of Lisbon

Guimarães is the cradle of Portugal. It was the birthplace of the country's founding father, King Afonso Henriques, in 1109, and the country's first capital. Its fortress was the base from where Afonso Henriques led the *Reconquista*, moving south to reclaim land taken

Minho & Trás-os-Montes

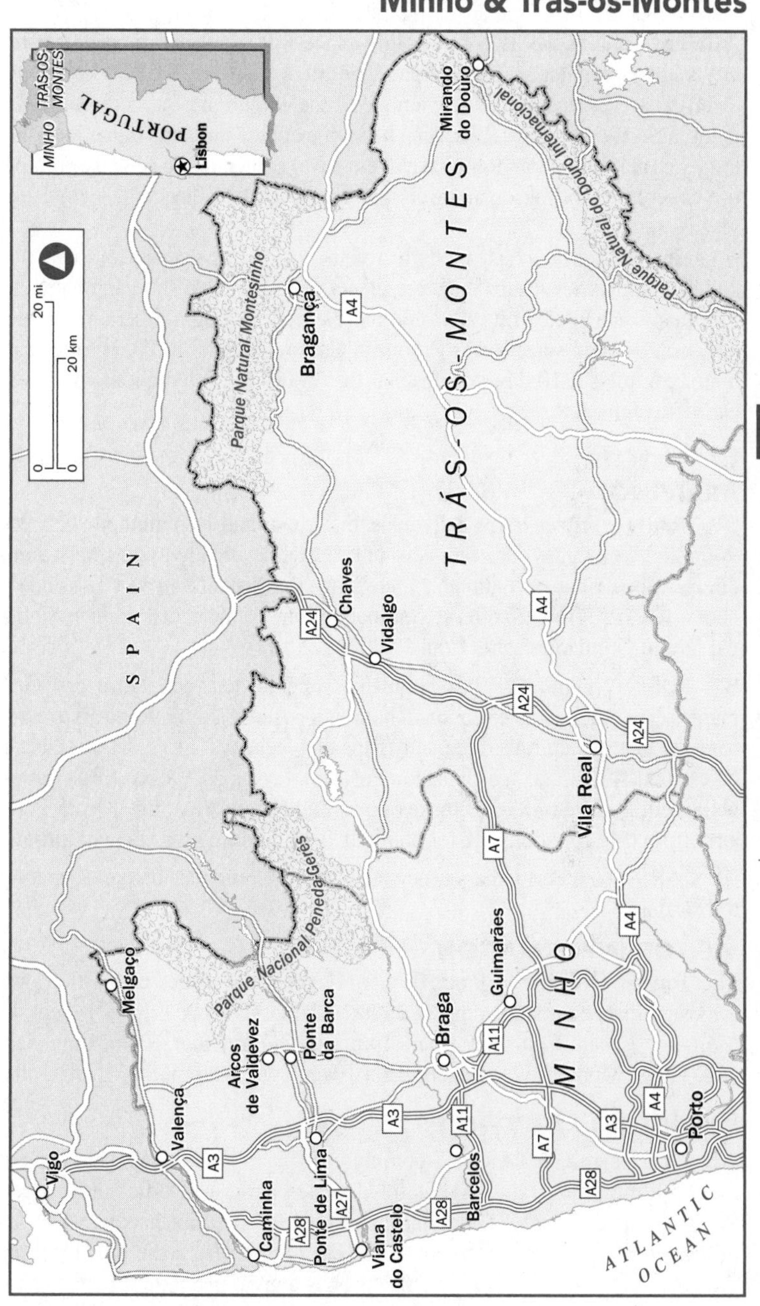

by Arab forces centuries earlier. "Guimarães is Portugal, the rest is just what we conquered," is a popular saying in the city.

Today's Guimarães is a fascinating place to visit. When it declared the city's historic center as a World Heritage Site in 2001, UNESCO called it a "well-preserved and authentic example of the evolution of a medieval settlement into a modern town." That can be seen from the ramparts of the founding king's castle through its Renaissance-era royal palace to the brightly colored, tile-covered town houses along its maze of cobbled alleys and picturesque plazas.

Guimarães is also a busy modern city. Its position as a center for the textile and shoe industries means there are plenty of fashionable shopping bargains. Its squares are lined with cafes, and its role as a leading northern arts center has been boosted since it was European Cultural Capital in 2012. Among its major events is a 10-day jazz festival that draws big international names in early November.

Essentials

ARRIVING

BY TRAIN Fifteen trains daily make the 1 hour and 10 minute run between Porto and Guimarães. The fare is usually 3.10€. There are two express trains direct from Lisbon to Guimarães, covering the distance in just less than 4 hours; fares are from 25.80€. If you pick up one of those fast trains in Porto, the fare to Guimarães starts from 11.70€.

BY BUS A number of bus companies operate between Porto and Guimarães. The journey takes about an hour and costs 6€ on the **Rede Expressos** national line, which runs three daily trips on weekdays. From Lisbon the trip takes about 4 hours with a change in Porto, and costs 20.50€. **Get Bus** (www.getbus.eu; ✆ **25/326-23-71**) makes up to eight daily trips direct from Porto airport for 14€ for adults, 8€ for children 4–14, and free for younger kids.

BY CAR From Porto, the journey takes about 45 minutes on the A3 and A7 toll roads.

VISITOR INFORMATION

The **Tourist Office** is at Praça de São Tiago in the center of the old town (www.guimaraesturismo.com; ✆ **25/342-12-21**). It's open June 1–Sept 15 Mon–Fri 9:30am–7pm, Sat 10am–1pm and 2–7pm, Sun 10am–1pm; Sept 16–May 31 Mon–Fri 9:30am–6pm, Sat 10am–1pm, 2–6pm, Sun 10am–1pm.

Exploring Guimarães

Alto da Penha ★ PARK Looming over the city, 620m (2,000 ft.) up at the top a mini-mountain range is this forested park, a favorite summer getaway for the citizens of Guimarães, particularly on summer days when the hilltop air stays cooler. There's a cable car running from the city. Once up there, the views are magnificent. The park is a great place for a picnic or for wandering among the woods, clambering around boulders, and exploring grottos. Above it all is a church built in the 1940s that looks like it's been carved from a solid block of local granite and is the destination of a pilgrimage held the second Sunday of September.

Santuário da Penha, Penha-Costa. www.penhaguimaraes.com. ✆ **25/341-41-14.** Mon–Fri 10am–6pm, Sat–Sun 9am–7pm. Admission free. For the cable car: Rua Aristides Sousa Mendes, 37. www.turipenha.pt. ✆ **25/351-82-39.** Return trip 5€ adults, 2.5€ children 4–11, 4€ seniors. Nov–Mar Fri–Sun 10am–5pm; Apr, May, Oct daily 10am–6:30pm; Sept daily 10am–7pm; Aug daily 10am–8pm.

Castelo ★ CASTLE This striking hilltop fortress is revered as the birthplace of the nation. King Afonso Henriques was reputedly born here and the citadel was his base as he declared his lands an independent kingdom in 1139 and fought off the advances of Spanish overlords. The castle is even older, founded in 958 by Countess Mumadona of Galicia to protect her subjects from raids by Vikings and Moors. Its battlements still dominate the Guimarães skyline and offer panoramic views over the city and surrounding hills. Amid the gardens beside the castle is the squat, rectangular 12th-century Romanesque **Igreja de São Miguel de Castelo,** where Afonso Henriques was supposed to have been baptized. Nearby there's a heroic **statue** of the mustachioed, armor-clad king, helmeted with sword and shield in hand—an obligatory selfie opportunity for visiting schoolchildren.

Rua Conde Dom Henrique. www.pduques.culturanorte.pt. ✆ **25/341-22-73.** Admission 2€ adults, 1€ seniors, free for children under 12. Daily 10am–6pm.

Centro Cultural Vila Flor ★ ARTS CENTER This ultra-modern cultural center incorporating a renovated 18th-century palace spearheaded Guimarães' re-emergence as a center for the arts. One outside wall of the old palace is lined with baroque granite statues of Portugal's early kings overlooking formal gardens. They are planted with camellias and boxwood hedges around fountains and water basins. The building holds exhibition spaces and concert halls, plus a cafe and restaurant.

Avenida D. Afonso Henriques, 701. www.ccvf.pt. ✆ **25/342-47-00.** Admission prices depend on events. Tues–Sun 10am–1pm, 2–9pm.

Citânia de Briteiros ★ HISTORICAL SITE Before the Romans invaded the Iberian Peninsula, Celtic peoples lived in hilltop fortress settlements across the northwest of Spain and Portugal. A half-hour's drive north of downtown, this is a remarkably well-preserved example. The cluster of ruined, round, and rectangular dwellings shows a well-organized civilization, with a network of streets, protective walls, barns for cattle, and a ceremonial crematorium. Some of the buildings have been reconstructed to give visitors an idea of what they were like at the settlement's Iron Age peak. The site is located on a hillside giving striking views over the valley of the River Ave. Back in the city, the **Museu Martins Sarmento,** Rua Paio Galvão, has a collection of archeological artifacts found at the site.

Monte de São Romão. www.csarmento.uminho.pt. ✆ **25/341-59-69.** Admission 3€. Daily Apr–Sept 9am–6pm; Oct–Mar 9am–5pm.

Largo da Oliveira ★★ PLAZA At the center of the old city is Guimarães' most distinctive plaza. "Olive tree square" is surrounded by brightly painted three-story houses in typical Minho style, with an arcade at street level to allow pedestrians to pass by in the dry during the winter rainy days responsible for the region's famed greenery. The square's Gothic shrine was built to commemorate a 14th-century victory over the Emirate of Granada. Other medieval monuments include the multi-arched former city hall and the **Igreja de Nossa Senhora da Oliveira** church, both Gothic works from the 14th century. For all its ancient, history, the square remains a center for social life and is lined with bars and cafes. In old monastery buildings attached to the church is the **Alberto Sampaio Museum** (www.masampaio.culturanorte.pt; ✆ **25/342-39-10;** open Tues–Sun 9am–6pm; admission 3€), which, amid a collection of silverware, ceramics, and medieval sculpture, contains the chain-mail tunic worn by King João I at the fateful battle of Aljubarrota, where Portugal secured its independence from Spain in 1385.

Largo do Tourel ★ PLAZA This spacious square was laid out in the 18th century and contrasts with the narrow, medieval streets around Largo da Oliveira and Largo de São Tiago. Its eastern edge is lined with tall, glass-fronted houses that glitter in the evening light. The plaza is a city meeting place where folks gather to talk, get a shoe shine, grab an almond pastry from the 60-year-old **Pastelaria Clarinha** cake shop, or take a coffee at the timeless **Café Milenário,** which opened in 1953, the year Guimarães celebrated 1,000 years since its founding. Next door, the slogan "Here Portugal was Born" adorns one of the surviving towers of the **city walls** standing among a row of houses covered with multicolored ceramic tiles.

Paço dos Duques de Bragança ★ PALACE This massive, four-winged palace was built in the early–15th century by an illegitimate son of King João I as a love nest for his mistress. With its stone towers, soaring chimneys, and steeply sloped tile roofs, it's an unusual example of a French-style Renaissance palace on the Iberian Peninsula. The place fell into disrepair when the Bragança family moved elsewhere, but it was heavily restored in the 1930s when dictator António de Oliveira Salazar turned it into his northern retreat. Today's it's a museum where you can view royal portraits, medieval weapons, Persian hangings, Indian urns, and Chinese porcelain. Enormous tapestries depict warlike Portuguese activity in North Africa. There's also a room dedicated to José de Guimarães, one of Portugal's best-known modern artists.

Rua Conde Dom Henrique. www.pduques.culturanorte.pt. ✆ **25/341-22-73.** Admission 5€ adults, 2.5€ seniors, free for children under 12. Daily 10am–6pm.

Rua de Santa Maria ★★ NEIGHBORHOOD If you'd like to step into the Middle Ages for an hour or two, stroll down Guimarães' oldest street, built to link the castle to the convent opened by Countess Mumadona in the 10th century. The narrow lane is flanked by solid granite houses both noble and humble. There are plenty of fascinating shops and cafes to stop in along the way: The **Casa Costinhas** at No. 70 is a cafe/pastry shop founded by nuns that still sells almond-and-pumpkin treats based on recipes from the neighboring Santa Clara convent; **Chafarica** at No. 29 is an emporium of local textile products; **Meia Tigela** at No. 35, in the shadow of the stone arch over the street, specializes in ceramics and other handicrafts. Rua de Santa Maria passes through a succession of pretty plazas like **Largo do Cónego,** where the baroque convent is now occupied by city hall; or **Largo de São Tiago,** lined with 16th- and 17th-century homes fronted by hand-carved wooded balconies, usually hung with flowers or washing. Much of the city's nightlife is around Largo de São Tiago, with bars like **Tásquilhado,** Rua Santa Maria 42, and **El Rock,** Praça de São Tiago 31, among the hotspots.

Shopping

Guimarães and the surrounding area is a center for the textile and shoe industries, as well as being home to a strong handicraft tradition. There are several stores selling homemade gifts in the historic center, but the city-run **Loja Oficina,** Rua Rainha D. Maria II, 126 (www.aoficina.pt; ✆ **25/351-52-50;** Mon–Sat 9am–1pm, 5–7pm) stands out for promoting local products like embroidered linen and the red-clay *cantarinhas dos namorados* jugs traditionally offered by young men to their intended fiancés. Portugal is second only to Italy in exporting high-quality shoes, and Guimarães is a good place for fashionistas to bag a bargain. The **Kyaia** factory store, Rua 24 de Junho 453, Penselo (www.kyaia.com; ✆ **25/355-91-40;** Mon–Sat 10am–1:30pm, 3–6pm) selling shoes from the hip Portuguese brand **Fly London,** is just outside the city in the village of Penselo. Downtown, **Fenui,** Rua Dr. Avelino Germano 84/86 (www.fenuishoes.com; ✆ **96/003-02-86;** Tues–Fri noon–7pm; Sat 10am–1pm and 2:30–7pm) and **Eureka,** Rua Paio Galvão 7 (www.eurekashoes.com; ✆ **25/343-81-82;** Mon–Sat 10am–7:30pm) sell a range of handmade Portuguese shoes.

Where to Stay

MODERATE

Casa de Sezim ★★★ This extraordinary country manor has been in the same family since 1376. The center of an estate producing *vinho verde* wines, it is 4km (2½ miles) outside Guimarães. Behind the noble, rose-painted facade, the interior decoration is notable for its murals—intensely colored paintings showing scenes of colonial life in India and the Americas, or historic events. Antique furnishings, traditional Portuguese fabrics, subtle lighting, fresh flowers from the garden, and a library of venerable leather-bound volumes (where you'll take breakfast) all combine to make this a very special place to stay. Guest rooms are spacious and decorated in tune with the house. There's a winery and bougainvillea-rich garden to explore, and a warm welcome from the owners. There's no restaurant, but evening meals can be taken in the dining room if ordered in advance.

Rua de Sezim, São Tiago de Candoso. www.sezim.pt. ✆ **25/352-30-00.** 8 units. 110€–115€ double, including breakfast. Free parking. **Amenities:** Bar; outdoor pool; garden; terrace; games room. Free Wi-Fi.

Pousada Mosteiro Guimarães ★★★ Overlooking the city on the slopes of the Penha hill, this luxury inn is located in a monastery dating back to the origins of Portugal. It once belonged to Queen Mafalda, wife of the country's first king. There's history all around you. Noble salons and the old library feature oak paneling and portraits of local nobles, vast panels of *azulejos* (tiles) show scenes of battles and hunting, ancient stonework frames the doors and windows, and antique furniture lines the bar, restaurant, and other public rooms. The attached church is a flamboyant granite-and-gold baroque wonder. Esplanades give views over the lights of Guimarães and the hotel's 10 hectares (25 acres) of garden and woodland. Guest rooms blend old stonework, regional fabrics, and Portuguese lithographs. About half are in a modern wing (added in 1985); ask to stay in the original house. The restaurant is renowned for its take on traditional Minho cooking served under medieval stone arches.

Largo Domingos Leite de Castro, www.pousadas.pt. ✆ **25/351-12-49.** 51 units. 99€–168€ double, including breakfast. Free parking. **Amenities:** Restaurant; bar; outdoor pool; garden; terrace. Free Wi-Fi.

INEXPENSIVE

Casa do Juncal ★★ This noble 18th-century manor in the heart of the old city has been transformed into a chic boutique hotel, with wooden floors, natural stone or pure white walls, and soft gray fabrics. Its modern, glass-fronted breakfast room opens onto a garden—the ideal place to relax after a hard day's sightseeing. The hotel is suite-only and the units range from 28 sq. meters to 32 sq. meters (300 sq. ft. to 344 sq. ft.). Some are split level, with the beds upstairs. Sheets are Egyptian cotton and duvets are stuffed with Hungarian goose down.

Rua Dr. Avelino Germano, 65. www.casajuncal.com. ✆ **25/204-21-68.** 6 units. 95€–110€ double, including breakfast. Free public parking nearby. **Amenities:** Terrace; garden; bike hire. Free Wi-Fi.

Hotel da Oliveira ★★ If you want to be in the thick of things, this is the place. Occupying a landmarked 16th-century building overlooking Largo da Oliveira in the heart of the historic center, this sophisticated option was recently renovated by interior designer Paulo Lobo under the slogan "Feel Guimarães." Rooms are each themed around a character or event out of the city's history. Original stone doorways and wooden ceiling beams are combined with stacks of old books, modern art, and natural cotton and linen bedclothes to create an ambience that is cool but comfy, and jibes with the history of the house. The ground-floor restaurant serving regional and international food has a terrace spilling over onto the square. Orchids and scented Portuguese toiletries in the bathrooms are a thoughtful touch.

Largo da Oliveira. www.hoteldaoliveira.com. ✆ **25/351-41-57.** 20 units. 76€–168€ double, including breakfast. Free parking, reservations recommended. **Amenities:** Restaurant; bar; bike hire; terrace. Free Wi-Fi.

Where to Eat

Cor de Tangerina ★ VEGETARIAN Something of a surprise amid the meat-driven traditional restaurants of the region, this delightful organic-vegetarian place is set in an old house up on the hill beside the castle. Decor is rustic-chic, with raw wooden floors and furniture; there's a splendid garden out back, perfect for summer lunches. As much as possible, they grow their own food or source from local producers (the delicious breads and pastries are baked on-site). Inventive dishes include creamy rice with wild mushrooms and cheese from the Azores, followed by carob mousse with pineapple, coconut cream, and nuts.

Largo Martins Sarmento, 89. www.cordetangerina.pt. ✆ **96/687-61-65.** Main courses 9.90€–11.90€. No credit cards. Tues–Wed noon–3:30pm; Thurs–Sat noon–3:30pm, 7:30–10pm; Sun 12:30–3:30pm.

Florêncio ★★ PORTUGUESE Entering this restaurant in the northern suburbs is bit of a shock. From outside, it's a rustic house built of massive blocs of stone, but walk through the door and you're amid sophisticated modern decor, with walls in crimson and lemon-yellow, decorated with award certificates, press clippings, and row upon row of wine bottles. There's no confusion about the food, though: This is a bulwark of traditional Minho cooking. Pork offal dishes such as *bucho* (stuffed stomach) and *rojões* (cubes of marinated pork fried with blood sausage and tripe), or salt cod in a cornbread crust are among the treats that secure its loyal local following. Many dishes are cooked in a wood-fired oven.

Madre-de-Deus, Azurém. www.restauranteflorencio.pt. ✆ **25/341-58-20.** Main courses 9€–15€. Daily noon–10pm.

São Gião ★★ PORTUGUESE The village of Moreia de Cónego is a 20-minute drive south from downtown, but it's worth the trip to eat in this restaurant that many consider the region's best. Chef Pedro Nunes' cooking is firmly rooted in northern Portuguese traditions, but he brings his own touch to the classics or experiments with some French or Italian touches. The restaurant has its own smokery, making hams and sausages served as appetizers, and even some main courses such as smoked duck breast served with red fruit sauce. The roast kid and wine-stewed pigs' cheeks are famed, and there are game dishes and fresh river fish in season. A classic.

Avenida Comendador Joaquim Almeida Freitas 56, Moreira de Cónego. www.restaurantesaogiao.pai.pt. ✆ **25/314-10-86.** Mains 17.50€–23€. Tues–Sat 12:30–3pm, 7:30–11pm; Sun 12:30–3pm.

Solar do Arco ★ PORTUGUESE A solid choice in the historic center. The dining room is in an antique house under the stone arches that give the place its name. White-painted wood panels are covered with big black-and-white pictures of city sights. The food is based on local products. *Vitela assada* is a signature dish. *Vitela* is usually translated as "veal," but is actually beef from a younger animal, rather than the white meat of very young calves served as veal in France or Italy. Here it's oven roasted and served with the

LAND OF green wine

There is some question over how ***vinho verde*** got its name. *Verde* means "green" in Portuguese, but although the crisp, fresh wines produced in the Minho region come in white, rosé, and red varieties, none are green. Some say *verde* in this case means "young" or "immature," since the wines are generally consumed shortly after bottling rather than being left to mature for years. Others suggest the name comes from the landscape where the vines are grown—**verdant hills** facing the Atlantic that owe their lush green hues to the winter rain.

Whatever the interpretation, the wines are a pleasure to drink and the **region ★★★** that produces them is a pleasure to explore. Portugal's biggest wine region covers almost all of the historic Minho province and spills over its borders. The vines are often grown on trellises that cover the hillsides, interspersed with forests or fields of corn. Scattered through the region are pretty towns and **aristocratic wine estates** known as *solars* or quintas, many dating back centuries and offering boutique accommodations to travelers.

Most *vinho verde* is white, usually blends of the Alvarinho, Arinto, Avesso, and Loureiro grape varieties, although single-variety wines—particularly **Alvarinhos**—are often considered the best. Some *vinho verdes* are slightly bubbly. The producers' association **CVRVV** has an informative website explaining about the wine and giving tips on where to stay, visit, and taste in the region: www.vinhoverde.pt.

The perfect base is **Ponte de Lima ★★**, one of the oldest and most charming towns in Portugal. Its two halves linked by an ancient stone bridge over the River Lima, the town has existed since Roman times, when wine was already being produced around here. The view of the elegant riverside church of Santo António beside the bridge is one of Portugal's most iconic. Ponte de Lima is filled with historic mansions whose verandas brim with summer flowers. The surrounding hills are packed with baroque wine estates. Among those where you can stay is **Paço de Calheiros ★★** (www.pacodecalheiros.com; ✆ **25/894-71-64**), where Count Francisco welcomes guests to the manor that's been his family's home since the 16th century.

Another must-see estate is the **Palácio da Brejoeira ★★★** (www.palaciodabrejoeira.pt; ✆ **25/166-61-29**), a magnificent palatial residence built in 1806 near the fortified border town of **Monção.** It doesn't have accommodations, but visitors can tour the house and vineyards, which produce one of the best Alvarinho wines and some tasty brandy.

Along the valleys of the Lima and Minho rivers, visit enchanting wine towns like **Arcos de Valdevez ★**, **Melgaço ★**, or **Ponte da Barca ★**, where you should try a steak from the locally raised Barrosã cattle breed in **O Moinho ★** (www.restauranteomoinho.pt; ✆ **25/845-20-35**), a restaurant in an old water mill. Don't miss the fortified frontier town of **Valença ★★**, which stares across the River Minho at its Spanish twin **Tui** on the north bank.

traditional accompaniments of roast potatoes and greens. Other recommended dishes include salt cod with cornbread and rice with octopus. As with many Portuguese restaurants, portions will be huge and it's perfectly okay to ask for a half-portion (*meia dose*) or to share a main.

Rua da Santa Maria 48–50. ✆ **25/351-30-72.** Reservations recommended. Mains 9€–28€. Wed–Mon noon–midnight.

BRAGA ★★

55km (35 miles) N of Porto; 370km (230 miles) N of Lisbon

The Minho's capital manages to be one of Europe's oldest and youngest cities: Oldest because it was founded by the Romans as Bracara Augusta in 20 B.C. on a site already occupied by Celtic tribes; youngest because of its youthful population—almost one-third are under 25—thanks in part to the University of the Minho, which injects a fresh vitality into the city's cultural life.

Since Roman times, Braga has been a center for Christianity. It's been the seat of a bishopric since A.D. 45 and remains one of Portugal's three archdioceses, along with Lisbon and Évora. A Portuguese saying has it that "Braga prays, Coimbra sings, Lisbon has fun, and Porto works." There are churches everywhere, some dating back to the Dark Ages. It has Portugal's oldest cathedral, as well as several splendid baroque temples. Easter Week celebrations are the most intense in Portugal, culminating in processions led by barefoot, black-hooded penitents.

Braga, however, is much more than a religious center. As the biggest city north of Porto, it's an important regional hub. Within the city walls are bright, sunny plazas filled with flowers; cobbled alleys, and streets of sturdy granite houses, many clad in bright *azulejos*. There are atmospheric old cafes, trendy boutiques, and one of the world's oddest soccer stadiums carved into a mountainside.

Essentials

ARRIVING

BY TRAIN It takes about 1 hour from Porto's Campanhã station to Braga, with about 30 trains making the trip daily. Tickets usually cost 3.10€, although there are six fast express trains that make the trip in 39 minutes with fares of 11.70€. There are five daily direct trains from Lisbon. The fastest takes just over 3 hours and costs 32.80€.

BY BUS The bus journey from Lisbon lasts about 4 hours and costs 21€. There are at least 15 buses making the trip for the Rede Expressos company. From Porto there are at least 18 daily buses. The trip takes 1 hour and costs 6€. **Get Bus** (www.getbus.eu; ✆ **25/326-23-71**) makes up to 10 daily trips direct from Porto airport for 14€ for adults, 8€ for children aged 4–14, and free for younger kids.

BY CAR From Porto, the drive takes about 45 minutes on the A3 toll highway. The journey from Lisbon is about 3½ hours. Guimarães is 30 minutes away on the A11.

VISITOR INFORMATION

The **Braga Tourist Office** is in a lovely 1930s building at Av. da Liberdade 1 (www.cm-braga.pt; ✆ **25/326-25-50**), open Mon–Fri 9am–1pm and 2 to 6:30pm; Sat–Sun 9am to 1pm and 2 to 6pm.

Exploring Braga

Braga is an easy place to explore on foot, with most of the sights in the historic center between the gardens of Praça da República in the east and Jardim da Casa dos Biscaínhos to the west. Beside the main sights, the streets around here are perfect for strolling among the old granite town houses and retro stores.

Capela de São Frutuoso ★ CHURCH Amid modern high-rise housing projects in Braga's northern suburbs is a cluster of stone-built religious buildings. Among them is this gem of a chapel, dating back to the 10th century or even earlier. It was built by the German tribes who settled in northern Portugal during the decline of the Roman Empire. It's a rare example of church architecture of that era, built on a Greek-cross layout with four stubby arms. Inside there are traces of Byzantine, Islamic, and Visigoth-influenced decoration. Unfortunately, the opening hours are limited and can be erratic. It's best to phone in advance to make sure the chapel is open.

Avenida São Frutuoso. www.culturanorte.pt/pt/patrimonio/capela-de-sao-frutuoso-de-montelios/. ✆ **92/721-18-12.** Admission free. Daily 10am–4pm (with reservation).

Mosteiro de São Martinho de Tibães ★★ MONASTERY This sprawling monastery is a 15-minute drive from downtown. It was founded in the 11th century and in 1569 became the headquarters of the Benedictine order in Portugal and Brazil. The buildings you see today date mainly from the 17th and 18th centuries and make up one of the biggest and most spectacular religious complexes in Portugal. On the grounds are armies of baroque statues; a rococo church adorned with gold, silver, and marble; and cloisters lined with *azulejos* and carved wooden ceilings. Beyond the opulence of the decoration, a visit also gives visitors the opportunity to glimpse the lives of the monks who lived there, peeping into their cells, dining rooms, even the barber's. It's located in acres of landscaped parkland.

Rua do Mosteiro, Mire de Tibães. www.mosteirodetibaes.org. ✆ **25/362-26-70.** Admission 4€ adults, 2€ students and seniors. Tues–Sun Apr–Oct 10am–7pm; Nov–Mar 10am–6pm.

Museu dos Biscainhos ★ MUSEUM How did the other half live in the 18th century? This well-preserved noble home has some answers. You'll stroll below ornamented ceilings and past walls with panels of tiles and paintings, through collections of Portuguese furniture, glass, silverware, textiles, and porcelain. Most impressive: the entry hall, with geometric patterns carved into its granite floor, and the vaulted painted ceiling of the ballroom. If you don't want pay the entry fee for the museum, you can walk through for free to gardens filled with sculptures, pavilions, and fountains among vegetation, which includes a 300-year-old American Tulip tree that bursts into flame-colored flower every spring.

Rua dos Biscainhos. www.museus.bragadigital.pt/Biscainhos/. ✆ **25/320-46-50.** Admission 2€, free for children under 15. Tues–Sun 10am–12:45pm and 2–5:30pm.

Praça da República ★★ PLAZA A broad, garden-filled plaza, the Praça da República is flanked by stately old buildings housing stores, cafes, and restaurants, plus the occasional grand bank or 18th-century church. Especially fun: the **ID Concept Store ★★**, Avenida Central, 118-120 (✆ **92/571-21-94,** Tues–Sat 10am–8pm), an extensive collection of Portuguese fashion and design; and its neighbor in the same splendid 18th-century silk merchant's house, the **Centésima Página ★★** (www.centesima.com; ✆ **25/326-76-47**) bookstore, cafe, and cultural hub.

Tunnels built in the 1990s took traffic underground, so the square is again a place to stroll, window-shop, or admire the flowers and fountains. Locals refer to the plaza simply as *Arcada*, referring to the arcades running along the neoclassical building on the western edge of the square.

Under those arcades are a couple of the city's historical cafes: **Café Vianna ★★** (✆ **25/326-23-36;** Mon–Thurs 8am–midnight, Fri–Sat 8-2am, Sun 9am–7pm), opened in 1871, and its neighbor **Café Astoria ★** (✆ **91/901-18-90;** Mon 8:30am–midnight, Tues–Thurs 8am–midnight, Fri–Sat 8am–2am), a relative newcomer from 1928. The square is particularly charming when the lights come on at dusk.

Rua do Souto ★★ NEIGHBORHOOD Braga's most iconic cafe is just west of Praça da República in a building covered in deep-blue *azulejos*. **A Brasileira ★★**, Largo do Barão de São Martinho 17 (✆ **25/326-21-04;** daily 7:30am–midnight), has been serving up shots of coffee since it was opened in 1907 by a trader importing beans from Brazil. It remains the city's favorite meeting place.

Beyond A Brasileira, **Rua do Souto,** the long, pedestrian-only street, is a center of social and commercial life. It and the lanes and plazas off it are packed with cute stores, cafes, and restaurants. For real local color, pop into **Mercado de São João ★★**, Rua de São João 5-9 (www.bacalhau-portugal.com; ✆ **25/327-88-60;** Mon–Fri 9am–7pm and Sat 9am–1pm), a grocer since 1894 which, among the spices, freshly ground coffee, and dried fruits, is where locals come to buy *bacalhau*, the salted cod that is a staple across Portugal and a particularly important part of the diet in Braga, where it's traditionally served pan-fried with onions and olive oil.

Also worth noting along the street: the **Arco da Porta Nova ★**, a baroque triumphal arch; the **archbishop's palace ★**, dating back to the 14th century and the neighboring **Santa Barbara gardens ★**; and the **Casa do Passadiço ★**, Largo de São João do Souto (www.casadopassadico.com; ✆ **25/361-99-88;** Mon–Sat 10am–1pm and 3pm–7pm), one of the city's finest old mansions, which now houses a stylish interior design store.

Santuário Bom Jesús do Monte ★★★ CHURCH This hilltop pilgrimage site is Braga's best-known landmark. It's 300m (983 ft.) above the city, but you can reach it by car up a tree-lined drive; take the oldest funicular in the Iberian Peninsula (for 1.20€) or climb on foot up the **monumental granite double staircase** dating from the 18th century, pausing to admire the baroque sculptures, chapels, and grottoes along the way. At the top is a twin-towered neoclassical church in white plaster and gray stone. The views are magnificent. There is also a leafy park with a boating lake, gazebos, and shady spots where locals come to picnic.

Bom Jesus do Monte, Tenões. www.bomjesus.pt. ✆ **25/367-66-36.** Free admission. Summer 8am–7pm; winter 9am–8pm.

Sé ★★ CHURCH When something is very old, Portuguese will say "It's older than Braga cathedral." An 11th-century building whose towers loom over downtown, it was built by Count Henry of Burgundy and his wife Dona Teresa, parents of Portugal's first king, Afonso Henriques. Their tombs are in the Gothic Chapel of Kings. Architecture buffs can read history in the building: The Romanesque structure has accumulated add-ons in just about every style over the centuries, from Gothic-arched entrances to the frame of Manueline cupolas topping the towers. Among the greatest treasures inside are the choir benches, made from ornately carved Brazilian hardwood coated with gold; and the magnificent organ installed in the 1730s. The cathedral's position as an integral part of downtown is increased by the habit locals have of using its front and side entrances as shortcuts when walking around the city. Attached to the cathedral is the **Museu do Tesouro da Sé,** containing a rich collection of religious artifacts, including the **iron cross** carried by Pedro Álvares Cabral when he discovered Brazil and used in the first mass held there in 1500.

Rua Dom Paio Mendes. www.se-braga.pt. ✆ **25/326-33-17.** Daily 9:30am–12:30pm, 2:30–5:30pm; in summer until 6:30pm. Free admission to the cathedral, but you need to pay to visit the treasury museum, choir, and royal tombs. A combined ticket granting access to everything costs 5€, for the museum alone 3€. Children under 12 go free.

Where to Stay

EXPENSIVE

Meliá Braga ★ This 12-story block of shining blue glass, a 35-minute walk from downtown, may lack some of the charm of boutique options but offers wall-to-wall comfort. Rooms are spacious and modern, decorated in soft grays and relaxing green. Many have views over the city from the floor-to-ceiling windows. There's a state-of-the-art health club, outdoor pool, and a spa covering 800 sq. meters (8,600 sq. ft.) including a heated indoor pool, Jacuzzi, sauna, Turkish bath, and range of massage services. The lobby, bar, and El Olivo restaurant (serving international and modern Portuguese food) are designed along clean, contemporary lines and bathed in natural light.

Av. General Carrilho de Silva Porto 8. www.meliabraga.com. ✆ **25/314-40-00.** 182 units. 87€–169€ double, including breakfast. Free parking (reservation recommended). **Amenities:** Restaurant; 2 bars; fitness center; outdoor and indoor pools; spa; babysitting; beauty salon. Free Wi-Fi.

MODERATE

Hotel do Parque ★ One of Braga's oldest hotels, opened in 1870 up on the Bom Jesús do Monte hilltop overlooking the city, it underwent a major overhaul in 2014 which preserved the original granite-and-white facade but

BRAGA'S modern side

Ancient it may be, but it would be a mistake to leave Braga without a glimpse at its modern side. The capital of the Minho has cutting-edge architectural surprises and a bubbling contemporary arts scene. A good place to start is **GNRation,** Praça Conde de Agrolongo 123 (www.gnration.pt; ✆ **25/314-22-00;** Mon–Fri 9:30am–6:30pm, Sat 2:30–6:30pm), a hip space for digital art exhibitions, modern dance, and concerts that opened in 2013 in a former National Guard headquarters, which the architects transformed by fixing dozens of potted plants to the patio walls.

Braga's soccer stadium is unique: the **Estádio Municipal,** Parque Norte, Dume (www.scbraga.pt; ✆ **25/320-68-60;** guided tours in winter Mon–Fri at 10:30am and 3pm, in summer at 10:30am, 2:30, and 3:30pm; 6€, reservation needed) was built by Pritzker Prize–winning architect Eduardo Souto Moura in 2003. He carved a space out of a hillside, leaving a wall of rock behind one goal. It's picked up rather more international prizes than the local club Sporting Braga.

In complete contrast is the **Árvore da Vida** (Tree of Life), Largo de Santiago 47 (✆ **25/320-33-00;** Fri 5–6pm), a tiny chapel crafted of 20 tons of bare wooden planks, fitted together without nails to build an intimate place of worship within the vast 16th-century São Pedro e São Paulo seminary. Local architects worked with a Norwegian sculptor to build the interlocking curving timbers; the chapel was voted 2011's religious building of the year worldwide by the website ArchDaily.com.

Braga's modern art galleries include **Galeria Emergentes dst,** Rua do Raio 175 (www.galeriaemergentesdst.com; ✆ **25/311-66-20;** Tues–Fri 11am–8pm, Sat 3–8pm; free admission), which promotes local artists and is a driving force behind the innovative www.shairart.com project that links galleries around Europe through online exhibitions and art sales. On a hillside just north of Braga, **Galeria Mário Sequeira,** Rua da Galeria, 129, Parada de Tibães (www.mariosequeira.com; ✆ **25/360-25-50;** Mon–Fri 10am–1pm, 3–7pm; free admission) has showcased international names such as Andy Warhol, Richard Long, and Gilbert and George, as well as leading Portuguese artists. The works are handsomely presented in a cool, low white building fused into the surrounding gardens, and a 19th-century farmhouse.

transformed the interior into a showcase for modern design. The rooms are bright and airy, and most offer views over the gardens, hilltop church, and city below. Decor is predominately soft grays and cream, with rich textile features in mauve or crimson. The lounge, games room, and spa offer a modernized take on grand-old-hotel elegance. The gardens filled with palm trees, statues, and grottoes are a treat. Guests can also use the spa at the next-door Hotel do Templo, which belongs to the same group.

Parque do Bom Jesús do Monte, 4700 Braga. www.hoteisbomjesus.pt. ✆ **25/360-34-70.** 44 units. 75€–106€ double, including breakfast. Free parking (reservation recommended). **Amenities:** Bar; games room; sauna; garden. Free Wi-Fi.

Villa Garden ★★ A palatial 19th-century villa surrounded by gardens about 20 minutes' walk from the cathedral, the Villa Garden is an island of calm in the city. Rooms are spacious, with rich, dark fabrics contrasting with the overall white, modern design. Throughout the hotel there's a scattering of antiques and modern artworks, along with vintage tiled floors, hardwood staircases, and chandeliers. In some bathrooms, the bare stone of the original walls has been exposed. The bar has a clubby feel with dark wood panels and black-and-white photos. Next door, the Migaitas Salão Champagne is a separate restaurant run by the hotel. In summer, the outdoor pool is a major attraction. Suites and family rooms are available. Be sure to visit the charming multilevel chapel.

Largo de Infias. www.villagarden.pt. ✆ **25/368-00-21.** 26 units. 59€–134€ double, including breakfast. Free parking. **Amenities:** Restaurant; bar; outdoor pool; terrace; garden; free bikes; babysitting. Free Wi-Fi.

INEXPENSIVE

Domus Guesthouse 26 ★★ Smack in the center of town, this sweet little B&B is a great bargain. It has just four rooms, each individually furnished in pastel shades featuring wallpaper with subtle floral or geometric patterns. It opened in 2015 in a restored, cream-colored, four-story 19th-century house adorned with flower-filled balconies. The welcome is friendly with great attention to detail, from scented made-in-Porto Castelbel soaps and body creams in the bathrooms, to orchids in the lounge and homemade preserves with breakfast. All rooms have cable TV, tea and coffee facilities, plus a sound system where you can plug in your tablet or smartphone. We recommend the Cathedral room, which has the most space and a view over the facade of Portugal's oldest cathedral.

Avenida São Miguel o Anjo, 26. www.domus26guesthouse.pt. ✆ **91/733-90-95.** 4 units. 60€–80€ double, including breakfast. Free parking nearby (reservation recommended). **Amenities:** Lounge. Free Wi-Fi.

InBraga Hostel ★ Braga's reputation as a lively student town and its location on the pilgrimage route to Santiago de Compostela across the border in Spain's Galicia region means there's plenty of good, cheap hostel accommodations. Among the advantages of this place is a central location—just around the corner from the Biscainhos museum—friendly welcome, and peaceful garden out back. Cheap, cheerful, and youthful, the hostel is housed in a restored 19th-century row house. Beds are covered with bright orange duvets. The lounge, opening onto the garden, is filled with recycled wooden furniture. Previous guests have left multicolored, multilingual graffiti messages on the walls. There are mixed and female-only dorms with private lockers and bunks, plus a couple of small but private rooms.

Rua da Boavista, 21. www.inbragahostel.com. ✆ **25/303-35-46.** 5 units. 25€–32€ double; 12€–15€ bunk in dorm. Rates include breakfast. No parking. **Amenities:** Garden; terrace; barbeque; shared kitchen; bike hire; games room. Free Wi-Fi.

Where to Eat

Arcoense ★★ PORTUGUESE For 30 years, this has been hallowed ground for fans of traditional Portuguese food. Fresh fish is brought in daily from the coast, the pork comes from their own hand-raised pigs, and the wine selection is enormous. It's hidden away on a nondescript side street in a modern neighborhood 20 minutes by foot from the cathedral, but is well worth the trip. The roomy interior is modern and refined, with wooden floors, wall paneling, and plenty of glass cabinets showing off all that wine. Braga-style cod with onions, mixed grill with baked rice, and ox stew are among the specialties. Most dishes come with a half-portion option.

Rua Eng. José Justino de Amorim, 96. www.arcoense.com. ✆ **25/327-89-52.** Reservations recommended. Main courses 10€–30€. Mon–Sat 12:30–4pm and 7:30–11pm, Sun 12:30–4pm.

Félix Taberna ★ PORTUGUESE There's a quirky bohemian feel to the pair of bric-a-brac–filled dining rooms that make up the restaurant in an old, yellow-painted house in the heart of Braga's old town. This is another holdout of the city's robust local cuisine; aficionados wax lyrical over its oven-baked rice with duck and *chouriço* sausage (*arroz de pato*). In summer, the outside tables offer a chance to dine alfresco on one of Braga's most handsome plazas.

Largo da Praça Velha 18/19. ✆ **25/361-77-01.** Reservations recommended. Main courses 10€–13€. Mon–Fri noon–3pm and 7pm–1am, Sat 7pm–1am.

O Inácio ★★ PORTUGUESE In an old stone building just outside the Arco da Porta Nova city gate, O Inácio has thrived since 1934 by providing authentic Minho regional cuisine. The decor features rugged walls and hand-hewn beams from the 1700s, regional pottery, and oxen yokes. In colder months a fire burns in an open hearth. Specialties include kid and young beef roast in the wood-fired oven; codfish dishes; and the regional winter favorite, *papas de sarrabulho* (a rich, cumin-flavored pork-based stew thickened with blood), which is often served alongside the marinated pork dish *rojões à moda do Minho*—best with red *vinho verde*. A main course is often enough for two. If you haven't had enough pork, a typical dessert here is *pudim abade de Priscos*—an egg and cinnamon pudding with a touch of melted bacon fat.

Campo das Hortas 4. www.restauranteinacio.com. ✆ **25/361-32-35.** Reservations recommended. Main courses 16€–20€. Wed–Mon noon–3pm and 7:30–10pm.

BARCELOS ★

23km (14 miles) W of Braga; 60km (37 miles) N of Porto; 380km (235 miles) N of Lisbon

Barcelos is an attractive riverside town ringed by green hills. Within its walls are a scattering of medieval and baroque churches, stately palaces, and fine houses. But the town is best known for its outdoor markets, handicrafts, and the legend that bequeathed Portugal one of its most enduring symbols—*O Galo de Barcelos* (the Rooster of Barcelos). The black cockerel with a red crest and flower-and-heart bedecked wings and tail is found transformed into refrigerator magnets, key rings, and ceramic statuettes of every size in souvenir shops around the country.

Essentials

ARRIVING

BY TRAIN There are six direct trains every day from Porto on the line heading to the Spanish city of Vigo. The journey takes about 45 minutes and costs around 5€. There are slower trains that involve a change at the station of Nine. If you want to travel from Braga to Barcelos, you also change in Nine.

BY BUS The station is on Avenida das Pontes (✆ **25/382-58-15**). The TransDev company operates buses almost hourly from Braga between 6:36am and 7:20pm on weekdays. The journey takes an hour and costs 2.65€. The same company operates three buses a day on the 2-hour run from Porto.

BY CAR From Braga it's 25 minutes on the A11 toll highway. From Porto it takes 50 minutes north on the A28, then east on the A11.

VISITOR INFORMATION

The **Barcelos Tourist Office** is at Largo Dr. José Novais 27 (www.cm-barcelos.pt; ✆ **25/381-18-82**). It's open Mar 15–Sept 30 Mon–Fri 9:30am–6pm, Sat 10am–1pm and 2–5pm, and Sun 10am–1pm and 2–4pm; Oct 1–Mar 14 Mon–Fri 9:30–5:30pm, and Sat 10am–1pm and 2–5pm.

Exploring Barcelos

Try to visit Barcelos on Thursday, when the **weekly outdoor market ★★★** (7am–6pm) takes over the vast **Campo da República.** The market dates back to the Middle Ages and draws busloads from around Portugal. Farmers bring in their produce, Roma women hawk cut-price clothes, and stands offer roast sausage and cups of local *vinho verde* wines. What interests most visitors are the handicrafts for which Barcelos is famous—rugs, shawls, embroidered linen, painted wooden ox yokes, handwoven baskets, and most of all, pottery. Local earthenware plates, pots, and jugs in red or yellow clay are renowned, but the real attractions are the **sculptured figures:** brightly colored marching bands, guitar-playing oxen, grotesque demons, and saints with oversize heads.

If you can't make it on a Thursday, look for the ateliers around town and in the surrounding villages. The tourist board has a list and can help organize visits. **Júlia Ramalho** is a leading artist who carries on a tradition started by her grandmother, Rosa Ramalho (1888–1977), considered the greatest of the clay sculptors. Her studio in the village of Galegos São Martinho can be visited by appointment (✆ **93/650-44-26**). Another option is to drop into the **Museu de Olaria ★** or Pottery Museum, Rua Cónego Joaquim Gaiola (www.museuolaria.pt; ✆ **25/382-47-41;** Tues–Fri 10am–5:30pm, Sat–Sun 10am–12:30pm and 2–5:30pm; free admission—although that may change soon). It showcases local artists, giving an overview of the handicraft traditions, as well as organizing regular temporary exhibitions and workshops.

One unavoidable handicraft item is the **Galo de Barcelos.** Reproductions of the renowned rooster are everywhere around Portugal. The country's best-known contemporary artist, Joana Vasconcelos, in 2016 installed what's believed to be the biggest ever—10m (33 ft.) high—and covered with thousands of ceramic tiles and LED lights on the banks of the River Tagus in Lisbon. The legend that launched a million souvenir roosters is set in medieval Barcelos. It seems a pilgrim passing through town was accused of stealing and sentenced to hang. Proclaiming his innocence, the man pointed to a cockerel carcass being prepared for the judge's table and said the deceased bird would crow three times. Surprise, surprise: As the rope was placed around the pilgrim's neck, the judge's lunch produced a cock-a-doodle-do that won the man a reprieve. The Barcelos rooster became a symbol of justice restored. If you buy one, better to get a handcrafted version made by a local artist in the hometown of this miraculous poultry, rather than any of the countless mass-produced varieties found in tacky stores nationwide.

A medieval stone cross, with carvings depicting the story, is said to have been erected by the pilgrim himself on a return visit. It can be seen in the archaeological museum, **Museu Arqueológico ★**, Rua Dr. Miguel Fonseca (✆ **25/380-96-00;** open daily summer 9am–7pm, winter 9am–5:30pm; free admission). The museum is housed within the ruins of the Counts' Palace (**Paço dos Condes**), a medieval hangout of the Bragança family, who went on to become kings of Portugal. Still one of the town's most distinctive sights, it overlooks the fast-flowing River Cávado and the **14th-century stone bridge** that crosses it.

Adjoining the palace is the **Igreja Matriz ★** (parish church), whose interior contains an unusual and lovely mix of stone Gothic arches framed with blue painted tiles.

Barcelos' other notable church buildings include the 18th-century **Igreja de Nossa Senhora do Terço ★**, Av. dos Combatentes da Grande Guerra (www.igrejadoterco.org; ✆ **25/381-70-91;** daily 9am–5pm; free admission), a church that boasts a spectacular gold and *azulejo*-filled interior beneath a ceiling covered with painted wooden panels depicting biblical scenes. Nearby is the small octagonal **Igreja do Bom Jesús da Cruz ★**, Largo da Porta Nova (✆ **93/918-70-71;** daily 7:30am–7pm; free admission), which shows the Italian influence on Portuguese architecture in the 1700s and features a sumptuous crystal, marble, and gilt interior. The church is the hub of one of the Minho's most important pilgrimages in late April and early May, the **Festa das Cruzes ★★**, accompanied by a week of festivities, when the city is strung with fairy lights, streets are strewn with flowers, fireworks light up the river, and big-name singers come to play in town. Check with the tourist office for dates and details.

Where to Eat & Stay

Bagoeira Hotel ★ Barcelos isn't overflowing with good places to stay, but this is the best in town, meaning that it is comfortable, functional, and centrally located (but rather dowdy, with a distinct 1970s vibe). Still, it has the advantage of a rooftop bar with views over the city and an excellent restaurant serving traditional regional cuisine: renowned for roast meats and grandma-style dishes such as *pica-no-chão*—a chicken and rice stew made with the bird's blood.

Av. Dr. Sidónio Pais 495. www.bagoeira.com. ✆ **25/380-95-00.** 54 units. 55€–75€ double, including breakfast. Free parking. **Amenities:** Restaurant; bar. Free Wi-Fi.

PORTUGAL'S wild north

Mountain ranges, bleak plateaus, forests where wolves roam, stone villages where time seems to have stood still—these are the hallmarks of the far north. The biggest and best wilderness area is the **Parque Nacional da Peneda-Gerês ★★★**. Portugal's only national park covers over 700km (over 270 sq. miles) curled around the Spanish border northwest of Braga. Its mountains soar 1,559m (5,115 ft.), sheltering plunging waterfalls, flower-filled valleys, crystalline lakes, and enigmatic ruins.

Unmissable sights include the **Miradouro Pedra Bela ★★**, a rocky outcrop providing breathtaking views over the forests and lake below; the **Cascatas do Tahiti ★★**, a series of waterfalls ending in a pool of transparent water; the 500-year-old **Ponte da Ladeira ★** bridge; and the villages of **Lindoso ★★** and **Soajo ★**, hewn from the rock and surrounded by ***espigueiros***—spooky tomblike granite structures that are actually grain stores, raised off the ground on pillars to deter vermin.

You may catch a glimpse of golden eagles, **gray wolves,** or Spanish ibex. More likely, you'll bump into the local long-horned cattle; powerful ***cão de Castro Laboreiro*** dogs are used by local herdsmen to keep the wolves at bay. You'll also likely spot the ***garrano*** ponies that roam wild here.

Even if soccer superstar **Cristiano Ronaldo** hasn't invited you to stay at his lakeside villa near the village of Valdosende, there are plenty of great places to sleep in and around the park. Cream of the crop is the **Pousada Mosteiro Amares ★★★** (www.pousadas.pt; ✆ **25/337-19-70**), situated in a former monastic retreat dating back to the 12th century. Just slightly more modest is its sister hotel, the **Pousada do Gerês-Caniçada ★★** (www.pousadas.pt; ✆ **21/040-76-50**), a rock-hewn luxury hilltop hideaway. Alternatives include the **Quinta da Mouta ★★** (www.quintadamouta.com; ✆ **92/439-10-76**), a family-run guesthouse in a restored farm complex, or the **Moinhos da Corga ★** (www.moinhosdacorga.com; ✆ **91/830-61-58**), modern wooden cabins near the castle village of Montealgre.

Pedra Furada ★★ PORTUGUESE A 15-minute drive south from downtown is the village of Pedra Furada, with this eponymous restaurant that has become something of a local legend—not least because of its roast rooster, a dish inspired by the bird that put Barcelos on the map. The beast is cooked slowly, filled with a smoked meat stuffing, and served with roast potatoes. They say one bird will feed six people, but you can order a half. It's only on the menu on Friday and Saturday lunchtimes, but Senhor António will make one special if you order a day in advance. Other specialties, served between the handicraft-laden granite walls of the cozy dining room, include marinated pork (*rojões*) and the traditional boiled dinner of meats, smoked sausages, and vegetables (*cozido*). Open since the 1940s, the place is a traditional stopover for pilgrims headed for Santiago de Compostela, the Spanish city 200km (120 miles) to the north.

Rua Santa Leocádia, 1415. Pedra Furada. www.pedrafurada.com. ✆ **25/295-11-44.** Main courses 9€–16€. Tues–Sun noon–3pm and 7–10pm; Mon noon–3pm.

VIANA DO CASTELO ★★

75km (50 miles) N of Porto; 390km (240 miles) N of Lisbon; 60km (40 miles) W of Braga

The highlight of the Minho coast, Viana do Castelo is a fishing port at the mouth of the River Lima. It's an appealing hodgepodge, with an historic downtown filled with medieval and Renaissance buildings overlooked by a spectacular mountaintop basilica; some of northern Portugal's best beaches on its doorstep; great seafood; and a vibrant folk tradition that sees female locals take to the streets in an August festival clad in layers of golden jewelry over gloriously colorful costumes. On top of all that, the maritime city in recent years has sprouted some of Portugal's most noteworthy modern architecture.

Essentials

ARRIVING

BY TRAIN There are eight direct trains a day from Porto. The trip lasts around 1 hour and 20 minutes, and costs 7.85€. Some trains are operated by the Spanish rail company Renfe and after Viana head north into Spain's Galicia region.

BY BUS Local company **AV Minho** (www.avminho.pt; ✆ **25/880-03-40**) has at least four trips from Porto on weekdays (more on Friday, fewer at weekends). The trip costs 6.50€ one-way and takes 1½ hours. They also operate buses from Viana's bus station on Av. dos Combatentes da Grande Guerra, 181, around the Minho region. The national Rede Expressos line has at least four daily journeys from Lisbon. The quickest lasts 4½ hours and costs 22€.

BY CAR From Porto the A28 toll highway gets you to Viana in about 1 hour.

VISITOR INFORMATION

The **Viana Welcome Center** is on Praça do Eixo Atlântico (✆ **25/809-84-15**). It's open Jul–Aug daily 10am–9pm; Mar–June and Sept–Oct Tues–Sun 10am–1pm, 2–6pm; Nov–Feb Tues–Sun 10am–1pm and 2–5pm. The city council has a useful, multilingual website: www.cm-viana-castelo.pt.

Exploring Viana do Castelo

The place to start is **Praça da República ★★**, one of Portugal's most handsome squares. At its heart is the much-photographed 16th-century **Chafariz Fountain.** The most striking building is the **Igreja da Misericórdia ★★** (www.scmviana.pt; ✆ **25/882-23-50;** Sat 10am–12:30pm and 2:30–6:30pm, Mon–Fri 10am–noon and 3–5pm). Beyond its three-tiered Renaissance facade, the inside is a riot of baroque gold work, floor-to-ceiling blue-and-white tiles showing scenes of biblical charity, and a glorious painted ceiling.

The other building dominating the square is the 1502 **Paço do Concelho ★** (✆ **25/880-93-51;** open during exhibitions daily 10am–6pm). This fortresslike former town hall is constructed over an arcade made up of three wide, low, Gothic arches. The crenulated facade displays a royal coat of arms and wrought-iron balcony windows above each arch. It is used now to host art shows.

Praça da República and the narrow streets running from it are a center for the **Romaria de Nossa Senhora d'Agonia ★★★** (www.romariadagonia-mag.pt), the city's biggest party. Built around a religious pilgrimage dating back at least to the 17th century, the 4-day festival takes over the city in late August. Streets are covered with flower petals and churches strung with lights, a flotilla of flower-decked fishing boats carries holy statutes to bring blessings to the sea, giant figures with papier-mâché heads stumble around the square, and fireworks light up the harbor. The main attraction is the procession of **Mordomas,** where over 500 local women parade in the local costume: a blaze of color with bodices, embroidered blouses, striped skirts, shawls wrapped around their heads, and layer upon layer of necklaces laden with the region's filigree gold work. It is a spectacular sight.

To find out more about Viana's costumes, jewelry, and rich folk tradition, visit the costume museum, **Museu do Traje ★**, Praça da República (✆ **25/880-93-06**; Tues–Sun 10am–1pm and 3–6pm; admission 2€ adults, 1€ students and seniors, free for children under 12). Located in a 1950s former bank building, the museum showcases the costumes and explains their place in the city's history and culture.

Viana's downtown is ideal for strolling. Among the lanes there's plenty to please the eye: the 15th-century **Igreja Matriz ★**, which serves as the town's cathedral; the mighty **Castelo de Santiago da Barra ★** fortress guarding the mouth of the River Lima since 1589; a cluster of palaces and churches, among which standouts include the 16th-century **Igreja de São Domingos ★** and the **Capela das Malheiras ★**, a little baroque gem. There's also an iron bridge across the Lima built in 1878 by the firm of Gustave Eifel. To understand Viana's position as the base for fishing armadas that once trawled the farthest reaches of the north Atlantic in search of cod, visit the **Gil Eannes ★**, Doca Comercial (www.fundacaogileannes.pt; ✆ **25/880-97-10**; daily 9:30am–6pm in winter, until 7pm in summer; admission 3.50€, children under 6 free), a former hospital boat that accompanied the cod fleets on their journeys to Greenland or Newfoundland. Now it's a floating museum moored in the harbor.

For one of the great panoramas in the north of Portugal (in fact, *National Geographic* called it one of the greatest views in the world), you can visit the **Miradouro de Santa Luzia ★★★**, a belvedere on the hill of Santa Luzia, where the view of Viana is especially stunning at night when all the lights go on. To the north of town, the viewpoint is topped by the **Basilica de Santa Luzia** (www.templosantaluzia.org; ✆ **25/882-31-73;** daily, summer 8am–7pm, winter 8am–5pm; admission free), constructed in a neo-Byzantine style in the early–20th century; its towers and domes recall Paris' Sacré-Coeur. For an even better view over the city and coast, climb the 142 steps up to the

THE GREEN coast

North and south of Viana, the Minho's shoreline is known as the **Costa Verde ★★**, or "Green Coast," named for the forests that spread down to the broad sandy beaches. The area has a reputation for chilly water and strong surf, but it has some beautiful, uncrowded beaches. Just keep an eye on the lifeguards to see if the currents are making it unsafe for swimming—red flags mean keep out of the water, yellow means take care, green indicates it's safe to go in and have fun. The beaches have always been popular with families from Porto and other northern cities, but they are increasingly drawing an international following—not least among surfers and other water sports enthusiasts.

Many rate **Praia de Moledo ★★★** as the region's best. It's Portugal's northernmost beach and draws a fashionable crowd from Porto. The wide sandy strand curls southward from the River Minho, which forms the Spanish frontier. Beyond is the conical Mount Santa Tecla, and there's a 15th-century fort on a small offshore island just to add to its scenic appeal. If all that sea air gives you an appetite, the **Pra Lá Caminha** (✆ **25/872-26-06** beach bar is renowned for its sandwiches. For something more serious, try **Restaurante Ancoradouro ★★** (✆ **25/872-24-77**), a block inland and renowned for its fresh fish served with potatoes baked in their skins.

The nearby town of **Caminha ★** has a lovely location where the River Minho meets the ocean, and is a picturesque old town reflecting its golden age trading with Portugal's Africa and Asian outposts during the 15th and 16th centuries. Staying the night? **Design & Wine Hotel ★★**, Praça Conselheiro Silva Torres (www.designwinehotel.com; ✆ **25/871-90-40**) offers a cool mix of 18th-century and ultra-modern buildings on the waterfront with a spa and wine cellar that serves as a reminder that we're still in *vinho verde* territory.

Other top beaches include **Praia de Ofir ★★**, backed by dunes and pine forests (and a trio of ugly tower blocks) just south of the resort town of Esposende, and **Praia de Afife ★★**, an endless stretch of fine white sand north of Viana, which boasts a celebrated restaurant, **Mariana ★★** (✆ **25/898-13-27**), serving divine sea bass steamed with algae.

cupola. Portugal's longest **funicular railway,** Av. 25 Abril (✆ **96/177-31-64;** June–Sept daily 9am–8pm, Mar–May and Oct Mon–Fri 10am–noon and 1–5pm, Sat–Sun 9am–6pm, Jan–Feb and Nov–Dec Tues–Fri 10am–noon and 1-5pm, Sat–Sun 10am–5pm; 2€ one-way, 3€ return) will haul you the 650m (2,130 ft.) to the hilltop.

Lately, Viana has gained a reputation for its **modern architecture** with internationally celebrated designers of the Porto school laying down major new works in the city. Highlights include the riverside **Praça da Liberdade ★** plaza by Fernando Távora; the **municipal library,** Alameda 5 de Outubro (✆ **25/880-93-40;** Mon–Sat 9am–7pm) designed by Álvaro Siza Vieira; and the **Centro Cultural,** Praça Marques Júnior (✆ **25/880-93-51**), opened in 2013 by another Pritzker Prize laureate from Porto, Eduardo Souto de Moura, which is used for concerts and theater performances.

Where to Stay

MODERATE TO EXPENSIVE

Casa Melo Alvim ★★ The oldest urban mansion in Viana do Castelo is today an inn of antique charm. Built in the Manueline style in 1509, it retains its baroque stairwell, which features a row of original stone pillars. Rooms range from 21 to 43 sq. meters (226 to 462 sq. ft.) and are individually decorated to illustrate the evolution of Portuguese styling from 17th-century baroque to contemporary. That might mean chestnut furniture typical from the region or rooms in the colonial Indo-Portuguese style using tropical hardwoods (these are particularly charming). A peaceful garden and a restaurant serving regional dishes with a classical French influence add to the inn's allure. Breakfast features local cold cuts, cheeses, fresh fruit, and breads. The hotel displays an extensive collection of Viana's filigree gold jewelry.

Av. Conde da Carreira 28. www.meloalvimhouse.com. ✆ **25/880-82-00.** 20 units. 75€–180€ double, including breakfast. Free parking. **Amenities:** Restaurant; bar; free bikes; library; babysitting. Free Wi-Fi.

Fábrica do Chocolate ★★ Yep, this is a hotel in a chocolate factory—the ideal place to unleash your Willy Wonka fantasies. In fact, there's a Willy Wonka–themed room featuring a giant mural inspired by Roald Dahl's character and a bedstead in the form of his "golden ticket." Rooms are all chocolate-themed, ranging from romantic to playful. One is inspired by the movie *Chocolat* staring Juliette Binoche and Johnny Depp. A suite with families in mind is made up like the candy house from Hansel and Gretel. It's all in a restored chocolate factory built in 1914, which also includes a chocolate museum, a store, and a revived factory where you can attend chocolate-making workshops. Naturally, the restaurant maintains the spirit, serving the likes of duck with pear purée and chocolate gravy, or sea bass rice with cocoa butter, as well as a cornucopia of chocolatey desserts. Nicely located on a quiet street a block from the riverside gardens and a short walk to Praça da Republica.

Rua do Gontim 70 a 76. www.fabricadochocolate.com. ✆ **25/824-40-00.** 18 units. 105€–137€ double, including breakfast. Public car park nearby from 8€ per day. **Amenities:** Restaurant; bar; massage service; shop; babysitting. Free Wi-Fi.

Flôr de Sal ★★ This modern three-story hotel in steel and glass stands right at the edge of the Atlantic's waters and most of its rooms have balconies with wooden decks offering uninterrupted ocean views. (The others look up to Santa Luzia mountain.) Bedrooms are elegant, tasteful, and supremely comfortable, with state-of-the-art bathrooms. An excellent spa and fitness center makes it fun to sweat: You can gaze out over the waves from the Jacuzzi or running machines. If it's too chilly for the beach, the hotel has two heated, indoor saltwater pools. The restaurant provides regional cooking with a seafood accent and more panoramic sea views.

Av. de Cabo Verde, 100 Praia Norte. www.hotelflordesal.com. ✆ **25/880-01-00.** 60 units. 145€–195€ double, including breakfast. Free parking. **Amenities:** Restaurant; health club and spa; 2 indoor pools; free bikes; babysitting. Free Wi-Fi.

Pousada Viana do Castelo ★★★ A jewel in the Pousada chain of luxury boutique digs, this Belle Epoque palace is surrounded by lush landscaped gardens and boasts some of the finest views in Portugal, looking down on the domes of Santa Luzia church with Viana, the River Lima, and the sweeping curve of the Atlantic coast laid out before you. It will be hard to drag yourself away from your balcony, but rest assured that you can also enjoy the panorama from the outdoor pool, while getting a massage in the gardens, or from amid the crystal and chintz of the spacious lounge and gourmet restaurant. Built in 1895, the hotel has neoclassical details and granite balconies and looks especially good when floodlit at night. Winding cobblestone roads run through a forest to the entrance, which is a 15-minute taxi ride from downtown.

Monte de Santa Luzia. www.pousadas.pt. ✆ **25/880-03-70.** 50 units. 89€–204€ double, including breakfast. Free parking. **Amenities:** Restaurant; bar; exercise room; outdoor pool; tennis court; garden. Free Wi-Fi.

Where to Eat

A Laranjeira ★ PORTUGUESE A friendly, family-run restaurant in the heart of downtown, the "orange tree" is devoted to preserving traditional Minho cooking, with recipes handed down from generation to generation. Menus change with the season, but signatures include deep-fried hake filets with Russian salad, roasted salt cod with kale, or pork with chestnuts. Vegetarian options are available; and a dessert trolley loaded with temptations ("golden soup" is a must-try) makes the rounds at the end of the meal. The decor is bright and modern. It's located in a town house fronted with green ceramic tiles that also contains Viana's oldest guesthouse, whose recently restored rooms provide bargain accommodations. There's an excellent wine list with a focus on local *vinho verde* and Douro reds.

Rua Manuel Espregueira, 24. ✆ **25/882-22-58.** Main courses 10€–14.50€. Thurs–Tues noon–3pm and 7–10pm.

Camelo ★★ PORTUGUESE Nationally renowned for its Minho cuisine, this country-style house on the road leading east out of Viana is located where the suburbs start to give way to vine-covered hills. The owners raise their own pigs; the vegetables come from their plot. And that's a LOT of pigs: Some 350 people can fit in the dining rooms, which quickly fill with families gathering for Sunday lunches or workmates out for celebration. In summer, the coveted tables are in the vine-shaded back garden. Camelo always has fresh fish, but salt cod and roast meat dishes are what the place is best known for, along with seasonal specials like marinated pork served with blood-thickened rice or lamprey—an eel-like fish that's pulled from the rivers of the Minho between January and April. It might be ugly, but it's a big favorite up here.

Rua de Santa Marta 119, Santa Marta de Portuzelo. ✆ **25/883-90-90.** Main courses 8.50€–23€. Tues–Sun noon–3:30pm and 7–11pm.

Os 3 Potes ★ PORTUGUESE/FRENCH Off Praça da República, "the 3 buddies" was an old bakery before its conversion into one of the best regional dining rooms in Viana. The grandma's-house decor includes sturdy granite walls mounted with traditional crockery, embroidered table coverings, and lighting by coach lamp. Diners can sometimes catch fado music on Fridays, and there's regular folk dancing on Saturday evenings. To start, try *caldo verde* (a regional soup made from cabbage and potatoes with a slice of *chouriço* sausage). Mains include all the Minho regional favorites, plus French *fondue bourguignon.*

Beco dos Fornos 7–9. ✆ **25/882-99-28.** Reservations recommended. Main courses 13€–17€. Thurs–Tues noon–3:30pm and 7–10:30pm.

CHAVES ★

125km (77 miles) E of Braga; 150km (96 miles) NE of Porto; 440km (275 miles) N of Lisbon

High up on the Spanish border, Chaves has its roots in Roman times. It was founded by Emperor Flavius Vespasian in A.D. 79 and prized by the Romans both as military strongpoint and bath resort, thanks to its hot springs. The arched bridge across the River Tâmega, which is still a symbol of the city, was built during the reign of the Iberian-born Emperor Trajan. Today Chaves is an attractive town of narrow streets and noble buildings clustered on the riverbank beneath the keep of its 14th-century castle. It's renowned for culinary delights such as smoked ham and puff-pastry meat pies, but the main attraction are those hot springs, making Chaves, and its surrounding resorts, a major spa center.

Essentials

ARRIVING

BY BUS There's no rail link, but plenty of bus options. Local operator **AV Tâmega** (www.avtamega.pt; ✆ **27/633-23-51**) has at least two daily runs from Lisbon, charging 22.50€ for the trip that lasts around 6 hours. It makes six trips every weekday from Porto, taking just less than 3 hours and charging 13.80€. Other companies, including **Rodonorte** (www.rodonorte.pt; ✆ **25/934-07-10**) and the national **Rede Expressos** also provide links to Lisbon, Porto, Braga, and other cities. Many trips to Chaves involve a change in the regional center of Vila Real.

BY CAR From Porto, it should take about 1½ hours along the A3 and A7 toll highways passing by Guimarães. From Lisbon, the journey is 4 hours: Take the A1 to Coimbra, the IP3 to Viseu, and the A24, which takes you to Chaves. If you are coming from the Douro Valley wine region, the A24 gets you from Peso da Régua in less than 1 hour.

VISITOR INFORMATION

The **tourist office** is at Terreiro de Cavalaria (www.chaves.pt; ✆ **27/634-81-80**). It's open Mon–Sat 9am–12:30pm and 2–5:30pm.

Exploring Chaves

Start out on the **Ponte Romana ★★**, or Roman Bridge, which runs for 150m (almost 500 ft.) over 12 arches across the Tâmega. It was built on the orders of Emperor Trajan in A.D. 104 and was a major link between the Roman cities of Braga and Astorga (in Spain). Today it's pedestrian-only and the perfect place to admire the outline of old Chaves with its churches, fortifications, and mansions on the west bank; the quaint **Madalena** neighborhood to the east; and leafy riverside gardens on both sides. In the center of the bridge are two engraved **Roman columns** dedicated to the city, which the Romans called *Aquae Flaviae* (Flavius' Waters) in honor of its founding emperor and the hot springs. For the adventurous, an alternative way across the river is the row of stepping stones or **Poldas ★** just downstream, which locals have long used as a shortcut.

From the bridge, the **Rua de Santo António ★** is the main commercial street running up to the center of town. It's lined with brightly painted granite-and-glass town houses dating back to the 18th century and earlier. At the top is the **Forte de São Francisco ★**, Rua do Terreiro da Cavalaria (www.fortesaofrancisco.com; ✆ **27/633-37-00**), a mighty star-shaped fortress built around a 15th-century convent in 1658 to bolster the frontier defenses during the war against Spain to restore Portugal's independence. It was the scene of a notable battle in 1809, when Portuguese troops dislodged Napoleon's invading French troops. These days, the hilltop fortress contains a hotel, but non-guests are welcome to pay a discreet visit inside the battlements.

Heading back downtown, many of the houses are cracked with age and maintain centuries-old wooden verandas decorated with flowers on the upper floors. **Rua Direita ★** is one of the best places to spot them. **Praça de Camões ★** is the city's monumental heart. It contains the **Igreja de Santa Maria Maior ★** (✆ **27/632-13-84;** daily 9am-6pm; free admission), a church dating back to the 12th century, on the site where a Roman temple and Swabian basilica once stood. There's also the handsome 19th-century **City Hall,** the baroque facade of the **Igreja da Misericórdia** and the imposing **Paço dos Duques de Bragança,** a ducal palace built between the 15th and 18th centuries and now housing the **Museu da Região Flaviense ★** (http://museus.chaves.pt; ✆ **27/634-05-00**; Mon–Fri: 9am–12:30pm and 2–5:30pm, Sat–Sun: 2–5:30pm; admission 1€ adults, 0.50€ students and seniors, free for children under 12), a museum containing Roman and prehistoric artifacts from around the region. The museum ticket also includes entry to the nearby military, religious arts, and railway museums.

Next door to the museum are the remains of Chaves' medieval castle, also built to deter Spanish incursions. Its 14th-century donjon, the **Torre de Menagem ★**, rises out of neatly tended gardens. It contains a military museum, but its main attraction is the view from the ramparts. Admission is included in the price of the regional museum and it keeps the same hours.

If you are not staying at one of the spa hotels, you can sample the benefits of Chaves' hot springs by popping into the **Termas de Chaves ★**, Largo das Caldas (www.termasdechaves.com; ✆ **27/633-24-46;** Mon–Sat 9am–7pm, Sun 9am–1pm), the modern municipal spa, which offers a range of health treatments and wellness packages using the waters that spring to the surface here at a constant 73°C (163°F). Day-long spa packages cost from 60€; a 45-minute massage, 26€; a 15-minute sauna, 7€. In the rotunda outside, you can drink the mineral-rich waters, said to be very good for the health, if not so easy on the taste buds.

Where to Stay

Forte de São Francisco ★★ The best choice in the center of town. A family-run hotel, it opened in 1997 within the massive walls of the 17th-century fortress built to defend Portugal's northern borders. The rooms are decorated in a restrained modern style, but with antique touches such as wooden bedsteads. Rooms are mostly in the old convent around which the defensive complex was raised. The broad parade grounds now hold gardens with palm, olive, and citrus trees; a tennis court; and an outdoor dining area. One of the corner bastions has an outdoor pool built into the roof that offers views over the city and surrounding hills.

Rua do Terreiro da Cavalaria. www.fortesaofrancisco.com. ✆ **27/633-37-00.** 58 units. 63€–128€ double, including breakfast. Free parking. **Amenities:** 2 restaurants; 2 bars; outdoor pool; spa; fitness room; garden; games room; tennis. Free Wi-Fi.

Hotel Casino Chaves ★ For a touch of Vegas in Trás-os-Montes, this brash modern place has roulette, blackjack, poker, and lots of slots. Just north of downtown, it's 8km (5 miles) from the border and popular with visitors from Spain, who nip over for a flutter. They can hardly miss it; the architecture resembles a pile of irregular shaped white boxes balanced precariously on top of each other. Inside, it's a riot of color. Rooms come in bright candy hues. All offer city or mountain views. Black and amber shades predominate in the bathrooms. There's a seriously large outdoor pool from which you can gaze across the hills, and a wide range of spa, fitness, restaurant, and bar options. Big-name Portuguese music stars give frequent performances.

Lugar do Extremo, Valdanta. www.hotelcasinochaves.solverde.pt. ✆ **27/630-96-00.** 78 units. 74€–153€ double, including breakfast. Free parking. **Amenities:** 3 restaurants; 6 bars; outdoor and indoor pools; spa; fitness room; terrace; garden; games room; squash courts; babysitting. Free Wi-Fi.

Pedras Salgadas Spa & Nature Park ★★★ Wherever you go in Portugal, cafes serve little green bottles of sparkling mineral water called "Agua das Pedras." This is where it comes from, a spa resort that was all the rage in the years before World War I, set in a forest of redwood, pine, and cypress and 30 minutes' drive south from Chaves. Revamped and reopened in 2012, its accommodations comprise slate-covered treehouses—space-age, tubular contraptions propped up among the branches. It's not exactly living Tarzan-style, however, the houses come will all mod cons, including lounge rooms and kitchenettes, all decked out in Nordic-style minimalism. Vertigo sufferers can relax, there are also roomy ground-based "eco houses" in a similar style planted among the trees. The resort includes a scattering of delightful original buildings like the pink-painted former casino and the white stucco spa pavilion from 1912, renovated by Pritzker-Prize–winning architect Álvaro Siza Vieira, which provides posh pampering.

Parque Pedras Salgadas, Bornes de Aguiar. www.pedrassalgadaspark.com. ✆ **25/943-71-40.** 7 units. 160€–270€ double, including breakfast. Free parking. **Amenities:** Restaurant; bar; outdoor pool; spa; garden; free bikes; games room; tennis. Free Wi-Fi.

Vidago Palace ★★★ This extraordinary place was commissioned in 1908 on the orders of King Carlos I, who wanted Portugal endowed with a grand spa resort to compete with the best of Europe. He never saw it completed, assassinated by gunmen later that year in Lisbon. Portugal became a republic the year it opened in 1910. Over the next century, the palace had its ups and downs, but it reopened in 2010, restored to all its Belle Epoque glamour, and is one of the best hotels in the country. Siza Vieira oversaw the restoration of the spa and Club House bar and restaurant. Behind the 100-plus windows of its vast salmon-pink facade, there are monumental staircases, marble columns, silk wall hangings, rooms fit for royalty, and chandelier-lit restaurants in the hands of Michelin-starred chef Rui Paula. Outside are 100 hectares (250 acres) of forested parkland and a golf course laid down in 1935 by the legendary Scottish designer Philip Mackenzie Ross.

Parque de Vidago, Vidago. www.vidagopalace.com. ✆ **27/699-09-00.** 70 units. 170€–424€ double, breakfast included. Free parking. **Amenities:** 3 restaurants; 3 bars; spa; outdoor pool; free bikes; garden; terrace; tennis; golf; babysitting. Free Wi-Fi.

Where to Eat

Adega Faustino ★★ PORTUGUESE Over a century ago this solid single-story stone building opened as a wine store and tavern. It's still in the same family and the great oak wine casks still stand proudly behind the bar, but its role has evolved over the decades. These days, Faustino serves up hearty plates of homemade local *petiscos*—Portugal's version of tapas. It's a no-frills place with plain whitewashed walls, cobbles on the floor, and plastic cloths on the long wooden tables. But the food is an authentic taste of Trás-os-Montes (with the occasional dish from Angola showing up sometimes on the menu—a reminder of many Portuguese families' links with the African former colony). Liver with bacon, garlicky *alheira* sausages, lamb chops, and tripe with chick peas are some of the treats you can wash down with a jug of red wine from those casks.

Travessa Cândido Reis. www.adegafaustino.pt. ✆ **27/632-21-42.** *Petiscos* 4€–9€. Mon–Sat noon–midnight.

ROSÉ palace

If you discovered wine in the 1960s or 1970s, chances are you're already familiar with the **Casa de Mateus** ★★★ (www.casademateus.com; ✆ **25/932-31-21**), a wonderful baroque palace just outside Vila Real on the road between Chaves and Régua. Back then, a slightly sweet pink fizz called **Mateus rosé** was the world's best-selling wine. Fans ranged from Jimi Hendrix and Queen Elizabeth II to countless students for whom Mateus was the beverage of choice for first dates—cheap sophistication, with an exotic curved bottle you could convert into a romantic candle holder. Tastes have evolved, and although Mateus has made something of a comeback as an icon of 1970s nostalgia (and sells 20 million bottles a year), serious wine buffs tend to be scornful. The palace that inspired its label, however, has a timeless appeal.

Built in the early–18th century, it is the most perfect of all the country's baroque manors. In contrasting white-painted plasterwork and soft gray granite, the main building is accessed by a balustraded double staircase flanked by twin wings advancing toward an ornamental pool that perfectly reflects the facade. A flurry of chimneys, decorative pinnacles, and pediments project over the roof. There's a splendid chapel off to one side and a row of stately cypress trees providing shade along the path from the remarkable **gardens.** The architect is unknown, but Nicolau Nasoni, the Italian behind much of Porto's baroque skyline, is thought to have had at least a hand in the design.

Inside, the house is richly furnished with silk hangings, high wooden ceilings, paintings of bucolic scenes, and an early illustrated edition of the Portuguese classic poem *Os Lusíadas*. Descendants of the original owners still live in one wing, but the rest of the house and the gardens are open to the public. Regular concerts of jazz, classical, and Portuguese music take place here during the summer.

It's located at Largo Morgados de Mateus in the village of Mateus, just over 3km (almost 2 miles) east of Vila Real. It's open daily May–Oct: 9am-7:30pm, Nov–Apr 9am-6pm. Admission to house and gardens is 11.50€ including a guided tour; just the gardens is 8€. The estate does produce excellent Douro wines in conjunction with other local wineries, which are on sale in the **on-site store.** Don't expect to find Mateus rosé, however; it is made elsewhere.

Carvalho ★★ PORTUGUESE Occupying the ground floor of a modern apartment block next to the thermal baths, this restaurant doesn't look much on the outside. Inside, too, the decor is not that exciting unless floral tablecloths and a collection of oversized clocks are your thing. The food, however, is something else. The mother and daughter team in the kitchen have made this place the restaurant of reference for regional cooking in Chaves for over 30 years. There's always fresh fish for the grill and typical dishes based on locally raised livestock. *Naco de vitela* (a hunk of young beef) served with rice baked with smoked meats, salt cod broiled over hot coals, or roast kid are among the specialties. The guestbook bears witness to Carvalho's fame—from Olympic champions to presidents of the republic—everybody eats here when they are in town.

Alameda de Tabolado, Largo das Caldas 4. www.restaurante-carvalho.com. ✆ **27/632-17-27.** Reservations recommended. Main courses 8.50€–18.50€. Tues–Sat noon–3pm and 7–11pm; Sun noon–3pm.

BRAGANÇA ★

210km (130 miles) E of Porto; 490km (310 miles) NE of Lisbon

Bragança (or Braganza, as it's sometimes written) is the historic capital of Portugal's Trás-os-Montes region. The heart of the city is a fortified citadel built in the early–12 century. From its sturdy walls you get an overarching view across the chestnut forests, desolate plateaus, and hill ranges that are snow-covered in winter. Natives call the county here *terra fria* (cold land). Inside the battlements are the narrow lanes of one of Portugal's best-preserved medieval cities, where ancient buildings and traditions survive. Despite its remoteness, Bragança played a key role in Portugal's history: Local lords bearing the city's name formed Portugal's royal family from 1640 until the fall of the monarchy in 1910.

Essentials

ARRIVING

BY BUS The rail network doesn't make it up here. Rede Expressos runs at least six daily buses from Lisbon. The trip takes around 6 hours and 40 minutes and costs 23€. From Porto there are also at least six buses making the 3½-hour trip for 14.50€.

BY CAR It should take less than 2½ hours from Porto along the A4 toll highway. From Lisbon, the journey should take around 5 hours: Take the A1 to Coimbra, the IP3 to Viseu, and the A24 to Vila Real, where you pick up the A4.

VISITOR INFORMATION

The **tourist office** is at Avenida Cidade de Zamora (www.cm-braganca.pt; **✆ 27/338-12-73**). It's open June–Sept Mon–Sat 9am–1pm and 2–6pm; Oct–May Mon–Fri 9am–1pm and 2–5:30pm, Sat 9am–12:30pm.

Exploring Bragança

The **Cidadela ★★** is the place to start. Fortified in the 12th century and strengthened in the 15th, it was long a stronghold to deter incursions from Spanish neighbors. Within the walls the medieval atmosphere is preserved. One- or two-story homes, with gray stone door and window frames, whitewashed walls, and clay-tiled roofs cluster beneath the donjon, the **Torre de Menagem ★**, which broods over the city and the surrounding plateau. An army outpost until the 1920s, it now holds a military museum, the **Museu Militar** (**✆ 27/332-23-78;** open Tues–Sun 9am–noon and 2–5pm; admission 2€), with displays that range from medieval suits of armor to a mockup of a World War I trench and material from Portugal's colonial wars in Africa. As much as the exhibits, it's worth the admission price to see the medieval architecture from the inside and climb to the roof for the stunning views.

In the garden besides the tower is a Gothic **stone pillory ★**. Such symbols of municipal power are found in towns across Portugal. This one stands out because it emerges from a statue of a *berrão*—an ancient statue representing a boar, sculptured by tribespeople who inhabited these lands before the

Romans. Hundreds of them were planted in the northwest of the Iberian Peninsula between the 4th and 1st centuries B.C. This is one of the best preserved. Nobody is quite sure what they meant to the Iron Age people who made them.

Another historical mystery is in the nearby Municipal House, or **Domus Municipalis ★,** Rua da Cidadela (✆ **27/332-21-81;** open daily 9:30am–6:30pm). A squat granite structure ringed with little arched windows, it is a rare surviving civil building from the Romanesque era of the early Middle Ages. Its original use is uncertain. One theory is that the first floor served as a cistern for the town water supply, while the chamber above was a meeting place for a prototype municipal council. Before leaving the walled upper town, cast your eyes inside the citadel's church, **Igreja da Santa Maria ★** (✆ **27/332-55-10;** daily 9am–noon and 2–5pm; free), distinguished by its twisted columns and vividly painted barrel-vaulted ceiling.

Down the hill from the castle, the lower part of Bragança's old town is a pleasing mix of handsome plazas, granite mansions, and white-painted churches. Its wealth reflects the 16th-century influence of the Bragança family and the city's establishment as the region's main administrative and religious center following a devastating Spanish attack on the border town of Miranda do Douro in 1762. **Praça da Sé ★** is the main square flanked by the 18th-century **Sé Velha,** or Old Cathedral, used as a cultural center since a new cathedral was built in 2001. The square forms a hub for the city's main commercial streets. A yellow building with the rounded facade and balcony at the eastern end of the square houses the **Chave d'Ouro** cafe, where locals have gathered to sip coffee, gossip, and argue soccer and politics since the 1920s.

Close by are a couple of museums that are well worth a visit. The **Museu Abade de Baçal ★,** Rua Abílio Beça 27 (www.mabadebacal.com; ✆ **27/333-15-95;** Tues–Fri 10am–5pm, Sat–Sun 10am–6pm; admission 2€), occupies a former bishop's palace built in the late 1600s. The expertly presented collection ranges from masks and costumes used in local folklore to Renaissance church sculptures; prehistoric boar statues, regional landscape paintings, silver plates, antique furniture, and ceramics. Down the road is the **Centro de Arte Contemporânea Graça Morais ★**, Rua Abílio Beça, 105 (www.centroartegracamorais.cm-braganca.pt; ✆ **27/330-24-10;** Tues–Sun 10am–6:30pm; admission 2€ adults, 1€ students and seniors, free for children under 10), a modern gallery dedicated to one of Portugal's best-known living artists, Graça Morais (b. 1948), who was born in Trás-as-Montes and frequently takes her inspiration from the region's landscapes, people, and traditions. It also shows works by other contemporary Portuguese artists and runs regular temporary exhibitions.

Bragança sits on the southern edge of the **Parque Natural de Montesinho ★★**, a forbidding but beautiful nature reserve of rolling hills and high plains, covered with forests of oak and chestnut. Almost 10% of the world's chestnut forest lies in Portugal, and 80% of the country's production is in Trás-as-Montes. Through fall and winter, carts of roasting chestnuts are a common street-corner sight in cities around the country. The park, which stretches almost 750 sq. kilometers (290 sq. miles) along the Spanish border, has some of southern Europe's wildest terrain. Temperatures range from –12°C (10°F) in winter to searing summers of 40°C (104°F). The Iberian wolf and rare black stork are among the wildlife. In the granite-and-slate villages spread through the park, shepherds, cattle herders, and small holders eek out an existence, many continuing centuries-old communal farming practices. Information, maps, and ideas for car, bike, or hiking tours can be found at the tourist office in Bragança or from the park authorities (www.natural.pt; ✆ **27/330-04-00**).

Other attractions close to Bragança include the **Basílica Menor de Santo Cristo** ★ (✆ **96/004-15-67**), an outsize baroque church that towers over the tiny village of Outeiro. It was built in 1698 to celebrate a miracle reported in the village when blood was supposed to have seeped from a statue of Christ. It's a 20-minute drive southeast from the city. Opening hours can be unpredictable, so it's best to call ahead if you want to view the golden altar and painted wooden panels inside. Just to the west of Bragança, the village of **Castro de Avelãs** contains a **church** ★ built partly in the 12th century that is one of the best-preserved examples in Portugal of the Mudéjar style of Christian buildings influenced by Arab architecture. Check opening times with the Bragança tourist office, but it's the exterior of the building that is most striking.

Where to Stay

A Montesinho ★ In the riverside village of Girmonde, a 15-minute drive from the center of Bragança at the entrance of the Montesinho Natural Park, the owners of a famed local restaurant have restored a bunch of rural dwellings that are now guesthouses. You can rent rooms or a whole house. The Casa da Mestra, once the schoolteacher's house, has five double rooms. The solid stone building was given a daring makeover, with a glass and wood-board front revealing a display of local handicraft products. It's not grand luxury, but makes a cozy, inexpensive base for exploring the park (the owners will be happy to guide your tracks). There's a shared kitchen and a lounge that integrates the bare stone walls into a modern design, warmed by a blazing fireplace. In summer, guests can use the outdoor pool belonging to another of the family's properties in the village. Dine at Dom Roberto's restaurant. A tavern since the 1930s, it does wonders with local meat, trout, and game.

Rua Coronel Álvaro Cepeda, 1, Girmonde. www.amontesinho.pt. ✆ **27/330-25-10.** 22 units. 38€–66€ double, breakfast extra. Free parking. **Amenities:** Restaurant; bar; Jacuzzi; sauna; bike hire; outdoor pool. Free Wi-Fi in public areas.

Pousada Bragança ★★ On the heights of the Serra da Nogueira, with panoramic views of the castle of Bragança and the old city, this lodging is at its best at night or emerging from the morning mist. The *pousada* was built in the 1950s, using local stone and natural wood. A vintage feel is maintained

BUONOS DIES miranda

Portuguese is the world's 6th-most-spoken language, used by 250 million people from Mozambique to Macao, Brazil to Braga. Up in Portugal's remote northeast, however, a few speak something different. The country's second official language is **Mirandese,** spoken by 15,000 people living around the city of **Miranda do Douro ★★**.

The language is closely related to Portuguese: "Good day" is *buonos dies* rather than *bom dia*; "thank you" is *oubrigado* instead of *obrigado*. But local people are proud of their distinct tongue, which has been making a comeback since schools began teaching it in the 1980s.

Miranda sits above the Douro. Up here, the river carves a deep canyon into the land, forming the border between Portugal and Spain. Once a thriving regional center, the city slipped into obscurity after 1762, when most of it was destroyed by shelling from an invading Spanish army during the Seven Years' War. Local bigwigs decamped to Bragança, farther from the frontier, and Miranda was left to its own devices.

Isolation maintained not only the language, which still resounds within the surviving medieval streets around the 16th-century canyon-side **Cathedral ★★**, but also other traditions. Inside the cathedral, look for the tiny statue of a boy sporting a top hat, frock coat, and sword strapped to his belt. Revered by locals, the **Menino Jesus de Cartolinha** is supposed to represent a youthful Jesus who, legend has it, appeared in the city in the 17th century waving a sword to inspire resistance against besieging Spaniards. An even older bellicose tradition are the ***pauliteiros*** **★★** (www.pauliteiros.com), groups of men who perform a war dance that involves bashing sticks together while dressed in frilly white skirts, striped stockings, and brightly colored shawls to a beat of drums and bagpipes. The origins are lost in time, but the local museum, **Museu da Terra de Miranda ★**, Praça D. João III 2 (www.culturanorte.pt/pt/patrimonio/museu-da-terra-de-miranda; ✆ **27/343-11-64;** open Wed–Sun 9am–1pm and 2–8pm, Tues 2–6pm; admission 2€) explains about the dance and other local traditions. Check your hotel or the local tourist office, Largo do Menino Jesus da Cartolinha (www.cm-mdouro.pt/;

with furniture and artwork from that period. The spacious guest rooms are well furnished and maintained, with private balconies. Beds feature covers with traditional Tràs-os-Montes patterns. Bathrooms come in granite and marble. In winter the open fireplace (and in summer the outdoor pool) are much appreciated. The restaurant draws raves from Lisbon food critics for its modern take on regional cuisine. It's a 15-minute walk to downtown.

Estrada de Turismo. www.pousadas.pt. ✆ **27/333-14-93.** 28 units. 90€–175€ double, including breakfast. Free parking. **Amenities:** Restaurant; bar; outdoor pool; garden; terrace. Free Wi-Fi.

Solar de Santa Maria ★ In the center of town, this graceful house built in 1639 served as a convent, school, and residence for the district police chief before being turned into a guesthouse. It still has the feel of a noble family home and is packed with antique wooden furniture, framed prints, and comfortable sofas. Rooms are a decent size, with wooden floors and high ceilings.

✆ **27/343-00-25**), for dates of *pauliteiro* performances.

The climate here is extreme. Locals say they get *nove meses de inverno e três de inferno* (9 months of winter and 3 of hell). Snow frequently covers the austere landscape of rocky plateaus and rolling hills. Stretching for 130km (80 miles) along the Portuguese bank of Douro is a nature reserve, the **Parque Natural do Douro Internacional ★★**. It's a paradise for bird-watchers. They can spot shaggy-headed Egyptian vultures, black storks, pink hoopoes, and blue rock thrushes. For the most spectacular ornithological encounters, head to **Penedo Durao ★★★**, a rocky outcrop towering over the river, which is a favored hangout for Griffon vultures, one of the largest raptors. You can look them in the eye as they glide past on 3m (9-ft.) wingspans.

Many of the villages around here have kept winter festivities rooted in ancient pagan rites. Around Christmas, Twelfth Night, or Mardi Gras, young men dress up in devilish masks and outlandish costumes and run riot through the streets. The most remarkable is in the village of **Podence,** a half-hour drive south of Bragança, where during the week of Mardi Gras, a masked, bell-ringing gang called the ***carretas*** **★★** take the streets, making merry mischief while draped in shaggy hooded suits striped with yellow, green, and scarlet.

The best place to stay in Miranda is the **Hotel Parador Santa Catarina ★**, Largo da Pousada (www.hotelparador santacatarina.pt; ✆ **27/343-10-05**), where the rooms have plunging views over the canyon. Among the many eateries serving the local delicacy *posta mirandesa* (a thick-cut steak from the local breed of cattle), try **La Balbina ★**, Rua Rainha Dona Catarina 1 (✆ **27/343-23-94**), where they grill them in the fireplace while you watch. The region's most original accommodation is 40km (25 miles) south of Podence, **Bela Vista Silo Housing ★★**, Quinta da Bela Vista 176, Eucisia, Alfândega da Fé (www.belavista-silohousing.pt; ✆ **27/946-32-80**), which has rooms in converted grain silos. Go in late February and March and it will be too cold for the outdoor pool, but perfect for seeing the countryside whitened by the blooming of countless almond trees.

The patio garden, with its renaissance arcades and shady orange trees, is a treat. Fresh bread, cheeses, homemade cakes, and jams are served at breakfast.

Rua Eng José Beça, 39. www.solarsantamaria.pt. ✆ **27/333-31-61.** 5 units. 75€ double, including breakfast. Free public parking nearby. **Amenities:** Garden; library. Free Wi-Fi.

Where to Eat

O Javali ★★ PORTUGUESE There's authenticity in overdrive at this roadside eatery, a 10-minute drive from downtown. The name means "the wild boar" and the highland cooking here is game-heavy. Boar stew with chestnuts or boar steak on the wood-fired grill are specialties. In Europe, chestnuts were a staple before traders introduced the potato from the New World. Here they still are. You can start your meal with chestnut soup and finish with chestnut pudding. Naturally, there's a boar's head mounted on the wall. If neither boar nor chestnuts are to your taste, they serve trout from the fast-flowing local streams and baby goat raised in the hills of Montesinho. Portions are massive; you may want to share a main.

Estrada do Portelo, km 5. ✆ **27/333-38-98.** Main courses 13€–20€. Daily 12:30–10pm.

Solar Bragançano ★★★ PORTUGUESE A legend. For many, this is the epitome of what a Portuguese regional restaurant should be. Located in a three-centuries-old house on the main square of town, it serves the best, most flavor-filled regional dishes with a true taste of Trás-os-Montes. A tiled stairway leads to a dining room lined with cabinets filled with wine and crystal. There are handwoven regional rugs and the occasional stag's head, sword, or portrait of a notable local on the walls. It's fabulous to eat here at any time, but autumn and winter are when game takes over the menu—the pheasant with chestnuts or hare with rice draw fans from all over the country. In summer, you can dine in the leafy garden.

Praça da Sé. ✆ **27/332-38-75.** Reservations recommended. Mains 10.50€–18.50€. Tues–Sun noon–3pm and 7–10pm.

MADEIRA (& THE AZORES)

The island of Madeira, 850km (528 miles) southwest of Portugal, is the mountain peak of an enormous volcanic mass. The island's craggy spires and precipices of umber-dark basalt end with a sheer drop into the blue water of the Atlantic Ocean, which is so deep near Madeira that large sperm whales often come close to the shore. If you stand on the sea-swept balcony of Cabo Girão, one of the world's highest ocean cliffs (590m/1,936 ft. above sea level), you'll easily realize the island's Edenlike quality, which inspired Luís Vaz de Camões, the Portuguese national poet, to say Madeira lies "at the end of the world."

The summit of the mostly undersea mountain is at Madeira's center, where **Pico Ruivo,** often snowcapped, rises to an altitude of 1,860m (6,102 ft.) above sea level. It is from this mountain peak that a series of deep, rock-strewn ravines cuts through the countryside and projects all the way to the edge of the sea.

The island of Madeira is only 56km (35 miles) long and about 21km (13 miles) across at its widest point. It has nearly 160km (99 miles) of coastline, but it's mostly rocks and just a few beaches. In Madeira's volcanic soil, plants and flowers blaze like creations from Gauguin's Tahitian palette. With jacaranda, masses of bougainvillea, orchids, geraniums, whortleberry, prickly pear, poinsettias, cannas, frangipani, birds of paradise, and wisteria, the land is a veritable botanical garden. Custard apples, avocados, passion fruit, mangoes, and bananas grow profusely throughout the island. Fragrances such as vanilla and wild fennel mingle with sea breezes and permeate the ravines that sweep down the rocky headlands.

In 1419, João Gonçalves Zarco and Tristão Vaz Teixeira of Portugal discovered Madeira after being diverted by a storm while exploring the west coast of Africa, some 564km (350 miles) east. Because the island was densely covered with impenetrable virgin forests, they named it Madeira (wood). Soon it was set afire to clear it for habitation. The blaze is said to have lasted 7 years, until all but a small northern section was reduced to ashes. Today the hillsides are so richly cultivated that you'd never know there had been such extensive fires. Many of the island's groves and vineyards, protected by buffers of sugarcane, grow on stone-wall ledges next to the cliff's edge. Carrying water from mountain springs, a complex network of man-made *levadas* (water channels) irrigates these terraced mountain slopes.

The uncovered *levadas*, originally constructed of stone by slaves and convicts (beginning at the time of the earliest colonization in the 16th century and slowly growing into a huge network), are most often .3 to .6m (1–2 ft.) wide and deep. By the turn of the 20th century, the network stretched for 1,000km (621 miles). In the past century, however, the network has grown to some 2,140km (1,330 miles), of which about 40km (25 miles) are covered tunnels dug into the mountains. The big development was during 1940 to 1950, when this network of canals was developed and increased.

The Madeira wine and the sugarcane production attracted many British traders to the islands since the 17th century—many English names are still found in wineries. They controlled the wine trade and sugar trade for years, and had considerable domain of the island's economy. Many English traditions have survived—including afternoon tea. The British influence is big in the architecture and decorative arts.

Madeira is both an island and the name of the autonomous archipelago to which it belongs. The island of Madeira has the largest landmass of the archipelago, some 460 sq. km (178 sq. miles). The only other inhabited island in the Madeira archipelago is **Porto Santo ★** (about 26 sq. km/10 sq. miles), 40km (25 miles) to the northeast of the main island of Madeira. *Réalités* magazine called Porto Santo "another world, arid, desolate, and waterless." Unlike Madeira, it has beautiful sandy beaches.

A series of other islands populate the archipelago, including the appropriately named *Ilhas Desertas*, or the Desert Islands, 19km (12 miles) southeast of Funchal (the capital of the island of Madeira), and even more remote islands, called *Selvagens*, or Wild Isles, which lie near the Canary Islands. None of these is inhabited and they are protected by the government for their flora and fauna—Selvagens is totally closed to visits, but Desertas can be visited on licensed boat trips.

Madeira can be a destination unto itself, and, in fact, many Europeans fly here directly, avoiding Portugal altogether. Most North Americans, however, tie in a visit to Madeira with trips to Lisbon. It isn't really suited for a day trip from Lisbon—the island deserves a minimum of 3 days, if you can afford that much.

MADEIRA ESSENTIALS

853km (530 miles) SW of Portugal; 564km (350 miles) W of the African coastline

Essentials

ARRIVING

The quickest and most convenient way to reach Madeira from Lisbon is on a 90-minute **TAP** or an **easyJet** flight. The daily flights stop at the Madeira airport and some go to Porto Santo. Flying is affordable, especially if you fly aboard any TAP plane into Lisbon from anywhere outside of Portugal and

Madeira

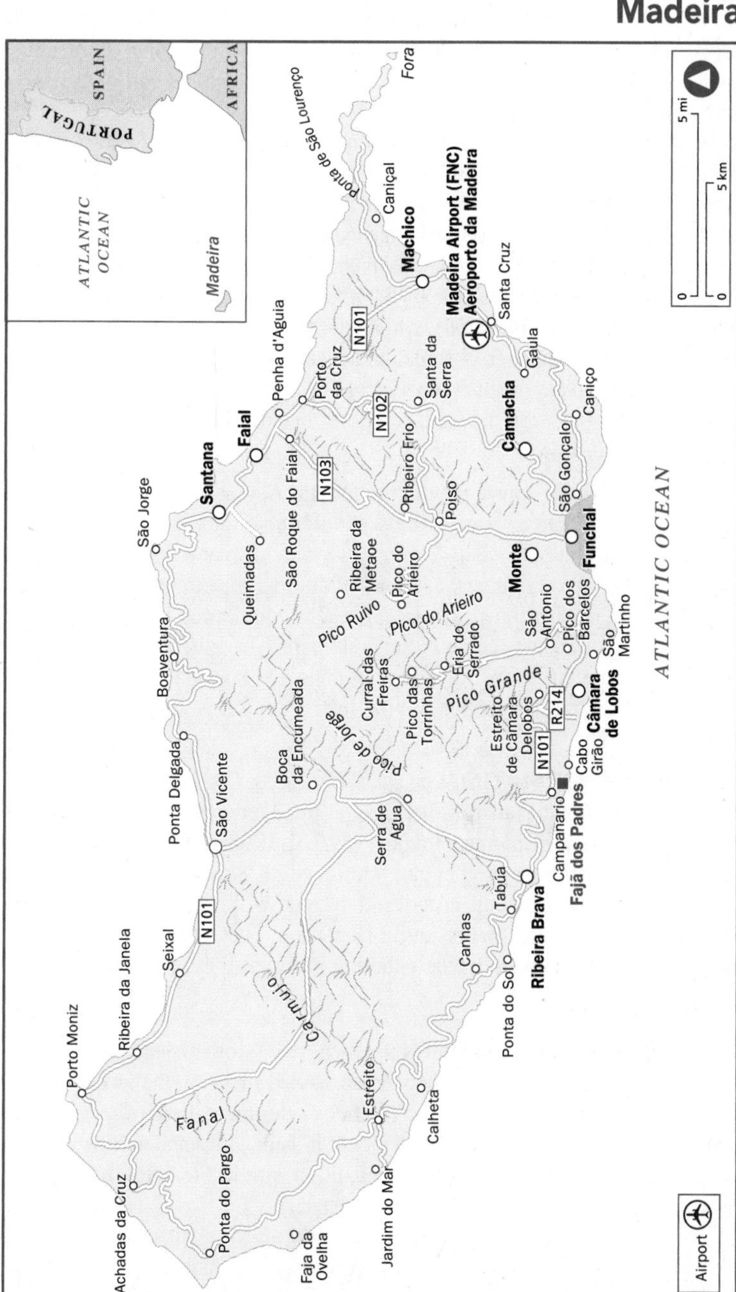

PORTUGAL
SPAIN
AFRICA
ATLANTIC OCEAN
Madeira
Ponta de São Lourenço
Fora
Caniçal
Machico
Madeira Airport (FNC)
Aeroporto da Madeira
Santa Cruz
Gaula
Caniço
Santa da Serra
Camacha
São Gonçalo
Funchal
Monte
ATLANTIC OCEAN
Penha d'Aguia
Porto da Cruz
N101
N102
N103
Faial
Santana
São Jorge
São Roque do Faial
Ribeiro Frio
Poiso
Queimadas
Ribeira da Metaoe
Pico do Arieiro
Pico Ruivo
Pico do Arieiro
São Antonio
Pico dos Barcelos
São Martinho
Boaventura
Curral das Freiras
Eria do Serrado
Pico das Torrinhas
Pico Grande
Estreito de Câmara Delobos
R214
Câmara de Lobos
Cabo Girão
Ponta Delgada
Boca da Encumeada
Pico de Jorge
São Vicente
Serra de Agua
Campanario
Fajã dos Padres
Ribeira Brava
Tabúa
Canhas
Ponta do Sol
Seixal
Ribeira da Janela
Porto Moniz
Carmujo
Fanal
Estreito
Calheta
Achadas da Cruz
Ponta do Pargo
Faja da Ovelha
Jardim do Mar
Airport
0
5 mi
5 km

then connect with a TAP commuter flight from Lisbon to Funchal. The supplement you'll pay for the final round-trip leg into Funchal rarely exceeds $100 and, in many cases, might be under $50. If you're going to Madeira, your best bet is to book all legs of your trip to Portugal as part of the same ticketing process.

In Madeira, planes arrive at **Aeroporto de Madeira** (www.aeroportos damadeira.pt; ✆ **29/152-07-00**), east of Funchal, at Santa Cruz. **Taxis** into Funchal's center take from 15 to 20 minutes and typically cost 25€. However, the taxis that wait at the airport take airline passengers anywhere they want to go on the island. If you're going to Funchal or from Funchal back to the airport, you can also take a **bus,** run by the Sociedade de Automóveis de Madeira (www.sam.pt; ✆ **29/120-11-50**), which can take from 40 minutes to 1 hour (depending on the number of stops) and costs only 5€ one-way. These buses run as needed and are timed to meet incoming and outgoing flights. They stop at three or four places in the town center as the need arises.

WHEN TO VISIT

Madeira enjoys year-round popularity, though April through May and September through October are the most comfortable and, in many ways, the most beautiful times to visit. You might want to avoid visiting in August because that's when *capacete*, a shroud of cooling mist, tends to envelop the island. If you're visiting in the summer, air-conditioning might be vital to you—unless you're at a retreat in the mountains—because the island is often quite hot. Temperatures are not as high as mainland Portugal, but the humidity makes it feel hotter. December and the festive season is also a great time to visit the island.

VISITOR INFORMATION

An English-speaking staff runs the desk at the **Madeira Tourist Office,** Av. Arriaga 16 (www.turismomadeira.pt; ✆ **29/121-19-00**), in Funchal. It's open Monday to Friday 9am to 7pm and Saturday and Sunday 9am to 3pm. The office distributes maps of the island, and the staff will make suggestions about the best ways to explore the beautiful landscape. They also have information about ferry connections to the neighboring island of Porto Santo.

Island Layout

The capital of Madeira, **Funchal** is the focal point of the island and the gateway to its outlying villages. When Zarco landed in 1419, the sweet odor of wild fennel led him to name the town after the aromatic herb (*funcho* in Portuguese). Today this southern coastal city of hillside villas and narrow winding streets is the island's most luxuriant area, filled with fertile fields, hundreds of flowering gardens, and numerous exotic estates.

A long, often traffic-clogged street, **Avenida do Mar,** runs east-west along the waterfront. North of this is **Avenida Arriaga,** the "main street" of Funchal. At the eastern end of this thoroughfare is the Sé (cathedral), and at the western end is a large traffic circle that surrounds a fountain. As Avenida Arriaga, site of several hotels, heads west, its name changes to **Avenida do Infante.** As it

FROMMER'S favorite MADEIRA EXPERIENCES

Riding a toboggan. Madeira's most fabled activity is taking a ***carro de cesto*** ride in a wicker-sided sled from the high-altitude suburb of Monte to Funchal. Two drivers run alongside the sled to control it as it careens across slippery cobblestones. It's a great joy ride that lasts 20 minutes.

Escaping to the golden beaches of Porto Santo. Pirates of the Atlantic once romped on the 6.5km (4 miles) of beaches in this relatively forgotten part of the world.

Spending a morning at the Mercado dos Lavradores (Market of the Workers). Go early—between 7 and 8am if you can—to see this market come alive. Flower vendors, fishermen, and farmers sell an array of local wares (clothing, flowers, baskets, ceramics, prepared food, crafts) not seen anywhere else on Madeira. Check out the fish, everything from tuna to eel, from scabbard fish (*espada*) to limpets that you'll be served later in local restaurants. It's open Monday to Saturday 7am to 8pm.

Tasting the local wines. At the islands wineries you'll have a ball acquainting yourself with the array of local wines, all fortified with grape brandy. These include the world-renowned, light-colored **Sercial,** the driest of the Madeira wines; the golden-hued, slightly sweeter **Verdelho;** the decidedly sweet **Boal,** a dessert wine that's good with cheese; and the sweetest: rich, fragrant **Malmsey,** which is served with dessert. Madeira wine has been long appreciated in the U.S.: It was the wine used for toasting in the celebration of Declaration of Independence in 1776.

Walking on a *levada* trail. Try to walk on at least one *levada*. These mostly flat walkways are up in the mountains in the heart of the splendid laurel forest, with scintillating views, and, sometimes, waterfalls.

Attending the end-of-the-year festival. The most exciting (and most crowded) time to visit Funchal is during this festival, December 30 to January 1, when live music, food stalls, dancing, costumes, and parades fill the streets. At night, fireworks light up the bay, with the mountains in the background forming an amphitheater.

runs east, it becomes **Rua do Aljube.** Running north-south, the other important street, **Avenida Zarco,** links the waterfront area with the heart of the old city.

But there's much to see beyond Funchal. Active visitors should hike one of the many trails strewn around the island. Hand-hewn stones and gravel-sided embankments lead you along precipitous ledges, down into lush ravines and across flowering meadows. These dizzying paths are everywhere, from the hillsides of the wine-rich region of Estreito de Câmara de Lobos to the wickerwork center of Camacha. If this is more walking than you can handle, organized tours, local buses, and rental cars will also whisk you around the island.

For a circular drive of the entire island, take N101 either east or west of Funchal. Heading west from Funchal, you'll pass homes so tiny that they're almost like dollhouses, and banana groves growing right to the edge of the cliffs that overlook the sea. Less than 10km (6¼ miles) away is the coastal village of **Câmara de Lobos (Room of the Wolves),** the subject of several paintings by Sir Winston Churchill. A sheltered, tranquil cove, it's set amid rocks and towering cliffs, with hillside cottages, terraces, and date palms. Churchill painted a species he (and others) called sea wolves, really a seal species known on Madeira as *lobo marinho* or *foca monge*, that used to be abundant in the bay. Nowadays these seals are an endangered species, but there's a colony living in the Desertas Islands that sometimes swims to Madeira.

The road north from Câmara de Lobos, through vineyards, leads to **Estreito de Câmara de Lobos** (popularly known as Estreito), an important winegrowing region. Along the way you'll spot women and men wearing brown stocking caps with tasseled tops as they cultivate the ribbonlike terraces; sometimes farmers sell fruit at small roadside stalls. (Incidentally, the islanders' blond locks were inherited from early Flemish settlers.)

Lying 16km (10 miles) west of Câmara de Lobos, **Cabo Girão** is one of the highest ocean-side cliffs in the world. You can stand here watching the sea crash 580m (1,903 ft.) below while also taking in a panoramic sweep of the Bay of Funchal. The viewpoint's new platform is all glass—challenging for those afraid of heights—but the sights are impressive, including the *fajãs*, fertile areas at the bottom of the cliff, where farmers grow vegetables and fruit.

From **Cabo Girão,** return to Funchal by veering off the coastal road past São Martinho to the belvedere at **Pico Dos Barcelos.** It is one of the most idyllic spots on the island, with vistas that take in ocean, mountains, orange and banana groves, bougainvillea, and poinsettias, as well as the capital.

By heading north from Funchal, you can visit some outstanding spots in the heart of the island. Past São António is **Curral das Freiras,** a village huddled around an old monastery at the bottom of an extinct volcanic crater. The site,

A hike TO REMEMBER

Southwest of Santana is **Queimadas,** rising to an altitude of 900 meters (2,953 ft.). From here, many people make the 3-hour trek to the apex of **Pico Ruivo (Purple Peak),** the highest point on the island, 1,860m (6,102 ft.) above sea level. This is a difficult, long, hot climb, and is recommended only for the hearty. The best access to Pico Ruivo is from Pico do Arieiro (see "Pico do Arieiro," later in this chapter) because the trail from there is the most scenic. Still, in **Queimadas Park** you can start the walk toward **Caldeirão Verde levada,** one the most scenic and adventurous treks, with tunnels and a beautiful waterfall at the end. It's 6.5km (4 miles) each way and you'll have to return to the same starting point.

Get there early, before 9am, when the crowds arrive. And don't forget the golden rules of hiking: Never walk alone; take a flashlight; and bring water, food, and a mobile phone. If you're not comfortable with hiking, hire a guide—the *levada* is flat but still physically challenging.

For more info and trail maps, visit www.visitmadeira.pt.

whose name means "Corral of the Nuns," was originally a secluded convent that protected the nuns from sea-weary, women-hungry mariners and pirates. The best view of the valley is from **Eira do Serrado** viewpoint, 1,095m (3,593 ft.) high.

If you go north, be sure to visit the **Santana** area. With an alpine setting, waterfalls, cobblestone streets, green meadows sprinkled with multicolored blossoms, thatched cottages, swarms of roses, and plunging ravines, it just about defines the word "picturesque." The novelist Paul Bowles wrote, "It is as if a 19th-century painter with a taste for the baroque had invented a countryside to suit his own personal fantasy."

Southeast of Santana, head for **Faial,** a colorful hamlet with tiny A-frame huts (the road descends in a series of sharp turns into a deep ravine). The lush terraces here were built for cows to graze on, not for farming.

In the east, about 30km (19 miles) from Funchal, is historic **Machico,** where Portuguese explorers first landed on Madeira. The town is now visited mainly because of the legend of "the lovers of Machico," an English couple who were running away to get married but whose ship is said to have sank here in 1346. In the main square of the town stands a Manueline church constructed at the end of the 15th century, supposedly over the tomb of the ill-fated pair. The facade contains a lovely rose window. In the interior are white marble columns and a frescoed ceiling over the nave. Try to view the village from the belvedere of **Camões Pequeno.** You can walk uphill to the belvedere by following a signpost in the center of Machico.

On the way back from Machico, you can detour inland to the village of **Camacha,** perched in a setting of flowers and orchards. It's the center of the wickerwork industry. You can shop here or just watch local craftspeople making chairs and other items. You'll find that though the stores in Funchal are amply supplied, some items are as much as 20% cheaper in Camacha.

GETTING AROUND MADEIRA

Though distances are short on Madeira, you should allow plenty of time to cover them because of the winding roads.

BY BUS The cheapest, albeit slowest, way to get around Madeira is by bus. Local buses go all over the island at a fraction of the cost the tour companies charge, but you will miss the commentary of an organized tour, of course. A typical fare in Funchal is 1.50€ to 2.50€; rides in the countryside can cost 5€. Sometimes only one bus a day runs to the most distant points. Some of the rides into the mountains can be quite bouncy and uncomfortable. There is no bus station in Funchal, but you can buy tickets for anywhere on the island at any of the newsstands in the center of Funchal. For schedules, go to www.madeira-island.com/bus_services.

Most buses depart from the large park at the eastern part of the Funchal waterfront bordering Avenida do Mar. Buses to Camacha or Caniço leave from a little square at the eastern sector of Rua da Alfândega, which runs parallel to Avenida do Mar near the marketplace.

BY TAXI The going taxi rate is about 90€ per day, but three or four passengers can divide the cost. Always negotiate (many taxi drivers speak English) and agree on the rate in advance. Most taxis are Mercedes, so you'll ride in comfort (and won't have to worry about navigating the nightmarish roads). If you're in Funchal, you'll usually find a line of taxis across from the tourist office along Avenida Arriaga—unlike mainland Portugal, they are painted in yellow and blue.

BY CAR Unless you're a skilled driver used to narrow roads and hairpin turns, you should not rent a car on the island. In this case you can hire a car for 1 or 2 days and use it to explore the beautiful north coast, with some of the most scenic drives. In recent years highways and tunnels have been built, making the drives shorter and safer. However, the highways don't go everywhere, and often the most scenic drives are the old narrow roads.

Avis (www.avis.com) has offices at the Aeroporto da Madeira, in Santa Cruz (© **29/152-43-82**), and in Funchal, at Largo António Nobre 164 (© **29/176-45-46**). **Hertz** (www.hertz.com) has a kiosk at Aeroporto da Madeira, in Santa Cruz (© **29/152-30-40**). **Budget Rent-a-Car** (www.budget.com) has an outlet at Estrada Monumental 182 (© **96/857-47-98**). You can also rent vehicles at **Europcar,** Aeroporto da Madeira (www.europecar.com).

Note on parking: Street-side parking on the narrow streets of Funchal is notoriously difficult to find, almost never free, and requires returns virtually every hour to feed the meter. Even large hotels in the city center maintain very few parking spaces, directing their clients instead to the nearest of many covered or underground parking lots in the city center. Rates vary with the location and the time of day you opt to park, but you can expect to pay between 1€ and 1.30€ per hour. Two of the most central of the parking lots include the ones associated with the **Anadia Shopping Center,** Rua Anadia (no phone), and with the **Dolce Vita Shopping Center,** on the Rua Dr. Brito Câmara (no phone) near the seafronting Ribera de São João. Parking at hotels and restaurants on the outskirts of town is plentiful and invariably free.

ORGANIZED TOURS If you don't care to venture out on your own, you can take one of the many organized bus tours that cruise through the valleys and along the coast of Madeira. You can arrange to be picked up at your hotel or at the tourist office; if you're staying at a hotel outside of Funchal, you must usually pay a small surcharge to be picked up. **Daniel Madeira Táxis** (www.danielmadeirataxis.com) does tours and transfers around the island. **Hit the Road Tours** (www.hittheroadmadeira.com) specializes in small-group tours in a Land Rover, visiting less explored parts of the island on day trips. They lead tours to some *levadas* (the aquaducts that were built to bring water from the north to south coast of the island and are now a network of hiking trails in the mountains), as well to the east and west of the island. In Funchal, students from Madeira University lead walking tours in the city, under the name

History Tellers (http://historytellers.pt; ✆ **29/170-50-60**); these cover tales about the old neighborhoods of Funchal and, to a lesser extend, the history of the island. Tours run Monday to Friday, 10am to 6pm.

[Fast FACTS] MADEIRA

Area Codes The country code for Portugal is ✆ **351.** The local area code is ✆ 291.

Automated Teller Machines (ATMs) Most ATMs (available 24 hours a day) are located in Funchal, but you can also find ATMs in towns throughout the island.

Business Hours **Shops** are usually open Monday to Friday 9am to 1pm and 3 to 7pm, and Saturday 9am to 1pm. Most are closed on Sunday. **Municipal buildings** are open Monday to Friday 9am to 12:30pm and 2 to 5:30pm. All **banks** are open Monday to Friday 8:30am to 3pm.

Consulates The Consulate of the **United States** is on Rua da Alfândega 10 (✆ **29/123-56-36**), off Avenida do Infante. The Consulate of the **United Kingdom** is on Rua da Alfândega 10, third floor (✆ **29/121-28-60**). All other consulates are located only in Lisbon.

Dentists A good English-speaking dentist, **John de Sousa,** has an office in Marina Shopping on the third floor, office 304, Avenida Arriaga (✆ **29/123-12-77**), in Funchal.

Doctors **Francis Zino,** in the Edificio Zino, Avenida do Infante (✆ **29/174-22-27**), in Funchal speaks English and has an excellent reputation.

Drugstores Drugstores (chemists) are open Monday to Friday 9am to 1pm and 3 to 9pm. The rotation emergency, night service, and Sunday schedules are posted on the doors of all drugstores. A reliable, centrally located chemist is **Farmácia Honorato,** Rua da Carreira 62 (✆ **29/120-38-80**).

Emergencies Call ✆ **112** for a general **emergency,** ✆ **29/120-84-00** for the **police,** ✆ **29/174-11-15** for the **Red Cross,** and ✆ **29/170-56-00** for a **hospital** emergency.

Hospital The island's largest hospital is the **Hospital Distrital do Funchal,** Cruz de Carvalho (✆ **29/170-56-00**).

Laundry & Dry-Cleaning Try **Lavandaria Donini,** Rua das Pretas (✆ **29/122-44-06**), Funchal. Clothing can be laundered or dry-cleaned in 1 or 2 days. It's open Monday to Saturday 9am to 7pm.

Lost Property The Lost Property office is located at the airport in the police building, next to the passenger terminal (✆ **29/152-08-90**).

Police Dial ✆ **29/120-84-00** or **112** for an emergency.

Post Office Funchal's main **Zarco Post Office** is at Av. Zarco 9 (✆ **29/120-28-30**), near the tourist office. Other post offices include **Calouste Gulbenkian,** Avenida Calouste Gulbenkian (Mon–Fri 9am–6:30pm), near the Monument of the Infante Dom Henrique; **Monumental,** on Estrada Monumental, near the Lido swimming pool (Mon–Fri 8:30am–6:30pm); and **Mercado,** Rua do Arcipreste, near the Municipal Market (Mon–Fri 8:30am–6:30pm). Signs in the center of Funchal that read CORREIOS point the way to the nearest post office.

Safety In terms of crime statistics, Madeira is safer than mainland Portugal, especially Lisbon. However, as in any area that attracts tourists, a criminal element preys on visitors. Pickpockets and purse-snatchers are the major culprits. Protect your valuables as you would at any resort.

Taxes Madeira imposes no special taxes other than the value-added tax (VAT) on all goods and services purchased in Portugal. Refer to "Fast Facts" in chapter 16.

Tipping Similar to mainland Portugal, we give some change on a restaurant or taxi. If the restaurant has good service, people will give 5 to 10%.

WHERE TO STAY IN FUNCHAL

Madeira's hotels range from some of the finest deluxe accommodations in Europe to attractively priced, old-fashioned quintas (manor houses) for budget travelers. Chances are you won't be staying in the center of Funchal, but on the outskirts, where many of the best hotels with pools and resort amenities are. However, these make travelers dependent upon transportation into town, and only the first-class hotels lying outside of Funchal offer vans that take guests into town at frequent intervals. Staying in the center of town has its downside as well; because heavy traffic fills the center of Funchal most of the day, hotels there tend to be noisy. Nevertheless, for shopping and the widest selection of restaurants, Funchal is your best bet.

Expensive

Belmond Reid's Palace ★★★ The iconic place to stay in Funchal is Reid's, founded in 1891 by William Reid. Its position is "smashing," as the British say, along the coastal road at the edge of Funchal, on 4 hectares (10 acres) of terraced gardens that descend the hillside to the rocky ocean shores. The prime location was also handy when, in those times, guests arrived by ship. The English, who frequent the hotel in large numbers (Sir Winston Churchill stayed here), spend their days strolling the walks lined with hydrangeas, geraniums, gardenias, banana trees, ferns, and white yuccas. The lush gardens give access to swimming in the tepid ocean, while the large swimming pool is perfect for relaxation.

The expansive guest rooms are conservative in the finest sense, with well-chosen furnishings (antiques or reproductions), sitting areas, desks, and plenty of storage space. Their style is as British as the hotel founder. Even the unmissable afternoon tea on the terrace, graced with delicious scones, finger sandwiches, cakes, and a piano player, seems more a scene for an Agatha Christie novel than a Madeira balcony. The bathrooms have marble and beautiful tile walls and floors, plus tub/shower combinations and luxurious toiletries. All bedrooms have a balcony and all face the Atlantic—the ocean view can be total or partial. The dining room and the lounges are superbly decorated. The latest renovation kept the turn-of-the-century glamour and the service is old school, impeccable, and friendly. The gourmet restaurant, William (see "Where to Dine in Funchal," later in this chapter), is on the sixth floor, in the garden wing, and has a Michelin star.

Estrada Monumental, 139. www.reidspalace.com. ✆ **800/223-6800** in the U.S., or 29/171-71-71. 163 units. 315€ classic double; 585€ superior double; 875€ junior suite; 1,130€ superior suite; 2,360€ executive suite. Rates include buffet breakfast. Bus: 4, 6, 48, or 61. Free parking. **Amenities:** 4 restaurants; 2 bars; airport transfers (57€); babysitting; children's programs; concierge; health club & spa; 3 outdoor pools; room service; 2 outdoor tennis courts (lit); watersports equipment/rentals; pets allowed at extra cost. Free Wi-Fi.

The Cliff Bay ★★★ One of the island's top lodgings, rivaled and surpassed only by Reid's (see above), this nine-story hotel is dramatically located

Funchal

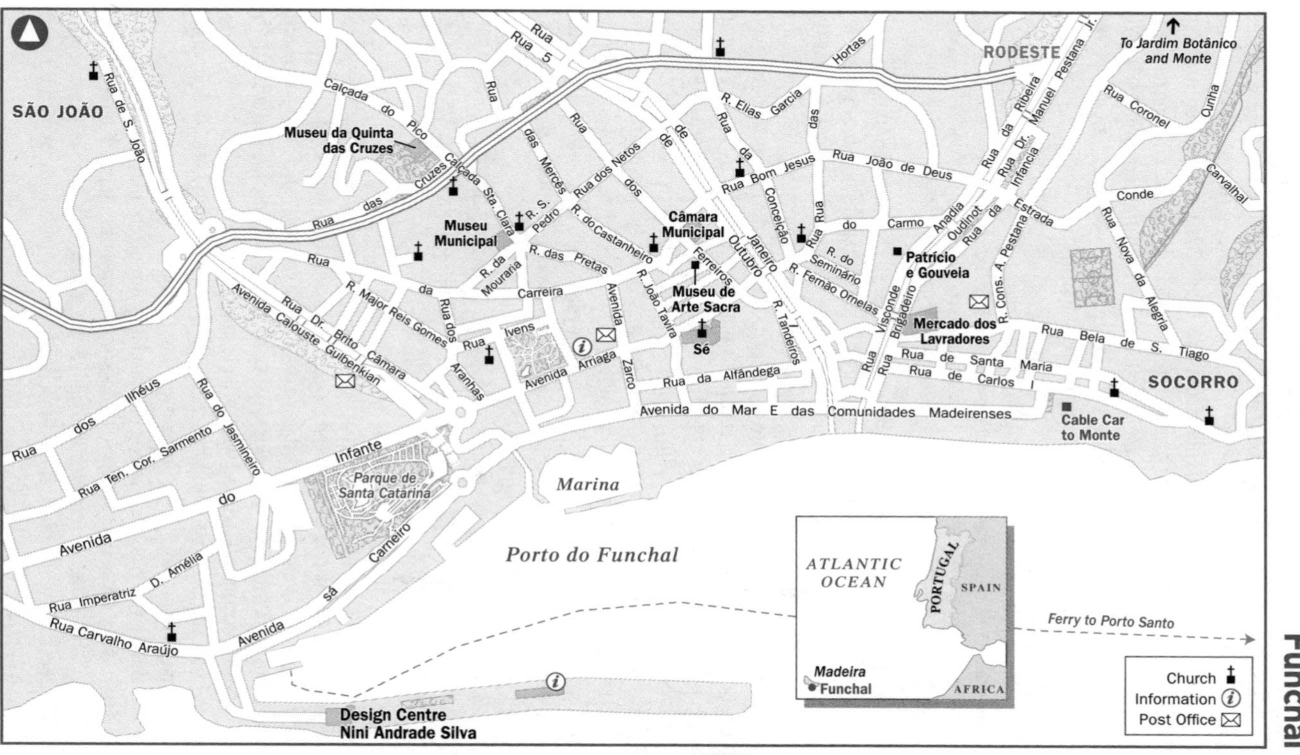

To Jardim Botânico and Monte
SÃO JOÃO
RODESTE
SOCORRO
Museu da Quinta das Cruzes
Museu Municipal
Câmara Municipal
Museu de Arte Sacra
Sé
Patrício e Gouveia
Mercado dos Lavradores
Cable Car to Monte
Parque de Santa Catarina
Marina
Porto do Funchal
Design Centre Nini Andrade Silva
Ferry to Porto Santo
Avenida do Mar E das Comunidades Madeirenses
Rua Nova da Alegria
Rua Bela de S. Tiago
Rua de Santa Maria
Rua de Carlos I
Rua João de Deus
Rua Bom Jesus
Rua dos Netos
Rua das Mercês
Rua de S. João
Calçada do Pico
Calçada Sta. Clara
R. Elias Garcia
R. do Castanheiro
R. das Pretas
R. João Tavira
R. Tanoeiros
R. Fernão Ornelas
R. do Seminário
Rua da Alfândega
Avenida Arriaga
Avenida Zarco
R. Major Reis Gomes
Rua Dr. Brito Câmara
Avenida Calouste Gulbenkian
Rua dos Aranhas
Rua do Jasmineiro
Rua dos Ilhéus
Rua Ten. Cor. Sarmento
Avenida do Infante
Avenida Sá Carneiro
Rua Imperatriz D. Amélia
Rua Carvalho Araújo
Rua Coronel Cunha
ATLANTIC OCEAN
PORTUGAL
SPAIN
AFRICA
Madeira
Funchal
Church
Information
Post Office

on a craggy bluff towering over wave-lashed rocks, 1.5km (1 mile) west of Funchal's center (a setting that is the site of a former banana plantation.) All but a dozen or so of the handsome rooms have ocean or harbor views. Units are generally spacious, with sitting areas and roomy marble bathrooms with deluxe toiletries. The restaurants, from the Rose Garden to Il Gallo d'Oro (Michelin starred) to the Blue Lagoon (featuring Portuguese and international cuisine), are among the finest on the island. Babysitting and children's programs make this place appealing to families with young children, but the bend-over-backward service is sure to appeal to all.

Estrada Monumental 147, Madeira. www.cliffbay.com. ✆ **29/170-77-00.** 201 units. 180€–395€ double; 400€–482€ junior suite; from 525€ suite. Bus: 1 or 2. Free parking. **Amenities:** 3 restaurants; 4 bars; airport transfers (29€); babysitting; children's programs; concierge; exercise room; 2 pools (1 indoor, 1 outdoor); room service; spa; outdoor tennis court (lit); watersports equipment/rentals. Free Wi-Fi.

Estalagem Quinta da Casa Branca ★★★ This grand country manor, surrounded by its own manicured grounds, is the personification of estate living on the island, the quinta. You'll be close to the city center but vastly removed from the hectic activity of Funchal. An old mansion dominates the grounds, but the guest rooms are entirely modernized and up to date, well integrated in the landscape and complete with spacious bathrooms. You can expect the services and comfort of a first-rate hotel here. The dining room and bar area in a restored outbuilding and a swimming pool in the middle of the garden are the perfect excuses to spend some more hours in the hotel. The restaurant is quite good, and on a balmy night the food tastes even better on the terrace. The quinta used to be a banana plantation and vineyard, and the ancestor of the current owners was John Leacock, founder of one of the important Madeira wine companies.

Rua da Casa Branca, 7. www.quintacasabranca.pt. ✆ **29/170-07-70.** 29 units. 180€–290€ double; from 320€ suite. Rates include buffet breakfast. Bus: 6. Free parking. **Amenities:** Restaurant; 2 bars; babysitting; health club & spa; outdoor heated pool; room service. Free Wi-Fi.

Meliá Madeira Mar ★★ The Meliá opens onto the small pebble beach of Corgulho and is one of the most elegant resorts in Funchal, though not quite up there in the ranks of the Cliff Bay or Reid's (see above). Guest rooms are capacious and modern, with plenty of configuration choices, including twin or superior accommodations, with private furnished verandas, some offering a sea view. Suites come with kitchenettes and roomy living areas. Room amenities range from safes to beverage-making facilities.

You have two restaurant options: Mare Nostrum offers themed hot and cold buffets, often with live shows; Il Massimo serves Italian and international cuisine. The Ilheu Deck Bar (designed by Madeira's top designer, Nini Andrade Silva) is the place to go for a drink and a snack with a splendid view of the Atlantic.

The spa is one of the finest on island, complete with sauna and Jacuzzi, along with various therapy treatments. The diverse buffet breakfast can be eaten on the terrace facing the ocean.

Rua de Leichlingen 2. www.meliahotels.com. ✆ **29/172-41-40.** 220 units. 110€–230€; from 205€ suite. Free parking. **Amenities:** 2 restaurants; 3 bars; babysitting; concierge; exercise room; 2 pools (indoor and outdoor); room service; spa. Free Wi-Fi.

Pestana Casino Park Hotel & Casino ★ Part of Madeira's Casino and Conference Centre, this deluxe citadel is a 7-minute walk from the town center, nestled in a subtropical garden overlooking the harbor. Designed by Oscar Niemeyer—one of the architects of Brasília, Brazil—the gray-concrete main building is low (only five stories) and undulating. The complex consists of the hotel as well as a conference center and a casino.

The small to midsize guest rooms—tastefully decorated in bright, sunny colors—have balconies with panoramic views over the harbor and town. Most rooms have only twin beds, but all boast first-class furnishings. Bathrooms have dual basins and bidets. ***A small warning:*** Walls can be thin, meaning sound can carry between guest rooms, particularly those with connecting doors. Bring earplugs if you're sensitive to noise.

Two comfortable lounge areas grace each floor. The luxurious dining room overlooks the port and town of Funchal, and the international Grill Room has an extensive wine cellar.

Rua Imperatriz Dona Amélia, Madeira. www.pestana.com. ✆ **29/120-91-00.** 379 units. 90€–163€ double; 189€–326€ suite. Rates include buffet breakfast. Bus: 1, 2, 10, 12, or 16. Free parking. **Amenities:** 3 restaurants; 3 bars; babysitting; exercise room; room service; spa; 2 outdoor tennis courts (lit). Free Wi-Fi.

Quinta da Bela Vista ★★ The core of this hotel in the hills above Funchal dates to 1844, when it was built as a private villa. Its owner has added two outlying annexes in the Portuguese colonial style. A verdant garden surrounds the annexes, which hold comfortable guest rooms that are slightly larger than the older accommodations in the main villa. Furnishings include high-quality mahogany reproductions and a scattering of English and Portuguese antiques—in fact, the family that owns this quinta has the most complete collection of old furniture on Madeira. Some of the higher rooms have one of the best views of Funchal, perfect to watch the famous New Year's fireworks. A well-staffed formal restaurant, Bella Vista, is in the original villa. The more relaxed Avista Navios offers sweeping views and regional and international cuisine.

Caminho do Avista Navios 4. www.belavistamadeira.com. ✆ **29/170-64-00.** 90 units. 170€–340€ double; from 480€ junior suite. Rates include buffet breakfast. Bus: 3 or 8. Free parking. **Amenities:** 2 restaurants; 3 bars; babysitting; concierge; exercise room; outdoor freshwater heated pool; room service; outdoor tennis court (lit). Free Wi-Fi.

Suite Hotel Eden Mar ★ This well-run hotel rises six floors from its swimming complex (the Lido). Though often booked by tour groups from England, it is still suitable for the individual traveler, especially families that like its rooms with kitchenettes. The midsize to spacious guest rooms open onto views of the sea. Decorated in neutral tones but with sunny pops of color (a burnt orange throw blanket here, an ochre pillow there), the hotel has of-the-moment furnishings and excellent tiled bathrooms. The restaurant serves international and Portuguese cuisine; there's a supermarket right next to the hotel for those who want to whip something up themselves.

Rua do Gorgulho 2. www.portobay.com. ✆ **29/170-97-00.** 146 units. 105€–149€ double; 135€–159€ junior suite. **Amenities:** Restaurant; 6 bars; airport transfers (29€); babysitting; children's center; exercise room; 3 pools (1 heated indoor); room service; spa; outdoor tennis court (lit). Free Wi-Fi in lobby.

Moderate

Enotel Quinta do Sol ★★ Among the best in its category on Madeira, the Enotel Quinta do Sol boasts an attractive setting and comfy guest rooms with marble bathrooms. Rooms are not big but are sun-flooded, with large windows and contemporary furniture; some have balconies with views of the sea. (***Tip:*** Units without balconies are both larger and less expensive.) The hotel has a bar-restaurant, Magnolia, which offers Portuguese and international food and is close to the beautiful park Quinta Magnólia, worth a visit for its collection of plants.

Rua Dr. Pita 6. www.enotelquintadosol.com. ✆ **29/170-70-10.** 156 units. 55€–85€ double; 70€–159€ triple. Rates include buffet breakfast. Bus: 2, 8, or 12. Free parking. **Amenities:** Restaurant; 2 bars; airport transfers (32€); babysitting; exercise room; Jacuzzi; 2 pools (outdoor, 1 for kids); room service. Free Wi-Fi.

Hotel do Carmo ★★ This hotel provides spiffy accommodations in the center of Funchal and so is ideal for travelers who want to be within walking distance of the city's attractions. It's laid out in a honeycomb fashion, and most guest rooms open onto balconies overlooking the busy street scene below. (***Tip:*** Rates for rooms with and without balconies are the same cost, so ask for a balcony room when you book.) Room design is quirky, with massive black-and-white photos of celebrities on the walls (such as the Beatles or Laurel and Hardy), and contemporary but (often) well-used furnishings. Guests gather at the rooftop pool, which affords a good view of the harbor. Meals are served in a spacious dining room or can be taken on a terrace on the second floor. The menu specializes in Portuguese and international cuisine, making use of the rich produce of Madeira.

Travessa do Rego, 10. www.hoteldocarmomadeira.com. ✆ **29/120-12-40.** 80 units. 60€–99€ double; 90€–130€ triple. Rates include buffet breakfast. Bus: 1, 2, 4, 6, 8, 9, or 10. Parking in a public park nearby costs 6€ per day. **Amenities:** Restaurant; bar; babysitting; outdoor pool; sauna. Free Wi-Fi.

Hotel Girassol ★★ Hotel Girassol was given a top-to-bottom refurbishment in the autumn of 2016, which has given the old girl a new swing in her step. The bar was redone, as were the two swimming pools and all the guest rooms, which are now quite spiffy. The bones of the place were always excellent: spacious double rooms that were, in reality, suites with a bedroom, sitting room, and veranda or terrace—ideal for families. The setting, too, has always been quite nice: on the outskirts of Funchal, overlooking the Tourist Club (a small complex with a restaurant, pool, and platform for swimming in the sea), where guests can access the sea for a small charge. The dining room still serves regional cuisine, has sea views, and, at dinner, live music. Return guests should be happily surprised.

Estrada Monumental 256, Madeira. www.hotelgirassolmadeira.com. ✆ **29/170-15-70.** 136 units. 65€ double; 90€–135€ suite. Rates include buffet breakfast. Bus: 1, 3, or 6. **Amenities:** Restaurant; 3 bars; babysitting; exercise room; 2 outdoor pools; room service. Free Wi-Fi.

Quinta da Penha de França ★★ This gracious old quinta house is now a guesthouse, with an annex containing 33 sea-view rooms, a balcony, and a terrace. Rooms in the older section have high ceilings, thick walls, casement windows, and a scattering of old-timey furniture, including some family heirlooms. Rooms in the annex are more contemporary, with traditional country-house designs. Like a family home, the quinta is chock-full of antiques, paintings, and silver. Near the Royal Savoy, it stands in a garden on a ledge almost hanging over the harbor. It's a short walk from Funchal's bazaars and is opposite an ancient chapel. Unlike most hotels on Madeira, many of this hotel's rooms have connecting doors, which can be opened and rented as two rooms for families with one to three children. Surrounded by lovely gardens, the property has an ocean-facing swimming pool.

Rua da Penha de França 2 and Rua Imperatriz da Amélia. www.penhafranca.com. ✆ **29/120-46-50.** 109 units. 65€–116€ double; 85€–157€ triple. Rates include buffet breakfast. Bus: 2, 12, or 16. Free parking. **Amenities:** 2 restaurants; 2 bars; airport transfers (32€); babysitting; outdoor seawater heated pool. Free Wi-Fi in lobby.

Inexpensive

Dorisol Estrelícia ★ This hotel lies on the upper floors of a high-rise building, constructed up a hill from the main hotel drag. The location is a bit inconvenient and the furnishings are dated, but that keeps this lodging squarely in the realm of the affordable. All of the rooms have a view of the sea—a nice perk. The hotel minibus runs to the center of Funchal several times a day.

Caminho Velho da Ajuda and Rua Casa Branca. www.dorisol.com. ✆ **29/170-66-00.** 148 units. 45€–120€ double. Rates include buffet breakfast. Bus: 1, 2, 4, or 6. Free parking. **Amenities:** Restaurant; 3 bars; airport transfers (32€); babysitting; children's center; health club with sauna and Jacuzzi; 2 pools (1 indoor); outdoor tennis court (lit). Free Wi-Fi.

Hotel Madeira ★★ This five-story hotel sits in the very center of Funchal, behind the tranquil park of S. Francisco. The rooftop pool has an extraordinary panoramic view of the town, mountains, and sea, and there's a solarium area with a bar and snack services. The small to midsize guest rooms can't compete with the views, but they're kept spotless and are quite comfortable. They're also quiet as they surround a plant-filled atrium; sheltered sun windows attached to each unit (they're one of the hotel's nicest features). Some rooms have balconies—the ones in the front overlook buildings and have no view, but those in the rear have views of the mountains above Funchal. Finally, we must acknowledge the staff, who are wonderful human beings.

Rua Ivens 21. www.hotelmadeira.com. ✆ **29/123-00-71.** 53 units. 66€ double; 74€ junior suite. Rates include buffet breakfast. Bus: 2, 12, or 16. **Amenities:** Bar; outdoor pool. Free Wi-Fi.

Hotel Windsor ★ The main reason to stay at the Windsor can be summed up in one word: location. The two buildings (connected by an aerial passage) that make up the hotel are in the heart of old Funchal, just a few cobblestone steps from restaurants, shops, and attractions (the free parking garage is another excellent perk). As for the rooms, they aren't memorable, but are comfortable enough in the cooler months (we'll come to that in a sec), with wall-to-wall carpeting and wooden furniture. But woe betide those who chose this place when a heat wave hits: There is no a/c in the rooms, and street noise means a sleepless night if you keep your windows open (in fact, some might say it's noisy even with the windows closed). The other downside: iffy Wi-Fi in the rooms. The hotel has a cafe/bar and a more formal restaurant.

Rua das Hortas 4C. www.hotelwindsorgroup.pt. ✆ **29/123-30-81.** 67 units. 50€-65€ double. Rates include buffet breakfast. No credit cards. Bus: 1, 12, or 16. Free parking. **Amenities:** Restaurant; 2 bars; outdoor pool. Free Wi-Fi.

On the Outskirts of Funchal

EXPENSIVE

Casa Velha do Palheiro ★★★ This unique inn was constructed in 1804 as a hunting lodge for the first Count of Carvalhal and then was restored in 1996 to become Madeira's first government-rated five-star country-house hotel, a type of accommodation more common in England. The hotel, a member of the Relais & Châteaux chain, adjoins the par-71 championship Palheiro golf course, about a 15-minute drive from Funchal. It is the only hotel on Madeira on a golf course. Rooms vary in shape and size, but all are richly furnished in an old-fashioned but restful way, with first-class furnishings and neatly kept bathrooms. The gorgeous garden can be visited separately and is itself a major attraction. The inn owns a yacht and organizes fishing trips, as well as dolphin watching.

Rua da Estalagem 23, São Gonçalo. www.casa-velha.com. ✆ **29/179-03-50.** 37 units. 190€–328€ double; 363€–419€ suite. Rates include buffet breakfast. Bus: 33. Free parking. **Amenities:** Restaurant; bar; babysitting; exercise room; golf course nearby; outdoor heated pool; room service; sauna. Free Wi-Fi.

Quinta Jardins do Lago ★★ Set in luxuriant botanical gardens, this elegant hotel lies in the S. Pedro district of Funchal, one of the hills enveloping the city. A little over 5km (⅓ mile) from the center, its landscaped grounds open onto panoramic vistas of both the Atlantic and the mountains in the distance. The gardens alone are reason enough to stay here, containing 495 different species of plants on 2.5 hectares (6¼ acres) of landscaped beauty, including rare trees from Africa, China, Japan, and even a jacaranda from Argentina.

At the time of Britain's wars with France under Napoleon, General Beresford commanded his country's forces on Madeira and selected this 1700s mansion as his private residence. Much of what he enjoyed remains to delight visitors today—a library, antiques, a billiard room, and a breakfast area with a rare ceramic wall panel hand-painted and glazed in the 1500s. The guest rooms, annexed to the 1750 manor house, are generously sized and beautifully furnished, offering traditional comfort but modern amenities as well. The Beresford restaurant offers formal service and refined continental and Portuguese cuisine. Among the mango trees is a large semicovered heated pool with a bistro, Jacuzzi, sauna, and steam bath.

Rua Dr. João Lemos Gomes 29. www.jardinsdolago.com. ✆ **29/175-01-00.** 40 units. 91€–169€ per person double; 135€–328€ per person suite. Bus: 15. Free parking. **Amenities:** 2 restaurants; bar; exercise room; Jacuzzi; outdoor freshwater heated pool; room service; sauna; outdoor tennis court; shuttle service to the city. Free Wi-Fi.

MODERATE

Quinta Bela São Tiago ★★ Here's another traditional Madeiran manor house from 1834 that has been successfully converted into a hotel of considerable charm. Until the early–20th century, this manor house was the private residence of Madeira's vice-governor. Surrounded by extensive gardens, the manor has expanded over the years from its original core. But the modern extension is in keeping with the original architectural plan. Rooms open onto the view of the mountains as a backdrop or the bay of Funchal in the distance. Guest rooms are suitably grand and carefully restored, with high ceilings and heavy draperies; many have balconies with panoramic views.

Rua Bela de São Tiago. www.quintabelasaotiago.com. ✆ **29/120-45-00.** 64 units. 90€–150€ double; 250€–350€ suite. Bus: 40. Free parking. **Amenities:** Restaurant; bar; airport transfers (32€); exercise room; Jacuzzi; 2 outdoor pools (1 for kids); room service; sauna. Free Wi-Fi.

Quinta Perestrello Heritage House ★★ Standing in well-manicured gardens, this is a good value restored manor house with much of its traditional architecture, including high ceilings, remaining intact. To its original core, modern extensions have been added. The roomy guest rooms are tastefully furnished, with wooden floors and tapestries, many of them opening onto superb views. All rooms have a terrace or balcony. Guests can take a dip in the heated swimming pool or simply soak up the sun on the terrace. An on-site restaurant serves excellent island meals for hotel guests.

Rua Dr. Pita 3, www.quintaperestrellomadeira.com. ✆ **29/170-67-00.** 36 units. 72€–135€ double; 126€–189€ triple. Free parking. **Amenities:** Restaurant; bar; airport transfers (32€); health club & spa; outdoor pool; room service. Free Wi-Fi.

Quintinha de São João ★ Dating from 1900, this quinta (manor house) is one of the best preserved in the Funchal area, surrounded by age-old trees and graced with classic architecture. Once an elegant private residence, it has been successfully converted into a family inn. Most of the standard guest rooms contain twin beds; some suites are available. All rooms are handsomely outfitted, often with traditional embroidery and Madeiran handiwork covering the beds. Old-style furnishings and antiques appear throughout. The restaurant, A Morgadinha, offers regional and international dishes, and features unusual Goan specialties. The terrace bar, Vasco da Gama, overlooks the Bay of Funchal and is one of the most scenic places in town for a drink.

Rua da Levada de São João and Estalagem Quintinha São João 4. www.quintinhasaojoao.com. ✆ **29/174-09-20.** 43 units. 95€–150€ double; 145€–180€ junior suite; 179€–210€ suite. Rates include buffet breakfast. Bus: 11. Free parking. **Amenities:** Restaurant; bar; babysitting; exercise room; 2 heated pools (1 indoor); room service; outdoor tennis court (lit). Free Wi-Fi in lobby.

INEXPENSIVE

Quinta da Fonte ★★★ This is a favorite B&B on the island, a converted 1850 manor house lying midway between Monte and Funchal. Set in the midst of landscaped gardens with tropical fruit trees, the hotel has a museum-like atmosphere, every corner beautified with art and artifacts—grandfather clocks, oil paintings, spool-columned four-poster beds, and more. Staying here is like living in an old family home owned by Madeiran aristocrats of long ago. (Prettiest of all is the Dona María bedroom; see if it is available when you book.) Breakfast is offered on a family-style table built in 1854 of preciously rare Madeira *pau santo,* or holy wood. A shared veranda and reading room are on the second floor, and a living and dining room are downstairs. Another smaller veranda is ideal for sunset watching. For what it offers, this quinta is startlingly well priced.

Estrada dos Marmeleiros 89. www.madeira-island.com/hotels/quintas/quintadafonte. ✆ **29/123-53-97.** 4 units. 50€–70€ double. Rates include continental breakfast. No credit cards. Bus: 20, 21, 21C, 22, 23, or 26. Free parking. **Amenities:** Chapel. Free Wi-Fi.

WHERE TO DINE IN FUNCHAL

Many visitors to Madeira dine at their hotels, but there's no reason you can't sneak away for a regional meal at one of the Funchal restaurants listed below. This list begins with the pick of the hotel restaurants.

Expensive

Casa Velha ★★ MEDITERRANEAN The setting for this first-class dining choice is lovely, and so is the carefully prepared food. On a cold day off-season you can enjoy the big log fire and drinks in the wood-paneled bar. In fair weather, diners take to tables in the courtyard, catching the night's breeze.

The dishes change with the season to take advantage of the best produce of any given month. Seafood and fish are always a feature, and the chefs work wonders with sea bass, fresh tuna, and a superb grilled scabbard fish. A vegetarian risotto is superbly prepared if you don't want fish or meat. For a starter, try the freshly caught swordfish, a tantalizing opening. If you have room, the desserts are top-notch, especially the crêpes suzette prepared at your table. Wine prices are reasonable, and many in-the-know diners sip offerings from Madeira, especially the island's white wine, which pairs nicely with the fish dishes. The excellent service is a plus.

Rua Imperatriz D. Amélia 69. www.casavelharestaurant.com. ✆ **29/120-56-00.** Reservations required. Main courses 18€–32€. Daily noon–2:30pm and 7–10pm.

Il Gallo d'Or ★★★ MEDITERRANEAN/PORTUGUESE Not surprisingly, the island's finest restaurant (2 Michelin stars) is found at the Cliff Bay hotel (p. 418). For the award-winning French chef Benoît Sinthon, the island's fresh produce plays a key role in his oeuvre, but he also draws on regions throughout Iberia for high-quality ingredients. These he tailors into sophisticated food sculptures that are as pretty to look at as they are delightful to eat. The menu changes with the seasons, but you might start with lobster cunningly wrapped around green asparagus with orange vinaigrette artfully swirled along the bottom of the plate—the prettiest "salad" you'll ever see. Other recent winners we tried include scarlet shrimp and tender suckling pig; each paired a delicate presentation with the boldest of flavors. For dessert, we're partial to the jellied pyramid of passion fruit and the gooseberries with avocado foam. If it's a balmy evening, ask to be seated outside on the terrace (a sexier space than the classic if somewhat boring-looking dining room). ***Note:*** Il Gallo d'Or hosts a weekly dinner dance.

In the Cliff Bay, Estrada Monumental 147. ✆ **29/170-77-00.** Reservations required. Main courses 35€–54€; fixed-price tasting menus 105€–130€. Daily 7–10pm.

William ★★★ PORTUGUESE/INTERNATIONAL Try to dine at least once at William, a fine hotel dining room in Reid's Palace (p. 418). Live piano music accompanies your meal, and winter guests often dress for dinner, the men in black tie. It's a swellegant scene if there ever was one.

As for the fare, chef Luís Pestana offers a variety of French specialties alongside typical but extremely well-executed Portuguese dishes. These include the chef's own smoked fish and a chunky seafood soup. Favorite entrees include langoustine with almonds, tuna tataki, and the excellent red mullet with tapenade. For dessert, the geometry of chocolates is irresistible. The restaurant won its first Michelin star in 2017.

In Reid's Palace, Estrada Monumental 139. www.reidspalace.com. ✆ **29/171-71-71.** Reservations required. Jacket and tie required for men. Main courses 32€–44€. Tues–Sat 7:30–10pm.

Moderate

Casa Madeirense ★ INTERNATIONAL/PORTUGUESE Owner Filipe Gouveia extends a hearty welcome to this wonderfully evocative restaurant with its *azulejos* (tiles) and hand-painted murals. His lively bar evokes a thatched-roof house in the village of Santana. Fresh fish and shellfish dominate the menu, with dishes like *cataplana de marisco* (shellfish stew steamed in a traditional copper pot) and tuna steak grilled to perfection. But the other type of steak is smashing here, too, especially the tender, expertly seasoned peppercorn steak.

Estrada Monumental 153. www.casamadeirense-funchal.com. ✆ **29/176-67-00.** Reservations recommended. Main courses 15€–30€. Daily noon–3:30pm and 6–10:30pm. Closed Aug.

Nini Andrade Silva Design Centre ★★ FUSION Chef and cookbook author Júlio Pereira knows how to make the most of the island's local ingredients, from passion fruit, and bananas to fresh fish and shellfish plucked from Madeira waters. But that doesn't mean the food is wholly traditional; our favorites include the red snapper braised in soy with samphire rice and the tempura-style black scabbard fish. For dessert, most find they can't pass up the brulée of passion fruit with apple and basil ice cream.

The restaurant is set on the top floor of this ancient fortress in the harbor, called Molhe or Fortaleza Nossa Senhora da Conceição, with spectacular views of Funchal. The old fort, once home to navigator and colonizer of Madeira João Gonçalves Zarco, is now dedicated to the local designer Nini Andrade Silva, internationally awarded for her work in interior design. Make sure to see her permanent exhibition. There's also a cafeteria and a bar.

Estrada da Pontinha, Forte de Nossa Senhora da Conceição. www.niniandradesilva.com. ✆ **29/164-15-51.** Reservations recommended. Main courses 21€–25€. Daily noon–3:30pm and 6–11:30pm.

Inexpensive

Dos Combatentes ★★ TRADITIONAL PORTUGUESE At the top of the Municipal Gardens, this simple restaurant serves well-prepared local specialties like rabbit stew, roast chicken, stewed squid, and scabbard fish with bananas. Most dinners begin with a bowl of the soup of the day. Portions are ample, and two vegetables and a green salad come with the main dish. Desserts are usually not as appealing as the mains (we recommend getting fresh fruit). The service is efficient and the waiters are very welcoming.

Rua Ivens 1. ✆ **29/122-13-88.** Main courses 8€–18€. Mon–Sat 11:45am–3pm and 6:00–10:30pm.

O Celeiro ★ TRADITIONAL PORTUGUESE O Celeiro attracts visitors and businesspeople with its reasonable prices and big helpings of the type of fare the people of Madeira eat (albeit for special occasions). Freshly caught scabbard fish is cooked with bananas, a longtime island favorite. Tuna steak is marinated in wine and garlic sauce and served with fresh mushrooms. Our pick on the menu is *cataplana de marisco*, a copper pot of seafood stew that tastes different every time we sample it. With the traditional *espetada* (skewered beef on a spit), you'll want crusty bread for soaking up the juices.

Rua das Aranhas 22. www.restauranteoceleiro.com. ✆ **29/123-06-22.** Reservations recommended. Main courses 12€–28€. Mon–Sat noon–3pm and 6–11pm. Bus: 2, 12, or 16.

Taberna Madeira ★★★ TRADITIONAL PORTUGUESE A new restaurant in the old town of Funchal, Taberna Madeira serves up local *petiscos* (small plates and snacks) with top ingredients at affordable prices. The cod or the scabbard fish filet is scrumptious, as is the duck breast with orange sauce. But if you don't want a full meal, you'll have many *tasca* (tapas) choices, like tuna stew with onions, squid, or mackerel with vinaigrette. There are also daily specials. ***Tip:*** This is an excellent pick for vegetarians as they can make a delightful meal from the side dishes, including the traditional fried corn (*milho frito*), the local sweet potatoes, and the garlicy and buttery flat bread (*bolo do caco*). The atmosphere is relaxed and the place is always chockablock with locals.

Travessa João Caetano, 16. www.tabernamadeira.com. ✆ **29/122-17-89.** Main courses 6€–16€. Mon–Sat noon–11:30pm; until 2 am Fri–Sat.

On the Outskirts of Funchal

A Seta ★ TRADITIONAL PORTUGUESE "The arrow" is a mountainside tavern known for its inexpensive yet tasty meals. Its rustic decor incorporates burned-wood trim, walls covered with pinecones, and crude pine tables.

All meals start with a plate of homemade coarse brown bread still warm from the oven. Above each table is a hook with long skewers (*espetadas*) of charbroiled meat, usually beef or chicken, seasoned with olive oil, herbs, garlic, and bay leaves. You slip off chunks while mopping up juices with the crusty bread. Other specialties served on platters (not skewers) include grilled steaks and several kinds of fish, including cod. Fried potatoes are executed perfectly here (ask for some hot sauce). The restaurant is almost midway between Funchal and Monte, 4km (2½ miles) from either, along winding roads.

Estrada do Livramento 80, Monte. ✆ **29/174-36-43.** Reservations recommended. Main courses 14€–24€. Thurs–Tues noon–3pm and 6–11pm. Bus: 19 or 23.

EXPLORING MADEIRA

Seeing the Sights in Funchal

Funchal's stately, beautiful **Praça do Município (Municipal Square)** is a study in light and dark; its plaza is paved with hundreds of black-and-white half-moons made from lava. (Masonry is a well-rehearsed Madeiran art form, and in Funchal, many of the sidewalks are paved with cobblestones that are arranged into repetitive patterns defined by contrasting colors.) The whitewashed buildings surrounding it have black-stone trim and ochre-tile roofs. On the south side of the square is a former archbishopric, now devoted to a museum of religious art (see Museu de Arte Sacra, below). Rising to the east is the **Câmara Municipal** (city hall), once the 18th-century palace of a rich Portuguese nobleman. It's noted for its distinctive palace tower rising over the surrounding rooftops.

Jardim Botânico ★★ GARDEN On the road to Camacha, about 4km (2½ miles) from Funchal, this botanical garden is one of the best in Portugal. Opened by the government in 1960 on the grounds of the old Quinta do Bom

Sucesso plantation, the grounds host virtually every tree or plant growing on Madeira. A heather tree, discovered near Curral das Freiras, is said to be 10 million years old. In addition, subtropical plants were imported from around the world, including anthuriums and birds of paradise from Africa and South America. The gardens open onto panoramic views of Funchal and its port. ***Note:*** The garden was partially affected by fire in August 2016, but it's being replanted in those areas and has re-opened to the public.

Caminho do Meio. ✆ **29/121-12-00.** Admission 4€ adults, 2€ children under 14. Daily 9am–6pm. Bus: 29, 30, or 31.

Museu da Quinta das Cruzes ★★ MUSEUM Set in the former residence of João Gonçalves Zarco, who discovered Madeira in 1419, the museum houses many fine examples of English furniture and China-trade porcelains brought to Madeira by expatriate Englishmen in the 18th century. You'll see rare Indo-Portuguese cabinets and the unique chests native to Madeira, fashioned from *caixas de açúcar* (sugar boxes, dating from the 17th century). A highlight: the superb collection of antique Portuguese silver. The surrounding park is of botanical interest and contains a noteworthy collection of orchids.

Calçada do Pico 1. www.museuquintadascruzes.com. ✆ **29/174-06-70.** Admission 3€, free entrance on Sun and for those under 18. Tues–Sun 10am–12:30pm and 2–5:30pm. Bus: 1, 2, 4, or 6.

Museu de Arte Sacra ★ MUSEUM The Museum of Sacred Art occupies an old bishop's house in the center of town. Many of its exhibitions came from island churches, some of which are no longer standing. Its most intriguing collections are a series of paintings from the Portuguese and Flemish schools of the 15th and 16th centuries. The paintings are on wood (often oak); an outstanding example is the 1518 *Adoration of the Magi.* A rich merchant commissioned it and paid for it with sugar. A triptych depicts St. Philip and St. James, and there's an exceptional painting called *Descent from the Cross.* Ivory sculpture, gold and silver plate, and gilded wood ornamentations round out the collection.

Rua do Bispo 21. www.museuartesacrafunchal.org. ✆ **29/122-89-00.** Admission 3€, seniors 1.5€. Tues–Sat 10am–12:30pm and 2:30–6pm, Sun 10am–1pm. Bus: 1, 2, 4, or 6.

Museu Municipal do Funchal ★ MUSEUM The Municipal Museum displays land and aquatic animal life of the archipelago. Specimens include moray eels, eagle rays, scorpion fish, sea cucumbers, sea zephyrs, sharp-nosed puffers, and loggerhead turtles. Also on display are many of the beautifully plumed birds seen around Madeira, although the most interesting exhibit (to us) is the collection of ferocious-looking stuffed killer sharks, evocative of the film *Jaws.* This museum is a favorite with families, although the curator says that very small children are sometimes afraid of the exhibitions. The museum, a minor attraction, need not take up much more than 30 minutes of your time, not counting the time it takes to get here. The buses listed below will take you to a stop where you get off and follow the signs to the museum grounds. It's a pleasant 10-minute walk to the entrance.

Rua da Mouraria 31. ✆ **29/122-97-61.** Admission 3€ adults, free for children under 12. Tues–Fri 10am–6pm, Sat–Sun noon–6pm. Bus: 1, 2, 4, or 6.

Quinta Palmeira Gardens ★★★ GARDENS Only a 5-minute ride from the center of Funchal, these carefully restored gardens are one of the botanical highlights of Madeira. The gardens were once owned by the well-known sugar industrialist Harry Hinton, and most were designed at the beginning of the 20th century. They have undergone an extensive restoration and are more gorgeous than ever, featuring a large collection of exotic plants, some unique to Madeira. The gardens are filled with curiosities, including a stone window in the Manueline style salvaged from the house where Columbus once lived on the island.

Rua da Levada de Santa Luzia, Funchal. ✆ **29/122-10-91.** Tues–Wed 10am–4pm. Closed in winter months. Bus: 26.

Sé (Cathedral) ★★ RELIGIOUS SITE The island's rustic 15th-century Sé is an unusual collection of architectural elements with a Moorish carved cedar ceiling, stone floors, Gothic arches, stained-glass windows, and baroque altars. The cathedral is at the junction of four busy streets in the historic heart of town. Note that open hours are subject to change depending on church activities. Once the center of the church outside mainland Portugal, Funchal's diocese was, during the 15th and 16th centuries, the biggest in the world, leading all the parishes from Funchal to Goa.

Rua do Aljube, Funchal. www.sefunchal.com. ✆ **29/122-81-55.** Free admission; donation suggested. Mon–Sat 7am–1pm and 4–7pm, Sun 8am–8:30pm. Bus: 1, 2, 4, or 6.

Exploring the Rest of the Island

Funchal is an excellent launching pad for exploring the island's mountainous interior and lush coastlines. During your exploration of Madeira, you're likely to see many banana, date, and fruit trees. Please remember that local farmers rely on these trees to make a living, and the fruity bounty should not be "harvested" for a picnic while touring the island.

THE OUTSKIRTS OF FUNCHAL

Immediately east of Funchal, the **Quinta do Palheiro Ferreiro** ★★ (www.palheirogardens.com; Mon–Fri 9am–4:30pm; admission 10.50€, 4€ for those 14–17) is a beautiful spot for a stroll. The mansion is the private property of the Blandy wine family, former owners of Reid's Palace. The 12-hectare (30-acre) estate has some 3,000 plant species, including camellia blooms that burst into full flower from Christmas until early spring and are reason enough to visit. You'll also see many rare flowers (several from Africa) and exotic trees.

You must get permission to picnic on the grounds: Ask at the gate upon your arrival. Bus no. 36 from Funchal runs here. By car, drive 5km (3 miles) northeast of Funchal, following N101 toward the airport. Fork left onto N102 and follow signposts toward Camacha until you see the turnoff to the quinta.

The grandest *miradouro* (or belvedere) on Madeira is **Eira do Serrado ★★★**, at 1,175m (3,855 ft.). This belvedere looks out over the Grande Curral, which is the deep crater (nicknamed "the belly button" of the island) of a long-extinct volcano in the center of Madeira. Down in this awesome crater, you'll see farms built on terraces inside the crater itself. The panorama takes in all the craggy mountain summits of Madeira if the day is clear. The location is 16km (10 miles) northwest of Funchal. To reach the lookout point, head west out of Funchal on Rua Dr. João Brito Câmara, which leads to a little road signposted to Pico Dos Barcelos. Follow the sign to Eira do Serrado until you reach the parking lot for the belvedere.

After taking in the view at the belvedere, head north along N107, which is signposted, to the stunningly situated village of **Curral das Freiras ★**, 6.5km (4 miles) north of Eira do Serrado. Meaning "Corral of the Nuns," the village used to be the center of the **Convento de Santa Clara,** where the sisters retreated for safety whenever Moorish pirates attacked Funchal. On the way to the village, the road goes through two tunnels cut through the mountains. Curral das Freiras sits in almost the exact geographic center of the island, lying in a valley of former volcanoes (all now extinct). The volcanoes surrounding Curral das Freiras were said to have been responsible for pushing up the landmass that is now Madeira from the sea. At the heart of this village of whitewashed houses is a small main square with a church of only passing interest. Most visitors stroll around the village, take in views of the enveloping mountains, have a cup of coffee at one of the cafes, and then head back to Funchal. Allow about 2 hours to make the 36km (22-mile) circuit of Eira do Serrado and Curral das Freiras.

WESTERN MADEIRA

If time is limited, head for the western part of Madeira, where you'll find panoramic views along the coastlines, dramatic waterfalls, and cliffs towering over the ocean. Leave Funchal on the coastal road, N101, heading west for 19km (12 miles) to the village of Câmara de Lobos, beloved by Sir Winston Churchill.

Câmara de Lobos ★

You approach Câmara de Lobos, meaning "Room of the Wolves," after passing terraces planted with bananas. The little fishing village of whitewashed red-tile-roofed cottages surrounds a cliff-sheltered harbor and rocky beach. If you come here around 7 or 8am, the fishermen will be unloading their boats after a night at sea. There's not a lot to do here beyond walking along the harbor to take in the view or perhaps following Churchill's example and becoming a Sunday painter. You can, however, stop for lunch nearby at **Santo António** (**© 29/191-03-60**), some 5km (3 miles) from Câmara de Lobos in the tiny village of **Estreito de Câmara de Lobos** (popularly known as Estreito). Near the little village church, owner Manuel Silvestro offers mostly grills, including golden chicken, cooked over an open hearth. A specialty is *espetada,* Madeira's most famous dish—delicately flavored skewered beef on a laurel spit. Don't expect elegance—you dine at simple paper-covered tables and mop up juices with crusty bread, the local *bolo do caco.* Santo António is open daily from noon to midnight; main courses cost 9€ to 18€.

Cabo Girão ★★★

These are the cliffs you might have seen from Câmara de Lobos; they lie 16km (10 miles) west of the village. To get to Cabo Girão, take R214 up a hill studded with pine and eucalyptus. From the 570m (1,870-ft.) belvedere, the panorama down the almost-sheer drop to the pounding ocean is thrilling. The terraced farms you'll see clinging to the cliff edges (called *fajãs*) are cultivated entirely by hand because the plots are too small for either animal or machine.

Ribeira Brava ★

Continuing on the coast road west, you'll come to Ribeira Brava, which lies 15km (9⅓ miles) west of Cabo Girão and 48km (30 miles) west of Funchal. Meaning "Wide River," Ribeira Brava is a lovely little Madeiran village (founded in 1440) and the sunniest spot on the island. It even has what locals refer to as a "beach," although you might view it as a strip of pebbles along the water.

We like to visit the village for its bustling seafront fruit market, which is active every morning except Sunday. Even if you don't buy anything, it's delightful to stroll through, seeing (and smelling) the amazing bounty grown in the mountains of Madeira. It also provides a great photo opp. As you wander through the village, you'll encounter locals selling island handicrafts. Be sure to visit the little 16th-century church in the center of the village. It has absolutely no artistic treasures, but somehow manages to feel tremendously spiritual nonetheless. There is one more sight, the ruins of the 17th-century **Forte de São Bento.** This towered fort once protected the fishing village against pirates from the African coast to the east.

Calheta ★★★

From Ribeira Brava, driving past Ponta do Sol, you'll find pretty Madalena do Mar and then Calheta, in the sunniest part of the island. The contemporary museum **Casa das Mudas Arts Centre ★★**, Vale dos Amores, Estrela à Baixo (✆ **29/182-09-00**) is here, with a stunning new building designed by local architect Paulo David. Besides the bold architecture, there's much to admire in the collection, which includes Portuguese art from 1960s to the present, with remarkable works from Lourdes de Castro, an artist born on Madeira. Other artists on display include Helena Vieira da Silva, Pedro Cabrita Reis, Pedro Calapez, and Ana Hatherly. There's a cafeteria if you wish to enjoy the view with a cup of coffee.

Bunk down for the night if you'd like a different perspective of the island. The quiet **Quinta das Vinhas ★★**, Lombo do Serrões, Estreito da Calheta (www.qdvmadeira.com; ✆ **29/182-40-86**), a small country house surrounded by vineyards, is a relaxing spot with guest rooms in a 17th-century house along with more modern small villas to rent. Quinta das Vinhas offers wine tastings as well as culinary and *poncha* (cocktail) workshops.

If you prefer a more conventional hotel, the **Savoy Saccharum ★★★**, Rua Serra d'Água, 1, Arco da Calheta (www.savoyresorts.com; ✆ **29/182-08-00**) is your place. Opened in 2015 on the site of a former sugarcane refinery, it boasts interior design by Nini Andrade Silva, the renowned Madeira designer. She took inspiration from the site's former use, so scattered here and there are tools from the former factory, as well as black-and-white photos of the island companies that produced sugar and distilled rum. Besides its wonderful location on the waterfront, the Saccharum has a well-equipped spa, two restaurants, and four pools (three outdoor and one indoor). The hotel has a garden where vegetables are fruits are grown organically. You can see also sugarcane in its natural environment.

Serra de Água ★★

Surrounded by abundant crops, jade-green fields, ferns, bamboo, weeping willows, and plenty of waterfalls, the village enjoys one of the loveliest settings on Madeira. Come here not for attractions, but for pure scenic beauty, though you should be warned that mist and clouds often shroud the town.

You reach Serra de Água, a little village 6.5km (4 miles) north of Ribeira Brava, by traversing a sheer canyon. From Ribeira Brava, head north along N104 to the center of the island. One of the best centers for exploring Madeira's lush interior, it has a worthy dining spot: the **Dorisol Pousada dos Vinháticos ★★**, Estrada de São Vicente Serra de Água (www.pousadadosvinhaticos.com; ✆ **29/195-23-44**). It sits near the top of a pass on the winding road to São Vicente. The solid stone inn, a tavern-style building with a brick terrace, opened in 1940. The tasty food is hearty and unpretentious. Specialties include *espetada* (a swordfish version), ox tongue with Madeira sauce, and local beef flavored with regional wines. Main courses cost 10€ to 22€; hours are daily from noon to 6pm and 7 to 9pm.

From Serra de Água, the route climbs to the 990m (3,248-ft.) **Boca da Encumeada ★**, or Encumeada Pass, 6.5km (4 miles) north of Serra de Água. It's one of the island's best centers for hiking (information about hiking is available from the tourist office in Funchal), and a belvedere affords great panoramas over both sides of Madeira.

Following the route northwest of Boca da Encumeada, you reach the village of São Vicente, 14km (8⅔ miles) northwest of Boca da Encumeada and 56km (35 miles) northwest of Funchal.

São Vicente ★★

One of the best-known towns on the north coast lies where the São Vicente River meets the ocean. Again, you come here for the sweeping views, some of the most dramatic on the island. Part of the fun of going to São Vicente is taking the one-lane north-coast route. It's a miraculous and costly feat of engineering, chiseled out of the cliff face. (The only nightmare: Encountering one of the bloated tour buses taking this highway. You'll often have to back up because the drivers rarely give way.) Constructed in 1950 and nicknamed the "gold road," the drive offers views of water cascading down the slopes. Many locals have planted vineyards in this seemingly inhospitable terrain.

In such a remote outpost, an inn comes as a welcome relief. You'll find good food and lodging at **Estalagem do Mar,** Juncos, Fajã da Areia (www.estalagemdomar.com; ✆ **29/18-4-00-10**). Most visitors pass through here only to dine on the excellent regional and international cuisine (scabbard fish prepared in almost any style, many versions of sea bass, and mouthwatering beef filet in mushroom cream sauce are among the top choices here). Main courses cost 10€ to 25€; it's open daily noon to 3pm and 7 to 10pm. Reservations are recommended.

If you decide to spend the night, the 91-room inn will do well by you. It has a provincial look, with flowery curtains and spreads, but rooms are modern, with tiled bathrooms, TVs, many outlets, and phones. On the premises are an indoor and outdoor pool, a tennis court, a Jacuzzi, a sauna, a gym, and a game room. Limited room service is available. The three-floor hotel was built in the early 1990s. A double costs 45€ and a suite costs 66€, including breakfast. Parking is free.

From São Vicente, you can continue west along N101 to the town of Porto Moniz, 16km (10 miles) away in one of the remotest parts of Madeira.

Porto Moniz ★★

This portion of the "gold road" is one of the most difficult but dramatic drives in Portugal, requiring nerves of steel. Though some of the parts have been closed due to erosion (and other issues), some are still open. The road is boldly cut into the side of a towering cliff that plunges vertically into the ocean below. Eventually you arrive at Porto Moniz, a fishing village of great charm built at the site of a sheltered anchorage shaped by a slender peninsula jutting out toward an islet, Ilhéu Mole. This is the only sheltered harbor on the north coast of Madeira. Porto Moniz has awe-inspiring lava pools, carved in the rocks and facing the wild Atlantic waves. It's great fun to swim in these ocean pools with the waves coming in but still protected by a wall. Entrance is 1.50€.

For the best food in the area, head to **Restaurante Orca**, Vila do Porto Moniz, Porto Moniz 9270 (✆ **29/185-00-00**). Stars on the menu are swordfish in mushroom and cream sauce, filet of beef served with dates, and fresh tuna steak breaded in corn flour and then sautéed and served with country cabbage and potatoes. Main courses cost 12€ to 33€. Food is served daily from noon to 4pm and 6:30 to 9pm. Major credit cards are accepted, and reservations are recommended.

After leaving Porto Moniz, you can continue southwest along N101, going back along a winding road via Ribeira Brava and Câmara de Lobos until you finally make the full circuit back into Funchal.

SANTANA & CENTRAL MADEIRA

For a final look at Madeira, you can cut through the center of the island, heading north from Funchal. This route takes you to such scenic highlights as Pico do Arieiro and Santana, and is one of the finest parts of Madeira for mountain hiking.

Pico do Arieiro ★★

This mountain and the settlement built on its side, 36km (22 miles) north of Funchal, really evoke the island's volcanic nature. When the 1,780m (5,840-ft.) peak is not covered by clouds (it's likely to be obscured Dec–Mar), the panoramic views are stunning. Pico do Arieiro is the third-tallest mountain on the island. To reach it, follow Rua 31 de Janeiro out of Funchal, and take N103 as it climbs to Monte. When you reach the pass at Poiso, some 10km (6¼ miles) north of Monte, take a left and continue to follow the signposts into Pico do Arieiro.

Once at the **miradouro** (belvedere) ★ at Pico do Arieiro, you'll have a sweeping view of the central mountains of Madeira. To the southeast is the village of Curral das Freiras (see above). To the immediate northeast you can take in a panorama of Penha d'Águia (Eagle's Rock), a rocky spike that is one of the most photographed sites on Madeira. You will also have a view of Pico Ruivo to the northwest (Madeira's highest point, at 1,860m/6,102 ft.), which can be accessed from Pico do Arieiro by a difficult 8km (5-mile) hill walk that takes approximately 4 hours.

Ribeiro Frio ★★

Instead of taking the left fork at Poiso and heading for Pico do Arieiro (see above), you can go straight to reach Ribeiro Frio, an enchanting spot 11km (6¾ miles) north of Poiso.

Ribeiro Frio (Cold River) is a little village in the **Madeira Forest Park** (a protected area of trees and mountains in the center of Madeira that is spared from development) that occupies a dramatic setting in view of waterfalls, jagged peaks, and sleepy valleys.

The area is the site of one of the most dramatic walks on Madeira. Just follow the signposts from Ribeiro Frio to the **Balcões** ★★. The walk passes along Levada do Furado and then on footpaths cut out of basalt rock to a belvedere, whose dizzying perch overlooks the jagged peaks of the Pico do Arieiro, Pico das Torres, and Pico Ruivo. This 40-minute walk is of only moderate difficulty and is suitable for the average visitor with no special hiking skills. It allows visitors to appreciate the amazing laurel forest, a UNESCO World Heritage Site since 1999. This forest is thought to be millions of years old and was destroyed on the continent. It only survives on Madeira (with the biggest area), the Azores, the Canary Islands, and Cape Verde.

If the mountain air gives you an appetite, head south from Balcões toward **Abrigo do Pastor** ★★, which will be past Ribeiro Frio, between Poiso and Camacha Estrada das Carreiras 209 (http://abrigodopastor.com; ✆ **29/192-20-60**). It serves hearty mountain food and is one of the most traditional restaurants on the island (you'll likely be the only nonlocal there). It's set in a former shepherd's shelter.

Follow N103 out of Ribeiro Frio, heading north toward the coast. In the village of Faial, you'll find a connecting route, signposted west, to the village of Santana.

Santana ★★★

Eighteen kilometers (11 miles) northwest of Ribeiro Frio and 40km (25 miles) north of Funchal, Santana is the most famous village on Madeira and certainly the prettiest. It is noted for its A-framed, thatched-roof cottages called *palheiros.* Painted in bright, often flamboyant colors, they are the most-photographed private residences on the island. On a coastal plateau, Santana lies at an altitude of 742m (2,434 ft.).

Outside Santana is the **Madeira Theme Park** ★, at Estrada Regional 101, Fonte da Pedra (www.parquetematicodamadeira.pt; ✆ **29/157-04-10**), set on 2.8 hectares (7 acres). This immense park and garden explores island history, culture, and tradition through various exhibits, including typical Santana houses. It is also riddled with amusements, everything from a lake to a watermill to a kiddie playground. The park is open daily 10am to 7pm (closed Mon in winter) and charges 10€ for adults and 8€ for seniors and children ages 5 to 14; children ages 4 and under are admitted for free.

For food and lodging, head to the most-frequented establishments on the north coast, **Quinta do Furão** ★★, Achada do Gramacho (www.quintadofurao.com; ✆ **29/157-01-00**). The 43-unit inn lies in a vineyard on a cliff-top setting that opens onto a panorama of the ocean. Most visitors stay just for the day to sample the cuisine, which is the finest on the north coast. The rustic dining room serves Madeiran, Portuguese, and international cuisine. Dishes include swordfish cooked with bananas, grilled T-bone steak in garlic butter, and filet of beef baked in a pastry case and served with Roquefort sauce. You *must* try the local goat cheese. Main courses cost 10€ to 25€. Hours are daily from noon to 3:30pm and 7 to 9:30pm. Reservations are recommended.

The inn is also a delightful place to stay, with ample guest rooms, handsomely furnished in the regional style, with excellent mattresses. Some accommodations open onto sea views, and others face the mountains. The inn has a swimming pool, gym, Jacuzzi, and pub. Doubles with half-board cost 140€; a suite costs 190€, including breakfast. Parking is free.

SPORTS & OUTDOOR ACTIVITIES ON MADEIRA

DEEP-SEA FISHING A popular sport on Madeira, the catch is mainly longtail tuna, blue marlin, swordfish, and several varieties of shark. Most boat rentals are moderately priced. The tourist office (see "Essentials," earlier in this chapter) can supply information about boat rentals and rates; or try such boat marketplace websites as GetMyBoat.com or Sailo.com.

GOLF The island maintains two 18-hole courses, both open to the public and accustomed to foreigners. The easier and better established is the **Clube de Golf do Santo da Serra** in the hamlet of Santo da Serra (www.santodaserragolf.com; ✆ **29/155-01-00**), on the island's northeastern side, about 24km (15 miles) from Funchal. Greens fees are 110€ for 18 holes. On rocky, steep terrain that some golfers find annoying is the **Palheiro Golf Course** in the hamlet of **São Gonçalo** (www.palheirogolf.com; ✆ **29/179-01-20**), about 5km (3 miles) north of Funchal. It charges 110€ for 18 holes. Both establishments rent clubs and carts and provide local caddies; both also feature a clubhouse with a bar and restaurant, abundantly accented with mimosas, pines, and eucalyptus trees.

SWIMMING Madeira doesn't have beaches. If your hotel doesn't have swimming facilities, you can use those at the **Complexo Balnear do Lido (Lido Swimming Pool Complex),** Rua do Gorgulho (✆ **29/110-51-63**), which has an outdoor Olympic-size pool as well as a spacious outdoor pool for children, both with ocean water. There's also an access if you wish to dive in the Atlantic. It's open daily in summer from 8:30am to 8pm, and off-season from 8:30am to 7pm. Adults pay 5€. Children under 11 swim free with parents; otherwise, they pay 3€ to use the pool. You can rent lounge chairs or umbrellas for 2€ each. The complex has a cafe, a restaurant, an ice-cream parlor, bars, and facilities for exercising in the water. To get there from Funchal, take N101 west for 5 minutes until you see the turnoff for Rua do Gorgulho, at which point you head south along this road to the Lido complex. The Lido is signposted from N101—you shouldn't have any trouble finding it. By public transit, take bus no. 6.

TOBOGGAN RIDES By far the most entertaining rides on the island are on the two- or three-passenger toboggans, which resemble big wicker baskets resting on wooden runners. You get into one of the cushioned passenger seats for a ride down the slippery-smooth cobblestones, which takes about 20 minutes to reach Funchal from Monte. Runners are greased with suet to make them go smoother. Trained sled drivers run alongside the sled. If the sled starts to go too fast, they can hop on the back of it and slow it down. Originally, these sleds were used to transport produce from Monte to Funchal, but over the years tourists began to request rides in them, and an island attraction was born. When you pass Terreiro da Luta, a point along the way of your ride (at a height of 875m/2,871 ft.), you'll enjoy a panoramic view of Funchal and see monuments to Zarco and Our Lady of Peace.

Before you begin your descent, visit the **Church of Nossa Senhora do Monte,** which contains the iron tomb of the last of the Habsburgs, Emperor Charles, who died of pneumonia on Madeira in 1922. From a belvedere nearby, you can look down on the whole of Funchal.

Toboggan rides from Monte to Funchal cost 25€ for one, 30€ for a couple, and 45€ for four people and end up at Estrada do Livramento, in Funchal. For more information, contact **Carreiros dos Montes** (http://carreirosdomonte.com/pt/home.php; ✆ **29/178-39-19**).

WATERSPORTS The activities desks of several major hotels, including **Reid's Palace** (p. 418), can arrange water-skiing, windsurfing, and rental of boats or sailing dinghies for guests and nonguests. If you want to go snorkeling or scuba diving, check with the **Madeira Carlton Hotel,** Largo António Nobre (www.pestanacarltonmadeira.com; © **29/123-95-00**).

SHOPPING ON MADEIRA

Crafts are rather expensive on the island, but collectors will want to seek out exquisite Madeira embroidery or needlework. Check to see that merchandise has a lead seal attached to it, certifying that it was made on Madeira and not imported. The businesses listed in this section are all in Funchal.

Craft Shops & Factories

At the factory **Patricio & Gouveia ★★★**, Rua do Visconde de Anadia 33 (© **29/122-29-28**), you can see employees making stencil patterns on embroidery and checking the quality of materials, though the actual embroidery is done in private homes (this process is not likely to be of great interest to anyone not seriously interested in embroidery). That being said, of the several embroidery factories of Funchal, this is not only the most famous, but also the best place to *buy* embroidery. Many of the routine souvenir shops scattered throughout the island sell embroidery from Taiwan and other places, but the embroidery at Patricio & Gouveia is the real thing—every item is guaranteed to be handmade on the island. **Bordal-Bordados da Madeira ★**, Rua Doctor Fernão Ornelas 77 (© **29/122-29-65**), also carries an outstanding selection of island-made embroidery.

Casa do Turista ★★ Though it looks hokey on first glance, this shop, on the waterfront in Funchal, is the best place on the island for Madeira handicrafts. On the patio, with a fountain and semitropical greenery, is a miniature village, with small-scale typical rooms furnished in the local style. The merchandise includes handmade embroideries in linen or cotton (the fabric is often imported from Switzerland and Ireland), tapestries, wickerwork, Portuguese pottery and ceramics, Madeiran wines, fruit, and flowers. You'll find all types of embroidery and appliqués, as well as "shadow work" (a technique in which stitching takes place on the reverse of a transparent fabric, with the design showing through to the front in a very subtle manner). Prices are determined by the number of stitches. Rua do Conselheiro José Silvestre Ribeiro 2. © **29/122-49-07.**

Casa Oliveira ★ The store is primarily a retail outlet for one of the largest embroidery manufacturers in town, and everything sold in the shop is handmade on the island. In fact, there's a workshop on-site that turns out everything from embroidered towels to delicate negligees to elegant "heirloom" tablecloths. The outlet is also known for its handmade and hand-painted ceramics. If you're seeking island souvenirs such as T-shirts, you'll find a large selection here, too. Rua da Alfândega 11. © **29//22-93-40.**

Madeira Wine

Every Madeira wine is fortified, brought up to full strength, with high-proof grape brandy. The distinctive flavor of Madeira comes from being kept for months in special rooms called *estufas*. These *estufas* have high temperatures instead of the cool chambers where most bottles of wine are stored. *Madeira* refers to a whole body of wines that ranges from very sweet to very dry. Even the cheapest Madeira is quite remarkable, and the French, among others, use the least expensive Madeira for cooking, which adds more flavor than sherry or Marsala. In the U.S., Madeira wine used to be very popular and it was with a glass of this wine that the Declaration of Independence was celebrated.

The light-colored **Sercial** has a very dry taste and is gently scented. This wine is often compared to a Fino sherry, although Sercial has its own special bouquet and character. **Bual** (sometimes known as Boal) is more golden in color and is a medium sweet wine, sometimes served as a dessert wine. It is velvety in content, its color ranging from a dark gold to a brown. Mainly a dessert wine, **Malmsey** is a sweet, chestnut-brown Madeira. The grapes that today produce Malmsey were the first ever shipped to the island.

Funchal is the center of Madeira's **wine industry.** Grapes have grown in the region since the early–15th century, when Henry the Navigator introduced vines and sugarcane to the island's slopes. If you're searching for a bottle in the city, we recommend the following two shops:

Blandy Wine Lodge ★★, Av. Arriaga 28 (www.blandyswinelodge.com/pt; ✆ **29/174-01-00**), a well-stocked wine shop next to the tourist office, offers samples from its diverse stock, which covers virtually every vintage produced on the island for the past 35 years. The shop is housed in a former convent dating from 1790. The building contains murals depicting the wine pressing and harvesting processes, which proceed according to the traditions established hundreds of years ago. You can savor a wide range of Madeira wines in a setting of old wine kegs and time-mellowed chairs and tables made from kegs. Admission is free; it's open Monday to Friday 9:30am to 6:30pm and Saturday from 10am to 1pm. **Guided tours** cost 5.90€. Tours last around 1 hour and take visitors into a museum of antique winemaking equipment and past displays of some of the oldest bottles of Madeira wine. The highlight of the tour, however, is when visitors are taken into a cellar bodega for an actual wine tasting. Visitors are escorted through the premises Monday to Friday at 10:30am 2:30pm, 3:30pm, and 4:30pm, and again on Saturday at 11am.

D'Oliveiras ★, Rua Ferreiros, 107 (✆: **29/174-01-00**) is one of the oldest wine companies on Madeira. It has an old cellar in central Funchal, founded in 1619, where wine tastings are organized.

Visiting a vineyard is highly recommended, and making that vineyard **Fajã dos Padres ★★★** (www.fajadospadres.com; ✆ **29/174-01-00**), is highly, *highly* recommended—it has a dream location near Cabo Girão. A cable car takes visitors up to the vines; a lovely restaurant on the oceanfront is waiting for you at the bottom. ***Tip:*** If you are afraid of heights, know that the new cable car is a much smoother ride than the old frightening one was. Or you can skip it altogether and take a boat ride instead from Funchal and Câmara de Lobos to Fajã dos Padres.

Tasting Madeira wines in a wine bar, where you can try different brands, is another excellent and fun way to get acquainted with the islands specialty. We're partial to **Paixão do Vinho** (Wine Passion), Av. do Infante, 22 (www.paixaodovinho.com; ✆ **29/101-01-10**). With wines from small producers and his own wines, owner Filipe Santos (originally a doctor) leads the very interesting tastings with expertise and passion.

Markets & Bazaars

The Farmers Market, **Mercado dos Lavradores ★**, at Rua Hospital Velho is held Monday through Saturday from 7am to 8pm but is liveliest in the morning. Flower vendors dressed in typical Madeiran garb of corselets, leather boots, and striped skirts will generally let you photograph them if you ask them—especially if you buy some flowers. The market is filled with stalls selling island baskets, crafts, tropical fruits, exotic chilies, and vegetables, and offers Madeira's largest array of that day's fish catch.

In Funchal's **bazaars,** found throughout the center of town, you can purchase needlepoint tapestries, Madeiran wines, laces, molasses cakes, and biscuits, as well as local craft items such as goatskin boots, Camacha basketry, and other eclectic merchandise. The colorful handicraft market at the square in the old town, close to the cable-car entrance, is open Monday through Saturday and offers a wide array of handicrafts, including products in wicker and leather, as well homemade jams and molasses cakes.

At these bazaars, you can find good deals on handmade shoes and tooled leather. However, prices on other items (embroidery, needlework, table linens, and tropical flowers) can be high, so have an idea of what you want to pay for certain items and sharpen your bargaining skills before going. Madeira is an excellent place to buy tropical (though expensive) flowers such as orchids and birds of paradise, all of which can be shipped to the United States. U.S. Customs allows flowers from Madeira into the United States, as long as they are inspected at any American airport upon arrival.

MADEIRA AFTER DARK

The glittering **Entertainment Complex at the Pestana Casino Park Hotel & Casino ★★**, Avenida do Infante, Funchal (www.casinodamadeira.com; ✆ **29/114-04-24**), is the most obvious entertainment venue for first-time visitors. The complex offers an array of options. Foremost is a **casino,** the only one on Madeira, which offers roulette, French banque, craps, blackjack, and slot machines. To be admitted you must be 21 and present a passport or other form of identification. You cannot be wearing flip-flops, sneakers, Crocs, or other "sports gear." The casino is open daily from 4pm to 3am, until 4am Friday and Saturday.

Inside the casino, on Avenida do Infante, is a dance club, **Copacabana ★** (✆ **29/114-04-24**), that's at its liveliest after 11pm Thursday through Saturday; it charges a cover (including one drink) of 5€. Wednesday to Saturday at 9pm, the hotel offers a Las Vegas–style cabaret show. For the show only, there's a minimum bar tab of 25€ per person; dinner, two drinks, and a view of the show costs 45€. In addition, the complex contains bars, kiosks, and boutiques. You must be 18 or older to enter.

Options outside the casino complex are limited, although some hotels present dinner shows. Funchal isn't the best place in Portugal to hear fado, but you can sample the music at **Arsenios Restaurant,** Rua de Santa Maria 169 (✆ **29/122-40-07**), which serves dinners ranging in price from 15€ to 30€. It's open daily from 8 to 10pm.

Teatro Municipal Baltazar Dias, Avenida Arriaga (✆ **29/123-35-69**), in the center of Funchal, presents plays (in Portuguese only) and occasional classical music concerts. The tourist office has information, and you can purchase tickets at the box office.

The town's dance club action is fairly limited. **Vespas,** Av. Sá Carneiro 7 (https://www.facebook.com/VespasClub; ✆ **29/123-48-00**), a warehouse-like club near the docks, attracts a young crowd. It's open Thursday through Saturday from 10pm to either 2 or 3am, depending on business. If you're over 35, you might head for the spacious **The Pub,** Largo António Nobre (✆ **29/123-95-00**) in the Pestana Carlton Madeira. Veddy British, it features modern dance music and hits from the 1970s and 1980s. Hours are Thursday to Saturday 10:30pm to 2am. Neither club has a cover charge.

The terrace rooftop bar of **Hotel The Vine,** Rua dos Aranhas 27A (✆ **29/100-90-00**) is another great spot to enjoy a cocktail, namely the traditional drink of Madeira *poncha*—local rum with orange or lemon juice.

You also might try the restaurant/*taverna* **A Seta** (p. 429), where you can sample the local wine until 11pm.

PORTO SANTO ★

39km (24 miles) NE of Madeira

The second major island of the Madeira archipelago is Porto Santo, an arid landmass that presents a marked contrast to the lushness of the main island. It is 14km (8⅔ miles) long and 5km (3 miles) wide, with a 6.5km (4-mile) strip of fine sandy beach along the southern shore. The island is not as hilly as Madeira: Its highest elevation is about 509m (1,670 ft.) above sea level, at **Pico do Facho.**

João Gonçalves Zarco and Tristão Vaz Teixeira, who discovered Madeira, landed on Porto Santo in 1418 when they took refuge from a storm. To express gratitude for their survival, they named the island Porto Santo (Holy Port). It was not until 1419 that the men were able to sail on and make landfall on the main island. Prince Henry the Navigator gave Teixeira and Zarco authority to run Madeira, but he placed Porto Santo in the hands of Bartolomeu Perestrello.

The island gets very dry in the summer, which makes it popular with beach-goers, but not good for crops. The foodstuffs grown on Porto Santo in the winter include grain, tomatoes, figs, and melons, as well as grapes, from which sweet wines are made. A few remaining windmills crown the island's low hills.

The water of Porto Santo supposedly has therapeutic value. It's a popular drink not only on the island, but also on Madeira and in Portugal. The water-bottling plants, fish canneries, and a limekiln make up the island's industries.

Essentials

ARRIVING

BY PLANE The flight from Madeira to the little **Campo de Cima** airport (www.aeroportosdamadeira.pt; © **29/198-01-20**), Estrada Regional 101, at Porto Santo, takes only 15 minutes and offers spectacular views. Always reserve well in advance for July and August, when beach lovers descend en masse. In peak season, count on eight flights per day; frequency diminishes in the off-season. For ticket reservations and information, go to www.aeroporto portosanto.pt (see "Essentials," earlier in this chapter, for information on arriving from Lisbon or international destinations). The airport lies right outside of town, a 30-minute walk from the center. Taxis (© **29/198-23-34**) meet all arriving flights, and a fare into town typically costs 10€. There is no bus service from the airport to the center of town.

BY BOAT Regularly scheduled ferry service connects Madeira and Porto Santo. The Lobo Marinho departs Funchal Harbor daily. Tickets cost 47€ to 58€ round-trip, depending on the season.

Saturday to Thursday, the ferry usually departs Madeira at 8am and arrives in Porto Santo at 10:15am. The departure from Madeira on Friday isn't until 7pm. During the month of August, a ferry departs Madeira at 8am daily. Always check the schedules for return trips from Porto Santo, which vary. You can purchase tickets at the **Lobo Marinho** office, Rua da Praia, Funchal (www.portosantoline.pt; © **29/121-03-00**), Monday to Friday from 9am to 12:30pm and 2:30 to 6pm. On weekends, you can buy a ticket at any travel agency in Funchal.

The boats arrive at a little port about a 15-minute walk from the center of town. Taxis await arriving boats and will take you into the center or to one of the nearby hotels for 5€.

VISITOR INFORMATION

The **tourist office** is at Avenida Dr. Manuel Gregório Pestana Junior (www.visitmadeira.pt; © **29/198-52-44**). It's open Monday to Friday 9am to 5:30pm and Saturday 10am to 12:30pm.

Getting Around

Most visitors get around on foot or rely on a **taxi** (© **29/198-23-34**) for excursions. In town, you can usually pick up a taxi along Rua Doctor Nuno Teixeira. Car rentals can be arranged at **Moinho,** at Porto Santo Airport (© **29/198-31-60**).

Exploring the Island

Most visitors come here strictly for the wide beach of golden sand along the southern coast. It's ideal for swimming or for long strolls. If you tear yourself from the beach for a day, you will find some minor attractions. **Vila Baleira,** a sleepy town of whitewashed stucco houses, merits an hour of your time. You'll be following in the footsteps of Christopher Columbus as you make your way along its cobblestone streets.

Locals call the town Vila, and it lies at the center of the 6.5km (4-mile) long beach. Stop for a drink at Café Ballena on **Largo do Pelourinho ★**, the main square. Shaded by palm trees, it is the center of life on the island. To the right of the Church of Our Lady of Piedad, follow a sign along the alley to the **Casa de Cristovão Colombo,** Travessa da Sacristia 4 (www.museucolombo-portosanto.com; ✆ **29/198-34-05**). The explorer is said to have lived here with his wife, Isobel Moniz. Documentation about the Columbus visit to Porto Santo is skimpy, but it appears that he did live here for a short time. In an annex, you can view maps and engravings depicting major events in his life. The museum is open Monday to Friday from 10am to noon and 2 to 5:30pm, Saturday and Sunday from 10am to 1pm. Admission is 2€, 1€ for seniors and students.

Later you can follow Rua Infante Dom Henrique, off Largo do Pelourinho, to a beach-surrounded, flower-filled **park** with a statue dedicated to Columbus. This is one of the most restful and scenic spots on the island.

After seeing the town and its meager attractions, you can visit some of the island's scenic highlights. They include **Pico do Castelo,** north of Vila Baleira, on a small and difficult road. It affords a perspective on the whole island and endless views of the sea. Pick up picnic provisions at one of the little shops in Vila Baleira. A fortified castle once stood here to guard Vila Baleira from attacks by pirates. Only four cannons remain—islanders removed most of the castle's stone for building materials. The island government has planted pine trees to keep the air moist, but they never grow beyond 3m (9¾ ft.), so as not to obscure the view. From Pico do Castelo, you can follow signs to **Pico do Facho,** the tallest point on the island.

At the southwestern tip of the island, **Ponta da Calheta** is another scenic destination. To get there, take the road west out of Vila Baleira. It has a view of the little offshore island of Baixo, across a dangerous channel riddled with reefs. The beach is made of black basalt rocks, so it's not suitable for swimming.

Directly north lies another of the island's great lookout points, **Pico dos Flores.** Access is over a pothole-riddled dirt road. The cliffs here also have a panoramic view of the islet of Baixo to your left. The tiny islet to your right is Ferro.

While in the southwestern part of the island, you can also follow the signs to **A Pedreira ★** on the slopes of Pico de Ana Ferreira. The amazing basalt rock formation brings to mind organ pipes stretching toward the sky.

Where to Stay

MODERATE

Porto Santo Hotel & Spa ★ Right on the beach, a 15-minute walk from the center of town, this is one of the most popular hotels on the island. The two-story building is set in a peaceful garden. Its midsize rooms can be a bit old-fashioned looking, but they're kept spotlessly clean. Make reservations far in advance if you plan to visit in August. The restaurant serves regional and international cuisine; in the summer, the lavish Wednesday night buffet is the hottest ticket on the island. The hotel has two bars, one in the restaurant and the other on the beach.

Campo Baixo. www.hotelportosanto.com. ✆ **29/198-01-40.** 97 units. 118€–266€ double. Rates include buffet breakfast. **Amenities:** Restaurant; 2 bars; babysitting; exercise room; 3 pools (1 heated indoor); spa; 2 outdoor tennis courts (lit). Free Wi-Fi.

Torre Praia Hotel ★★ On the outskirts of Vila Baleira, but more importantly, just adjacent to its own beach, the Torre Praia is a good pick for sun worshippers. Spread over three stories, the rooms are pleasantly furnished, with excellent beds, tile floors, and state-of-the-art plumbing. Most have water views. The restaurant, constructed around an old watchtower, is one of the island's best. Head to the bar on top of the hotel for great views.

Rua Goulart Medeiros. www.hoteltorrepraiaportosanto.com. ✆ **29/198-04-50.** 66 units. 100€–235€ double; 130€–400€ suite. Rates include buffet breakfast. **Amenities:** 2 restaurants; 3 bars; babysitting; exercise room; Jacuzzi; outdoor pool; room service; sauna. Free Wi-Fi in lobby.

Vila Baleira Thalassa ★★ A favorite for families, this hotel lies 4km (2½ miles) from the center of Vila Baleira, opening onto a long, sandy beach with a playground and beach room. The largest on Porto Santo, the hotel is linked by an underground tunnel to an outdoor leisure area with pool and various drinking and eating facilities. There's beach equipment, a spa, a gym, and a diving center.

The hotel itself contains restaurants, bars, shops, public lounges, and an indoor pool connected to a kiddie pool. Many take the all-inclusive plan so that they don't have to worry about extra costs (good when you have wee ones in tow). The guest rooms, often furnished in wicker, are midsize and some of the best on the island (32 of the units are junior suites). Most of the airy bedrooms open onto private balconies overlooking the water.

The on-site Atlantic Restaurant in the main building serves only buffets, which are wide-ranging in scope and cuisine, with a variety of regional and international specialties.

Cabeço da Ponta-Apartado 243. www.vilabaleira.com. ✆ **29/198-08-00.** 256 units. 85€–187€ double; 120€–290€ suite **Amenities:** 2 restaurants; 2 bars; babysitting; bikes; children's center; concierge; exercise room; 2 seawater pools (1 heated indoor); room service; spa. Free Wi-Fi in lobby.

the azores: THE GREEN ISLANDS

One of the most offbeat travel experiences in Europe is a trip to these nine Portuguese islands. Conspiracy theorists believe the remote Azores are the only remnants of the lost continent of Atlantis. For hundreds of years these islands were considered the end of the earth, the outer limits of the European sphere of influence beyond which ships could not sail. Even today, they're a verdant but lonely archipelago in the middle of the ocean, seemingly more tuned to Boston more than Lisbon. The cluster of islands is the place where the winds off the Atlantic meet; and visiting urbanites can lose themselves in the often fog-bound volcanic islands occupied by 245,000 hearty people.

The autonomous archipelago spans a distance of more than 805km (500 miles) from the southeastern tip of Santa Maria to the northwestern extremity at Corvo. The main island of **São Miguel** lies about 1,223km (760 miles) west of Portugal (3,396km/2,110 miles east of New York), making the Azores the most isolated islands in the entire Atlantic.

Completely uninhabited when discovered, the Azores were named by Diogo de Silves (a captain of Henry the Navigator) after the hook-beaked açor (compared to both a hawk and an eagle), which sailed on the air currents over the coast. The date: 1427 (give or take a year or two). It wasn't long before settlements sprang up. Besides the Portuguese settlers, Flemish immigrants came to the central Azores, and today's place and family names show this influence.

Eventually it was learned that the entire island group was actually composed of three distinct archipelagos: the eastern section of **Santa Maria** and **São Miguel;** the central section with **Terceira** (the scene of bullfighting in the streets), **Graciosa,** cigar-shaped **São Jorge** (Raul Brandão's ethereal island of dust and dream), **Pico** (with a cloud-capped mountain and a very different, volcanic landscape that has vineyards), and **Faial** (vulnerable to earthquakes and known for the eerie crater of the extinct volcano, Caldeira, and a famous marina); and the western group made up of **Flores** (flowers), where the vegetation runs riot in a setting of lakes, waterfalls, and valleys, and **Corvo** (the smallest member—everybody knows everybody else—and a visit by a foreigner is an occasion).

The unknown writer who once made the much-publicized characterization the

INEXPENSIVE

Praia Dourada Hotel ★ This cheery hotel lies within the center of Vila Baleira. It opened in 1980 and has been renovated several times since. Its three floors contain standard, motel-like rooms. But that being said, rooms are light and airy, though they lack any particular luster. Many units have private balconies. The hotel, about a 5-minute walk from a beach, attracts many frugal Madeirans in the summer. Breakfast is the only meal served.

Rua D. Estêvão de Alencastre. www.booking.com/hotel/pt/praia-dourada. ✆ **29/198-04-50.** 100 units. 70€–125€ double. Rates include buffet breakfast. **Amenities:** Bar; outdoor pool. Free Wi-Fi.

"Gray Azores" must have been color-blind. Much of the color of the archipelago comes from the flowers that grow rampant in its volcanic soil: azaleas, camellias, heather, agapanthus, and rhododendrons. Although very occasionally lashed by violent storms, these enchanted isles enjoy a mild climate year-round: The temperature averages around 58°F (14°C) in winter and only 75°F (24°C) in the summer.

Even though one might expect these isolated islanders to be insular, the rugged people here, who contend with the elements of nature daily, are hospitable to strangers. Coming back from a walk in the São Miguel hills, we were stopped by a boy riding a mule. Under a straw hat with a hoe slung over his shoulder, the boy smiled as he bid us *boa tarde.* The world YALE was written across his sweatshirt. It seemed that his uncle had attended Yale. "Do you know him?" the boy asked. "He now lives in Boston."

Many on the island seem to have relatives living in the United States. Many settled in New Bedford, Massachusetts (of *Moby-Dick* fame), during the whaling heyday of that port, taking jobs as sailors, fishermen, whalers, and caulkers. Others settled in Newark. Many of the immigrants returned to the Azores, however, after earning their fortunes across the sea.

For a first introduction to the archipelago, stay in São Miguel and enjoy the quiet pace of the island. You can stay in the long-time favorite **Hotel do Colégio,** Rua Carvalho Araújo,39 (www.hoteldocolegio.com; ✆ **29/630-66-00;** doubles 60€–100€). A newer option is **Casa das Palmeiras,** Rua dos Açores, 26 (✆ **29/670-99-03;** doubles 70€–120€). Don't miss the fresh produce market, **Mercado da Graça,** which also sell fish, Azorean cheese (many varieties), and exotic fruits. Have dinner at **Calçada do Cais**, Rua dos Mercadores, 27 (✆ **29/628-10-52**) and visit **Gorreana** (http://gorreana.pt; ✆ **29/644-23-49**), the oldest and only tea plantation in Europe. Finally, visit the volcanic geysers in Furnas and the **Terra Nostra park** (www.parqueterranostra.com). Besides the thermal pool there's a stunning park with plants and trees from all the continents.

There's more information at the **Azores Tourist Board** (www.visitazores.com; ✆ **29/220-05-00**). A division of SATA Airlines, **Azores Express** (www.sata.pt) has direct flights from Boston to the Azores.

Where to Dine

Most guests dine at their hotels, which are also open to nonguests. Some little eateries around the island specialize in fresh fish.

Pita ★ STEAK Simple food done well—that's the secret to the success of Pita, which is the clear locals' favorite. That may have to do with the warm welcome the owner/host gives each and every guest. Or it could be the excellent steaks, which are lathered with a just-right house-made pepper sauce and come with proper french fries. Yes, you can go for the fish, and it's good, and comes in many preparations, but it is the beef that has guests raving. The hotel is very near the Pestana Hotel.

Rua D. Estêvão de Alencastre. ✆ **92/787-04-10.** Tues–Sun 6–11pm. Mains 13€–16€.

16 PLANNING YOUR TRIP

This chapter addresses the where, when, and how of visiting Portugal—all the logistics of putting your trip together and taking it on the road.

GETTING THERE

By Plane

Portugal has five international airports: three on the mainland, the others on Madeira and the Azores. The biggest is Lisbon, recently named **Aeroporto Humberto Delgado** (LIS; www.aeroportolisboa.pt/en/lis/home). **Porto's Francisco Sá Carneiro Airport** is the second largest, serving the north (OPO; www.aeroportoporto.pt/en/opo/home), followed by **Faro** (FAO; www.aeroportofaro.pt/en/fao/home), gateway to the Algarve's beaches.

João Paulo II Airport (PDL; www.aeroportopontadelgada.pt/en/pdl/home), serving **Ponta Delgada,** the capital of the mid-Atlantic Azores Islands, saw a 25% increase in traffic in 2015, thanks to an opening up to European low-cost carriers. It also receives direct flights from some North American airlines.

Madeira Airport (FNC, www.aeroportomadeira.pt/pt/fnc/home) lies just outside the capital city of Funchal and is famous for its sea-level runway.

Most flights from North America land in Lisbon. Portuguese carrier **TAP Portugal** (www.flytap.com ✆ **21/843-11-00**) operates regular direct flights from Boston, Miami, Newark, New-York, and Philadelphia. Flying time from New York to Lisbon is about 6½ hours. It also has flights from Montreal and Toronto, which last about 8 hours.

TAP is a members of the **Star Alliance** frequent flyer program, to which United Airlines and Air Canada also belong. TAP is also strong on African and Latin American routes, particularly to Brazil.

United flies to Lisbon direct from Newark, and **American Airlines** has direct flights from Philadelphia to the Portuguese capital. Portugal's **Azores Airlines** (www.azoresairlines.pt, ✆ **29/620-97-20**) also has flights from Boston to Lisbon and to Ponta Delgado.

Canada's **Air Transat** and **Azores Airlines** also operate flights to Portugal from Montreal and Toronto.

Portugal is very well connected with flights to the rest of Europe. Lisbon, for example, has around 15 daily flights to London. Faro has 10 weekly non-stop flights to Paris. Low-cost companies led by Ireland's **Ryanair** (www.ryanair.com) and Britain's **Easyjet** (www.easyjet.com) have many flights from cities around Europe to Portugal, making it easy and cheap to connect. Ryanair has flights from Lisbon to around 25 European destinations in 10 countries from as little as 15€.

Lisbon airport is conveniently close to the city center. There is a metro line heading into town and a convenient and relatively fast shuttle bus (www.aerobus.pt/en), which is not part of the regular bus network.

Porto airport also has good subway and bus links to the city center.

From Faro airport you can catch a city bus that connects the train and bus station, where you can catch lines running to resorts along the coast, if your hotel does not offer a pickup service.

If you are traveling in a group, taxis—which are relatively cheap compared to most other European countries—can be a convenient alternative without adding too much to the cost.

For details, see regional chapters.

By Car

There are **fast highways** linking Portugal to the rest of Europe. If you are making the 2,180km (1,355-mile) drive from London to Lisbon, after crossing into France, you take the A16 and A28 *autoroutes* toward Rouen, then onward south via Le Mans and Tours. There, you join the A10 that takes you to Bordeaux, then the A63 to the Spanish border at Hendaye. From there, take the A8 along the Basque coast, before turning south to Burgos on the AP-1. From Burgos, turn west on the A62 that takes you all the way to the Portuguese border via Valladolid and Salamanca. If you are heading to Porto and the north, turn off at Burgos onto the A231 toward León.

Beware that the French and northern Spanish highways can be very crowded at peak seasons, particularly in August, when vacationers heading south. Especially long lines can build up at the toll booths on the *autoroute*.

From London, the trip will cost you around 140€ in **highway tolls** and 120€ in fuel. If you have time, you can avoid the toll roads, but it will add at least another day to your trip. There are plenty of splendid places—from the pastures of Normandy to the mountains of the Basque Country—where you can break the trip.

If you are driving to the Algarve, turn south at Salamanca toward Cáceres and Seville.

There is also a direct highway linking Madrid to Lisbon in 5½ hours.

One way of reducing the drive is by taking a car ferry from England to the north coast of Spain. **Brittany Ferries** (www.brittany-ferries.co.uk; ✆ **44 330 159 7000**) operates six weekly crossings from Plymouth and Portsmouth on the English south coast to the Spanish ports of Santander and Bilbao. The crossing time is around 24 hrs. From Santander, it's a 6-hour drive to Porto; 8 hours to Lisbon.

By Train

International rail connections are limited. Portuguese governments have been talking for years about building a high-speed train line that would link into the European system in Madrid, but the plans have yet to get off the drawing board.

You can travel on France's high-speed train network to Irun/Hendaye on the France-Spain border and connect with the **Sud Expresso** sleeper train that runs nightly to Lisbon operated by the Portuguese rail company **CP** (www.cp.pt; ✆ **70/721-02-20**). The journey takes around 12 hours. There's a dining car and first-class private cabins for two with showers; cheaper berths are available in four-person cabins. One-way prices range from 69€ for a seat to 198€ for a "grand class" single cabin complete with private bathroom. Adult prices on the French **TGV** high-speed train from Paris to Hendaye start from 91€.

If you are coming from Madrid, the train can be a good option. The base single tariff for the 10-hour Madrid-Lisbon overnight **Lusitania Comboio Hotel** ranges from 60€ to 177€, depending on whether you get a regular seat or a luxury sleeping berth.

Cut-price ways of touring in Europe include **Eurail** (www.eurail.com) for non-European residents, and **Interrail** (www.interrail.eu) for European residents, which offers passes allowing for unlimited rail travel in a number of countries for a specific period of time. Eurail, for example, offers a family 10-day pass for two adults and two children for 998€. Interrail has an adult monthly pass for up to 30 countries for 532€. There are discounts for young people and seniors.

By Bus

If you're not in a hurry or you really don't like flying, the bus can be a cheap alternative for getting to Portugal. Europe's largest coach line is **Eurolines** (www.eurolines.com), which is a network of operators in 33 countries serving over 660 cities. Their Portuguese partner is **Internorte** (www.internorte.pt; ✆ **70/720-05-12**). Eurolines operates bus routes to Portugal from dozens of European cities, including London, Paris, and Madrid. There are three per week leaving from London to Lisbon. The journey takes about 35 hours with a change of coach at an interchange in Spain; one-way adult tickets cost around 120€. A 16-hour trip from Barcelona to Lisbon costs around 75€.

GETTING AROUND

By Car

Portugal has one of Europe's highest densities of motorways, most built in the last 30 years or so thanks to European Union investment funding. That means it's usually quick and easy to get between the main cities. Beyond them, drivers used to long, straight North American highways may find some of the narrower country roads and the intricate street patterns of city centers a challenge.

The fastest roads are ***autostradas***, toll highways mostly four- or six-lane, linking the main cities. They are designated by an A; for example, the A1 links Lisbon to Porto via Coimbra and Aveiro, the A2 runs from the capital to the Algarve, the A3 heads north from Porto to Braga and on to the Spanish border at Valença, and so on.

Other major roads are designated *itinerários principais* (IP) or *itinerários complementares* (IC), which may involve sections of highway and stretches of single track. They mostly don't carry tolls. *Estradas nacionais* (EN) tend to be older roads, less used and replaced by highways, although many drivers prefer to use them to avoid tolls. *Estradas regionais* (R) connect smaller towns.

Confusingly for the uninitiated, Portugal has two types of **toll systems** on its roads. In the classic type, used, for example, on the A1 Lisbon-Porto autostrada or the A2 Lisbon-Algarve road, there are **toll booths** where you pick up a ticket when you enter and pay when you leave, either by handing over cash to a cashier or paying by credit card at a machine. Toll gates will usually have one or two lanes marked by green signs bearing a white V standing for **Via Verde.** They are reserved for vehicles fitted with automatic electronic toll collection, a system pioneered by Portugal in the 1990s. If you are renting a car in Portugal, check whether your vehicle is fitted with Via Verde. If it is, you won't have to stop to pay at toll gates, but the toll will be added to your rental bill.

In 2011, Portugal introduced an exclusively **electronic toll system** on a number of highways, including the A22 running east-west along the Algarve coast and the A25 leading to Aveiro from the Spanish frontier. Here there are no toll gates, but electronic sensors are posted over the road. Once again, if you are renting a car, you should check that it is equipped with a Via Verde mechanism so you can travel on these roads; most are, and in that case the tolls will be added to your rental bill. If you are driving into Portugal on a highway from Spain, the best way to deal with the system is to stop off at one of the **"Welcome Points"** just past the border posts and register your license plate and credit card. Tolls you incur will be charged directly to your card. Alternatively, you can buy a **pre-paid toll card** online on www.tollcard.pt, which will be activated by a cellphone text message. The highway authority makes an attempt to explain the whole messy system at www.portugaltolls.com, and there is an information line at ✆ **70/750-05-01** from within Portugal or ✆ **+351 212 879 555** from outside.

Lisbon to Porto on the A1 costs around 21€ in tolls; Lisbon to Faro on the A2 and A22, 22€; and a trip along the Algarve coast from Lagos to Castro Marim on the Spanish border, 10€. Fuel prices in Portugal are among Europe's highest. In November 2016 a liter of unleaded gasoline averaged 1.5€. Diesel is cheaper at 1.2€ per liter.

The minimum age for driving a car in Portugal is 18. If you are a European Union citizen and are over 18, your license is valid for Portugal. U.S. and Canadian licenses are also valid for 180 days driving in Portugal. You may want, but are not obliged, to get an **International Driving Permit**, which contains a translation of your license in various languages. You can get it for $20 from the **AAA** (www.aaa.com) in the United States, or $25CDN from the **CAA** (www.caa.ca) in Canada.

DRIVING RULES Although there has been a marked improvement in road safety over recent years, that's due to better highways and stricter law enforcement, Portugal's roads remain dangerous compared with most places in Western Europe. The death rate is above the European Union average and more than double that of the safest countries like Sweden, the Netherlands, or Britain. Care is therefore needed when driving, particularly on narrower rural roads and on busy suburban highways. Speeding and tailgating on highways are particular problems.

The official **speed limits** are 120 kph (75 mph) on most highways, 90kph (54 mph) on two-lane roads, and 50kph (31 mph) in urban areas. Although they are frequently disregarded, if you are caught speeding fines can be high, from 60€ to 2,500€ depending on how fast you are going and where. As with other traffic violations, the police can fine you on the spot. If you don't have cash, they carry credit card–reading machines. You also have to carry your passport or ID cards, as well as ownership documents for the vehicle, and prove that it's insured, as well as your license.

Speed limit signs are round with black numbers on a white background in a red circle. The end of a speed zone is a round white sign with a black slash.

Drivers and passengers must wear **seat belts** in front and back seats. Children under 12 or shorter that 135cm (53 inches) must ride in the back and in special **child seats.** Exceptions are made for children under 3, who can sit in the front if they have a proper child's seat and the airbag has been deactivated.

It is also obligatory to carry a red **warning triangle** and a yellow or orange **reflective vest,** which must be warn if you have to get out of the vehicle on the highway. Drivers are not allowed to use mobile phones.

Portugal's **drunk driving** rules are strict, with a maximum of 0.05%, less than in England or most U.S. states; it means a single drink may push you over the legal limit.

PARKING Street parking is difficult in big city centers. You'll often need to pay by purchasing a ticket from coin-operated dispensing machines. There is normally a 2-hour maximum limit. Common in many cities are people, often homeless, who will guide you to a parking spot. Usually they are content with a few cents in return, but in some places—Aveiro has been a black spot—gangs have taken over, aggressively demanding several euros. They also have no scruples in guiding unsuspecting drivers to illegal places, where they face fines. **Car parks** are plentiful but may be more expensive. A city-run car park in central Lisbon will charge 1.45€ for an hour, with a daily maximum of 13.05€. Exit booths in car parks are usually automatic. You'll need to exchange the ticket you pick up at the barrier on your way in for an exit ticket after paying at a coin- or card-operated automated payment machin returning to your vehicle.

RENTALS Generally you'll get the best rates if you book your weeks in advance. Major international rental companies are present in Portugal, including Avis (www.avis.com; ✆ **80/020-10-02**), Budget (www.budget.com.pt; ✆ **21/754-78-54**), Sixt (www.sixt.pt; ✆ **25/578-81-99**), and Hertz (www.hertz.com; ✆ **21/942-63-85**). As well as booking directly, you can search for rental bargains through websites such as www.autoeurope.com, www.rentalcars.com, or www.kayak.com. If you are unfamiliar with stick drives, don't forget to request an automatic, although that may be considerably more expensive, especially if you are renting a compact or mid-range model. Drivers below 25 are likely to face a surcharge of around 10€ a day.

BREAKDOWNS Rental car companies will usually offer 24-hour breakdown service. Otherwise, if you belong to major automobile club such as AA, CAA, or AAA, you can get aid from the **Automóvel Club de Portugal** (www.acp.pt; ✆ **70/750-95-10**). Check also if your credit card or insurance company offers free breakdown assistance.

By Plane

Portugal is a small country, but there are regular internal flights between the three mainland airports and to the islands. TAP runs hourly shuttle flights between Lisbon and Oporto, sometimes for less than 10€ each way. Ryanair has fewer flights on the same route, but can be even cheaper. TAP also has three daily flights to Faro. Check regional chapters for more details.

By Train

Trains are operated by the **CP** rail company (www.cp.pt; ✆ **70/721-02-20**) company. There are regular, fast, and comfortable trains between Lisbon and Porto, particularly the **Alfa Pendular** service that links the two cities in 2½ hours, stopping in Coimbra and Aveiro.

Elsewhere, the mainline system is limited. Porto is a hub for trains heading farther north to Guimarães, Braga, and up to Vigo in Spain. The picturesque line connecting the wine towns along the Douro River is an excellent way to discover the region. There are occasionally special trains along the Douro that use historic cars and serve gourmet lunches.

The Beira line heading inland from Coimbra to Guarda and occasionally to Madrid is slow, but provides an alternative to driving.

To get to the Algarve, there's a train from Lisbon that takes just over 2½ hours to reach the junction from Tunes where the mainline connects with the line running along the south coast from Vila Real de Santo António, on the Spanish border, to the western town of Lagos.

There are also trains that chug through the countryside from Lisbon to the inland cities of Évora, Beja, Portalegre, Castelo Branco, and Covilhã.

Both Lisbon and Porto have extensive networks of urban electric trains running out to the suburbs. In Lisbon the lines to Cascais from the **Cais do Sodré** station and to Sintra from the **Rossio** station are the most useful for visitors.

Many of Portugal's railway stations are decorated with beautiful *azulejos* (tiles) that make them attractions in their own right. São Bento in Porto is the most spectacular, but many small rural stations, particularly those along the Douro, are worth stopping to look at, if you are not rushing.

See regional chapters for more details of services, times, and prices.

CP offers significant discounts for tickets purchased in advance and for young and senior passengers. Full details can be found on the company's excellent English-language website (above), where you can also buy tickets online.

By Bus

The **Rede Expressos company** (www.rede-expressos.pt; ✆ **70/722-33-44**) runs a national network of intercity buses, which are a cheap, air-conditioned way of getting around. Lisbon to Bragança, in the far northeast, takes 7 hours and costs 23€; to reach Tavira in the Algarve takes just over 4 hours and costs 20€. There are also regional networks such as **EVA** (www.eva-bus.com; ✆ **28/951-36-16**) in the Algarve, which, for example, runs a 2-hour route from Faro to Lagos for 5.90€ one-way.

See regional chapters for more details.

[FastFACTS] PORTUGAL

Area Codes The country code for Portugal is ✆ **351.** Portugal scrapped area codes and incorporated them into subscribers' numbers. Portuguese fixed numbers are nine digits long. Fixed numbers generally begin with a 2, mobile numbers with a 9.

Business Hours Banks generally are open Monday to Friday from 8:30am to 3pm. Some smaller branches will also take a break for lunch, usually from noon to 1pm or 2 to 3pm. Shop hours vary. In the centers of big cities, they tend to open Monday to Saturday between 9 and 10am and stay open until 7 or 8pm. Shopping malls stay open longer, often until 11pm, and are usually open Sundays. Out of centers and in rural areas, stores tend to close earlier, around 5 to 6 pm, and close on Saturday afternoon and Sunday.

Note that almost all museums are closed on Mondays. The Gulbenkian in Lisbon is a notable exception, taking its weekly break on Tuesday. For the rest of the week, museums are generally open 10 am to 6 pm, although some smaller ones may break for lunch.

Most restaurants serve lunch from noon until 3pm and dinner from 7:30 until 10pm, although in cities it's not hard to find places that serve food all day and until midnight or later. On Sundays many restaurants close or only open for lunch. Several take their weekly break on Mondays. Many nightclubs open at 10pm, but the action doesn't really begin until after midnight and often lasts until between 3 and 5am.

Customs Travelers from outside the European Union should declare any currency above 10,000€ when they are leaving or entering Portugal. Duty-free goods you can carry to and from Portugal include a maximum of 2 liters of wine or 1 liter of spirits; 200 cigarettes, or 50 grams of perfume. You are generally not allowed to bring meat or dairy products from non-EU countries.

There are few restriction when traveling to or from another EU country, but you may face questioning if you are carrying more than 10 liters of spirits, 90 liters of wine, or 800 cigarettes.

Heading home to the United States you are required to declare food products. You'll generally be okay with things like olive oil, hard cheese, canned fish, honey, and cakes. Hams and sausage may be more problematic; certain types of hams and cured deli products are allowed, others are illegal. Be sure to look at the U.S. Customs' website before purchasing. Canada has similar rules. Remember that any liquids will have to packed be in your checked luggage.

Disabled Travelers

With their steep hills and cobbled sidewalks that are often narrow, uneven, and blocked by scaffolding or illegally parked cars, the centers of Lisbon, Porto, and other Portuguese cities can be challenging for people with disabilities. Portuguese authorities woke up late to the idea of accessibility, but there has been significant progress in recent years.

Many more modern hotels and other forms of accommodation have accessible rooms. The **Associação Salvador** (http://portugalacessivel.beta.due.pt; ✆ **21/318-48-51**) has information in English on the accessible options in hotels, transport, beaches, and so on.

There are also travel agencies that specialize in travel for people with disabilities that can help plan trips to Portugal. Many are based in the UK, where Portugal has long been a popular destination. They include **Enable Holidays** (www.enableholidays.com; ✆ **+44 203 598 3865**) and Disabled Holidays (www.disabledholidays.com; ✆ **+44 1457 833 444**). Within Portugal, **Adapted & Senior Tours** (www.adaptedtoursportugal.com; ✆ **91/619-04-14**) and **Accessible Portugal** (www.accessibleportugal.com; ✆ **92/691-09-89**) organize tours and transfers.

The "**Praia Acessível–Praia para Todos!**" (Accessible Beach – Beach for All) program launched in 2005 and covered 209 beaches in 2016, which means they must have accessible parking spaces, toilet facilities, lifeguards, and unimpeded access, usually wooden pathways leading down to the water. Many also have amphibious wheelchairs, available from the lifeguards, to ease entry into the sea.

Lisbon's public bus company **Carris** (www.carris.pt/en/reduced-mobility) says 80% of its vehicles are equipped with ramps for ease of access for wheelchair users, and 50% also have spaces for wheelchairs. All buses have seats reserved for disabled travelers. Carris also has adapted minibuses at the disposal of special-needs passengers, but they must be reserved 2 days in advance (✆ **21/3-61-3141**).

Lisbon's **Metro** (www.metrolisboa.pt/eng/customer-info/accessibility) stations have special wide access gates for disabled customers and ticket vending machines are adapted for visually impaired users. Newer stations have elevators. The company says 36 of its 56 stations offer full accessibility.

The railway company **CP** (www.cp.pt/passageiros/en/passenger-information/Special-needs-customers) has a 24-hour help line for passengers with special needs (✆ **70/721-07-46**). It also offers discounts of up to 75% on tickets for disabled passengers and smaller discounts for their companions. Most taxi companies have adapted vehicles available. **Cooptaxis,** which operates in Lisbon and the Algarve (http://cooptaxis.pt; ✆ **21/799-64-75**) is among the best equipped. In Porto, try **Raditaxis** (www.raditaxis.pt; ✆ **22/507-39-00**).

Doctors & Hospitals

European Union citizens should apply for the free **European Health Insurance Card.** It grants access to medically necessary, state-provided health care in Portugal and the other EU nations under the same conditions as local people. That means free or low-cost treatment under Portugal's **national health service.** It won't give you access to private health care or expatriation services.

Travelers from the United States and other non-EU nations should check with their insurer to see what coverage they have; most

U.S. insurance plans do not cover accidents in Europe, so it's a good idea to get medical insurance before you hit the road.

Portuguese doctors and nurses are much sought after in other countries, but years of underfunding mean state hospitals and health centers, although generally well equipped in the big cities, often have long waits for all but the most urgent cases.

If your insurance covers it, private hospitals in big cities are often very well equipped with English-speaking staff, and many offer 24-hour emergency services. Among the best prepared for international visitors are **Hospital da Luz** (www.hospitaldaluz.pt; ✆ **21/710-44-00**), which is based in Lisbon but operates a number of hospitals and clinics around the country; **CUF** (www.saudecuf.pt/en/; ✆ **21/112-17-17**); and **Lusíadas** (www.lusiadas.pt/en; ✆ **21/770-40-40**).

The U.S. embassy has a list of hospitals and doctors in Lisbon and the Azores (https://portugal.usembassy.gov/medical_information.html).

In the summer, authorities in the Algarve set up special consultation times for tourists with nonemergency health issues at a number of clinics across the region with a special hotline for inquiries (www.arsalgarve.min-saude.pt/portal/?q=node/4881; ✆ **80/824-24-24**). There are also first-aid posts installed on 32 of the region's beaches.

Check our regional chapters for more details.

Drinking Laws The legal age for drinking in Portugal is 18. Beer, wine, and liquor are on sale in markets, cafes, restaurants, and liquor stores. There are no restrictions on when you can purchase alcohol. In an effort to curb noise and antisocial behavior, Lisbon city council in 2014 banned drinking in the street after 1am in areas with a high concentration of bars like Bairro Alto and Cais do Sodré, but the rules are rarely enforced.

Drugs In 2001, Portugal decriminalized possession of drugs for personal use. That's all drugs, from cannabis to heroin. The law was ground-breaking, but it does not mean that drugs are legal. Possession is still an offense, but if you are caught with small amounts you will not be arrested or prosecuted, although you may have the drugs confiscated, receive a citation, and be ordered to attend counseling sessions. You can also be fined and have other "administrative" restrictions, such as being banned from attending bars and clubs, or being suspended from working in certain professions.

Supporters of the policy claim it has been successful in reducing HIV infection, overdose deaths, and addiction rates by encouraging users to seek medical treatment. Portugal's drug-induced death rate is five times lower than the EU average.

There are still strict criminal penalties for selling, producing, or trafficking drugs, including prison terms of up to 12 years. Nevertheless, in Lisbon, Porto, and some other places, it is quite common for foreigners to be approached by shady-looking characters in the street, even in broad daylight, offering to sell cocaine or marijuana. Often what they sell is fake—making it hard for police to prosecute them. They will usually move on if you ignore them.

Electricity Voltage is 200 volts AC (50 cycles) as opposed to the U.S. 110-volt (60 cycles) system. Portugal uses plugs with two round pins like the rest of continental Europe. You'll need a simple converter for devices using flat-pin North American plugs or the UK-style three-pin plugs. Most electronics are dual-voltage—check to see if they have 110–220 on the plug. If not, you may want to buy a current converter. Hardware stores, travel and luggage shops, and airports should be able to meet your converter needs before you leave.

Embassies & Consulates The **U.S. Embassy** in Lisbon on Avenida das Forças Armadas (www.portugal.usembassy.gov; ✆ **21/727-33-00** or 21/094-20-00) is open Monday through Friday from 8am to 5pm. For U.S. citizens' consular services, call ✆ **21/770-21-22.** There is also a U.S. Consulate on São Miguel island in the Azores, Avenida Príncipe do Mónaco, 6-2 F, Ponta

Delgada; ✆ **29/630-83-30;** open Monday to Friday, 8:30am to 12:30pm and 1:30 to 5:30pm.

The **Canadian Embassy** in Lisbon is at Av. da Liberdade 198–200, 3rd Floor (www.canadainternational.gc.ca; ✆ **21/316-46-00**). It's open Monday through Thursday from 8am to 12:30pm and 1 to 5:15pm; consular services for Canadians are open 9am to noon. Canada also offers consular services in the Algarve at Rua Frei Lourenço de Santa Maria 1, 1st Floor, Faro; ✆ **28/980-37-57;** open Monday to Friday 2 to 5:30 pm; and in the Azores at Rua Carvalho Araujo, 94, Ponta Delgada on São Miguel island; ✆ **29/628-14-88;** Monday to Friday 9:30am to noon and 2 to 4 pm.

The **U.K. Embassy** in Lisbon is on Rua de São Bernardo 33 (www.gov.uk; ✆ **21/392-40-00**), open Monday to Friday 9am to 1pm and 2:30 to 5:30pm. There is a British Vice Consulate in the Algarve in Portimão at Edificio A Fábrica Avenida Guanaré (✆ **28/249-07-50**), open 9:30am to 2pm.

The **Irish Embassy** is at Av. da Liberdade 200, 4th Floor, Lisboa (✆ **21/330-82-00**), open Monday through Friday 9:30am to 12:30pm.

The **Embassy of Australia** is in the same building, Av. da Liberdade 200, 2nd Floor, Lisboa (www.portugal.embassy.gov.au; ✆ **21/310-15-00**), open Monday through Friday 10am to 4pm.

New Zealand is represented in Portugal by its embassy in France (✆ **+33 1 450 14343**).

Emergencies For emergencies needing police, ambulance, or firefighters, call ✆ **112,** the European Union–wide equivalent to North America's 911.

Family Travel Portugal is a good place to travel with kids. Most beaches on the south coast are gently sloping with shallow water and small waves. On the west coast, you'll need to be aware that there can be heavy surf and riptides; check with the lifeguards, and never let your children (or yourself) go into the water if red flags are flying. They should also be protected against the sunshine, which will beat down hard during the middle of the day in summer.

Portugal has enticing attractions and activities for children, from the delights of the **Oceanário** in Lisbon, where kids can overnight next to the shark tank, to dolphin safaris or surf school in the real-life ocean. Most museums offer free entry to small children and half-price admission to students.

Portuguese families eat out with their children even late in the evening. Kids usually get a warm welcome, with most places offering special kid's menus and almost all offering half-portions of dishes on the menu.

Children get discounts on public transport. On the **CP** rail network, for example, children under 3 travel free if they don't take up a seat. Kids age 4 to 13 pay half-price.

Many hotels have family rooms, suites, or apartments and babysitting services. Particularly along the coast, there are family-friendly resorts. The wide availability of self-catering accommodations, both in traditional aparthotels and villas, and through agencies like **Airbnb**—which is thriving in Portugal—has also made it easier to travel with kids.

Children need a **passport** to travel to Europe. Minors under 18 must be accompanied by a parent or guardian to enter Portugal or be met at the airport by a parent or guardian. If not, they will need a **letter of permission** to travel signed by their parents or guardians. Children traveling with just one parent should have a letter dated and signed by the other parent. In both cases the letter should be authorized by a notary. U.S. Customs and Border Protection offer advice on how to draft such a letter (https://help.cbp.gov/app/answers/detail/a_id/268/kw/1254/related/1/sno/1) as do the authorities in Canada (https://travel.gc.ca/travelling/children/consent-letter). If in doubt, it's best to contact the Portuguese Embassy in your country.

Health You should encounter few health problems while traveling in Portugal. The tap water is generally safe to drink; milk is pasteurized, and health services are good. Occasionally, the change in diet can cause stomach upsets, so you might want to take along some anti-diarrheal medicine.

There is a very wide network of **pharmacies** (*farmácias*). They are normally open Monday to Friday 9am to 7pm and Saturdays 9am to 1pm. However, they take turns staying open later and on Sundays, serving as *farmácias de serviço.* These are listed on a notice posted in the windows of all pharmacies and on the website, www.farmaciasdeservico.net, which is in Portuguese only, but quite straightforward since you only have to click on the name of towns and districts to get a list. The site also lists a number of pharmacies that are routinely open until late at night or 24 hours.

Insurance For information on traveler's insurance, trip cancellation insurance, and medical insurance while traveling, please visit www.frommers.com/planning.

Internet Access Portugal is a wired-up country. Most hotels and hostels have free Wi-Fi in rooms and public spaces. It's also common in cafes and restaurants; just ask the staff for the password. Museums, libraries, railway stations, and other public spaces will have it. In the airports, there is unlimited free Wi-Fi, although you will need to set up an account to access it. Public transport networks such as the buses in Porto, Lisbon metro, and certain CP trains offer free Wi-Fi, although the connection can be up-and-down when busy. If you buy a Portuguese SIM card or don't mind paying roaming charges, you can connect with tablets and smartphones via 3G or 4G in all but the most remote places.

Language English is widely spoken, especially among younger people in the cities, much more so than in France, Spain, or Italy. If you speak Spanish, most people will understand you and reply in a hybrid, jokingly known as *portunhol.*

LGBT Travelers Portuguese attitudes to homosexuality have undergone a sea change in the past couple of decades. It was one of the first countries in Europe to outlaw workplace discrimination based on sexual orientation, and legalized **gay marriage** in 2010. In 2016, gay couples were given equal adoption rights and lesbians granted access to medically assisted fertilization. Lisbon, Porto, and the Algarve have thriving gay scenes. Overt homophobia and hate crimes are rare. Attitudes tend to be more conservative in rural areas. The annual **Pride** festivals are major events on the Lisbon and Porto social calendars, and **Queer Lisbon,** held in September, is the city's oldest film festival. The main gay rights organization, ILGA Portugal (http://ilga-portugal.pt), apologizes for not having all of its website translated into English, but welcomes calls (✆ **21/887-39-18**) and promises to answer emails (ilgaportugal@ilga-portugal.pt). Other sites offering information for LGTB travelers include http://gay.portugalconfidential.com and http://portugalgay.pt.

Mail & Postage Sending postcards and standard letters from Portugal costs 0.75€ to elsewhere in Europe, 0.80€ to the rest of world. Post office opening hours vary, but bigger branches are usually open 9am to 6pm; smaller ones close for an hour at lunchtime. The mail company CTT (www.ctt.pt) has a list of post offices on its website and a phone line for enquiries in English (✆ **70/726-26-26**).

Mobile Phones Most modern North American cellphones will work in Europe, but roaming charges can be high. Check with your provider to make sure yours will work and if you can activate their international service to cut costs.

If you plan on making regular calls in Portugal, it can be cheaper to buy a local phone or a Portuguese SIM card. The process is generally hassle-free and offered by the three main telecom companies: Vodafone (www.vodafone.pt), MEO (www.meo.pt), and NOS (www.nos.pt), which have shops around the country, including in airport arrival lounges. Vodafone has an easy-to-understand English language section on its website that explains what you need to do and how much it costs. A prepaid, rechargeable SIM card with 500 minutes/text messages to Portuguese numbers and three gigabytes of data costs 17.49€.

What Things Cost in Lisbon (Hotel Prices Are High Season)

Bus ticket (bought on board)	1.85€
Double room with breakfast at Pestana Palace (expensive)	285€
Double room with breakfast at Ispira Santa Marta (moderate)	169€
Double room at Casa São Mamede (inexpensive)	110€
Dinner for one with wine at Belcanto (expensive)	180€
Dinner for one with wine at Ramiro (moderate)	35€
Dinner for one with wine at Zé Varunca (inexpensive)	17€
Pastel da nata at Manteigaria	1€
Espresso at A Brasileira (at bar/seated outside)	0.70€/1.50€
Glass of wine at Pensão Amor	3€–5.50€
Adult admission to Ocenário	14€
Stall seat for an opera at São Carlos theater	60€

Wi-Fi is widely available in hotels, cafes, and other public places in Portugal.

Money & Costs Frommers lists exact prices in the local currency. The currency conversions quoted below were correct at press time. However, rates fluctuate, so before departing, consult a currency exchange website such as **www.xe.com** to check up-to-the-minute rates.

Portugal is one of 19 countries in the euro-zone. The **euro** is divided into 100 cents. Euro coins are issued in denominations of 0.01€, 0.02€, 0.05€, 0.10€, 0.20€, 0.50€, 1€, and 2€; bills come in denominations of 5€, 10€, 20€, 50€, 100€, 200€, and 500€.

THE VALUE OF THE EURO VS. OTHER CURRENCIES

Euro (€)	US$	UK£	C$	AUS$	NZ$
1	1.07	0.86	1.43	1.43	1.51

The easiest way to get **cash** is to take it directly from your bank account in euros by using your debit card at one of Portugal's 12,400 **ATMs.** They have multilingual machines that enable you to carry out transactions in English; they are found in shopping malls, railway stations, airports, and other public spaces as well as in banks. Your bank may charge you a small commission (around 1 to 3%) on the exchange. Rates are less favorable if you exchange money at exchange bureaus and even worse if you use hotels or stores.

Credit cards are accepted almost everywhere, apart from some budget and remote places. Visa and MasterCard are the most widely used. You will sometimes see MULTIBANCO FORA DE SERVICO signs up in some places, meaning the card service is out of order. Some stores won't allow card transactions for less than 5€. Credit card transactions in Europe are usually by the "chip and PIN" system, meaning you type in your PIN code rather than signing a receipt. Most places will still allow signature payments by U.S. cardholders, but you should check with your bank to make sure you have your four-digit PIN code. It's always a good idea to let your bank and credit card provider know when you are traveling to avoid them blocking the card through fear that it's being used fraudulently.

Newspapers & Magazines There's a weekly English-language newspaper, the ***Portugal***

News, which updates national events and focuses mostly on the British community in the Algarve and around Lisbon. It's distributed free in some hotels and stores in the Algarve and other areas and is also available online at http://theportugalnews.com. British newspapers and *The New York Times, Wall Street Journal*, and *USA Today* are widely available at newsstands in the big cities and in the Algarve. Many newsstands also have a wide range of international magazines. One of the biggest selections of the international press in Lisbon can be found at **Livraria Sunrise,** 9 Avenida da Liberdade ✆ **21/347-02-04.**

Passports & Visas For visits of less than 3 months, U.S., Canadian, Irish, Australian, New Zealand, or British citizens need only a valid passport.

Police Portugal has three main police bodies. The **Public Security Police** (PSP), in dark-blue uniforms, are the ones you are most likely to see patrolling the streets and take a lead role in law enforcement in cities. The **National Republican Guard** (GNR), who wear gray, are a paramilitary unit and generally perform more "high-end" public-order work, such as riot control, although they are active in traffic policing, particularly in rural areas, and their work overlaps with the PSP. The **Judicial Police** (PJ) is a plainclothes investigative force. In emergencies, call ✆ **112.** The PSP run special **tourist police** units for dealing with travelers' problems. In Lisbon they are based in the pink **Palácio Foz** building in Praça dos Restauradores (✆ **21/342-16-23** or 21/340-00-90); in Porto they are next to City Hall at Rua Clube dos Fenianos, 11 (✆ **22/208-18-33**).

Safety Portugal is a low-crime country. Violent crime against tourists is rare. **Pickpocketing** and theft from parked cars are the biggest problems. Don't leave valuables in cars, even during daylight. Pickpockets and bag snatchers tend to focus on crowded areas where there are lots of tourists. The Chiado district and the Portas do Sol viewpoint in Lisbon are hotspots. They also operate on public transport: take special care on packed Lisbon streetcars. If you're robbed, report it to the police. They may not put out an all-points alert for the culprit, but they will return stolen documents, which frequently show up dumped by criminals after they've emptied purses of cash.

Take care on the roads. Many Portuguese males, who take pride in their nation's laid-back, relaxed reputation, turn into stressed, macho **speed freaks** when they get behind a wheel. Those owning big German cars tend to behave particularly badly. Tailgating at high speed and overtaking on the inside are common problems.

In the summer season, almost all of Portugal's beaches are staffed with **lifeguards.** They hoist red flags or yellow flags if the water is deemed dangerous for bathing: Red means don't go in the water at all; yellow allows you to walk into the water, but swimming is not allowed. It's best to follow their advice. As a general rule, south coast beaches tend to be gentle and sheltered; some of the more exposed places on the west can have strong currents and big waves. Jellyfish (*alforreca*) can be an occasional annoyance, as are **weaver fish** (*peixe aranha*). These small fish live along the western and southern coasts of Europe. They bury themselves in sand below shallow coastal waters but leave venomous spines exposed on their back. Stepping on one is very painful, but generally not dangerous. If it happens, go to the lifeguard. Plunging the foot in hot water usually brings quick relief. In rare cases, fever, chills, or nausea occur. If so, head to a hospital.

Senior Travel Portugal has long been a draw for senior travelers. Madeira, the Algarve, and the Cascais area west of Lisbon, in particular, have attracted retirees from Britain, other places in northern Europe, and, recently France, with their mild climate, relaxed lifestyle, and plethora of golf courses. Many decide to stay, buying vacation or retirement homes there.

Of particular interest is the **Golden Age** program of the **Pestana Pousadas de**

Portugal chain (www.pousadas.pt; ✆ **888/441-4421** in the U.S., or ✆ 21/844-20-01), which offers discounts of up to 35% for those over 55 in some of Portugal's best small luxury hotels. It allows seniors to stay in palaces, castles, or 500-year-old convents for as little as 55€ a night.

Those over 65 can travel for half-price on Portugal's **CP rail network** and get significant reductions on **Rede Expresso**'s buses. There are also discounts of up to 50% on admission to most museums and attractions. In all cases, you must show a valid ID proving your age.

Smoking Smoking is banned in most public buildings and transport. Under certain conditions, restaurants and bars can set aside smoking rooms, and hotels can assign up to 40% of rooms for smokers. The rules are generally applied strictly in restaurants, less so in some bars. If you want to dine or drink alfresco, be aware that many smokers will head to outside tables to escape the ban.

Student Travel Students can get discounts on everything from museums to haircuts. In most cases your university's student ID will work, but to be on the safe side, get an **International Student Identity Card** (www.isic.org). In some places, you must be under 30 to get the discounts. Trains in Portugal don't offer discounts for students, but if you are under 25, you get a 25% reduction. To get reductions on **Rede Expresso** buses, you need to be below 30.

Taxes Sales tax, known as **IVA,** is included in the price of almost everything you buy in Portugal. The standard rate is 23%, although reduced rates apply to some purchases. In restaurants, for example, the rate on food is 13%, but on liquor the full 23% rate will apply. Your receipt will usually tell you how much you've given to the government. Residents outside the EU can get **a sales tax refund** when they leave on purchases they are taking home over 50€ to 60€ depending on the type of product. Look for stores displaying tax-free shopping signs and ask them to hand you a refund form. In some places, you can be refunded in the store. In others, you'll need to get the form stamped by a customs official at the airport and pick up your money from a refund desk in departures. For more details, check out **www.premiertaxfree.com** or **www.globalblue.com.**

Taxes are usually included in the price of your hotel room, but in Lisbon, the City Hall has controversially introduced a special **tourism tax,** meaning you'll have 1€ per person per night added to your bill, up to a maximum of 7€. It does not apply to children under 13.

Time Portugal keeps the same time as Britain and Ireland, an hour behind Spain and most of western Europe. It is 5 hours ahead of U.S. Eastern Standard Time. Portugal has daylight saving time. It moves its clocks ahead an hour in late spring and an hour back in the fall. Exact dates vary.

Tipping Service charges are rarely included in restaurant bills, but tipping is optional. In fancy places, people may leave up to 10%; elsewhere, rarely more than 5%, and only then if you've appreciated the service. Often people will just use a couple of coins or nothing. In bars and cafes it's rare to tip more than a few coins. In taxis, too, tipping is optional, although people will often round up the bill to the nearest euro or two, likewise with hairdressers or barbers. In hotels with porters or valet parking, you might want to tip 0.50€ or 1€.

Toilets Public toilets exist but are rare. If you are caught short, nip into a cafe, pay 0.60€ for an espresso or bottle of water, and use facilities as a paying customer.

Water Tap water is drinkable throughout Portugal, but many people prefer the taste of bottled water and it's commonly drunk and served in restaurants and cafes. Portugal's wealth of springs means there's a variety of still brands on the market. If you order water (*água*) in a cafe, you'll always be asked if you want still (*sem gás*) or sparking (*com gás*), chilled (*fresca*) or room temperature (*natural*).

Most beaches in season fly a blue flag signaling the water has been certified as clean for bathing by European Union inspectors, as well as have adequate lifeguard services. Several inland bathing spots on rivers and lakes have similar blue-flag certification.

Websites The national tourist board has a good multilingual website, **www.visitportugal.com**. The quality of regional tourism sites is patchy. Among the best are www.visitcentro.com on the center, www.visitmadeira.pt, http://visitportoandnorth.travel, www.visitazores.com, and www.visitlisboa.com.

Some interesting blogs and private guides in English giving tips and insight into the country include **www.saltofportugal.com**, which is produced by a group of enthusiastic young Portuguese and offers tips on everything from poetry to *pasteis da nata;* **www.portugalconfidential.com**, which claims to cover "everything cool in Portugal"; and **www.nelsoncarvalheiro.com**, for great food, recipes, and travel ideas.

Index

See also Accommodations and Restaurant indexes, below.

General Index

T

U

V

W

Y

Z

Accommodations

Restaurants

Map List

Photo Credits

© Agnieszka Skalska/Shutterstock.com: p. xi top right; © Aki Shi/Shutterstock.com: p. xii top; © Alvaro German Vilela/Shutterstock.com: p. xiv top left; © AngeloDeVal/Shutterstock.com: p. xvi middle; © Anton_Ivanov/Shutterstock.com: pp. xii middle, xv top; © Aureliy: p. xvi top; © Cenz07/Shutterstock.com: p. xiii bottom right; © Chris Brown: p. vii top; © Christophe Cappelli/Shutterstock.com: p. xiv top right; © Cris: p. xv bottom; © dynamosquito: p. viii top left; © Eduardo Estellez/Shutterstock.com: p. xiv bottom; © ESB Professional: p. v top; © Filipe Pimentel: p. ix top; © Gary Yim/Shutterstock.com: p. xv middle; © Jessica Spengler: p. xi bottom right; © joyfull: p. ii; © Junior Braz/Shutterstock: pp. vi bottom left, viii bottom; © kps1664: p. vi bottom right; © Kravtsov_Ivan/Shutterstock.com: p. ix bottom right; © Landscape Nature Photo/Shutterstock.com: p. xi top left; © Marc Venema: p. xii bottom; © Mauro Rodrigues/Shutterstock.com: p. xiii bottom left; © Meghan Lamb: pp. v bottom left, v bottom right; © monysasu/Shutterstock.com: p. ix bottom left; © Nacho Pintos: p. x top; © Pawel Kazmierczak: p. iv; © Pedro Ribeiro Simões: p. vii middle; © Photo and Vector/Shutterstock.com: p. iii; © ribeiroantonio/Shutterstock.com: p. vii bottom; © Sean Pavone: p. i; © Sean Pavone/Shutterstock.com: p. x bottom; © senai aksoy: p. viii top right; © Sergio Stakhnyk: p. xvi bottom; © StockPhotosArt/Shutterstock.com: p. vi top; © Tatiana Popova: p. xiii top; © Vector99: p. x middle; © Zacarias Pereira da Mata/Shutterstock.com: p. xi bottom left.

Published by
FROMMER MEDIA LLC

ISBN 978-1-62887-308-5 (paper), 978-1-62887-309-2 (e-book)

Editorial Director: Pauline Frommer
Developmental Editor: Pauline Frommer
Production Editor: Lynn Northrup
Cartographer: Roberta Stockwell
Photo Editor: Meghan Lamb
Indexer: Kelly Henthorne

For information on our other products or services, see www.frommers.com.

Frommer Media LLC also publishes its books in a variety of electronic formats. Some content that appears in print may not be available in electronic formats.

Manufactured in the United States of America

5 4 3 2 1

ABOUT THE AUTHORS

Paul Ames has been enchanted by Portugal since he first arrived as a child in 1975 and found the country gripped by revolutionary fervor. He lives in Lisbon, works as a freelance journalist, and never tires of exploring the delights of his adopted homeland, from the vine-covered hills of the Minho to Madeira's rocky shores, and all the beaches in between.

Célia Pedroso is a Portuguese journalist specializing in travel and food. She is the co-author of the book *Eat Portugal* and head of Culinary Backstreets, Lisbon, for whom she writes and leads culinary tours. Her work has been featured in the *Guardian, DestinAsian, Sunday Times,* and other international travel magazines. She never says no to a pastry or to a weekend outside the big city.

ABOUT THE FROMMER'S TRAVEL GUIDES

For most of the past 50 years, Frommer's has been the leading series of travel guides in North America, accounting for as many as 24 percent of all guidebooks sold. I think I know why.

Though we hope our books are entertaining, we nevertheless deal with travel in a serious fashion. Our guidebooks have never looked on such journeys as a mere recreation, but as a far more important human function, a time of learning and introspection, an essential part of a civilized life. We stress the culture, lifestyle, history, and beliefs of the destinations we cover, and urge our readers to seek out people and new ideas as the chief rewards of travel.

We have never shied from controversy. We have, from the beginning, encouraged our authors to be intensely judgmental, critical—both pro and con—in their comments, and wholly independent. Our only clients are our readers, and we have triggered the ire of countless prominent sorts, from a tourist newspaper we called "practically worthless" (it unsuccessfully sued us) to the many rip-offs we've condemned.

And because we believe that travel should be available to everyone regardless of their incomes, we have always been cost-conscious at every level of expenditure. Though we have broadened our recommendations beyond the budget category, we insist that every lodging we include be sensibly priced. We use every form of media to assist our readers, and are particularly proud of our feisty daily website, the award-winning Frommers.com.

I have high hopes for the future of Frommer's. May these guidebooks, in all the years ahead, continue to reflect the joy of travel and the freedom that travel represents. May they always pursue a cost-conscious path, so that people of all incomes can enjoy the rewards of travel. And may they create, for both the traveler and the persons among whom we travel, a community of friends, where all human beings live in harmony and peace.

Arthur Frommer

NOTES

NOTES